HUMAN RESOURCE MANAGEMENT

A global and critical perspective

HUMAN RESOURCE MANAGEMENT

A GLOBAL AND CRITICAL PERSPECTIVE

2nd edition

JAWAD SYED & ROBIN KRAMAR

macmillan education   palgrave

First edition 2012
Second edition 2017

Published by PALGRAVE

Palgrave in the UK is an imprint of Macmillan Publishers Limited,
registered in England, company number 785998, of 4 Crinan Street,
London, N1 9XW.

Palgrave is a global imprint of the above companies and is represented
throughout the world.

Palgrave® and Macmillan® are registered trademarks in the United States,
the United Kingdom, Europe and other countries.

ISBN 978–1–137–52162–0 paperback

This book is printed on paper suitable for recycling and made from fully
managed and sustained forest sources. Logging, pulping and manufacturing
processes are expected to conform to the environmental regulations of the
country of origin.

A catalogue record for this book is available from the British Library.

A catalog record for this book is available from the Library of Congress.

To all teachers, practitioners and students of HRM, especially the great ones.

BRIEF CONTENTS

PART 3

3   HRM AND CONTEMPORARY ISSUES   **277**

LONG CONTENTS

PART I

① THE HRM ARENA   **1**

PART 2

2 **HRM IN PRACTICE** **109**

PART 3

HRM AND CONTEMPORARY ISSUES   277

LIST OF FIGURES

LIST OF TABLES

CASE STUDY GRID

ACKNOWLEDGEMENTS

I would like to thank all the authors for their valuable contributions to this book including a wealth of organisational examples and theoretical insights from across the globe, my colleagues at the Suleman Dawood School of Business (Lahore University of Management Sciences) and University of Huddersfield for their support of my research endeavours, and my parents - Khalida Sarwar Malik and Ghulam Sarwar Syed (late) - whose teachings and character continue to inspire, invigorate and guide me. Special thanks are also due to Ursula Gavin and her team at Palgrave Macmillan for their support in publishing the second edition of this book.

Jawad Syed

The publisher and editors would like to thank the following reviewers for their constructive feedback and suggestions for the development of this textbook:

Almina Bešić – ICF International, UK
Charmi Patel – Henley Business School, UK
Claudia Buengeler – University of Amsterdam, the Netherlands
Estelle Toomey – Zayed University, UAE
Ezaz Ahmed – Central Queensland University, Australia
Henrik Holt Larsen – Copenhagen Business School, Denmark
Jenny Rodriguez – Manchester Business School, UK
Jie Shen – University of South Australia, Australia
Khaldoun Ababneh – American University in Dubai, UAE
Louise Møller Pedersen – Aalborg University, Denmark
Monika Huesmann – Berlin School of Economics and Law, Germany
Helen De Cieri – Monash University, Australia
Ulke Veersma – University of Greenwich, UK
Monika Hamori – IE Business School, Spain
Wayne Cascio – University of Colorado Denver, USA
Chris Rowley – Cass Business School, UK
Miao Zhang – Kingston Business School, UK
Paul Sparrow – Lancaster University Management School, UK
Elaine Farndale – The Pennsylvania State University, USA, and Tilburg University, the Netherlands

The publisher and the editors would like to thank the organisations listed below for permission to reproduce material from their publications:

John Wiley & Sons, Inc. for Figure 7.2. Original source is Oldham, G. (1996) Job design. In Cooper, C. L. and Robertson, I. T. (eds), *International Review of Industrial and Organisational Psychology*. New York: John Wiley, 11: 33–60.

Sage Publications, Inc. for Figure 7.3. Original source is Vandenberg, R., Richardson, H. & Eastman, L. (1999), The Impact Of High Involvement Work Processes on Organizational Effectiveness; *Group & Organization Management*, Vol. 24 No. 3, 300–339.

CIPD for Table 10.3 and 10.6. Original source is the CIPD Annual Survey Report: Reward Management 2014–15, Issued: July 2015, Reference: 7042.

Every effort has been made to trace all copyright holders, but if any have been inadvertently overlooked, the publishers would be pleased to make the necessary arrangements at the first opportunity.

NOTES ON EDITORS

JAWAD SYED is Professor of Organisational Behaviour and Dean of the Suleman Dawood School of Business at Lahore University of Management Sciences. Previously he held the positions of Reader in Human Resource Management at University of Kent and Professor of Organisational Behaviour and Diversity Management at University of Huddersfield. Jawad received his PhD in Business from Macquarie University, Australia, and completed a Postgraduate Certificate in Higher Education at University of Kent, UK. In addition, he received a Masters of International Business from University of Western Sydney, Australia. With a professional and academic career that spans over 25 years in academic institutions and business organisations in the UK, Australia and Pakistan, Jawad examines HRM, organisational behaviour and diversity from relational, contextual and interdisciplinary perspectives, and focuses on critical integration of theory with organisational practice.

ROBIN KRAMAR is Professor of Human Resource Management at the Faculty of Business, Australian Catholic University, Australia. Professor Kramar is the co-author of Human Resource Management in Australia (McGraw-Hill), now in its 5th edition, and she has also authored or edited five other books on aspects of human resource management.

NOTES ON CONTRIBUTORS

Fida Afiouni is Associate Professor of Human Resource Management at the Olayan School of Business, American University of Beirut, Lebanon. She also serves as an AE in Business Ethics: A European Review. Her current research and teaching focus on the interplay of HRM, careers, and gender in the Arab Middle East.

Chris Brewster is Professor of International Human Resource Management at Henley Business School, University of Reading, UK; Nijmegen University, the Netherlands; the University Vaasa, Finland; and ISCTE-Instituto Universitário de Lisboa, Portugal. He had substantial experience as a practitioner and gained his doctorate from the LSE before becoming an academic. He researches in the field of international and comparative HRM; and has published more than thirty books and over two hundred articles. He has taught in many countries around the world. In 2006 Chris was awarded an Honorary Doctorate by the University of Vaasa, Finland.

Julie Davies is HR Subject Group Leader at the University of Huddersfield Business School, UK. She is a Fellow of the Chartered Institute of Personnel and Development and gained her PhD at Warwick University. Julie's research interests include international business education, research impact, strategy-as-practice, HR in SMEs, and professional ethics.

Michael Dickmann is Professor of International HRM at Cranfield University, School of Management, UK. His work focuses on human resource strategies, structures and processes of multinational organisations, cross-cultural management, international mobility, global careers and change management. Michael has published more than 100 academic and professional papers and reports. He is the lead author/editor of three books on international HRM and global careers. Since 2012 he is also the Editor of *The International Journal of Human Resource Management*. Having worked as the Head of HRM for a German multinational and as a management consultant he combines pragmatic understanding and intellectual rigour to solve international people challenges.

Yu Fu is Senior Teaching Associate in the Department of Organisation, Work and Technology at Lancaster University, UK. She delivers lectures and seminars in the areas of HRM and Organisational Behaviour. Her research interests lie in international HRM, particularly national cultural factors in employment.

Janet Handley is Head of Department of Management at the University of Huddersfield Business School, UK. She is an experienced interviewer of senior public and private sector professionals using a socio-biographic narrative interview approach and is currently researching the constitution, maintenance and contribution to organisational practice of talent management within a large public sector organisation.

Peter Holland is Associate Professor in Human Resource Management and Employee Relations at Monash University, Australia. He is the Co-Director the Faculty research centre – The Australian Consortium for Research on Employment and Work (ACREW) and Acting Head of the Human Resource and Employee Relations Discipline in the Department of Management.

Dima Jamali is Professor at the Olayan School of Business, American University of Beirut and currently holding the Kamal Shair Chair in Responsible Leadership and serving as Associate Dean for Research and Faculty Development. Her research and teaching revolve primarily around Corporate Social Responsibility (CSR) and Social Entrepreneurship (SE) and she is winner of several prestigious awards and honors pertaining to her work in this domain.

Andrew Jenkins is Subject Leader and Principal Lecturer at the Business School, the University of Huddersfield, UK. He has written extensively on employment issues and his research has been published in Employee Relations, Equality, Diversity and Inclusion, International Journal of Contemporary Hospitality Management, Journal of Human Resources in Hospitality and Tourism and Tourism Management. He is co-author of the textbook "Introducing Human Resource Management" (2016), published by Pearson, and he is the author of a chapter on "Human Resource Strategy and Talent Management" for a book on "Talent Management in Hospitality and Tourism", edited by Susan Horner and published by Goodfellow. He is an Academic Member of the Chartered Institute of Personnel and Development (CIPD), Member of the Chartered Management Institute (CMI) and Fellow of the Higher Education Academy (HEA).

Nicolina Kamenou-Aigbekaen is Professor in International Human Resource Management and Diversity Management at the College of Business, Zayed University, Dubai, UAE. Her research lies in the area of diversity management primarily with regard to race, ethnicity, culture and gender in employment. She also conducts research on cross-cultural management and HRM policies and practices in non-western regions, work-life balance and human rights. Her recent work focuses on gender and culture in organisations in the Middle East.

Olivia Kyriakidou is Assistant Professor of Management and Organizational Behavior at Athens University of Economics and Business, Greece. Her current research interests are focused on the field of equality, diversity and inclusion at work with a special and the management of organizational and social change.

Diannah Lowry is Lecturer in HRM at the Faculty of Business and Law at The Open University, UK. She is an experienced academic who has taught and researched in areas within Human Resource Management in universities in both Australia and the United Kingdom. Diannah has held a variety of different positions both in the commercial sector and in higher education.

Liisa Mäkelä is Associate Professor at the University of Vaasa, Department of Management, Finland. Her research interests focus on the international workforce and related career paths, work-life interface, and occupational well-being.

Jane Maley is Senior Lecturer in Management at the School of Management and Marekting, Charles Sturt University, Australia. Jane has held managing director roles for UK, US and Japanese biotech multinational corporations.

Peter A Murray is currently Professor of Management at the University of Southern Queensland, Australia, with previous affiliations at Macquarie University and University of Western Sydney, Australia. He is an applied researcher in strategic change and diversity management and lectures more broadly in strategic management, change management and human resource management. He is also an associate editor and editorial board member of many leading journals and journal reviewer for top ranked outlets.

Amanda Pyman is Professor and Head of Department of Management, Faculty of Business and Law at Deakin University, Australia. Her research interests include employee voice, privacy in the workplace and Australian and international employment relations. Amanda has published widely and is also a Fellow at Warwick Business School in the UK.

Liz Rivers is Senior Lecturer of Human Resource Management at the University of Huddersfield, UK. She spent the first 17 years of her career in Human Resource Management and Development posts in the private sector. Her current research interests centre on emotions and the working lives of Human Resource practitioners.

Jim Rooney is Senior Lecturer at the University of Sydney, Australia, within the Discipline of Accounting at the School of Business. His research and teaching interests include corporate governance, risk management, management control, supply chain and management decision-making.

Cathy Sheehan is Associate Professor in the Department of Management at Monash University in Australia. She has conducted research with the Australian Human Resource Institute (AHRI) and led an Australian Research Council–funded project to review the role of the HR function. More recently she has worked with Worksafe Victoria to isolate and measure OHS lead indicators. Her publications have regularly appeared in international peer reviewed journals.

John Shields is Professor of Human Resource Management and Organisational Studies at The University of Sydney Business School, Australia, and is the School's Deputy Dean (Education). John holds a PhD in Economic History from the University of Sydney, Australia (1990). His principal areas of research and teaching include performance management, reward management, executive remuneration, corporate governance, leadership, and labour history.

Vesa Suutari is Professor of International Management at the Department of Management at University of Vaasa, Finland. He has also acted as Dean of the Faculty of Business Studies and the Vice Rector of the University for over six years. His research interests are on international human resource management and cross-cultural management.

Stephen Swailes is Professor of Human Resource Management in The Business School, University of Huddersfield, UK. His research interests include organizational commitment, the roles that people display in teams and more recently developing a more critical understanding of organizational approaches to the management of high performing employees.

Tracy Wilcox is Senior Lecturer at UNSW Australia Business School. Her research interests include responsible management practice, business ethics, and business ethics education. She has published in edited collections and international journals including the Journal of Business Ethics, the Asia Pacific Journal of Human Resources, and the Routledge Companion to Philosophy in Organization Studies.

Tour of book

Learning outcomes

At the start of every chapter, learning outcomes guide your reading and provide a useful reference for revision

LEARNING OUTCOMES:

After reading this chapter, you should be

➤ Understand and distinguish between d
➤ Understand how demographic transfor sity management in the workplace.
➤ Understand various forms of employm
➤ Know about various laws and regulati
➤ Distinguish between the business ca
➤ Understand methodological consi

Critical Thinking boxes

Develop your critical thinking skills by exploring contemporary debates in HRM and some of the issues facing human resources managers in the global workplace

? **Critical Thinking 1.1** **Parochia**

In the 'mainstream' English-language te guages (Özbilgin, 2004; Sheldon et al., 2 French-, German- and Spanish-language texts. The inclusion of materials not writte petence of individual authors. As a conse and dominated by the English-speaking w

Adler (1991) refutes any claims of univers Clark et al. (1999) identify two forms of English-language sources poses a ma logical complexities of studying cros English language appears to be th elated to HRM practice to tho

the difficulty

HRM in the news

Each chapter includes issues from the media that are relevant to the chapter topic

HRM AND CONTEMPORA

📖 **HRM in the news**

7-Eleven is the largest retail convenience ABC, and the Fairfax Media exposed socia payroll compliance issues and falsification permitted to work 40 hours per fortnight; ho to work more hours, paying them half the le dents did not comply, they were threatened

The Fair Work Ombudsman is the regula have conducted audits on a number of ered that this level of underpaying wa regulator has taken legal action aga employees at the legal minimum

ing Chairman of 7-E

Stop and reflect

Thought-provoking questions encourage you to development critical thinking skills

STOP AND REFLECT

Consider the bund tices that have been Performance Work Pr or High Performance W (HPWS). These practi widely discussed in the Consider the practices organisations discuss and reflect on wheth HRM is just anothe HPWS.

Class Activity

A class activity in every chapter gives you the chance to test your understanding and apply your reading to your own experiences

🖉 **Class Activity**

Choose one of the micro-orga that impact on employee invol by Dundon and Gollan (2007). know, and your knowledge an how this dimension affected e

rchington and V

For discussion and revision

Assignments, revision questions and topics for discussion at the end of each chapter help guide your class discussion and revision

tual issues and deal w strategic manner.

FOR DISCUSSION AND REVISION

1 How do macro-contextual factors affect the design and operationalisation of the following HRM functions:
   • recruitment and selection;
   • training;
   • performance management;
   • reward management;
   • career management.
2 Make a study of HRM policies and practices in a spe-cific company. Identify the various ways in which the HRM policies and practices in that company ar affected by its sociocultural, political, legal, and e nomic contexts.

What are various tensions between the glob d contextualisation of HRM? What are i tensions for the future of HRM

Case studies

Chapter opening cases and extended end of chapter cases give insight into HRM in practice in companies and countries around the world

Case Study HRM in Brunei's pu

Brunei is a monarchical government that
who has executive authority and is assiste
Islamic Monarchy' (MIB) is often thought o
guage, culture and customs and the impor

In October 2013, the Sultan announced h
which represent around 78 per cent of th
Asia to introduce Sharia law into its per
human rights and minority rights (USA
about 9 per cent of the country's t
Brunei will enforce fines and pri
ligions other than Isl

Mini case studies

There are also mini case studies throughout the book, providing a glimpse into real-world HRM in a global context

cts of HRM in multinationa

Mini Case Study 2.1 HRM at Algorithi

Algorithm is a pharmaceutical plant operating
firm's business line is manufacturing pharmace
ers (it does not handle any distribution activitie
employing a total of 320 employees, 170 of wh
licence, as well as its own generic products. It
but this mainly copies generic products and d
does not outsource any technical or product
This means that it manufactures, analyses
the-counter (OTC) and prescription drugs

interview was conducted with Mrs
l a member of Algorithm's
ter import

Glossary

Key terms are explained at the end of each chapter

es and create partic
social responsibility and sustai

GLOSSARY

Coordinated Market Economies (CMEs) ar
mies that acknowledge the diversity of stakeh
in the economy and society. These interests ca
in arrangements such as government regulatic
representatives on Workers Councils within c
Dialogue involves two or more groups wor
a collaborative way to come to a commo
Global Reporting Initiative (GRI) es
Principles for organisations that w
gories of sustainability: e
Six groups

INTRODUCTION

THEORY AND PRACTICE OF HRM IN THE CHOPPY WATERS OF A COMPLEX GLOBAL CONTEXT

Jawad Syed and Robin Kramar

WELCOME AND OVERVIEW

Welcome to *Human Resource Management: A Global and Critical Perspective*, which is a revised, updated and slightly restructured second edition of our book *Human Resource Management in a Global Context: A Critical Approach*. The book covers the core topics of human resource management (HRM) but situates the discussion within a global perspective. Two key features of the revised edition are its global orientation, and a critical approach to HRM theory and practice.

In terms of the global approach, the current edition focuses on the implications of globalisation for HRM, the ways in which HRM theory has addressed these implications, and the way HRM works in multinational corporations. A non–Western-centric approach is maintained throughout. In terms of the critical approach, the chapters are woven to encourage readers to question assumptions that underpin managing people within organisations. The text examines the subject through a critical lens that brings readers to a deeper understanding of the complexities of HRM.

Together, the global and critical elements of the text challenge readers both to think about the various alternative ways of looking at aspects of HRM and to consider the management and organisational implications of a globalised workforce. This makes the text much more relevant to the needs of lecturers who increasingly include international and critical material in their HR modules.

EVOLVING THEORY AND PRACTICE OF HRM

In an increasingly complex global context, characterised by international mergers and acquisitions, migration and diversity (Gomes et al., 2013; Ravasi et al., 2015), HRM is often seen as the major factor distinguishing successful from unsuccessful organisations, an integral element in achieving and maintaining competitive advantage. In the manufacturing sector, it serves to enhance employee productivity, quality, and motivation at work. In the service sector, it may result in improved customer satisfaction where workers are the primary source of contact with customers, either face-to-face or through the telephone or the Internet (Den Hartog et al., 2013). Much of this revolves around the extent to which HRM is designed to maintain international competitiveness and quality while also being sensitive and responsive to contextual environment and requirements.

While HRM is expected to be aligned with strategic organisational objectives, as it should be, its strategies are also influenced by wider societal factors, legislative and political frameworks, social and economic institutions, and a range of different stakeholder interests. For example, a key challenge for HRM in multinational companies (MNCs) is to balance the interplay between home- and host-country influences.

The book has been written with the aim of developing our understanding and practice of HRM in an increasingly globalised world of work. It uses a critical lens to develop an approach to HRM that is not only business-focused but also context-sensitive and socially responsible – we will explain our rationale for this below.

The emergence of HRM in the 1980s was accompanied by a sustained theoretical assault on its pretensions, highlighting the gap between the rhetoric of HRM and the reality, which was focused on impersonal economic rationalism. The reconstruction of the employment relationship as a singularly individual market exchange did not go uncontested in management education. However, whereas the proponents of HRM once felt the need to engage with and respond to criticism, the field now seems to have narrowed as the major concerns relate merely to strategic 'fit' and identifying mechanisms to facilitate 'high-commitment' and 'high-performance' organisations.

We consider the overemphasis of HRM on strategic performance to be problematic in view of the considerable gap between the policy and practice of strategic HRM. Vaughan (1994) argues that although organisational mission statements usually hold that employees are their most important asset, organisational reality is characterised by impersonal economic rationalism. However, Kay (2011) argues that profit as a 'direct goal' is overrated, and that business problems cannot be solved by drawing a straight line between cause and long-term effect because they are so complex, a manager's information so incomplete, the competitive environment so complicated, and analytic techniques so inadequate that it is impossible to draw a credible connection. Wilmott (1993) asserts that the rhetoric of HRM tends to turn employees into 'willing slaves' who negate their own interests, assuming the organisation will take care of them. Seen from this angle, HRM's unitary rhetoric may compromise the individual and collective needs of employees and may instil an HRM culture that advantages organisations at the expense of employees. This is particularly true in periods of economic recession and instability. Although the economic gains for the organisation are always a priority, issues related to individuals and societies remain subject to various concerns and tensions. Furthermore, a number of changes have occurred in factors influencing the way people are used in organisations, for example globalisation, migration, environmental sustainability, governance, ethics, work–life balance, and workforce diversity.

CULTURAL AND INSTITUTIONAL PERSPECTIVES,

A key implication of globalisation for the discipline of HRM is the need to provide managers, particularly those working in MNCs, with insights on how to design and implement an effective HRM system in diverse national, cultural, and institutional contexts. This notion has generated critical debates on localisation versus standardisation and the possibilities and implications of transferring HRM policies and practices across nations.

From a cultural perspective, HRM practices need to be designed in view of the cultural distinctiveness of beliefs, practices, and values shared by a community. Bartlett and Ghoshal (1998) suggest that the history, infrastructure, resources, and culture of a nation state permeate all aspects of life, including the behaviour of managers and employers. Scholars have analysed the influence of national cultural values on styles of business and management (Hofstede, 1980; Trompenaars and Hampden-Turner, 1997). At the same time, the movement of human resources across national borders, together with differences in social and economic experiences, indicates the complexity of HRM in a global context and also highlights that subcultures can coexist within a macro-culture.

Indeed, an important limitation of culturalist approaches is their tendency to oversimplify national cultures and promote cultural stereotypes.

From an institutional perspective, there are differences between countries and societies that may result in specific models of HRM. Indeed HR practice, such as recruitment and selection techniques, performance appraisal, and approach to diversity, may have a different focus or shape due to institutional and societal differences. Given that much of the research relates to Western models of HRM, it may be naïve to expect that these ideas will be easily transported into Africa, South America, South Asia, or the Middle East. Indeed, a complete convergence or universality of HRM practices is highly unlikely. Differences in HR practices between countries are caused not only by national cultural differences but also by the institutional forces. Forces such as the education and training system, the legal and political framework, and the social and economic environment affect the nature and practices of HRM and employment relations. While all societies might face similar pressures as a consequence of greater international integration and globalisation, 'these pressures will lead to modification and change of societal institutions, but the particular form of the response will reflect each country's own societal logic' (Rubery and Grimshaw, 2003: 39).

Scholars have also identified how cultural and institutional contexts are interlinked. Dore (1973) suggests that institutions are created or perpetuated by powerful actors following their interests and cultural orientations. Hofstede (1980) argues that culture reflects institutions. Whitley (1992) points towards strong cultural features within his dominant contingency institutional perspective, arguing that institutions include cultural attitudes (cited in Reiche et al., 2012). However, Gerhart and Fang (2005) suggest that while national cultural differences are important and must be understood, their role needs to be put in the context of other important contextual factors, including organisational culture.

A MULTILEVEL APPROACH TO HRM

Understanding HRM in a globalised world requires acknowledging complexity, and the coexistence of institutions with competing approaches (Kramar, 2013). This complexity can be framed and understood in terms of a multilevel model that identifies the macro-context, the meso-organisational context, and the micro-individual level (Syed and Özbilgin, 2009). By identifying these each level, this model enables the explicit consideration of the complex interplay of a number of factors operating at the three levels. It also acknowledges the interaction of these factors across levels.

At the macro level, legislation and the state play a crucial role in shaping HRM policies. Market conditions influence employee rights, level of employment, and the adoption of particular HRM policies. Cultural dynamics, social practices, religious beliefs, and demographics influence national institutions as well as organisational practices and employee behaviour. The explicit recognition of these factors enables the identification of the assumptions that inform national institutions that influence HRM. For instance, in the USA, UK, and Australia, an understanding of the economic system is framed in terms of primarily neo-economic assumptions (MacEwan, 1999). In comparison, many countries in Europe, such as Germany, Norway and Poland, adopt an approach that involves the interests of a variety of stakeholders.

At the meso- or organisational level, the framework allows the identification of the formal policies and the actual practices that constitute HRM. Intended and realised HRM practice can be different and there are many reasons for this, such as individual preferences and social networks, changes in direction, and senior management support (Bartram et al., 2007; Kramar, 1992; Truss and Gratton, 1994).

These factors are not independent of the broader macro-level influences and will therefore vary between countries. In addition, when identifying HRM at this level, the assumptions that inform the analysis of the organisation can be made explicit. Many HRM frameworks adopt a mechanical view of organisations, rather than seeing organisations as organic, nonlinear, evolving institutions and examples of a complex adaptive system reflecting power inequities. For instance, in many countries with equal employment opportunity legislation and organisational policies, there are still adverse gender stereotypes and managerial practices that may impede women's participation in employment and leadership in organisations. In cultures with strong emphasis on women's nurturing roles in traditional families, flexible working practices may enable women's employment in formal organisations. For example, in India, Maruti Suzuki has introduced customised office hours wherein employees can choose from seven time slots depending on work commitments (Chaturvedi and Verma, 2014).

At the micro- or individual level, the framework takes into account the individual impacted by and also influencing HRM practices. For instance, at this level, demographic differences and responses of individuals to HRM, issues of individual identity and diversity, and the difficulties associated with the implementation of HRM policies can be taken into account. Therefore, analysis at this level enables the identification of the assumptions about individuals in the workplace to be made explicit. It enables an assessment of the influence of macro-factors on individuals and enables individuals to be regarded as active players in HRM, not just receivers of the policies. Here, the issues of individual agency and employee voice become relevant to effective design and implementation of HRM practices. Employee voice, a two-way communication between management and employees that enables employees to participate in decision-making, is particularly important to boost employees' motivation and engagement. It is also a core feature in research on high performance work systems which points to links between 'high involvement' management and performance (CIPD, 2015).

Consideration of HRM at the micro-individual level enables the adoption of more realistic assumptions about the way people behave in the workplace, including the behaviour associated with the execution of HRM policies. Rather than assuming that people are value-creating assets, who may be readily influenced by HRM policies, when the micro-level is explicitly acknowledged, it is possible to make more realistic assumptions about the emotional, political, social, and spiritual dimensions of individuals (Zappala, 2010).

When examining HRM at this micro-level in a globalised world, HRM becomes particularly complex. Macro-level factors such as culture, values, and religion play out at the micro-level through individual actions and behaviours. For instance, in Muslim majority countries (MMCs), the Islamic religion has an important influence on the practice of HRM, such as in approaching gender equality or creating workplace routines that accommodate religious practices of employees (Ali and Kramar, 2015; Syed and Metcalfe, 2015).

As the demographic composition of employees continues to change, their motivations and expectations evolve too. It is imperative that HRM understands what is most valued by these workers. Is it compensation, or prestige, or perhaps autonomy at work? To what extent do their cultural values and individual identity and circumstances affect their relationships at work and affect their corporate citizenship and productivity? In diverse industries and national settings, organisations may have to adapt their HRM incentives, benefits policies, and retention strategies for workers who are not just driven by financial compensation.

The multilevel view enables the expansion of HRM beyond a specific organisation and an acknowledgement of multiple constituencies. HRM can make a strategic contribution by engaging multiple stakeholders both inside and outside the employing organisation in decision-making. Such an approach facilitates the acknowledgement of performance outcomes that move beyond organisational goals, the existence of alliances, and partnership arrangements between organisations.

CONTEXTUAL VARIANCES

In a globalised context, in which there is an interdependence of countries, industries, and companies reflected in the cross-border flow of goods and services, capital and knowhow, confront HRM with complexities associated with multiplicity, interdependence, and ambiguity. HRM in a global context requires an understanding of the opportunities and risks across national and functional boundaries. This is not transferring knowledge from the parent organisation to a subsidiary; rather it reflects a process of distinguishing between situations in which it is appropriate to emphasise global integration and other situations when it is appropriate to respond to local conditions. HRM needs to take into account the diverse and heterogeneous nature of the people doing its work, national and local requirements such as laws, and the need for integration across countries. These requirements pose challenges to the development and execution of HRM policies and they also provide the opportunity for HRM to recast itself as the terrain of organisations and industry change (Kramar, 2013).

For instance, Chinese societies attach great importance to cultivating and maintaining *guanxi*, i.e. connection or relationship. Although societies such as Taiwan, Hong Kong, and China have been rapidly modernising, the influence of the cultural value of relationship-building, guanxi, is still an important influence in managing relationships and conducting HRM policies in the workplace. A similar notion of *wasta* is seen in Arab countries in the Middle East, which may mean anything from networking to nepotism. It refers to using one's connections and/or influence to get things done, including finding a job or securing a contract (Smith et al., 2012).

A particular challenge for HRM is posed by cultural factors and national values. For instance, culture is a significant constraint on the evaluation of employee performance and the feedback process. It has been found that Western style performance appraisals are difficult to transfer to non-Western countries (Vance, 2006; Rubera and Kirca, 2012).

Acceptance of performance appraisal, the purpose of appraisals, the conduct of the feedback session, and the nature of errors experienced during an appraisal process vary between countries (Maley, 2012). For instance in some cultures, such as Japan, the appraisal process can be interpreted as a sign of distrust and is not accepted by employees, while in Chinese MNCs appraisals are primarily used to determine pay.

Determining a reward strategy also poses challenges in a global context (Shields, 2012). The issues of integration and localisation are again crucial. Each country has its own legal, economic, and political institutional contexts that can provide a framework for reward determination. In addition, employees will have different expectations. In some countries, such as India, Indonesia, and China, employees have a strong respect for hierarchy which is rooted in their culture. These employees also favour long-term employment relationships, customary allowances and benefits. On the other hand, the head office of the organisation might not have employment principles that endorse long-term stable employment or the provision of allowances. Once again, the pressures of localisation and uniformity require careful evaluation. This has been found in relation to employee share-ownership schemes and profit-sharing schemes. Government policy and promotion of financial participation plans, such as employee share-ownership and profit-sharing schemes, strongly influence the adoption of these schemes (Poole and Jenkins, 2013; Poutsma, 2006). In addition these schemes are more common in workplaces with employee involvement structures.

Employee involvement in decision-making has been linked to a number of organisational benefits, particularly improved employee productivity and organisational performance. It has been found that involvement can result in improved communication, cooperation, co-ordination of tasks, improved information sharing and flows, and reduced turnover (Poutsma et al., 2006; Zopiatis et al., 2014). Employee involvement is shaped by a range of national factors such as market forces, industrial relations, technology, regulations, policy environment, the financial system, and social forces (Boxall and Purcell, 2008). It is also influenced by organisational factors such as organisational size and workplace factors (Dundon and Gollan, 2007. Therefore when considering employee involvement in a global context, the issues of local forces and pressures for uniformity and consistency require attention. Although there is evidence for country of origin influences on patterns of employee involvement (Pyman, 2012), the nature of employee involvement will vary according to country and institutional factors (Marginson et al., 2010).

Cultural and linguistic differences may present a key challenge for team management, particularly when managing virtual teams (Klitmøller and Lauring, 2013). Differences in culture appear in a broad range of attitudes and values and may greatly increase the potential for a breakdown in team cohesiveness and productivity. Such differences may span a wide range of areas, including attitudes toward authority, teamwork, and working hours.

CHALLENGES OF GLOBALISATION

Just as the transformation of people management from personnel administration to HRM posed many challenges and opportunities to practitioners and theorists, so does the management of people in a globalised world (Jackson et al., 2013). Existing modes of conceptualising HRM, such as through contingency, configurational and universalistic frameworks have limited to capacity to explain the need to satisfy a variety of stakeholder requirements, rather than primarily shareholder requirements. This raises the need to reconsider the measures and metrics of organisational and HRM performance. Similarly, the most compelling opportunities are to consider HRM at a number of levels simultaneously – the national, organisational, and the individual – and to accommodate the complexities and ambiguities of doing this (Kramar, 2013).

In recent decades, significant demographic changes – such as increased participation of women, migrants, and older workers – have placed greater pressure on both governments and the private sector to initiate and implement creative solutions to train, integrate, and retain a rapidly changing and diverse working population. The scenario is further compounded by the on-going quest for competitive advantage while hiring temporary and part-time workers to respond to individual and organisational needs of flexibility.

As mergers, acquisitions, and joint ventures increase around the world, HRM will be expected to exercise cultural, institutional, and legal due diligence, in line with strategic organisational objectives, in the way it approaches and manages employees. This is especially true for Western MNCs that spread their operations or acquire companies across Asia, Latin America, Africa, and other parts of the developing world, where firms' cultural, institutional, and industrial practices may be much different (EIU, 2014).

BOOK'S OVERVIEW AND FOCUS

Bringing together eminent international scholars, this book places a premium on the critical thinking and analytical abilities that can be successfully applied to HRM. We take a different view of HRM theory and practice from that of often mechanically prescriptive orthodox texts. Our take on the theory and practice of HRM is far from US- or UK-centric: our choice of the topics as well as geographies covered in the text (that is, continental Europe and Asia-Pacific) is an attempt to situate the critical issues facing HRM in a global context.

Each chapter in this volume addresses a core topic and reflects the current state of critical scholarly activity in the field, highlighting some enduring theories and approaches and then pushing the boundaries of HRM beyond those ideas. Our approach differs most widely when we consider that the practice and theory of HRM involve a number of key issues, including but not limited to managing diversity, ethics, corporate social responsibility, national context, knowledge management, relationship between work and non-work, implementing HRM (which often requires managing change), understanding the expectations and motivations of individuals and groups, and the role of external factors, for example legal and regulatory requirements, in influencing HRM. We consider these topics to lie at the heart of real-life HRM situations, and we believe that a critical approach offers a more effective outcome. We identify and challenge assumptions, develop an awareness of the context, seek alternative ways of seeing a situation and relate these to real-world examples in contexts as diverse as Europe and the Asia–Pacific region.

Each chapter follows a common structure by first identifying learning outcomes, and then moving on to a discussion of fundamental theories and key concepts related to the chapter, an integration of contextual and critical insights with the HRM literature, and one or more case studies exemplifying the application of theory to the world of HRM practice.

Each case study is designed for students who are taking a course in HRM with a significant international component. The aim is to provide a dynamic example and critical illustration of the HRM theory that readers are studying. As a learning tool, Clegg et al. (1984) and Hoffman and Ruemper (1991) identify several advantages of the case study approach:

- For students, case studies provide an opportunity to think logically and imaginatively, to experiment, and to debate ideas free of risk.
- Cases provide an opportunity for experiential learning with particular reference to interpersonal skills and group work.
- Cases provide an opportunity to evaluate critically some of the theories covered in the textbook and on the course.
- A series of set case tasks typically provides an opportunity to improve a student's ability to write business communications.

The case studies we present in this book are expected to encourage students to integrate knowledge and skills relating to HRM and to avoid 'compartmentalising' or 'silo' thinking and action. They also encourage students to look for multicausality when examining workplace problems and solutions, to think across disciplines and subdisciplines, and to think logically. We hope that students and practitioners alike will find these cases useful for testing and developing human resources theories, stimulating a critical insight into and a contextual understanding of this subject.

STRUCTURE OF THE BOOK

There are 17 chapters in this book, and these are divided into three parts: The HRM Arena (five chapters), HRM in Practice (six chapters) and HRM and Contemporary Issues (six chapters). The first part discusses the broader issues and contextual factors within which HRM operates, focusing on issues such as contextual influences on HRM, strategic direction, HRM in MNCs, diversity as well as issues of ethnic and corporate social responsibility. The second part deals with practicalities of HRM focusing on human resource planning, job and work design, recruitment and selection, performance management and training and development. The third part focuses on contemporary issues facing HRM across the world such as talent, productivity, employee involvement, international assignments, global and migrant workers and the issues of work life balance and sustainability. A detailed description of the book's various chapters is provided below.

Part I: The HRM arena

Jawad Syed's chapter on 'Context-specific human resource management' (Chapter 1) focuses on contextual influences on HRM and how it may be designed taking into account institutional, cultural, socioeconomic and other contextual factors. The chapter begins with a literature review of the contextual forces that influence the design and practice of HRM. It also considers certain latent tensions between globalisation and HRM. The case study presents an empirical study of HRM practices in Brunei Darussalam. It describes the influence of the macro-environmental context on the design and implementation of HRM strategies, policies, and practices in government sector organisations. The case study reveals that culture, especially the Malay Islamic Monarchy ideology, plays a significant role in shaping HRM in Brunei.

In their chapter on 'A critical perspective on strategic human resource management' (Chapter 2), Fida Afiouni and Dima Jamali provide a critical assessment of strategic HRM (SHRM), shedding light on its differentiating attributes and theoretical foundations, as well as on the lingering gaps and challenges in this rapidly growing field. Their chapter shows that SHRM presents significant advances and new insights in relation to people management, but it

is still plagued by both conceptual ambiguity and a dearth of empirical support. These challenges, coupled with the difficulty of translating theory into practice, are possibly stumbling blocks in the way of a full-fledged maturation of SHRM and are fleshed out and discussed in detail in Chapter 2. The chapter also discusses how human resources can be a source of sustainable competitive advantage within a global context, and it offers a critical examination of choices and contingencies in the HRM field.

In her chapter on 'HRM in MNCs: A critical approach (Chapter 3), Julie Davies highlights decisions such as on standardisation and localisation of international human resource management, vertically and horizontally, that HR professionals make. The chapter considers the dual logics of local integration and responsiveness, hybridisation, and optimised forms of global best practice or guiding principles by drawing on theories of convergence, divergence, universalism, and contingency theory. The chapter also discusses the diffusion of ideas, postcolonial theory, impact of national institutional and cultural differences and cross-convergence. In particular, it explores the job roles and behaviours of global HR professionals and international HR departments.

Nicolina Kamenou-Aigbekaen and Jawad Syed's chapter on 'Diversity management in a global context' (Chapter 4) explains the concepts of managing diversity and equal opportunities in employment. Given the demographic transformation of the population and the labour force in many countries, workforce diversity is a major issue facing managers and organisations. There is, however, evidence of an application of unrelenting stereotypes and discriminatory attitudes and behaviours that not only permeate the workplace but are also found in abundance on a societal and institutional level. The authors introduce students to various forms of employment discrimination, as well as legislation in various countries to tackle discrimination. With respect to theorising diversity management, two key approaches are discussed: the business case approach and the social equity approach. The authors also discuss some methodological issues in conducting research on diversity and equal opportunity and present a case study on ethnic minority women in the UK.

In their chapter on 'HRM, ethics, and corporate social responsibility' (Chapter 5), Tracy Wilcox and Diannah Lowry discuss human resources practices from an ethical perspective. The authors identify how and why human resources activities have an ethical dimension and also highlight the connections between ethical human resources practices and ethical global business operations. In addition, the chapter identifies some key distinctions between ethical relativism (the view that the definition of right or wrong depends on culture, history, and the individual) and ethical pluralism (the view that there are multiple, possibly incompatible definitions of right or wrong that may be equally correct and fundamental), and describes some of the features of critical business ethics.

Part II: HRM in practice

In her chapter on 'Human resource planning' (Chapter 6), Cathy Sheehan explains how current changes in socio-economic circumstances require innovative responses and careful HRM planning. The author explains that, as a custodian of the people resource in organisations, it is the function of the HRM to assist in the development of human resource planning initiatives that match changes in the supply and demand for labour and also manage initiatives for attracting and retaining talent strategically rather than reactively. Sheehan's chapter broadly reviews approaches to human resource planning and also critically analyses some of the strategic responses to issues associated with the supply and demand of labour that impact on talent management.

Peter Holland, in his chapter on 'Job and work design' (Chapter 7), examines the development of modern job and work design to better understand the contemporary nature of work organisation. The chapter reviews the literature on work organisation and provides a contextual analysis for the development of 'modern' job and work design, explaining how it has already evolved and continues to evolve.

In her chapter on 'Recruitment and selection' (Chapter 8), Olivia Kyriakidou explores the classical theories and current research that underpin the three basic elements of a personnel selection system: (1) studying the job to be performed, (2) recruiting a pool of applicants for the job, and (3) selecting the 'best' people from the applicant pool. Such an exploration is enriched by international considerations and implications for recruitment and selection, with a special focus on expatriate managers. Finally, the author adopts a critical perspective that tries to reveal the ethical issues underpinning personnel staffing and questions the current emphasis on connecting selection practices with performance.

Jane Maley's chapter on 'Performance management' (Chapter 9) discusses an organisation's most critical procedures, that is, the performance management system. These systems are now widely and routinely used for many employees. Their use increased through the 1990s as a result of the pressures of globalisation, increased competition, and a greater analysis of all the characteristics of employee performance. Performance management systems were originally used for managers, professionals, and technical employees, but today they are frequently used to appraise staff at all levels in many parts of the world. The author explains the purpose, criteria and ethics of

performance management, and also considers approaches to and effective methods of conducting appraisals, the limitations of the process, and the value of multiple sources. The chapter includes various suggestions to help improve the performance management process and evaluates performance management in an international context. Finally, the chapter discusses the need for a critical evaluation of and future direction for performance appraisal.

In their chapter on 'Reward management' (Chapter 10), John Shields and Jim Rooney explain how reward strategies, programmes, and policies are structured in both domestic and international contexts. The chapter discusses the variety of reward possibilities and practices covered by the notion of 'total reward' and the different motivational and behavioural assumptions associated with particular types of reward. It also explains how social and cultural factors affect employees' perceptions of pay fairness and how these perceptions affect the design and effectiveness of pay programmes. Finally, the chapter explains the worth of a constructively critical (pluralist) approach to understanding reward management theory and practice.

Peter Murray's chapter on 'Training, development, and learning' (Chapter 11) discusses and explores a number of critical issues related to training, development, and learning in organisations. It does so by highlighting the differences between the terms, reflecting on older, more classical approaches to training compared with more contemporary and recent trends that are more situation- or context-specific. The latter mean that the older approaches to training, albeit useful, have to be rethought. More recent trends in global organisations, such as technological advances, human expectations of what constitutes a valuable job, the organisation's expectations related to capabilities that match strategic business needs, and increased social interaction, have meant that the older approaches are less valuable. The chapter explores the nuances and differences between individual and organisational learning, including, but not limited to, developing versus recruiting workers, needs assessments linked to training design and performance issues, various training and learning methods, the link between learning and knowledge, and critical issues within an international context. The chapter is designed to take the reader from existing normative and traditional views of training, development, and learning to a more critical creative view that is context-specific.

Part III: HRM and contemporary issues

In their chapter on 'Talent management' (Chapter 12), Stephen Swailes, Janet Handley, and Liz Rivers compare and critique definitions of talent management and also explain the reasons for the growth of corporate interest in talent management. The chapter discusses rational and critical approaches to talent management and also outlines the difficulties of identifying talent fairly and reliably.

Jawad Syed and Andrew Jenkins in their chapter on 'International assignments' (Chapter 13) explain the notion of international assignments, in relation to HRM in a global context and discuss how international assignments are different from domestic staffing. The chapter critically examines the nature and evolution of international assignments and also outlines the range of options available to organisations in terms of deployment of expatriates or local employees. It discusses the issues of expatriate selection and adjustment and also identifies some of the competencies, along with antecedents, needed for successful expatriation.

Amanda Pyman's chapter on 'HRM, productivity and employee involvement' (Chapter 14) deals with a critical evaluation of the relationship between employee involvement (EI) and productivity. The chapter focuses on direct and indirect means of EI, which can take a wide variety of forms. EI is management-initiated and management-led and has a number of objectives. Some examples of the objectives of EI are summarised for the reader. The chapter demonstrates that managements introduce EI for a variety of reasons, with the overarching objective of improving productivity and competitiveness.

In their chapter on 'Work–life balance in the twenty-first century' (Chapter 15), Nicolina Kamenou-Aigbekaen and Yu Fu engage in key debates on work–life balance through a global context perspective, acknowledging national and cultural differences in how work–life balance is perceived and how flexible working arrangements are negotiated. The chapter examines the diverse legal frameworks and workplace practices involved in dealing with work and employment, as well with rights for parents, carers, and so on. The experiences of social groups, including, among others, women, older workers, and ethnic minority groups, in relation to work–life balance issues are also explored. A range of work–life balance organisational initiatives and flexible working types are presented, together with the legal protection associated with these practices. A discussion of the social and economic benefits of a healthy, fulfilled workforce is presented, as is an evaluation of the costs of inaction by organisations and the government, such as the costs of high absenteeism and work-related stress.

In their chapter on 'Managing global and migrant workers' (Chapter 16), Chris Brewster, Michael Dickmann, Liisa Mäkelä, and Vesa Suutari recognise that the international workforce has existed since slaves built the pyramids. But international work has been increasing substantially in recent decades. With it, the interest in how to manage international workers, their talent, and global careers has grown. The chapter explores key forms of international work. The authors use the length of international assignment as their template and concentrate on international business travellers, short-term assignees, company-sponsored long-term expatriates, self-initiated expatriates, and global careerists. The chapter also discusses immigration-related mobility of labour. It investigates contextual, strategic, operational, and individual influences and puts a particular focus on how organisations can manage their international workers.

In her chapter on 'Sustainable HRM' (Chapter 17), Robin Kramar explains the factors contributing to the development of Sustainable HRM and discusses the role of contextual factors in shaping an understanding of Sustainable HRM. The chapter identifies the key features of each of main categories of Sustainable HRM, outlines the major characteristics of the emerging Sustainable HRM approach to management, and also discusses the measurement of the outcomes of Sustainable HRM.

In the next section, we provide a critical synthesis of the various topics and themes covered in the book and highlight a number of challenges and opportunities for HRM scholars and practitioners.

KEY THEMES IN HRM

HRM is not what it used to be – the developments of the last two to three decades have changed the face and practice of business. These changes have confronted managers with many opportunities and challenges, and nowhere are these opportunities and challenges more pronounced than in the area of HRM.

The chapters in this book highlight ten recurring themes that have emerged in HRM. These themes define the domain of HRM and confront academics and practitioners with many theoretical and practical issues. The chapters clearly highlight that these themes and issues are not mutually exclusive but interact and overlap. Among the most powerful themes to emerge include:

- the powerful role of factors in the external, international environment on business, management and HRM;
- a need to consider HRM at a number of levels, particularly at the macro or national level, the meso or organisational level, and the micro or individual level;
- the continuing debate surrounding the convergence and divergence of HRM practices across the globe;
- the framework of strategic HRM (SHRM);
- the theoretical explanations of the links between organisational performance and HRM practice, as

- captured in the universalistic, configurational, and contingency theories;
- the role of ethics in HRM including issues of corporate social responsibility and sustainability;
- debates about measuring the effectiveness of HRM;
- the difficulties surrounding the implementation and consistency of human resources policies within organisations;
- the need to manage workforce diversity and talent;
- the complexities of managing international assignments and global workforce.

Although scholars differ in their views about the extent to which HRM should serve different stakeholders, there is consistent agreement that the interests of the owners of an organisation are supported by HRM (Beer et al., 2015; Kramar et al., 2011). In their recent analysis of implications of the multistakeholder perspective for HRM, Beer et al (2015) highlight the need to consider a wider view of stakeholders and argue that while the HRM studies have given us much valuable learning, the subject has now reached a point where there is a need to take a more contextual, more multilayered approach founded on the long-term needs of all relevant stakeholders. During the last three decades, there have been developments, such as the policies of the World Trade Organisation and the European Union, that have championed business interests (Bakan, 2004; Gooderham et al., 1999). In addition, the deregulation of many economies has encouraged an emphasis on financial returns to shareholders.

This view is most sharply brought out in the SHRM approach, which represents a distinctive approach to the management of people doing the work of an organisation so that the organisation achieves competitive advantage as well as financial and, possibly, other results in both the short term and the longer term (Kramar et al., 2011; Zikic, 2015). However, the approaches to SHRM and the involvement of various stakeholders in the process of formulating and implementing HRM policy vary between organisations. Although there are converging forces of international legislation such as the International Labour Organisation Conventions and Declarations that have specific implications for employment relations (Kellerson, 1998), the enactment of such laws, the roles of trade unions and governments and their agencies are not consistent across national contexts. For instance, in private sector companies in the USA, trade unions play a more limited role in HRM formulation than they do in private sector organisations in some Australian industries. Other contextual factors such as culture and values are equally relevant. For example, based on their comparative study of work-related attitudes and organisational change in post-socialist countries, Alas and Rees (2006) highlight

that HRM practices are inextricably linked to conceptions surrounding culture and society, as well as to variables such as job satisfaction and organisational commitment.

In this book, Chapter 1 provides useful frameworks that identify aspects of the 'macro-environment'. This chapter argues that HRM strategies and practices need to be understood in the context of their legal and political, economical, sociocultural, and technological environments. This theme is consistent with the institutional theory proposing that the institutional environment, consisting of regulative, normative, and cultural-cognitive aspects and their activities, will influence the organising principles and shape the behaviour of stakeholders in an economy and labour market (Di Maggio, 1988; Reay and Hinings, 2009). This does not, however, preclude complexity in the environment, which enables the coexistence of institutions with competing approaches; this complexity is reflected throughout many of the other chapters of the book.

An explicit acknowledgement of these macro-contexts provides insights into the convergence/divergence debate. Although globalisation of business, culture, information transfer, technology, and international standards has occurred and has contributed to some convergence of HRM, the chapters in this book demonstrate that the particular arrangements in national economies and societies are effective in maintaining divergent HRM policies in different countries. This is clearly brought out in the chapters on 'Performance management' and 'Reward management' (Chapters 9 and 10, respectively), which identify the influential role of cultural factors in the conduct and process of evaluating performance and designing rewards. These chapters also highlight the difficulties of conducting evaluations and designing reward strategies in an international context, particularly in multinational corporations.

A very strong theme running through the book is the importance of understanding HRM in terms of not only the macro-environment, but also the meso-organisational and micro-individual levels. This approach enables us to consider the influence of collective factors operating within the organisation, such as teams, people on different terms of engagement (for example, subcontractors) and employees, as well as individual differences and characteristics. By acknowledging the influence of these three levels, it is possible to explicitly think about the influence of nonrational responses and influences on the development and implementation of HRM policies and practices (Syed and Özbilgin, 2009). Such an approach enables explanations for the difficulties associated with implementing HRM policies, which are frequently based on assumptions about individuals being rational rather than complex social, emotional, and political creatures. It enables a consideration of the rhetoric of HRM (Legge, 1995) and the reality of HRM. The chapter on training, development, and learning (Chapter 11) implicitly acknowledges the influences of these three levels, while other chapters such as those on diversity (Chapter 4) and human resource planning (Chapter 6) explicitly use this framework.

The book clearly highlights the fact that management adopts varies approaches to HRM in different organisations, as well as for different employees in the same organisation. Managers therefore make choices about HRM policies and practices. Two approaches that are often referred to either explicitly or implicitly are the 'hard' HRM and the 'soft' HRM approaches. Hard HRM focuses on the development of HRM strategies that further business strategy and consistently support its achievement. Soft HRM, however, focuses on using HRM to develop employee commitment, flexibility and highly competent staff. An acknowledgement of the various HRM approaches highlights how HRM policies and practices are not value-neutral; instead, they involve making choices about the development of policies that have different outcomes for the various stakeholders of an organisation, and different ethical implications for these stakeholders and the broader society.

The chapter on HRM, ethics and CSR (Chapter 5) provides the basis for considering the ethical dimensions of all areas of HRM and reveals some of the assumptions embedded in HRM practices. It also emphasises that ethical practice is broader than just applying to current employees and the current generation: it also involves taking future generations and world ecology into account. When this broad approach to HRM is adopted, it has implications for the nature of the metrics used to measure the effectiveness of HRM policies and practices (Syed and Kramar, 2009). Metrics will also vary according to the theoretical approaches that are used to explain the link between HRM and organisational performance. These metrics could include a range of mediating factors that, according to the theories, will influence business performance. The chapter on Strategic HRM (Chapter 2) discusses the ambiguity surrounding performance metrics.

A number of the chapters, particularly 'A critical perspective on strategic human resource management', refer to three popular theoretical explanations known as the universalistic, the contingency, and the configurational or resource-based views. These theories explain the link between HRM and organisational performance and focus on business outcomes as measures of organisational performance. These theoretical explanations are not, however, mutually exclusive. They also accord alignment with business strategy and other mediating factors different weights of influence. For example, according to the configurational view, HRM policies and practices are critically important for developing a unique culture that is unique and inimitable. Although culture is the mediating factor in this approach, behaviours required to achieve the strategy are frequently identified by writers on contingency as the mediating factor. The universalistic approach is somewhat diverse and incorporates writers on high-performance work systems, 'high-involvement management' and 'high-commitment management'. According to these writers, particular HRM practices such as sharing information, teamwork, involving employees in decision-making and selective hiring are able to develop employee motivation and commitment (Boxall and Purcell, 2008), and these will contribute to organisational outcomes.

These theories are based on assumptions about the economy, organisations, and individuals that are similar to the assumptions informing the SHRM framework. All of these theories and the SHRM framework itself assume that people are value-creating assets, that they are rational and that they can be influenced by HRM policies and practices. In reality, however, people are often irrational, emotional, political and social individuals (Kramar, 1992; Thory, 2013). People also have qualities that are ignored by these explanations, such as passion, spirituality, and creativity (Zappala, 2010). Similarly, these theories are framed within the context of a mechanical view of organisations, rather than a view that sees organisations as organic, nonlinear, evolving, and one form of a complex adaptive system. Finally, the explanations are framed within the context of a neoliberal economy in which the interests of the owners of the business are accorded priority over those of other stakeholders.

Ideas about the nature of individuals and the implications for HRM developed during the twentieth century, and these ideas are addressed in some of the chapters. Although the complex motivations and needs of individuals were identified in classical approaches to motivation, the contemporary complexities are not captured or explicitly addressed in the approaches that inform the theory and frameworks of HRM.

A major theme emerging from this book concerns the variety of stakeholders who have interests in HRM and its outcomes. For instance, stakeholders such as employees, the community, and governments have a stake in the outcomes. The pluralist view confronts the unitarist view that informs most of the theoretical frameworks on HRM. This pluralist view highlights possibilities that different stakeholders could have different interests and/or different priorities. The chapters highlight that it is essential to adopt a pluralist view when considering HRM in a global environment. In particular, the chapters on 'Diversity management' (Chapter 4), 'Work–life balance in the twenty-first century' (Chapter 15), 'HRM, ethics, and corporate social responsibility' (Chapter 5), 'Talent management' (Chapter 12), 'International assignments' (Chapter 13) and 'Managing global and migrant workers'

(Chapter 16) indicate that when HRM operates in an international labour market and a global business, it is essential to adopt a pluralist view.

The chapters in this book highlight a number of challenges and opportunities for scholars and practitioners of HRM. The development and growth of business, especially developments emerging from globalisation and technological advances, suggest that the existing approaches to HRM require re-evaluation. In addition, ecological developments and the impact of business on the environment raise issues about appropriate measures of organisational performance and whether the focus and priority should remain on financial measures of success. It also raises debates about the time frames that should be used to assess organisational outcomes – should the focus be predominantly on short-term outcomes, or would it be more appropriate to consider outcomes in the longer term? These challenges have implications for both scholars and practitioners.

Similarly, the transformation of people management to SHRM and the development of universalistic, contingency, and configurational theories have a limited capacity to explain the role of HRM in satisfying stakeholder requirements in the twenty-first century. These theories adopt a narrow view of the contribution of HRM to organisational outcomes and their impact on a range of stakeholders. This raises a need to reconsider the measures and metrics of not only organisational performance but also the performance and effectiveness of HRM.

The opportunities raised for scholars and practitioners of HRM are numerous. The most compelling opportunities are the need to consider HRM at a number of levels simultaneously – national, organisational, and individual – and to integrate these levels into a framework acknowledging the complexities of individuals, the diverse processes and cultures in organisations, and the varying institutional arrangements operating in different national contexts. The ability to do this will become even more important as business continues to internationalise and companies need to manage global workforces. This provides practitioners and scholars with the opportunity to integrate a wide range of knowledge available from disciplines as diverse as psychology, chaos theory, politics, and economics.

The book also challenges the traditional terrains of international HRM (IHRM) and HRM. It highlights that the globalisation of business has also globalised HRM. Although this book does not explicitly deal with the difference between IHRM and HRM, it does reveal the fact that global HRM is not synonymous with IHRM. This poses further exciting opportunities for HRM scholars to recast the scope of HRM and its many representations.

We anticipate that this book will provide insights into the framing and operation of HRM in a global environment. Although not all organisations have a global workforce, all organisations now operate in a global, international labour market. This raises the opportunity for HRM to be reconceptualised, and provides many wonderful opportunities for scholars and practitioners.

CIPD MAPPING OF THE BOOK

Table 1 provides a mapping of the book chapters for the professional HRM areas outlined by the Chartered Institute of Personnel and Development (CIPD, 2016). It outlines key learning outcomes of each area and links them to relevant chapters in this book. It sets out what students need to do (activities) and what they need to know (knowledge) for each area of the HR Profession.

KEY FEATURES OF THE BOOK

Here is a brief overview of key features of this book:

Extent

With a total of 17 chapters, the book is designed for a 12-lecture course in HRM which may also be expanded to 24 lectures depending upon the choice and depth of topics covered. Some competitor texts can be quite encyclopaedic in their coverage of the minutiae of HRM, and students can get lost in the detail. Lecturers consistently say that HRM textbooks go into too much detail and students lose sight of what is important. In contrast, some other texts miss out on certain key topics relevant to HRM in the current global era, such as the need for contextualising HRM and the issues of diversity and sustainability. The present book is a manageable length – leaving out excessive detail on the lifecycle of an employee and focusing instead on contemporary debates in HRM – and will help students to pick out the key areas of importance. It also responds to a growing trend for modules to be shortened to one term or semester. This means that lecturers only have about 11 to 12 weeks teaching and so find it impossible to cover all of the material contained in a large textbook. Lecturers often complain that new editions grow as new material is added but little is removed. In light of extensive feedback received from students and instructors, a few topics have been updated or removed while new topics such as managing global and migrant workers, sustainable HRM, international assignments, and talent management have been incorporated in the present text.

Table 1 Professional area map of the book

CIPD's professional area / theme	Key learning outcomes	Chapters
HRM in Context	Understand the contemporary business and external environment within which HR professionals work; the extent to which organisational and HR strategies and practices are shaped by and developed in response to internal and external environmental factors; examine demographic, social, legal, technological and international trends and how they shape and impact on organisational and HR strategies and practices.	1, 3, 4, 13 and 16
Resourcing and Talent Planning	Ensure that the organisation has the right resources, capability, and talent to achieve immediate and strategic ambitions now and in the future.	6, 8 and 12
Organisational Design	Ensure the organisation is appropriately designed to deliver maximum impact in the short and long term.	7, 2 and 17
Performance and Reward	Help create and maintain a high-achieving organisation culture by delivering programmes that reward and recognise key employee capabilities, skills, behaviours, experience and performance, and ensure that reward systems are market-relevant, fair and cost-effective.	9 and 10
Learning and Development	Build individual and organisational capability and knowledge to meet current and strategic requirements and create a learning culture to embed capability development.	11 and 12
Organisation Development	Identify organisational and individual capability requirements and align strategy, people and processes to optimise effectiveness and achieve organisation goals. Design interventions to drive the appropriate culture, behaviours, skills, and performance and provide insight and leadership on change management strategy, planning and implementation.	11, 2 and 9
Employee Engagement	Ensure that the individual and collective relationship between the organisation and its employees are managed appropriately within a clear framework underpinned by organisation, culture, practices, polices and, ultimately, by relevant law.	14 and 1
Employee Relations	Ensure that the individual and collective relationship between the organisation and its employees are managed appropriately within a clear framework underpinned by organisation, culture, practices, polices and, ultimately, by relevant law.	14, 9, 10, 15 and 4
Service Delivery and Information	Ensure customer-focused HR service delivery excellence across the entire employee lifecycle, applying exceptional process and project management to enable effective and cost-efficient HR service delivery; provide the organisation with meaningful analytics to enable business improvement.	15, 2, 6 and 9
HR Management, Development and Leadership in Practice	Review and critically evaluate major contemporary research and debates in the fields of HRM and human resource development (HRD). Promote professionalism and an ethical approach to HRM/D practice in organisations. Develop insights into the creation and delivery of effective HR strategies, practices and solutions in different national and global organisational contexts. Evaluate theories of employee involvement and productivity. Understand the roles of flexible working and work life balance in organisations. Understand ethical and legal obligations, such as diversity, social responsibility and sustainability.	Introduction, 2, 5, 1, 6, 7, 8, 9, 10, 11 and 17
Developing Skills for HRM	Develop research and generic study skills in the field of general and HR management. Develop students' interpersonal and management skills to enable them better to lead and influence others more effectively through enhanced IT proficiency and better management of organisational information, people and other resources. Display an enhanced understanding of the role of leaders in ethically managing people and act ethically and professionally with a demonstrated commitment to leadership and management practice	Case studies, news reports and critical thinking boxes in chapters 1-17
Investigating Business Issues from a Human Resources Perspective	Critically analyse and discuss existing literature, contemporary HR policy and practice. Identify and justify HRM issues that are of strategic relevance to contemporary organisations. Draw realistic and appropriate conclusions and make recommendations based on HRM case studies and organisational analysis.	Introduction, 2, 14, 15, 16 and 17

Academic rigour

In terms of academic rigour and latest research, the text has a thorough, academic approach, which complements its critical focus well. Chapters are supported by detailed references and guides for further reading, grounded in the latest research in HRM, and combine coverage of 'the basics' with a style that is user-friendly for upper-level undergraduates and postgraduates.

International case studies

In terms of international coverage, the case studies in this book – looking at HRM in companies based in countries around the globe – were also identified by reviewers as a major strength of the first edition against its competitors. The cases for the second edition are entirely new or updated and have a wide geographical spread, particularly in BRICS countries (Brazil, Russia, India, China, and South Africa). As with the first edition, there is a case study grid at the beginning of the book to highlight the global spread of cases.

Pedagogical framework

In terms of pedagogical framework, the academic approach in the text is combined with a thorough pedagogical framework designed to help students by checking understanding, developing critical thinking skills, and ensuring that the book is consistent and cohesive. Each chapter has a clear structure that outlines theory, context, and practical relevance and highlights 'key points' throughout the chapter. Students should be able to digest the theory before going on to examine a global situation or context to explore how the theory relates to a real-world situation. Students are challenged to consider alternative theoretical positions as they engage with the material. Each chapter then considers a range of practical recommendations that will help readers to see how theory and analysis can be used to form practical strategies that can help manage people.

In terms of pedagogical features and consistent structure, each chapter has:

- a list of learning objectives;
- a brief summary of chapter contents;
- an opening case study (The case studies provide a real-world context from an emerging or BRICS economy and discuss a key concept of HRM in practice, as relevant to the chapter. Written in a lively and accessible style, they pique interest and draw the reader into the chapter.);
- a critical thinking box (The boxes discuss a key issue or debate in HRM and challenge the student to think

critically about the topic. The feature is supported with critical questions to stimulate debate and encourage reflection);
- a class activity/exercise (These boxes stimulate action-oriented interaction with the material, help the students apply theory to a real-life situation, and test their understanding of what they have read. They are engaging and action-orientated and help develop transferable skills);
- 'In the News' (These highlight a contemporary HR topic from the mainstream media or web sites, demonstrate the real-world relevance of HRM, and link to topical contemporary themes);
- 'Stop and Reflect' (Thought-provoking questions that encourage students to think critically about an aspect of HRM);
- end of chapter case study (A detailed case examining a global company/example and a topic relevant to the chapter);
- end of chapter questions (for discussion and revision);
- further reading and web resources (These highlight areas for further study and research.);
- defined glossary terms (These define key terms from the chapter.).

By virtue of the range of topics as well as the geographical regions covered in the theoretical discussions and practical examples offered in the various chapters, we believe that this volume will be equally beneficial for undergraduate and postgraduate students in business and management studies, particularly those pursuing a major in HRM. Courses on HRM or/and employment relations or/and international HRM are generally compulsory in undergraduate and postgraduate management programmes across a number of universities in the UK, Australia, and other countries. This book will be useful for students enrolled on such programmes.

Although the book is primarily designed for students, it will be of equal interest to research scholars as well as practitioners of HRM. Academic as well as governmental libraries and academic associations, such as the Chartered Institute of Personnel and Development, the Australian Human Resources Institute, and the Society for Human Resource Management, may be interested in procuring copies of this book.

In addition to those outlines above, the book has several important features:

- It has been specially designed to relate to HRM in the UK, continental Europe, Australia and Asia, but with many case studies and examples from BRICS countries, the book is accessible to a wider international audience.

- It is suitable for undergraduate and graduate teaching programmes on general HRM, as well as for specialist modules on critical HRM and international HRM.
- It is suitable as a core text for general business and management degrees, specialist HRM degrees and international business degrees. It is suitable for both undergraduate and postgraduate levels.
- It can be adopted as a core text on the following modules: second-year undergraduate HRM modules (general/introductory modules on business and management degrees and international business degrees); specialist HRM modules at the postgraduate level (MSc/PGDip); HRM modules in MBA programmes (the international angle will particularly appeal here, given the global orientation of MBA programmes); International HRM modules (UG and PG) where the topic coverage is largely HR principles with a global focus.
- It is an international text, written for an international audience, with the ability to be adapted for various countries and continents.
- It offers a critical perspective on HRM, integrating fundamental theories and practices of HRM with critical insights.
- Original case studies provide critical and contextual insights into HRM practice.
- The text is jargon-free but deals with cutting-edge research, and it is easily accessible to scholars from non-English-speaking backgrounds.
- The book has a logical structure and pedagogy that is useful for teachers, students and practitioners alike.
- Contributions have been made by eminent scholars in the field.
- There is a common structure for all the chapters.

With a view to reconnecting a critical HRM perspective to the mainstream, we feel that the time is right for an in-depth evaluation of the phenomenon of HRM. Although old debates cannot be ignored, our concern is to provide a critical text integrating the fundamental theories and practices of HRM with critical insights and relevant practical examples from a variety of international contexts. This book is expected to stimulate a discussion of how to destabilise the prevailing orthodoxy in the field of HRM and deconstruct some aspects of the HRM paradigm. While the book has been designed and written primarily for students, we believe that it will be equally useful for academics and practitioners who want to understand and meet the increased challenges facing HRM in the current global crisis and beyond.

REFERENCES

ALAS, R. AND REES, C. (2006) Work-related attitudes, values and radical change in post-socialist contexts: A comparative study. *Journal of Business Ethics*, 68(2): 181–189.

ALI, F. AND KRAMAR, R. (2015) An exploratory study of sexual harassment in Pakistani organisations. *Asia Pacific Journal of Management*, 32(1): 229–249.

BAKAN, J. (2004) *The Corporation*. London: Constable.

BARTLETT, C. A. AND GHOSHAL, S. (1998) *Managing across borders: The transnational solution*. Boston, MA: Harvard Business School Press.

BARTRAM, T., STANTON, P., LEGGAT, S., CASIMIR, G. AND FRASER, B. (2007) Lost in translation: Exploring the link between HRM and performance in healthcare. *Human Resource Management Journal*, 17(1): 21–41.

BEER, M., BOSELIE, P. AND BREWSTER, C. (2015) Back to the future: Implications for the field of HRM of the multi-stakeholder perspective proposed 30 years ago. *Human Resource Management*, 54(3): 427–438.

BOXALL, P. AND PURCELL, J. (2015) *Strategy and Human Resource Management*. Basingstoke: Palgrave Macmillan.

CHATURVEDI, A. AND VERMA, P. (2014) India Inc allows staff to 'compress' work week, helping them balance work and home. *Economic Times*, November 18. Available at: http://economictimes.indiatimes.com/articleshow/45183825.cms.

CIPD (2015) Employee voice. *CIPD Factsheet*, December. Available at: http://www.cipd.co.uk/hr-resources/factsheets/employee-voice.aspx.

CIPD (2016) CIPD HR Profession Map. *Chartered Institute of Personnel and Development*. Available at: http://www.cipd.co.uk/cipd-hr-profession/cipd-hr-profession-map/default.html

CLEGG, C., KEMP, N. AND LEGGE, K. (1984) *Case Studies in Organisational Behaviour*. London: Paul Chapman Publishers.

DEN HARTOG, D. N., BOON, C., VERBURG, R. M. AND CROON, M. A. (2013) HRM, communication, satisfaction, and perceived performance: A cross-level test. *Journal of Management*, 39(6): 1637–1665.

DI MAGGIO, P. J. (1988) Interest and agency in institutional theory. In Zucker, L. (ed.) *Institutional Patterns and Organizations: Culture and Environment*. Cambridge, MA: Ballinger, pp. 3–21.

DORE, R. (1973) *British factory, Japanese factory: The Origins of National Diversity in Industrial Relations*. Los Angeles: University of California Press.

DUNDON, T. AND GOLLAN, P. (2007) Re-conceptualising voice in the non-union workplace. *International Journal of Human Resource Management*, 18(7): 1182–1198.

EIU (2014) Challenges for human resource management and global business strategy. *The Economist Intelligence Unit.* Available at: http://futurehrtrends.eiu.com/report-2014/challenges-human-resource-management/.

GERHART, B. AND FANG, M. (2005) National culture and human resource management: Assumptions and evidence. *International Journal of Human Resource Management*, 16(6): 971–986.

GOMES, E., ANGWIN, D., PETER, E. AND MELLAHI, K. (2013). HRM issues and outcomes in domestic mergers and acquisitions: A study of the Nigerian banking sector. In *Effective people management in Africa*. Basingstoke: Palgrave Macmillan, pp. 17–52.

GOODERHAM, P. N., NORDHAUG, O. AND RINGDAL, K. (1999) Institutional and rational determinants of organizational practices: Human resource management in European firms. *Administrative Science Quarterly*, 44(3): 507–531.

HOFFMAN, R. AND RUEMPER, F. (1991) *Organizational Behavior: Canadian Cases and Exercises*. Whitby, ON: Captus Press.

HOFSTEDE, G. (1980) *Culture's Consequences: International Differences in Work-Related Values*. Beverly Hills, CA: Sage.

JACKSON, G., KURUVILLA, S. AND FREGE, C. (2013) Across boundaries: The global challenges facing workers and employment research. *British Journal of Industrial Relations*, 51(3): 425–439.

KAY, J. (2011) *Obliquity: Why Our Goals Are Best Achieved Indirectly*. Profile Books.

KELLERSON, H. (1998) The ILO declaration of 1998 on fundamental principles and rights: A challenge for the future. *International Labour Relations Review*, 137(2): 223–235.

KLITMØLLER, A. AND LAURING, J. (2013) When global virtual teams share knowledge: Media richness, cultural difference and language commonality. *Journal of World Business*, 48(3): 398–406.

KRAMAR, R. (1992) Strategic human resource management: Are the promises fulfilled? *Asia Pacific Journal of Human Resources*, 30(1): 1–15.

KRAMAR, R. (2013) The challenges and opportunities for human resource management in a globalised world. *European Financial Review*, December 2. Available at: http://www.europeanfinancialreview.com/?p=1260.

KRAMAR, R., BARTRAM, T. AND DE CIERI, H. (2011) *Human Resource Management in Australia*. Sydney: McGraw-Hill.

LEGGE, K. (1995) *Human Resource Management: Rhetoric and Realities*. London: Macmillan Business.

MACEWAN, A. (1999) *Neo-liberalism or Democracy? Economic Strategy, Markets, and Alternatives for the 21st Century*. Zed Books.

MALEY, J. (2012) Performance management. In Kramar, R. and Syed, J. (eds) *Human Resource Management in a Global Context: A Critical Approach*. Basingstoke: Palgrave Macmillan, pp. 211–242.

MARGINSON, P., EDWARDS, P., EDWARDS, T., FERNER, A. AND TREGASKIS, O. (2010) Employee representation and consultative voice in multinational companies operating in Britain. *British Journal of Industrial Relations*, 48(1): 151–180.

POOLE, M. AND JENKINS, G. (2013) *The Impact of Economic Democracy: Profit-Sharing and Employee-Shareholding Schemes*. Routledge.

POUTSMA, E. (2006) *Changing Patterns of Employee Financial Participation in Europe*. Nijmegen School of Management, Nijmegen.

POUTSMA E., KALMI, P. AND PENDELTON, A. (2006) The relationship between financial participation and other forms of employee participation: New survey evidence from Europe. *Economic and Industrial Democracy*, 27(4): 181–197.

PYMAN, A. (2012) Human resource management, productivity and employee involvement. In Kramar, R., and Syed, J. (eds), *Human Resource Management in a Global Context: A Critical Approach*. Basingstoke: Palgrave Macmillan, pp. 345–373.

RAVASI, C., SALAMIN, X. AND DAVOINE, E. (2015) Cross-cultural adjustment of skilled migrants in a multicultural and multilingual environment: An explorative study of foreign employees and their spouses in the Swiss context. *International Journal of Human Resource Management*, 26(10): 1335–1359.

REAY, T. AND HININGS, C. R. (2009) Managing the rivalry of competing institutional logics. *Organizational Studies*, 30(6): 629–652.

REICHE, B. S., LEE, Y. AND QUINTANILLA, J. (2012) Cultural perspectives on comparative HRM. In Brewster, C. and Mayrhofer, W. (eds), *Handbook of Research in Comparative Human Resource Management*. Cheltenham: Edward Elgar.

RUBERA, G., AND KIRCA, A. H. (2012) Firm innovativeness and its performance outcomes: A meta-analytic review and theoretical integration. *Journal of Marketing*, 76(3): 130–147.

RUBERY, J. AND GRIMSHAW, D. (2003) *The Organisation of Employment: An International Perspective*. London: Palgrave.

SHIELDS, J. (2012) Reward management. In KRAMAR, R., AND SYED, J. (eds), *Human Resource Management in a Global Context: A Critical Approach*. Basingstoke: Palgrave Macmillan, pp. 243–284.

SMITH, P. B., TORRES, C., LEONG, C. H., BUDHWAR, P., ACHOUI, M. AND LEBEDEVA, N. (2012). Are indigenous approaches to achieving influence in business organizations distinctive? A comparative study of guanxi, wasta, jeitinho, svyazi and pulling strings. *International Journal of Human Resource Management*, 23(2): 333–348.

SYED, J. AND KRAMAR, R. (2009) Socially responsible diversity management. *Journal of Management and Organization*, 15(5): 639–651.

SYED, J. AND METCALFE, B. D. (2015) In pursuit of Islamic akhlaq of business and development. *Journal of Business Ethics*, 129(4): 763–767.

SYED, J. AND ÖZBILGIN, M. (2009) A relational framework for international transfer of diversity management practices. *International Journal of Human Resource Management*, 20(12): 2435–2453.

THORY, K. (2013) A gendered analysis of emotional intelligence in the workplace issues and concerns for human resource development. *Human Resource Development Review*, 12(2): 221–244.

TROMPENAARS, F. AND HAMPDEN-TURNER, C. (1997) *Riding the Waves of Culture: Understanding Cultural Diversity in Business*. London: McGraw-Hill.

TRUSS, C. AND GRATTON, L. (1994) Strategic human resource management: a conceptual approach. *International Journal of Human Resource Management*, 5(3): 663–686.

VANCE, C. M. (2006) Strategic upstream and downstream considerations for effective global performance management. *International Journal of Cross Cultural Management*, 6(1): 3137.

VAUGHAN, E. (1994) The trial between sense and sentiment: A reflection on the language of HRM. *Journal of General Management*, 19(3): 20–32.

WHITLEY, R. (1992) Societies, firms and markets: The social structuring of business systems. In Whitley, R. (ed.), *European Business Systems: Firms and Markets in Their National Contexts*. London: Sage, pp. 5–45.

WILMOTT, H. (1993) Strength is ignorance; slavery is freedom: Managing culture in modern organizations. *Journal of Management Studies*, 30(4): 515–553.

ZAPPALA, G. (2010) *Beyond Corporate Responsibility: The Spiritual 'Turn' and the Rise of Conscious Business*. CSI Background Paper No. 6. Sydney: Centre for Social Impact.

ZIKIC, J. (2015). Skilled migrants' career capital as a source of competitive advantage: Implications for strategic HRM. *International Journal of Human Resource Management*, 26(10): 1360–1381.

ZOPIATIS, A., CONSTANTI, P. AND THEOCHAROUS, A. L. (2014) Job involvement, commitment, satisfaction and turnover: Evidence from hotel employees in Cyprus. *Tourism Management*, 41: 129–140.

part

1

The HRM Arena

1

CONTEXT-SPECIFIC HUMAN RESOURCE MANAGEMENT

Jawad Syed

LEARNING OUTCOMES

After reading this chapter, you should be able to:

➤ Understand the importance of local context and its implications for HRM
➤ Identify the external contexts that affect the policies and actions involved in HRM
➤ Learn how to design context-appropriate HRM
➤ Understand the pros and cons of a cross-cultural transfer of HRM practices
➤ Identify future directions for contextualising HRM.

SUMMARY OF CHAPTER CONTENTS

➤ **Opening Case Study**: Employees' rights and labour disputes in China
➤ Introduction
➤ Contextualising HRM in a global village
➤ Contextual influences on HRM
➤ Critical discussion and analysis
➤ Conclusion
➤ **End of Chapter Case Study**: HRM in Brunei's public sector
➤ For discussion and revision
➤ Glossary
➤ Further reading
➤ Web resources
➤ References

Opening Case Study **Employees' rights and labour disputes in China**

Workers in China do not have much choice when it comes to forming or joining a trade union. There is only one lawful trade union – the government-controlled All China Federation of Trade Unions (ACFTU) – that acts as the federating and representative body of all local union organisations. A 2012 report published by the Brussels-based International Trade Union Confederation lamented that with the majority of their officials directed and indirectly appointed by the central government, the level of autonomy of most local unions in China remained low. The report alleged that many of the unions were controlled by factory managers. This in turn results in tight governmental and organisational control over unions' stances on issues of concern to employees. In January 2016, Chinese authorities detained seven labour activists in the southern province of Guangdong, alleging that they were 'inciting workers to go on strike', and 'disturbing public order'. In recent years, labour disputes have arisen in some industries due to an increase in workers' layoffs. The phenomenon is particularly evident in Guangdong province where a total of 412 strikes were recorded in 2015. The total number of strikes across the country grew from 1,379 incidents in 2014 to a total of 2,741 in 2015. The government data also indicate an upsurge in labour disputes, with the country's Ministry of Human Resources and Social Security stating that there were 1.56 millions registered cases in 2014, an increase of 4.1 per cent compared to that of 2013. Overall, this indicates how China's unique sociopolitical and legal context affects employees' ability to safeguard their interests, particularly during economic recession and layoffs (Chan, 2016). Cheng Zhenqiang, the lawyer representing Zeng Feiyang, one of the activists arrested in Guandong, suggests that while the present crackdown is related to the economic downturn, the authorities have never really felt easy about nongovernmental organisations, especially labour rights NGOs (Clover, 2016).

Questions

1   How does China's unique context affect the shape of employment relations in that country?
2   Identify two or three key differences between employees' rights and choices in China and those in a Western democratic country?

INTRODUCTION

Human resource management (HRM) as a management concept originated in the 1950s in North America with the seminal works of Drucker (1954) and McGregor (1957), and it has subsequently been adopted and widely used across the world. HRM is defined as the managing of people within employer–employee relationships. This usually involves maximising employees' performance (Harris, 2002), and effective utilisation of human resources to enhance productivity and other organisational outcomes. By the 1980s, the concept of HRM had gained wider international recognition, particularly in English-speaking countries (Sparrow and Hiltrop, 1994; CIPD, 2015).

Around the mid-80s, the concept arrived in the UK. The term 'human resources' captured much interest: it seemed to suggest that employees were an asset or resource, but at the same time it also appeared to emphasise employee commitment and motivation (CIPD, 2015).

The theories and practices of HRM have since made inroads into continents other than North America and Europe, such as their adoption and integration into Asia and Africa (see, for example, Bennington and Habir, 2003; McCourt and Foon, 2007; Syed et al., 2014; Zhou et al.,

2012). However, despite more than two decades of academic research and practice, the HRM literature has been only partly successful in offering a universal solution for the complexities of managing people that can transcend national, institutional, cultural, and economic divides. Özbilgin's (2004) survey of academic scholarship and journals in the field of international HRM points towards a limited geographical coverage by the 'mainstream' scholarship in HRM, which remains dominated by North American and Western European theorisations and empirical studies. In other words, HRM is not culturally neutral. The limited geographical reach of HRM is also highlighted by Baruch (2001) and Clark et al. (2000) who have argued for an ethical duty on the part of HRM scholars and journals to widen their geographical spread. Critical Thinking 1.1 highlights the parochial nature of HRM resulting from its geographical and theoretical limitations.

Although HRM is today an international phenomenon, the nature and scope of its links with local institutions, labour laws, corporate strategies, and trade unions vary greatly across national borders (Özbilgin, 2004). Despite the fact that the mainstream HRM theories, which were overwhelmingly formulated in management schools in North America (see, for example, Beer et al., 1985; Schuler and Jackson, 1987) and the UK (Storey, 1992) in the 1980s, quickly found their way to other developed countries (Maurice et al., 1986; Tung, 1993) and later to developing countries (Budhwar and Debrah, 2001), few models of HRM found in the mainstream literature derive from outside the English-speaking world. This is despite an increasing consensus that mainstream human resources theories and practices are inadequate in addressing the human resource issues facing international and multinational companies (Clark et al., 2000). As a result, and also because of a growing pursuit of effective ways of managing human resources in cross-cultural contexts (Taylor et al., 1996), it is important to develop a contextualised understanding and operationalisation of HRM.

For example, Zhou et al. (2012) offer a contextualised approach to examine the structures, measures, and predictive value of HRM in China. Synthesising the established HRM concepts in the Western literature with the indigenous practices in the Chinese workplace, the authors contextually adapt the conceptual components of commitment-based, collaboration-based, controlled-based, and contract-based HRM systems. Using data from 224 organisations, their study indicates a pluralistic structure of the HRM systems in China. The interest of scholars and practitioners in this topic is expected to grow further due to the relevance of issues such as cross-national and comparative HRM, expatriate management, and diversity management (Caligiuri, 1999).

This chapter begins with a literature review on the adoption and implementation of HRM and the contextual forces that influence it. We also consider certain latent tensions between globalisation and HRM. The case study at the end of the chapter presents a real-life example of HRM practices in Brunei Darussalam, describing the influence of the macro-environmental context on the design and implementation of HRM strategies, policies, and practices in government sector organisations.

(?) **Critical Thinking 1.1 Parochialism in the HRM literature**

In the 'mainstream' English-language texts on HRM, there are hardly any references to resources in other languages (Özbilgin, 2004; Sheldon et al., 2014). Exceptions to this rule are some European languages, for example French-, German- and Spanish-language publications, which are very occasionally cited in English-language texts. The inclusion of materials not written in English is hardly encouraged and is often left to the linguistic competence of individual authors. As a consequence, the mainstream writing in the field of HRM remains influenced and dominated by the English-speaking world.

Adler (1991) refutes any claims of universal reach and offers the notion of 'parochialism' in management writing. Clark et al. (1999) identify two forms of parochialism in the international HRM texts: (1) that a sole reliance on English-language sources poses a major challenge; and (2) that the texts often fail to acknowledge the methodological complexities of studying cross-national and international management issues. The limiting impact of the English language appears to be the most insidious as it simply demarcates our knowledge of and imagination related to HRM practice to those geographies where the English language is spoken.

Similarly, the difficulty of formulating overarching conceptual frameworks, theoretical models, and critical approaches is a recurring theme in the international HRM literature. Large-scale empirical studies in this field are rare, and such studies come with long descriptions of the limitations of their method and analysis. However, due to their rarity, great significance is attributed to the studies that are available, and their findings are often overstated, misinterpreted, or used out of context. For example, although Hofstede's work in the 1960s and 1970s challenged the assumption that the theoretical frameworks developed in the USA would be universally applicable (Schneider, 2001), Hofstede's IBM studies were later quoted as a clear indicator of the convergence and divergence of management practices, without much questioning of the nature of his study. Recently, Chung et al. (2014) through their study of nine major Korean MNEs' approaches to subsidiary-HRM, argued that the firms pursue hybridisation through a blending of localisation and global standardisation across various HRM practice areas.

Questions

1 What are the implications of the dominance of English-language literature for theories and practices in HRM?
2 How can scholars and practitioners of HRM benefit from the literature on HRM that has been published in languages other than English?

Source: Adapted and updated from Özbilgin (2004)

CONTEXTUALISING HRM IN A GLOBAL VILLAGE

Global integration has driven dramatic changes in the economic and institutional contexts of HRM. Globalisation refers to the shift to a more integrated and interdependent world economy (Hill, 2009; also see Afiouni et al., 2014). It focuses on the maximisation of profits and, as an economic driver, has had a significant effect on the way in which human resources are managed. Globalisation has also changed the image of a company. Companies have become multinational, each one seeking to attain the competitive advantage, and the human resources of a company may just be the key to that. For this reason, HRM policies are changing in order to better respond to different cultural and institutional contexts.

Context is multilayered, multidimensional, and interwoven (Collin, 2007), and different contexts may have dynamic and divergent influences on the organisation of work within their sphere of influence. Globalisation has steadily and gradually created a world in which:

> barriers to cross-border trade and investment are declining; material culture is starting to look similar the world over; and national economies are merging into an interdependent, integrated global economic system. (Hill, 2009: 4)

During current times, when the world economy and businesses are shaped and structured by the process of globalisation, it is imperative to understand and contextualise the policies and practices of HRM.

Although it is no longer possible to divide the world economy into separate, distinct national economies isolated from foreign markets and influences, it would be wrong to ignore the fact that employment relationships in almost all countries remain largely shaped by national systems of employment legislation and the cultural contexts in which they are operationalised. Critical Thinking 1.2 highlights the case of varying perspectives on working hours in the European Union (EU).

Although factors such as culture, history, and language underlie much of the variation in management practices, the practice of HRM is, more than that of any other business function, closely linked to national culture (Gaugler, 1988). Culture can mean many different things for people with different backgrounds. Culture, according to Tylor (1924: 1), is 'that complex whole which includes knowledge, belief, art, morals, law, custom, and any other capabilities and habits acquired by man as a member of society'. Within employment contexts, there is ample evidence that people's behaviours are affected by specific national cultures. Hofstede (1991) suggests that the

significance of national culture is that most inhabitants of a country share the same mental programme. Based on that, other researchers have sought to discover to what extent individuals' national culture influences their way of working and thinking and to identify how people in different countries may have a collective programming, that is, a predisposition to behave in a certain way (Stredwick, 2005).

Although globalisation is pervasive, it is not without serious criticism. Critics argue that globalisation has demoted national governments as regulators of the free market system (Chomsky, 1999). Among other things, globalisation may at times create inequality and environmental challenges. In 1996, the United Nations reported that the assets of the world's 368 billionaires exceeded the combined incomes of 45 per cent of the planet's population (Faux and Mishel, 2001). The Kyoto Protocol in 1997 and subsequent agreements at the Copenhagen climate summit in 2009 have highlighted issues (the need to reduce emissions of carbon dioxide and greenhouse gases) that directly affect the behaviour of organisations and countries. Organisations will lobby their governments to prevent the ratification of such treaties and lessen other external pressures that may affect their economic interests. For example, in 2002, Canada potentially faced unemployment losses through plant closures and costs in the manufacturing sector relating to curbing their emissions (Chase, 2002). When firms seek foreign investment or outsourcing to take advantage of economies of scale, lay-offs of workers in the home country may drain the economy through welfare benefits, and the demand for cheaper services in the host country of globalising firms may entail making adjustments in the local labour markets.

Globalisation has created dynamic alternatives for multinational firms. Corporations can outsource production and services to more economically viable locations, allowing multinational enterprises to drive down costs and increase their efficiency. For example, several clothing giants in the UK and the USA now outsource much of their manufacturing to South Asia, where production costs are much lower. And the displacement of workers caused by transferring resources away from Europe to Asia is not occurring just in the clothing industry. Many telecommunication firms too are transferring their back-office operations to India and other countries where costs are cheaper. This adversely affects the labour market in home countries that may face unemployment of the manual working classes.

In recent years, it has become increasingly evident that the global economic crisis that began in 2008 may leave many nations in recession. Many firms have reacted to this by making thousands of workers redundant, especially in

---

(?) Critical Thinking 1.2 Geographical variation in philosophy

Scholars and scientists list a large number of variations between countries and point towards a 'wide diversity in philosophies of people management' (Price, 1997: 122; Kaufman, 2016). When comparing one country with another, certain tasks that need to be completed within a line of work are given different priorities and are completed in a different way (Price, 1997). An example of this is the EU voting for a decree stating that its Member States should introduce legislation to decrease the number of working hours for employees. Every country then had to set a chosen number of hours, and it was apparent that the number of working hours thought suitable was different between different countries: the UK believed that 48 hours was reasonable, whereas France decided 35 hours was enough (Stredwick, 2005).

Questions

1   Why is it important to consider a country's sociocultural context when designing HRM?
2   What factors affect the number of working hours per week in a country?

---

sectors where the recession has hit hardest, for example financial services and the construction industry in 2009. This approach places pressure on organisations in terms of issues outside of their control, at times forcing them to relocate or restructure their operations. In these circumstances, it is essential to consider how HRM can be contextualised in its design and implementation.

CONTEXTUAL INFLUENCES ON HRM

This section highlights different contextual forces that may influence HRM – we will start with a discussion of sociocultural context. Hofstede (1980) identified five dimensions of culture, and culture serves as an umbrella for all other contexts: legal, political, economic, and technological contexts are all influenced by the role culture plays in a society. Noe et al. (2008) state that culture shapes people's respect and obedience for laws and regulations, hence affecting a country's legal and political system. And the way in which human capital and technology are valued by a particular society influences the economy of that country. Various HRM practices, such as recruitment and selection, training and development, compensation systems, performance appraisal, and the employment relationship, are affected by the macro-contextual factors that this section will cover (Table 1.1).

Table 1.1 suggests that the strategies and practices of human resources ought to be examined in a broader context and that social, legal, economic, political, and technological influences all have a different impact when putting HRM into a context. For example, the global economic crisis and the near collapse of the banking system in 2008 are powerful contextual events that affect both national economies and organisations. Macro-contextual analysis

Table 1.1 An organisation's macro-environment

Legal and political factors	Economic factors
National legislation (current and future)	Home economy
International legislation	Trends in the economy
Regulatory bodies and processes	Overseas economies
Government policies	General taxation
Government term and change	Taxation specific to the product/service
Trading policies	Seasonality issues
Funding, grants and initiatives	Market/trade cycles
Home market pressure groups	Specific industry factors
International pressure groups	Distribution trends
Ecological/environmental issues	Customer/end-user drivers
Wars and conflicts	Interest/exchange rates
	International trade and monetary issues

Sociocultural factors	Technological factors
Lifestyle trends	Information and communications
Demographics (age, gender, literacy)	Development of competing technology
Language	Associated/dependent technologies
Ethnicity/race	Replacement technology/ solutions
Religion/sect	Maturity of technology
Ethical issues	Manufacturing maturity and capacity
Social policy	Research funding
Technology	Technology legislation
Media views	Innovation potential
Consumer attitudes and opinions	Intellectual property issues
Company image	Global communications
Fashion, brand, role models	
Major events and influences	

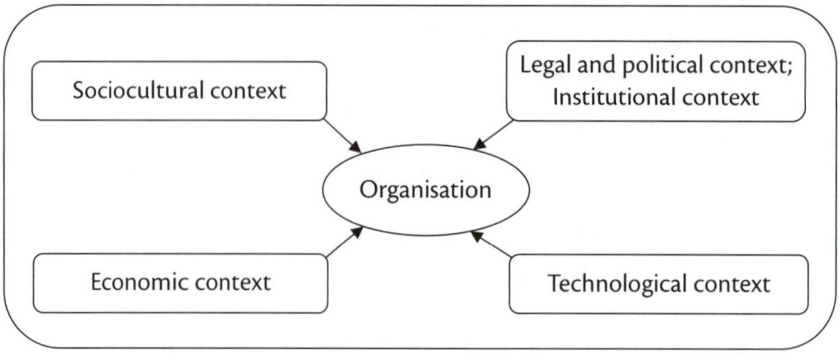

Figure 1.1 Key factors of the macro-environment

will lay the groundwork for an investigation of the extent to which and how local cultural and institutional contexts affect HRM (Figure 1.1).

Sociocultural context

Several elements in the sociocultural context have consequences for the design and efficacy of HRM. Culture dynamics and population demographics affect many aspects of the business environment. Rousseau (1990) argues that culture is a set of common values, beliefs, expectations and understandings that are obtained through socialisation; it is learnt and shared by the members of the community (Noe et al., 2008). Culture can be defined as a system of values and norms that are shared among a group of people (Hill, 2009). It is dynamic and changes over time, for example when a nation becomes more affluent.

According to Tayeb (2005), HRM is a 'soft' aspect of an organisation. Hence it is more influenced by culture than are financial and technical matters, which are considered to be the 'hard' aspects of an organisation. Culture has a significant role in attracting, motivating and retaining individuals in organisations. Other key areas that are usually influenced by culture are training, performance management, and compensation.

Cultural context may also explain differences in national practices in HRM. However, the intangible nature of culture makes it difficult to clearly map out its influences on HRM. Geert Hofstede (2001), a seminal writer on culture, refers to culture as the 'software of the mind'. Hofstede's (1984) six dimensions of culture (including a new dimension highlighted in Hofstede's later work) can influence management practices and the culture of organisations. The six categories are outlined in Table 1.2 and are also discussed below.

Table 1.2 Hofstede's cultural dimensions

Individualism	The degree to which individuals are integrated into groups.
Power distance	The extent to which the less powerful members of organisations and institutions accept and expect that power is distributed unequally.
Uncertainty avoidance	A society's tolerance for uncertainty and ambiguity.
Masculinity	The distribution of emotional roles between the genders.
Long-term orientation	Long-term-oriented societies foster pragmatic virtues oriented towards future rewards, in particular saving, persistence, and adapting to changing circumstances. Short-term-oriented societies foster virtues related to the past and present, such as national pride, respect for tradition, preservation of 'face', and fulfilment of social obligations.
Indulgence	Indulgence is a characteristic of a society that allows relatively free gratification of basic and natural human drives related to enjoying life and having fun.

Source: Adapted from http://geert-hofstede.com/national-culture.html. Accessed 28 January 2016.

Individualism versus collectivism

This dimension describes the strength of the relationship between individuals in a society, that is, the degree to which people act as individuals rather than as members of a group, or the extent to which the individuals are integrated into groups. In individualist cultures such as the USA, the UK, and the Netherlands, people are expected to look after their own interests and the interests of their immediate families. South-East Asian countries are more collectivist – they look after the interests of the larger community. Collectivist cultures tend to owe total loyalty to their group.

Low versus high power distance

This cultural dimension concerns hierarchical power relationships and refers to the unequal distribution of power. It describes the degree of inequality among people that is considered to be normal in different countries. For example, Denmark and Israel have a small power distance, whereas India and the Philippines have a larger one. Another obvious example is the way people are addressed. In a business context, Mexican and Japanese people always address each other using titles, for example Señor Smith or Smith-San, but in the USA, first names are preferred. The reason for this is to minimise power distance.

Low versus high uncertainty avoidance

This dimension deals with the fact that the future is not perfectly predictable. For example, in Singapore and Jamaica, cultures of weak uncertainty avoidance, individuals are socialised to accept uncertainty and take each day as it comes. However, Greek and Portuguese culture socialises people to seek security through technology, law, and religion.

Masculinity versus femininity

This dimension indicates the extent to which the dominant values in a society tend to relate to assertiveness and a greater interest in things than in people and quality of life. A 'masculine' culture is one in which dominance and assertiveness are valued, as is evident in the USA, Japan, and Venezuela, for example. A 'feminine' culture, as can be found in the Netherlands and Sweden, promotes values that have been traditionally regarded as feminine, leaning more towards quality of life and relationships in society. Hofstede (1984) notes that most South-East Asian countries fall the between the masculine and feminine poles.

Long-term versus short-term orientation

Long-term orientation focuses on the future and holds values in the present that will not necessarily provide an immediate benefit; examples of countries adopting this approach are Japan and China. The USA, Russia, and West Africa have a short-term orientation, being oriented towards the past and present and promoting respect for tradition and the fulfilment of social obligations.

Indulgence versus restraint

Indulgence is a feature of a society that allows or encourages frequent and unrestrained gratification of basic and natural human drives related to enjoying life and having fun. Restraint stands for a society that suppresses gratification of needs and regulates it by means of strict social norms.

It is, however, important to acknowledge the criticism raised by some authors who view Hofstede's conceptualisation of culture as static and essential. For example, Ailon (2008) and McSweeney (2002) caution against an uncritical reading of Hofstede's cultural dimensions, particularly because of their allegedly ethnocentric interpretations, which may lead to stereotyping.

Other scholars have identified additional dimensions of culture, including its informal, material or dynamic orientation (Adler, 1991; Ronen, 1994). They have compared HRM across countries and observed that cultural values and orientations are determinants of the differences found between them (see, for example, Arvey et al., 1991; Brewster and Tyson, 1991; Triandis et al., 1994; Brewster, 2007). However, culture may not explain all the differences in HRM found across countries (Lincoln, 1993; Jackson and Schuler, 1995) – such differences may also be an outcome of variations in economic and political conditions (see, for example, Carroll et al., 1988), laws and social policies (see, for example, Florkowski and Nath, 1993), industrial relations systems (Strauss, 1982) and labour market conditions (see, for example, Levy-Leboyer, 1994).

Cultural dimensions and differences have also been investigated by other scholars. For example, the GLOBE (Global Leadership and Organisational Behavior Effectiveness Research) project further explored the cultural differences initially identified by Hofstede (1980). The GLOBE Project studied 62 of the world's cultures and collected data from 17,300 middle managers in 951 organisations. The research identified nine cultural competencies and grouped the 62 countries into ten convenient societal clusters (Javidan and Dastmalchian, 2009). The nine GLOBE cultural competencies are described below.

- Performance orientation: the extent to which an organisation or society encourages and rewards group members for performance improvement and excellence.
- Assertiveness orientation: the degree to which individuals in organisations or societies are assertive, confrontational, and aggressive in social relationships.
- Future orientation: the degree to which individuals in organisations or societies engage in future-oriented behaviours such as planning, investing in the future, and delaying gratification.

- Humane orientation: the degree to which individuals in organisations or societies encourage and reward individuals for being fair, altruistic, friendly, generous, caring, and kind to others.
- Institutional collectivism: the degree to which organisational and societal institutional practices encourage and reward collective distribution of resources and collective action.
- In-group collectivism: the degree to which individuals express pride, loyalty and cohesiveness in their organisations or families.
- Gender egalitarianism: the extent to which an organisation or a society minimises gender role differences and gender discrimination.
- Power distance: the degree to which members of an organisation or society expect and agree that power should be unequally shared.
- Uncertainty avoidance: the extent to which members of an organisation or society strive to avoid uncertainty by reliance on social norms, rituals, and bureaucratic practices to alleviate the unpredictability of future events.

GLOBE's major finding and contribution is that leader effectiveness is contextual and is embedded in the societal and organisational norms, values, and beliefs of the people being led. Indeed, countries and regions vary based on their approach to and norms of several cultural dimensions of leadership, such as performance orientation, power distance, and collectivism.

Legal and political context

The legal and political context is represented by national laws and sociopolitical policies and norms. Given that culture is a codification of right and wrong that exists in a country's laws, political systems and laws often reflect what constitute the legitimate behaviour and norm of a particular country (Tayeb, 2005; Noe et al., 2008; Syed et al., 2014). These contexts have the power to shape the nature of the employment relationship and the way in which HRM practices and policies are enacted (Bratton and Gold, 2007). Jackson and Schuler (1995) claim that almost all aspects of HRM are influenced by political and legal regulations, and Noe et al. (2008) have identified training, compensation, hiring and lay-offs as some of the HRM practices most commonly affected by this context.

The UK, the USA, and most European countries, for example, place a strong emphasis on eliminating discrimination in the workplace; hence, equal employment regulations are put into effect. To focus on one example, in the UK the Sex Discrimination Act 1975, the Disability Discrimination Act 1995, the Race Relations Act 1976, the Employment Equality (Age) Regulations 2006, the Employment Equality (Religion or Beliefs) Regulations 2003, and the Equality Act (Sexual Orientation) Regulations 2007 are the laws that are included under the heading of Equality Employment Regulations. These regulations play a major role in developing HRM policies in relation to recruitment and dismissal procedures (Noe et al., 2008). Not only that, but pay and compensation can also be affected, with the setting of minimum wages for employees and

In the News Emiratisation of Etihad Airways

Since 2007, Etihad Airways has embarked on its Emiratisation programme which is aimed at replacing migrant workers with local workers of the United Arab Emirates (UAE). According to Etihad's vice-president of Emiratisation strategy, Ali Al Shamsi, it was not always easy to convince prospective employees to work the odd hours required by the aviation industry. 'As a culture, we weren't really in favour of letting our daughters and sons to work outside of normal hours, especially in the middle of the night,' Al Shamsi said. 'We started to communicate with families, and sometimes we would invite them to the airport to see the work environment, to see our employees wearing the Etihad Abaya, doing their job,' he said. Apparently, the programme has been successful. On 27 January 2016, the company announced that it now employed more than 3,000 Emirati staff, 40 per cent of whom were hired in 2015, including 26 Emirati executives and senior managers. The airline plans to employ a further 5,000 Emiratis by 2020. In reaching its long-term goal, the airline recently marked the graduation of 280 Emiratis from its development programme. More than 400 cadets are also enrolled in the Etihad Airways' cadet pilot programme (Adapted from Samoglou, 2016).

Questions

1 How does the legal and political context shape the Emiratisation programme in Etihad?
2 What are possible implications of Emiratisation for the Emirati and migrant workers?

a determination of the extent to which unions have the legal right to negotiate with the management.

One recent example of legal implications on employment is the legal challenge that the multinational online transportation network company Uber is currently facing from drivers who say that they should be recognised officially as workers at the company instead of being treated as self-employed. Uber drivers argue that the terms and conditions of their work with the company mean that they are not technically self-employed and should be entitled to a range of benefits that they currently do not receive. The case highlights the challenges associated with the growth of the so-called 'gig economy', where companies use self-employed workers rather than keeping people on their books (Osborne, 2016).

The role of the state and its political system is crucial in determining the nature of employment relations in a country. Tayeb (2005) points out that workers in Germany have a legal right to 'co-determination', in which their participation in management is ensured; therefore, any HRM matter must abide by such laws (Noe et al., 2008). The Brunei case study at the end of this chapter provides another example of how the state impacts on employment relations. Furthermore, the European Economic Community can also affect the political-legal system relating to HRM because it provides workers' fundamental social rights. These rights include freedom to be fairly compensated, freedom of association and collective bargaining, and equal treatment for men and women.

Legal influences affecting HRM practices can take the form of how local regulations affect the labour market (see Critical Thinking 1.3). Different countries will impose regulations on minimum wages and working hours as well as the involvement of trade unions, as has been seen in most Western developed economies. In the UK, government legislation has gradually worn down the power of trade unions and given rise to managerial flexibility and decentralised employment regulation. Although it is employers who control the design of HRM practice at an organisational level, managers need to be aware or informed of external developments in the legal context.

Politically related external conflicts may have acute implications for firms operating in a particular country, and managers need to be aware of political manoeuvrings relevant to their interests. The state does not, however, have a monopoly of control over the conduct of business – firms too can lobby and influence state policies to meet their needs (Needle, 2004). This was the case with the USA's mohair farmers, who were paid numerous cash payments from the Federal budget (Wheelan, 2003). The mohair agricultural subsidy has now disappeared, but it highlights the importance and power of organised institutions.

External pressures in the global political environment may directly affect how business and employee relationship are conducted. The collapse of the Communist system in 1989 in East Europe and Central Asia paved the way for new market economies based on the Western capitalist market system. Employment regulation and managerial responsibility were taken away from government and replaced by the power of institutions and organisations.

Institutional context

Institutions represent the structures and activities that give shape and stability to a society, such as education, economic, religious, social, political, and family systems. Organisations in turn are shaped by institutions because of their embedded nature in the fabric of society. HRM is influence by institutions in terms of three mechanisms. Coercive mechanisms are more powerful than the organisation and force their norms, rules, and expectations on it. Mimetic mechanisms represent an organisation's desire to respond to uncertainty and its tendency to imitate another organisation's structure because of the belief that the structure of the latter organisation is beneficial. Normative mechanisms result from adopting standards or expectations associated with an industry or profession.

A common set of institutions can be found in most societies, including public and private enterprises, financial establishments, educational institutions, trade unions, and government agencies (Hollinshead, 2010). The relative strength of these institutions can vary, as can the manner in which they interact. In some societies, as a result of sociopolitical traditions, institutions operate in a mutually supportive fashion, while in others, there is an emphasis on institutional autonomy and self-support. From an HRM perspective, it is important to take into account the role of the state and related institutional arrangements on human resources and employee relations. Moreover, differences in business systems from region to region also depend on patterns of ownership such as neoliberalist (privatisation of public enterprises, deregulation of the economy, liberalisation of trade and industry), neocorporatist (an active role for the state in seeking to mediate and integrate the interests of various groups, particularly those representing labour and capital), and Marxist views (the conviction that unequal power relations in industry are enabled by patterns of institutional inequality in education, health, and housing).

Economic context

Although the economic context of a country is hardly predictable and stable, it is most likely to have long-term consequences for HRM (Tayeb, 2005). The attitudes and

(?) Critical Thinking 1.3 **Employment relations in India**

Labour unrest haunts auto sector in India

2014 Strike in Bangalore

Toyota's twin plants at Bidadi, Bangalore remained shut for 36 days owing to a workers' strike for a wage hike. More than 4,000 members of the trade union went on strike as they demanded a rise in wages, holidays, and housing. The union also demanded that the automaker reinstate 30 employees who were suspended on charges of causing disruption to work. While the plants continued to work with 700–800 contract labourers, there was a 40 per cent decrease in production capacity. Toyota is the fifth largest automaker in India. Its two plants have an installed capacity to produce about 310,000 units annually. The unionised employees called off their strike after the state government intervened and directed the management and the union to restore normalcy and harmony in operations.

2010 Strike in Tamil Nadu

In recent decades, the Indian State of Tamil Nadu has been attracting enormous investment into automobile and accessories manufacturing. However, investors and manufacturers have of late become quite worried about repeated labour unrest, which is also impeding future investment in the state.

Hyundai, the second largest car maker in the country, is facing a similar situation. In May 2010, Hyundai employees threatened a sit-in strike after the company refused to reinstate 35 employees who had been dismissed for alleged misconduct. According to a news report, the company was not able to meet the agreed deadline to reinstate the dismissed workers. The company has been making frantic efforts for a possible settlement with the dismissed employees, offering them certain financial compensation as a part of the settlement.

If the strike announced in May 2010 does go ahead, it will be the third strike at Hyundai over the past year. Previously, in April 2009, employees went on strike for 18 days after the company laid off 65 workers. Then again, in July 2009, employees went on strike protesting a wage agreement that had allegedly been signed by a minority union (or pocket union).

However, Hyundai is not the only company suffering as a result of labour unrest. In May 2009, workers at MRF struck work for several months, demanding recognition of their union. In September 2009, a senior official at Pricol was killed in workers' unrest in the auto-ancillary hub of Coimbatore, which resulted in a work closure lasting more than a month.

According to Abdul Majeed, an auto sector leader at PWC, labour laws are to be blamed: 'Our labour laws need an amendment. No one wins when it comes to dealing with labour. There has to be a give and take to some level amongst everyone. But our labour laws are the biggest of problems.'

The existing labour laws in India require large companies to seek prior permission from state governments before laying off workers or hiring workers on contract. These laws have been blamed by managers for encouraging workers to go on frequent strikes. With India positioning itself as the hub of small car production, such labour unrest may not send the right message to international investors.

Questions

1   In the light of this example, is it correct to blame laws for encouraging workers to strike?
2   Is it okay for a government authority to intervene for industrial peace and operational normalcy?
3   Is it always possible to reconcile the ethical and business implications of labour laws?

Source: Adapted from NDTV Profit, May 4 2010; Zee News, April 22 2014

values that are embedded in every individual are formed by culture (Noe et al., 2008); hence the claim of human capital theory that a culture that encourages continuous learning is most likely to contribute to the success of the economy. Jackson and Schuler (1995) argue that skills, experience and knowledge are of significant value for the economy, and enhancing them can make individuals more productive and more adaptable to changing economic conditions.

The need to improve human capabilities relates back to whether the economic system supplies sufficient incentives for developing human capital. For example, Tayeb

(2005) found that socialist economies offer a free education system, which provides an opportunity for human capital to be developed, thus enabling employees to obtain greater monetary rewards based on their competencies. This is evident in the USA, where levels of human capital are reflected in the differences in individuals' salaries, higher skilled employees, for example, earning better compensation than lower skill ones (Noe et al., 2008). In fact, it has been discovered that for each additional year of schooling, individuals' wages increase by about 10–16 per cent (Noe et al., 2008). Conversely, the opportunity to enhance human capital is smaller in capitalist systems due to the high costs of training employees; hence, human resource development is lower in capitalist countries (Tayeb, 2005).

Tayeb (2005) highlights the role of market conditions in determining employees' rights in capitalist countries that have 'centre right' policies. According to Flamholtz and Lacey (1981), investments in human capital are usually made in anticipation of future returns; besides improving employees' competencies, the costs also include factors such as motivating, monitoring, and retaining these employees in order to benefit from their gains in productivity (Jackson and Schuler, 1995). Chapter 3 in this book offers a detailed discussion of HRM in contemporary multinational businesses.

Of course, different forms of political capitalism, for example in terms of their socialist or free-market orientation, will have different effects on the way in which HRM is practised domestically as well as internationally. Even the most global of companies may be deeply rooted in the national business systems of their country of origin. For example, Edwards (2004), Hu (1992), and Ruigrok and van Tulder (1995) have argued that, on several dimensions, multinational corporations exhibit national characteristics.

There are various ways in which HRM can increase organisations' human capital, for instance offering attractive compensation and benefits packages to individuals, what Jackson and Schuler (1995) claim is 'buying' human capital, which is apparent in recruitment and selection processes. Creating equal opportunities in training and development can also help to 'make' human capital in an organisation; at times of tight labour supply, this method is usually adopted. Training and developing existing employees' capabilities, as well as enhancing their wages, benefits, and working conditions, can help in retaining them, especially when there is a scarce supply of human capital in the economy.

At times of economic boom and similarly in times of recession, the supply and demand of labour forces may vary in relation to a country's unemployment level. When the economy is booming and the level of unemployment is low, employees have much greater power and influence over their working conditions, pay, and other employment rights (Tayeb, 2005). Having said that, managers in return gain more prerogatives during recessions and periods of high unemployment by controlling employees' working conditions and compensation, thus weakening the power and influence of both workers and trade unions. Jackson and Schuler (1995) note that it is common in such periods for absenteeism and turnover rates to fall because competition for jobs is more intense and employees' poor performance may result in retrenchment. It has been identified that, in the USA, excess demand typically relates to low unemployment, whereas high unemployment is reported to be associated with excess supply (Jackson and Schuler, 1995).

Technological context

Technology has evolved along with globalisation, which is often associated with advances in communication and information technology. The way people throughout the world communicate, exchange information, and learn about their world has changed as computer usage has become more prevalent in almost every part of the globe, further enhanced by the increase in the number of information technology-literate individuals (Burton et al., 2003). The influence of technology is also apparent in HRM (Critical Thinking 1.4), especially with the transformation of traditional HRM to IT-based HRM, or what is known as e-HRM (Bondarouk and Ruel, 2009), as a result of the growing sophistication of IT.

For example, e-HRM deals with the implementation of HRM strategies, policies and practices through the full use of web-based technologies. Bondarouk et al. (2009) believe that e-HRM can reduce the cost of traditional methods of processing and administration of paperwork, as well as speeding up transaction processing, reducing information errors, and improving the tracking and control of human resources actions. However, the effectiveness of e-HRM may depend upon the types and levels of knowledge that are required by the system and the extent to which tasks and people are interdependent (Jackson and Schuler, 1995).

When face-to-face HRM services become obsolete, higher levels of motivation and commitment are required (Othman and Teh, 2003). This is because employees are expected to work independently with little supervision, so the supervisor's role is greatly reduced as control over employees' work behaviour can no longer be exerted through direct observation. According to Bondarouk and Ruel (2009), e-HRM eliminates the 'human resources middleman' who is initially responsible for dealing with human resources matters.

Besides ensuring independent work through the introduction of e-HRM, IT also enables organisational learning to help employees improve their capability, adaptation, knowledge and understanding (Othman and Teh, 2003) because the use of teams is practised, which helps the transfer of learning from the individual to the organisation. Othman and Teh claim that, with the growing usage of IT, people are expected to think critically, be able to solve problems, communicate and work in teams, creatively and proactively, as well as bring diverse and newer perspectives to their work. This requires a change in organisational structures and processes, for example selection processes, training, performance appraisals and rewards. Put simply, this means that the way employee performance is monitored has to rely on data interpretation and on assessing outputs.

There are, however, some critiques of the usage of IT in organisations. Based on findings from Othman and Teh (2003), the workforce is deskilled and controlled by managers through the use of IT. There is less chance for employees to develop their intellectual skills when their role has already been weakened by IT. Additionally, while most management invests heavily in acquiring technology, insufficient resources tend to be allocated to managing the organisational change process; thus HRM issues are neglected, and technology usage fails to meet expectations.

CRITICAL DISCUSSION AND ANALYSIS

HRM is constantly being reshaped by new economic, institutional, sociocultural, and political realities. Changes in the levels of unemployment, structural transformation (for example, privatisation and deindustrialisation),

---

? Critical Thinking 1.4 Technological context and HRM

Organisations across the world are currently exploring ways to integrate digital and other modern technology into organisational systems and operations. In particular, employers are interested in exploring the workforce impacts of artificial intelligence, wearable technologies and automation, among other fundamental shifts in the working world. Many companies are introducing the existing and start-up technologies to revolutionise work and job designs and processes (HRM Asia, 2016). The correlation between new technology and work can be identified in many different forms. Academics have, however, pinpointed three specific areas in which HRM practices are directly affected (Millward and Stevens, 1986):

▸ *Advanced technology change:* new plant machinery and equipment that has incorporated microprocessor technology.
▸ *Conventional technological change:* machinery and equipment not aided by microprocessor technology.
▸ *Organisational change:* substantial changes in work organisations not involving new plant, machinery or equipment (Bratton and Gold, 2007).

Across many workplaces, micro-processor technology plays an active role: in 1998, 87 per cent of manufacturing workplaces in the UK used micro-processor–based technology, a large jump from 44 per cent in 1984 (Bratton and Gold, 2007). This reflects how great an influence the technological context may have on designing HRM. Entire organisations are administered based on their information systems. In addition, manufacturing process concepts are part of the technological context that are able to directly impact upon organisations. Similarly, performance enhancement and organisational restructuring have vigorously shaped business processes in order to gain a competitive advantage.

Total quality management (TQM) focuses on maximising profits by increasing service and product quality and decreasing costs (Hill, 2005). TQM and other quality management innovations such as Six Sigma are groundbreaking institutional approaches to improving organisations and are an example of how the technological context has influenced the design of HRM. However, quality management may also pose a problem for managers and organisations: although the system welcomes key aspects of quality – between suppliers and customers – it demands mutual commitment from every party involved in the organisation and requires rigorous implementation and corporate governance, which may cause a hegemonic conflict between top and mid-level management and the workforce whom they direct.

Questions

1 Do technological advances always have positive implications for employees in organisations?
2 What role can HRM play in coping with changes in the technological context of an organisation?

and social trends (an ageing population) will all shift the balance of power in individual and collective contract negotiations.

It is possible to link cultural traits and orientations theorised by Hofstede (2001), Trompenaars and Hampden-Turner (1997), and other scholars with the observed manifestations of HRM across regions. Although such linkages are not always empirically proven, certain organisational practices may be regarded as being influenced by culture. For example, whether pay is individually or collectively determined (individualism versus collectivism); preferred organisational structures – flat/tall, consultative/authoritarian (power distance); short-term profit focus or sustainability focus (short-term versus long-term orientation).

While cultural theory is useful to examine comparative manifestations of HRM across countries, it is also valuable in avoiding cross-cultural misunderstandings in an international HRM context. Indeed, individuals are generally embedded in specific national-level cultures and are shaped by and express their cultural orientation in their attitudes and behaviours at the workplace.

Furthermore, increasing globalisation and advances in information and communication technologies are fast transforming the world into a global village in which management practices cannot remain isolated from external influences. As demonstrated in this chapter, we would be ill-advised to believe that globalisation will cause organisations to become isolated or aloof from the society in which they operate. Conversely, local contexts will remain a key influence on the way in which human resources are treated and managed.

It is, however, a fact that some types of HRM system may be used effectively across countries that are culturally quite dissimilar (Wickens, 1987; MacDuffie and Krafcik, 1992), and that organisational and industry characteristics remain key determinants of managerial practices and employee behaviours (Hofstede, 1991). Our understanding of the role of national culture in HRM could also benefit from investigations examining how multinational corporations develop HRM systems that are simultaneously consistent with multiple and distinct local cultures and yet internally consistent in the context of a single organisation (cf. Heenan and Perlmutter, 1979; Tung, 1993; Jackson and Schuler, 1995).

From an academic perspective, certain specialised fields, for example industrial-organisational psychology and social work psychology, may be very useful in advancing our understanding of HRM in context. In this age of unprecedented internationalisation as well as sociocultural specificity, the dearth of comparative publications in HRM is both surprising and alarming (Özbilgin, 2004). Several shifts in approach may be required: from treating organisational settings as sources of error variance to attending as closely as possible to individual characteristics; from focusing on individuals to

treating social systems as the target for study; from focusing on single practices or policies to adopting a holistic approach to conceptualising HRM systems; from research conducted in single organisations at one point in time to research comparing multiple organisations across time, space, and culture; and from a search for the 'one best way' to a search for the many possible ways to design and maintain effective HRM systems (Jackson and Schuler, 1995).

STOP AND REFLECT

Questions

1 Is national culture dynamic or static?
2 Are national cultures converging in the current global era?
3 Can it then be assumed that after a few decades national variances in HRM will disappear?

CONCLUSION

In conclusion, it is imperative that contextual factors are considered when designing and operationalising HRM policies. While HRM is evolving due to the evolving nature of globalisation and the digital era, culture continues to have a vital effect on people and organisations. As Stredwick notes 'indeed to the observer in one country, the workplace practices in another might seem downright absurd...any attempt to impose the ways and methods that he or she knows best in that other national context might be doomed to failure' (2005: 442).

This chapter has demonstrated that the field of HRM will have limited value if it does not adequately take into account cultural and institutional contexts. Global policies may seem an easy solution, but the issues of expatriate workers, diversity and institutional and cultural variances must not be neglected. As Sparrow and Hiltrop (1994) suggest, care must be taken to escape the trap of ignoring significant differences between national cultures. More recently, Vaimin and Brewster (2015) have argued that while much of the national differences in HRM are generally determined by institutional factors, management has more influence over the effect of national cultural differences than it has over institutional differences. The authors argue that where institutions are less constraining, cultural differences may be the appropriate template.

In this chapter, we have identified a number of elements in the macro-level environment, that is, the sociocultural, legal, political, economic, and technological contexts, that affect HRM in different ways. Economy is an important context that influences the design and outcomes of HRM; the financial crisis occurring at the time of writing this book has affected employment environments across many nations, and this is in turn affecting the behaviour of local labour markets. Similarly, cultural values, such as age and gender traditions and stereotypes, are significant social contexts relevant to HRM.

Managers need to be aware of legal contexts that have the potential to affect employment relations. Local culture and other external pressures will influence the design of HRM, but institutions can, in their turn, influence the contexts affecting them – political leveraging and lobbying has, for example, been conducted by corporations against agreements that have had the potential to affect employment behaviour, such as the Kyoto Protocol (UN, 1992) which calls for a reduction of greenhouse gases emissions.

External contexts can also be linked to the pursuit of competitive advantage, as is usually emphasised in organisations in industrialised Western economies linking HRM strategy to competitive advantage. Towards that end, HRM practitioners will need to analyse and respond to external contextual issues and deal with them in a coherent and strategic manner.

End of Chapter Case Study HRM in Brunei's public sector

(Authors: Jawad Syed and Dk Nur'Izzati Pg Omar)

Brunei is a monarchical government that is governed by Sultan Haji Hassanal Bolkiah Mu'izzaddin Waddaulah, who has executive authority and is assisted and advised by five constitutional bodies. The concept of 'Malay Islamic Monarchy' (MIB) is often thought of as a 'national philosophy', incorporating both the official Malay language, culture and customs and the importance of Islam as a religion and a set of guiding values.

In October 2013, the Sultan announced his intention to impose Islamic Sharia law on the country's Muslims, which represent around 78 per cent of the country's population. This would make Brunei the first country in East Asia to introduce Sharia law into its penal code. The move attracted international criticism and concerns about human rights and minority rights (USA Today, 2013). Christians represent 9 per cent and Buddhists represent about 9 per cent of the country's total population (*CIA Factbook*, 2016). The Sharia law being introduced in Brunei will enforce fines and prison sentences for 'crimes' such as pregnancies outside of wedlock, propagating religions other than Islam, and not attending mandatory Friday prayers. Further it introduces harsh punishments such as floggings and cutting off hands for property offences, and in its final phase it will also introduce executions, including stoning, for offences such as adultery, abortion, homosexuality/sodomy, and blasphemy (Ozanick, 2015).

Brunei, situated in South-East Asia, has an estimated population of 429,000, of whom 66 per cent are Malay and 10 per cent are Chinese, the remaining 24 per cent comprising indigenous groups, expatriates, and immigrants. About 54 per cent of the overall population is made up of the 20–54 age group, which is the economically productive group. The main source of income for Brunei is the oil and gas industry, followed by the private and government sectors. The public sector is the main employer for the majority of citizens and residents of Brunei (Brunei Economic Development Board, n.d.).

Owing to Brunei's distinct political system, it has different employment structures from those of other South-East Asian countries. Brunei is ruled by a strict essence of conformity and consensus that does not allow organisations or individuals to challenge the government and its policies. Brunei's public sector may be seen as a 'model employer' (Beattie and Osborne, 2008), in the sense that the public sector sets an example to the private sector in terms of the fair treatment of employees and providing good conditions of service – this includes high levels of job security, better leave entitlement, and generous pensions (Black and Upchurch, 1999). This case study sheds light on how HRM policies and practices in the public sector are shaped by contextual influences in Brunei.

In the public sector, the *General Order and State Circulars* shape HRM practices. The General Order dates back to 1962; its content covers many key elements of HRM, for example appointments, promotions, benefit entitlement, work etiquette and discipline, although certain current issues related to HRM may not be present in the booklet. State Circulars cover more current HRM issues not addressed in the General Order, including those that have just arisen. All government bodies are sent Circulars whenever any new issues arise. Circulars often call upon the command of the Sultan of Brunei, who holds absolute power over the way that Brunei should be managed.

All civil servants are required to have a detailed knowledge of – and abide by – both the General Order and State Circulars in order to carry out their jobs and to progress in their careers. Every officer, supervisor, or clerk who is aspiring towards promotion or a rise in salary will have to sit a written examination based on the content of both these sets of government policies.

A recent innovation within HRM in the Brunei public sector is the *Government Employee Management System* (GEMS), which is currently being trialled. This is a web-based system that enables efficient data input and greater transparency, which allows a better management of HRM practices such as recruitment and selection, compensation and benefits, as well as human resources administration. In addition, this will reduce paper usage and help Brunei to become more 'green'. Human resources administrators, government employees, and the public are the three main stakeholders that GEMS is focusing on.

GEMS allows human resources administrators to manage job advertisements and update and approve allowance and benefit applications. Government employees can apply for allowances and benefits online, retrieve useful information such as the latest policies that have been introduced, check their balance of leave entitlement, and participate in surveys and forums where they can express their suggestions for how to improve the civil service. The public, on the other hand, can check job vacancies online, submit job applications and track their progress (Government Employee Management System, 2014).

Interviews conducted with a number of managers and nonmanagerial staff in three departments within the Brunei public sector have provided an insight into how the local context has an impact on the design and implementation of HRM practices.

Socioculture

Many interviewees felt that Brunei's close-knit socioculture was an important factor in HRM practices. In particular, family relationships have a significant impact on workplace relations with supervisors and colleagues alike. As one interviewee stated:

> Working in the public sector, we are expected to respect our supervisors and officers. Supervisors and officers, regardless of their age, are like a father or leader to us; we share an informal relationship and talk to them in person if we have any issues or problems. A very family-like relationship is what motivates me, in particular, because it gives me a feeling of belonging and security. Although we have an informal relationship, it does not mean that we respect our superiors any less.

Previous research in other countries has highlighted that close-knit relationships often result in subjective and informal recruitment and selection processes (see, for example, Myloni et al.'s [2004] research in Greece). The majority of the employees interviewed for this case study claimed that family connections do not influence the way people are employed. This is evident in the following excerpt:

> Yes we have a very close relationship in our culture, but I must say that it has no direct influence on the way we recruit and select applicants. Because everyone goes through the same procedure, that is, a written exam and then interviews for short-listed applicants. Furthermore, there are guidelines and procedures that need to be followed when recruiting people. Also, there is a group of committee members who decide on the final result'; this is based on consensus agreement. There is no room for favouritism.... Personally, when the one who is newly recruited happens to be the son/daughter of an authority figure in the public sector, it is because he/she is qualified for the position, he/she might have already been trained with the kind of traits and skills that we are looking for. That is not nepotism.

However, the above account contradicts statements made by at least three other participants, who felt that 'nepotism' is still the essence of recruitment and selection, particularly in the government sector. Overall, the interviews suggest that close-knit social relationships in Brunei society have an impact on employment relationship in the workplace. However, the impact is moderated in HRM practices, particularly in recruitment and selection, because governmental regulations still affect HRM policies.

Law and politics

While full implications of Islamic Sharia law remain yet unknown, the national philosophy of MIB has an important influence on the way HRM works in the public sector. One interviewee noted that:

> Malay culture teaches us to be respectful and courteous to others. Islam instills honesty, trust, loyalty and good faith in oneself. Monarchic government means that His Majesty the Sultan holds the ultimate power in decision-making; no one is allowed to go against His Majesty's command. So, basically MIB influences us, in terms of the way we bring ourselves, the way we perform our work as a loyal subject of His Majesty. Every aspect of government affairs revolves around the concept of MIB.

The political influence of the state has in other studies been shown to either strengthen or undermine the role of HRM (Tayeb, 2005): a more cooperative government will have a better chance of adopting HRM efficiently, and vice versa. When asked whether monarchical government hinders employee participation in decision-making, one interviewee stated that:

> Any grievances, complaints or suggestions that are made by employees are attended to by respective supervisors or officers. Obviously in a monarchical government like Brunei, His Majesty holds the absolute powers in major decisions. But other than that, we do value employees' suggestions and points of view. We always take their opinions into consideration. In my position as an officer, I make sure that my door is always open for them to come in and express any problem or suggestion that they may have. We ensure that we include them into any problem-solving and decision-making, because it is important that they feel included.

When asked about how the General Order and State Circulars are dealt with by public sector workers, managers underlined the critical importance of these, not only for their own careers, but also to provide a basis for all government servants for what should and should not be done while working in the public sector. As one interviewee noted:

> Every circular is by command of His Majesty The Sultan; we are obliged to obey them. Officers are directed to encourage and make employees aware of existing circulars.

Nonmanagerial staff, however, tended to take a less rigorous approach and were sometimes unfamiliar with the content of these documents. Regulations were still poorly enforced regardless of the availability of the General Order and State Circulars.

With regards to the content of the General Order, benefits entitlements and working hours are usually included and practised in workplace policies. Participants generally felt that the policies adopted by the government are flexible and family-friendly. For example, one married female participant stated that:

> Yes it is very family-friendly. One of the most obvious aspect is the working hours in the government sector. In the regulation book, General Order, it states that one should work maximum 8 hours from 7.45 am to 4.30 pm, but there is some flexibility when it comes to family responsibility, such as sending or picking up children to/from school. Also, in terms of leave entitlement, a married woman can take unpaid leave to follow her husband who was sent to work abroad and her job is still available when she comes back.

Of late, there is some indication that at least some of the Islamic laws being enforced in the country are discriminatory or repressive in nature. In 2014, the Brunei Sultan announced the enforcement Islamic law (sharia) in the country, announcing fines and prison sentences for propagating religions other than Islam and punishment for the violation of Islamic laws. The UN urged Brunei to delay the changes so they could be reviewed to make sure they complied with international human rights standards (BBC, 2014).

Economics

Research suggests that, for individuals to be more productive and adaptable to changing economic conditions, experience and knowledge have to be significantly valued (Jackson and Schuler, 1995). In the Brunei public sector, this valuation of education and human capital seems to have been achieved. When asked whether different economic situations influenced the need for an educated or experienced workforce, one manager noted that:

> In the government sector education plays a very important role because we believe fresh graduates have new ideas, which would ultimately benefit the organisation, over a person with experience who might not have anything new to bring to the organisation.

From an economic perspective, Brunei is currently facing an excess supply of labour in the job market. An officer thus explained this:

> This is a very challenging issue Brunei is facing. The demand for jobs is overwhelmingly high, but the supply of jobs to accommodate the demand is rather low. This is because a new post will only be available when someone retires, resigns, there is end of contract of an employee, or a budget is allocated to create new posts.

This is consistent with Jackson and Schuler's observation that a country is likely to experience high unemployment in times of oversupply of its labour force. Brunei is currently experiencing this problem, and thus many students are sponsored to study abroad to temporarily alleviate the number of workers currently seeking jobs. The problem with an oversupply of labour is that very few vacant positions are usually available in the government sector. For example, in response to a recent advertisement (at the time of this research) for a clerical position, 1,000 applications were received for only four vacancies.

Technology

Technology is a new element in the government sector in Brunei. The Sultan has allocated billions of dollars for IT to be used effectively. In particular, the introduction of GEMS, described above, is indicative of a new approach to technology in HRM practice. Public sector workers have mixed reactions to this new system. One manager noted that:

> It's very convenient because there's less paperwork and sharing of documents will be easier as it is computerised. Leave applications, benefits entitlement, car and house loans, all are accessible any time and anywhere.

Another, less positively, argued that:

> We currently have an online method of inputting data called SIMPA; it is in Malay and it is very straightforward. But it is only for data entry and nothing else. Well, GEMS from what I have tried is a bit too complex for me because there are so may folders to click on and most importantly, it is in English. To be honest, I am not good in English language, so I don't know how I will be able to get used to the changes.

Officers in general tend to agree with the technological changes that the government intends to implement, whereas the staff are slightly hesitant about the changes. For example, a training officer stated that:

> Every human resource development representative of each government department is given courses to train their respective employees on the usage of this new system. Emphasis is given to clerical positions as they are the ones who handle most paperwork.

From the interview data, one obvious challenge facing HRM in Brunei relates to how well individuals can adjust themselves to technological changes. Moving away from the traditional face-to-face HRM services may cause some difficulty and stress for some employees. Training, on the other hand, may assist staff and officers to adapt effectively to such changes.

Conclusion

This study of HRM in Brunei makes clear that the macro-environmental context has a huge impact on the way HRM polices are designed and implemented. Culture serves as the overarching umbrella for all the other contexts, such as the legal and political system, the economy, and adaptation to technology. In the main,

HRM in Brunei revolves around the MIB ideology, which signifies the extent to which Western-originated HRM practices are customised and applied in the country. Human capital is given great importance and has high value in the job market; incentives are, therefore, given to improve human capital. However, the monarchical government of Brunei limits the ability for freedom of speech, freedom of associations, and collective bargaining. Such limitations have become further restricting due to promulgation of Islamic Sharia in recent years.

A hierarchical relationship is present in the government sector, but power distance is not a key concern, as is evident from the interview data. These show that Brunei does have a hierarchical relationship as claimed by Hofstede (1984) but that the power distance is not very great and is often a sign of respect for authority and for one's superiors. The relationship shared between officers and subordinates positively affects employees' participation rates in problem-solving and decision-making. However, close-knit relationships seem not to excessively influence the recruitment and selection process, which is regulated by state laws and procedures.

From a legal and political context perspective, the MIB ideology seems to have a visible impact on HRM. It enhances the initiatives of various departments in ensuring that everyone gets 100 hours of training and development. It also prohibits employees from setting up or joining trade unions; instead encouraging a more peaceful and harmonious negotiation with officers and supervisors. The General Order and State Circulars are still weakly enforced, although superiors tried to stress their importance. In addition, MIB and state laws help to create a family-friendly policy that is flexible for working parents and employees with dependants.

From an economic context perspective, human capital, education, knowledge and skills are encouraged through continuous learning for all employees and officers. The benefits offered by the public sector create the perception of its being the most stable and secure workplace and hence provide an advantage when recruiting and retaining human capital. Oversupply of the workforce is a prominent issue in Brunei. This affects HRM processes in making sure that the public sector recruits the right people for the right jobs.

Technology seems to be an upcoming aspect in the government sector. Not much information could be gleaned, except for the perceptions of older workers that there is a shift towards an online-based system of HRM. Some older workers find it difficult to adjust to this, but they are still able to do so slowly. Also, when officers and staff were asked whether this would increase convenience, most participants answered positively, saying that IT is helping to speed up their work and lessen their workload.

It can be concluded that local culture and politics (MIB) have a significant impact on the implementation of HRM in Brunei. We recommend that further research be conducted on a larger scale to explore the contextualisation of HRM in Brunei and other national contexts. Preferably, academia–industry partnership-based research in these government departments might allow for a deeper understanding of the topic.

Questions

1   How do culture and politics affect the design and implementation of HRM in Brunei?
2   Culture serves as the overarching umbrella for all the other contexts, such as the legal and political system, the economy, and adaptation to technology. Critically discuss this.
3   How can HRM enable individual employees to adjust themselves to technological changes in their organisations?
4   How does HRM in Brunei differ from HRM in a Western country?
5   What are the likely implications of the enforcement of Islamic Sharia for HRM?

FOR DISCUSSION AND REVISION

1   How do macro-contextual factors affect the design and operationalisation of the following HRM functions:
   - recruitment and selection;
   - training;
   - performance management;
   - reward management;
   - career management.

2   Make a study of HRM policies and practices in a specific company. Identify the various ways in which the HRM policies and practices in that company are affected by its sociocultural, political, legal, and economic contexts.
3   What are various tensions between the globalisation and contextualisation of HRM? What are implications of such tensions for the future of HRM?
4   Identify at least one resource in a language other than English that deals with issues related to HRM.

Feel free to seek help from a friend who speaks a language other than English. What can you learn from this resource?

5 How does the dominance of US and UK literature in the field of HRM affect the contextualisation of HRM?

6 According to Hofstede (1991), organisational and industry characteristics may be more important than national cultures as determinants of managerial practices and employee behaviours. Discuss.

GLOSSARY

Context: Environment, framework, setting, or situation surrounding an event, function or organisation.

Culture: The way of life, especially the general customs, social behaviour and beliefs, of a particular people or society.

Employee relations: The contractual, emotional, physical, and practical relationship between employer and employee.

Globalisation: The process of international integration arising from the interchange of worldviews, ideas, culture, products, and knowledge sharing. The process by which businesses or other organisations develop international influence or start operating on an international scale.

Institutions: Systems of established and prevalent social rules that structure social interactions.

Macro-environment: The major external and uncontrollable factors that influence an organisation's decision-making, performance, choices and strategies.

Stereotype: A widely held but fixed, sweeping, and over-simplified image or idea of a particular people or society.

FURTHER READING

Books

DOWLING, P. J., FESTING, M. AND ENGLE, A. D. (2008) *International Human Resource Management: Managing People in a Multinational Context* (5th edn). London: Thomson Publishing.

PRICE, A. (2007) *Human Resource Management in a Business Context* (3rd edn). London: Thomson Learning.

QUINN, J. B., MINTZBERG, H. AND JAMES, R. M. (eds) (1988) *The Strategy Process: Concepts, Context, and Cases.* Englewood Cliffs, NJ: Prentice Hall International.

Journals

BUDHWAR, P. AND KHATRI, P. (2001) HRM in context: the applicability of HRM models in India. *International Journal of Cross Cultural Management*, 1(3): 333–356.

JACKSON, S. E. AND SCHULER, R. S. (1995) Understanding human resource management in the context of organizations and their environment. *Annual Review of Psychology*, 46: 237–264.

KAMOCHE, K. (2002) Introduction: Human resource management in Africa. *International Journal of Human Resource Management*, 13(7): 993–997.

KHATRI, N. (1999) Emerging issues in strategic HRM in Singapore. *International Journal of Manpower*, 20(8): 516–529.

SCHMIDT, V. (1993) An end to French economic exceptionalism? The transformation of business under Mitterand. *California Management Review*, (Fall): 75–98.

SELMER, J. AND LEON C. D. (2001) Pinoy-style HRM: Human resource management in the Philippines. *Asia Pacific Business Review*, 8(1): 127–144.

WAN, D. (2003) Human resource management in Singapore: Changes and continuities. *Asia Pacific Business Review*, 9(4): 129–146.

WEB RESOURCES

The Hofstede Centre (2016). Available at: http://geert-hofstede.com/. Accessed 28 January 2016.

Jabatan Perkhidmatan Awam (2015). Available at: http://www.jpa.gov.bn/Theme/Home.aspx. Accessed 31 December 2015.

The Negara Brunei Darussalam Government (2016). Available at: https://www.brunei.gov.bn/en/SitePages/Home-Government.aspx. Accessed 26 January 2016.

REFERENCES

ADLER, N. J. (1991) *International Dimensions of Organizational Behavior*. Boston, MA: PWS-KENT Publishing.

AFIOUNI, F., RUËL, H., AND SCHULER, R. (2014) HRM in the Middle East: Toward a greater understanding. *International Journal of Human Resource Management*, 25(2): 133–143.

AILON, G. (2008) Mirror, mirror on the wall: Culture's consequences in a value test of its own design. *Academy of Management Review*, 33(4): 885–904.

ARVEY, R. D., BHAGAT, R. S. AND SALAS, E. (1991) Cross-cultural and cross-national issues in personnel and human resources management: Where do we go from here? *Personnel and Human Resource Management*, 9: 367–407.

BARUCH, Y. (2001) Global or North American top management journals? *Journal of Cross-cultural Management*, 1(1): 131–147.

BBC (2014) Brunei introduces tough Islamic penal code. *BBC News*, April 30. Available at: http://www.bbc.co.uk/news/world-asia-27216798.

BEATTIE, R. S. AND OSBORNE, S. P. (2008) *Human Resource Management in the Public Sector*. London: Routledge.

BEER, M., LAWRANCE, P. R., MILLS, D. Q. AND WALTON, R. E. (1985) *Human Resource Management*. New York: Free Press.

BENNINGTON, L. AND HABIR, A. D. (2003) Human resource management in Indonesia. *Human Resource Management Review*, 13(3): 373–392.

BLACK, J. AND UPCHURCH, M. (1999) Public sector employment. In HOLLINSHEAD, G., NICHOLLS, P. AND TAILBY, S. (eds), *Employee Relations*. London: Financial Times Management.

BONDAROUK, T. V. AND RUEL, H. J. M. (2009) Electronic human resource management: Challenges in the digital era. *International Journal of Human Resource Management*, 20(3): 505–514.

BONDAROUK, T., RUEL, H. AND HEIJDEN B. V. D. (2009) e-HRM effectiveness in a public sector organization: A multistakeholder perspective. *International Journal of Human Resource Management*, 20(3): 578–590.

BRATTON, J. AND GOLD, J. (2017) *Human Resource Management: Theory and Practice* (6th edn). New York: Palgrave Macmillan.

BREWSTER, C. (2007) Comparative HRM: European views and perspectives. *International Journal of Human Resource Management*, 18(5): 769–787.

BREWSTER, C. AND TYSON, S. (eds) (1991) *International Comparisons in Human Resource Management*. London: Pitman.

Brunei Economic Development Board (n.d.) Introducing Brunei. Available at: http://www.bedb.com.bn/. Accessed 21 November 2015.

BUDHWAR, P. S. AND DEBRAH, Y. A. (2001) *Human Resource Management in Developing Countries*. London: Routledge.

BURTON, J. P., BUTLER, J. E. AND MOWDAY, R. T. (2003) Lions, tigers and alley cats: HRM's role in Asian business development. *Human Resource Management Review*, 13(3): 487–498.

CALIGIURI, P. M. (1999) The ranking of scholarly journals in international human resource management. *International Journal of Human Resource Management*, 10(3): 515–519.

CARROLL, G. R., DELACROIX, J. AND GOODSTEIN, J. (1988) The political environments of organizations: an ecological view. *Research in Organizational Behavior*, 10: 359–392.

CHAN, C. (2016) Labor rights movements gaining momentum in China. *DW*, January 5. Available at: http://www.dw.com/en/labor-rights-movements-gaining-momentum-in-china/a-18959557.

CHASE, S. (2002) Ratifying Kyoto. *Globe and Mail*, 27 February, p. B6.

CHOMSKY, N. (1999) *Profit over People: Neoliberalism and the Global Order*. New York: Seven Stories Press.

CHUNG, C., SPARROW, P. AND BOZKURT, Ö. (2014) South Korean MNEs' international HRM approach: Hybridization of global standards and local practices. *Journal of World Business*, 49(4): 549–559.

CIA Factbook (2016) Brunei. Available at: https://www.cia.gov/library/publications/the-world-factbook/geos/bx.html.

CIPD (2015) History of HR and the CIPD. CIPD Factsheet, October 2015. Available at: http://www.cipd.co.uk/hr-resources/factsheets/history-hr-cipd.aspx.

CLARK, T., GOSPEL, H. AND MONTGOMERY, J. (1999) Running on the spot? A review of twenty years of research on the management of human resources in comparative and international perspective. *International Journal of Human Resource Management*, 10(3): 520–544.

CLARK, T., GRANT, D. AND HEIJLTJES, M. (2000) Researching comparative and international human resource management. *International Studies of Management and Organization*, 29(4): 6–17.

CLOVER, C. (2016) China police arrest activists in campaign against labour unrest. *Financial Times*, January 11. Available at: http://www.ft.com/cms/s/0/7ae19510-b85e-11e5-b151-8e15c9a029fb.html.

COLLIN, A. (2007) Contextualising HRM: Developing critical thinking. In Beardwell, J. and Claydon, T. (eds), *Human Resource Management: A Contemporary Approach*. Harlow: FT Prentice Hall, pp. 83–116.

DRUCKER, P. (1954) *The Practice of Management*. New York: Harper and Row.

EDWARDS, T. (2004) The transfer of employment practices across borders in multinational companies. In Harzing, A.-W. and Ruysseveldt, J. V. (eds), *International Human Resource Management*. London: Sage, pp. 389–410.

FAUX, J. AND MISHEL, L. (2001) Inequality and the global economy. In Hutton, W. and Giddens, A. (eds), *On the Edge: Living with Capitalism*. London: Vintage Books.

FLAMHOLTZ, E. G. AND LACEY, J. M. (1981) Personnel management, human capital theory, and human resource accounting. Cited in Jackson, S. E. and Schuler, R. S. (1995), Understanding human resource management in the context of organizations and their environments. *Annual Review of Psychology*, 46: 237–264.

FLORKOWSKI, G. W. AND NATH, R. (1993) MNC responses to the legal environment of international human resource management. *International Journal of Human Resource Management*, 4: 305–324.

GAUGLER, E. (1988) HR management: An international comparison. *Personnel*, August: 24–30.

Government Employee Management System (2014) About GEMS: GEMS background. Available at: http://www.jpa.gov.bn/Theme/Home.aspx. Accessed 20 January 2014.

HARRIS, L. (2002) The future for the HRM function in local government: Everything has changed – but has anything changed? *Strategic Change*, 11(7): 369–378.

HEENAN, D. A. AND PERLMUTTER, H. V. (1979) *Multinational Organization Development*. Reading, MA: Pearson Addison Wesley.

HILL, C. (2009) *International Business: Competing in the Global Marketplace* (7th edn). New York: McGraw-Hill.

HILL, T. (2005) *Operations Management*. Basingstoke: Palgrave Macmillan.

HOFSTEDE, G. (1980) *Culture's Consequences: International Differences in Work Related Values*. Beverly Hills: Sage.

HOFSTEDE, G. (1984) Cultural dimension in management and planning. *Asia Pacific Journal of Management*, 1(2): 81–99.

HOFSTEDE, G. (1991) *Cultures and Organizations*. London: McGraw-Hill.

HOFSTEDE, G. (2001) *Cultures' Consequences: Comparing Values, Behaviors, Institutions, and Organizations across Nations* (2nd ed.). Thousand Oaks, CA: Sage Publications.

HOLLINSHEAD, G. (2010) *International and Comparative Human Resource Management*. McGraw-Hill.

HRM Asia (2016) Technology and HR leaders gather for Smart Workforce Summit. HRM Asia, June 21. Available at: http://www.hrmasia.com/content/technology-and-hr-leaders-gather-smart-workforce-summit.

HU, Y. S. (1992) Global or stateless corporations are national firms with international operations. *California Management Review*, Winter: 107–126.

JACKSON, S. E. AND SCHULER, R. S. (1995) Understanding human resource management in the context of organizations and their environments. *Annual Review of Psychology*, 46: 237–264.

JAVIDAN, M., AND DASTMALCHIAN, A. (2009). Managerial implications of the GLOBE project: A study of 62 societies. *Asia Pacific Journal of Human Resources*, 47(1): 41–58.

KAUFMAN, B. E. (2016). Globalization and convergence–divergence of HRM across nations: New measures, explanatory theory, and non-standard predictions from bringing in economics. *Human Resource Management Review*. doi:10.1016/j.hrmr.2016.04.006.

LEVY-LEBOYER, C. (1994) Selection and assessment in Europe. In TRIANDIS, H. C., DUNNETTE, M. D. AND HOUGH, L. M. (eds), *Handbook of Industrial and Organizational Psychology* (2nd edn, vol. 4). Palo Alto, CA: Consulting Psychology Press, pp. 173–190.

LINCOLN, J. R. (1993) Work organization in Japan and the United States. In Kogut, B. (ed.), *Country Competitiveness: Technology and the Organizing of Work*. Oxford: Oxford University Press, pp. 93–124.

MACDUFFIE, J. P. AND KRAFCIK, J. (1992) Integrating technology and human resources for high performance manufacturing. In Kochan, T. and Useem, M. (eds), *Transforming Organizations*. New York: Oxford University Press, pp. 210–226.

MAURICE, M., SELLIER, F. AND SILVESTRE, J.-J. (1986) *Bases of Industrial Power*. Cambridge, MA: MIT Press.

MCCOURT, W. AND FOON L. M. (2007) Malaysia as model: Policy transferability in an Asian country. *Public Management Review*, 9(2): 211–229.

MCGREGOR, D. (1957) *The Human Side of Enterprise*. Fifth Anniversary Convocation of the MIT School of Industrial Management. Cambridge, MA: MIT Press.

MCSWEENEY, B. (2002) Hofstede's model of national cultural differences and their consequences: A triumph of faith – a failure of analysis. *Human Relations*, 55(1): 89–118.

MILLWARD, N. AND STEVENS, M. (1986) *British Workplace Industrial Relations 1980–1984*. Aldershot: Gower.

MYLONI, B., HARZING, A. K. AND MIRZA, H. (2004) Host country specific factors and the transfer of human resource management practices in multinational companies. *International Journal of Manpower*, 25(6): 518–534.

NEEDLE, D. (2004) *Business in Context* (4th edn). London: Thomson.

NOE, R. A., HOLLENBECK, J. R., GERHART, B. AND WRIGHT, P. M. (2008) *Human Resource Management: Gaining a Competitive Advantage* (6th edn). New York: McGraw Hill.

OSBORNE, H. (2016) Uber faces court battle with drivers over employment status. *Guardian*, July 19. Available at: https://www.theguardian.com/technology/2016/jul/19/uber-drivers-court-tribunal-self-employed-uk-employment-law.

OTHMAN, R. AND TEH, C. (2003) On developing the informated work place: HRM issues in Malaysia. *Human Resource Management Review*, 13: 393–406.

OZANICK, B. (2015) The implications of Brunei's Sharia Law. *Diplomat*, May 21. Available at: http://thediplomat.com/2015/05/the-implications-of-bruneis-sharia-law/.

ÖZBILGIN, M. (2004) Inertia of the international human resource management text in a changing world: An examination of the editorial board membership of the top 21 IHRM journals. *Personnel Review*, 33(2): 205–221.

PRICE, A. (1997) *Human Resource Management in a Business Context*. London: International Thomson Business Press.

RONEN, S. (1994) An underlying structure of motivational need taxonomies: A cross-cultural confirmation. In TRIANDIS, H. C., DUNNETTE, M. D. AND HOUGH, L. M. (eds), *Handbook of Industrial and Organizational Psychology* (2nd edn, vol. 4). Palo Alto, CA: Consulting Psychology Press, pp. 241–270.

ROUSSEAU, D. M. (1990). Assessing organizational culture: The case for multiple methods. In Schneider, B. (ed.),

Organizational Climate and Culture. San Francisco: Jossey-Bass, pp. 153–192.

RUIGROK, W. AND VAN TULDER, R. (1995) *The Logic of International Restructuring.* London: Routledge.

SAMOGLOU, E. (2016) Etihad celebrates Emirati staff target. *National UAE,* January 27. Available at: http://www.thenational.ae/uae/transport/etihad-celebrates-emirati-staff-target.

SCHNEIDER, S. (2001) Introduction to the international human resource management special issue. *Journal of World Business,* 36(4): 341.

SCHULER, R. S. AND JACKSON, S. E. (1987) Linking competitive strategies with human resource management practices. *Academy of Management Review,* 1(3): 207–219.

SHELDON, P., SUN, J. J. M. AND SANDERS, K. (2014). Special issue on HRM in China: Differences within the country. *International Journal of Human Resource Management,* 25(15): 2213–2217.

SPARROW, P. R. AND HILTROP, J.-M. (1994) *European Human Resource Management in Transition.* London: Prentice Hall.

STOREY, J. (1992) *Developments in the Management of Human Resources: An Analytical Review.* Oxford: Blackwell.

STRAUSS, G. (1982) Workers participation in management: An international perspective. *Research in Organizational Behavior,* 4: 173–265.

STREDWICK, J. (2005) *An Introduction to Human Resource Management* (2nd edn). London: Elsevier.

SYED, J., HAZBOUN, N. G. AND MURRAY, P. A. (2014) What locals want: Jordanian employees' views on expatriate managers. *International Journal of Human Resource Management,* 25(2), 212–233.

TAYEB, M. H. (2005) *International Human Resource Management: A Multinational Company Perspective.* New York: Oxford University Press.

TAYLOR, S., BEECHLER, S. AND NAPIER, N. (1996) Toward an integrated model for strategic international human resource management. *Academy of Management Review,* 21(4): 959–971.

TRIANDIS, H. C., DUNNETTE, M. D. AND HOUGH, L. M. (eds) (1994) *Handbook of Industrial and Organizational Psychology* (2nd edn, vol. 4). Palo Alto, CA: Consulting Psychology Press.

TROMPENAARS, F. AND HAMPDEN-TURNER, C. (1997) *Riding the Waves of Culture: Understanding Cultural Diversity in Business* (2nd ed.). London: Nicholas Brealey Publishing.

TUNG, R. L. (1993) Managing cross-national and intra-national diversity. *Human Resource Management Journal,* 23(4): 461–477.

TYLOR, E. B. (1924). *Primitive Culture* (7th ed., vols 1 and 2). New York: Brentano's.

UN (1992) Kyoto Protocol to the United Nations Framework Convention on Climate Change. United Nations Framework Convention on Climate Change. Available at: http://unfccc.int/essential_background/kyoto_protocol/items/1678.php.

USA Today (2013). Brunei's sultan to implement Sharia penal code. October 22. Available at: http://www.usatoday.com/story/news/world/2013/10/22/brunei-sharia-law/3162127/.

VAIMAN, V. AND BREWSTER, C. (2015) How far do cultural differences explain the differences between nations? Implications for HRM. *International Journal of Human Resource Management,* 26(2): 151–164.

WHEELAN, C. (2003) *Naked Economics: Undressing the Dismal Science.* New York: W. W. Norton.

WICKENS, P. (1987) *The Road to Nissan.* London: Macmillan.

ZHOU, Y., LIU, X. Y. AND HONG, Y. (2012) When Western HRM constructs meet Chinese contexts: Validating the pluralistic structures of human resource management systems in China. *International Journal of Human Resource Management,* 23(19): 3983–4008.

2

A CRITICAL PERSPECTIVE ON STRATEGIC HUMAN RESOURCE MANAGEMENT

Fida Afiouni and Dima Jamali

LEARNING OUTCOMES

After reading this chapter, you should be able to:

➤ Recognise recent transformations and dynamic change in the human resources management (HRM) field
➤ Demonstrate good knowledge of the various theoretical approaches to strategic HRM
➤ Discuss how human resources can be a source of sustainable competitive advantage within a global context
➤ Critically examine choices and contingencies in the HRM field
➤ Recognise the significant advances brought about by the strategic HRM paradigm, as well as lingering challenges, particularly the gap that remains between human resources policies and practices.

SUMMARY OF CHAPTER CONTENTS

➤ **Opening Case Study**: Boecker
➤ Introduction
➤ From personnel management to SHRM: An evolutionary road map
➤ Differentiating attributes, key contributions and underlying theories
➤ Critical analysis and discussion
➤ Conclusion
➤ **End of Chapter Case Study**: Strategic human resource management: Insights from Deloitte ME's experience
➤ For discussion and revision
➤ Glossary
➤ Further reading
➤ Web resources
➤ References

Opening case study Boecker

Boecker Public Health is the Middle East's largest Pest Management group providing World Class pest control, pest management, professional disinfecting, and pest control equipment and chemicals. Founded in 1993, Boecker provides World Class quality services for commercial and residential clients including Pest Management, Food Safety Training and Consulting, Fumigation and Heat Treatment as well as professional disinfecting services. Boecker's offices are active in Lebanon, United Arab Emirates, Kuwait, Qatar, Jordan and Nigeria.

Boecker's clients include various residential, institutional, and commercial accounts. Boecker services the most vital sectors of the economy; from airports to large urban projects, as well as medical facilities, food processing plants, catering and food manufacturing, hotels, restaurants, universities and schools, as well as commercial and residential facilities.

Boecker provides an excellent work environment; the Boecker team is a professional, highly trained group of specialists in the fields of Environmental Health, Entomology, Marketing and Business Development.

Furthermore, Boecker has developed the 'Boecker Academy', a specialised centre for the formation and training of professional pest management technicians. The Academy is run by accredited trainers with strong background in Entomology, Environmental Health, Agricultural Sciences and Field Experience.

Boecker has realised that in order to fulfil its vision to become one of the World's leading players in the Pest Management and Food Safety Industries, it has to build on providing World Class services through exceptional management skills. That's why the HR function's role is crucial to ensure that Boecker has the needed capabilities to provide high quality services globally while at the same time building capabilities for the future to ensure and sustain the growth of the company globally.

Questions

1   Highlight the strategic role that HRM is playing in fulfilling Boecker's global vision.
2   Find examples of two companies in your own city or country where HR is playing a strategic role. Prepare to share your findings with your classmate and discuss the importance of the HR function in supporting business strategy.

INTRODUCTION

Over the past three decades, there has been a vibrant change and evolution in the field of human resource management (HRM). Schuler and Jackson (2007) categorise changes in the field into two major transformations. The first has entailed a transformation from personnel management to HRM, and the second constituted a leap forward into what is commonly referred to today as strategic HRM (SHRM). More recently, we are witnessing a third transformation in the field that is driven by the increasingly global nature of HRM activities and the war for talent leading to a focus on global talent management (GTM). According to its proponents, SHRM constitutes a new orthodoxy and is mainly differentiated by its macro or strategic orientation, as well as its focus on outcomes and performance (Buyens and De Vos, 2001; Delery and Doty, 1996; Jackson, Schuler, and Jiang, 2014). SHRM also emphasises that the people or staff are core assets rather than a cost to the organisation (Armstrong, 2006; Redman and Wilkinson, 2009). Although it is certainly a discipline that is still taking shape and form, SHRM has enjoyed an astounding ascendancy in recent years, and has attracted significant interest from the academic and practitioner community (Becker and Huselid, 2006; Jackson, Schuler, and Jiang, 2014).

The aim of this chapter is to provide a critical assessment of SHRM, shedding light on its differentiating attributes and theoretical foundations, as well as the persistent gaps and challenges in this rapidly growing field. SHRM undoubtedly presents significant advances and new insights in relation to people management, but it is not a panacea and there is still no consensus on an exact definition of SHRM among scholars. These challenges, coupled with the difficulty of translating theory into practice, are possible stumbling blocks in the way of the full fledged maturation of SHRM and will be fleshed out and discussed further in the sections below.

The structure of this chapter is as follows. First, we will explore the evolutionary road map from personnel management to SHRM and examine the various theoretical approaches to SHRM, namely the resource-based view (RBV) as well as the universalist, contingency and configurational approaches. This exploration will be enriched by practical exercises and critical questions that allow for a better understanding of the strategic role of HRM in a global context. Finally, we will adopt a critical perspective that aims to reveal the global and ethical issues that underpin SHRM and sensitise the reader to the potential gaps that remain between the policy and practice of SHRM.

FROM PERSONNEL MANAGEMENT TO SHRM: AN EVOLUTIONARY ROAD MAP

The traditional personnel management approach was prevalent in the first part of the twentieth century and reflected management currents revolving around Weberism, Taylorism, and scientific management. Engineers such as Frederick W. Taylor were the actual designers of processes of production, and their focus was on developing collaboration among workers and machines to maximise labour productivity and efficiency. The purpose of HR was to address organisational challenges, add value via management, and streamline the employment relationship. During World War One, and with labour shortage, oversupply of immigrant workers, and increased demand for wartime production, employers were forced to make use of workers' labour more efficiently by establishing personnel departments (Ulrich and Dulebohn, 2015). The personnel management function adopted a uniquely inward and operational focus, with an obsessive concern with legal compliance and streamlining basic administrative and personnel processes. Personnel management was therefore commonly characterised as a transactional, low-level, record-keeping and maintenance function with a short-term micro-orientation and a preoccupation with operational issues, practices and policies, to the neglect of broader business issues and the overall direction of the organisation (Guest, 1987; Redman and Wilkinson, 2009). This approach to the management of people was essentially anchored in a view of labour as a commodity to be used efficiently and discarded as appropriate.

The first major transformation or turning point came about in the 1970s and reflected the ascendancy of the human relations and organisational behaviour paradigms (Anthony, Kacmar, and Perrewe, 2002; Mahoney and Deckop, 1986). These new theoretical traditions highlighted the complexity of human behaviour and the importance of soft aspects of management, including leadership and motivation, in impacting work outcomes in a positive way. The challenge for HRM was therefore to reposition 'employees as valued organisational resources' (Dunn, 2006: 71) and to better orchestrate policies and

practices that affected their behaviour and productivity at work (Schuler and Jackson, 2007).

Although HRM retained essentially its tactical short-term orientation, it was heralded as 'a new era of humane people oriented employment management' (Keenoy, 1990: 375) capitalising on systematic and professional management practices and the improved coordination and integration of human resources practices. Valuing employees as an important human capital – an investment rather than a cost (Wright et al., 2001) – was the prevailing assumption permeating this first transformation of the function. This transformation of the HRM function was in turn accompanied by the emergence of the total quality management (TQM) paradigm. Despite differences in the nature of and approaches to TQM and HRM, both concepts share the paramount importance of people-focused organisational efforts. These shared characteristics of the two concepts suggest a resurgence of the value attached to managing human resources, as both focus on a systematic and careful approach to the recruitment of employees, the use of teamwork and group problem-solving, egalitarian work structures, a commitment to training, and performance and reward systems.

The second major transformation in the field occurred more recently, starting in the 1990s in response to large-scale organisational change and an intensely competitive global economic environment (Colakoglu, Lepak, and Hong, 2006). In the context of new trends including organisational transience, corporate restructuring (for example, mergers and acquisitions, and downsizing), a renewed focus on quality and customers, and the war for talent among others (Amit and Belcourt, 1999; Conner and Ulrich, 1996; Pilbeam and Corbridge, 2006), the need for agility and efficiency has been accentuated. In addition, the role of human resources has been brought to the fore as it has been realised that employees can have a significant impact on the overall success of the organisation. SHRM is therefore anchored in a recent appreciation that human resources and the effective management of people are critical to profitability (Boxall and Purcell, 2011) and the overall ability of a firm to thrive and compete (Meilich, 2005). As suggested by Boxall and Purcell (2011), the adjective 'strategic' implies a concern with the ways in which HRM is critical to the firm's survival and relative success, and SHRM has come to denote 'a strategic and coherent approach to the management of an organisation's most valued assets – the people working there, who individually and collectively contribute to the achievement of its objectives' (Armstrong, 2006: 3).

Figure 2.1, adapted from Brockbank (1999: 340) and Pilbeam and Corbridge (2006: 10), outlines this ongoing process of transformation or evolution from traditional personnel management to SHRM. Figure 2.1

Degree of Competitive Advantage

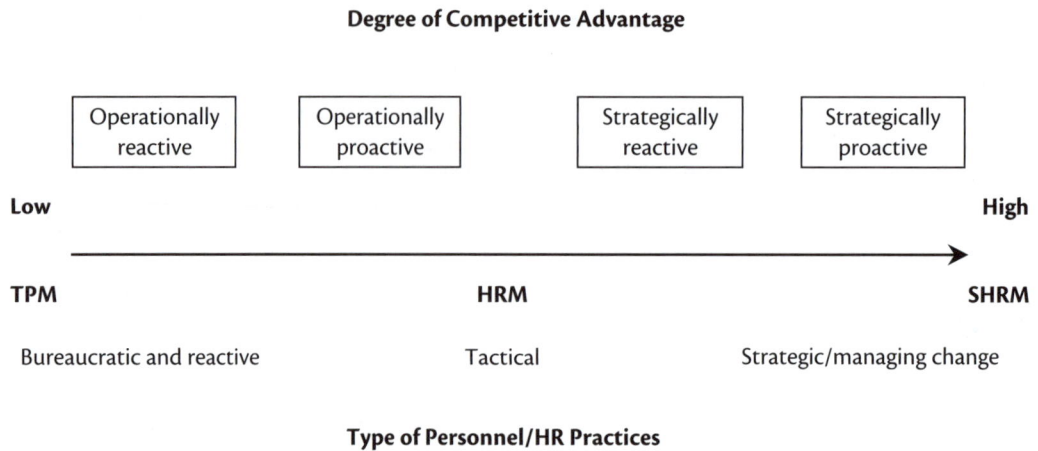

Operationally reactive	Operationally proactive	Strategically reactive	Strategically proactive

Low   High

TPM   HRM   SHRM

Bureaucratic and reactive   Tactical   Strategic/managing change

Type of Personnel/HR Practices

Figure 2.1 From traditional personnel management (TPM) to strategic human resource management (SRHM)
Source: Adapted from Brockbank (1999: 340), and Pilbeam and Corbridge (2006: 10)

also highlights interesting nuances at both sides of the continuum. On the left-hand side, we can note nuances between reactive and proactive operational orientations with an operationally reactive human resources function focused on day-to-day demands and implementation of the regular and mundane; this contrasts with a more proactive orientation concerned with improving the basics, as suggested by Brockbank (1999). We can also highlight interesting nuances between strategically reactive and strategically proactive human resources orientations on the right-hand side of the continuum, with the strategically reactive human resources generally concerned with implementing and realising strategy, and more strategically proactive human resources concerned with creating and forging strategic alternatives (Brockbank, 1999).

The third major transformation in the field has started over the turn of the century and is mainly driven by the increasingly global nature of HRM activities and the war for talent. As a matter of fact, the issue of global talent management (GTM) has gained a rising importance which also implies new roles for the corporate HR function, in addition to many challenges. In fact, the most daunting challenges currently facing the HR profession is the competition for highly skilled talents, managing international mobility, and dealing with emerging markets difficulties. Farndale et al. (2010) identified as a result four changing roles of corporate HRM in GTM in MNCs: champions of processes, guardians of culture, network leadership and intelligence, and managers of internal receptivity.

Most recently, the forces of globalisation have changed the business world in terms of increased competition for quality products and customer care, continuous technological innovations, a more mobile and diverse workforce,

growth in part-time and flexible work, and an increase in numbers of women joining the workforce (Sparrow, Brewster, and Harris, 2004). All of this led to further developments in HRM and placed more emphasis on people management (Huczynski and Buchanan, 2001). Many factors are driving globalisation, such as shortage of talent in developed countries mainly due to ageing and retirement of baby boomers while there is availability of low-cost labour from emerging countries, in addition to continuous technological progress (Kapoor, 2011). Therefore, only those multinational companies that are willing to adapt to all such changes in the labour market through working on their global staffing and management of a workforce diverse in culture and language skills and dispersed across various nations will survive and gain competitive advantage (Kapoor, 2011).

International Human Resource Management (IHRM) has gained increased interest among scholars and practitioners due to the rapid rise of globalisation of the world economy and the competitive challenges of attracting and retaining global qualified talents. IHRM entails how employees are managed in multinational corporations (MNCs) and the outcomes of such policies and practices (Schuler, Budhwar, and Florkowski 2002). IHRM thus involves the effective management of human resources in global markets for MNCs, in order to gain competitive advantage and be globally successful (Schuler and Tarique 2007). The concept of IHRM has developed throughout the years from being mainly concerned with managing expatriates towards a broader field that considers organisational and contextual issues, such as transferring HR practices into subsidiary units, or HRM's role in international mergers and acquisitions (M&As) (Björkman and

Welch, 2015). It has matured to a broader field of three approaches (Budhwar, Schuler, and Sparrow, 2009; Dowling, Festing, and Engle, 2013; Festing et al., 2013). The first approach revolves around cross-cultural management, meaning studying human behaviour within organisations from an international, intercultural perspective. The second approach describes, compares, and analyses HRM systems in various countries to provide, for instance, information on best practice and comparative performance (developed from the comparative industrial relations and HRM literature). The third approach focuses on aspects of HRM in multinational firms and considers the management of expatriates as well as the challenges of global standardisation and local adaptation of HRM in multinational firms.

According to Ulrich and Dulebohn (2015), to succeed in its new roles the HR function will need to adopt an outside/inside that connects HR to the broader context in which business operates and to external stakeholders. This approach allows HR to go beyond prior efforts to add value inside the organisation, through serving employees and line managers, to creating value by aligning HR services and activities to meet expectations of external stakeholders including customers, investors, and

---

Mini Case Study HRM at Algorithm: good strategic alignment

Algorithm is a pharmaceutical plant operating in the Middle East, having existed under this name since 1989. The firm's business line is manufacturing pharmaceutical products and sending them to its distributors and exporters (it does not handle any distribution activities itself). Algorithm belongs to a group of three sister companies employing a total of 320 employees, 170 of whom are employed by Algorithm. It manufactures products under licence, as well as its own generic products. It has a development laboratory – the Product Development Lab – but this mainly copies generic products and designs new products without creating molecules. The organisation does not outsource any technical or production activities as it has all the necessary departments and assets. This means that it manufactures, analyses and registers all its products. The plant's production includes over-the-counter (OTC) and prescription drugs, but no cosmetic products.

An interview was conducted with Mrs Nicole Bakhache, the HR and administration manager at Algorithm Lebanon and a member of Algorithm's strategy-setting team. The human resources function at Algorithm has been given much greater importance over the past five years, and no major decision related to people or structure is taken without human resources input. Mrs Bakhache explained that some personnel activities involve a more reactive role (for example, benefits and payroll), whereas other activities, such as recruitment, training, and career planning, involve a more proactive and strategic role.

At Algorithm, the human resources department also plays a substantial role in ensuring the success of general business strategies and helping to accomplish business goals. It is expected to translate business strategy into action and to focus on aligning human resources strategies and practices with business strategies. The department has forged a partnership with line managers, and together they formulate and manage processes to help meet business objectives. Furthermore, line managers now view human resources as a partner and are themselves involved in the management of human resources – working along with the human resources function on activities such as recruitment, people development, and personnel-related issues.

The human resources manager explained that the strategies of the human resources function are aligned with the general business strategies and that line management involves human resources in meetings where future strategies are being formulated. They are, for example, involved in strategic meetings discussing company expansion (since they will have to recruit the qualified staff needed for this), budgeting and planning. Mrs Bakhache explained that the technical departments do not have regular meetings with human resources, but hold periodic meetings to discuss budgets, management reviews, expansion plans, recruitment, and a review of training needs. The input of human resources is required when discussing issues related to staff, such as filling internal vacancies and retaining key staff if ever they should consider leaving the company.

Questions

1 How does the human resources department at Algorithm help to accomplish its business goals?
2 Use Figure 2.1 to evaluate the role of the human resources department in terms of its strategic/operational orientation as well as proactive/reactive orientation.
3 Explain why it is important for Algorithm to adopt an outside-in approach to HRM?

the community. To do that, HR will need to focus on the business context and external stakeholders (customers, investors, and community) while being also able to identify and build organisational capabilities that will support organisational strategy, add value, and increase the performance of the firm. In sum, the most recent developments within Strategic HRM currently look at HR as a complex group, taking into consideration the organisation's external and internal environments, the multiple players who enact HRM systems, and the multiple stakeholders who evaluate the organisation's effectiveness and determine its long-term survival (Jackson, Schuler, and Jiang, 2014). Indeed effective SHRM, endorsed by both line managers and HR professionals, can lead to various outcomes such as strategy execution, administrative efficiency, employee contribution, and capacity for change which will lead to gaining competitive advantage over others, especially in an increasingly global environment (Ulrich, 2013).

DIFFERENTIATING ATTRIBUTES, KEY CONTRIBUTIONS AND UNDERLYING THEORIES

At the heart of SHRM lies the idea that the way in which people are managed is one of the most crucial factors in the array of competitiveness-inducing variables, with a view that labour is an asset that should be leveraged in the pursuit of competitive advantage (Boxall and Purcell,

2011). Strategic choices associated with labour processes in turn reflect on the firm's performance. Hence, human resource policies need to be integrated with each other, as well as linked to the strategies and overall direction of the organisation (Schuler and Jackson, 2007). In this context, the core differentiating attributes of SHRM have come to be theorised as revolving around commitment, flexibility, quality, and integration (Guest, 1987), a strategic thrust informing decisions about people management and a new set of levers to shape the employment relationship (Storey, 2001). Moreover, Armstrong (2006) identifies core differentiating features of SHRM revolving around strategic orientation, commitment, people as a core asset, and business values/results. Some of these core themes are reflected in Table 2.1. which was compiled following a review of the SHRM literature.

In essence, SHRM is more fluid, organic and strategy-driven practice and is associated with *commitment*-based systems of control (Guest, 1990: 152). SHRM is therefore based on the assumption that people are not only assets but also have value-creating properties. This insight derives essentially from the RBV of the firm, a concept that emerged in 1984 and has enjoyed increasing popularity within the strategic management and HRM literatures. According to Wright et al. (2001), the RBV has been clearly instrumental to the development of the SHRM field of study, primarily because it has promoted a rebalancing of the strategy literature away from external factors (such as industry position) towards the firm's internal resources as sources of competitive advantage.

Table 2.1 Definitions and differentiating attributes of strategic human resource management (SHRM)

Author(s)	Definition of SHRM
Guest (1987)	SRHM has four key dimensions: commitment, flexibility, quality, and integration.
Boxall and Purcell (2000)	A concern with the ways in which HRM is critical to organisational effectiveness
Buyens and De Vos (2001)	The linking of the human resources function with the strategic goals and objectives of the organisation in order to improve business performance and develop organisational cultures that foster innovation and flexibility
Storey (2001)	Four key aspects of SHRM entailing a particular constellation of beliefs and assumptions, a strategic thrust informing decisions about people management, the central involvement of line managers, and a reliance upon a new set of levers to shape the employment relationship
Armstrong (2006)	SHRM is differentiated by its strategic thrust, emphasis on integration, commitment orientation, belief that people are core assets and focus on business values and results.
Redman and Wilkinson (2009)	A concept entailing strategic integration and a positive approach to the management of employees, with an emphasis on staff as a resource rather than a cost
Ulrich (2013)	Strategic HR often connects business strategies to HR actions by defining the critical capabilities required for an organisation to succeed.
Jackson, Schuler, and Jiang (2014)	SHRM is the study of HRM systems (and/or subsystems) and their interrelationships with other elements comprising an organisational system, including the organisation's external and internal environments, the multiple players who enact HRM systems, and the multiple stakeholders who evaluate the organisation's effectiveness and determine its long-term survival.

Indeed, one of the key contributions of the RBV to date has been a theory of competitive advantage and how firms can achieve and sustain their competitive advantage (Fahy, 2000). The RBV contends that the answer to this question lies in the nurturing and deployment of certain key resources. From an RBV perspective, not all resources are of equal importance – certain resources have an edge in terms of creating competitive advantage (Fahy, 2000). Barney (1991) posits that desirable resources must meet four conditions, namely value, rareness, inimitability, and non-substitutability. Collis and Montgomery (1995) suggest along the same lines that value-creating resources are characterised by inimitability, durability, appropriability, non-substitutability and competitive superiority. The RBV has therefore contributed significantly in terms of putting people on the strategy radar screen and highlighting the importance of people to competitive advantage.

Following the logic of the RBV, human capital constitutes a very important intangible asset or resource that is resistant to duplication by competitors. However, what is equally important from this perspective is the way in which this asset is deployed and managed, which has been captured through the notion of 'capabilities' that was introduced by Leonard-Barton as early as 1992. Capabilities are the tangible and intangible assets that firms use to develop and implement their strategies (Wernerfelt, 1995). Essentially, capabilities encompass the skills of individuals and groups, as well as the organisational routines and interactions through which all the firm's resources are coordinated (Grant, 1991). Typical of the latter are, among others, teamwork, communication, collaboration, learning, knowledge management, work design, organisational culture, trust between management and workers, and leadership. In this respect, human resources is not limited to its effects on employee skills and behaviour. Instead, its effects are more encompassing in that they help weave those skills and behaviours within the broader fabric of organisational systems, processes, and ultimately competencies (Wright et al., 2001). Thus, in a global context, the ultimate target of MNCs is to transfer capability across multiple countries through monitoring the implementation for relevant policies and practices and creating an appropriate culture at the organisation while staying responsive to employees' needs (Farndale et al., 2010).

Capabilities that give an organisation a strategic advantage over its competitors have been called core capabilities (Leonard-Barton, 1992), although a number of alternative terms have been used to refer to the same or similar concepts. An important article by Prahalad and Hamel (1990) that helped to disseminate the RBV refers to developing core competence within an organisation. Core competence develops from collective learning in an organisation, especially from being able to coordinate diverse sets of skills and integrate different technologies. Teece, Pisano, and Shuen (1997) define dynamic capabilities as the ability to integrate, build, and reconfigure internal and external competencies to address rapidly changing environments. Similarly, Leonard-Barton (1992) posits that dynamic capabilities reflect an organisation's ability to achieve new and innovative forms of competitive advantage given path dependencies and market positions.

In other words, human resources do not automatically confer a sustainable competitive advantage, and the managerial role is critical in nurturing, deploying, and protecting key firm resources over time (Williams, 1992). Whereas exceptional human talent confers human capital advantage (HCA), firms need to supplement or pair the latter with what has been referred to as human process advantage (HPA), through the nurturing of specific processes, routines and practices, and their constellation, operation and application over time (Boxall, 1996). Therefore, organisations face a dual challenge – or the management of mutuality (Wright et al., 2001) – that entails the creation of a committed and talented workforce, as well as nurturing the right processes to support this talent and shape its competencies, cognitions, and attitudes (Boxall, 1996). The contemporary theories of job design, as outlined by Holland in Chapter 7 in this book, are important in conferring such a HPA in the sense that they focus on human needs and psychological aspects of job content. In other words, SHRM needs to take into account job design aspects relating to variety and challenge, continuous learning, decision-making autonomy, and social relationships, particularly in creating HPA.

These two sources of competitive advantage, when effectively combined, reinforce the systemic quality of highly effective human resources architectures and confer human resource advantage, as illustrated in Figure 2.2. SHRM posits in turn a relationship between a firm's

STOP AND REFLECT

Barney (1991) posits that desirable resources must meet four conditions – value, rareness, inimitability and non-substitutability – in order to be a source of sustainable competitive advantage. Based on these characteristics, critically examine how human resources are a possible source of competitive advantage.

Questions

1 Where does the advantage come from?
2 Is it a human capital advantage deriving from the quality of the employees, or is it a human process advantage deriving from the set of human resources policies and practices that has been applied?

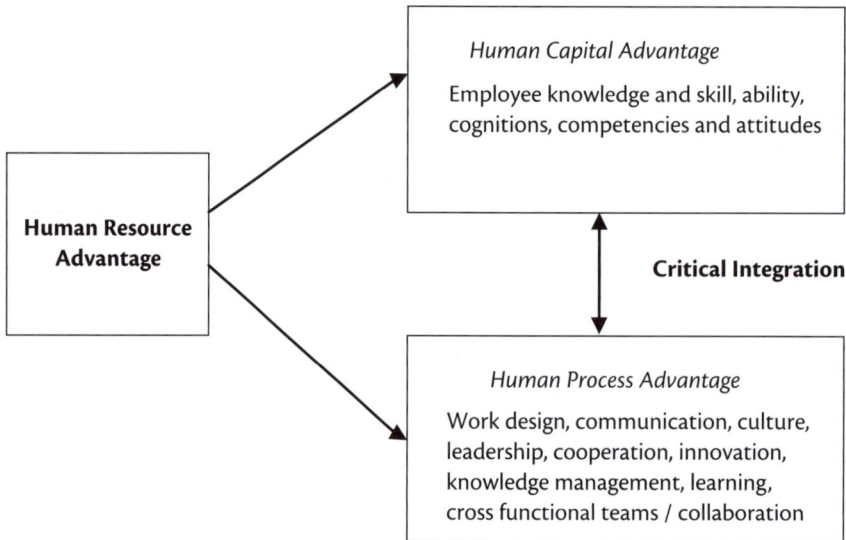

Figure 2.2 The resource-based view and human resource advantage
Source: Adapted from Boxall (1996: 66–67)

human resources architecture and that firm's perfor-mance (Becker and Huselid, 2006).

The link between the human resources architecture and the firm's performance is not direct but is usually mediated by an appropriate match between the human resources architecture and strategic choice – what is com-monly referred to as the human resources–strategy fit (Schuler and Jackson, 1987). In other words, the human resources architecture needs to be aligned with the larger competitive strategy of the firm. As Mohrman and Lawler (1997, 160) write, 'in order for the human resources func-tion to contribute to its organisation's performance, it must ensure that all of its human resources practices "fit with each other and with the strategy and design of the organisation"'. Although the latter has tended to be a sali-ent underlying premise of SHRM – that firms adopting a particular strategy require human resources practices that are different from those required by organisations adopt-ing alternative strategies (Delery and Doty, 1996) – there is no consensus on this point. This is reflected in the emer-gence of three different modes of theorising in the field of SHRM:

- the universalistic perspective;
- the contingency perspective;
- the configurational approach.

These are described briefly below.

The universal approach, also commonly referred to as the best practice approach, to SHRM posits that some

human resources practices are always better than others and that all organisations should adopt these best prac-tices (Delery and Doty, 1996). The logic is that all firms are likely to see improvements in their performance if they identify and implement best practice and that the link between human resources and the firm's perfor-mance is universal across the population of organisa-tions. The most renowned model in the best practice approach is that of Pfeffer (1994), who argued that the greater adoption and use of 16 management practices, such as employment security, selectivity in hiring, incen-tive pay, high wages, empowerment, participation, train-ing and skill development, and promotion from within, would result in higher productivity and profit across firms. Osterman (1994) similarly suggested that inno-vative work practices, such as teams, quality circles, job rotation, and TQM, stimulate productivity gains across companies. These practices identified by Pfeffer (1994) and others have been labelled as high-performance work practices as they induce higher performance (Delery and Doty, 1996).

Contingency theorising, or what is commonly referred to as the best-fit approach, argues that the human resources strategy will be more effective when it is appro-priately integrated with its specific organisational and broader environmental context (Boxall and Purcell, 2011). For example, the rate of product, service, or market inno-vation has frequently been treated as a critical contingency, with firms that are highly innovative considered as pros-pectors, firms that are moderately innovative considered

? Critical Thinking 2.1

Google and Apple have become 'innovation companies' and talent magnets. Both have moved from literally nowhere in the competitive landscape to market cap and product domination within the last decade due to their ability to attract and manage innovators, which is at the source of their success.

Questions

1 Look up the HR practices at both Google and Apple.
2 Do you think that these set of best HR practices would yield positive results if applied in a different company setting and in a different context (for example in an industrial company in a country with high power distance)?

as analysers, and firms that rarely innovate considered as defenders (Miles and Snow, 1984). Basically, the successful implementation of any of those business strategies relies heavily on human resources and its moulding of appropriate employee behaviour (Delery and Doty, 1996). Schuler and Jackson (1987), for example, argue that human resources practices should be designed to reinforce the behavioural implications of the various generic strategies defined by Porter (1985), as illustrated briefly in Figure 2.3 and Table 2.2. Therefore, to the extent that an organisation's strategy demands behavioural requirements for its success, the use of human resources practices can reward and control employee behaviour (Delery and Doty, 1996).

A third approach, the configurational approach to HRM, bridges the gap between the universal and the contingency approaches and suggests that a firm will perform better through an appropriate internal fit between its HRM practices (the configuration fit) and an appropriate external fit between the firm's business strategy and its HRM practices. MacDuffie (1995) argues that the appropriate unit of analysis for studying the strategic link between different HRM practices and performance does not involve individual practices as much as interrelated and internally consistent practices, called 'bundles'. He explains that a bundle creates the multiple, reinforcing conditions that support employee motivation, given that employees have the necessary knowledge and skills to perform their jobs effectively.

Moreover, global companies must make critical decisions because the diversity of the workforce presents unique challenges to the development and implementation of HR strategy. Companies should adapt their HR structure to fit the demands of globalisation while being reactive to specific cultural requirements (Bamberger, Biron, and Meshoulam, 2014). Decisions need to be made with regards to staffing, performance management,

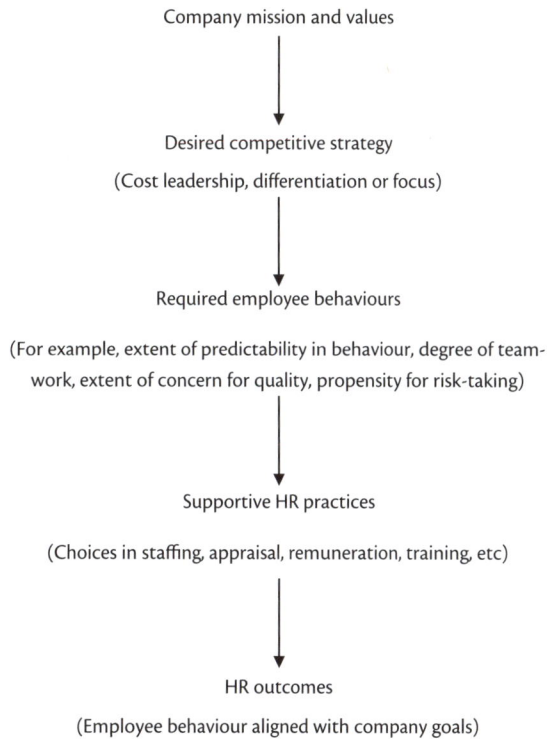

Company mission and values

↓

Desired competitive strategy

(Cost leadership, differentiation or focus)

↓

Required employee behaviours

(For example, extent of predictability in behaviour, degree of teamwork, extent of concern for quality, propensity for risk-taking)

↓

Supportive HR practices

(Choices in staffing, appraisal, remuneration, training, etc)

↓

HR outcomes

(Employee behaviour aligned with company goals)

Figure 2.3 Linking human resources (HR) practices to competitive strategy
Source: Adapted from Schuler and Jackson (1987, 208)

Table 2.2 Different competitive strategies and different employee competitive role behaviours

Strategy	Employee role behaviours needed
Innovation	• Highly innovative behaviour • Very long-term behaviour • Highly cooperative behaviour • Moderate concern for quality • Moderate concern for quantity • Equal concern for process and results • Flexibility for change and risk-taking • High tolerance for ambiguity and unpredictability
Cost leadership	• Repetitive and predictable behaviour • Short-term behaviour or focus • Autonomous or individual activity • Modest concern for quality • High concern for quantity of outputs • Primary concern for results • Low risk-taking activity • High degree of comfort with stability

Source: Adapted from Schuler and Jackson (1987: 209)

Mini Case Study HRM at Fattal: A continuous improvement journey

Fattal Holding is a regional organisation operating in the Middle East and North Africa region, with a total of 932 employees in Fattal Lebanon, 220 in Syria, 140 in Jordan, 110 in Iraq, 50 in the UAE, and 50 in Sudan. It specialises in distribution, sales, and marketing. The human resources director at Fattal, Mr Samir Messara, has worked there for 24 years, for the last 6 years as human resources director, reporting to the chief operating officer, and previous to that as a line manager.

The human resources department at Fattal has existed since 1982, and has developed from a personnel department in charge of administrative activities to a strategic human resources department that started off in 1996–1997. There are currently seven employees in the human resources department working in the following divisions: personnel administration, training, compensation and benefits, recruitment, and communication and bonding – better known in Fattal as 'the five pillars of human resources', as Mr Messara describes them.

In the past three years, the human resources function has shifted its techniques and adopted a competency-based approach in which all functions (for example, recruitment, selection and performance appraisal) are linked back to core skills and competencies. Mr Messara explained that Fattal's CEO has announced to all the directors that the human resources department is the most strategic asset in the company because it deals with people. Mr Messara asserted that senior management, as well as line management, at Fattal recognise the significance of the human resources function and appreciate its added value, considering it to be as important as the other functions in contributing to the organisation's performance. He also stressed that the operational and strategic pillars are equally important parts of the human resources department: 'operational does not mean that it is not important, and strategic does not mean that it is theoretical'. Subdividing functions into operational and strategic is thus a secondary issue as one without the other does not work or succeed – in other words, there is a 'duality'.

The human resources function therefore plays both a reactive and a proactive role. A reactive role is adopted when a decision is taken and the human resources department 'cascades it' through its systems and procedures; human resources monitors its execution and follows it to completion or finalisation. Human resources operations are now expanding in terms of new people – new assignments and recruitment for human resources in Syria and Iraq – a reactive role in which human resources has been deeply involved.

The proactive role comes from the strategic part of human resources. Human resources is always invited to be part of the 'think-tank' of the company and is invited by the CEO and Director to join in the decision-making about the next steps to be taken. Human resources is involved in the organisation's major business decisions and takes part in strategy-setting meetings wherein HR staff offer their own input. Their input is considered in the final outcome, and the department also maintains open lines of communication with the Chairman, CEO, and all the general managers and country managers.

The proactive role of human resources can therefore be seen to be quite important in Fattal. For example, the firm had an issue regarding whether or not to open a subsidiary in Libya – this would need investment, the country was new to the firm's operations, and it would need new suppliers. Mr Messara explained that the human resources department was involved from day one in discussing the viability, feasibility and implications of opening up in Libya, as well as in how to go about it.

Questions

1 How has the human resources department evolved at Fattal during the last 28 years?
2 Mr Messara stressed that the operational and strategic pillars are equally important parts of the human resources department: 'operational does not mean that it is not important, and strategic does not mean that it is theoretical'. Critically examine this statement and elaborate more on the 'duality' of HRM's role, as well as on factors critical to success.

---

compensation, and employee relations. More specifically, these include decisions about global 'work systems, cross-national and virtual teams, global talent management, the management of expatriates, and the cross-national pay differentials in the context of global compensation' (Bamberger et al., 2014: 15).

CRITICAL ANALYSIS AND DISCUSSION

The succinct review presented above clearly highlights new directions and a significant advance in the scholarship of SHRM. SHRM has partly evolved in response to a dramatically more competitive economic environment. But there are those who argue that the ascendancy of SHRM should be viewed in the context of the long-standing battle that the human resources function has faced in justifying its position and demonstrating its value to business firms (Wright et al., 2001). At the heart of SHRM is the question of how much of a difference HRM can make in terms of organisational performance, and more specifically how the management of human capital can make this difference (Colakoglu et al., 2006). SHRM has certainly matured over the past few years, and has benefited from some empirical support and from the reinforcement provided by the RBV; however, there are lingering issues that are worth accounting for when discussing SHRM, most notably the frequently raised criticism that the field still lacks a solid theoretical foundation, as highlighted below (Delery and Doty, 1996; Dyer, 1984). According to Wright and McMahan (1992: 297):

> Without good theory, the field of SHRM could be characterised as a plethora of statements, regarding empirical relationships and prescriptions for practice that fail to explain why these relationships exist or should exist.

The RBV of the firm has provided a core theoretical rationale for the potential role of human resources as a strategic asset in the firm, and has broadened the foundation for exploring the impact of human resources on strategic resources. Several authors have, however, expressed concern about the level of abstraction in RBV theory and in SHRM theory in general (Priem and Butler, 2001; Becker and Huselid, 2006). According to Becker and Huselid (2006), the link between the human resources architecture and most RBV concepts remains too abstract and too indirect to explain the link between that architecture and a firm's subsequent performance, or how human resources contributes to a firm's sustained competitive advantage. Implementation from this perspective should be given more attention in SHRM theory because the link between the human resources system and the firm's performance is not as direct as suggested by previous SHRM literature (Wright and Sherman, 1999). There are also intermediate outcomes that are central and crucial to a more complete understanding of how the human resources architecture drives a firm's performance, and very few attempts have been made to demonstrate that the human resources practices actually impact the skills or behaviours of the workforce and that these skills or behaviours are related to concrete performance measures (Becker and Huselid, 2006; Wright et al., 2001).

Another common criticism is the reliance in the RBV on constructs that are difficult to operationalise in practice, which limits the prescriptive value of the theory for

Class Activity

Today, there has been clear evidence supporting a positive link between HR practices and firm's performance. There is however a little understanding of the mechanisms through which HRM influence performance and multiple potential explanations exist.

- ▸ Working in a group of two to four people, try to identify the mechanisms through which HRM affects performance.
- ▸ Present your findings to the class and compare your findings to other groups' findings.
- ▸ What conclusions can you draw? How do these conclusions connect with the SHRM concepts explained in this chapter?

managers (Priem and Butler, 2001). What we need, according to Priem and Butler (2001), is a more careful delineation of the specific mechanisms purported to generate competitive advantage and more actionable prescriptions. According to Wright et al. (2001), a major step forward in the SHRM literature will be simply to move beyond the application of RBV logic to human resource issues, and towards research that directly tests the core concepts of the RBV. According to Fahy (2000), the vast majority of contributions within the RBV have been of a conceptual rather than an empirical nature, with the result that many of its fundamental tenets remain to be validated. Colbert (2007) posits that although the RBV has been helpful and relevant to the field of SHRM, there are aspects of the view that scholars have deemed critical but that are difficult to deal with in research and practice. Another important and salient criticism relates to the preoccupation of the RBV with internal resources, undermining the fact that countries provide variable contextual inputs and resources in terms of physical infrastructure, sociopolitical systems, and educational and technical infrastructure. Hence, there is a danger of becoming too absorbed with the firm as the unit of analysis (Boxall and Purcell, 2011).

There is also a continuing debate and various expressed concerns about best practice (universal) versus best fit (contingency) streams of theorising in SHRM. A common concern with the best practice approach is whether there is indeed a best human resources architecture that creates value for all firms. Despite the appeal of the notion of universally applicable HRM practices, some problems persist including the following:

- subjectivity and a lack of agreement on a definitive prescription of the best bundle;
- the implicit assumption that a particular bundle of practices is feasible for all organisations;

- the way in which best practices sometimes become ends in themselves dissociated from company goals (Boxall and Purcell, 2011).

Moreover, research suggests that national context matters, and the wide variations in labour laws and unionism across nations undermine support for best practice models. There are also salient differences across sectoral and organisational contexts (for example, sectors exposed to international competition). Generally, the evidence points to the adoption of innovative human resources bundles or high-performance work systems in sectors where quality is a major competitive factor and where firms need to exploit advanced technology. Cost-effectiveness is also certainly an important consideration in the limited diffusion of best practice models (Boxall and Purcell, 2011).

There is also a parallel set of concerns with best fit or contingency models. The most important concern relates to the purported simplicity of arranging a firm's assets and resources given a specific choice of strategy (Wright et al., 2001). Specifically, according to Cappelli and Singh (1992), most SHRM models based on fit assume: (1) that a certain business strategy demands a unique set of behaviours and attitudes on the part of employees; and (2) that certain human resources policies produce a unique set of responses from employees. But both assumptions are simplistic. There is also a lack of sophistication in existing descriptions of competitive strategy in the sense of concrete evidence that resilient firms in some sectors tend to successfully and simultaneously pursue different kinds of strategy (for example, cost leadership and differentiation). In addition, there are concerns that best fit models emphasising the alignment of HRM and competitive strategy tend to overlook employee interests (Boxall and Purcell, 2011). In other words, the strategic goals of HRM are plural. Although they do involve supporting the firm's competitive objectives, they also involve meeting employee needs and complying with social requirements for labour management (Boxall and Purcell, 2011). Multiple fits are required, and there is always a strategic tension inherent in a changing environment between

performing optimally in the present context and building the capacity of the organisation and preparing for the future.

One of the main reasons for lingering ambiguity and complexity in this area is that the choice of performance measures used in SHRM research studies varies widely. SHRM tries to link and synthesise multiple metrics, but this has been neither simple nor straightforward. Whereas traditional HRM research has tended to focus on individual-level outcomes such as job performance, job satisfaction, and motivation, SHRM has focused on firm-level outcomes related to labour productivity, sales growth, return on assets, and return on investment. This latter category of financial and accounting outcomes is less familiar to human resources practices than individual-level employee outcomes (Colakoglu et al., 2006). Although corporate- or firm-level performance metrics are important to examine, they are, according to some authors, not definitely and necessarily more important than others. The focus on organisational performance is illuminating and convincing for managers looking for concrete evidence of a significant impact of human resources on less familiar outcomes such as market or financial performance (Colakoglu et al., 2006). But these organisational performance outcomes are inevitably rooted in lower-level outcomes to which SHRM does not seem to accord enough attention.

These complexities become even more accentuated in the context of international SHRM research, which considers the growing importance of multinational corporations (MNCs) and the influence of complex global strategic business decisions on the human resource activities of these MNCs (Sparrow and Braun, 2007). Complexity arises from the multiplicity of independent variables as influencing factors and from the importance of linking HRM policies and practices with the organisational strategies of the MNC. This is rooted in the realisation that MNCs are geographically dispersed and vary in their goals and that different levels of integration and responsiveness are also invariably affected by whether or not the parent company actually has a global strategy, or more specifically 'a strategic international HRM system orientation'. In addition, it comes from the degree of similarity of affiliates' human resources systems to those of the parent company and the extent to which top management believes that HRM capability is indeed a source of strategic advantage (Sparrow and Braun, 2007).

On a final note, there is also enduring concern about whether human resources strategy theories developed in Western countries do actually apply to other cultures and how human resources strategies may be made to apply better in other cultures, which has been the domain of comparative HRM research. The answer to the first part of the question is clearly no, in the sense that human resources theories developed in Western countries do not necessarily apply universally and there are important contingency variables and institutional realities and multilevel factors

STOP AND REFLECT

Many qualified human resources managers often fail to manage the function strategically.

Questions

1 Who is to blame?
2 The human resources manager?
3 Organisational factors?
4 Environmental factors?
5 List and discuss all possible factors that might impede the implementation of proper SHRM initiatives.

that affect the practice of SHRM. Generally, the conclusion reached is that companies are not as global or international as is often assumed and that a clear country-of-origin effect is still evident (Sparrow and Braun, 2007). US MNCs, for example, tend to be more formalised and centralised than others in the management of HRM issues ranging from pay systems to collective bargaining and employee recognition. There is also a stream of literature that considers how the transfer of human resources practices can happen successfully, with convergence of practice depending, according to Kostova (1999), on internationalisation and the implementation of human resources rules by subsidiaries. Understanding the global effects on SHRM, such as diversity recruitment, push for professional development, greater emphasis on training, and management of laws across jurisdictions, can aid managers in better equipping their firms for the escalating global business environment (Choo, Halim, and Keng-Howe, 2010).

such as social and political systems, legislation and the power of labour unions and trade associations have on the adoption of human resources practices (Chow, 2004). The rationale of institutional theory is, according to Paauwe and Boselie (2003), that organisations are embedded in a wider institutional context that plays a role in shaping HRM practices and policies. Institutional mechanisms (for example, legislation with respect to conditions of employment, collective bargaining agreements, employment security, trade union influence and employee representation) shape employment relationships and human resources decision-making in organisations. Paauwe (2004) acknowledges institutional differences at both a country level and an industry level. Institutional mechanisms (mimetic, normative, and/or coercive) affect the relationship between HRM and performance and should therefore be taken into account in future research (Paauwe and Boselie, 2003).

? Critical Thinking 2.2

Multinational corporations operating in a global context face additional challenges when it comes to managing their human resources. For example, HR managers need to decide what standards and practices should be standardised across countries and which should be localised within each country.

Questions

1   Identify five challenges HR managers need to deal with when operating in a global context.
2   Working alone or in group, try to critically reflect about possible actions HR managers can undertake to address these challenges.

Looking back on the last two decades, Paauwe and Boselie (2005) point to major similarities between the development of HRM and the developments in strategic management theorising. In the 1980s, HRM was influenced by Porter-like outside–in approaches, for example reflected in the work of Schuler and Jackson (1987), emphasising the necessity of strategic fit – the fit between the overall strategy (based on the external environment) and the human resources strategy. The introduction of the RBV in the 1990s also led to a transition from the former outside–in approaches (based on contingency assumptions) to an inside–out approach, in which human resources play a key role in the search for the sustained competitive advantage of an organisation (Paauwe and Boselie, 2005).

Recently, institutional theory has been increasingly used as a framework to analyse human resource practices. It looks at the influence that environmental factors and institutions

---

✐ Class Activity

Defining the effective human resource manager

Based on what you have learned above about SHRM, What skills, competencies, and knowledge does an HR manager require to become a strategic business partner and impact the company's performance positively, namely in a global context? Try to collect information from a range of sources, for example corporate websites, human resources practitioner journals (*HR magazine, Personnel Today, People Management*), other journals (*Human Resource Management Journal, International Journal of Human Resource Management, Personnel Review*), the Chartered Institute of Personnel Development and The Society for Human Resource Management websites, and HRM textbooks to develop a profile of an effective human resources manager in the twenty-first century.

▸ Discuss your findings with other students in your class. What conclusions can you draw?

CONCLUSION

The aim of this chapter was to provide a critical assessment of SHRM, shedding light on its differentiating attributes and theoretical foundations, as well as on the lingering gaps and challenges in this field. The opening sections highlighted the evolution in the field from personnel management to HRM and, most recently, SHRM. Although some suggest that the changes in the field are revolutionary (Hope-Hailey et al., 1997; Hoque and Noon, 2001; Storey, 1993), it is more accurate to characterise the change process as one of metamorphosis, evolution, or adaptation rather than of completely new creation (Redman and Wilkinson, 2009; Torrington, Hall, and Taylor, 2002). Each phase basically constitutes an improvement that has effectively leveraged or built on, rather than replaced, the preceding knowledge base of the discipline (Schuler and Jackson, 2007).

SHRM is essentially posited as constituting the highest level of sophistication or maturation in the field, and as an apt response to existing business trends and challenges. It has brought to the fore a set of new assumptions relating to strategic thrust, an emphasis on integration, an orientation towards commitment, a belief that people are the core assets, and a focus on business values and results. In the process, SHRM has raised and addressed an array of important questions, probing the link between HRM and organisational effectiveness. For example, which human resources practices lead to greater organisational performance? How does a firm ensure that its human resources practices fit with its strategy? How does it ensure that its individual human resources practices fit with each other? The key constructs and central debates in SHRM have grown out of the above questions: best practice versus best fit, horizontal and vertical fit, fit versus flexibility, univariate and multivariate effects, and appropriate theoretical frames (Colbert, 2007). What is common to all this work though is a focus on the links between human resources practices, the human resource pool and organisational outcomes (Colbert, 2007).

The applications and implications of the RBV within the SHRM literature have clearly led to an increasing convergence between the fields of strategic management and SHRM (Snell, Shadur, and Wright, 2001). In relation to both areas of the literature, the RBV has helped to put people on the radar screen and to highlight the importance of human knowledge and a firm's processes and capabilities in general as sources of competitive advantage. With its emphasis on the firm's internal resources as sources of competitive advantage, the RBV has gained increasing popularity within SRHM and has become by far the most often used theory within SHRM, both for the development of theory and for the rationale underlying empirical research. The RBV has triggered at the very least a deeper understanding of the interplay between HRM and competitive advantage, as well as a substantial advance in the SHRM literature.

But although the RBV has formed an integrating ground or backdrop for most of the work in SHRM over the past decade, it offers little in an explicit sense in the way of prescriptions for managers, thus not answering the 'how' questions central to SHRM. Delery (1998) notes that while the RBV provides a nice backdrop explaining the importance of human resources to a firm's competitiveness, it does not specifically deal with how an organisation can develop and support the human resources it needs for competitive advantage.

Although many continue to refer to best practice versus best fit, perhaps a broader conceptualisation, as suggested by Wright et al. (2001) and also nicely captured in Figure 2.2 above, is to focus on the people management system within an organisation. The word 'system' denotes attention to the importance of understanding the multiple practices that impact employees, rather than focusing on a single practice. The term 'people', rather than 'human resources', expands the relevant practices to those beyond the direct control of the human resources function, such as to communication, work design, culture, leadership, and a host of others that affect employees and shape their competencies, cognitions, and attitudes. In other words, sustained competitive advantage is not just a function of single or isolated components but rather a combination of human capital elements such as the development of stocks of skills, strategically relevant behaviours, and supporting people management systems. The recognition of the systemic quality of highly effective human resources and people management systems has been a key insight brought to the fore through the RBV and SHRM paradigm.

In the News How Netflix Reinvented HR

Netflix have adopted a truly unconventional approach to managing their Human Resources. As Patty McCord's (former Chief Talent Officer at Netflix) recent article in the *Harvard Business Review* tells it, everything came down to the motto: 'Be honest, and treat people like adults.' McCord carefully breaks down the basic elements of Netflix's talent philosophy:

> Performers Only. The best thing you can do for employees—a perk better than foosball or free sushi—is hire only 'A' players to work alongside them.

> Keeping High Standards. Let go of people whose skills no longer fit and provide compassionate severance packages to those who served you well.

> Kill the Performance Improvement Plan and formal performance reviews. They are inefficient, ineffective, and born of a fear of litigation.

McCord ends with a call to arms that HR teams need to be as innovative as other teams at their company, and in the market at large. There is no excuse for 'mimicking other companies' best practices (most of them antiquated)' when you could create something meaningful to propel your company forward.

Adapted from: McCord, P. (2014). How Netflix Reinvented HR, https://hbr.org/2014/01/how-netflixreinvented-hr. Harvard Business Review, 92(1), 70–76.

End of Chapter Case Study **Strategic human resource management: Insights from Deloitte ME's experience**

The Deloitte Middle East Firm (Deloitte ME) is a member of the global professional services firm Deloitte Touche Tohmatsu, which employs 169,000 people in 140 countries and had revenues of US$27 billion in the 2009 fiscal year. Deloitte ME is one of the longest established professional services firms in the region and has been operating since 1926 in 15 countries with 26 offices and a team of over 2,300 professionals. It has enjoyed a compounded revenue growth rate of 31 per cent in the region over the three years to 2010.

This case study is based on several rounds of interviews with Mrs Rana Ghandour Salhab, the first woman admitted as partner in the Middle East in the 80-year history of the firm in the region. She is currently the partner in charge of human resources and communications in the Middle East and a member of the Deloitte ME Board Advisory Council and the Deloitte ME Partner Screening Committee. It is worth noting that, in April 2009, Deloitte ME was recognised as one of the 10 best employers in the Middle East by Hewitt Associates, the global human resources consulting firm that runs best employer surveys across the world.

Based on a recent survey asking Deloitte employees what they expect from their employer, Deloitte ME adopted a 'develop, deploy, and connect' model as a talent strategy and a Career Value Map tool to reinforce the steps that individuals can take to own their careers and leverage Deloitte's resources and tools within each of the model areas. According to Mrs Salhab, organisations can, by focusing on these three elements, generate capability, commitment, and alignment in key workforce segments (Figure 2.4), which in turn improves business performance: 'When this happens, the attraction and retention of skilled talent largely take care of themselves'.

Deloitte has an interesting regional Talent Attraction Program and e-recruitment, revolving around a Middle East referral scheme, university relationships, an alumni and experienced hire programme, supplier relations, web and social networks sourcing, and Google ad words. The Deloitte Invites Top Talent programme also aims to attract top students from leading universities around the region to source offices with nationals of the Gulf Cooperation Council and Arabic-speaking professionals. The company's screening techniques focus on assessment centres, competency-based behavioural interviewing, psychometric testing, and a global development programme for its workforce. The Deloitte performance management system is

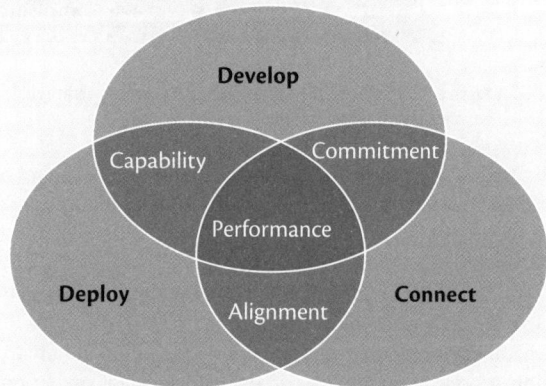

Figure 2.4 The Deloitte ME 'develop, deploy, and connect' model
Source: Deloitte office, Lebanon

the key development employee tool, with a technical and shared skills competency model that facilitates year round career conversations and a coaching culture. Through the ME Deloitte Retention and Advancement for Women Program, the firm is committed to creating an environment where high achieving women and men both reach leadership roles.

Deloitte ME has been striving for a balance between a strategic human resources agenda with a long-term impact and operational day-to-day human resources activities. The company realises that the drivers and challenges for the business are transitioning the core efforts of human resources towards providing the business with a competitive advantage. This will happen by moving away from a focus on administration (for example, payroll, benefits, compliance, and record-keeping), or what they refer to as value maintenance, to a focus on value creation through the selection and design of human resources practices that support the firm's strategy (Figure 2.5). Mrs Salhab recognises that assuming the human resources partner role depends on the level of maturity of the organisation; it also illustrates nicely how the Deloitte ME function has made a successful transition from roles revolving around analyst and advisor to human resources roles entailing effective advocacy and partnering. This transformation has, according to Mrs Salhab, required a proactive approach combining flexible and specialist human resources orientations, combined with the redirecting of administration queries and a more active involvement of line managers in different sorts of people management activities.

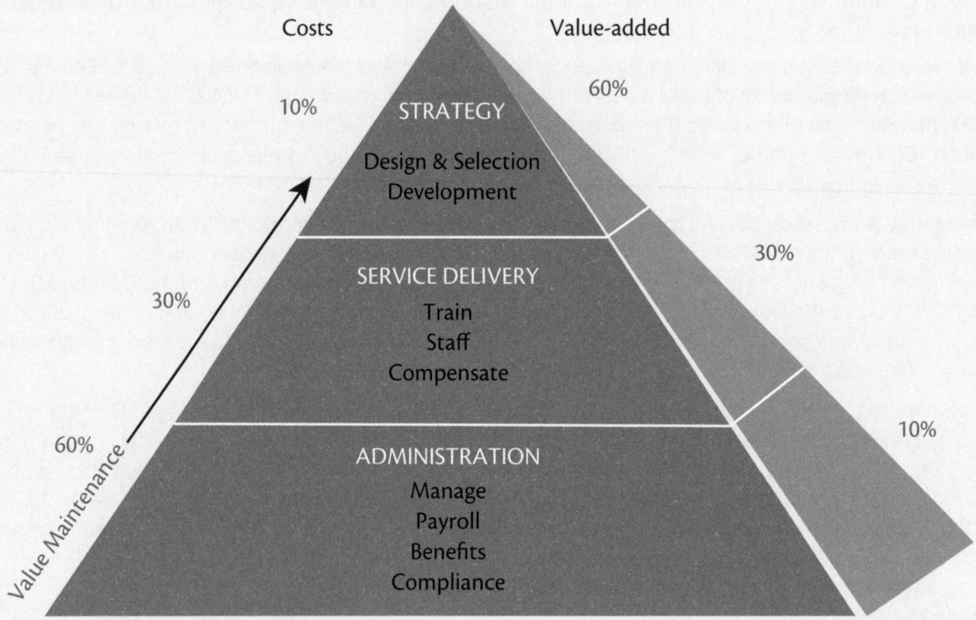

Figure 2.5 Deloitte ME value creation through strategic human resources
Source: Deloitte office, Lebanon

Mrs Salhab admits that the transformation of human resources into strategic roles is not always easy and may in some companies be typically undermined by a number of risks and pitfalls that have to be avoided. These may be, for example:

▸ reduced client satisfaction (in the sense that a one-size-fits-all approach to service delivery may not recognise the diversity of employees);
▸ insufficient market insight into and innovation in human resources policies;
▸ low morale in human resources, with no clear career path or longer-term development programme for some human resources professionals;
▸ overly expensive running costs and poor-quality outsourcing contracts;
▸ ineffective human resources business partners who are unable and ill-equipped to deliver the level of business advice expected;
▸ a continued erosion of data quality, and therefore human resources credibility, as a result of poorly constructed processes;
▸ dissatisfaction with self-service technologies due to their low-quality implementation and the poor education of line managers.

These failings have led the business to question whether human resources is best placed to fix the issues or whether the business itself should take control and address them. Mrs Salhab also admits that, despite the global change in paradigms of SHRM, human resources professionals are still spending too much time on low-impact activities (for example, responding to queries, responding to complaints, enforcing policies, managing conflicts, and basic administrative transactions) as opposed to forging strategy, developing metrics, and nurturing talent and leaders.

According to Mrs Salhab, human resources cannot just become strategic overnight. They have to drive a strategic agenda around things that matter, strengthen leadership capability, create an adaptable workforce, and advise on strategies that can maintain and enhance performance. This requires a number of key organisational and cultural changes that need to be crafted together, revolving around establishing the role of the chief human resources officer, optimising shared service centres, measuring success through value operation centres, and freeing business partners and the chief human resources officer to reflect the strategic focus. Other important changes revolve around adjusting human resources strategies to respond to changing needs, identifying critical human resources metrics and business strategies, identifying talent issues and prioritising human resources needs, redesigning structures around strategic objectives and, importantly, understanding the talent needs of the business. In this context, the onus also falls on human resources to nurture the right skills and competencies, including, among others, the following:

▸ behavioural competencies as in leadership skills, negotiation and conflict resolution, change leadership and communication skills;
▸ technical competencies, as in functional human resources knowledge, project management and the management of strategic resources;
▸ business competencies, as in business acumen, industry and organisational awareness, strategy and business planning, and consulting skills.

In conclusion, for Mrs Salhab, human resources is clearly at a turning point. For a decade now, it has been undergoing a process of transformation. But for many, this has been a process that has increasingly failed to produce the results expected of it: 'During these times of rapidly changing economics, we believe human resources is faced with a stark choice. It can either evolve and make a significant contribution, or be diminished and dispersed in the business.'

Questions

1   Mrs Salhab stated that 'During these times of rapidly changing economics, we believe human resources is faced with a stark choice. It can either evolve and make a significant contribution, or be diminished and dispersed in the business.' Use Figures 2.4 and 2.5 to explain how the human resources department at Deloitte adds value to the business.
2   Mrs Salhab is the first woman admitted as a partner in the Middle East in the 80-year history of the firm in the region. What additional challenges and opportunities can this provide for the successful development of the human resources department?
3   Do some further research and investigate whether the same human resources practices and policies are applied at Deloitte in various regions of the world. What lessons can you draw?

FOR DISCUSSION AND REVISION

1   Explain the evolutionary road map from personnel management to SHRM. What are the factors that triggered this evolution?
2   Why is the application of 'best practice' models of SHRM in organisations problematic?
3   In what way have the contingency and the configurational approaches to HRM contributed to your understanding of SHRM?
4   How does the RBV contribute to your understanding of SHRM?
5   Despite the fact that SHRM has evolved over the past few years, it continues to face a lot of criticism surrounding its theoretical and practical perspectives. List and discuss some of these criticisms.
6   What are some of the current challenges facing organisations today? How can a strategic approach to HRM aid MNCs to gain competitive advantage?

On February 2013, Maryssa Mayer, the new CEO of Yahoo has decreed there will be no more working from home for Yahoo staff. She mentioned that 'To become the absolute best place to work, communication and collaboration will be important, so we need to be working side-by-side. That is why it is critical that we are all present in our offices. Some of the best decisions and insights come from hallway and cafeteria discussions, meeting new people, and impromptu team meetings. Speed and quality are often sacrificed when we work from home. We need to be one Yahoo!, and that starts with physically being together.'

● Do you agree with the decision of Maryssa Mayer to stop telecommuting i.e. working from home) at yahoo?
● Working alone or in a group, identify some of the drivers (both at the country level and organisational level) for telecommuting.

- Working alone or in a group, critically reflect on the advantages and disadvantages of telecommuting for both the employees and the organisation.
- Reflecting back on Maryssa Mayer's decision described above, do you think it was a good decision to make at that time? Explain.

GLOSSARY

Configurational approach to SHRM: The configurational perspective posits a simultaneous internal and external fit between a firm's external environment, business strategy and HR strategy, implying that business strategies and HRM policies interact, according to organisational context in determining business performance.

Contingency approach to SHRM: The contingency perspective emphasises the fit between business strategy and HRM policies and strategies, implying that business strategies are followed by HRM policies in determining business performance.

Global Talent Management (GTM): global talent management involves the systematic identification of key positions which differentially contribute to the organisation's sustainable competitive advantage on a global scale, the development of a talent pool of high potential and high performing incumbents to fill these roles which reflects the global scope of the MNE, and the development of a differentiated human resource architecture to facilitate filling these positions with the best available incumbent and to ensure their continued commitment to the organisation.

Intangible Assets: the definition of 'intangible' comes from the field of accounting. Intangibles are organisational resources that do not appear on the balance sheet. On average, roughly 80 per cent of the value of today's corporation is intangible. Intangible assets (also called Intellectual capital) represent the intangible value of a business, covering its people (Human Capital), the value inherent in its relationships (Relational Capital), and everything that is left when the employees go home (Structural Capital). Human Capital is thus a form of intangible capital and includes all the talent, competencies, and experience of employees and managers.

Organisational Capabilities: An organisational capability is a company's ability to manage resources, such as employees, effectively to gain an advantage over competitors. The company's organisational capabilities must focus on the business's ability to meet customer demand.

Resource-Based View: The resource-based view states that organisational resources and capabilities that are rare, valuable, non-substitutable, and imperfectly imitable form the basis for a firm's sustained competitive advantage. The resource-based view of the firm provides therefore a conceptual basis for asserting that key human resources are sources of competitive advantage.

Strategic Human Resource Management: Strategic HRM covers the concepts and practices that guide and align Human Resource Management philosophy, tactical planning, and practice with the strategic and long-term goals of the organisation, with a particular focus on human capital. It deals with the macro-concerns of the organisation regarding structure, quality, culture, values, commitment, matching resources to future needs and other longer-term people issues.

Universalist Approach to SHRM: Universalistic or 'best practice' approach to HRM relates to the viewpoint that there is a set of best HRM practices and that their adoption is going to generate positive results regardless of the circumstances associated with organisations.

FURTHER READING

Books

BOXALL, P. AND PURCELL, J. (2015) *Strategy and Human Resource Management* (4th edn). New York: Palgrave Macmillan.

> This book is a classic work integrating HRM and strategic management, explaining the latest theoretical and practical developments in this fascinating area, and bridging the gap between theory and practice. It also integrates both HRM and employment relations in a critical and constructive way.

SCHULER, R. AND JACKSON, S. (2007) *Strategic Human Resource Management* (2nd edn). Malden, MA: Blackwell Publishing.

> This book provides students with a complete and updated guide to the latest work in the field. This selection of important and highly readable articles from authors around the world charts key developments that have changed the theory and practice of SHRM over the last decade.

Journals

LEGNICK-HALL, M. L., LEGNICK-HALL, C. A., ANDRADE, L. S. AND DRAKE B. (2009) Strategic human resource management: The evolution of the field. *Human Resource Management Review*, 19: 64–85.

> This article takes an evolutionary and chronological perspective on the development of the SHRM literature. The authors trace how the field has evolved to its current state, articulate many of the major findings

and contributions, and discuss how they believe it will evolve in the future. This approach contributes to the field of SHRM by synthesising work in this domain and by highlighting areas of research focus that, while promising, have remained largely unexamined.

PAAUWE, J. AND BOSELIE, P. (2003) Challenging 'strategic HRM' and the relevance of the institutional setting. *Human Resource Management Journal*, 13(3): 56–70.

In this article, the authors use the theory of new institutionalism as a better way to understand the shaping of human resources policies and practices in different settings. After a concise review of the latest debates in the area of SHRM, in which the RBV is the dominant perspective, they turn to an analysis of HRM in different institutional settings, which suggests the need for additional theory – that is, new institutionalism.

WRIGHT, P. M., MCMAHAN, G. C. AND MCWILLIAMS, A. (1994) Human resources and sustained competitive advantage: A resource-based perspective. *International Journal of Human Resource Management*, 5(2): 301–326.

The RBV of the firm has influenced the field of SHRM in a number of ways. This paper explores the impact of the RBV on the theoretical and empirical development of SHRM. It explores how the fields of strategy and SHRM are beginning to converge around a number of issues and proposes a number of implications of this convergence.

WEB RESOURCES

- The society of Human Resource Management: www.shrm.org.
- The Chartered Institute of Personnel and Development: http://www.cipd.co.uk/.
- The RBL group: http://rbl.net/.
- International Labour Organisation, Bureau for Employers' activities: http://www.ilo.org/public/english/dialogue/actemp/.
- Bayt: http://www.bayt.com/en/research-reports/.

REFERENCES

AMIT, R. AND BELCOURT, M. (1999) Human resources management processes: A value-creating source of competitive advantage. *European Management Journal*, 17(2): 174–181.

ANTHONY, W., KACMAR, M. AND PERREWE, P. (2002) *Human Resource Management: A Strategic Approach* (4th edn). Cincinnati, OH: South-Western.

ARMSTRONG, M. (2006) *Strategic Human Resource Management: A Guide to Action* (3rd edn). London: Kogan Page.

BAMBERGER, P. A., BIRON, M., AND MESHOULAM, I. (2014) *Human Resource Strategy: Formulation, Implementation, and Impact*. New York: Routledge.

BARNEY, J. (1991) Firm resources and sustained competitive advantage. *Journal of Management*, 17(1): 99–120.

BECKER, B. AND HUSELID, M. (2006) Strategic human resources management: Where do we go from here? *Journal of Management*, 32(6): 898–925.

BJÖRKMAN, I. AND WELCH, D. (2015) Framing the field of international human resource management research. *International Journal of Human Resource Management*, 26(2): 136–150.

BOXALL, P. (1996) The strategic HRM debate and the resource-based view of the firm. *Human Resource Management Journal*, 56(3): 59–75.

BOXALL, P. AND PURCELL, J. (2000) Strategic human resource management: Where have we come from and where should we be going? *International Journal of Management Reviews*, 2(2): 183–203.

BOXALL, P. AND PURCELL, J. (2011) *Strategy and Human Resource Management* (3rd edn). New York: Palgrave Macmillan.

BROCKBANK, W. (1999) If HR were really strategically proactive: Present and future directions in HR's contribution to competitive advantage. *Human Resource Management*, 38(4): 337–352.

BUDHWAR, P., SCHULER, R. AND SPARROW, P. (eds.) (2009) *Major Works in International Human Resource Management*. London: Sage (4 volumes).

BUYENS, D. AND DE VOS, A. (2001) Perceptions of the value of the HR function. *Human Resource Management Journal*, 11(3): 70–89.

CAPPELLI, P. AND SINGH, H. (1992) Integrating strategic human resources and strategic management. In LEWIN, D., MITCHELL, P. AND SHERER, P. (eds), *Research Frontiers in Industrial Relations and Human Resources*. Madison, WI: IRRA, pp. 165–192.

CHOO, S. S., HALIM, H. AND KENG-HOWE, I. C. (2010) The impact of globalisation on strategic human resources management: The mediating role of CEO in HR. *International Journal of Business Studies: A Publication of the Faculty of Business Administration, Edith Cowan University*, 18(1): 101–124.

CHOW, I. (2004) The impact of institutional context on human resource management in three Chinese societies. *Employee Relations*, 26(6): 626–642.

COLAKOGLU, S., LEPAK, D. AND HONG, Y. (2006) Measuring HRM effectiveness: Considering multiple stakeholders in a global context. *Human Resource Management Review*, 16: 209–218.

COLBERT, B. (2007) The complex resource-based view: Implications for theory and practice in strategic human resource management. In SCHULER, R. AND JACKSON,

s. (eds), *Strategic Human Resource Management* (2nd edn). Malden, MA: Blackwell Publishing, pp. 98–123.

COLLIS, D. AND MONTGOMERY, C. (1995) Competing on resources: Strategy in the 1990s. *Harvard Business Review*, 73: 118–128.

CONNER, J. AND ULRICH, D. (1996) Human resource roles: Creating value, not rhetoric. *Human Resource Planning*, 19(3): 38–49.

DELERY, J. (1998) Issues of fit in strategic human resource management: Implications for research. *Human Resource Management Review*, 8: 289–309.

DELERY, J. AND DOTY, D. (1996) Modes of theorising in strategic human resource management: Tests of universalistic, contingency, and configurational performance predictions. *Academy of Management Journal*, 39 (4): 802–835.

DOWLING, P. J., FESTING, M. AND ENGLE, A. D. (2013) *International Human Resource Management* (6th edn). London: Cengage.

DUNN, J. (2006) Strategic human resources and strategic organization development: An alliance for the future? *Organizational Development Journal*, 24(4): 69–76.

DYER, L. (1984) Linking human resource and business strategies. *Human Resource Planning*, 7(2): 79–84.

FAHY, J. (2000) The resource-based view of the firm: Some stumbling blocks on the road to understanding sustainable competitive advantage. *Journal of European Industrial Training*, 24: 94–104.

FARNDALE, E., SCULLION, H. AND SPARROW, P. (2010) The role of the corporate HR function in global talent management. *Journal of World Business*, 45(2): 161–168.

FESTING, M., BUDHWAR, P. S., CASCIO, W., DOWLING, P.J. AND SCULLION, H. (2013) Current issues in International HRM: Alternative forms of assignments, careers and talent management in a global context. *Zeitschrift für Personalforschung / German Journal of Research in Human Resource Management*, 27(3): 161–166.

GRANT, R. (1991) The resource-based theory of competitive advantage: Implications for strategy formulation. *California Management Review*, 33: 114–135.

GUEST, D. (1987) Human resource management and industrial relations. *Journal of Management Studies*, 24(5): 503–521.

GUEST, D. (1990) Personnel management: The end of orthodoxy? *British Journal of Industrial Relations*, 29(2): 149–175.

HOPE-HAILEY, V., GRATTON, L., MCGOVERN, P., STILES, P. AND TRUSS, C. (1997) A chameleon function: HRM in the '90s. *Human Resource Management Journal*, 3(3): 5–18.

HOQUE, K. AND NOON, M. (2001) Counting angels: A comparison of personnel and HR specialists. *Human Resource Management Journal*, 11(3): 5–22.

HUCZYNSKI, A., AND BUCHANAN, D. (2001) *Organizational Behaviour: An Introductory Text*. Financial Times/Prentice Hall..

JACKSON, S. E., SCHULER, R. S. AND JIANG, K. (2014) An aspirational framework for strategic human resource management. *Academy of Management Annals*, 8(1), 1–56.

KAPOOR, B. (2011) Impact of globalization on human resource management. *Journal of International Management Studies*, 6(1): 1–8.

KEENOY, T. (1990) HRM: Rhetoric, reality, and contradiction. *International Journal of Human Resource Management*, 23(1): 363–384.

KOSTOVA, T. (1999) Transnational transfer of strategic organizational practice: A contextual perspective. *Academy of Management Review*, 24(2): 308–324.

LEONARD-BARTON, D. (1992) Core capabilities and core rigidities: A paradox in managing new product development. *Strategic Management Journal*, 13: 111–125.

MACDUFFIE, P. (1995) Human resource bundles and manufacturing performance: Organizational logic and flexible production systems in the world auto industry. *Industrial and Labor Relations Review*, 48(2): 197–221.

MAHONEY, T. AND DECKOP, J. (1986) Evolution of concept and practice in personnel administration/human resource management. *Journal of Management*, 12(2): 223–241.

MEILICH, O. (2005) Are formalization and human asset specificity mutually exclusive: A learning bureaucracy perspective. *Journal of American Academy of Business*, 6: 161–169.

MILES, R. AND SNOW, C. (1984) Designing strategic human resource systems. *Organizational Dynamics*, 13(1): 36–52.

MOHRMAN, S. AND LAWLER, E. III (1997) Transforming the human resource function. *Human Resource Management*, 36(1): 157–162.

OSTERMAN, P. (1994) How common is workplace transformation and who adopts it? *Industrial and Labor Relations Review*, 47: 173–188.

PAAUWE, J. (2004) *HRM and Performance: Unique Approaches for Achieving Long-Term Viability*. Oxford: Oxford University Press.

PAAUWE, J. AND BOSELIE, P. (2003) Challenging 'strategic HRM' and the relevance of the institutional setting. *Human Resource Management Journal*, 13(3): 56–70.

PAAUWE, J. AND BOSELIE, P. (2005) HRM and performance: What's next? *Human Resource Management Journal*, 15(4): 68–83.

PFEFFER, J. (1994) *Competitive Advantage through People: Unleashing the Power of the Workforce*. Boston, MA: Harvard Business School Press.

PILBEAM, S. AND CORBRIDGE, M. (2006) *People Resourcing: Contemporary HRM in Practice* (3rd edn). London: Prentice Hall.

PORTER, M. (1985) *Competitive Advantage*. New York: Free Press.

PRAHALAD, C. K. AND HAMEL, G. (1990) The core competence of the corporation. *Harvard Business Review*, May–June: 79–91.

PRIEM, R. AND BUTLER, J. (2001) Is the resource-based view a useful perspective for strategic management research? *Academy of Management Review*, 26(1): 22–40.

REDMAN, T. AND WILKINSON, A. (2009) *Contemporary Human Resource Management: Text and Cases* (3rd edn). Harlow: Prentice Hall.

SCHULER, R. AND JACKSON, S. (1987) Linking competitive strategies with human resource management practices. *Academy of Management Executive*, 1(3): 207–219.

SCHULER, R. AND JACKSON, S. (2007) Preface. In *Strategic Human Resource Management* (2nd edn). Malden, MA: Blackwell Publishing.

SCHULER, R. S., BUDHWAR, P. AND FLORKOWSKI, G.W. (2002), International human resource management: Review and critique. *International Journal of Management Reviews*, 4: 41–70.

SCHULER, R .S. AND TARIQUE, I. (2007) International human resource management: A North American perspective. *International Journal of Human Resource Management*, 18(5): 717–744.

SNELL, S., SHADUR, M. AND WRIGHT, P. (2001) The era of our ways. In Hitt, R., Freeman, R. and Harrison, J. (eds), *Handbook of Strategic Management*. Oxford: Blackwell Publishing, pp. 627–629.

SPARROW, P. AND BRAUN, W. (2007) Human resource strategy in international context. In Schuler, R. and Jackson, S. (eds), *Strategic Human Resource Management* (2nd edn). Malden, MA: Blackwell Publishing, pp. 162–199.

SPARROW, P., BREWSTER, C. AND HARRIS, H. (2004) *Globalizing Human Resource Management*. Routledge,, London..

STOREY, J. (1993) The take-up of human resource management by mainstream companies: Key lessons from research. *International Journal of Human Resource Management*, 4(3): 529–533.

STOREY, J. (2001) *Human Resource Management: A Critical Text* (2nd edn). London: Routledge.

TEECE, D. J., PISANO, G. AND SHUEN, A. (1997) Dynamic capabilities and strategic management. *Strategic Management Journal*, 18(7): 509–533.

TORRINGTON, D., HALL, L. AND TAYLOR, S. (2002) *Human Resource Management*. London: FT/Prentice Hall.

ULRICH, D. (2013) *Human Resource Champions: The Next Agenda for Adding Value and Delivering Results*. Cambridge, MA: Harvard Business Press.

ULRICH, D. AND DULEBOHN, J. H. (2015) Are we there yet? What's next for HR? *Human Resource Management Review*, 25(2): 188–204.

WERNERFELT, B. (1995) The resource based view of the firm: Ten years after. *Strategic Management Journal*, 16: 171–174.

WILLIAMS, J. (1992) How sustainable is your competitive advantage? *California Management Review*, 34: 29–51.

WRIGHT, P. AND MCMAHAN, G. (1992) Theoretical perspectives for strategic human resource management. *Journal of Management*, 18: 295–320.

WRIGHT, P., MCMAHAN, G., SNELL, S. AND GERHART, B. (2001) Comparing line and HR executives' perceptions of HR effectiveness: Services, roles, and contributions. *Human Resource Management*, 40(2): 111–123.

WRIGHT, P. AND SHERMAN, W. (1999) Failing to find fit in strategic human resource management: Theoretical and empirical problems. *Research in Personnel and Human Resources Management*, Supplement, 4: 53–74.

3

HRM IN MULTI-NATIONAL COMPANIES – A CRITICAL APPROACH

Julie Davies

LEARNING OUTCOMES

This chapter explores the complexities and challenges in managing HR strategy and functions across borders in multinational corporations. Brewster et al. (2015: 463–464) suggest that 'MNCs may have much greater influence in countries where foreign direct investment is vitally important. They may be free to act almost as mini-states. Or they may be constrained by their greater visibility'.

After reading this chapter, you should be able to:

➤ Understand dynamic globalised contexts for MNCs, HR professionals, workers, line managers, employee representatives, and policy-makers
➤ Frame dilemmas and decisions using relevant theoretical concepts and models
➤ Discuss the behaviours and roles of transnational HRM professionals
➤ Reflect critically on challenges within MNCs for HR strategies and future prospects.

SUMMARY OF CHAPTER CONTENTS

➤ **Opening Case Study**: Banking on professional HR
➤ Introduction
➤ Integration versus differentiation, convergence v. divergence; best practice versus best fit
➤ Are we all global now?
➤ MNCs – Benefactors or villains? Ethical issues
➤ National culture versus dominance effect model
➤ Influence on HR in MNCs
➤ Developing cross-cultural skills, global HR professionals and departments
➤ HR careers in MNCs
➤ Behaviours of global professionals
➤ IHRM futures
➤ Conclusion
➤ **End of Chapter Case Study**: Xiaoinc: An HR professional on a long-distance assignment
➤ For discussion and revision
➤ Glossary
➤ Further reading
➤ Web resources
➤ References

This chapter highlights decisions that international HR professionals make such as on standardisation and localisation of international human resource management (IHRM) vertically and horizontally (Evans et al., 2011). We consider the dual logics of local integration and responsiveness (Rosenzweig, 2007), hybridisation (Gamble, 2010), and optimised forms of so-called global 'best practice' (Martin and Beaumont, 1998). We also reflect on guiding principles by drawing on theories of convergence, divergence, universalism, and contingency theory. We consider the diffusion of ideas, postcolonial theory, the impact of national institutional and cultural differences, and cross-vergence. In particular, we explore the job roles and behaviours of global HR professionals (Thite et al., 2014) and international HR departments (Stiles, 2012).

You are asked to reflect critically on the benefits and limitations of different approaches to managing human resources in MNCs. This entails delicate balancing acts when competing against the home advantage of local companies (Bhattacharya and Michael, 2008) and dealing with ethical pluralism. HR professionals in MNCs must be alert to the rapidly changing rules of the game, for example Brexit, Trans-Pacific Partnership, a Trump presidency.

Finally, we discuss HR careers, talent and risk management (Deloitte, 2014). Future trends relate to the value of HR strategies and functions (see Sparrow et al., 2014), changing business models and the influence of MNCs worldwide.

Opening Case Study Banking on professional HR

Ari worked as a senior HR Manager in a global bank on a two-year secondment in the Middle East and North Africa region. At the end of this assignment, Ari recounted several critical episodes:

In the HR team we faced some quite tricky situations. One day, a male staff member who is a local citizen stormed into my office. He said that his wife, another employee, had left the country with an expatriate who had been working in our bank as a consultant. The husband demanded that I call the police to arrest the consultant (who no longer worked for us). All I could say was that while I was concerned about the welfare of the man's wife as our employee, I could not interfere in domestic matters.

On another occasion, an employee marched into my office wielding confidential data from another global bank, one of our competitors. We were making this employee's job redundant because our retail branches were closing. I called the competitor bank in front of him to ask them where they would like me to deliver the stolen information. I assured them that I would not look at it. Curiously, the employee thought I was going to reward him for this unethical behaviour and save his job!

Another very difficult issue for us was that the bank's licence to operate in this particular country depended on us employing 75 per cent local citizens. When we ran the retail side of the business, this was possible but when we only operated the investment arm, then we needed higher qualified staff. The problem is that local banking specialists prefer to work for national or Islamic banks because of shorter working hours and better job security and not for a European bank/MNC.

Finally, two catastrophic events really tested my professionalism. The first was a fire in our document repository which destroyed personnel files and other important records just before we had a merger. The second incident was the alleged rape of one of our female staff. During a very hot summer, a leading client said he was too busy and tired to travel to the bank to sign some papers. He requested that a member of the bank's staff visit his home to explain the contracts. Unfortunately, a woman employee agreed to this request and we had to deal with accusations that she was molested during the visit.

Overall it's been very interesting working on this overseas assignment as we've restructured our operations and hired more local talent. It's also been highly stressful. I'm ready to return to HQ for a while and take stock of my next career move!

Questions

1 Why do you think the HR matters Ari dealt with were more complex in an MNC context than in a purely domestic organisation?
2 Provide examples in the diagram below of HR functions in this bank that might be adopted from different

sources and applied to different types of staff, for example planning, policy development, payroll, benefits, resourcing, induction, learning and development, performance management, talent management, reward, employee relations, employee exit, HR systems, employee survey, relocations:

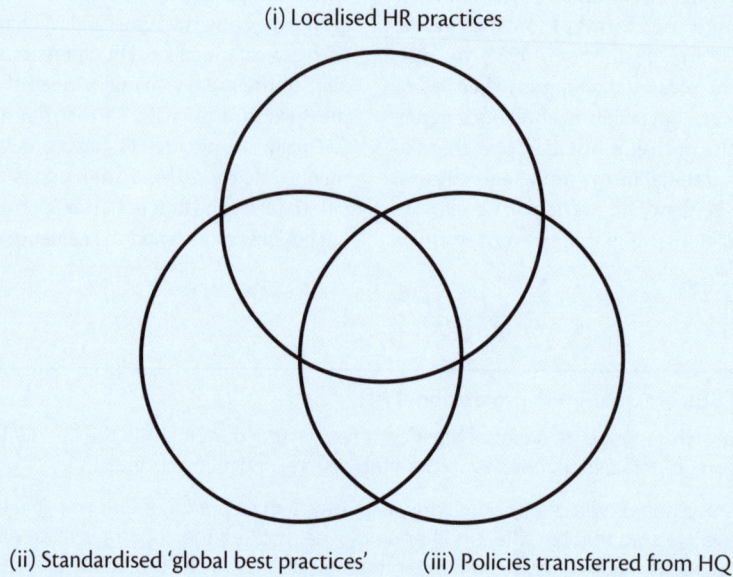

(i) Localised HR practices

(ii) Standardised 'global best practices'   (iii) Policies transferred from HQ

Figure 3.1 HR practices in context

INTRODUCTION

A multinational company or enterprise (MNC/MNE) 'owns, controls and manages income generating assets in more than one country' (Dunning, 1992: 34). A transnational corporation (TNC) operates its HQ functions in several countries (e.g. GlaxoSmithKline). UNCTAD (2015: ix) reported that the number of emerging market MNCs (EMMNCs) is the highest ever. Indeed, there are increasing opportunities for them to employ Western talent (Alkire, 2014). Dobbs et al. (2015: 53) argue that 'companies in the emerging world are catching up with Western multinationals on pay and career opportunities'.

First in this chapter we consider the complexities of HRM in MNCs compared with domestic only firms. We critique useful theoretical models to frame key challenges, particularly concepts of best practice, best fit, and configurational approaches. You are asked to reflect on the benefits and limitations of globalisation with respect to cross-cultural management, differences in national business systems, power inequalities, and ethics within MNCs.

Finally, we discuss the capabilities of global HR practitioners and departments in MNCs. Future prospects are reviewed with the growth and dominance of new models of EMMNCs and the UN's 2015–2030 sustainable development goals.

Taylor et al. (1996: 960) broadly define IHRM as 'the aggregate of the various HRM systems used to manage people in the MNC, both at home and overseas'. Domestic HRM is concerned with one country whereas IHRM relates to how employees are managed across borders and in different national country systems. Taylor et al. (1996: 980) emphasize the dynamic nature of MNC SIHRM (strategic international HRM) systems and, drawing on the resource based view of the firm, they observe that 'because the MNC is a complex organisational network consisting of many subunits, resources can exist at multiple levels within the firm and may or may not be useful outside a given level or context'.

While working in an MNC may appear exciting, the reality of communicating across multiple cultures, national systems, time zones, and different perceptions of what is ethical may present enormous challenges for HR practitioners, quite apart from (cyber)security and risk management. It is useful, therefore, for global HR professionals to be aware of relevant theoretical concepts to understand key debates and the inherent complexity of global HRM. Delery and Doty (1996) provided three ways of theorising strategic HRM performance in terms of (i) universalistic 'best practices' (Pfeffer, 1994), (ii) contingency approaches (Schuler and Jackson, 1987), i.e. 'best fit', and (iii) a configurational perspective, 'the pattern of planned human resource deployments and activities intended to enable an organisation to achieve its goals' (Wright and McMahan, 1992: 298) through both horizontal and vertical fit. In the past, best practices in MNCs have tended to emanate from the high quality HR practices of leading US/Western or dominant parent-country policies. However, they can be risky (Marchington and Grugulis, 2000). Typically, 'best fit' additionally relies on a pragmatic degree of local adaptation. A configurational view is an ideal arrangement that supports high performance and may result in hybridisation.

INTEGRATION VERSUS DIFFERENTIATION, CONVERGENCE, VERSUS DIVERGENCE; BEST PRACTICE VERSUS BEST FIT

MNCs adopt different types of staffing policies (Heenan and Perlmutter, 1979). These are integrated with or diverge from home country HRM depending on central controls, best practices, best fit, or hybrid approaches:

(i)   Ethnocentric – PCNs, parent company nationals, occupy key positions in subsidiaries.
(ii) Polycentric – HCNs, host, country nationals, dominate.
(iii) Regiocentric – involves hiring personnel from a region of the world that closely resembles approaches in the host country (O'Connell, 2015).
(iv) Geocentric – the most suitable people are employed to staff foreign subsidiaries regardless of their nationality (Banai and Reisel, 1999) which may include third-country nationals (TCNs).

Variations in the staffing of subsidiaries with parent-country nationals can be influenced by the extent to which the HQ differs culturally from the host company. Other influences include the industry sector, types of management functions and levels of seniority, size, and whether the subsidiary was a green-field site or acquisition (Harzing, 2001). Theoretically, in subsidiaries where HCNs

determine local HR strategy, staffing is more locally embedded and autonomous than when PCN led. This means that when planning, designing, and delivering operating standards, interventions, knowledge networks, innovations, and reporting, global HR managers must deal with the dilemmas of integration and differentiation (Kamoche, 1996). HR managers in MNCs are constantly grappling with home, host, and macro-influences and micro-politics (e.g. Heikkilä et al., 2013). Power issues of country of origin effects (Almond, 2011; Ferner, 1997), localisation and dominant country effects (Pudelko and Harzing, 2007) need to be considered. While centralised HR may drive economies of scale (Evans et al., 1989), it neglects the need for flexibility in local markets and specific legal and regulatory requirements of the host country. Zhang and Edwards (2007) acknowledge the limitations of attempting to diffuse 'best practice' in Chinese MNCs. In polycentric organisations, HR practitioners should guard against duplication and fragmentation of resources. Prahalad and Doz's (1987: 255ff) integration—responsiveness model suggests that the dualities of a global—local dilemma can be overcome through organisational culture acting like a corporate 'glue' to integrate disparate elements. Indeed, the dualities of a monolithic 'and/or' approach may in reality be realised through hybrid systems (e.g. Zhu et al., 2007) within and between subsidiaries.

In addition to central efficiencies and local responsiveness, successful MNCs must be innovative (Pucik, 1992) through knowledge creation and transfer. The type and speed of cross-national knowledge transfer in MNCs depend on the drivers, context, and mechanisms for dissemination, motivations, capabilities and the feasibility and value given to 'the travel of ideas' (Czarniawska and Joerges, 1996). Gratton (2007) provides interesting examples where managers in MNCs are able to create 'hot spots' of cooperative attitudes across boundaries. These are characterised by rewards for supporting a clear purpose to enhance productivity between teams located in different parts of the globe. Minbaeva et al. (2003) found that transfer of HRM practices within MNCs depended on the employees' ability and motivation (i.e. absorptive capacity) within subsidiaries. HRM in MNCs is enabled by the use of communications technology for HR professionals to keep in regular touch with employees, even those in remote locations, to enhance flexible working and support e-learning (e.g. InterContinental Hotels, see Marsh, 2011).

Importantly, Bartlett and Ghoshal (1989: 71) argued that a 'fundamental prerequisite for the normative integration a transnational seeks is a sophisticated HRM system… to help individuals to cope with its diversity and complexity'. Yet, Brewster and Sparrow (2007) state that in many organisations, HR is the least globalised management function. HR professionals in MNCs need to facilitate reciprocal information flows (Gupta and Govindarajan, 1991) and opportunities to make real differences to working lives and communities. Bartlett and Ghoshal (1995) suggested that an ideal transnational company is highly innovative, globally efficient, and locally responsive. This is achieved by granting subsidiaries considerable autonomy, integrating activities to minimise costs with global economies of scale, and developing knowledge jointly through lateral and vertical communications internationally. It may depend, however, on the levels of confidence and experience the parent company has in managing HR internationally.

Hedlund (1994) proposes that knowledge networking is supported by a heterarchical (non-hierarchical) structure based on distributed power, horizontal communications, and temporary projects teams. In the past, forms of 'Anglo-Saxonisation' (Ferner and Quintanilla, 1998) and corporate 'Englishisation' (Boussebaa et al., 2014) may have been regarded as appropriate but no longer. Bartlett and Ghoshal (1989, 1998) suggest that an MNC can overcome the global–local dilemma through high levels of innovation to gain supranational competitive advantage. Dualities of integration and differentiation are being replaced by discourses of paradox (Ehnert, 2013), ambiguity, complexity, and 'hybridity' in terms of IHRM systems as well as at the level of the individual, for example the English-language-educated Indian call centre worker (Das and Dharwadkar, 2009).

ARE WE ALL GLOBAL NOW?

While Friedman (2005) subscribes to a convergence view that the world is flat because technology is enabling a level playing field for businesses to cross geographical boundaries, Ghemawat (2007) contends that on the contrary, the world is not flat. He argues that globalisation is fragile and still strongly influenced by cross-border protectionism. Ghemawat points out that most phone calls, internet traffic, and investments are still very localised despite the rhetoric of globalisation. In a digitally connected world, many organisations in the developed world that are not MNCs are internationally oriented. For example, local hospitals in developed countries may rely on nurses from third world countries. Local universities often develop international partnerships and branch campuses, for example Murdoch University and INSEAD operate in Singapore and Dubai. *The Economist* (2015) notes that Amity University, founded in India, has ambitious worldwide development plans and there are significant 'south-to-south' growth opportunities for higher education institutions. A restaurant might differentiate itself based on sourcing locally produced products. Yet supply chains are so globally networked that

a volcanic ash cloud over Europe that halts all flights can soon result in supermarket shortages of commonly purchased fresh produce sourced from Africa, the Caribbean, South America, etc. where labour is cheap. Reliance on foreign workers in GCC (Gulf Cooperation Council) countries suggests high levels of multinational connectivity. In 2011, foreigners comprised over 65 per cent of Kuwait's population and 87 per cent of the total population in Qatar (Emirates 24|7, 2013). Even Cuba, Iran, and Myanmar are opening up to international markets. Interdependencies between countries, companies, and governments provide interesting opportunities for MNCs.

> **(?) Critical Thinking 3.1**
>
> Thinking on HRM in MNCs has shifted from calls to be more locally considerate and globally integrated (Prahalad and Doz, 1987) to a more hybrid approach (Chung et al., 2014; Shimoni and Bergmann, 2006). The notion that MNCs always dominate local competition is also being questioned. Santos and Williamson (2015) found that local companies were two-and-a-half times more likely to gain superior performance over MNCs in the same locality because indigenous organisations are often much better at engaging with customers and users, suppliers, talent, regulators, and institutions and contribute greater social value. Kwan (2015: 51) reminds us to avoid monolithic approaches; for instance he argues that it is important for HR professionals not to aggregate national cultural or managerial behaviours throughout Asia and to ask particular questions to understand differences. For instance, working conditions in Laos, Indonesia, and South Korea are quite different.

MNCS – BENEFACTORS OR VILLAINS? ETHICAL ISSUES

MNCs are variously depicted as heroes and villains (Segal-Horn, 2002). On the one hand, MNCs distribute wealth and jobs globally and create inward investment with foreign currency and economies of scale. They may raise standards and invest significantly in research and innovation. MNCs can be very powerful in building social capital and supporting workers. Gomez and Sanchez (2005) found positive examples of progressive HR practices in MNCs that were able to create a family-like corporate culture in Mexico. On the other hand, MNCs have been criticised for acting as monopolies, exploiting customers (e.g. Nestlé), disregarding

In the News Stakeholders and challenges

Working in groups of at least three, nominate individuals to represent key stakeholders from each organisation:

Human Resources in the Volkswagen Group

Our success is based on the qualification and personal commitment of approximately 610,000 people who are employed by the Volkswagen Group. A company will only be able to survive in the face of international competition if it has a top team characterised by a high level of competence, dedication, inventiveness and fitness. Competence is created from good basic training and a life-long willingness to learn. Dedication ideally means entrepreneurial thinking and actions, not only by management staff. Active contribution of ideas and participation are expected of all members of staff. The success factors are encouraged in our human resources processes and in projects.

Source: http://www.volkswagenag.com/content/vwcorp/content/"en/human_resources.html?ShowPrint=true.]

HR and Corporate Services in FIFA

Human Resources and Corporate Services is part of the Finance and Administration Division. The seven departments within the Human Resources and Corporate Services Division are Delegation and Event Services, Facility Management, Human Resources, Information and Communication Technology, Language Services, Logistics and Reception. The focus and objectives of the Human Resources and Corporate Services Division are to provide all kinds of services for the Home of FIFA and FIFA events worldwide to enhance and enable FIFA's football mission and to ensure that FIFA's corporate services are provided efficiently and effectively for all the FIFA employees, partners and customers.

Source: http://www.fifa.com/about-fifa/home-of-fifa/fifa-divisions.html.

National Health Service Wales Human Resources Mission Statement

We will provide a high quality, approachable and confidential service to managers, staff and clients. We will stay in touch with staff needs, offering support and advice to improve staff working lives and in turn patient care. Our values are to: provide a quality effective service through team work; provide support, advice and guidance to our customers and HR colleagues in line with customers' needs, with regard to work life balance; promote ourselves and our business' value and continually develop ourselves and others; treat each other fairly as we would like to be treated ourselves with dignity and respect; promote a blame free, non-bullying culture and a secure working environment; be open and approachable; be knowledgeable and have a professional understanding of each department in HR; maintain confidentiality.

Source: http://www.wales.nhs.uk/sites3/Documents/115/HR%20Mission%20Statement.pdf.

Questions

1 Compare the cultural, structural, and systems challenges for HR managers, line managers, employee representatives, and employees for the three organisations.
2 What might the first two companies learn from the third example in terms of HR practices to rectify reputational damage caused by employees and senior executives?

---

human rights (Ruggie, 2013), treating employees as slaves (Foxconn making iPads for Apple, see Chakrabortty, 2013), harming communities and the environment (BP, Shell), squeezing out local businesses (the Wal-Mart effect of closing smaller retailers – see Basker, 2005), and evading taxes (Facebook, Starbucks). Managers in MNCs must be simultaneously controlling and flexible to deal with such issues. Whatever your views on and experiences of MNCs, we assume here that HRM practices can make a difference to a firm's competitive strategy (Schuler and Jackson, 1987).

HR staff in MNCs must be alert to public relations and corporate social responsibility issues and unethical behaviours, as we have seen at HSBC, Monsanto, Nestlé, Nike, Phillip Morris, and Ryanair. Elayan et al. (2014) found that a favourable Covalence Ethical Quote (CEQ), an index of MNCs' ethical performance, positively impacted investors. Unethical employee practices can seriously harm an organisation's reputation, bottom line, and sustainability, as we have seen in organisations such as Enron, major global banks, and the Volkswagen Group. Employees' class-actions against Wal-Mart on issues based on gender discrimination, wage theft, and gay rights tarnished the employer brand (see for example Sethi, 2013). How do HR professionals actively promote integrity and ethical pluralism (DeGeorge, 1993) in an MNC's diverse contexts? Schneider et al. (2014) recommend that values must be clearly articulated despite heterogeneous cultures and inherent contradictions in understanding the nature of ethical global capitalism. Yet what may be perceived as acceptable high performance work systems in one context may increase employee turnover in overseas subsidiaries (Yalabik et al., 2008) where these types of activities are instead perceived as bullying.

Class Activity

Working in pairs or small groups, select at least **TWO** MNCs in different industry sectors from lists of global top 100 companies or the *World's Best Multinational Workplaces* on the internet. You have been seconded with your colleague to compare HR policies and practices globally in these two organisations. Consider the following questions in relation to your chosen organisations based on your research in the media and in the companies' annual reports:

▸ What are the organisations' corporate strategies and competitive advantages?
▸ What external factors are impacting on these MNCs?
▸ What evidence is there about the internal corporate and business unit strategies, integrating mechanisms, and relationships between the HQ and subsidiaries?
▸ How do the MNCs trade-off global standardisation with being responsive to local conditions in their subsidiaries?
▸ In which one of the two MNCs would you prefer to work as an HR manager and why?

Class Activity

In small groups, look at the rankings of the world's best multinationals and the most unethical, for example on the web site for *Great Place to Work* http://www.greatplacetowork.com and http://www.ethicalquote.com/.

▸ How do you build a strong sense of community and culture, competent managers, effective leadership, and a supportive working environment with flexibility for employees as an HR professional in an MNC?
▸ What do you consider to be the main business and HR challenges going forward for two MNCs ranked in the top 10 on each list?
▸ Debate why you would and would not recommend a career in HR working in MNCs in TWO of the following sectors: advertising, airlines, deep water oil extraction, food snacks, fracking, management consulting, mining, tobacco.

(Pudelko and Harzing, 2007), home country HRM practices dominate. However, for a subsidiary based in a host country that represents a more dominant economy, then local HRM best practices may prevail (Smith and Meiksins, 1995).

MNCs must balance institutional tensions between (i) the *push* of transferring and localising home HRM practices and (ii) and *pull* of host-country HRM. A 'best fit' approach indicates that MNCs adapt HRM to external multicultural conditions to achieve legitimacy (Rosenzweig and Singh, 1991; Sayım, 2010). Ghoshal and Nohria (1993) highlighted the importance of MNCs adopting appropriate forms to fit the environment. Hayden and Edwards (2001) noted the dilution of the country of origin's influence over time. Rosenzweig and Nohria (1994) found that an MNC may implement different policies for different subsidiaries.

NATIONAL CULTURE VERSUS DOMINANCE EFFECT MODEL

When are HR practices from an organisation's headquarters more likely to be imposed on a subsidiary and why might they be adapted and localised? The national culture model emphasises the prevailing local sociocultural and legal and economic context so that HRM is adapted to the host country's practices (Vo and Stanton, 2011). In contrast, the dominance effect model suggests that when the home country such as the USA is more economically and technically advanced than the host country

INFLUENCES ON HR POLICIES AND PRACTICES IN MNCS

Some MNCs transfer HR practices from one national system to another context. For example, KPMG in the UK established a version of the German *Kurzarbeit* or 'short-time' working week. The OECD (2012) estimated that this initiative saved a significant number of layoffs during the recession. HRM in MNCs is evolving from paternalistic modes (Bae et al., 2011) to an awareness that Western HRM practitioners may learn from MNCs in other parts of the world (Chen and Easterby-Smith, 2009). Inevitably, hybrid forms of HR are evolving (Zhu et al., 2007), particularly with the growth in EMMNCs that may adopt mixed IRHM practices. There is also 'reverse diffusion' (Edwards and Ferner, 2004) from East to West. Thite et al. (2012: 253) provide a useful model of external and internal factors acting on direct and indirect HR strategies and practices in EMMNC subsidiaries.

How do HR specialists deal simultaneously with managing global efficiencies and innovations worldwide? How do they remain responsive to national contexts, respect diversity, communicate and coordinate initiatives across national boundaries? How do they optimise economies of scope, scale, cost, and information (Ghoshal and Nohria, 1993) while adhering to local employment laws and regulations and tax regimes and strengthening relations with local customers and markets? A heterogeneous HRM model of some HQ centralisation combined with localised policies with power distributed through networks that enhance mutual support may evolve as HR departments in the HQ and subsidiaries develop greater trust. Over time, IHRM in some sectors develops faster than in others. For instance the Indian IT sector is ahead of its manufacturing sector. Indian IT has required a shift from mass recruitment of coders in Indian subsidiaries to a situation where there is high turnover and dissatisfied workers just abandon their jobs (Demirbag et al., 2012). Customers in India are now demanding more sophisticated HRM concentrated on talent management as customers expect higher levels of IT services.

DEVELOPING CROSS-CULTURAL SKILLS AND GLOBAL HR PROFESSIONALS AND DEPARTMENTS

How do HR managers navigate multicultural pluralism? Adler and Bartholomew (1992) suggest that global managers should adopt broad, open-minded perspectives and value diversity. In contrast, Janssens and Cappellen (2008) recommend that global employees gain specific in-depth knowledge. Earley and Mozakowski (2004) instead emphasize cultural intelligence (CQ). They acknowledge that not all employees possess CQ and organisations should judiciously deploy those who do demonstrate these skills.

Convergence theory focuses on individuals aligned to values common to capitalist, industrialised countries. Divergence theory is based on how individuals hold on to their own society's values and behaviours. Cross-vergence theory is concerned with dynamic interactions between social influences and business ideology to create unique value systems different from parent cultures

and not just conforming to traditional Western models (Guo, 2015). Cross-vergence occurs 'when an individual incorporates both national culture influences and economic ideology influences synergistically to form a unique value system that is different from the value set supported by either national culture or economic ideology' (Ralston et al., 1997: 183). Cross-vergent behaviour is useful for IHRM professionals to display in their bridging and translating roles.

In terms of practical examples to enhance cross-cultural movement where traditional expatriate programmes are being replaced by alternatives (Collings et al., 2007), KPMG offers 'tax treks', short overseas placement opportunities for its recently qualified tax accountants. McDonald's provides adventurous European employees with a 'McPassport' which enables them to work in its restaurants anywhere in Europe.

HR CAREERS IN MNCS

The status and credibility of HR professionals in MNCs will depend on how they demonstrate their added value (Sparrow et al., 2014). They need to manage dynamic changes such as digital disruptions, employee mobility, safety and security. Hewlett and Rashid (2010) are concerned about the war for talent for college-educated women in emerging markets, while Hill (2015) believes that some companies are just too big to manage. Furthermore, Handy (2015) states quite clearly that a job for life at an MNC like Shell as he envisaged when he first started work is now an unlikely option for most people. He argues that we must be 'second curvers'. As the Sigmoid curve of company lifespans is shortening, we have to reinvent ourselves continually by jumping to a second curve of a career before the current one dips.

Class Activity

▸ How might you advise an HR student who is considering a career in a multinational organisation?

BEHAVIOURS OF GLOBAL PROFESSIONALS

Global HR directors may be charged with promoting a strong employer brand based on best practices within an MNC. At the same time they have to implement best fit with local laws and markets and to guard against accusations of social injustice by imposing or failing to implement centralised standards. A win-win might be achieved by adopting leading HR practices and raising standards in countries where there has traditionally been low employee protection. A corporation, however, may impoverish a local community ironically by raising its standards to prevent child labour (Khan et al., 1997), thereby eliminating vital sources of income. MNCs might lower HR standards to align with local pay and conditions to achieve cost benefits.

HR managers in MNCs need to consider different approaches depending on various HR functions and integration with other support functions. Harzing et al. (2016) explored how knowledge transfer in MNCs is facilitated by different types of expatriates and inpatriates (employees from foreign subsidiaries transferred to the HQ). They found that expatriates tend to facilitate the knowledge transfer from HQ to subsidiaries. With respect to resourcing, Caligiuri (2012) suggests that global professionals with effective intrapersonal and interpersonal competencies are in great demand. In relation to talent management, Adler and Bartholomew (1992) stress an ethnocentric perspective with five effective cross-cultural competences: (1) understanding business, political and cultural environments worldwide; (2) learning tastes, trends, technologies of other cultures; (3) working with people from other cultures; (4) adapting to lifestyles and communications in other cultures; and (5) relating to people as equals. In contrast to conflict avoidance, Friedman and Berthoin Antal (2005) emphasise adaptation and the value of 'negotiating reality' by learning from cultural conflict rather than avoiding it.

Class Activity

What are the similarities and differences in the following two job advertisements for senior HR roles in MNCs? What further information would you find useful to include?

(1) Dynamic generalist role supporting a complex MNC in Singapore

Our client is a global MNC with a broad and varied product itinerary. You will be a seasoned ASEAN HR Business Partner used to working in a fluid, complex, highly matrixed environment supporting demanding business leads. This role is to support the Singapore based businesses with around 700 staff in sales/revenue generating roles.

Key responsibilities are:

▸ Acting as a strategic HR business partner to support the business in formulating HR strategies, goals, and objectives that are aligned with the company's business strategies.
▸ Provide HR expertise and partner with functional HR Solutions and HR Services teams in areas such as succession planning, talent management, talent acquisition, employee learning and development, employee relations, compensation and benefits, etc.
▸ Provide guidance to management on a wide range of matters, including employee engagement, HR processes and/or company guidelines and programmes.
▸ Ensure flawless execution of a key leadership development programme to optimise performance and build up future pipeline of leaders. Review/develop HR best practices to bridge current abilities to future talent needs.
▸ Align HR practices and policies with Corporate HR where applicable.
▸ Lead/support organisational development strategies including change management, conflict resolution, team-building, coaching, work-climate studies, and/or other necessary strategies.
▸ Able to coach and develop all levels of management through performance feedback and effective management processes.
▸ Monitor local environment to maintain competitive compensation and benefits, in compliance with local legislations.

Key experience sought:

▸ 10+ years' experience in an HR Business Partner role in an MNC setting, preferably with ASEAN experience.
▸ Superior organisational skills, including the ability to prioritise and anticipate the needs of multiple client groups.
▸ Demonstrated ability to influence senior business leaders.
▸ Ability to be flexible in operational style to meet the needs of a multicultural and diversified, matrix organisation.
▸ Ability to interpret data and provide meaningful analysis of employee engagement survey; staff turnover, salary surveys, etc.

Our clients offer extremely attractive salary and perks and career growth opportunities.

(2) HR Director for MNC, Cairo, Egypt

The role

Must have international experience. The client is a multinational company and they are currently looking to appoint an HR Director based in Cairo. The person will be responsible for a team of five. Some of the primary duties would be the following:

▸ Coach, build, enable manager capability and effectiveness.
▸ Ensure programmes and processes delivered are aligned with the business and HR strategies.
▸ Drive execution of annual and daily processes and provide timely and effective coaching to managers on the following HR processes and programmes.
▸ Implement people strategy and HR aspects for business priorities that are efficient, consistent, and legally sound.
▸ Employee relations/industrial relations: develop and implement the industrial relations strategy at the country level.
▸ Mergers, acquisitions, and divestitures (restructuring, corporate-wide initiatives, strategic business unit initiatives, union-related work).
▸ Drive global standardisation, alignment, and operational efficiency.
▸ Ensure understanding, alignment, and adherence to all company's global and regional policies.

Requirements

▸ Bachelor's degree;
▸ MBA, MA in Organisational Development, HRM or related field preferred;
▸ At least 10+ years of HR experience with increasing responsibility;
▸ Excellent communication skills in English;
▸ Ideally, the person should be able to speak some Arabic or be willing to learn.

---

⑦ Critical Thinking 3.2 Power inequalities

Clearly, multinational enterprises do not exist in a vacuum. HR professionals, therefore, need to be aware of geo-political events and may become embroiled in power struggles, as well as CSR (corporate social responsibility) and PR (public relations) matters. An employer brand is important and organisations need to be seen not to be doing harm. Dunning (2003: 13) defines responsible global capitalism (RGC or societal/democratic capitalism) as 'a system made up of individuals, private commercial corporations, NGOs, governments, and supranational agencies… [whose roles] include the transformation and upgrading of the economic structure and social fabric of societies'. He warns of MNCs being 'in cahoots' with governments that neglect democratically elected institutions and civil society. Critical management scholars view 'globalisation' in a post-colonial era as the subjugation of emerging economies by developed countries (Banerjee and Linstead, 2001). Frenkel (2008) observes how the colonised imperfectly imitate the coloniser in an attempt to gain legitimacy.

MNCs may achieve competitive advantage through low-cost wages, goods, production, and standards in a race to the bottom. For example, an MNC might site operations in Chinese Special Economic Zones or in Mexico in maquiladora zones, thereby avoiding high medical and insurance costs and US labour unions (Nissen, 2002). Meardi et al. (2013) compared the approach to employee relations by MNCs in Eastern Europe in car making and finance sectors. They found in the former unilateral management and in the latter anti-union practices were adopted to improve firm advantages. Traxler and Woitech (2000) discuss opportunities for MNCs to engage in 'regime shopping' by targeting countries with low labour costs and weak employment regulations.

Tarique et al. (2016) consider the degree of internationalisation an MNC demonstrates over its evolution, acknowledging that some companies are born global. They ask how IHRM in MNCs can support 'global competitiveness, efficiency, local responsiveness, flexibility, and organisational and transfer of learning…across geographically dispersed units' (Tarique et al., 2016: 59). The authors suggest four different types of HQ-subsidiary structures depending on various levels of integration of central HR and local responsiveness: (i) transnational structure, integrated network; (ii) global structure, centralised hub; (iii) multi-domestic structure, decentralised federation; or (iv) international structure, coordinated federation.

Differences in IHRM in various physical locations or hierarchies may be explained by local cultural values, acceptable national norms, or trade blocs. The nature of IHRM in various MNCs is both shaped by and shapes their environment (Djelic and Quack, 2003). 'Cultural values' models that draw on frameworks such as Hofstede's (1980) dimensions have been used to explain how HR practices are transferred (Ngo et al., 1998) and how reward systems are developed cross nationally (Schuler and Rogovsky, 1998). Newman and Nollen (1996) found that performance related pay is more acceptable in individualistic societies such as the USA and UK.

Issues of (de)centralisation have been addressed in studies of performance appraisals. Lindholm et al. (1999) noted the importance of contextualisation to accommodate loss of face for employees in the Chinese-based subsidiaries of Western MNCs caused by different cultural values. Such models, however, are limited by universalistic approaches based on ideal cross-cultural archetypes and stereotypes. Paradigms of IHRM that adopt 'institutionalist' frames influenced by business systems, governance, legislation, labour markets within particular nations explain how different economic ecosystems shape behaviours. For instance, Almond et al. (2006) adopted a framework focused on institutional differences to explain pay and performance in MNCs. The extent of local modification of centralised HRM and degree of hybridisation may also depend on micro-political behaviours (Geppert and Williams, 2006; Gamble, 2010).

Class Activity

Compare and contrast the experiences of three HR directors in MNCs in interviews available on the internet and by searching on LinkedIn profiles. Several examples are provided below:

Gina Qiao, Lenovo

http://www.hrmagazine.co.uk/article-details/exclusive-interview-with-gina-qiao-senior-vp-hr-at-lenovo.

https://www.linkedin.com/pub/gina-qiao/17/a94/5a.

Isabelle Minneci, L'Oréal

http://www.hrmagazine.co.uk/article-details/interview-with-isabelle-minneci-hr-director-at-loreal-uk.

https://www.linkedin.com/pub/isabelle-minneci/2/66a/b97.

Hugh Mitchell, Royal Dutch Shell

http://www.hrmagazine.co.uk/article-details/exclusive-interview-with-hugh-mitchell-chief-hr-and-corporate-officer-at-royal-dutch-shell.

https://www.linkedin.com/in/hugh-mitchell-15b39817.

IHRM FUTURES

What are the future prospects for IHRM professionals? How can they navigate complex, turbulent, and hyper-competitive terrains? How can HRM facilitate multi-country collaboration and innovation (Berry, 2014)? Gartside et al. (2015: 2) suggest that in future to gain competitive advantage HR managers will have to reconceptualise talent management to an 'extended workforce' of 'a global network of outside contractors, outsourcing partners, vendors, strategic partners and other nontraditional workers'. HR professionals in MNCs need to be aware of

business strategies and processes and how HR might be aligned in what Zakaria (2011) terms 'the post-American world' where China and India are world powers. Singapore's first Prime Minister, Lee Kwan Lee, warned of China's rise: 'It is vital that the younger generation of Chinese, who have only lived through a period of peace and growth and have no experience of China's tumultuous past, are made aware of the mistakes China made as a result of hubris and excesses in ideology' (Allison et al., 2013: 48). MNCs compete in volatile circumstances of trade and budget deficits, social inequality, low savings and social mobility, where middle classes in the West are being hollowed out and experiencing unsustainable medical costs and youth unemployment. HR managers need to consider general trends such as mobile technology; the cloud; wearables; virtual reality; gamification; agile, closer links with marketing and IT: http://hrtrendinstitute.com/wp-content/uploads/2016/01/HR-Trends-2016-Summary1.png.

Tarique et al. (2016: 484) suggest that the twentieth-century model of the multinational enterprise is being replaced by a 'globally integrated enterprise'. HR specialists need to understand centres of excellence, in-sourcing for shared services, and outsourcing, employee rights in different countries, the legal frameworks of free trade agreements. Tarique et al. (2016) argue for more local leadership, greater respect between HQ and subsidiary HR staff, involvement of subsidiaries in corporate planning, and employee engagement internationally. They warn against MNC policies of confining locals to merely local concerns. Global HR managers will need to deal with HR analytics, e-HR, green-HR, and global mind-sets focused on performance measurement, including how the international HR department is performing. Tarique et al. (2016: 489–490) suggest that successful IHRM in MNCs requires individuals with international experience.

These specialists should be widely dispersed, sourced, and assigned globally with exposure to developmental projects and business challenges. Such HR experts need a global HR balanced scorecard; they must communicate company and global issues proactively, and train 'everyone in cross-cultural communication, etiquette, protocol, negotiation styles, and ethics'. Additionally, Tarique et al. (2016) recommend the professionalisation of MNC IHRM specialists so they understand finances, manage vendors for outsourced HR, and master cross-border HR responsibilities, policies, and initiatives to support organisational global growth, retention, organisational programmes, processes and tools as validated by HR credentials awarded by professional bodies. Moore (2006) suggests that HQ HR professionals who are working in subsidiaries should use 'dynamic negotiation' strategically to navigate between central and local expectations. Stiles (2012) argues that international HR departments must be strategic in demonstrating their power and value. Boudreau and Rice (2015) advise HR leaders to integrate research insights on talent management in organisations that compete on the basis of innovation. Moreover, Ghemawat and Vantrappen (2015) note that many CEOs and other executives in MNCs are born in the country of the firm's headquarters which suggests the need for greater diversity in the leadership of MNCs.

Mini Case Study   Infosys role and career enhancement (i-Race) initiative and head of HR role

Nandita Gurjar was Head of HR for 10 years at the Indian MNC Infosys, a global business technology consulting services provider. She led the Infosys Role and Career Enhancement (i-Race) initiative to create high performance from October 2009. The changes took place in the context of India's IT sector post-recession shifting from recruiting masses of basic coders to a more volatile environment of customers requiring IT staff with high levels of interpersonal and consultancy skills.

Gurjar explained the rationale for the i-Race programme: 'we have told employees that growth will be slower, promotions will be restricted, there will be lower salary hikes and fewer onsite assignments. Employees need to be aware that the days of a 50 per cent plus growth rate for the industry are over'.

Within the i-Race programme, employees could be promoted at any time of the year. The initiative attracted considerable criticism as some employees were adversely affected. It resulted in high staff attrition and employee dissatisfaction.

At the 2010 World HRD Congress (https://www.youtube.com/watch?v=yjQ_IcBlaE8), Gurjar commented: 'Somewhere the employee decided to believe that "because I spend nine to 10 hours of my working day in an organization, HR is responsible for everything in my life".… We forget to mention that someone in the chain is called a client who allows you to bring the bread to the table. We are apologetic to talk about a client. There are lots of theories about the employee coming first [Nayar, 2010]. First where? I think it is HR's job first to bring the fundamentals back: you come here to create a career, we promise to create a career, we promise you investment and learning. Beyond that, you are as capable as you make yourself to be'.

In a surprise move in April 2013, Gurjar stepped down from her role, and she left Infosys a year later. Srikantan Moorthy (Tan) replaced her as Group Head of HRD with responsibility for several facets of the employee lifecycle including compensation and benefits, performance management, career development, and employee engagement. Tan subsequently moved to a non-HR role at Infosys.

In March 2015 it was announced that Infosys would separate the role of Head of HR into two. One role concentrates on strategy, succession planning, and leadership development in line with the CEO's interest in artificial intelligence and new technology. The other role is responsible for HR operations and mass recruitment. In August 2015, Infosys appointed Krish Shankar as Executive Vice President (EVP) and Group Head of Human Resources from Philips, South Asia.

Questions

1 What were the external and internal contexts driving i-Race?
2 How do you think Gurjar could have formulated and implemented the programme differently?
3 Reflect on the evolution of the head of HR role at Infosys as the IT sector has matured.
4 What lessons can you draw personally about the political and personal aspects of working in HR in such a large firm?
5 Read the 2014 Knowledge@Wharton article on leadership at Infosys. Write your manifesto as a prospective Head of HR in the company: *Will a Change in Leadership Turn Around Infosys?* 19 June, http://knowledge. wharton.upenn.edu/article/icon-idle-leadership-challenges-facing-infosys/.

CONCLUSION

This third chapter has demonstrated that HRM in MNCs is multifaceted and challenging. There are problems in power asymmetries and multicultural working and differences in national institutions and sensitivities. These demands require open systems and mind-sets and a willingness to change. Sacred cows in MNCs may suddenly be overturned. For instance, in redesigning its performance management system and ending the practice for each employee of 'a single year-end rating' (Buckingham and Goodall, 2015: 42), Deloitte set a trend for other MNCs in the same sector such as Accenture which is also abandoning annual performance appraisals (Vara, 2015).

An MNC is only as ethical as its employees in terms of their activities in establishing systems, implementing, monitoring, and evaluating practices. HR jobs in MNCs for mobile transnational professionals can offer rewarding career paths provided the individuals demonstrate appropriate cultural intelligence and the ability to negotiate multiple realities, cultures and systems successfully.

In applying Schuler's (1992) '5-P model' of strategic HRM of philosophies, policies, programmes, practices, and processes, we might conclude that traditional perspectives of first world dominance are being eroded by hybrid forms. In future, Western IHRM professionals may actively seek EMMNCs as employers of choice.

Managing IHRM in an MNC is complex and demanding. There is considerable competition and there are high

Class Activity

▸ Using Deloitte's interactive dashboard for its most recent annual *Global Human Capital Trends*, report, compare and contrast metrics for THREE different size organisations and industry groups on three continents.

▸ What conclusions can you draw for current issues facing HR managers in MNCs? http://public.deloitte.com/media/human-capital/main-dashboard.html.

Mini Case Study Chinese MNCs (CMNCs) in Africa

China represents Africa's most significant trading partner. Managers in Africa must deal with relatively poor infrastructure and political, economic, and social instability and poverty. Performance management in Chinese MNCs is characterised by Confucian values of hierarchy (*jie ji*), seniority, *guanxi* (social networks that influence business), teamwork, subjective group evaluations and processes rather than outcomes (Cooke, 2009). In Africa, there tends to be a focus on the individual in relation to the collective (*Ubuntu*), maintaining face (*mianzi*), favouring family members (nepotism) (Kamoche et al., 2004), and an interest in basic salary levels rather than employees' intrinsic motivation. The Chinese telecom giants Huawei and ZTE have had considerable success in Africa through strong local partnerships and R&D activities in Nigeria and South Africa, combined with effective political and economic diplomacy. Deloitte's *Global Human Capital Trends 2015* report highlights in order of priority key HR issues in Africa. These include leadership, culture and engagement, learning and development, performance management, and workforce capability.

Questions

1 What HR policies and practices might you expect in a Chinese-owned copper mine in Zambia that differ from a mine in a developed economy?

2 How equitable do you think reward systems for parent-country nationals (PCNs), host-country nationals (HCNs), and third-country nationals (TCNs) might be in a Chinese oil MNC in Tanzania?

3 If you were in a Chinese telecoms HQ, what IHRM policies and practices might you (a) transfer or (b) not transfer to an African subsidiary?

4 How can you apply the ILO's 'decent work' guidance to a Chinese textile factory in Kenya? http://www.ilo.org/global/topics/decent-work/lang--en/index.htm.

5 How useful do you think the following guidelines might be if you were an HR manager working in a CMNC building African transport systems?
OECD's 2011 *Guidelines for Multinational Enterprises*
http://www.oecd.org/corporate/mne/
UN's 2008 '*Protect, Respect and Remedy*' *Framework and Guiding Principles*
http://business-humanrights.org/en/un-secretary-generals-special-representative-on-business-human-rights/un-protect-respect-and-remedy-framework-and-guiding-principles.

6 What are the risks of applying the questions above and further reading below uncritically in practice?

expectations with particular issues of risk management, terrorism, safety and security as well as reputational issues to consider. The Economist Intelligence Unit (2010: 7) predicted key challenges for global firms in 2020: more contingent workers, localised managers, workforce flux, international and ethnic diversity, and the need for soft skills in conditions of constant disruption. Dobbs et al. (2015: 62) contend that 'North American and European multinationals have enjoyed an exceptional three-decade ride; [however] the competition will be relentless and less predictable, and the operating environment not nearly as supportive.... Over the next decade…as headwinds break up the perfect non-storm'. Yet MNCs are powerful players. Apple is richer than New Zealand and most African countries (Bartlett, 2014). Sharma (2015: 589) argues that the outlook of nation states is too parochial and that MNCs instead are best placed as powerful players to address the UN's 2015–2030 sustainable development goals such as gender and diversity: 'in the face of critical global challenges, this private sector intervention is preferable to government inaction'. The MNC HR professional is, therefore, charged with considerable responsibility.

Critical analysis of this case study

This case demonstrates the psychosocial impact of a global HR role on an overseas posting in terms of stresses, self-identity, cognitive dissonance, and family arrangements as well as HR careers. It highlights the HR practitioner's orientations, the ability to reflect and learn from experience while balancing career and organisational commitment with personal wellbeing and the positive aspects of cross-cultural working.

The vignette illustrates a central HQ perspective on HR. It neglects less empowered voices on the ground, the views of unions or customers or members of communities and governments located close to overseas subsidiaries.

End of Chapter Case Study Xiaoinc: An HR professional on a long-distance assignment

Xiaoinc began as a mobile telephone manufacturer in 1999. Following the acquisition of overseas subsidiaries, Xiaoinc is now a hi-tech multinational with 4,500 employees and activities in 70 countries. Its headquarters are in Suzhou, 100 km west of Shanghai. It has subsidiaries in R&D, manufacturing, sales, and customer support in Europe, the Middle East, and Asia-Pacific.

Xiaoinc operates a matrix structure with six functional divisions: R&D, operations, finance, HR, sales, marketing. HQ coordinates strategic planning and outsourced and shared services. Centres of excellence are located where there is a critical mass of local expertise, for example Silicon Fen in Cambridge, UK.

In the past, Chinese expatriates managed Xiaoinc's overseas subsidiaries. Currently, shorter postings and self-initiated expatriates (Cerdin and Selmer, 2014) abroad are mainly used to provide employees with international exposure and to reduce disruption and overheads. The company is now investigating new ways of supporting employees' transitions with its global expansion by providing an HR toolkit of templates and shared/outsourced services to enable HR practitioners in the company to focus on strategic, legal, and other complex issues to enhance performance.

Xiaoinc plans to expand into Africa by opening new laboratories, factories, and offices in South Africa, Ethiopia, and Ghana. The company's CEO has invited the Deputy Global HR Director Jo, whose children are now at university, to oversee the planning and implementation of these and future projects in Africa by establishing a solid HR function regionally. Jo considers this an important career opportunity and has agreed to commute monthly over the next year. Although Jo retains the family home in Suzhou, the assignment requires extended periods of living in serviced apartments. Jo had mixed feelings about the experience:

> My family was not really interested in travelling to see me during that year. Although we regularly communicated by Skype, I felt really, really isolated. I tended to work 15-hour days, eat at strange times, and found it difficult to exercise – there was nowhere to walk safely. I missed many family occasions and company briefings. I felt out of sight, out of mind. I was wary about socialising with local work colleagues. After all that, I wasn't sure whether my year-long sojourn in Africa was actually beneficial or harmful for my CV.

> I love travelling to our sites all over the world and teleconferencing with colleagues. There's lots of knowledge-sharing and rich social interaction. It's fascinating to work in cross-cultural teams, and I am much more confident about mentoring others who are working globally. It can be thrilling for a while to be a road warrior like the George Clooney frequent flier type in the movie Up in the Air. But it can also be distracting and disorienting and completely exhausting – making important decisions that affect people's lives with lost sleep, lost appetite, jet lag. However, nothing can replace face-to-face contact. At the same time, you need to avoid 'going native' entirely.

I'm really interested in national cultural differences. It's hugely rewarding figuring out ways to be flexible and to work as a genuine HR business partner at a senior level across boundaries.

Questions

1 How would you advise Xiaoinc to address/prevent some of the frustrations Jo experienced?
2 Reflect on what lessons Jo has learned from this overseas posting.
3 What specific support do you think mobile global HR professionals require for their continuous professional development?

FOR DISCUSSION AND REVISION

1 As a parent or third-country national HR professional in a foreign subsidiary, how would you reassure HQ that you are implementing corporate standards and why might you negotiate changes in HQ controls?
2 How would you guard against 'going native' as an HR professional during a five-year overseas assignment in relation to HR policies and practices?
3 What learning interventions do you think would be useful for your personal development as a global professional to demonstrate cultural sensitivity in managing the HR function of an overseas subsidiary remotely?
4 What HR advice would you give to a Japanese or French MNC in the fast fashion retail industry that is establishing a subsidiary in your country? Make reference to the Social and Labor Convergence Project facilitated by the Sustainable Apparel Coalition: http://apparelcoalition.org/.
5 How have social media and technology generally impacted on the ability of HR managers to influence employee engagement and satisfaction in MNCs?

Shell's Hugh Mitchell named most influential practitioner of the decade (Frith, 2015, Abridged: http://www.hrmagazine.co.uk/article-details/shells-hugh-mitchell-named-most-influential-practitioner-of-the-decade).

As he announces his retirement, Hugh Mitchell, Chief Human Resources and Corporate Officer for Shell, has been named the most influential HR practitioner of the decade. The expert panel that ranks the most influential HR practitioners described Mitchell as 'the right hand to his CEO'.

He is seen as having enormous longevity, working incredibly well at board level, being great at stakeholder management, and having a strong point of view about the role of HR. Publishing Director of *HR Magazine* Siân Harrington added of Mitchell: 'He manages HR in a highly complex and challenging company, contributes widely to the profession, and runs HR in a business that covers 90 countries and employs some 100,000 people. He champions progressive HR policies,

including flexible working in some of the most senior HR roles in the business, showing that mature corporations can successfully change and pioneer new approaches'. During his acceptance speech, Cassidy (a colleague who collected the award on Mitchell's behalf) drew attention to Hugh's irreverent sense of humour. He also praised Mitchell for his achievements in getting people management strategies on the very highest business agenda at Shell.

Questions

1 What do you find surprising about Hugh Mitchell's achievements as an HR practitioner?
2 What do you consider the benefits and risks of an HR specialist being a 'CEO's right hand person'?
3 What lessons do you find personally relevant from these insights?
4 What theoretical concepts can you apply to this excerpt?
5 Reflect on the 'dark side' of HR practices in the energy sector.
6 Search on the internet for *HR Magazine's* 'Most Influential Thinker' list of *practitioners*. Note individuals on the list who work in MNCs. Choose one to explore their career trajectory and thoughts on global HRM.
7 Search on the internet for *HR Magazine's* 'Most Influential Thinker' list of *academics* over the past three years and compare how the rankings have changed in terms of key themes.

Questions

1 What has happened in the news this week that might concern an HR Director of an MNC?
2 How do you think HR professionals might interact with marketing in a transnational company?
3 What are the limitations of national stereotypes when working across borders?
4 How do you think MNCs can collaborate with SMEs, start-ups, local communities, regulators, and governments?

5 How might you work with expatriates and with HR global professionals differently?

6 If you were in the HR department based in the HQ, meeting the HR Manager of an overseas subsidiary for the first time at HQ, how would you develop trust?

GLOSSARY

Absorptive Capacity: an organisation's ability to recognise the value of new information, to assimilate and commercialise it

CMNC: Chinese multinational corporation

EMMNC: emerging market multinational corporation

Ethnocentric Staffing: parent-country nationals dominate, centralised approach

Geocentric: subsidiaries combine worldwide and local objectives, staffing from the most suitable people globally

Guanxi: business networks from close social ties (China)

HCN: host-country national

IHRM: international human resource management

Jie Ji: hierarchy, seniority (China)

Mianzi: saving face (China)

MNC/MNE: multinational corporation/multinational enterprise

PCN: parent-country national

Polycentric: host (local) country focus, decentralised

Regiocentric: focused on a geographical region

TCN: third-country national (not parent or host countries)

TNC: transnational corporation

Ubuntu: 'I am because we are' (South African region)

UNCTAD: United Nations Conference on Trade and Development

FURTHER READING

CERDIN, J.-L. AND SELMER, J. (2014) Who is a self-initiated expatriate? Towards conceptual clarity of a common notion. *International Journal of Human Resource Management*, 25: 1281–1301.

COLLINGS, D. G., WOOD, G. T. AND CALIGIURI, P. M. (2014) (eds) *The Routledge Companion to International Human Resource Management*. Abingdon: Routledge.

COOKE, F. L. (2009) A decade of transformation of HRM in China: A review of literature and suggestion for future studies. *Asia Pacific Journal of Human Resources*, 47(6): 6–40.

DELOITTE (2011) *Global Business Driven HR Transformation*. London: Deloitte. http://www2.deloitte.com/content/dam/Deloitte/de/Documents/human-capital/global-business-driven-hr-transformation.pdf.

DELOITTE UNIVERSITY PRESS (2015) *Global Human Capital Trends 2015: Leading in the New World of Work*. Deloitte University Press: Westlake, TX. http://www2.deloitte.com/content/dam/Deloitte/at/Documents/human-capital/hc-trends-2015.pdf.

DICKMANN, M. (2015) Models of international HRM. In *Wiley Encyclopedia of Management* (3rd edn). Hoboken, NJ: John Wiley & Sons, 5: 1–3.

HARZING, A.-W. AND PENNINGTON, A. (2014) (eds) *International Human Resource Management*. London: Sage.

HAYTON, J. C. (2012) *Global Human Resource Management Casebook*. New York and London: Routledge.

HORWITZ, F. (2015) Human resources management in multinational companies in Africa: A systematic literature review. *International Journal of Human Resource Management*, 26: 2786–2809.

HORWITZ, F. AND BUDHWAR, P. (2015) (eds) *Handbook of Human Resource Management in Emerging Markets*. Cheltenham: Edward Elgar.

KAMOCHE, K., YAW, D., HORWITZ, F. AND MUUKA, G. N. (2004) (eds) *Managing Human Resources in Africa*. New York and London: Routledge.

PURCELL, J. (1999) Best practice and best fit: Chimera or cul-de-sac? *Human Resource Management Journal*, 9(3): 26–41.

TARIQUE, I., BRISCOE, D. AND SCHULER, R. (2015) *International Human Resource Management: Policies and Practices for Multinational Enterprises* (5th edn). New York and London: Routledge.

XING, Y., LIU, Y., TARBA, S. Y. AND COOPER, C. L. (2014) Intercultural influences on managing African employees of Chinese firms in Africa: Chinese managers' HRM practices. *International Business Review*, 25: 28–41.

WEB RESOURCES

Jack Welch: The role of HR
https://www.youtube.com/watch?v=rByDmC0SqtM

The role of HR Managers in driving ethics in the workplace
https://www.youtube.com/watch?v=YAgLSJxJNFw

5 'megatrends' for HR leaders, leadership 2030
https://www.youtube.com/watch?v=Q9nGRnUIr1M

Steve Jobs talks about managing people
https://www.youtube.com/watch?v=f60dheI4ARg

Clayton Christensen at the 2014 Drucker Forum
https://www.youtube.com/watch?v=amK8pOT-rsg

Child labor around the world
https://www.youtube.com/watch?v=PdmiUb9_E94

Henry Mintzberg Spring 2014 interview on why society must be rebalanced
https://www.youtube.com/watch?v=BQF6aVpJUic

Riding the waves of culture: Fons Trompenaars at TEDxAmsterdam
https://www.youtube.com/watch?v=hmyfjKjcbm0

REFERENCES

ADLER, N. J. AND BARTHOLOMEW, S. (1992) Managing globally competent people. *Academy of Management Perspectives*, 6(3): 52–65.

ALKIRE, T. D. (2014) The attractiveness of emerging market MNCs as employers of European and American talent workers: A multicultural study. *International Journal of Emerging Markets*, 9: 333–370.

ALLISON, G., BLACKWILL, R. D. AND WYNE, A. (2013) *Lee Kuan Yew: The Grand Master's Insights on China, the United States, and the World*. Cambridge, MA: Belfer Center for Science and International Affairs.

ALMOND, P. (2011) Re-visiting 'country of origin' effects on HRM in multinational corporations. *Human Resource Management Journal*, 21: 258–271.

ALMOND, P., MULLER-CAMEN, M., COLLINGS, D. AND QUINTANILLA, J. (2006) Pay and performance. In Almond, P. and Ferner, A. (eds), *American multinationals in Europe*. Oxford: Oxford University Press. pp. 119–145.

BAE, J., CHEN, S-J. AND ROWLEY, C. (2011) From a paternalistic model towards what? HRM trends in Korea and Taiwan. *Personnel Review*, 40: 700–722.

BANAI, M. AND REISEL, W. D. (1999) Would you trust your foreign manager? An empirical investigation. *International Journal of Human Resource Management*, 10: 477–487.

BANERJEE, S. B. AND LINSTEAD, S. (2001) Globalization, multiculturalism and other fictions: Colonialism for the new millennium? *Organization*, 8: 683–722.

BARTLETT, C. AND GHOSHAL, S. (1989) *Managing Across Borders*. London: Hutchinson.

BARTLETT, C. AND GHOSHAL, S. (1995) (eds) *Transnational Management: Text, Cases, and Readings in Cross-Border Management*. London: Irwin.

BARTLETT, C. AND GHOSHAL, S. (1998) *The Individualised Corporation: A Fundamentally New Approach to Management*. Heinemann: London.

BARTLETT, E. (2014) Apple makes more money each year than all of these countries. *The Independent*, September 19. http://i100.independent.co.uk/article/apple-makes-more-money-each-year-than-all-of-these-countries-gyJUU9BoEe.

BASKER, E. (2005) Job creation or destruction? Labor market effects of Wal-Mart expansion. *Review of Economics and Statistics*, 87: 174–183.

BERRY, H. (2014) Global integration and innovation: Multicountry knowledge generation within MNCs. *Strategic Management Journal*, 35: 869–890.

BHATTACHARYA, A. K. AND MICHAEL, D. C. (2008) How local companies keep multinationals at bay. *Harvard Business Review*, 86(3): 84–95.

BOUDREAU, J. AND RICE, S. (2015) Shiny objects and the future of HR. *Harvard Business Review*, 93(7/8): 72–78.

BOUSSEBAA, M., SINHA, S. AND GABRIEL, Y. (2014) Englishization in offshore call centres: A postcolonial perspective. *Journal of International Business Studies*, 45: 1152–1169.

BREWSTER, C. AND SPARROW, R. (2007) *Globalising HR: Roles and Challenges for the International HRM Function*. Lancaster: Lancaster University Management School.

BREWSTER, C., MAYRHOFER, W. AND COOKE, F. L. (2015) Convergence, divergence and diffusion of HRM in emerging markets. In Horwitz, F. and Budhwar, P. (eds) *Handbook of Human Resource Management in Emerging Markets*. Edward Elgar: Cheltenham, pp. 451–469.

BUCKINGHAM, M. AND GOODALL, A. (2015) Reinventing performance management. *Harvard Business Review*, 93(4): 40–50.

CALIGIURI, P. (2012) *Cultural Agility: Building a Pipeline of Successful Global Professionals*. Chichester: John Wiley & Sons.

CHAKRABORTTY, A. (2013) The woman who nearly died making your iPad. *The Guardian*, August 5.

CHEN, C. L AND EASTERBY-SMITH, M. (2009) Can Western HRM learn from Eastern MNCs? The case of Taiwanese/Chinese MNCs in the UK. *International Journal of Chinese Culture and Management*, 2: 333–351.

CHUNG, C., SPARROW, P. AND BOZKURT, Ö. (2014) South Korean MNEs' international HRM approach: Hybridization of global standards and local practices. *Journal of World Business*, 49: 549–559.

COLLINGS, D. G., SCULLION, H. AND MORLEY, M. J. (2007) Changing patterns of global staffing in the multinational enterprise: Challenges to the conventional expatriate assignment and emerging alternatives. *Journal of World Business*, 42: 198–213.

CZARNIAWSKA, B. AND JOERGES, B. (1996) Travel of ideas. In Czarniawska, B. and Sevon, G. (eds), *Translating Organizational Change*. Berlin: Walter de Gruyter, p. 13.

DAS, D. AND DHARWADKAR, R. (2009) Cultural mimicry and hybridity: On the work of identity in international call centres in India. In Bannerjee, S. B., Chio, V. C. M. and Mir, R. (eds), *Organisations, Markets and Imperial Formations: Towards an Anthropology of Globalization*. Cheltenham: Edward Elgar, pp. 181–197.

DEGEORGE, R. T. (1993) *Competing with Integrity in International Business*. New York: Oxford University Press.

DELERY, J. AND DOTY, D. (1996) Mode of theorizing in strategic human resource management: Tests of universalistic, contingency, and configurational performance predictions. *Academy of Management Journal*, 39: 802–835.

DELOITTE (2014) *Risk, Culture, and Talent in Global Financial Services*. Deloitte Development LLC. http://www2.deloitte.com/content/dam/Deloitte/pa/Documents/human-capital/2015-01-Pa-HumanCap-RiskCulture-TalentGFS.pdf.

DEMIRBAG, M., MELLAHI, K., SAHADEV, S. AND ELLISTON, J. (2012) Employee service abandonment in offshore operations: A case study of a US multinational in India. *Journal of World Business*, 47(2): 178–185.

DJELIC, M.-L. AND QUACK, S. (2003) (eds) *Globalisation and Institutions – Redefining the Rules of the Economic Game*. Cheltenham: Edward Elgar.

DOBBS, R., KOLLER, T. AND RAMASWAMY, S. (2015) The future and how to survive it. *Harvard Business Review*, 93(10): 48–62.

DUNNING, J. H. (1992) *Multinational Enterprises and the Global Economy*. Wokingham: Addison-Wesley.

DUNNING, J. H. (2003) Making globalization good: The moral challenges of global capitalism: An overview. In Dunning, J. H. (ed.), *Making Globalization Good: The Moral Challenges of Global Capitalism*. Oxford: Oxford University Press, pp. 11–40.

EARLEY, P. C. AND MOZAKOWSKI, E. (2004) Toward culture intelligence: Turning cultural differences into a workplace advantage. *Academy of Management Executive*, 18(3): 151–157.

Economist (2015) Indian private universities. *The Economist*, October 10.

Economist Intelligence Unit (2010) *Global Firms in 2020: The Next Decade of Change for Organisations and Workers*. London: EIU.

EDWARDS, T. AND FERNER, A. (2004) Multinationals, reverse diffusion and national business systems. *Journal of International Business*, 44: 49–79.

EHNERT, I. (2013) Paradox as a lens for theorizing sustainable HRM: Mapping and coping with paradoxes and tensions. In Ehnert, I., Harry, W. and Zink, K. (eds), *Sustainability and Human Resource Management*. Berlin Heidelberg: Springer, pp. 247–271.

ELAYAN, F. A., LI, J., ZHEFENG, F. L., MEYER, T. O. AND FELTON, S. S. (2014) Changes in the covalence ethical quote, financial performance and financial reporting quality. *Journal of Business Ethics*, 1–27.

Emirates 24|7 (2013) UAE, Qatar have highest expat ratio in GCC, Saudi Arabia has lowest expat ratio, September 11. http://www.emirates247.com/news/emirates/uae-qatar-have-highest-expat-ratio-in-gcc-2013-09-11-1.520659.

EVANS, P., LANK, E. AND FAQUHAR, A. (1989) Managing human resources in the international firm: Lessons from practice. In Evans, P., Doz, Y. and Laurent, A. (eds), *Human Resource Management in International Firms: Change, Globalization, Innovation*. Basingstoke: Macmillan, pp. 367–387.

EVANS, P., PUCIK, V. AND BJÖRKMAN, I. (2011) *The Global Challenge — International Human Resource Management*. New York: McGraw-Hill.

FERNER, A. (1997) Country of origin effects and HRM in multinational companies. *Human Resource Management Journal*, 7: 19–37.

FERNER, A. AND QUINTANILLA, J. (1998) Multinationals, national business systems and HRM: The enduring influence of national identity or a process of 'Anglo-Saxonization'. *International Journal of Human Resource Management*, 9: 710–731.

FRENKEL, M. (2008) The multinational corporation as a third space: Rethinking international management discourse on knowledge transfer through Homi Bhabha. *Academy of Management Review*, 33: 924–942.

FRIEDMAN, T. L. (2005) *The World Is Flat: A Brief History of the Twenty-First Century*. New York: Farrar Straus Giroux.

FRIEDMAN, V. J. AND BERTHOIN ANTAL, A. (2005) Negotiating reality: A theory of action approach to intercultural competence. *Management Learning*, 36: 69–86.

FRITH, B. (2015) Shell's Hugh Mitchell named most influential practitioner of the decade. *HR Magazine*, September 22.

GAMBLE, J. (2010) Transferring organizational practices and the dynamics of hybridization: Japanese retail multinationals in China. *Journal of Management Studies*, 47: 705–732.

GARTSIDE, D., SILVERSTONE, Y., FARLEY, C. AND CANTRELL, S. M. (2015) *The Future of HR: A Radically Different Proposition*. Dublin: Accenture.

GEPPERT, M. AND WILLIAMS, K. (2006) Global, national and local practices in multinational corporations: Towards a sociopolitical framework. *International Journal of Human Resource Management*, 17: 49–69.

GHEMAWAT, P. (2007) Why the world isn't flat. *Foreign Policy*, 159: 54–60.

GHEMAWAT, P. AND VANTRAPPEN, H. (2015) How global is your C-Suite? *MIT Sloan Management Review*, 56(4): 72–82.

GHOSHAL, S. AND NOHRIA, N. (1993) Horses for courses: Organizational forms for multinational corporations. *Sloan Management Review*, 34(2): 23–35.

GOMEZ, C. AND SANCHEZ, J. I. (2005) HR's strategic role within MNCs: Helping build social capital in Latin America. *International Journal of Human Resource Management*, 16: 2189–2200.

GRATTON, L. (2007) *Hot Spots: Why Some Companies Buzz with Energy and Innovation – and Others Don't*. Harlow: Financial Times/Prentice Hall.

GUO, C. (2015) Cultural convergence, divergence, and crossvergence. *Wiley Encyclopedia of Management* (3rd edn). Hoboken, NJ: John Wiley & Sons, 6: 1–2.

GUPTA, A. AND GOVINDARAJAN, V. (1991) Knowledge flows and the structure of control within multinational corporations. *Academy of Management Review*, 16: 768–792.

HANDY, C. (2015) *The Second Curve: Thoughts on Reinventing Society*. London: Random House.

HARZING, A.-W. (2001) Who's in charge? An empirical study of executive staffing practices in foreign subsidiaries. *Human Resource Management*, 40: 139–158.

HARZING, A.-W., PUDELKO, M. AND REICHE, S. B. (2016) The bridging role of expatriates and inpatriates in knowledge transfer in multinational corporations. *Human Resource Management*, 55: 679–695.

HAYDEN, A. AND EDWARDS, T. (2001) The erosion of the country of origin effect: A case study of a Swedish multinational company. *Relations Industrielles/Industrial Relations*, 56: 116–140.

HEDLUND, G. (1994) A model of knowledge management and the N-form corporation. *Strategic Management Journal*, 15: 73–90.

HEENAN, D. A. AND PERLMUTTER, H. V. (1979) *Multinational Organizational Development*. Reading, MA: Addison Wesley.

HEIKKILÄ, J-P., BREWSTER, C. AND MATTILA, J. (2013) Micropolitical conflicts and institutional issues during e-HRM implementation in MNCs: a vendor's view. In Machado, C. and Davim, J. P. (eds), *Human Resources Management and the Technological Challenge*. Cham: Springer, pp. 1–22.

HEWLETT, S. A. AND RASHID, R. (2010) The battle for female talent in emerging markets. *Harvard Business Review*, 88(5): 101–106.

HILL, A. (2015) When is a company too big to manage? *Financial Times*, February 27.

HOFSTEDE, G. (1980) *Culture's Consequences: International Differences in Work-Related Values*. Beverly Hills, CA: Sage.

ILO (2015). *World Employment and Social Outlook*. Geneva: International Labour Organization.

JANSSENS, M. AND CAPPELLEN, T. (2008) Contextualizing cultural intelligence: The case of global managers. In Ang, S. and Van Dyne, L. (eds), *Handbook of Cultural Intelligence, Theory, Measurement, and Applications*. Armonk: New York: M. E. Sharpe, pp. 356–374.

KAMOCHE, K. (1996) The integration-differentiation puzzle: A resource-capability perspective in international human resource management. *International Journal of Human Resource Management*, 7: 230–244.

KHAN, F. R., MUNIR, K. A. AND WILLMOTT, H. (1997) A dark side of institutional entrepreneurship: Soccer balls, child labour and postcolonial impoverishment. *Organization Studies*, 28: 1055–1077.

KWAN, C. W. (2015) What HR needs to do to help develop global Asian talent. In Ulrich, D., Schiemann, B. and Sartain, L. (eds), *The Rise of HR. Wisdom from 73 Thought Leaders*. Alexandria, VA: HR Certification Institute, pp. 57–54. http://hrleadsbusiness.org/docs/default-source/staff-directory-downloads/the_rise_of_hr_page_view.pdf?sfvrsn=2.

LINDHOLM, N., TAHVANAINEN, M. AND BJÖRKMAN, I. (1999) Performance of host-country employees: Western MNEs in China. In Brewster, C. and Harris, H. (eds), *International HRM. Contemporary Issues in Europe*. Oxford: Routledge, pp. 143–159.

MARCHINGTON, M. AND GRUGULIS, I. (2000) 'Best practice' human resource management: Perfect opportunity or dangerous illusion? *International Journal of Human Resource Management*, 11: 1104–1124.

MARSH, V. (2011) Human resources: Power to the people. *Financial Times*, May 17.

MARTIN, G. AND BEAUMONT, P. (1998) Diffusing 'best practice' in multinational firms: Prospects, practice and contestation. *International Journal of Human Resource Management*, 9: 671–695.

MEARDI, G., STROHMER, S. AND TRAXLER, F. (2013) Race to the East, race to the bottom? Multi-nationals and industrial relations in two sectors in the Czech Republic. *Work Employment & Society*, 27: 39–55.

MINBAEVA, D., PEDERSEN, T., BJÖRKMAN, I., FEY, C. F. AND PARK, H. J. (2003) MNC knowledge transfer, subsidiary absorptive capacity, and HRM. *International Journal of Business Studies*, 34: 586–599.

MOORE, F. (2006) Strategy, power and negotiation: Social control and expatriate managers in a German multinational corporation. *International Journal of Human Resource Management*, 17: 399–413.

NAYAR, V. (2010) *Employees First, Customers Second: Turning Conventional Management Upside Down*. Boston MA: Harvard Business School Publishing.

NEWMAN, K. L. AND NOLLEN, S. D. (1996) Culture and congruence: The fit between management practices and national culture. *Journal of International Business Studies*, 27: 753–779.

NGO, H. Y., TURBAN, D., LAU, C. M. AND LUI, S. Y. (1998) Human resource practices and firm performance of multinational corporations: Influences of country origin. *International Journal of Human Resource Management*, 9: 632–652.

NISSEN, B. (2002) (ed.) *Unions in a Globalized Environment: Changing Borders, Organizational Boundaries and Social Roles*. Oxford: Routledge.

O'CONNELL, J. (2015) Regiocentric approach to hiring. In Cooper, C. L. (ed.), *The Blackwell Encyclopedia of Management*. Oxford: Blackwell Publishing, Blackwell Reference Online.

OECD (2011) *Guidelines for Multinational Enterprises*. http://www.oecd.org/corporate/mne/.

OECD (2012) *OECD Employment Outlook 2012*. Paris: OECD. http://www.oecd.org/germany/Germany_final_EN.pdf.

PFEFFER, J. (1994) *Competitive Advantage through People: Unleashing the Power of the Work Force*. Boston, MA: Harvard Business School Press.

PRAHALAD, C. AND DOZ, Y. (1987) *The Multinational Mission*. New York: Free Press.

PUCIK, V. (1992) Globalization and human resource management. In Pucik, V., Tichy, N. M. and Barnett, C. K. (eds), *Globalizing Management*. New York: John Wiley & Sons, pp. 61–81.

PUDELKO, M. AND HARZING, A.-W. (2007) Country-of-origin, localization, or dominance effect? An empirical investigation of HRM practices in foreign subsidiaries. *Human Resource Management Journal*, 46: 535–559.

RALSTON, D. A., HOLT, D. H., TERPSTRA, R. H. AND YU, K-C. (1997) The impact of national culture and economic ideology on managerial work values: A study of the United States, Russia, Japan and China. *Journal of International Business Studies*, 39: 27–40.

ROSENZWEIG, P. M. (2007) The dual logics behind international human resource management: Pressures for global integration and local responsiveness. In Stahl, G. K. and Björkman, I. (eds), *Handbook of Research in International Human Resource Management*. Cheltenham: Edward Elgar, pp. 36–48.

ROSENZWEIG, P. M. AND NOHRIA, N. (1994) Influences on human resource management practices in multinational corporations. *Journal of International Business Studies*, 25: 229–251.

ROSENZWEIG, P. M. AND SINGH, J. V. (1991) Organizational environments and the multinational enterprise. *Academy of Management Review*, 16: 340–361.

RUGGIE, J. G. (2013) *Just Business: Multinational Corporations and Human Rights*. New York: W.W. Norton.

SANTOS, J. F. P. AND WILLIAMSON, P. J. (2015) The new mission for multinationals. *MIT Sloan Management Review*, 56(4): 45–54.

SAYIM, K. Z. (2010) Pushed or pulled? Transfer of reward management policies in MNCs. *International Journal of Human Resource Management*, 21: 2631–2658.

SCHNEIDER, S. C., STAHL, G. K. AND BARSOUX, J.-L. (2014) *Managing across Cultures* (3rd edn). Harlow: Pearson.

SCHULER, R. S. (1992) Linking the people with the strategic needs of the business. *Organizational Dynamics*, 18–32.

SCHULER, R. S. AND JACKSON, S. E. (1987) Linking competitive strategies with human resource management practices. *Academy of Management Executive*, 1: 207–219.

SCHULER, R. S. AND ROGOVSKY, N. (1998) Understanding compensation practice variations across firms: The impact of national culture. *Journal of International Business Studies*, 29: 159–177.

SEGAL-HORN, S. (2002) Global firms – heroes or villains? How and why companies globalise. *European Business Journal*, 14: 8–19.

SETHI, S. P. (2013) *The World of Wal-Mart*. New York: Carnegie Council for Ethics in International Affairs, May 8.

SHARMA, A. (2015) Who leads in a G-zero world? Multinationals, sustainable development, and corporate social responsibility in a changing global order. *Washington International Law Journal*, June: 1–25.

SHIMONI, B. AND BERGMANN, H. (2006) Managing in a changing world: From multiculturalism to hybridization – the production of hybrid management cultures in Israel, Thailand, and Mexico. *Academy of Management Perspectives*, 20(3): 76–89.

SMITH, C. AND MEIKSINS, P. (1995) System, society and dominance effects in cross-national organisational analysis. *Work Employment & Society*, 9: 241–267.

SPARROW, P., HIRD, M. AND COOPER, C. (2014) *Do We Need HR? Repositioning People Management for Success*. Basingstoke: Palgrave Macmillan.

STILES, P. (2012) The international HR department. In Stahl, G. K., Björkman, I. and Morris, S. (eds), *Handbook of Research in International Human Resource Management* (2nd edn). Cheltenham: Edward Elgar, pp. 36–51.

TARIQUE, I., BRISCOE, D. AND SCHULER, R. (2016) *International Human Resource Management: Policies and Practices for Multinational Enterprises* (5th edn). New York and London: Routledge.

TAYLOR, S., BEECHLER, S. AND NAPIER, N. (1996) Toward an integrative model of strategic international human resource management. *Academy of Management Review*, 21: 959–985.

THITE, M., BUDHWAR, P. AND WILKINSON A. (2014) Global HR roles and factors influencing their development: Evidence from emerging Indian IT services multinationals. *Human Resource Management*, 53: 921–946.

THITE, M., WILKINSON, A. AND SHAH, D. (2012) Internationalization and HRM strategies across subsidiaries in multinational corporations from emerging economies: A conceptual framework. *Journal of World Business*, 47: 251–258.

TRAXLER, F. AND WOITECH, B. (2000) Transnational investment and national labour market regimes: A case of 'regime shopping'? *European Journal of Industrial Relations*, 6(2). 141–159.

UN (2008) *'Protect, Respect and Remedy' Framework and Guiding Principles*. New York: UN. Available at: http://business-humanrights.org/en/un-secretary-generals-special-representative-on-business-human-rights/un-protect-respect-and-remedy-framework-and-guiding-principles.

UN (2015) *Sustainable Development Goals*. Available at: https://sustainabledevelopment.un.org/topics.

UNCTAD (2015) *Trade and Development Report, 2015 – Making the International Financial Architecture Work for Development*. Geneva: UNCTAD.

VARA, V. (2015) The push against performance reviews. *New Yorker*, July 24.

VO, A. AND STANTON, P. (2011) The transfer of HRM policies and practices to a transitional business system: The case of performance management practices in the US and Japanese MNEs operating in Vietnam. *International Journal of Human Resource Management*, 22: 3513–3527.

WRIGHT, P. M. AND MCMAHAN, G. C. (1992) Alternative theoretical perspectives on strategic human resource management. *Journal of Management*, 18: 295–320.

YALABIK, Z. Y., CHEN, S.-J., LAWLER, J. AND KIM, K. (2008) High-performance work system and organizational turnover in East and Southeast Asian countries. *Industrial Relations*, 47: 145–152.

ZAKARIA, F. (2011) *The Post-American World and the Rise of the Rest* (Release 2.0). New York: Penguin.

ZHANG, M. AND EDWARDS, C. (2007) Diffusing 'best practice' in Chinese multinationals: The motivation, facilitation and limitations. *International Journal of Human Resource Management*, 18: 2147–2165.

ZHU, Y., WARNER, M. AND ROWLEY, C. (2007) Human resource management with 'Asian' characteristics: A hybrid people-management system in East Asia. *International Journal of Human Resource Management*, 18: 745–768.

4

DIVERSITY MANAGEMENT IN A GLOBAL CONTEXT

Nicolina Kamenou-Aigbekaen and Jawad Syed

LEARNING OUTCOMES

After reading this chapter, you should be able to:

➤ Understand and distinguish between diversity management and equal employment opportunity
➤ Understand how demographic transformation of the population and the workforce affects the future of diversity management in the workplace
➤ Understand various forms of employment stereotypes and discrimination
➤ Know about various laws and regulations in place in several countries to tackle workplace discrimination
➤ Distinguish between the business case and social equity approaches to diversity management
➤ Understand methodological considerations in diversity management research.

SUMMARY OF CHAPTER CONTENTS

🔖 **Opening Case Study Oscars so white**

For a second year in a row, all of the 20 acting nominations for the Academy Awards 2016 went to white actors. As happened last year, this has resulted in a heated debate about racial bias in the Oscars, and the opinions of film artists and activists vary from a blatant denial of racial bias to an outright allegation of racism. The nomination process for the Oscars appears to reflect institutional bias, given that racial privileges, choices, and networks seem to perpetuate a dominantly white organisation in which the inclusion of non-whites is either an exception or a token. The Academy of Motion Picture Arts and Science, the organisation behind the Oscars, is by its very construction and perpetuation, an overly white organisation. Its membership is limited to mostly white actors, writers, directors, and other professionals. New members must be sponsored by two current members from within their own field or be nominated for an Oscar. There is further scrutiny involved, and the final decision lies with the Board of Governors. According to a 2012 study, with more than 6,000 voting members, the Academy is predominantly white (94 per cent of members) and predominantly male (77 per cent). Black members account for just 3 per cent. Moreover, within its various branches, whites represent 98 per cent of producers, 98 per cent of writers and 88 per cent of actors. Thirty-three per cent of members are previous winners of or nominees for Academy Awards. In other words, the dominance and perpetuation of whiteness are hard to ignore (adapted from Syed, 2016).

Questions

1 Read the entire article (see references) and discuss the extent to which institutional racism may be a factor in the nomination and award of the Oscars?
2 Critically discuss this statement: 'The dominance and perpetuation of whiteness in the Academy of Motion Picture Arts and Science are hard to ignore.'

INTRODUCTION

The aim of this chapter is to introduce students to the concepts of managing diversity and equal opportunities in employment. Given the demographic transformations of the general population and the labour force in many countries, workforce diversity is a major issue facing managers and organisations. There is, however, evidence of unrelenting stereotypes and discriminatory attitudes and behaviours that not only permeate the workplace but are also found in abundance on a societal and an institutional level. Chapter 15 further expands on issues related to diversity and the experiences of social groups in relation to balancing their work and personal life, and interested readers can review the related work in that chapter.

This chapter will introduce students to various forms of employment discrimination, as well as legislation in various countries to tackle discrimination. Chapter 15 also focuses on some equality legislation and the experiences of diverse groups, mainly in relation to work–life balance. With respect to theorising diversity management, here we discuss two key approaches: the business case approach and the social equity approach. Our chapter also discusses some methodological issues related to conducting research on diversity and equal opportunity and presents a case study on ethnic minority women in the UK.

KEY CONCEPTS OF DIVERSITY MANAGEMENT

In the last few decades, diversity management has been gaining increasing attention within the field of human resource management (HRM) and international HRM. Cox (1994) noted that diversity management was initially seen to be a 'North American affair' and that the emphasis in other countries (for example, Canada and the UK) was on learning lessons from the US experience. Local context, however, remains a major determinant of the approach to diversity and diversity management in any country. For example, British identity or Britishness is a key factor in diversity management in the UK 'because most of the disadvantaged women and men in our society have ancestral roots in the colonies of Britain's erstwhile empire, and it is they who bear the brunt of racism and discrimination' (Lorbiecki, 2001: 2).

Most definitions of and discussions related to diversity management focus on the organisational benefits it can provide, that is, the business case for diversity. A large number of organisations in the US, UK and elsewhere are now attempting to 'embrace diversity', not only as a result of the advocated benefits of having a diverse group of staff but also because of demographic changes. There are discussions within the 'inclusion' debate that engage with the need for 'real inclusion' that acknowledges and values diversity and the benefits this can bring not only to organisations but also society as a whole (for example, see Frost, 2014). Legislative pressures are also crucial in organisations' attempts to present themselves as diversity-friendly.

In the UK, there is extensive legislation covering equality diversity, with the first formal acts introduced in the 1970s and including the Race Relations Act 1976, the Race Relations Amendment Act 2000, and the Sex Discrimination Act 1975, as well as EU discrimination provisions that cover religion or belief, sexual orientation, and age. The new UK single Equality Act, which came into force in October 2010, brings together a number of existing laws and includes age, disability, gender reassignment, marriage and civil partnership, pregnancy and maternity, race, religion and belief, gender and sexual orientation. The general equality duty in the public sector is set out in the Equality Act 2010 (Equality and Human Rights Commission, 2011), which states that those subject to the equality duty must make efforts to:

- eliminate unlawful discrimination, harassment and victimisation and other conduct prohibited by the Act;
- advance equality of opportunity between people who share a protected characteristic and those who do not;
- foster good relations between people who share a protected characteristic and those who do not.

In New Zealand, institutions concerned with a single group in society have been replaced by an overarching human rights body that is concerned with various equality strands (Parker and Douglas, 2010).

With some notable exceptions, mainly in the US (for example, Nkomo and Cox, 1996; Thomas, 1992; Thomas and Ely, 1996) but also with some UK examples since 1990 (Dickens, 1994, 1999; Healy et al., 2010; Kamenou and Fearfull, 2006; Kamenou et al., 2013; Liff, 1997, 1999; Lorbiecki and Jack, 2000; Syed and Özbilgin, 2015), diversity management has received limited attention from academic scholars. This has been the case in other regions and in both developed and emerging economies, and examples in relation to diversity management will be cited throughout this chapter. There has been more sociological work on the effects of discrimination and prejudice in organisations and society as a whole (see, for example, Afshar and Maynard, 1994; Anthias, 1992; Brah, 1994; Blackstone et al., 1998) than on diversity management research within business or management schools, although this situation has slowly improved over the last few years. There is a dire need for more academic research on diversity and equality within the 'human-focused' management topics, such as HRM, and organisational behaviour, but also within more general management and business areas such as strategic management, economics, and critical accounting.

Discussions surrounding equality should be mainstream in both management research and teaching, instead of being considered as a 'soft extra' within more sociological aspects of the curriculum and of research.

THE DIVERSITY MANAGEMENT DISCOURSE AND ITS LIMITATIONS

In the literature addressing specific approaches to diversity and their limitations, 'equal employment opportunity' (EEO), 'affirmative action' and 'diversity management' are frequently used terms (see, for example, Deluca and McDowell, 1992; Syed and Kramar, 2009). Demographic changes in both the population in general and the labour market in many countries mean that employers today need to manage a far broader diversity of groups across Europe, Australia, BRICS countries, and other developed and emerging economies (Bisin et al., 2011) Accordingly, much literature has been becoming increasingly available to organisations informing them how best to handle a diverse workforce (see, for example, Ashkanasy et al., 2002; Bell, 2007; Ely and Thomas, 2001; Ferris et al., 1994; Härtel and Fujimoto, 2000; Murray and Syed, 2005; Thomas and Ely, 1996).

Figure 4.1 offers three popular approaches to workforce diversity in various international contexts. It highlights the key features of each approach, for example:

- the emphasis of EEO on eliminating discrimination in human resources policies and practices;
- the emphasis of affirmative action on equality of outcomes;
- the emphasis of diversity management on the inclusion of all forms of diversity and business outcomes.

All of these approaches have their origins in the US labour market. Whereas the first two approaches are generally legally mandated, the diversity management approach is based on voluntary corporate measures. Diversity management was adopted as an alternate approach to affirmative action because the realities facing organisations were 'no longer the realities affirmative action was designed to fix' (Thomas, 1990: 107). Affirmative action failed to 'deal with the root causes of prejudice and inequality and did little to develop the full potential of every man and woman in the company' (1990: 117).

Within the Australian context, diversity management has been described as 'second-generation' EEO opportunity that followed a wave of anti-discrimination legislation (Teicher and Spearitt, 1996). The diversity agenda has been

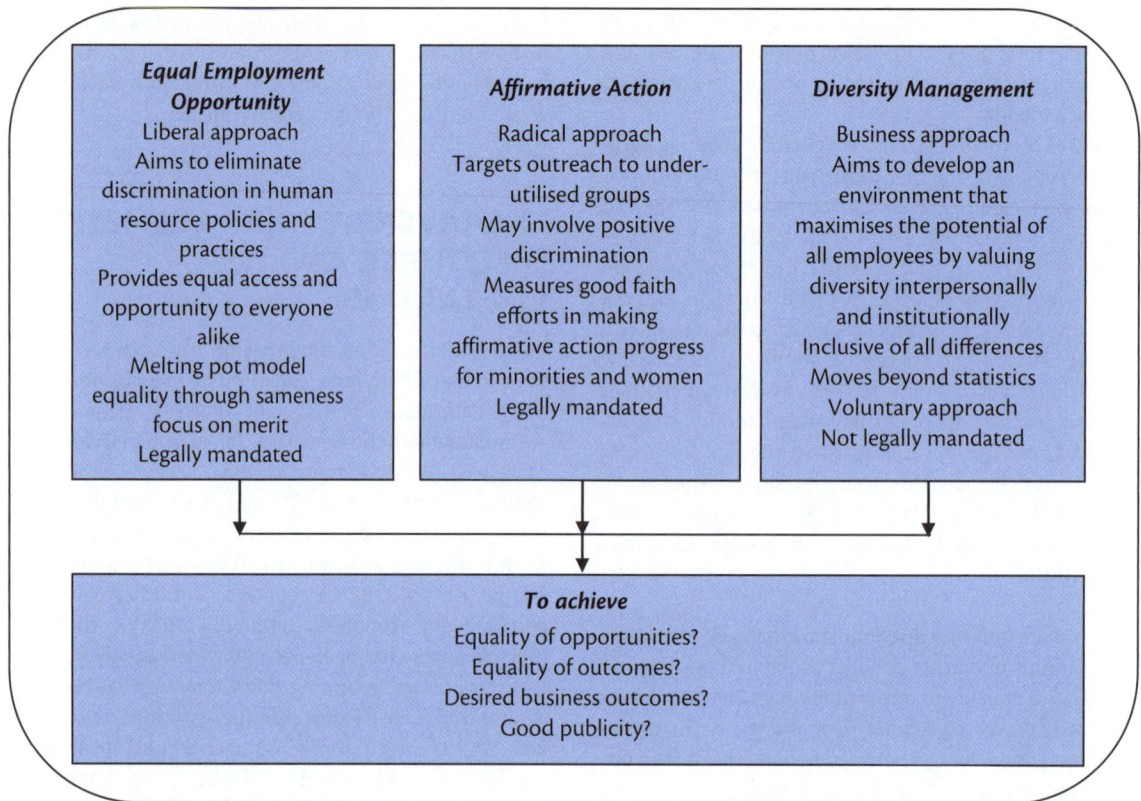

Figure 4.1 Usual approaches to managing diversity
Source: Based on University of California (1999) and Gagnon and Cornelius (2000).

described as one that 'has come to Australia from the USA as an HRM workplace strategy' (Strachan et al., 2004: 199), an agenda that has traditionally focused on gender (De Cieri and Kramar, 2005). However, certain other groups of people, such as indigenous Australians and persons from non-English-speaking backgrounds, continue to be disadvantaged in employment (Syed and Ali, 2005).

Traditionally, diversity policies have been externally driven, influenced by social responsibility doctrines. However, since the mid-1990s, there has been a shift in public policy towards the business case for diversity. Managing a diverse workforce is now closely linked to business performance (that is, it is internally driven) and is generally considered to be a part of corporate strategy (Bertone and Leahy, 2003). Accordingly, diversity management is described as a programme that was 'needed, not only to meet employee needs, but to reduce turnover costs and ensure that customers receive the best service possible' (De Cieri and Kramar, 2005: 28–29). In Chapter 15 of this book, Kamenou-Aigbekaen and Fu argue that government and organisational initiatives relating to work–life balance

are also often based on business case arguments, that is, how different social groups can be 'utilised' in a manner that is good for business and profitability. Syed and Özbilgin (2015) have argued that the need to understand and effectively manage diversity should not focus solely on the business case for diversity but that there should be an acknowledgement of the importance of creating a fair and socially inclusive society.

A RELATIONAL FRAMEWORK FOR DIVERSITY MANAGEMENT

In order to enable organisations to pursue an integrated approach, Syed and Özbilgin (2009) propose a relational framework that treats diversity management from a layered and intersectional perspective. The framework is informed by Bourdieu's relational sociology, which treats social reality as being layered across agency and structure (see, for example, Bourdieu, 1998). Syed and Özbilgin discuss the need for a relational framework with which

Ⓠ

Critical Thinking 4.1 The discourse of diversity management

Some scholars suggest that managers now talk about diversity both to keep on the right side of the law and to ensure the commitment of diverse employees to the organisation and its objectives (Dover et al., 2016). Employers' approaches generally range from a straight lack of interest to a more inclusive approach and positive potential for a long-term business strategy. Some organisations devote little attention to the area, whereas others devote much. There is also some evidence of a negative reaction against EEO endeavours. In particular, the emphasis on affirmative action has sparked most resistance (D'Netto et al., 2000). Previous research suggests that, in most organisations, diversity policies appear to represent a renaming of EEO rather than being an integrated management approach in their own right (Kramar, 2004). An integrated approach is, however, hard to achieve through single-level conceptualisations of diversity management (Syed and Kramar, 2009; Syed and Özbilgin, 2009).

Scholars have expressed some concern that a shift from social-equity-driven EEO to business-benefits-driven diversity management may exacerbate the disadvantaged employment conditions of women, ethnic minorities, and other disadvantaged groups. For example, Humphries and Grice (1995) argue that while diversity management may be seen as a new social division between the core, the periphery, and the unemployed, it ignores the categories that 'illustrate women and other people as not having achieved proportionate representation in the statistics of privilege' (1995: 30–31). The replacement of the discourse of equity with the discourse of diversity may relegate many people from diverse backgrounds to the 'insecure periphery' (1995: 31). In other words, there are serious concerns about the direction and scope of diversity management in improving the conditions of disadvantaged people in the workplace.

There are also some concerns about a predominant emphasis on individuality within the discourse of diversity management. Social identity theory proposes that individuals identify with groups that positively affect their self-esteem and evaluate their own groups by social comparisons to other groups (Tajfel and Turner, 1986). Previous research also suggests that organisational interventions that fail to address the underlying problem of cultural disintegration will not be able to alleviate social disadvantage within and outside organisations (Appo and Härtel, 2003).

Although collective identity is generally ignored in employment contexts, employers are reportedly more concerned about legal regulations. Managers generally seem to be driven by a legal compliance approach (Antonios, 1997), but legislation is generally limited in its ability to bring about cultural and attitudinal change in organisations (Pyke, 2005). Most probably, this is because of the narrow, single-level conceptualisations of diversity management, so that issues related to national culture, structural conditions, and intersectionality (overlapping) of various forms of identity remain generally neglected.

Questions

1 Is diversity management a repackaging of EEO to make it more attractive to business organisations while paying lip-service to disadvantaged workers?
2 What tangible differences in outcomes may be identified as a result of the change from EEO to diversity management?

equality of opportunities could be studied in dynamic (that is, always evolving), overlapping (in terms of structure and agency and of various forms of identity), and context-specific (instead of universalistic) terms. They argue that single-level conceptualisations of equal opportunities fail to capture the interplay between agentic and structural concerns of equality. Therefore, they propose a relational framework that bridges the divide between large-scale macro-national, medium-sized meso-organisational, and small-scale micro-individual insights to arrive at a realistic conceptualisation of diversity management.

At the *macro-national* level, the relational framework of diversity management discusses the impact of national structures and arrangements, such as laws, social organisation, national culture, and gender and race relations. At the *meso-organisational* level, the framework takes into account the organisational processes, rituals, and routinised behaviours at work that establish the rules of middle-level gender and race relations. An absence of debate on equality of rights at work and a lack of recognition of multicultural traditions mean that meso-level relationships may reflect a hierarchical organisation of discriminatory practices, embedded within broad social relations. At the *micro-individual* level, the relational framework deals with issues related to individual identity, aspirations, and agency that affect change, these phenomena also being viewed in terms of gender and race.

While organisations can play a key role in developing a diverse and inclusive culture in the workplace, there are numerous stereotypes, biases, and cultural and structural issues that continue to proliferate from the wider society. A relational, multilevel approach to managing diversity may help capitalise on the advantages of diversity while minimising its challenges and problems. However, despite the fact that many industrialised countries have anti-discrimination policies and laws to ensure equal opportunity, an integrated approach to understanding and managing diversity at multiple levels is lacking (Syed and Kramar, 2009). While there is an emphasis on the business benefits case of diversity, important structural and sociocultural challenges faced by ethnic minorities, women and other diverse groups remain generally ignored. A multilevel framework may capture both the business arguments and the social justice arguments for diversity management. The framework indicates the need to address the various contextual variables, such as anti-discrimination and human rights laws, and the way they affect actual and perceived limitations on employment opportunities available to diverse workers.

ADVANTAGES OF DIVERSITY

Cox and Blake (1991) identified six dimensions that help organisations to create a competitive advantage from effectively managing the diversity of their workforce, namely cost, human resource acquisition, marketing, creativity, problem-solving, and organisational flexibility. It can be argued that more than two decades later, this seminal work is still relevant in today's organisations.

Cost

Issues such as high employee turnover rates and absence from work cost businesses significant amounts of money. A lack of attention to issues such as diversity, equality, and inclusion means that individuals may feel isolated or disengaged in the workplace and in extreme circumstances may resign. A survey by Kronos (2008) showed that unplanned and extended absences cost companies 9.2 per cent of their payroll. According to Cox and Blake (1991), women and racial minority groups may experience high turnover rates and absenteeism in the workplace due to lack of inclusive approach towards issues such as pregnancy and work–life balance. Studies prove that

organisations have reduced women's turnover rates by 63 per cent as a result of providing in-house childcare facilities (Youngblood and Cook, 1984), and that introducing flexible working times has significantly reduced absenteeism (Kim and Campagna, 1981).

Resource acquisition

Organisations today are involved in a persistent struggle to attract and retain top-quality employees. Cox and Blake (1991) suggest that by using positive publicity to recruit women and individuals from racial minorities, companies can indirectly boost their recruiting efforts.

Marketing and creativity

Markets are becoming more diverse (Cox and Blake, 1991), and each market has its own cultural preferences and sensitivities (Hill, 2008). From a team perspective, a diverse mix of team members is likely to be more creative than a group of identical individuals. A diverse team holds different attitudes and perspectives that are not possessed by a homogeneous team. Therefore, discussions within a diverse group are likely to result in a higher level of analysis and lower conformity in thought, whereas the members of a homogeneous group may have little to talk about or may commit identical mistakes (Cox and Blake, 1991). Diversity encourages more creativity and innovation, which can in turn lead to more effective decision-making (Gibson and Gibbs, 2006).

Problem-solving and system flexibility

Companies such as HSBC Bank and Proctor and Gamble (P&G) have achieved global success by hiring talented employees and making sure they gain international experience by relocating them to countries with cultural identities completely different from their own (Ready and Conger, 2007). In this way, employees exchange information about each others' cultures. The knowledge gained in this way can help employees to understand subtle details such as valuable cultural dimensions and how business deals are negotiated (Hofstede, 1984). This can in turn lead to greater flexibility in the system and better problem-solving in organisations (Ready and Conger, 2007).

Discrimination is a major issue in organisations with a diverse workforce. International Labour Organisation (ILO, 2004) studies show that qualified migrants in Western industrialised countries face a discrimination rate of 35 per cent (that is, one in three is unfairly excluded in employment procedures). The social identity of employees is reported to be responsible for differing career path trajectories and significant income differences, for instance, for migrant workers who face both 'glass door'

? Critical Thinking 4.2 The challenges of managing diversity

Managing diversity is not an easy task. Several issues, such as conflict, isolation, and discrimination, may exist within diverse work groups.

In certain situations, diversity may trigger social isolation, which is probably caused by not only social stereotypes but also unique individual dispositions (Putnam, 2007). Kreitz (2008) suggests that managers in organisations should be able to identify whether people are keeping to themselves and rectify this by promoting an organisational culture in which each group is enabled to embrace others' identities rather than trying to 'make everyone the same' (Putnam, 2007).

In addition, conflict may arise in diverse groups. In-groups and out-groups can be created as a result of racial and gender differences. Richard et al. (2004) explain that strong identification between people of the same race and gender results in 'poor intergroup communication' and increased conflict during group work.

Research has also suggested that the majority group may feel resentful towards diversity initiatives, especially if these initiatives are not communicated sensitively and constructively by organisations. This often leads to resistance and tensions among different groups and also to a reluctance on the part of minority groups to engage with diversity initiatives, such as positive action, in case they are seen as 'tokens' (Kamenou, 2003).

Questions

1 If the majority group remains resentful towards disadvantaged employees, is it at all useful to implement diversity management in the workplace?

2 What can organisations do to alleviate any apprehensions in the majority group?

and 'glass ceiling' discrimination based on their race and gender (Syed, 2008).

FROM POSITIVE DISCRIMINATION TO POSITIVE ACTION

Although positive discrimination (or affirmative action) is now disallowed in many countries (for example, Australia, the UK, and the USA) because it allegedly violates the principle of merit and equality, there is evidence of governmental initiatives to encourage employment of previously disadvantaged groups. Positive action may take many forms, as seen, for example, in targeted advertising campaigns encouraging ethnic minority candidates to join the police force.

From a legal perspective, section 47 of the Sex Discrimination Act 1975 in the UK allowed for the use of 'positive action' in a number of specific circumstances. Similarly, sections 37 and 38 of the Race Relations Act 1976 allowed an employer to give special encouragement and to provide specific training for a particular racial group. These two Acts have now been replaced by the Equality Act 2010, which also provides for positive action in recruitment and promotion. From an organisational perspective, positive action may include initiatives such as the introduction of non-discriminatory selection procedures and training programmes or policies aimed at preventing sexual harassment.

Box 4.1 provides some examples of positive action in organisations and also a guide to assess the need for positive action.

Box 4.1 Does your company need positive action?

Before deciding to introduce positive action to encourage underrepresented groups to apply for jobs, employers must look at their own employees to establish how many underrepresented groups have been doing the kind of work in question during the previous 12 months. If the number of underrepresented groups is comparatively small, consideration can be given to encouraging them to apply for the relevant vacancies. For example:

▶ A local government authority in the UK used 'statements of encouragement' in adverts to women to encourage applications in areas where women had traditionally been underrepresented.

▶ London's Metropolitan Police has a positive action team who are undertaking a series of job fairs to encourage ethnic minority and female candidates to join their service.

Useful contacts

▶ See http://www.equalityhumanrights.com/ for further information on gender-positive action and other equality related policies and actions.

▶ For resources on Age Positive, a diversity-related initiative from the UK government, see http://www.dwp.gov.uk/age-positive/.

Source: Equality Advice Centre; http://www.equality-online.org.uk/equality_advice/index.html

📖

In the News Diversity and the backlash

There is also a need to manage those people who are not identified as 'diverse' groups but who may need policies that take into account their differences. In many countries and organisations, diversity policies remain mainly focused on only one or two dimension, such as women's participation and promotion in employment. Other dimensions of diversity, such as race, age, religion, sexual orientation, and disability, either remain completely ignored or do not see much action in terms of statistical patterns and positive action. Such groups who remain ignored in diversity programmes may in turn lose trust in organisational initiatives.

There is also an element of backlash that is more likely to emanate from the groups whose resources or power may be threatened due to diversity initiatives. For example, white men (and some white women) in the West, upper-caste Brahmins in India, and the tribal elite and the Wahhabi clergy in Saudi Arabia are some examples of powerful groups in their respective country. At times, such groups may be less sympathetic to diversity policies and may feel that their interests are at stake. One recent example is the reaction to the call for diversity at the Oscars by some white actors (Syed, 2016).

In an interview with French radio network Europe 1, Oscar nominee Charlotte Rampling said that complaining about the all-white acting nominees 'is racist to whites'. She added: 'One can never really know, but perhaps the black actors did not deserve to make the final list.' In response to a suggestion about affirmative or positive action, she said: 'Why classify people? These days everyone is more or less accepted.... People will always say: "Him, he's less handsome"; "Him, he's too black"; "He is too white".... someone will always be saying "You are too" [this or that].... But do we have to take from this that there should be lots of minorities everywhere?' (Addley and Child, 2016).

Michael Caine, another Oscar nominee, said that black actors needed to 'be patient'. Oscar nominations 'will come. It took me years to get an Oscar, years.' He also said 'There's loads of black actors. In the end you can't vote for an actor because he's black. You can't say "I'm going to vote for him, he's not very good, but he's black, I'll vote for him."' (Addley and Child, 2016).

SEXUAL HARASSMENT AT WORK

Sexual harassment refers to unwelcome sexual advances, requests for sexual favours, and other verbal or physical harassment of a sexual nature. It is a form of bullying or abuse (physical or psychological) and is illegal in most countries. In the workplace, harassment may result in a hostile or offensive work environment and may also result in an adverse employment decision. For many organisations, preventing sexual harassment is a key legal consideration.

In 1992, the European Union enacted the Commission code of practice on sexual harassment. The Act prohibits sexual harassment in the workplace and recommends that the employers should issue a policy statement that expressly states that sexual harassment will not be permitted or condoned and that employees have a right to complain about it should it occur (EUR-lex, 2007). In the Equality Act 2010 of the UK, sexual harassment is described as a form of discrimination (section 26) (UK Legislation, 2010). In 2005, China added new provisions to the Law on Women's Right Protection to include sexual harassment. The legal provisions were proposed in the backdrop of a national survey of 8,000 women that found 79 per cent of female respondents had experienced sexual harassment, compared to 22 per cent of men (BBC, 2005).

Ali and Kramar (2015) note that few studies have examined sexual harassment, its impact on victims, and redress processes in Muslim majority countries. In their study, the authors use neo-institutional theory to examine harassment experienced by women in the workplace in Pakistan. Drawing on interviews with working women and human resource managers in six Pakistani organisations, Ali and Kramar show that even when there are formal policies designed to prevent sexual harassment, cultural factors influence policy implementation. Their study identifies three major factors that influence sexual harassment redressal: socio-cultural factors (e.g. female modesty), institutional factors (e.g. inappropriate redress procedures), and managerial expertise/bias.

STRATEGIES TO MANAGE DIVERSITY

Managing diversity is not a 'one-off problem'. Hence, organisations need a coherent strategy to understand and manage it, for example in the shape of top management commitment, training, and extensive organisational knowledge (Kreitz, 2008). To be more specific, organisations need to create respect for all identity groups by valuing and respecting diversity (Cox and Blake, 1991; Kamenou and Fearfull, 2006; Syed and Özbilgin, 2015). Moreover, diversity should be represented at all levels and in all networks across the organisation (Ely and Thomas, 2001). Olsen and Martins (2012) have argued that there should be more engagement in understanding the benefits and challenges of diversity management programmes in organisations. Box 4.2

Box 4.2 Successful business stories of diversity management

It's not that difficult to find examples of good diversity practice. Here are a few.

▸ UK supermarket giant Tesco does not impose an age limit on its employees. They say that 'It's attitude not age that creates customer satisfaction'. Tesco recruits people from all ages since they believe that customers love to have people from different age groups dealing with them. Tesco's employees also report that they prefer working in an age-diverse team (Chartered Institute of Personnel and Development, 2005).

▸ BC Tel, a telephone company in Canada, set up an Indo-Canadian phone line. This helped the company to provide Indian- and Chinese-language services and fostered its relationship with diverse customers (AMSAA, 2000).

▸ Ebco Industries, Ltd., a Canadian manufacturing company, has received several prestigious awards, for example the federal government's Excellence in Race Relations Award and the Boeing Company's Eagle Award for Outstanding Cost Reduction and Quality Performance. The company has 900 employees from 48 nationalities. Hugo Eppich, the founder of the company, says that their philosophy is to respect individuals and their uniqueness; he also says that they focus more on strengths rather than differences. Among the diversity practices of this company are multicultural food festivals for all employees and displaying flags of all nationalities in the reception area (AMSAA, 2000).

▸ Corporate Rabobank (based in The Netherlands) has an intranet site that is dedicated to diversity management. This site gives information about the bank's policies, improvements, and planned activities. The most interesting thing about this site that it has a page called 'intercultural management', which talks about the reasons behind Rabobank choosing to adopt a multicultural environment (Subeliani and Tsogas, 2005).

▸ The military of a country usually reflects its society. The social composition of the US Air Force has altered in recent years as a result of increasing diversity of the USA's population. The military leadership is committed to education and training on equal opportunities and non-discrimination. Several short courses are offered on sexual harassment, equal opportunities, and cultural diversity. Moreover, two-day courses are offered to senior management on areas such as racism, cross-cultural socialisation, and others.

The US Air Force's leadership encourages contributions from all people without any regard to their origins (Moon, 1997).

Class Activity

Undertake the following as a class exercise. Based on your personal knowledge or research, identify a successful story of diversity management in a local or international organisation.

▸ What works well in that organisation?
▸ Where is there room for improvement?

provides some examples of best practices in diversity management.

The US Government Accountability Office (2005) has consulted experts on diversity and suggested nine leading practices organisations that should follow, as described below.

1. Leadership commitment

A good leader's commitment to diversity should be visible based on how well he or she communicates the vision of diversity in an organisation. The US Government Accountability Office (2005) further recommends that an organisation's support for diversity should be communicated in the form of policies, procedures, speeches, meetings and newsletters. Moreover, this support should exist throughout the organisation all the way from senior management to the lowest level (Kreitz, 2008). Roosevelt (2006) identifies the following three skills a leader should have for managing diversity, namely the ability to:

● recognise and analyse diversity in a group;
● determine whether action is required with respect to a particular group;
● respond appropriately to a problem.

2. Diversity as part of an organisation's strategic plan

Managing diversity is not an isolated issue (Kreitz, 2008): it can take five to seven years for an organisation to successfully integrate its related policies into the strategic plan (US Government Accountability Office, 2005). The strategic plan to manage diversity should be in line with the organisation's goals (Jayne and Dipboye, 2004).

3. Diversity linked to performance

Managing diversity should be effectively focused on increasing productivity and innovation. For example, positive promotion of diversity can boost an organisation's overall recruiting effort (Cox and Blake, 1991) and help a company to extend its services to a more diverse customer base (Ely and Thomas, 2001).

4. Measurement

Organisations can measure the impact of diversity on their performance by collecting and analysing empirical data drawn from interviews, focus groups, and surveys (US Government Accountability Office, 2005). In order to successfully measure the impact (for example, cost and effort) of diversity, managers must set goals at the start of the year and then review them at the end (Roosevelt, 1999).

5. Accountability

In order to promote the achievement of an organisation's diversity goals, managers should be rewarded through adequate performance management and reward systems (US Government Accountability Office, 2005). According to the US Government Accountability Office, this implies that managers at all levels of the organisation should be reviewed based on their ability to manage diverse teams and achieve diversity-specific goals.

6. Succession planning

Organisations should actively identify diverse talent pools and develop them into potential future leaders (US Government Accountability Office, 2005). For example, Ready and Conger (2007) explain how the banking organisation HSBC has a system of talent pools that tracks the careers of employees with good potential within the organisation. The selected candidates are first trained by local managers or business heads, after which they are given assignments overseas. Managers then identify the most capable candidates, who are put in a higher level pool of talent. These candidates can become executive managers in three to five years and may in the long term reach top management level.

7. Recruitment

In order to keep up with international competition and an increasingly diverse market place (Kreitz, 2008), firms need to attract a skilful and diverse workforce. This may help organisations to solve problems and achieve their goals using the multicultural exchange of knowledge, innovation and creativity (Cox and Blake, 1991; Richard et al., 2004).

8. Employee involvement

Organisations should involve employees in their diversity management efforts. According to the US Government Accountability Office (2005), this will lead employees to form networks, task forces, councils and committees that help an organisation to identify issues, raise opinions and so on, which will ultimately lead the organisation to recommend actions while keeping its employees' interest first.

9. Diversity training

To reap the benefits of diversity, organisations need to ensure that management and staff understand the advantages and challenges of diversity (US Government Accountability Office, 2005). According to Jayne and Dipboye (2004), the training provided needs to emphasise that a diverse group brings with it new skills and perspectives that can be used to improve task performance. Moreover, team-building exercises should be carried out in such a way that members are able to understand each others' cultural backgrounds. Training is essential as team members who are unaware of diversity and its complexities may not work together effectively and may instead contribute to negative stereotypes and discrimination in the workplace (Ely and Thomas, 2001).

So far, this chapter has provided an overview of important areas of diversity and equality, engaging with key concepts and frameworks and the advantages and challenges faced when managing diversity. The next section will focus on methodological issues that researchers should consider when conducting research on diversity management.

METHODOLOGICAL CONSIDERATIONS IN CONDUCTING RESEARCH ON DIVERSITY MANAGEMENT: THE CASE OF ETHNIC MINORITY WOMEN

This section presents some key methodological considerations to be taken into account when conducting research in the diversity management area. The discussion will engage with the career experiences of ethnic minority women as a means of illustrating key issues related to methodology and the position of the researcher and the researched. Reflexivity on the researchers' role and influence must be considered, particularly in situations where one group is historically seen as more dominant than another. Lorbiecki and Jack (2000: S22) have argued that reflexivity:

> encourages social actors, be they academics or practitioners, to look more deeply at what they are doing and to consider the political, cultural and social implications of the knowledge they are constructing.

Ethnic minority women are seen as social actors within organisational and social group structures and cultures that may affect their strategies and plans; in turn, they may also be affected by these structures and cultures. In the same vein, researchers are also seen as social actors placed within a specific context at a specific point in time, where their experiences may be informed by a number of factors, including their ethnicity, gender, class, education, and geographical location. An ethnic minority woman may have different realities from those of a white woman, a white man, an ethnic minority man, or an ethnic minority woman of a different ethnic group or class. At the same time, one should avoid essentialising (that is, stereotyping) groups as having specific traits – the above argument should be extended to remind researchers that ethnic minority women of the same ethnic group or class can still have different experiences.

If we acknowledge the fact that there is a need for a better understanding of how researchers can conduct work within diversity management, it is important to examine and identify appropriate methodologies that are sensitive to our topic of investigation and overcome biased perspectives that limit the validity and usefulness of the research.

In focusing on the career experiences of ethnic minority women, one should be aware of the dangers of adopting a feminist research methodology, since the second-wave Western feminist literature has been accused of ignoring the experiences of ethnic minority women (hooks, 1981, 1984, 1989, 1991; Collins, 1990; Maynard, 1994). For example, Finch (1984) and Oakley (1981, 1987) have been criticised for assuming unity by gender and ignoring other divisive factors (Lee, 1993). In some respects, however, a feminist methodology may be appropriate as it is open to giving participants voices to express themselves in their own words, and to setting up non-hierarchical relations between the researcher and the participants.

It is important to identify and engage with non-ethnocentric feminist methodologies that have been sensitive to multicultural studies and have allowed for an interaction of gender with other subidentities such as class, race, culture, and religion. The work of Edwards (1990, 1993) is especially useful in this respect, as she has provided a detailed discussion of feminist research methodologies that need to be sensitive to racial and class divisions. She has also discussed her own position as a white woman interviewing Caribbean women and has engaged with debates on how white researchers can conduct sensitive research on minority groups without imposing their own power or privilege.

Most feminist research writers agree that there is no one method that can be deemed 'the feminist methodology' – to use Edwards's (1993: 182) original emphasis. It seems that there is not one specific feminist philosophy or methodology, but rather a number of overlapping feminist methodologies. Thus, there are no feminist 'how-to-recipes' (Duelli Klein, 1983: 90). Nevertheless, Edwards (1990: 479) has argued that even though there is no single feminist methodology, there are certain elements that characterise the overall approach: 'a feminist methodology has as its base a critique of objectivity, of the supposedly rational, detached, value-free research as traditionally espoused'. Edwards goes to present three key principles that guide feminist research:

1 Women's lives need to be addressed in their own terms: 'women's round lives have been pushed into the square holes of male-defined theories, and where their experiences do not fit, those experiences have been invalidated, devalued, or presented as deviant' (Edwards, 1990: 479).

2 Feminist research should not just be 'on women' but 'for women' (Edwards's original emphasis). Edwards (1990) argues that the final aim of research should be to improve women's situations, and this raises concerns about the relationship between the researcher and the researched. The researched should not be treated as 'objects' of research, and their voices and concerns should be heard.

3 The researcher should locate herself (Edwards wrote from a perspective that women should interview women and therefore only acknowledges the female in her discussions) in the research and the process of production of results. She should do this by making explicit the reasoning procedures she has used in carrying out the research and, on a reflexive level, by focusing on the 'researcher's effect upon the actual process of the research, her class, race, assumptions, and beliefs', as well as the effect these have upon the research and its analysis (Edwards, 1990: 479).

Carrying out a study across racial and ethnic lines raises certain issues for the researcher, for example practical, strategic, ethical, and epistemological concerns (Stanfield and Dennis, 1993, cited in Kamenou, 2007). Andersen (1993) has argued that research focusing on race has often been distorted as it has been centred on the perspectives and experiences of dominant group members. This could have the unwelcome consequence that the production of knowledge has been 'ideologically determined and culturally biased' (Stanfield, 1993: 4).

Alvesson and Willmott (1992) argue that it is important, when conducting research, to allow people to speak for themselves through ethnographic studies. This 'is a vital means of moderating "totalising" accounts of management and organisation' (442) and of allowing a detailed analysis of perceptions of cultural life through the eyes of the participants (Hammersley and Atkinson, 1995). With regard to interviewing women from ethnic minority groups, some feminists have attributed to the open-ended interview 'an ability to help counter any implicit racism on the part of white researchers' (Edwards, 1993: 184). Open-ended interviews allow women to speak for themselves, and this can avoid the production of data that 'pathologise' women (Edwards, 1993: 184) and treat them as passive agents.

Edwards (1993: 184), however, goes on to discuss possible dangers if the female researcher and the female participant(s) derive from a different race or class:

> if we accept that there are structurally based divisions between women on the basis of race and/or class that may lead them to have different interests and priorities, then what has been said about woman-to-woman interviewing may not apply in all situations.

In terms of women interviewing women, Minister (1991) argued that women are not comfortable with hierarchical same-sex systems and that researchers should therefore attempt to minimise the hierarchical relationship. This argument is perhaps simplistic as it falls into the trap of stereotyping all women as behaving in a similar way and having similar preferences and goals. Some women may be comfortable in a given scheme of hierarchies and may even encourage a power relationship with other women, whereas some may not see themselves as having a bond with other women or as feeling any need to provide them with help or support.

It is important to look at some of the arguments proposed by black feminists who have criticised white feminists for attempting to involve themselves in research into black people's experiences. Black feminists have argued that white researchers are not capable of and should not be conducting research involving ethnic minority men and women as they do not have first-hand experience, insight or understanding. Carby (1982), a main voice in black feminism, argued that studies by white researchers involving black people are operating within white Western supremacist assumptions. A central argument lies in whether white researchers can contribute to the understanding of the experiences of different racial groups and whether dominant groups can comprehend the experiences of outsiders. Andersen (1993: 41), a white female researcher, suggested that there are certain problems in conducting research involving ethnic minority groups because of the social distance imposed by class and race relations when the interviewers are white and middle-class and those being interviewed are not:

> How can white scholars study those who have been historically subordinated without further producing sociological accounts distorted by the political economy of race, class and gender?

Standpoint feminists (that is, scholars who propose that feminist social science should be practised from the standpoint of women instead of men) have advocated that members of subordinated groups have unique viewpoints on their own experiences and on society as a whole, arguing that one's race, class, and gender are both the origin and the object of sociological knowledge (Andersen, 1993). Kamenou (2002, 2007) has contended, however, that people may be able to gain knowledge without having first-hand experience and be able to produce research and 'represent the other' (Kitzinger et al., 1996), provided they adopt reflexivity, being sensitive to their own position and the ways in which that position can affect their perceptions and attitudes.

When attempting to conduct culturally sensitive research, there are concerns over how researchers' identities and positions might affect their understanding of situations in which they are not involved. Andersen (1993) has contended that white academics conducting research on race and ethnicity need to acknowledge the influence of institutional racism in their research. This is a great challenge for researchers in white-dominated academic institutions. Academic scholars wanting to conduct research within the diversity management area need to understand the sensitivity of the topic if they want to embark on research involving groups that are diverse in terms of ethnicity, gender, culture, religion, and so on. In addition, this research needs to be placed within the broader historical and geographical context in which it is taking place.

To conduct research within the diversity management field and examine the work and life experiences of ethnic minority groups, we advocate for a non-hierarchical, empathy-driven approach in which participants are given a voice to express their opinions and discuss their experiences (Kamenou, 2002, 2007; Syed and Pio, 2010). One cannot deny that profit-making organisations will inevitably focus on any benefits they can accrue from diversity, as well as on cost–benefit analysis in relation to legal sanctions if they do not adhere to equality policies and practices. Management academics, however, need to look beyond the narrow spectrum of conducting research on yet another management topic and recognise that this research needs to be placed within its historical context and geographical location (Kamenou, 2007; Syed, 2009).

There is an urgent need for more work exploring *how* research in equality and diversity should be conducted. Again, work has been conducted in this area of studying 'others' (Davis et al., 2000) in anthropological and cultural studies (see, for example, Rosaldo, 1989; Alcoff, 1991/1992), but this has not occurred to any great extent within management studies. It is not suggested that there is one best model to be adopted when conducting research in this area, but it is important to highlight the fact that there are some methodological considerations that scholars ought to be aware of when working in the field of diversity management.

STOP AND REFLECT

The influx of migrants from Africa and the Middle East has caused a lot of political controversy and debates across many countries in Europe. Supporters of the mass migration say that migrants are a welcome boost as Europe's ageing society needs immigrants to keep its workforce from shrinking further. Germany, Italy, and Spain have some of the lowest birth rates in the region: the European Commission forecasts that Germany's population will shrink from 81.3 million in 2013 to 70.8 million in 2060 (Peston, 2015). Supporter of migration argue that fast-aging Europe could well benefit from the arrival of young, often relatively well-educated migrants. However, there are also questions of cultural differences, unemployment, and the ability to integrate migrants into the mainstream society.

CONCLUSION

This chapter has demonstrated that the current on-going demographic transformation of both the workforce and the general population in many countries has immense implications for the future of HRM, including diversity management, in the workplace. The chapter has discussed key concepts of diversity management and distinguished between the EEO and diversity management approaches to managing workforce diversity. It has also discussed the distinction between affirmative action and positive action and identified a gradual transition to the latter in many countries.

In our theorisation of diversity management, we criticised the usual organisation-focused approaches to diversity management and instead argued for a multilevel approach to diversity that takes into account the overlapping (macro-national, meso-organisational, and micro-individual) dimensions of diversity. We discussed the issue of the various laws and regulations in place in several countries to tackle workplace discrimination. Finally, we offered a detailed case study of ethnic minority women in the UK in order to highlight important methodological considerations in understanding and researching diversity management.

An understanding of or interest within management in research on equality and diversity, although fundamental, needs to be informed by historical, sociopolitical and economic factors, as well as by an understanding of post-colonialism and institutional racism in organisations. We explored here the methodological considerations of conducting research within the diversity management field, illustrating the key points through a focus on the work and career experiences of ethnic minority women. Certain issues have a universal appeal, for example:

- the need for an informed understanding of the context in which research is conducted;
- an acknowledgement of how this context affects participants from diverse social groups, in terms of, for example, gender, ethnicity, culture, age, and disability;
- an understanding of the issues surrounding reflexivity and self-awareness within research.

Conducting sensitive research within diversity management is therefore dependent on context, but the methodological process allows for some elements of convergence across locations and populations. There is a real need for more work in this area to improve the baseline of diversity and equality-related research within management settings so that such research will adopt a relevant and context-specific methodology and acknowledge the historical, political, and geographical context within which it functions.

End of Chapter Case Study Samina's career experiences in different contexts: UK and the Middle East

Samina recently relocated from the UK to Dubai after she was headhunted by a multinational retail organisation to work as a senior Retail Development Manager. Prior to that she had been working in Retail Co, a large British retail firm in the UK, for almost 12 years. At Retail Co, she rose through the organisational ranks and was promoted quickly to Store Manager in one of the company's stores in the North of England, the youngest ever store manager in the history of the organisation.

As she was having a quick lunch with some of her colleagues in a downtown Dubai cafe, she started reflecting on how different her experiences had been so far in Dubai in comparison to the UK. In a lot of ways, she missed England and her family tremendously, as she was born and raised on the outskirts of Bradford (a second-generation British Pakistani as her family had migrated from Pakistan to England in the 1970s). In other ways, she loved how much more multicultural Dubai was and the fact the she felt much more at ease as a South Asian woman in a senior position here than in the UK. She then felt that perhaps that sounded unfair, as if she didn't enjoy her work experiences back in the UK, which wouldn't necessarily be true. She had learnt a lot and had a number of supportive managers and mentors along the way who showed her 'the ropes' and helped her make smart career choices. She did however also face resistance from staff and managers when she was promoted to store manager at a young age, and she always felt that in addition to the age factor, this had a lot to do with her gender and ethnicity.

Although she had a good working relationship with most of the staff and managers at Retail Co, she was very aware of some resentment, especially from some older white managers who had assumed they would be made the store's manager once it opened. The focus of Retail Co on equality and diversity issues at that time had been great and, in Samina's opinion, much needed. There were very few ethnic minority staff in any management positions, but they were especially sparse at senior management levels. The Chief Executive had clearly communicated her commitment to equality in all areas – gender, ethnicity, disability, and age. She had focused on the benefits that diversity could bring to the organisation and the need for the stores to represent local communities. As part of these diversity initiatives, stores were given 'aspirational targets' to reach within two years, including a higher representation of ethnic minority male and female staff at management levels. Samina had all the right credentials for a store manager's post, as she had gained the required management experience in her time at Retail Co. She knew, however, that quite a few staff and managers were not supportive of her promotion, attributing it solely to an organisational focus on increasing diversity at senior levels. She remembered a comment she overheard a few years back, made by Tom, the Bakery manager at Retail Co: 'Everyone knows she was placed in that position to reach ethnic targets. Actually, it's one tick for race and one tick for gender. It's not right. Why can't they just promote people on merit?'

After a few years as store manager, Samina had achieved a lot and felt she had proven her critics wrong as the store's performance flourished. She felt more comfortable in her position and she became more involved in Diversity fora across the organisation and industry, discussing and debating the need for equal opportunities across the retail sector. At the same time, she was feeling more and more exhausted by the need to constantly 'defend' her talent and that of other minority staff. The opportunity for a position abroad came at the right time as she was ready for a change. The fact that the job she was offered was in Dubai was an added bonus. She had visited Dubai in the past as both her mum and dad had extended family who settled there 30 years ago, and she had always liked its vibe. She found it a very ambitious and entrepreneurial environment and, more importantly, she enjoyed working with other managers and staff from different parts of the world. There were many more senior managers who did not fall under the white western 'norm' of the UK and Samina found that comforting, especially after her own experiences in the UK. She wasn't naive however, and she was acutely aware that she was 'sheltered' as a senior manager in a multinational firm. She often heard stories of discrimination and racism in Dubai and across the Middle East faced by staff at lower levels of organisations across industries. She was very uncomfortable with this situation but felt helpless to address it in any constructive way. She also heard stories of racial hierarchies in Dubai and other Middle Eastern countries, where people of European and Arab origin are generally better treated and offered better jobs and salaries than people from Southeast Asia and South Asia. She knew that in the UK there were clearer processes in place to raise complaints against discriminatory managers and organisations and much more support was embedded in the legal and social system.

As she was finishing her lunch with her new colleagues, she reflected that her experiences in the UK had prepared her for this new and amazing opportunity. At the same time, she reminded herself that there are different forms of discrimination and prejudice, depending on where one lives, works, and the position one is in. She knew that by virtue of her British passport, British qualification, and English-language skills, she was in a position of privilege in a lot of ways and she wouldn't allow herself to forget that.

Questions

1   What are some of the issues that Samina faced in relation to her work and promotion to Store Manager when she worked in the UK?
2   What are your views on the positive action initiatives that Retail Co had put in place?
3   Do you think Samina's experiences were different from those of white women or ethnic minority men in Retail Co? Do you think they are different from other groups in her present position in Dubai?
4   How important do you think the location/region of one's work is in relation to one's career experiences? Are other factors more important?
5   Do you think some industries provide fairer opportunities than others for career development and progression irrespective of one's gender, ethnicity, age, and other diversity strands? Why or why not?
6   Consider the experiences of Samina in her new job in Dubai. Are her experiences more influenced by her passport, socioeconomic status, and organisational position than by her gender, ethnicity, or age? Critically discuss.

FOR DISCUSSION AND REVISION

Questions

1   Why is it inappropriate to treat diversity management as an organisation-specific issue?
2   Critically review the legislative framework of diversity management in your country. What are its strengths and weaknesses?
3   What key steps can an organisation take in order to manage diversity effectively?
4   Why is it important to understand the local context in order to manage or research diversity?
5   What are current best practices in organisations in your country to manage diversity?

Exercises

1   What are the pros and cons of affirmative action? Debate your answers.
2   Study diversity management policies and practices in a specific company. Identify the various ways in which diversity management policies and practices in that company are affected by its sociocultural, political, legal, and economic contexts.
3   Through an Internet search, identify and compare the diversity management policies or visions of at least three companies. Which policies or visions do you prefer, and why?

GLOSSARY

Affirmative Action: A strategy where women, racial minorities, and other historically disadvantaged groups are placed in specific organisational positions, with the key aim being to redress historical endemic disadvantage and discrimination (also referred to as Positive Discrimination). Quotas may be put in place with specific percentages of groups at different levels of the organisation.

Business case for diversity: The argument that having an inclusive, diverse workforce is good for business, i.e. it can be positive in terms of the organisation's performance and profitability.

Diversity Management: Inclusive equality practices that value diversity and acknowledge individual differences, skills and preferences. Diversity Management is seen as a way forward from the 'traditional' equal opportunities approach, with the latter seeking to redress discrimination through focusing on equal treatment of social groups and relying heavily on equality legislation.

Equal Opportunities: Treating individuals or groups equally in organisations (in relation to access to jobs, terms and conditions of employment, training, performance evaluations, rewards, termination of employment) irrespective of their social group membership.

Positive Action: Steps or initiatives that organisations can take to encourage increased participation of historically disadvantaged groups. Organisations can communicate aspirational targets of representation of these groups, but they cannot positively discriminate.

Relational framework: A model or framework that views diversity management from a layered and intersectional perspective acknowledging the interaction of macro-, meso-, and micro-levels.

Standpoint feminism: The proposition that feminist social science should be practised from the standpoint of women instead of men.

FURTHER READING

Books

ANTHIAS, F. AND YUVAL-DAVIS, N. (1992) *Racialised Boundaries: Race, Nation, Gender, Colour and Class and the Anti-racist Struggle*. London: Routledge.

BELL, M. (2007) *Diversity in Organizations*. Mason, OH: Thomson/South-Western.

BHAVNANI, R. (1994) *Black Women in the Labour Market: A Research Review*. London: Organisation Development Centre, City University.

BLAINE, B. E. (2007) *Understanding the Psychology of Diversity*. London: Sage.

DAVIDSON, M. J. (1997) *The Black and Ethnic Minority Woman Manager: Cracking the Concrete Ceiling*. London: Paul Chapman.

HARVEY, C. AND ALLARD, M. J. (eds) (2005) *Understanding and Managing Diversity: Readings, Cases, and Exercises* (3rd edn). New York: Prentice Hall.

KONRAD, A., PRASAD, P. AND PRINGLE, J. (eds) (2006) *Handbook of Workplace Diversity*. London: Sage.

MODOOD, T., BERTHOUD, R., LAKEY, J., NAZROO, J., SMITH, P., VIRDEE, S. AND BEISHON, S. (1997) *Ethnic Minorities in Britain: Diversity and Disadvantage. Fourth National Survey on Ethnic Minorities*. London: Policy Studies Institute.

ÖZBILGIN, M. (2009) *Equality, Diversity and Inclusion at Work: A Research Companion*. Cheltenham: Edward Elgar.

ÖZBILGIN, M. AND SYED, J. (eds) (2010) *Managing Cultural Diversity in Asia: A Research Companion*. Cheltenham: Edward Elgar.

ÖZBILGIN, M. AND TATLI, A. (2008) *Global Diversity Management: An Evidence-Based Approach*. New York: Palgrave Macmillan.

Journals

AMOS, V. AND PARMAR, P. (1984) Challenging imperial feminism. *Feminist Review*, 17: 3–20.

FEARFULL, A. AND KAMENOU, N. (2006) How do you account for it? A critical exploration of career opportunities for and experiences of ethnic minority women. *Critical Perspectives on Accounting*, 17(7): 883–901.

KAMENOU, N. (2008) Reconsidering work–life balance debates: challenging limited understandings of the 'life' component in the context of ethnic minority women's experiences. *British Journal of Management*, Special Issue on Gender in Management: New Theoretical Perspectives, 19: S99–S109.

MCGUIRE, G. M. (2000) Gender, race, ethnicity and networks: The factors affecting the status of employees' network members. *Work and Occupations*, 27: 500–523.

MCGUIRE, G. M. (2002) Gender, race and the shadow structure: A study of informal networks and inequality in a work organization. *Gender and Society*, 16(3): 303–322.

MASON, D. (1996) Themes and issues in the teaching of race and ethnicity in sociology. *Ethnic and Racial Studies*, 19(4): 789–806.

WHITE, Y. E. (1990) Understanding the black woman manager's interaction with the corporate culture. *Western Journal of Black Studies*, 14(3): 182–186.

WEB RESOURCES

Australian Human Rights Commission https://www.humanrights.gov.au/.

CIPD Fact Sheet: Diversity in the Workplace http://www.cipd.co.uk/hr-resources/factsheets/diversity-workplace-overview.aspx.

Equal Opportunities Commission (Hong Kong) http://www.eoc.org.hk/eoc/GraphicsFolder/default.aspx.

Equality and Human Rights Commission (UK) http://www.equalityhumanrights.com/.

Managing Diversity and Inclusion: Sage companion web site https://study.sagepub.com/syed.

REFERENCES

ADDLEY, E. AND CHILD, B. (2016) Charlotte Rampling finds herself outnumbered in Oscars diversity row. *Guardian*, January 22. Available at: http://www.theguardian.com/film/2016/jan/22/charlotte-rampling-finds-herself-outnumbered-in-oscars-diversity-row.

AFSHAR, H. AND MAYNARD, M. (1994) (eds) *The Dynamics of Race and Gender*. London: Taylor and Francis.

ALCOFF, L. (1991/1992) The problem of speaking for others. *Cultural Critique*, 20: 5–32.

ALI, F. AND KRAMAR, R. (2015) An exploratory study of sexual harassment in Pakistani organizations. *Asia Pacific Journal of Management*, 32(1), 229–249.

ALVESSON, M. AND WILLMOTT, H. (1992) On the idea of emancipation in management and organization studies. *Academy of Management Review*, 17(3): 432–464.

AMSAA (Affiliation of Multicultural Societies and Service Agencies) (2000) Cultural diversity in organizations and business: Gaining a competitive advantage. Vancouver, Canada. Available at: http://www.amssa.org/resources/ [accessed 10 January 2016].

ANDERSEN, M. L. (1993) Studying across difference: race, class and gender in qualitative research. In Stanfield, J. H. II and Dennis, R. M. (eds), *Race and Ethnicity in Research Methods*. California: Sage, pp. 39–52.

ANTHIAS, F. (1992) Connecting race and ethnic phenomena. *Sociology*, 6(3): 421–438.

ANTONIOS, S. (1997) *The CDEP scheme and race discrimination*. Sydney: Human Rights and Equal Opportunity Commission.

APPO, D. AND HÄRTEL, C. E. J. (2003) Questioning management paradigms that deal with Aboriginal development programs in Australia. *Asia Pacific Journal of Human Resources*, 41(1): 36–50.

ASHKANASY, N. M., HÄRTEL, C. E. J. AND DAUS, C. S. (2002) Diversity and emotion: the new frontiers in organizational behavior research. *Journal of Management*, 28: 307–338.

BBC (2005) China to outlaw sexual harassment. *BBC News*, June 27. Available at: http://news.bbc.co.uk/1/hi/business/4625913.stm.

BELL, M. P. (2007) *Diversity in Organizations*. Mason, OH: South-Western.

BERTONE, S. AND LEAHY, M. (2003) Multiculturalism as a conservative ideology: impacts on workforce diversity. *Asia Pacific Journal of Human Resources*, 41(1): 101–115.

BISIN, A., PATACCHINI, E. VERDIER, T., ZENOU, Y. (2011) Ethnic identity and labour market outcomes of immigrants in Europe, *Economic Policy*, 26 (65): 57–92.

BLACKSTONE, T., PAREKH, B. AND SANDERS, P. (eds) (1998) *Race Relations in Britain: A Developing Agenda*. London: Routledge.

BOURDIEU, P. (1998) *Practical Reason: On the Theory of Action*. Cambridge: Polity Press.

BRAH, A. (1994) Race and culture in the gendering of labour markets: South Asian young Muslim women and the labour market. In Afshar, H. and Maynard, M. (eds), *The Dynamics of Race and Gender*. London: Taylor and Francis, pp. 151–171.

CARBY, H. V. (1982) White women listen! Black feminism and the boundaries of sisterhood. In Centre for Contemporary Cultural Studies, *The Empire Strikes Back*. London: Hutchinson, pp. 45–54.

Chartered Institute of Personnel and Development (2005) *Diversity Management: Linking Theory and Practice to Business Performance*. London: CIPD.

COLLINS, P. H. (1990) *Black Feminist Thought*. London: Unwin Hyman.

COX, T. (1994) A comment on the language of diversity. *Organization*, 1(1): 51–57.

COX, T. H. AND BLAKE, S. (1991) Managing cultural diversity: implications for organizational competitiveness. *Academy of Management Executive*, 5(3): 45–56.

DAVIS, O. I., NAKAYAMA, T. K. AND MARTIN, J. N. (2000) Current and future directions in ethnicity and methodology. *International Journal of Intercultural Relations*, 24: 525–539.

DE CIERI, H. AND KRAMAR, R. (2005) *Human Resource Management in Australia: Strategy, People, Performance*. Sydney: McGraw-Hill.

DELUCA, J. M. AND MCDOWELL, R. N. (1992) Managing diversity: A strategic 'grass-roots' approach. In Jackson, S. E. and Associates (eds), *Diversity in the Workplace: Human Resources Initiatives*. New York: Guilford Press, pp. 227–247.

DICKENS, L. (1994) The business case for equal opportunities: Is the carrot better than the stick? *Employee Relations*, 16(8): 5–18.

DICKENS, L. (1999) Beyond the business case: A three-pronged approach to equality action. *Human Resource Management Journal*, 9(1): 9–19.

D'NETTO, B., SMITH, D. AND PINTO, C. (2000) *Diversity Management: Benefits, Challenges and Strategies*. DIMA Project No. 1. Carlton, Victoria: Mt Eliza Business School.

DOVER, T. L., MAJOR, B. AND KAISER, C. R. (2016) Diversity policies rarely make companies fairer, and they feel threatening to white men. *Harvard Business Review*, January 4. Available at: https://hbr.org/2016/01/diversity-policies-dont-help-women-or-minorities-and-they-make-white-men-feel-threatened.

DUELLI KLEIN, R. (1983) How to do what we want to do: Thoughts about feminist methodology. In Bowles, G. and Duelli Klein, R. (eds), *Theories of Women's Studies*. London: Routledge and Kegan Paul, pp. 88–102.

EDWARDS, R. (1990) Connecting method and epistemology: A white woman interviewing black women. *Women's Studies International Forum*, 13(5): 477–490.

EDWARDS, R. (1993) An education in interviewing: Placing the researcher and the research. In Renzetti, C. M. and Lee, R. M. (eds), *Researching Sensitive Topics*. California: Sage, pp. 181–196.

ELY, R. J. AND THOMAS, D. A. (2001) Cultural diversity at work: the effects of diversity perspectives on work group processes and outcomes. *Administrative Science Quarterly*, 46: 229–273.

Equality and Human Rights Commission (2011) Public Sector Equality Duty. Available at: http://www.equalityhumanrights.com/private-and-public-sector-guidance/public-sector-providers/public-sector-equality-duty. Accessed 28 January 2016.

EUR-lex (2007) Code of practice to clamp down on sexual harassment at work. Available at: http://eur-lex.europa.eu/legal-content/EN/TXT/?uri=URISERV:c10917b.

FERRIS, G. R., FRINK, D. D. AND GALANG, M. C. (1994) Diversity in the workplace: The human resources management challenges. *Human Resource Planning*, 16: 41–51.

FINCH, J. (1984) 'It's great to have someone to talk to': The ethics and politics of interviewing women. In Bell, C. and Roberts, H. (eds), *Social Researching: Politics, Problems, Practice*. London: Routledge and Kegan Paul, pp. 166–180.

FROST, S. (2014) *The Inclusion Imperative: How Real Inclusion Creates Better Business and Builds Better Societies*. London: Kogan Page Limited.

GAGNON, S. AND CORNELIUS, N. (2000) Re-examining workplace inequality: A capabilities approach. *Human Resource Management Journal*, 10(4): 68–87.

GIBSON, C. B. AND GIBBS, J. L. (2006) Unpacking the concept of virtuality: The effects of geographic dispersion, electronic dependence, dynamic structure, and national diversity on team innovation. *Administrative Science Quarterly*, 51(3): 451–495.

HAMMERSLEY, M. AND ATKINSON, P. (1995) *Ethnography: Principles in Practice*. London: Routledge.

HÄRTEL, C. E. J. AND FUJIMOTO, Y. (2000) Diversity is not a problem to be managed by organizations but openness to perceived dissimilarity is. *Journal of Australian and New Zealand Academy of Management*, 6(1): 14–27.

HEALY, G., KIRTON, G., NOON, M. (2010) (eds) *Equality, Inequalities and Diversity*. Basingstoke: Palgrave.

HILL, C. W. L. (2008) *International Business Competing in the Global Market Place* (7th edn). New York: McGraw-Hill.

HOFSTEDE, G. (1984) Cultural dimensions in management and planning. *Asia Pacific Journal of Management*, 1(2): 81–98.

HOOKS, B. (1981) *Ain't I a Woman?* London: Pluto.

HOOKS, B. (1984) *Feminist Theory: From Margin to Center*. Boston: South End Press.

HOOKS, B. (1989) *Talking Back: Thinking Feminist, Thinking Black*. London: Sheba Feminist Publishers.

HOOKS, B. (1991) *Yearning*. London: Turnaround.

HUMPHRIES, M. T. AND GRICE, S. (1995) Equal employment opportunity and the management of diversity: A global discourse of assimilation? *Journal of Organizational Change Management*, 8(5): 17–32.

ILO (International Labour Organisation) (2004) Facts on Migrant Labour. Available at: http://www.ilo.org/wcmsp5/groups/public/---dgreports/---dcomm/documents/publication/wcms_067570.pdf. Accessed 15 January 2016.

JAYNE, M. E. A. AND DIPBOYE, R. L. (2004) Leveraging diversity to improve business performance: research findings and recommendations for organizations. *Human Resource Management*, 43(4): 409.

KAMENOU, N. (2002) Ethnic minority women in English organisations: Career experiences and opportunities. Unpublished PhD thesis, University of Leeds.

KAMENOU, N. (2003) Critical issues in the implementation of diversity strategies: A case study of UK organisations. *International Journal of Knowledge, Culture and Change Management*, 3: 507–520.

KAMENOU, N. (2007) Methodological considerations in conducting research across gender, 'race', ethnicity and culture: a challenge to context specificity in diversity research methods. *International Journal of Human Resource Management*, 18(11): 1995–2009.

KAMENOU, N. AND FEARFULL, A. (2006) Ethnic minority women: A lost voice in HRM. *Human Resource Management Journal*, 16(2): 154–172.

KAMENOU, N., NETTO, G., FEARFULL, A. (2013) Ethnic minority women in the Scottish labour market: Employers' perceptions. *British Journal of Management*. 24 (3): 398–413.

KIM, J. S. AND CAMPAGNA, A. F. (1981) Effects of flexitime on employee attendance and performance: A field experiment. *Academy of Management Journal*, December: 729–741.

KITZINGER, D. P., BOLA, M., CAMPOS, A. B., CARABINE, J., DOHERTY, K., FRITH, H., MCNULTY, A., REILLY, J. AND WINN, J. (1996) The spoken work: speaking of representing the other. *Feminism and Psychology*, 6(2): 217–235.

KRAMAR, R. (2004) Does Australia really have diversity management? In Davis, E. and Pratt, V. (eds), *Making the Link 15: Affirmative Action and Employment Relations*. Sydney: CCH Australia, pp. 19–26.

KREITZ, P. A. (2008) Best practises for managing organizational diversity. *Journal of Academic Librarianship*, 34(2): 101–20.

KRONOS (2008) The total financial impact of employee absences. Available at: http://www.kronos.co.uk/showAbstract.aspx?id=23622324930&rr=1&sp=y&LangType=2057&ecid=ABEA-5W2GSQ. Accessed 15 December 2015.

LEE, R. M. (1993) *Doing Research on Sensitive Topics*. London: Sage Publications.

LIFF, S. (1997) Two routes to managing diversity: Individual differences or social group characteristics. *Employee Relations*, 19(1): 11–26.

LIFF, S. (1999) Diversity and equal opportunities: room for a constructive compromise? *Human Resource Management Journal*, 9(1): 65–75.

LORBIECKI, A. (2001) Openings and burdens for women and minority ethnics being diversity vanguards in Britain. Gender, Work and Organisation Conference, University of Keele, June 2001.

LORBIECKI, A. AND JACK, G. (2000) Critical turns in the evolution of diversity management. *British Journal of Management*, 11, Special Issue: S17–S31.

MAYNARD, M. (1994) 'Race', gender and the concept of 'difference' in feminist thought. In Afshar, H. and Maynard, M. (eds), *The Dynamics of Race and Gender*. London: Taylor and Francis, pp. 9–25.

MINISTER, K. (1991) A feminist frame for the oral history interview. In Gluck, S. and Patai, D. (eds), *Women's Worlds: The Feminist Practice of Oral History*. New York: Routledge, pp. 27–42.

MOON, M. M. K. (1997) Understanding the impact of cultural diversity on organizations. The Research Department Air Command and Staff College, Research Paper No. AU/ACSC/0607C/97-03. Maxwell, AB: Air University.

MURRAY, P. AND SYED, J. (2005) Critical issues in managing age diversity in Australia. *Asia Pacific Journal of Human Resources*, 43(2): 210–224.

NKOMO, S. AND COX, T. JR (1996) Diverse identities in organisations. In Clegg, S. R. et al. (eds), *The Handbook of Organisation Studies*. London: Sage, pp. 338–356.

OAKLEY, A. (1981) Interviewing women: A contradiction in terms. In Roberts, H. (ed.), *Doing Feminist Research*. London: Routledge and Kegan Paul, pp. 30–61.

OAKLEY, A. (1987) Comment on Malsteed. *Sociology*, 21: 63.

OLSEN, J.E. AND MARTINS, L. L. (2012) Understanding organizational diversity management programs: A theoretical framework and directions for future research. *Journal of Organizational Behavior*, 33 (8); 1168–1187.

PARKER, J. AND DOUGLAS, J. (2010) The role of women's groups in New Zealand, UK and Canadian trade unions in addressing intersectional interests. *International Journal of Comparative Industrial Relations and Labour Law*, 26(3): 295–319.

PESTON, R. (2015) Why Germany needs migrants more than UK. *BBC News*, September 7. Available from: http://www.bbc.co.uk/news/business-34172729.

PUTNAM, R. D. (2007) E pluribus unum: Diversity and community in the twenty-first century. The 2006 Johan Skytte Prize Lecture. *Scandinavian Political Studies*, 30: 137–174.

PYKE, J. (2005) Productive diversity: Which companies are active and why? Master's thesis, Victoria University, Melbourne, Australia.

READY, D. A. AND CONGER, J. A. (2007) Make your company a talent factory. *Harvard Business Review*, 85(6): 68–77.

RICHARD, O. C., BARNETT, T., DWYER, S. AND CHADWICK, K. (2004) Cultural diversity in management, firm performance, and the moderating role of entrepreneurial orientation dimensions. *Academy of Management Journal*, 47(2): 255–266.

ROOSEVELT, T. R. JR (1999) Diversity management: Some measurement criteria. *Employer Relations Today*, 25: 49–62.

ROOSEVELT, T. R. JR (2006) Diversity management: An essential craft for leaders. *Leader to Leader*, 41 (Summer): 45–49.

ROSALDO, R. (1989) *Culture and Truth: The Remaking of Social Analysis*. Boston: Beacon Press.

STANFIELD, J. H. (1993) Epistemological considerations. In Stanfield and Dennis, pp. 16–36.

STANFIELD, J. H. AND DENNIS, R. M. (eds) (1993) *Race and Ethnicity in Research Methods*. California: Sage.

STRACHAN, G., BURGESS, J. AND SULLIVAN, A. (2004) Affirmative action or managing diversity: what is the future of equal opportunity policies in Australia? *Women in Management Review*, 19(4): 196–204.

SUBELIANI, D. AND TSOGAS, G. (2005) Managing diversity in the Netherlands: a case study of Rabobank. *International Journal of Human Resource Management*, 16(5): 831–851.

SYED, J. (2008) Employment prospects for skilled migrants: A relational perspective. *Human Resource Management Review*, 18, 28–45.

SYED, J. (2009) Contextualising diversity management. In Özbilgin, M. (ed.), *Equality, Diversity and Inclusion at Work: A Research Companion*. Cheltenham: Edward Elgar, pp. 101–111.

SYED, J. (2016) Oscars so white: An institutional racism perspective. *CounterPunch*, January 29. Available at: http://www.counterpunch.org/2016/01/29/oscars-so-white-an-institutional-racism-perspective/.

SYED, J. AND ALI, F. (2005) Minority ethnic women in the Australian labour market. In Davis, E. and Pratt, V. (eds), *Making the Link: Affirmative Action and Employment Relations*. Sydney: CCH Australia, pp. 48–54.

SYED, J. AND KRAMAR, R. (2009) Socially responsible diversity management. *Journal of Management and Organization*, 15(5): 639–651.

SYED, J. AND ÖZBILGIN, M. (2009) A relational framework for international transfer of diversity management practices. *International Journal of Human Resource Management*, 20(12): 2435–2453.

SYED, J. AND ÖZBILGIN, M. (2015) Introduction: Theorising and managing diversity and inclusion in the global workplace. In Syed, J. and Özbilgin, M. (eds), *Managing Diversity and Inclusion: An International Perspective*. London: Sage, pp.1–10.

SYED, J. AND PIO, E. (2010) Veiled diversity: Workplace experiences of Muslim women in Australia. *Asia Pacific Journal of Management*, 27(1): 115–137.

TAJFEL, H. AND TURNER, J. C. (1986) The social identity theory of intergroup behaviour. In Worchel, S. and Austin, W. G. (eds), *Psychology of Intergroup Relations*. Chicago: Nelson, pp. 7–24.

TEICHER, J. AND SPEARITT, K. (1996) From equal employment opportunity to diversity management: The Australian experience. *International Journal of Manpower*, 17(4/5): 109–133.

THOMAS, D. AND ELY, R. (1996) Making differences matter: A new paradigm for managing diversity. *Harvard Business Review*, 74(5): 79–90.

THOMAS, R. R. (1990) From affirmative action to affirming diversity. *Harvard Business Review*, (March–April): 107–17.

THOMAS, R. R. (1992) Managing diversity: A conceptual framework. In Jackson, S. E. (ed.), *Diversity in the Workplace: Human Resource Initiatives*. New York: Guilford.

UK Legislation (2010) Equality Act 2010. Available at: http://www.legislation.gov.uk/ukpga/2010/15/section/26.

University of California (1999) *Staff Affirmative Action Office Policy*. Berkeley: University of California.

US Government Accountability Office (2005) Diversity management: Expert-identified leading practices and agency examples. Available at: http://www.gao.gov/new.items/d0590.pdf. Accessed 10 January 2016.

YOUNGBLOOD, S. A. AND COOK, K. C. (1984) Child care assistance can improve employee attitudes and behaviour. *Personnel Administrator*, (February): 93–95.

5

HRM, ETHICS, AND CORPORATE SOCIAL RESPONSIBILITY

Tracy Wilcox and Diannah Lowry

LEARNING OUTCOMES

After reading this chapter, you should be able to:

➤ Understand why and how human resources activities have an ethical dimension and identify various ethical issues in contemporary human resource management activities
➤ Recognise the connections among ethical human resources practices, corporate social responsibility, and ethical global business operations
➤ Describe the key features of ethical thinking in the context of ethics, business, and human resources
➤ Recognise some of the various ethical frameworks that can apply to human resources in a global context
➤ Distinguish between ethical relativism and ethical pluralism
➤ Describe some of the features of critical business ethics.

SUMMARY OF CHAPTER CONTENTS

➤ **Opening Case Study**: Ethics and HR practices
➤ Introduction
➤ Ethics and human resources
➤ Critical thinking and ethics
➤ Ethical thinking and behaviour
➤ Ethical theories and frameworks
➤ Corporate social responsibility and HRM
➤ Critical business ethics: The problem of being 'charmed'
➤ Conclusion
➤ **Fnd of Chapter Case Study**: Amazon's brutal workplace is an indicator of an inhumane economy
➤ For discussion and revision
➤ Glossary
➤ Further reading
➤ Web resources
➤ References

Opening Case Study Ethics and HR practices

For the past 45 years Bangladesh has been working towards a society that is poverty and hunger free. In more recent years, the political environment and economic approach has moved away from a subsidised socialist orientation towards a free market economy, which has resulted in significant economic growth. Bangladeshi factories are now considered key suppliers of products to MNCs in the garment, electronics, pharmaceutical, and other labour-intensive industries. Given limited natural resources and an abundance of human resources, the efficiency and efficacy of HRM practices within Bangladeshi organisations could play a crucial role in Bangladesh's further economic development.

Bangladeshi employers, however, are being blamed for unethical HRM practices, including labour exploitation, the provision of non-inclusive employment practices, and poor safety standards. The collapse of the Rana Plaza factory building in 2013, with a loss of more than 1,100 lives, brought these concerns to the world's attention (Lund-Thomsen and Lindgreen, 2014). Equal employment opportunities are also problematic in Bangladesh: indigenous minority groups and people with disabilities are often deprived of opportunities for employment. Another issue lies in the reward available to employees in certain industries, evidenced by Bangladesh having the lowest manufacturing wages in the world.

The labour market context also plays a role in the way employers view the importance (or in this case the unimportance) of sound HR practice. The high unemployment rate in Bangladesh means that there is a permanent over-supply of people looking for work, and organisations seldom find it difficult to recruit or retain suitable employees. Against this backdrop, the competition for limited job opportunities provides an impetus for management to engage in nepotistic practices, whereby friends and relatives are favoured in recruitment and selection practices. This is exacerbated by the lack of government regulation in place to control recruitment and selection activities.

Most organisations in Bangladesh are family owned and managed by family members resulting in a system of 'family or crony-capitalism'. Under such a system human resource management activities become the sole domain of owners and their idiosyncratic needs, with little or no regard to the needs of their workers. Employers have so far failed to understand that the adoption of systematic, fair and 'good' HR practices are in their best interest.

In recent years, however, there has been increasing pressure from outside the country, which is leading organisations to change their corporate culture and HRM practices. EU and North American countries have been putting pressure on labour-intensive and export-oriented industries to adopt ILO labour-rights standards and to improve their factories' working conditions. Arguably, improved HRM practices, working conditions, and better wage rates could improve the productivity and the profitability of organisations in Bangladesh.

Source: Adapted from: Mahmood, M. and Nurul Absar, N. (2015).

Questions

This case study raises important issues that are covered throughout this chapter. These include:

1 What are the long-term implications for both employees and employers of unfair HR practices in Bangladeshi organisations?
2 What are the implications of unethical HR practices for the way in which corporate social responsibility (CSR) in Bangladesh is viewed by the wider global economy?

INTRODUCTION

Ethical considerations emerge in most if not all areas of human resource management (HRM) practice, including performance management, work organisation, and workplace relations (Jamali, El Dirani, and Harwood, 2015; Voegtlin and Greenwood, 2016). Furthermore, human resources practitioners have what Kochan (2004) has called a 'special professional responsibility'. They are expected to act as stewards of the social contract, to uphold accepted social standards in workplaces and to 'balance the needs of the firm with the needs, aspirations, and interests of the workforce and the values and standards society expects to be upheld at work' (Kochan, 2004: 133).

In recent times, there has been much debate about the relationships between business and society and about the unintended consequences of the functioning of the global economic system (Jamali, El Dirani, and Harwood, 2015). Faced with economic and environmental uncertainty, recession and, in some regions, the near-collapse of national economies, some of the assumptions and practices we have taken for granted are showing their fragility.

The predominance of neoliberal economic logics, with its narrow view of corporate social responsibility (CSR), has been questioned (Lund-Thomsen and Lindgreen, 2014). The emergence of the 'sharing' or 'gig' economy and 'zero hours' employment contracts has also led to concerns being raised (Crane et al., 2014). We have seen supply-chain employment practices questioned in the aftermath of Rana Plaza and other disasters in Bangladesh and elsewhere. All of these questions and debates have provided an additional impetus for a more critical examination of human resources–related issues, such as the remuneration of executives and finance professionals, performance management systems, and downsizing and outsourcing practices.

Implicit in contemporary critiques of human resources practice are notions of trust, responsibility, rights, duties, and authority – all components of a frame of reference suggested by the study of *ethics*. Ethical inquiry is intrinsically concerned with *human actions and interactions, their effects and motivations*.

Human resources decisions and actions can have far-reaching consequences, and there is potential for the ethical treatment of employees within the discourse and practice of HRM. This is especially the case for human resources activities in the global sphere, as global business activities raise important and highly complex ethical issues. Tensions between the diversity of perspectives in international business considered to be 'ethical' can pose moral dilemmas with few easy solutions (Preston, 2014; Treviño and Nelson, 2013). Despite codes of conduct and various sanctions, multinational companies are able to use their economic might to pressure developing countries reliant on foreign investment to accept values that are not their own. Large global firms may, for example, employ local labour with inadequate health and safety provision, poor working conditions, and low pay rates.

In this chapter, we argue that the ethical dimensions of human resources practices in the arena of global business demands serious scrutiny, where the human and social embeddedness of human resources practice is typically viewed against a background of other market-oriented concerns. We argue that human resources practices are all too often underpinned by assumptions from Western popularist psychology that should be acknowledged and problematised. Hence we have 'absentee management' programmes based on assumptions that workers are absent due to lack of motivation or laziness, or recruitment centres perpetuating unjust assessment procedures, or attempts to engender 'organisational citizenship behaviours' which might include '[tolerating] the inevitable inconveniences and impositions of work without complaining' (Podsakoff et al., 2000: 517; Bolino et al., 2013).

This chapter starts with an examination of what is meant by the term 'ethics' and a discussion of the key elements of ethical thinking and behaviour. We will then review some of the key frameworks for identifying and making sense of ethical issues in business. These frameworks will provide us with a vocabulary for discussing business practices from an ethical perspective. The frameworks are grounded in the field of moral philosophy, much of which can be applied across cultures (Donaldson and Dunfee, 1994). Following this discussion, we will move to a consideration of contemporary critiques of traditional approaches to ethics. Finally, we will consider a case study of a contemporary human resources ethical issue.

ETHICS AND HUMAN RESOURCES

The word *ethics* comes from the Greek word *ethos*, meaning 'character' or 'custom'. Ethics can be defined, in action-oriented terms, as 'the principles, norms and standards of conduct governing an individual or group' (Treviño and Nelson, 2013: 17). Ethics places human beings, or humanity, centre stage. This is what makes ethics so important and in some senses countercultural, particularly in light of the changing expectations of human resource managers.

Ethics is underpinned by the discipline of moral philosophy, which provides theoretical tools and frameworks for reasoning and reflecting on whether something is right and good. Ethics differs from other areas of study such as psychology, science, sociology, or economics, in that understanding ethics entails adopting a *normative* perspective. The aim of ethical thinking is to discover what *ought to be*, rather than simply describing what is or predicting what will probably happen (Enderle, 2000). For example, although a great number of people around the globe are not protected from dangerous conditions in their workplace, whether this be exposure to harmful chemicals or unsafe practices on building sites, for example, this fact does not imply that things *ought* to be this way (Box 5.2). Thus, ethical reasoning involves an evaluation of a situation and its context and reaching conclusions about whether a particular action or decision *should* be taken.

STOP AND REFLECT

Consider the case of manufacturing in Bangladesh featured at the beginning of the chapter.

Questions

1 What are the ethical issues relevant to the case?
2 How do these issues relate to values?
3 The law?

? Critical Thinking 5.1

In understanding what ethics *is*, it is important to recognise what ethics *isn't*.

Ethics is not the same as *values*. While values are important in shaping ethical (and unethical) practice, prevailing social values may not further human 'good', or be 'right'. For example, in Western industrialised countries up until the mid-nineteenth century, it was widely held that the practice of slavery could be justified by solid economic arguments. The idea that the fundamental human rights of those enslaved were being violated gradually became more widely accepted, but it took centuries for the recognition that slavery was *wrong* to become the 'majority view'. So we cannot assume that just because the majority of members of a society consider something to be right, it is ethical. This is particularly the case in the business arena.

Similarly, *ethics* and the *law* are not equivalent. Legislation typically reflects a society's ideals, norms and values at a particular time and place. However, the law can be slow to change and often reflects only the values and norms of those in positions of power. Moreover, in business, legislation is generally *reactive*: laws are often triggered by problems that have already occurred, for better or for worse. Occupational health and safety laws, for example, have typically been developed in response to catastrophic industrial accidents and employee deaths – examples of laws developed *after* something has gone wrong.

Box 5.1 Ethical relativism: When in Rome...

The phrase 'When in Rome, do as the Romans do' implies that we should follow the customs and behaviours of the cultures we are visiting. For many elements of our life, this does not present problems, but what happens if a behaviour or practice has moral content? Or if someone might be harmed by the practice? This presents us with an ethical dilemma.

Some people may argue that we should adjust our ethical standards in accordance with the culture we are living in (or the culture our organisation is operating in). There may be practices that are common, and considered acceptable, in some places but not others (or in some industries but not others). Recognising and accepting this variation, or pluralism, constitutes what is known as *cultural relativism*.

But what if you were to translate this understanding of cultural differences to a stance that saw *any* action as ethically permissible, as long as it was in keeping with the cultural standards held by the majority of people in a society? This position is known as *ethical relativism*. Just because practices are widespread does not mean that they are right, or ethical. Cultural practices reflect *values* but not necessarily *ethics*. We have already considered the abhorrent practice of slavery, which was not only widespread in the Western business world in the eighteenth and nineteenth centuries but was also considered *right*.

There are a number of possible reasons why responses to ethical issues may differ across cultures, whether these are national cultures, industry cultures, or organisational cultures. Practices may differ because their moral content has not been recognised. For example, as recently as 25 years ago, chemical companies in Australia were dumping industrial waste in waterways and soil, with only the economic value of such practices being considered. Many managers simply did not recognise that such a decision had a moral content as people were likely to be harmed. (Others, of course, may have recognised the moral content but ignored the associated ethical dilemma.) Societies (or industries) can sometimes simply be wrong in evaluating whether something is ethical; the acceptance of slavery provides a good example in this case. Practices can also differ across cultures because of different (or incorrect) factual understandings. Differing responses to the issue of human-induced climate change provide an example of this, with some people still believing that there is insufficient evidence for action.

On the other hand, we need to beware of automatically judging the practices and behaviours of other cultures as wrong just because they are different. The idea that there is only ever *one* acceptable or right moral principle is known as *ethical absolutism*. In the early days of business ethics education, some Western educators were rightly criticised for adopting this perspective. Both ethical relativism and its flip side, ethical absolutism, involve the oversimplification of complex issues.

Ethicists argue that it is important to recognise that ethics should always be seen in the context of a particular situation. Although there is often no 'absolutely right' answer to an ethical question, there is usually a *better* answer, which involves finding the best or most fitting position in the circumstances. Basic principles can be shared across cultures, even though practices may differ. For example, perhaps the basic principle of respect for one another can be manifest in different ways, with, say, the right of individual liberty given more precedence in the USA than in some Pacific Island communities, where community wellbeing is considered more important when operationalising 'respect'.

The alternative to ethical relativism or ethical absolutism, one advocated by many business ethicists, is one in which social and cultural diversity is accepted, alongside *ethical pluralism*. Crane and Matten (2007: 84) explain ethical pluralism as a viewpoint that:

> accepts different moral convictions and backgrounds while at the same time suggesting that a consensus on basic principles and rules in a certain social context can, and should, be reached.

Ethical pluralism implies an acknowledgement that ethical decisions in fact involve balancing various demands and perspectives that are often in tension with each other. An understanding of ethical relativism, ethical absolutism, and ethical pluralism is particularly relevant to human resource practitioners in multinational organisations, or organisations where work is outsourced to contractors in other countries. Organisations such as Unilever, Pirelli, MSD, and The Body Shop, for example, have clearly defined guidelines for their global operations that are applied by local counterparts.

Ethical issues may present to the human resource practitioner at an individual, organisational, or macro-level, as Figure 5.1 shows:

- At the *individual* level fall questions about the rightness or wrongness of a person's decisions and actions, such as unfair recruitment or termination decisions.

- Ethical issues can also arise in the *organisational* realm and relate to an organisation's policies, practices, or culture. In the past, there has been some debate about the moral status (and responsibility) of organisations, but it is now widely held that organisations can make decisions and take action, just as individuals do, and can therefore be evaluated for the rightness or

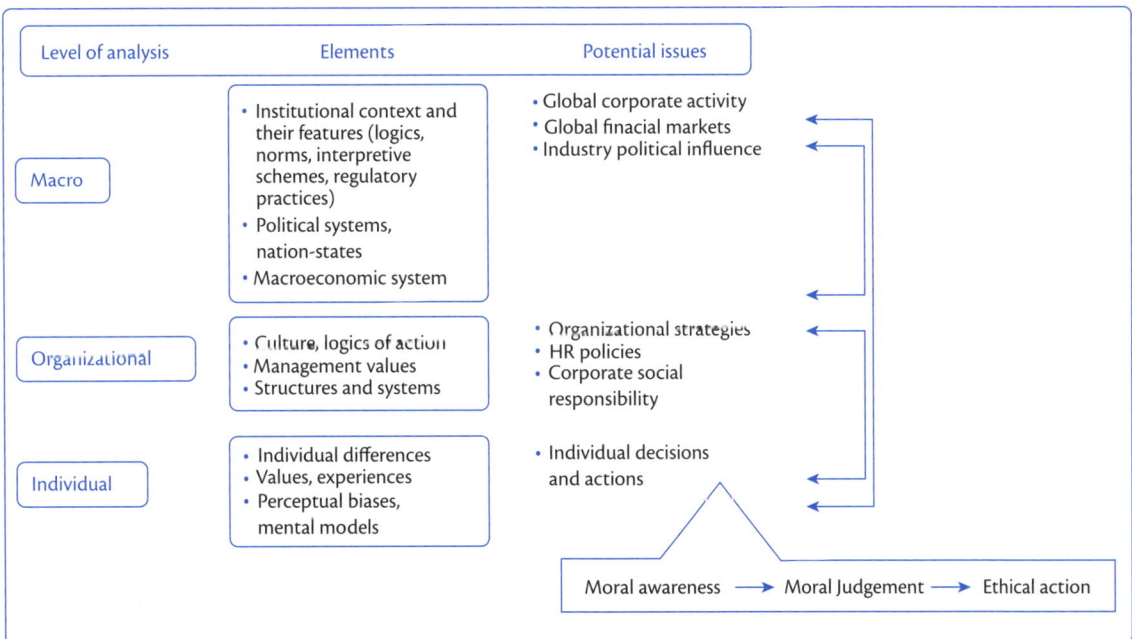

Figure 5.1 The interrelationships between ethical action and contextual issues
(adapted from Treviño and Nelson, 2013)

wrongness of those actions and decisions. The notion of CSR reflects this assumption.

- Finally, *macro-* or systemic ethical issues relate to ethical questions concerning the economic, political, legal, and social systems in which businesses operate. Systemic ethical issues include the negative consequences of political decisions reflecting the dominant logics of deregulation and financialised capitalism.

ETHICAL THINKING AND BEHAVIOUR

Ethics provides a means through which business practices can be critiqued and alternatives offered. The practice of ethical reasoning allows those interested in human resources decisions to evaluate a range of possible actions and determine what is 'right' in a particular set of circumstances. The three interrelated elements of ethical practice are thus:

1 *moral awareness* – recognising the existence of an ethical dilemma;
2 *moral judgement* – deciding what is right;
3 *ethical behaviour* – taking action to do the right thing (Treviño and Nelson, 2013).

As Figure 5.1 illustrates, the ethical (or unethical) behaviour of individuals is best viewed as the outcome of a process involving moral awareness and moral judgement, but shaped by the individual, organisational, and broader contextual features pertinent to a particular situation. It is important to situate this process of ethical thinking and action within the individual, organisational, and contextual features relevant to a situation. All of these features are interrelated. An individual's own value system and cultural background can influence the nature of the philosophical frameworks he or she chooses to resolve an ethical dilemma, whereas an organisation's culture or management systems can influence the type of action (or inaction) taken in response to an ethical dilemma. It is thus important to take into account the social, psychological, and political factors that can shape all three elements, or stages of reflective ethical practice. We will now consider each of these stages in turn.

Moral awareness

An important element of ethical practice is the ability to bring ethical issues and dilemmas to the foreground – to make the 'invisible' visible. Doing this entails *moral imagination* or *moral awareness* – the recognition that a particular action or decision could potentially harm others.

This in turn requires the ability to consider an issue and how others might be affected from various perspectives. Business issues with ethical or moral content can be distinguished from those without by considering the possible unintended consequences of a decision, particularly the question of whether someone might be harmed. In the case of HRM, a potential for affecting the welfare of others is inherent in the human resource manager's role, and many, if not most, HRM decisions have a moral content.

In business, it is not uncommon for managers to fail to 'see' the existence of an ethical issue in the first place. Sense-making practices – in other words, the ways in which people 'see' some elements of their immediate environment and fail to 'see' others, framing their responses according to this filtered perception – can render moral dilemmas 'invisible' to the managers in an organisation (Werhane, 2002). This is perhaps not surprising given the nature of the logics and systems of meaning that predominate in a particular business context. Human resource managers have, within organisations, the logics of capitalist markets, the logics of professional practice (if they consider themselves to be 'human resource professionals'), and the logics of state interpretations of the employment relationship as potential influences on their sense-making practices. As Thornton and Ocasio (2008) explain, these logics shape what is considered to be important, the 'rules of the game', and the kinds of answers and solutions are seen as available and appropriate to a given social actor – all of this influencing processes of moral awareness.

Moral judgement

Even if an ethical issue has been identified, resolving it may not be simple. So moral imagination – the ability to see an ethical dilemma in a particular situation – needs to be augmented by the practice of *ethical reasoning*. Ethical reasoning in turn involves the application of decision tools based on ethical theories, which provide a template or framework against which to evaluate a particular practice or decision. Some of the most well-known ethical frameworks will be considered below.

Ethical behaviour

Choosing to act ethically in a given situation is the third element of reflective ethical practice. Of course, this is not always easy due to the contextual constraints that may be present – including the cultures, norms and values that predominate in an organisation. But here we argue that human resource managers do not have to be 'morally mute' (Watson, 2003). An understanding of some of the key elements of ethical thinking, along with an appreciation of the contextual factors discussed here, will go some way towards enabling ethically 'assertive' behaviour on the part of managers (see Lowry, 2006).

Reflect on the activities associated with HRM in your own organisation or in one in which you have worked.

Questions

1 Can you identify any ethical issues (issues with moral content) associated with such activities?
2 What are they?

Box 5.3 Ethical thinking and behaviour

Ethical thinking implies the ability to:

▶ think critically;
▶ recognise issues or practices that have moral content;
▶ see beyond one's own personal experience;
▶ consider the interconnections between human resources decisions and the contexts within which they are made;
▶ address issues from all sides, considering the perspectives of a range of stakeholders;
▶ consider the consequences of decisions, whether intended or unintended, on all the stakeholders;
▶ evaluate the best arguments from each perspective;
▶ arrive at a conclusion based on a systematic analysis of these arguments;
▶ defend viewpoints, and analyse new information or perspectives.

Ethical thinking enables questions about the rightness or wrongness of organisational practice to be considered, in effect placing a critical lens on current business practice (Box 5.3). Ethics, as Preston (2014: 14) reminds us, can be a 'counter-hegemonic exercise built around a rhythm of action and reflection'. In the next section, we go on to consider some theoretical ethical frameworks that can be used as thinking tools to enable such reflection. A consideration of human resources practice informed by ethical reasoning enables a nuanced and action-focused critique of unethical human resources practice.

ETHICAL THEORIES AND FRAMEWORKS

Each of the frameworks discussed in this chapter is grounded in the field of moral philosophy, in the ideal moral perspectives that provide us with ways of thinking about moral issues. A knowledge of normative ethical theories provides a common language with which to debate and evaluate ethical issues and critically reflect on the way in which organisations are managed. There is no one right framework to adopt in all circumstances as each has its usefulness, and each has its limitations. They all contribute normative principles that can underpin moral judgement and moral behaviour (Cohen, 2004). In practice, when faced with ethical issues, more than one framework may be adopted. In the business world, many people do not think about which particular framework they are using when they are faced with an ethical issue. The approach they take will depend in part on their mental models and in part on their cultural and social development.

Consequences of actions (consequentialism)

Consequentialist frameworks enable ethical issues to be examined by *considering the consequences* (both intended and unintended) of decisions, in order to decide the right course of action. This approach is sometimes referred to as 'teleology', from the Greek word *telos*, which means 'end' or purpose. Consequentialism means deciding whether an action is right or wrong based on the possible consequences of that action.

The best-known consequentialist framework is utilitarianism. Adopting this framework, we would say that the best decision is that which maximises 'utility', or leads to the greatest good for the greatest number of people. The best course of action is, then, one that *brings about the best outcome for most people*, so that overall good (or utility) is maximised. Utilitarianism is based on writings of British Enlightenment philosophers Jeremy Bentham and John Stuart Mill. Both these philosophers thought about how to operationalise the idea of 'the good'. Bentham defined 'good' as pleasure, while Mill developed this further, defining good as the general happiness or wellbeing of society.

Using this framework, we can argue that certain actions are morally justifiable even if they violate a particular individual's rights. For example, a manager may argue that the construction of a new manufacturing plant in a disadvantaged area will provide employment for the local community, even if the buildings encroach on part of a nature reserve. The manager may argue that the overall benefits of the new facility (the good) outweigh the harm caused (environmental damage) and provide the greater good for the greater number of people. In this example, the employment needs of the local community would be given greater weight by the manager than the ecological needs of future generations (of both humans and animals).

Utilitarian thinking tools are familiar to most managers, and this framework is useful when working through complex issues with multiple stakeholders. Indeed, the idea of conducting a cost–benefit analysis is based on utilitarian thinking. In the business world, however, underlying assumptions about how 'the good' should be defined are not typically subject to critical examination. Cost–benefit analyses are congruent with economics, but 'the good' is traditionally assumed to be economic gain, with profit, return on investment or share price considered acceptable surrogate measures, particularly in Anglo-American cultures. See, for example, the approach of ethical egoism in Box 5.4. But whose good is this? Rarely are the total benefits and harms relating to *all* the stakeholders who are affected by a decision fully considered when cost–benefit analyses are undertaken. Similarly, public goods are not typically taken into account when calculating costs and benefits. This type of narrowly applied and hollow utilitarianism does not consider, at its core, *overall human wellbeing* as the 'good'.

Box 5.4 Ethical egoism: distorted consequentialism

Another type of consequentialist thinking – one that is in many ways 'anti-'ethical – is known as ethical egoism. This approach to resolving an issue holds that the best action is one that benefits oneself – as either an individual or an organisation. At the core of ethical egoism lies a desire to maximise self-interest, however it may be operationalised. Ethical egoism lies behind arguments that individuals should treat others well, not for any intrinsic reason, but because otherwise they may themselves be harmed. Similarly, claims of 'looking out for number one' or 'if we didn't do it, somebody else would' reflect the distorted consequentialism of ethical egoism. The neoclassical economic assumption that people will only act to pursue their own interests, which is particularly prevalent in Anglo-American capitalism, is based on an application of ethical egoism.

Another concern relating to utilitarian thinking is the implication that 'the ends justify the means'. Does this suggest that 'anything goes'? Or are there some things we should *never* do, regardless of the net benefits? These are valid questions. One of the criticisms of consequentialist utilitarian frameworks is that they can be used to rationalise actions that are clearly wrong. This brings us to the next framework.

Deontological principles

The second framework commonly used in ethical reasoning is sometimes known as 'non-consequentialism'. Using this framework, we can judge actions as *right or wrong in themselves*, regardless of the consequences. Ethicists refer to this approach as deontology, which derives from the Greek word *deon*, meaning duty. Deontology means deciding whether an action is right or wrong by considering the principles or duties that relate to that action. The essence of this approach to deciding what is right or good is that there are some universal, duty-based principles or rules that apply to everyone and should be used to guide our actions.

Religious ethics are probably the best-known examples of deontological rules. The so-called Golden Rule – treat others as you would like to be treated yourself – or versions of it, can, for instance, be found in religious traditions across the globe (Neusner and Chilton, 2008). People who follow religious maxims when faced with ethical issues are drawing on deontological ethical tools to guide their decision-making, even if they are not conscious of so doing.

Another well-known set of deontological principles are those developed by the German philosopher Immanuel Kant. Kant's moral philosophy focuses on humans as moral agents with the ability to make reasoned decisions about what is right or wrong. According to Kant, 'the first proposition of morality is that to have genuine moral worth, an action must be done from duty' (cited in Bowie, 1999: 120). He argued that we are all part of a moral community and hence have duties to one another.

Kant's approach to ethical decision-making revolves around his idea of a 'categorical imperative', which sets in place universal moral principles that should guide human behaviour:

- His first formulation of the categorical imperative holds that *any principle or maxim should be able to be applied universally*. This forces one to ask the question, 'What if everyone did this?' when considering a moral principle or duty. If, for example, you think it is acceptable to lie to someone, you should also accept his or her lying to you (Jones et al., 2005).
- The second formulation essentially states that *all people have an intrinsic humanity and should never be treated merely as a means to an end*. In other words, we should never 'use' other humans as instruments to achieve our own purposes, as humans possess an innate dignity that should not be violated. As Bowie (1999: 1) acknowledges, this 'respect for persons' principle has fairly radical implications for business and, we might add, human resources practice because '[at] a minimum, labour cannot be treated as a commodity like land, money, and machines'. Respect for humanity also implies that people should not be coerced or deceived by others in pursuit of their own ends (Bowie, 1999).

- Kant's third version of his categorical imperative in essence states that we should act as if *we are all part of a moral community* (what he called an ideal 'kingdom' where one is both 'ruler and ruled at the same time' (Jones et al., 2005: 46).

Kant's framework forms the basis of human rights arguments. It is generally accepted (by reasoning, autonomous people who 'look into their own hearts', as Kant would suggest; Jones et al., 2005) that *all people have rights*, by virtue of their intrinsic humanity – although there may be some debate about precise the nature and scope of those rights. Here we are interested in moral rather than legal rights. Rights can be *negative* – in other words, others are obliged *not* to interfere with a person's right to, for example, privacy or safety. *Positive* rights, on the other hand, relate to the *entitlements* that people have to necessities they may not be able to provide themselves (Velasquez, 2012). In the aftermath of World War II, the United Nations codified a set of universal (positive) human rights. Part of this declaration is reproduced in Box 5.5 below. Although the language is a reflection of the time it was written, the principles remain important.

Kant's moral philosophy, along with the notion of rights, provides a conceptual foundation for a critique and reformulation of human resources practices. Deontological approaches to ethical dilemmas are not, however, without their problems. There are instances, for example, when principles, rights or duties conflict with each other. For example, one person's right to a healthy workplace may contradict another's right to smoke cigarettes at his or her desk. Other ethical frameworks, such as utilitarianism, may be needed to resolve these types of conflict.

A consideration of rights leads us to another important derivative of deontological ethics, the idea of *justice* as a universal principle and a fundamental human right. What a person deserves or is entitled to can be evaluated using rules or laws that relate to principles such as equality, non-discrimination, fairness, and retribution. Employment laws and practices are heavily reliant on such rules. The word 'justice' is used broadly to cover both the principles and the specific rules derived from these principles (Arnold et al., 2012).

Some interesting ideas on justice have been set out by the contemporary philosophers John Rawls and, more recently, Amartya Sen (2009). Rawls's seminal theory

---

Box 5.5 Extract from the United Nations Universal Declaration of Human Rights

Whereas recognition of the inherent dignity and of the equal and inalienable rights of all members of the human family is the foundation of freedom, justice and peace in the world…

Article	Principle
1	All human beings are born free and equal in dignity and rights. They are endowed with reason and conscience and should act towards one another in a spirit of brotherhood.
2	Everyone is entitled to all the rights and freedoms set forth in this Declaration, without distinction of any kind, such as race, colour, sex, language, religion, political or other opinion, national or social origin, property, birth or other status. Furthermore, no distinction shall be made on the basis of the political, jurisdictional or international status of the country or territory to which a person belongs, whether it be independent, trust, non-self-governing or under any other limitation of sovereignty.
3	Everyone has the right to life, liberty and security of person.
4	No one shall be held in slavery or servitude; slavery and the slave trade shall be prohibited in all their forms.
5	No one shall be subjected to torture or to cruel, inhuman or degrading treatment or punishment.
6	Everyone has the right to recognition everywhere as a person before the law.
7	All are equal before the law and are entitled without any discrimination to equal protection of the law. All are entitled to equal protection against any discrimination in violation of this Declaration and against any incitement to such discrimination.
8	Everyone has the right to an effective remedy by the competent national tribunals for acts violating the fundamental rights granted him by the constitution or by law.

Source: United Nations: http://www.un.org/en/universal-declaration-human-rights/index.html.

of justice is focused on *justice as fairness*. Rawls uses an interesting thought experiment to convey his argument, challenging us to imagine a society where we are covered by a hypothetical 'veil of ignorance', which means that we would have no idea of our position in that society in terms of race, class, gender, intelligence, or physical ability, for example. Rawls called this situation the 'original position'. What kind of arrangements would we agree to if we did not know where in society we would be placed? We would be compelled to be impartial and to live by principles of fairness that might not favour our own situation. For Rawls (Velasquez, 2012: 96), justice means that:

1 Each person has an equal right to the most extensive basic liberties compatible with similar liberties for all; and
2 social and economic inequalities are arranged so that they are both:
   ● to the greatest benefit of the least advantaged persons and
   ● attached to offices and positions open to all under conditions of fair equality of opportunity.

Nobel Prize recipient Amartya Sen critiqued and extended Rawls's more theoretical treatment of justice in his 2009 book *The Idea of Justice*, which considers the global dimensions of social justice and injustice and examines justice in practice. Drawing on both Western and Eastern philosophical traditions to support his arguments, he challenges those who live in wealthy, powerful countries to consider the interests and perspectives of the poor and the powerless.

Both of these philosophers are primarily concerned with *distributive* justice, which, as the term suggests, relates to the distribution of resources and opportunities. *Procedural* justice, on the other hand, relates to the processes that are used to come to a decision and whether these processes themselves are intrinsically fair. The notion of due process is particularly applicable to HRM, as much unethical human resources activity relates to the absence of fair processes of recruitment, performance management, and termination. In human resources terms, procedural justice can be operationalised through the provision of employee voice, justifiable explanations of practices, and compassionate interpersonal treatment (Margolis et al., 2007). *Interactional* justice implies fairness in interpersonal relations, for example honest, respectful, and open communication (Barling and Phillips, 1993). This principle ties directly into Kant's 'respect for persons' dictum and into the need to avoid deception. In the business world, decisions to withhold information from employees prior to downsizing or failure to communicate known hazards in the workplace would violate interactional justice principles.

Virtues

Another important framework used in resolving ethical dilemmas in the workplace is known as virtue ethics. This framework, which has seen a resurgence in the past two decades, is based on the idea that humans should and do cultivate a set of virtues or qualities in their day-to-day living. Virtue ethics is hence concerned with *the actor rather than the action* (Treviño and Nelson, 2013); virtues are *practised* rather than thought about. Using this framework, we do not ask 'What should we do?' but 'Who ought we become?'(Preston, 2014). Virtues relate to a person's character and are qualities that can be admired in others. They are the qualities that help define what being a 'good person' entails.

This framework is commonly associated with the ideas of the ancient Greek philosopher Aristotle and religious thinkers such as Confucius or Thomas Aquinas. Aristotle argued that a life well lived was a virtuous one. Across most cultures, individual role models are often used to educate others in what it means to live a 'good' life, providing a grounding in virtue ethics. Virtues can be taught and are acquired through practice – the more someone practices the virtue of *honesty*, the more *honest* they become. As Velasquez (2012: 112) explains, moral virtues comprise 'those habits that enable a person to *live* a human life well and not merely to do well in social practices'. Every individual has the potential for virtue.

This approach to ethical thinking and, more accurately, *behaving*, overcomes the criticism that sometimes people know what is right but *choose* not to do it (Preston, 2014). It also precludes the more instrumental approach to character traits seen in models such as 'emotional intelligence'. In recent times, there has been a resurgence of interest in virtue ethics among business ethicists, particularly after the corporate scandals of the past 20 years (Moore, 2012).

Which virtues should be valued? Many philosophers and religious thinkers have tried to develop a list of those virtues necessary for individuals and communities to experience the good life. Such lists tend to include:

- honesty;
- generosity;
- courage;
- selflessness;
- compassion;
- empathy;
- self-control;
- justice;
- trustworthiness;
- prudence.

Contemporary philosopher Alasdair MacIntyre (1999) adds two core virtues to this mix: *integrity* in one's character across different social contexts; and *constancy*, or showing the same moral character across time.

Without most of these virtues, it would be difficult for people to live and work together or resolve day-to-day community issues. Virtue ethics tends to emphasis the interrelatedness of people rather than their status as impartial, rational individuals. In recent times, however, it has become clear that some of the role models and heroes of Western business culture have lived anything but 'the good life'. The virtues a society views as worthy (and the vices viewed as repellent) reveal much about the dominant values and mental models within that society.

The main shortcoming of a virtue ethics framework is that, like universal principles, virtues can sometimes contradict each other. Virtue ethics may be insufficient in themselves to resolve a dilemma. For example, human resource managers may be faced with a choice between acting with honesty or with loyalty. Other frameworks, such as justice or utilitarianism, would be needed to examine this dilemma from the perspective of those affected by the human resource manager's choices.

Care ethics

An alternative approach to resolving ethical dilemmas is what has been termed an ethic of care. Within this framework, the main considerations are a *recognition of, and responsiveness to, others' wellbeing needs*. The care framework is an important recent contribution to moral philosophy which, like virtue ethics, differs from more conventional approaches. Unlike deontological or utilitarian frameworks, this approach does not require impartiality when facing an ethical choice. Instead of considering an abstract or generalised 'other' in approaching an issue (for example, justice), the 'other' is seen as concrete, relational and specific to a particular context.

In care ethics, the *connection* between others is recognised and valued, which also distinguishes this approach from the moral philosophies of Kant and others, with their notions of an autonomous, rational individual (Borgerson, 2007). Finally, care ethics acknowledges the 'different voices' of males and females, an acknowledgement often missing in traditional philosophy (Gilligan, 1995).

Rather than restricting this conceptualisation of care to that of a mother–child relationship, as earlier formulations did, contemporary feminist philosophers see care ethics as 'something that develops out of a sense of obligation and the acceptance of responsibility towards the individual cared for' (Machold et al., 2008: 672). Care is seen to have multiple dimensions and is not simply based on familial relationships. The practice of care specifically involves:

- *caring about* – a recognition of another's need, which is a form of *moral awareness*;
- *taking care of* – acting when care is needed, entailing a sense of *responsibility*;
- *care-giving* – ensuring that care needs are met, entailing both *empathy* and *competence*;
- *care-receiving* – the interaction between the carer and the recipient, entailing *responsiveness* and *receptiveness* (Machold et al., 2008).

Like virtue ethics and *quanxi* ethics (Box 5.6), care ethics emphasises practice and social (rather than cognitive) processes, in this case with the aim of empowering and emancipating others (Machold et al., 2008). Both care-givers and care-receivers grow as a result. A consideration of rights is not excluded from this approach, but here rights are seen as *relational* in nature, depending in part on the power relationships between the care-giver and the care-receiver (Baier, 1995). Similarly, justice and care are seen as interconnected, as a just society would acknowledge the fact that all people are dependent (and need care) at some stage in their lives (Kittay, 1998). Care ethics' recognition of relationships, power, and needs has also been at the forefront of feminist philosophy, hence the association between the two; feminism, like other critical theories, also rejects the 'liberal individualism' that lies at the heart of conventional economics-informed conceptions of society (Nedelsky, 1998).

An example of care ethics in action can be seen in the actions of the Australian greengrocer chain Harris Farm Markets, who actively employ and train asylum-seekers across their operations, in addition to supporting their employees' religious observance. In choosing to assist the often traumatised refugees by providing them with training and meaningful work, they are exercising a care relationship. This was not an impartial decision for the Harris managers – they actively sought out a group of people whom they knew and whom they felt they could empower and emancipate through the care they could offer.

The concrete, relationship-specific features of care ethics have meant that this approach has sometimes been criticised as relativist. Box 5.6 outlines an example of how the notion of an emphasis on relationships can lead to different ethical positions. Care ethicists have, however, argued that, unlike ethical relativism (see Box 5.2), the *idea* of care itself can be universalised, because all humans are entitled to be cared for. Early versions of care ethics – now labelled 'feminine' rather than 'feminist' – have also

---

Box 5.6 Guanxi business practices and ethics

Like care ethics, *guanxi* ethics places an emphasis on the particulars of relationships and contexts when approaching a moral issue. *Guanxi*, which means 'interpersonal connectedness' or networks, is a central part of business culture in Chinese business (Po, 2009). Its key principles include an acknowledgement of interdependence, reciprocity, traditional social relationships, and the sharing of scarce resources (Su et al., 2003). Relationships are viewed in particularistic terms, with norms based on both the relative position and level of intimacy of individuals (Tan and Snell, 2002).

There has been much debate about whether *guanxi* practices encourage unethical behaviour or corruption in business practices (Zheng et al., 2014). While gift-giving and norms of reciprocity are indeed embodied in a *guanxi* orientation, this does not mean that *guanxi*-focused individuals necessarily make decisions that are less ethical (Su et al., 2003). This Confucian-influenced approach to social practice in fact discourages self-interested practice and recognises the interconnectedness of people within a differentiated society. Morality is seen as 'both role- and act-dependent', with Confucian virtues such as honesty, sincerity, loyalty, and benevolence expected to guide behaviour alongside particular role and relationship features (Po, 2009).

---

been criticised for conflating sex and gender and implying a type of biological determinism and essentialism in their insistence that caring is a uniquely female or 'mothering' quality (Borgerson, 2007).

Although a number of frameworks have been presented here, it is important to remember that ethical thinking is not:

> a set of absolute principles, divorced from and imposed on everyday life.... It is the awareness that one is an intrinsic part of a social order, in which the interests of others and one's own interests are inevitably intertwined. (Solomon, 1998: 89)

The ethical frameworks provided in this section can all be used as the basis for recognising and critiquing HRM practice. In the following section, we will explore alternative conceptions of ethics and how they may apply to human resources.

Class Activity

▸ In what ways may the care ethics framework be particularly applicable to HRM practice?
▸ Many organisations are now providing 'domestic violence leave' for employees suffering from the effects of domestic violence. How can the provision of this type of leave be justified using care ethics principles?

Mini-Case Study **Organisational restructuring in a multinational subsidiary**

Consider the following scenario:

The senior management within a subsidiary of a large multinational manufacturing organisation have decided that due to increased global competition, falling profits, and resultant shareholder dissatisfaction, a significant downsizing (up to 700 layoffs) will take place. The decision was arrived at by management's collective concern that if the down-sizing did not occur, the organisation would in time fail to operate at all and final closure would be the grim result.

The organisation is the main provider of employment in the region, which has in past years witnessed a high level of unemployment and a decline in living standards. Many of the workers employed by the organisation have been with the firm for over 20 years, are over 45 years of age, and are largely unskilled or semi-skilled. You, as the HR Manager, have been called in to discuss the design of the downsizing process and how decisions regarding who will be made redundant will be determined.

You attend the meeting and are told that management are keen to keep the production line in operation until just before the production will be closed. You are asked to restrict communication to the workers about the redundancies, so that they will be more likely to work harder; this means workers will receive minimal time notification of redundancy.

Questions

As you sit in the meeting, it becomes clear to you that management have not thought this through. They have not asked themselves questions such as:

1 What are the implications of minimal communication of the redundancy procedures?
2 How motivated will the surviving employees feel once their work colleagues have left?
3 Shouldn't there be some counselling offered to employees?
4 Shouldn't there be some effort made to relocate workers to other parts of the organisation, or assistance offered to them to reskill and find alternative work?

You realise there is much work to do with this management team in order to minimise the damage from the downsizing strategy.

Class Activity

▸ Are there ethical implications of the decision to downsize in the case study above? If so, what are they and how (if at all) can they be addressed? What might be the obstacles to ethical action being taken?
▸ How would each of the four ethical frameworks presented here view the situation in the case study:
  • A *utilitarian* perspective?
  • A *rights* perspective?
  • A *justice* perspective?
  • A *care* perspective?

CORPORATE SOCIAL RESPONSIBILITY AND HUMAN RESOURCE MANAGEMENT

Over the past two decades, we have seen a growing discontent with what appears to be a lack of social and ethical responsibility on the part of some organisations. This discontent has been exacerbated by the failure of some of the key players in the financial crisis of 2008–2010 and its aftermath to act responsibly, resulting in widespread harm to workers, communities, and nations (Donaldson, 2012; Stiglitz, 2009).

But what might CSR mean? Is it reasonable to expect that this responsibility encompasses not only an avoidance of harm to society, but also an active consideration of the public good? Argandoña and Hoivik (2009: 225) have noted difficulties in pinning down a universal, globally relevant notion of CSR given the differing views of the role of business in society. However, they go on to describe CSR in relational terms as:

the set of moral duties towards other social actors and towards society that the firm assumes...and...the set of moral duties that the other agents and society attribute to the firm as a consequence of the role it assumes and its relationships with those actors.

This *relational* conception of CSR is particularly relevant to human resource practitioners, whose daily work has, at its core, relational practices. The moral duties associated with CSR in this sense relate to how a company *makes* its money, rather than how it *spends* its money – in other words, philanthropic activities can never substitute for responsible business practice (Crane et al., 2014).

There are three ways of looking at the CSR-HRM nexus. The first concerns itself with socially responsible HR practices, such as ensuring freedom from discrimination, decent work, a living wage, and safe workplaces for all workers associated with a firm's operations. The second perspective considers how the human resources function can support corporate social (and environmental) responsibility within an organisation through, for example, employee involvement in CSR. The third perspective sees HRM and CSR as mutually dependent, with 'workers, worker representatives, and those who manage workers [seen as] actors in networks involving multiple stakeholders and institutions' (Voegtlin and Greenwood, 2016: 6).

For human resource practitioners, the social actors or stakeholders of most relevance are the organisation's employees, their families, contractors/outsourcing partners, trade unions or staff associations, and the state institutions concerned with regulation of the employment relationship. Distinct moral duties relate to each of these stakeholders, but for our purposes we are most concerned with those who may have limited power. As we saw earlier, the ethical treatment of employees, contractors, and other workers is a central element of socially responsible business practice, particularly given that they are significantly affected by their employer's success or failure; they often make a substantial investment in terms of experience, skills, and in some cases relocation; and they may depend on their work for income, identity, and social relationships (Greenwood and Anderson, 2009).

Building on the work of Margolis and Walsh (2003), Wilcox (2006) discusses three types of duty relevant to human resource practitioners:

1   A duty to respond to situations or conditions caused by the organisation, for example to prevent harm to employees working with hazardous materials through the provision of safe working environments or common safety training standards across all workplaces.

2   The duty owed when organisations benefit from unjust or harmful conditions. Wilcox cites the example of child labour in unregulated economies and the actions of some companies to mitigate the harm through the provision of on-site classrooms.

3   The duty of beneficence, the duty to aid others simply because one is in a position to do so. The earlier example of employment of asylum-seekers fits into this category.

In the case of human resources development, there are a number of socially responsible policies that human resource practitioners can introduce to enact their moral duties. Some of these can directly address broader social issues (Wilcox, 2006). Human resource managers also have a role to play in the promulgation of cultural norms and values that have social responsibility at their heart.

A number of organisations have responded to calls to move to socially responsible practices. In Europe, for example, the European Commission has instituted the 'European Alliance for CSR', which is composed of member organisations including Business Europe (https://www.businesseurope.eu/european-alliance-csr). Each of the member organisations has in turn developed policies and practices that directly relate to their duties towards employees, contractors' employees, and local communities. Similarly, the *United Nations Global Compact* commits organisations to adhering to the 10 principles shown in Table 5.1.

Table 5.1 United Nations Global Compact Principles for business practice

Category	Principle	
Human rights	1	Businesses should support and respect the protection of internationally proclaimed human rights; and
	2	make sure that they are not complicit in human rights abuses.
Labour standards	3	Businesses should uphold the freedom of association and the effective recognition of the right to collective bargaining;
	4	the elimination of all forms of forced and compulsory labour;
	5	the effective abolition of child labour; and
	6	the elimination of discrimination in respect of employment and occupation.
Environment	7	Businesses should support a precautionary approach to environmental challenges;
	8	undertake initiatives to promote greater environmental responsibility; and
	9	encourage the development and diffusion of environmentally friendly technologies.
Anti-corruption	10	Businesses should work against corruption in all its forms, including extortion and bribery.

Source: United Nations Global Compact Ten Principles (n.d.) Retrieved from http://www.unglobalcompact.org/AboutTheGC/TheTenPrinciples/index.html

There are over 8000 signatories to the Global Compact, from 162 countries, with companies including Unilever (UK), Volvo AB (Sweden), Carrefour (France), Copel (Brazil), Tata Teleservices (India), Mars Inc. (US), PGE (Poland), Endesa (Chile), Westpac Bank (Australia), and SAP (Germany). As indicated in Table 5.1, the first six principles relate directly to HRM practice, including basic human rights, elimination of forced labour and child labour, freedom of association, and elimination of employment discrimination. Frameworks such as these provide legitimacy for socially responsible human resources practice.

Vuontisjarvi (2006a, 2006b) has provided an overview of some practical strategies for socially responsible HRM, which are summarised in Table 5.2. Each of these elements can be translated into principles, process indicators, and performance indicators. For example, the principle of 'Long, secure contracts' has associated *process indicators* of 'proactive measures to avoid redundancies and professional support for redundant employees' and *performance indicators* including 'number of redundancies or dismissals, number of internal rotations, breakdown by fixed term or regular, and perception measures'.

Although these principles and their enactment reflect a particular contextual arena, they can be adapted for a broad range of social, political, and regional contexts. For example, international HR managers can operationalise a commitment to socially responsible HR practice by implementing a 'living wage' globally and ensuring that workers, regardless of their location or the nature of their employment contract, have workplaces that are safe and work that is decent. The conventions set down by the UN-affiliated International Labour Association (ILO), underpin many elements of the Global Compact, providing a baseline for ethical HRM practice. In addition, countries where the core ILO conventions have been ratified and supported through national laws can be given preference when sourcing products and services, for example. The core ILO conventions include:

- Freedom of Association and Protection of the Right to Organise, 1948 (No. 87);
- Right to Organise and Collective Bargaining, 1949 (No. 98);
- Forced Labour Convention, 1930 (No. 29);
- Abolition of Forced Labour Convention, 1957 (No. 105);
- Minimum Age Convention, 1973 (No. 138);
- Worst Forms of Child Labour Convention, 1999 (No. 182);
- Equal Remuneration Convention, 1951 (No. 100);
- Discrimination (Employment and Occupation) Convention, 1958 (No. 111).

Source: ILO (n.d.) Available at: http://www.ilo.org/global/lang--en/index.htm).

Research into the *political* aspects of the CSR-HRM relationship highlights the importance of representative bodies like the ILO and the role that CSR and HRM activities can play in advancing social and political conditions (Voegtlin and Greenwood, 2016).

When CSR and HRM are fully integrated, they can 'reinforce each other to create benefit for the firm and its stakeholders' (Voegtlin and Greenwood, 2016: 9); employees are recognised as valuable stakeholders (rather than instrumentally as a means to an end), engaged and involved in co-designing HRM and CSR practices such as community involvement, sustainability and environmental initiatives (2016: 11). To this end, the SHRM Foundation has put together a set of guidelines for integrating HRM and CSR practices (Cohen et al., 2012).

Table 5.2 Elements of socially responsible human resources practice

Element	Principle
Training and development	Life-long learning; employability of an employee
Pay and benefits	Just, equal pay
Participation and staff involvement	Open and two-way communication (for example, employee representation, trade unions and teams)
Values and principles	Values, mission, vision statements, and articulated ethical or social responsibility principles
Employee health and well-being	Stress on preventative activities; zero accidents
Measurement of policies	Job satisfaction or other internal surveys
Employment policy	Diversity; access for those who are unemployed or low-skilled (social inclusion)
Security in employment	Long, secure contracts
Equal employment opportunities	Non-discrimination; equal opportunities
Work–life balance	Support for work–life balance

Source: Vuontisjarvi (2006a, 2006b)

Class Activity

Visit the Website of the International Labour Organisation (ILO) at www.ilo.org/global/lang--en/index.htm. According to this website:

> The ILO was founded in 1919, in the wake of a destructive war, to pursue a vision based on the premise that universal, lasting peace can be established only if it is based on social justice…. Underlying the ILO's work is the importance of cooperation between governments and employers' and workers' organisations in fostering social and economic progress.

In your group, discuss the following:

▸ What can you find out about the ILO's 'Decent Work' agenda?
▸ How might it apply to an industry with which you are familiar?
▸ What are some of the challenges associated with implementing this agenda in your industry? How might they be overcome?

Find two other aspects of the ILO's work that relate to ethical HRM.

Critical Thinking 5.2 The problem of being 'charmed'

So far, we have presented the view that ethics is an essential part of any critical treatment of management practice. We have also argued the case for a potential and legitimate ethics of human resources *in action*. Furthermore, underpinning our discussion is the assumption that ethics has an essence and can be defined, albeit in many ways. But, as students of HRM, you need to explore alternative viewpoints. Consider the following two quotes:

> in its most visible manifestations, business ethics has become an exercise in proclamations: the publishing of admonitions, inducements, seductions. (Roberts, 2003: 250)

> ethical behaviour takes place within a complex interaction of social forces and vested interests…. Ethics as philosophical reflection is never enough but must interact with a realistic and accurate interpretation of social conditions and the prospects from their transformation. (Preston, 2014: 12)

The perspectives of Roberts (2003) and Preston (2014) provide us with some insight into the tension in any treatment of business ethics. In their engaging book, Jones et al. (2005) explore and discuss the 'charm of business ethics'. Drawing creatively on the writings of the French philosopher Bachelard, they argue that a definition of business ethics (and hence human resources ethics) is as elusive yet as charming as the notion of 'fire'. Following the reasoning of Bachelard, Jones et al. (2005: 70) argue that fire is difficult to treat objectively due to its seductive, almost hypnotic, charm and warming properties. In the same way, they argue, business ethics has its own particular charm, for after all, 'who could be against business ethics? Business ethics is a charming and attractive idea, seemingly irresistible to many' (Jones et al., 2005: 70).

The notion of Corporate Social Responsibility (CSR) also has its 'charmed' aspects. The idea of 'responsibility' goes beyond the requirements of the law, and as Jones et al. (2005) assert, is worthy of celebration. But when responsibility is codified, it is no longer an independent responsibility; it is no longer a moral choice. CSR is often treated as a strategic or marketing approach whereby customers are appeased by dealing with companies that market themselves as being 'ethical'. Whether or not firms are ethical in reality is not questioned. Under this approach, the prime concern of an organisation is conditional; the organisation wants to appear to be ethically responsible in order to secure market share. Another approach to CSR is the stakeholder approach, which is also a type of *conditional* responsibility'. Like the strategic approach to responsibility, it too is largely superficial. It 'is a responsibility that trades on the positive connotations of the word, but only loosely engages in anything that could be called responsibility in a stronger sense' (Jones et. al, 2005:123).

Charming? Business ethics and human resources ethics may well be charming, but we perhaps need to be aware of the potential pitfalls of charming objects. They may hold us 'spellbound', thus preventing us from reflecting on their meaning and significance and possible dangers. In the case of business ethics and indeed human resources ethics, the critical distance can be thwarted by the entrancement and 'warmth' of the phenomenon itself.

We are thus drawn into arguments about the very *meaning* of ethics. As discussed above, most ethical frameworks tend to assume the meaning of ethics. Yet the meaning of ethics does not lie solely within the object; rather – and here is the contentious proposition – ethics relates to the subject who observes ethics. In short, as Jones et al. (2005: 73) simply state, 'People disagree about ethics'. In other words, the essence of ethics is mutable. This stance implies a non-essentialist approach to ethics.

Questions

1 In what ways might human resource management ethics be 'charming'?
2 What are some of the dangers of unreflective consideration of HRM ethics?

CRITICAL BUSINESS ETHICS: AN ANTI-ESSENTIALIST VIEW

Ethics can be conceived in many different ways. The essence of, say, business ethics is not hiding waiting to be found, nor is it found in a *clear* code of rules prescribing specific forms of ethical behaviour.

The key proponent of a non-essentialist (or even anti-essentialist) ethics is Emmanuel Levinas (1906–1995). His works, which have had a profound impact on European philosophy, sought to critically transform and question the meaning of ethics. A comprehensive review of Levinas and his contribution to the notion of a 'critical business ethics' is far beyond the scope of this chapter, yet his ideas are important enough to warrant discussion. What is presented here is a distillation of his foundational thoughts related to an approach to the study of business ethics and the associated notions of ethics and human resources.

It is worthwhile knowing a little of Levinas's own personal history here. As a Jew in World War II, he was captured by German soldiers and sent to a prison camp, and while there he befriended a dog. He observed that the dog exhibited an openness to the prisoners that was of a higher ethical order than the German town folk, who treated the Jews as subhuman. The dog recognised him as human, unlike the townspeople whose 'expressions were clear' (Levinas, 2001: 41).

In order to understand where Levinas is 'coming from', it is most useful to consider a story offered by Levinas himself (1999). The story is the children's story of *The Little Prince*, in which the narrator finds himself in the company of a young boy. The narrator had hoped to be an artist but instead was made to learn other more concrete and diverse disciplines that led him to become a pilot. One day, he crashed his plane in the desert. There he met the special little boy (the prince), who insisted he draw a picture of a sheep. The pilot attempts this, but all of his efforts are disregarded by the little prince. In the end, the pilot draws a small box and explains to the little prince

that this box has little holes in it and that in the box is the sheep that he wanted. Happy, the prince does not disturb the sheep since he thinks it is sleeping.

In this story, Levinas attempts to relate his approach to ethics. Rather than drawing (or defining) ethics, an undertaking likely to be rejected by all the little princes and princesses who think they know what ethics 'is', he attempts to draw the box in which ethics may be sleeping. As Jones et al. (2005: 74) observe:

this suggests that ethics is not something that we can approach directly or something that is easy to represent, but neither should we deny that it is important, or give up because minor royalty are confidently telling us what is in the box.

CONCLUSION

This chapter has touched on many issues associated with HRM and ethics and the global context of HRM. We have outlined the complexities associated with ethics and human resources, and discussed the core issues related to HRM and CSR (see Jamali, El Dirani and Harwood, 2015; Voegtlin and Greenwood, 2016). Moreover, we have explored how HRM practices that enable individual, organisational and societal wellbeing can be framed as an element of socially responsible business practice (Wilcox, 2006). Throughout this chapter we have presented a critical perspective on human resources and ethics.

Fisher, Lovell and Valero-Silva (2013) suggest that when you start to think about an ethical issue in the workplace, there will be at least four questions through which the issue can be addressed:

1 What is it that is ethically (or morally) wrong about the situation? What has triggered the recognition of the issue as an ethical one? What in other words, has triggered your *conscience*?

2 What ideally can you do about the situation? When you apply your *ethical reasoning* to the situation, what will you think is the proper course of action?

3 What do you think all the other interested persons and parties think about the situation? What are the *demands and expectations* that other stakeholders in the situation wish to impose?

4 What, in practical terms, should be done about it, given all the constraints and complexities of the 'real' world? What are the *options for action*?

Despite the complexities and paradoxes inherent in any ethics of HRM, we do believe that there is the need, and potential, for ethical human resources practices. These could arguably be achieved through the embedding of ethical considerations into the human resources systems associated with performance management, recruitment and selection, termination, reward, human resources development, and the gamut of other such activities (CIPD, 2015). The design and operation of these systems could draw on multiple perspectives and recognise the important role that unions have to play in providing employees with a voice. If human resource managers were to bring a consideration of ethics as part of their role to a strategic level, they would presumably need to be able to challenge and critique strategies as they were formulated, as well as respond to any ethical dilemmas created after the fact by the need to implement predetermined strategies. An overarching aim, then, of *best* human resources practice is to ensure the ethical treatment of employees during the formulation and implementation of organisational strategies.

The question remains whether ethical human resources practices and outcomes are possible or simply quixotic musings. Do the harsh realities of global economic systems mean that human resources managers, as Watson (2007: 228) suggests, have little choice but to act as 'agents of industrial capitalist corporations'?

MacIntyre (1999) has argued that the ability of actors to transcend the narrow confines of their organisational roles depends on their habitual questioning of institutionalised social orders. Central to moral agency is a capacity to 'stand back from and consider [one's] engagement with the established role structures' (MacIntyre, 1999: 317) – in other words, the contexts within which individuals find themselves.

The importance of such critical and reflective questioning is also acknowledged by McKenna and Tsahuridu (2001: 71), who argue that individuals' ability to act ethically will typically depend on their 'freedom to rationally examine society's values, choose what values to make [their] own and use them in making ethical decisions'. Human resource practitioners can hence find space for ethically informed action, particularly if they are able to tap into their professional values (CIPD, 2015) and vocabularies and find 'relational spaces' where ethical concerns can be shared with like-minded professionals (Wilcox, 2012).

The sense of who one is as a human being also needs to remain solid in spite of pressures to 'be something else' in accordance with one's social role (in other words, integrity and constancy of character is needed). We would thus caution against overly deterministic conclusions; individuals continue to demonstrate this type of reflective practice. Here we have advocated an ethically pluralistic stand – one in which deontological principles, a sense of virtue, and considerations of care also have a place alongside calculations of consequences.

Acting ethically is not easy. As Jones et al. (2005: 51) put it, 'morality in daily life is a struggle'. However, as these authors also later assert, the struggle should not prevent us from trying to 'strive for the good' as we navigate our way through the dilemmas that human resources practice presents to us.

End of Chapter Case Study **Amazon's brutal workplace is an indicator of an inhumane economy**

The on-line retailer Amazon has recently come under scrutiny for the creation of a 'relentless work environment' characterised by excessive working hours, limited opportunity for holidays, poor work–life balance, and extreme demands for performance and output.

Critics argue that Amazon sets impossibly high goals while monitoring and measuring every aspect of an individual's productivity. Current and former Amazon employees spoke of colleagues weeping at their desks and of being pressured by their line managers to spend less time with their families. Examples include a woman who was expected to get back to work the day after her miscarriage, and other employees who were penalised for taking time to care for ailing parents. Those who resist sacrificing their personal lives for their work are quickly discarded.

Alongside these revelations, the founder of Amazon responded by arguing that it was never his intention for management to take such actions and that he advocated a zero tolerance for lack of empathy in the workplace.

Critics have argued that that the type of relentless work environment in Amazon is simply not humane; that it leads to high levels of burnout and pushes people to the margins of the economy.

Others argue that the founder of Amazon is free to run his organisation any way he wants, and that people can choose not to work at Amazon in such a 'pressure cooker' environment.

The type of work regime in place at Amazon potentially raises a serious precedent. It may be the case that Amazon is just the leading edge of a widespread phenomenon whereby employers and management see no need to treat workers as full human beings with lives outside of work.

We may be moving towards a world of work that treats workers purely as means to an end and where even committed, engaged, and competent employees are viewed as easily disposable.

Adapted from: Horsey, D., Amazon's brutal workplace is an indicator of an inhumane economy. Los Angeles Times, August 18, 2015. Available at: http://www.latimes.com/opinion/topoftheticket/la-na-tt-amazon-brutal-workplace-20150818-story.html.

Questions

1 What are the HRM ethical issues relevant to the case?
2 How would each of the four main ethical frameworks presented in this chapter view the situation in the case study?
3 Consider the treatment of workers in this case against the background of Table 5.2 in this chapter. In what ways can the treatment of workers in the case be considered a violation of socially responsible human resources practice?

FOR DISCUSSION AND REVISION

1 How has globalisation impacted on ethics and human resources?
2 In what realms may human resources decisions have an ethical impact?
3 What are the implications of CSR for the way HRM activities are enacted in organisations?
4 Discuss the relationship between ethical reasoning and moral imagination, using two human resources activities to illustrate your answer.
5 In what ways are neoclassical economics and 'ethical egoism' linked?
6 How do consequentialism and deontological principles differ?
7 How do both virtue and care ethics differ from utilitarian frameworks? Illustrate your discussion by reference to two human resources activities.

Questions

1 What are the ethical human resources implications of the growth of the 'share' or 'gig' economy and the rise of temporary labour hire organisations such as Uber or Airtasker?
2 Imagine you are the HR director of a fashion retailer and you have been asked by the company's board to comment on the retailer's supply chain practices. How would you go about responding to this request? What sources of information/references could you use? You will need to conduct an internet search on fashion supply chains to answer these questions.

GLOSSARY

Ethics: comes from the Greek word ethos, meaning 'character' or 'custom'. Ethics can be defined, in action-oriented terms, as 'the principles, norms and standards of conduct governing an individual or group'. Ethics places human beings, or humanity, centre stage.

Care ethics: the main considerations are a recognition of, and responsiveness to, others' wellbeing needs.

Consequentialist ethics frameworks: enable ethical issues to be examined by considering the consequences (both intended and unintended) of decisions, in order to decide the right course of action. This approach is sometimes referred to as 'teleology', from the Greek word telos, which means 'end' or purpose. The best-known consequentialist framework is utilitarianism. Adopting this framework, we would say that the best decision is that which maximises 'utility', or leads to the greatest good for the greatest number of people.

Corporate Social Responsibility: the social responsibility of business encompasses the economic, legal, ethical, and discretionary expectations that society has of organizations at a given point in time. It is the idea that corporations have an obligation to constituent groups in society, other than stakeholders and beyond that described by law. The obligation is a broad one and must be voluntarily enacted; it extends the traditional duty to shareholders to other societal groups such as customers, employees, suppliers, and neighbouring communities.

Deontological ethics: deciding whether an action is right or wrong by considering the principles or duties that relate to that action. The essence of this approach to deciding what is right or good is that there are some universal, duty-based principles or rules that apply to everyone and should be used to guide our actions.

Distributive justice: the fair distribution of resources and opportunities.

Ethical relativism: a stance that sees any action as ethically permissible, as long as it was in keeping with the cultural standards held by the majority of people in a society.

Ethical pluralism: the alternative to ethical relativism or ethical absolutism, one advocated by many business ethicists; one in which social and cultural diversity is accepted.

Ethical absolutism: the idea that there is only ever one acceptable or right moral principle is known as ethical absolutism.

Ethical practice: there are three interrelated elements of ethical practice moral awareness, moral judgement, and ethical behaviour.

Ethical egoism: a type of consequentialist thinking. This approach to resolving an issue holds that the best action is one that benefits oneself – as either an individual or an organisation. At the core of ethical egoism lies a desire to maximise self-interest.

Interactional justice: implies fairness in interpersonal relations, for example honest, respectful and open communication

Justice: in ethical terms this is a universal principle and a fundamental human right. What a person deserves or is entitled to can be evaluated using rules or laws that relate to principles such as equality, non-discrimination, fairness and retribution. Employment laws and practices are heavily reliant on such rules. The word 'justice' is used broadly to cover both the principles and the specific rules derived from these principles.

Normative perspective of ethics: the aim of ethical thinking is to discover what ought to be, rather than simply describing what is or predicting what will probably happen.

Procedural justice: the processes that are used to come to a decision and consideration of whether these processes themselves are intrinsically fair.

Utilitarianism: a consequentialist framework that holds that the best decision is that which maximises 'utility', or leads to the greatest good for the greatest number of people. The best course of action is, then, one that brings about the best outcome for most people, so that overall good (or utility) is maximised.

Virtue ethics: concerned with the actor rather than the action. Virtues are practised rather than thought about. Using this framework, we do not ask 'What should we do to be ethical?' but 'Who ought we to become?' Virtues relate to a person's character and are qualities that can be admired in others. They are the qualities that help define what being a 'good person' entails.

FURTHER READING

Books

BOLTON, S. C. AND HOULIHAN, M. (2007) *Searching for the Human in Human Resource Management: Theory, Practice and Workplace Contexts.* Basingstoke: Palgrave Macmillan.
Explores a variety of issues associated with ethics and HRM.

CRANE, A., MATTEN, D. AND SPENCE L. (2013) *Corporate Social Responsibility: Readings and Cases in a Global Context* (2nd edn.). Abingdon: Routledge
An excellent collection of chapters for readers interested in the wider subject of CSR. Crane and Matten also have a blog: craneandmatten.blogspot.com.

GRACE, D. AND COHEN, S. (2013) *Business Ethics* (5th edn). Oxford: Oxford University Press.
An interesting text on general business ethics.

JONES, C., PARKER, M. AND TEN BOS, M. (2005) *For Business Ethics.* London: Routledge.
A very readable text providing a critical approach to business ethics.

PINNINGTON, A., MACKLIN, R. AND CAMPBELL, T. (2007) *Human Resource Management: Ethics and Employment.* Oxford: Oxford University Press.
Covering a range of issues associated with ethics and HRM.

PRESTON, N. (2014) *Understanding Ethics* (3rd edn). Sydney: Federation Press.
Provides an accessible general introduction to ethical thinking and action in a variety of contexts.

TREVIÑO, L. K. AND NELSON, K. A. (2013) *Managing Business Ethics: Straight Talk About How to Do It Right* (6th edn). Hoboken, NJ: Wiley.
A text covering general business ethics.

WINSTANLEY, D. AND WOODALL, J. (2000) *Ethical Issues in Contemporary Human Resource Management.* Basingstoke: Macmillan.
This classic book brought ethics to the attention of the human resource management community.

WEB RESOURCES

The following web resources are useful for further exploring issues covered in this chapter:

The European Alliance for CSR (n.d.) Available at: https://www.businesseurope.eu/european-alliance-csr.

The ILO (n.d.) Available at: http://www.ilo.org/global/lang--en/index.htm.

United Nations Global Compact Ten Principles (n.d.) Available at: http://www.unglobalcompact.org/AboutTheGC/TheTenPrinciples/index.html.

United Nations Universal Declaration of Human Rights (n.d.) Available at: http://www.un.org/en/universal-declaration-human-rights/index.html.

REFERENCES

ARGANDOÑA, A. AND HOIVIK, H. VON W. (2009) Corporate social responsibility: One size does not fit all. *Journal of Business Ethics*, 89(3): 221–234.

ARNOLD, D. G., BEAUCHAMP, T. L. AND BOWIE, N. (2012) *Ethical theory and Business*. Basingstoke: Pearson Higher Ed.

BAIER, A. C. (1995) The need for more than justice. In Held, V. (ed.), *Justice and Care: Essential Readings in Feminist Ethics*. Boulder, CO: Westview, 47–58.

BARLING, J. AND PHILLIPS, M. (1993) Interactional, formal, and distributive justice in the workplace: An exploratory study. *Journal of Psychology*, 127(6): 649–656.

BOLINO, M. C., KLOTZ, A. C., TURNLEY, W. H. AND HARVEY, J. (2013) Exploring the dark side of organizational citizenship behavior. *Journal of Organizational Behavior*, 34(4): 542–559.

BORGERSON, J. (2007) On the harmony of feminist ethics and business ethics. *Business and Society Review*, 112(4): 477–509.

BOWIE, N. E. (1999) *Business Ethics: A Kantian Perspective*. Malden: Blackwell.

Business Europe (n.d.) European Alliance for CSR Available at: (https://www.businesseurope.eu/european-alliance-csr.

CIPD (2015) Ethical decision-making: Eight perspectives on workplace dilemmas. Chartered Institute of Personnel and Development Research Report, London.

COHEN, E., TAYLOR, S. AND MULLER-CAMEN, M. (2012) HRM's role in corporate social and environmental sustainability. *SHRM report*. Alexandria, VA: SHRM Foundation.

COHEN, S. (2004) *The Nature of Moral Reasoning*. Melbourne: Oxford University Press.

CRANE, A. AND MATTEN, D. (2007) *Business Ethics: Managing Corporate Citizenship and Sustainability in an Age of Globalization* (2nd edn). Oxford: Oxford University Press.

CRANE A., PALAZZO G., SPENCE L. J. et al. (2014) Contesting the value of 'creating shared value'. *California Management Review*, 56: 130–153.

DONALDSON, T. (2012) Three ethical roots of the economic crisis. *Journal of Business Ethics*, 106: 5–8.

DONALDSON, T. AND DUNFEE, T. (1994) Toward a unified conception of business ethics: Integrative social contracts theory. *Academy of Management Review*, 19(2): 252–284.

ENDERLE, G. (2000) Whose ethos for public goods in the global economy? *Business Ethics Quarterly*, 10(1): 131–144.

FISHER, C., LOVELL, A. AND VALERO-SILVA, N. (2013) *Business Ethics and Values* (4th edn). London, Pearson.

GREENWOOD, M. AND ANDERSON, E. (2009) 'I used to be an employee but now I am a stakeholder': Implications of labelling employees as stakeholders. *Asia Pacific Journal of Human Resources*, 47: 186–200.

GILLIGAN, C. (1995) Moral orientation and moral development. In Held, V. (ed.), *Justice and Care: Essential Readings in Feminist Ethics*. Boulder, CO: Westview, pp. 31–46.

DIMA, R., JAMALI, D., EL DIRANI, A. AND HARWOOD, I. (2015) Exploring human resource management roles in corporate social responsibility: The CSR-HRM Co-creation Model. *Business Ethics: A European Review*, 24(2): 125–143.

JONES, C., PARKER, M. AND TEN BOS, M. (2005) *For Business Ethics*. London: Routledge.

ILO (International Labour Organisation) (n.d.) Available at: http://www.ilo.org/global/lang--en/index.htm.

KITTAY, E. F. (1998) Human dependency and Rawlsian equality. In Gatens, M. (ed.), *Feminist Ethics*. Aldershot: Ashgate, pp. 445–492.

KOCHAN, T. (2004) Restoring trust in the human resource management profession. *Asia Pacific Journal of Human Resources*, 42(2): 132–146.

LEVINAS, E. (1999) *Alterity and Transcendence*, trans. Michael Smith. New York: Columbia University Press.

LEVINAS, E. (2001) *Is It Righteous to Be? Interviews with Emmanuel Levinas*, ed. Jill Robbins. Stanford, CA: Stanford University Press.

LOWRY, D. (2006) HR managers as ethical decision-makers: Mapping the terrain. *Asia Pacific Journal of Human Resources*, 44(2): 171–183.

LUND-THOMSEN, P. AND LINDGREEN, A. (2014) Corporate social responsibility in global value chains: Where are we now and where are we going? *Journal of Business Ethics*, 123(1): 11–22.

MACHOLD, S., AHMED, P. K. AND FARQUHAR, S. S. (2008) Corporate governance and ethics: A feminist perspective. *Journal of Business Ethics*, 81: 665–678.

MACINTYRE, A. (1999) Social structures and their threats to moral agency. *Philosophy*, 74(289): 311–329.

MAHMOOD, M. AND NURUL ABSAR, N. (2015) Human Resource Management practices in Bangladesh: Current scenario and future challenges. *South Asian Journal of Human Resources Management*, 2(2): 171–188.

MARGOLIS, J. AND WALSH, J. (2003) Misery loves companies: Rethinking social initiatives by business. *Administrative Science Quarterly*, 48: 268–305.

MARGOLIS, J., GRANT, A. AND MOLINSKY, A. (2007) Expanding ethical standards of HRM: Necessary evils and the multiple dimensions of impact. In Pinnington, A., Macklin, R. and Campbell, T. (eds), *Human Resource Management: Ethics and Employment*. Oxford: Oxford University Press, pp. 237–251.

MCKENNA, R. AND TSAHURIDU, E. (2001) Must managers leave ethics at home? Economics and moral anomie in business organizations. *Reason in Practice*, 1(3): 67–75.

MOORE G. (2012). The virtue of governance, the governance of virtue. *Business Ethics Quarterly*, 22: 293–318.

MORAN, S. (2009) More Hardie directors join bid to overturn court. *The Australian*, 17 October: 32.

NEDELSKY, J. (1998). Reconceiving autonomy: Sources, thoughts and possibilities. In Gatens, M. (ed.), *Feminist Ethics*. Aldershot: Ashgate, pp. 391–420.

NEUSNER, J. AND CHILTON B. D. (2008) *The Golden Rule: The Ethics of Reciprocity in World Religions*. London: Bloomsbury Publishing.

NIMBALKER, G., MAWSON, J., CREMEN, C., WRINKLE, H. AND ERIKSSON, E. (2015) *The Truth behind the Barcode: Australian Fashion Report 2015*. Melbourne: Baptist World Aid.

PO, K. I. (2009). Is Confucianism good for business ethics in china? *Journal of Business Ethics*, 88: 463–76.

PODSAKOFF, P. M., MACKENZIE, S. B., PAINE, J. B. AND BACHRACH, D. B. (2000) Organizational citizenship behaviors: A critical review of the theoretical and empirical literature and suggestions for future research. *Journal of Management*, 26(3): 513–563.

PRESTON, N. (2014) *Understanding Ethics* (4th edn). Sydney: Federation Press.

ROBERTS, J. (2003) The manufacture of corporate social responsibility: Constructing corporate sensibility. *Organization*, 10(2): 249–265.

SEN, A. (2009) *The Idea of Justice*. Harvard: Harvard University Press.

SOLOMON, R. C. (1998) The one-minute moralist. In Hartman, L. P. (ed.), *Perspectives on Business Ethics*. Chicago: McGraw-Hill, pp. 88–90.

STIGLITZ, J. E. (2009) The current economic crisis and lessons for economic theory. *Eastern Economic Journal*, 35: 281–296.

SU, C., SIRGY, M. J. AND LITTLEFIELD, J. E. (2003) Is Guanxi orientation bad, ethically speaking? A study of Chinese enterprises. *Journal of Business Ethics*, 44(4): 303–312.

TAN, D., AND SNELL, R. S. (2002) The third eye: Exploring Guanxi and relational morality in the workplace. *Journal of Business Ethics*, 41: 361–384.

THORNTON, P. H. AND OCASIO, W. (2008) Institutional logics. *Sage Handbook of Organizational Institutionalism*, 840: 99–128.

TREVIÑO, L. K. AND NELSON, K. A. (2013) *Managing Business Ethics: Straight Talk about How to Do It Right* (6th edn). Hoboken, NJ: Wiley.

United Nations Global Compact Ten Principles (n.d.). Available at: http://www.unglobalcompact.org/About TheGC/TheTenPrinciples/index.html.

United Nations Universal Declaration of Human Rights (n.d.). Available at: http://www.un.org/en/universal-declaration-human-rights/index.html.

VELASQUEZ, M. G. (2012) *Business Ethics: Concepts and Cases* (6th edn). Upper Saddle River, NJ: Pearson Prentice Hall.

VOEGTLIN, C. AND GREENWOOD, M. (2016) Corporate social responsibility and human resource management: A systematic review and conceptual analysis. *Human Resource Management Review*. Available at: http://dx.doi.org/10.1016/j.hrmr.2015.12.003.

VUONTISJARVI, T. (2006a) Corporate social reporting in the European context and human resource disclosures: An analysis of Finnish companies. *Journal of Business Ethics*, 69(4): 331–354.

VUONTISJARVI, T. (2006b) The European context for corporate social responsibility and human resource management. *Business Ethics: A European Review*, 15(3): 271–291.

WATSON, T. (2003) Ethical choice in managerial work: The scope for moral choices in an ethically irrational world. *Human Relations*, 56(2): 167–185.

WATSON, T. J. (2007) HRM, ethical irrationality and the limits of ethical action. In Pinnington, A. H., Macklin, R. and Campbell, T. (eds), *Human Resource Management: Ethics and Employment*. Oxford: Oxford University Press, pp. 223–236.

WERHANE, P. H. (2002) The very idea of a conceptual scheme. In Donaldson, T., Werhane, P. and Cording, M. (eds), *Ethical Issues in Business*. Upper Saddle River, NJ: Prentice Hall, pp. 83–97.

WILCOX, T. (2006) Human resource development as an element of corporate social responsibility. *Asia Pacific Journal of Human Resources*, 44(2): 184–196.

WILCOX, T. (2012) Human resource management in a compartmentalized world: Whither moral agency? *Journal of Business Ethics*; 111: 85–96.

ZHENG, Q., LUO, Y. AND WANG S. L. (2014) Moral degradation, business ethics, and corporate social responsibility in a transitional economy. *Journal of Business Ethics* 120(3): 405–421.

HRM in Practice

6

HUMAN RESOURCES PLANNING

Cathy Sheehan

LEARNING OUTCOMES

After reading this chapter, you should be able to:

➤ Discuss the rise of human resource planning (HRP) as a strategic priority
➤ Explain the techniques associated with forecasting the supply and demand of human resources
➤ Outline the role of job analysis in the HRP process
➤ Describe and analyse the impact of restructuring on HRP responses
➤ Explain the role of HRP in talent management
➤ Discuss international HRP considerations.

Changes to the nature of work, such as the shift to service delivery, have had strategic implications for the type of worker who is now in demand and the structure of work arrangements.

Forecasting labour demand can be undertaken either quantitatively or qualitatively.

Labour supply forecasting draws from both internal and external sources of HRM information.

Job analysis complements the HRP process by providing information about exactly what each job involves and the type of labour required.

Strategic initiatives such as restructuring and downsizing draw heavily on appropriate HRP responses.

Firms have become more mindful of the importance of attracting and retaining talent, even during periods of a slow-down in labour demand, so they are more careful about HRP reactive approaches.

The increase in the outsourcing of work and the resultant 'offshoring' of tasks to overseas providers requires additional monitoring to ensure that quality and service are being delivered in an appropriate manner.

Opening Case Study **Offshoring in the banking industry**

When ANZ, one of Australia's leading banks, advertised 55 jobs at its new Manila operation, ranging from a new head of human resources to credit-risk officers and business analysts, not a single job was advertised in Australia. Almost all jobs were classified as high skilled, requiring a high level of university education, two years of similar experience, and fluent written English (Wade and Hawthorne, 2012). The example reflects the trend of the major Australian banks, Westpac, NAB, and ANZ, to carry out functions overseas (Yeates, 2012).

Lower overseas wages that translate to lower business costs are a major reason for the decision to head overseas to source labour. As a high-wage developed nation, Australia struggles to compete with wage costs in developing nations. An Australian-based credit risk officer with the National Australia Bank told *The Saturday Age*, for example, that the wage for this position in Australia would be around $60,000 a year, ranging up to $80,000 for someone with more experience. In Manila, on the other hand, jobs for credit-risk officers working for overseas banks are being advertised at 20,000–30,000 Philippine pesos a month, equivalent to about $5000–$7800 a year. These jobs are skilled positions that require a university education and a minimum of four years of similar experience (Wade and Hawthorne, 2012).

New technologies have also meant that offshored work can be more easily transferred to home countries and communicated to other international sites. Technological innovations expand the range of activities that can be outsourced with an increasing number of service-sector jobs suitable for offshoring (Graham, 2012). Modelling commissioned by several unions, including the one representing the financial-sector workers, the Financial Sector Union (FSU) have predicted that at least 250,000 jobs across Australia's service sector are susceptible to outsourcing over time, especially in finance, telecommunications, and IT (Wade and Hawthorne, 2012).

A further reason given for the increase in offshoring is the Australian skills crisis that threatens business growth and expansion. If it is not possible to cater for business needs in Australia, then companies look elsewhere, especially when overseas wage rates are lower and potentially provide a greater return on investment (Graham, 2012). The increasing incidence of offshoring and the emerging sophistication in offshoring operations raises the sourcing of labour from overseas as a viable option for more organisations. The decision does however require considerable forethought, and it can take several years to successfully prepare and execute an offshoring initiative.

The big Australian banks have approached the offshoring of labour in different ways. NAB and Westpac have outsourced operations to specialist business-processing firms that have established reputations. ANZ on the other hand directly employs staff in lower-cost Asian countries as evidenced by the 'operations hubs' in Manila and the Chinese city of Chengdu and the long-established centre in Bangalore. ANZ chief Mike Smith has emphasised the importance of these operations hubs, which facilitate ANZ's operations across Asia, not just Australia. 'Our investment in our operations hubs continues to support our productivity agenda, and we're also placing a stronger emphasis on generating on-going efficiencies given the more constrained conditions.... This isn't a matter of reacting to events, but of dynamically managing our costs to reflect our business strategy and the market conditions' (Wade and Hawthorne, 2012).

There has been a lot of negative press about the impact of these outsourcing and offshoring strategies on Australian jobs with the FSU pushing for regulations to make offshoring more difficult for banks. Former Westpac chief Gail Kelly deflected negative perceptions by shifting the discussion of outsourcing to one of 'best sourcing'. 'It's called best sourcing rather than outsourcing because in some cases we insource as well.' A spokesman for National Australia Bank has also noted that with a workforce of 44,000 worldwide, numbers 'will fluctuate in various parts of the business at times due to the completion of programs, outsourcing of some projects and continuing focus on efficiency.' He said NAB always tried to redeploy people within the business if possible (Wade and Hawthorne, 2012). These comments reflect the need for financial institutions to become flexible and pragmatic in their decision-making about where they source labour and to remain responsive to changes in demand for their product.

Questions

1 As explained in the case, NAB and Westpac have outsourced operations to specialist business-processing firms, whereas ANZ directly employs staff in the targeted location. What would be the advantages/disadvantages of each approach?
2 What sort of jobs are best suited for offshoring?
3 What controls would an organisation need to put in place when offshoring work to ensure that jobs requirements are met?

INTRODUCTION

The opening case that considers responses by the banking industry to new sources of labour is an example of human resource planning (HRP). Part of the explanation for the rise in offshoring has been the difficulty in securing a locally talented skill set, or an appropriate supply of local labour, to meet demand for a company's product. The rise in the supply of an educated, relatively cost-effective labour source in countries such as India and the Philippines has changed business thinking and expanded options for meeting the demand for labour. These trends pose particular challenges for the human resource management (HRM) function, as it assists the organisation in remaining viable. Decisions associated with offshoring may require the HR function to manage local workforce reductions, all the time ensuring that the business attracts and retains critical talent in order to maintain business viability. These circumstances require innovative responses and careful HRM planning. As custodians of the people resource in organisations, it is the role of the HRM function to assist in the development of such human resource planning initiatives that match changes in the supply and demand for labour and also manage initiatives to retain and attract talent strategically rather than reactively.

The purpose of this chapter is, first, to broadly review approaches to HRP, and second, to critically analyse some of the strategic responses to issues associated with the supply and demand of labour. The chapter starts with a discussion of the emerging recognition of the strategic importance of this area. Techniques for HRP are then explored, including quantitative and qualitative approaches. Following on from this, a discussion of job analysis highlights the connections between the analysis of what a job involves and the HRP requirements for it. Having explained HRP techniques, the discussion will then move on to an examination of the more strategic issues associated with HRP, such as HRP as part of restructuring initiatives and the role of HRP in decisions related to talent management and globalisation.

APPROACHES TO HRP

The evolution of HRP

Huselid (1993: 36) has explained that HRP essentially matches 'projected human resource demand with its anticipated supply, with explicit consideration of the skill mix that will be necessary throughout the firm'. HRP is a dynamic process affected by both predictable and unpredictable forces. The economic change experienced during the global financial crisis, for example, in 2008–2009 impacted on markets and resulted in swings in consumer demand that affected the level of labour required to meet the product output thus needed. These unplanned changes in the demand for labour occurred at a time when there were on-going forecasted demographic shifts in the profile of the available workforce (Rudd et al., 2007). These environmental challenges potentially pose major threats to organisational viability, but careful management of the HRP process can make a substantial contribution to the ultimate success or failure of the business.

In Chapter 2, Afiouni and Jamali consider the change and evolution that have occurred in the field of HRM and the increasing awareness of the value of strategic HRM for improving organisational outcomes that has become apparent in the past two decades. HRP activity is a good example of how HRM can provide this strategic value. Industry shifts away from manufacturing to a greater focus on service and knowledge work have led to a recognition of the potential for human capital to make a substantial and lasting impact on sustainable competitive advantage (Barney and Wright, 1998; Wright et al., 1994; Zula and Chermack, 2007).

Historically, the manufacturing industry has provided a large source of work, but its contribution to the number of employed people has been in decline. As a result, the primary focus of employment in many developed countries has increasingly become service oriented. By the late 1980s, for example, more than 60 per cent of employees in the Organisation for Economic Co-operation and Development as a whole were working in the services sector (Blyton, 1989). The impact of this shift towards services has implications for the type of employee who is now in demand:

- As most service work requires *face-to-face or voice-to-voice interaction* with customers (Macdonald and Sirianni, 1996), the service interaction may involve high levels of emotional labour or 'the management of feeling to create a publicly observable facial and bodily display' (Hochschild, 1983: 7).
- Another feature of employment conditions in the service sector is *flexibility in work arrangements* (Smith, 2005). Australian studies suggest evidence of the common pattern also seen in other industrialised countries: employment is moving from the 'traditional' forms of full-time, permanent work towards a wider variety of working arrangements, including part-time work, temporary employment and contract employment (Kalleberg, 2000; Van den Heuvel and Wooden, 1997).

The growth in the service sector has therefore changed expectations of the type of worker who is now in demand and the structure of working arrangements. Firms that can effectively adjust their human capital base to meet these economic challenges and maintain a workforce mix that supports strategic priorities are well placed to maintain their competitive advantage.

Before moving on to a discussion of some of these strategic issues, it is useful to consider how the HRP planning process actually works. The next section will therefore review how an organisation can approach matching human resource demand to supply, before moving into a broader discussion of the strategic impact of HRP activity.

Techniques of human resources planning

Demand forecasting in HRM determines the quantity and quality of employees required to meet the organisation's goals. These forecasts are usually associated with particular job categories and skill areas that support the organisation's current and future goals. There are a variety of approaches that provide useful data, differing in their approach and level of sophistication. Demand forecasting may be undertaken either *quantitatively* or *qualitatively*.

Quantitative demand forecasting

Quantitative approaches rely on statistical techniques and mathematical modelling, whereas qualitative approaches gather expert opinions to determine possible changes in demand. Two forms of quantitative analysis include trend projections and multiple regression.

Trend projection is time series analysis that processes past and present information on the number of people hired in various departments, job categories, or skills areas and, based on any observed increases or decreases, forms predictions into the future. Although such information is quite easy to understand, the underlying assumption is that previous trends will determine future trends, which does not take into account unexpected environmental developments.

The aim of the *multiple regression* approach is to broaden the determinants of future demand to determine reliable indicators of future demand. Specific independent variables, or predictors, may include variables such as sales in a retail store, student numbers in a school, or hospital bed capacity in a hospital. In the situation facing Holden outlined in Box 6.1, for example, labour demand was impacted by adjustments to internal operating decisions as well as changes in consumer taste. The greater the number of independent variables that can be used to predict the labour demand, the more accurate will be the prediction. The restrictions on using multiple regression are, however, the availability of the data and also the size of the sample, with larger datasets providing more accurate information. There is also an expectation that those working in the HRM area are comfortable dealing with both datasets and the computer programmes that accompany the technique.

Qualitative demand forecasting

An alternative to the quantitative approach is provided by qualitative techniques that draw in information from key stakeholders. Data collection can be quite informal or can be structured in a formal manner using approaches such as the Delphi technique.

Using a Delphi survey, HRM planners contact a group of expert informants and ask them to respond anonymously to some questions on HRP. Responses are collected and fed back to respondents together with another set of questions. The process continues until a consensus has been obtained (Rothwell, 1995). The benefits of this approach are that expert information is gathered without face-to-face pressure within the group to conform to a particular line of thinking. The approach is also useful when conditions are changing and there are few existing precedents on how to proceed.

Class Activity

▸ Under what conditions would a qualitative approach to demand forecasting be more feasible or appropriate than a quantitative approach?

Supply forecasting

Supply forecasting draws from both internal and external sources of HRM information related to supply of employees. Internal labour supply information considers the range of people within the organisation who can be promoted, transferred, or developed to meet supply needs. When undertaking such a review, a skills inventory – a system for keeping track of employee skill development – is a useful source of information. These data can be kept manually, especially in smaller organisations, but in larger organisations well-developed human resources information systems and detailed performance management information may assist in identifying employees with high potential and the appropriate skills. Along with internal sources of supply, organisations scan labour supply sources external to the organisation. This sort of analysis takes into account environmental analysis relating to demographic trends in order to assess the qualitative and quantitative impacts.

In terms of the usefulness of efforts to match the demand and supply of labour, evidence suggests that firms adopting clear HRM planning objectives and a formal planning process obtain useful information for strategic planning (Huselid, 1995; Lam and Schaubroeck, 1998). Despite the logic of external and internal labour scanning, there is evidence that people planning is not always formally developed and implemented. The impact of unplanned

Factors impacting on labour demand at Holden

General Motors has announced it will close its Holden car-making operations in Australia by 2017, leading to a loss of 2,900 jobs when it closes its Port Melbourne engine plant at the end of 2016, and its engineering centre in 2017. An additional 1,600 jobs will be lost at Holden's Adelaide factory at the end of 2017 (Griffiths, 2014).

The decision comes after a long struggle by Holden to remain viable in Australia and adopt labour management strategies to handle the downturn in product demand. During March 2007, for example, Holden made a decision to cut 600 jobs at its assembly operations in Adelaide, Australia. The fall in labour demand was associated with a range of demand determinants including adjustments to internal operating decisions as well as changes in broader consumer demand (Dornin, 2007).

With respect to the internal operating changes, Director of Manufacturing Rod Keane said that the decision to reduce the workforce at the Elizabeth plant followed a major investment at the plant that had increased efficiencies and allowed the car maker to maintain production levels with fewer staff. It also came as the company moved to end the production of its older VZ range of vehicles and concentrate on the new VE models.

Broader reasons for the decline in labour demand were related to a slide in sales of the locally built Commodore range in 2006, with sales down 15.4 per cent. Holden had also cut 1,400 jobs in August 2005, when it axed its third shift at Elizabeth due to a falling local and global demand for large cars.

Ian Jones, federal secretary of the Australian Manufacturing Workers Union vehicle division, commented on environmental pressures that had contributed to this decline in sales. 'Petrol pricing, currency costs, unabated entry of imported products, declining assistance and increased cost of finance are all factors that by themselves would cause major problems for industry,' Mr Jones said.

Federal Industry Minister Ian Macfarlane confirmed that the global automotive industry was going through challenging times and that Australian car producers were not immune from this (Dornin, 2007).

HRP approaches. The most common use of HRP occurred in firms that were experiencing moderate levels of workforce volatility. Firms characterised by high or low levels of workforce volatility, however, tended to have a lower use of HRP. Huselid (1993) observed that higher levels of volatility may render HRP ineffective, whereas low levels of volatility make it unnecessary.

Rothwell (1995) also commented on the lack of HRP within the development of human resource strategy. Consistent with Huselid (1993), the argument is made that the rate of environmental change renders HRP so problematic that it becomes infeasible. Plans are developed but fail to be implemented as further internal or external changes negate the relevance of any proposed initiatives. Policy priorities may also shift as competing interest groups vie for primacy and existing plans are side-lined in the process.

Rothwell (1995) also suggests that the abilities and skills of those who are expected to take on these planning tasks may impact on the quality of HRP. Line managers who are given the task of making planning projections, for example, may not have the background skills or the time to dedicate to developing labour models. Kulik and Bainbridge (2006), in a survey of both HRM professionals and line managers covering a range of HRM responsibilities, established that with respect to HRP, the collective view confirmed that HRP is best managed centrally by HRM rather than by the line. Although this assigns responsibility to those who may have the skills, line managers often still need to be involved as the decisions ultimately impact on the capacity of line management to complete the organisation's output requirements.

Job analysis

Within the HRP process, matching the demand and supply of labour informs decision-makers about potential trends and changes in labour requirements and also provides information about the best labour mix. Job analysis refines and complements this information to determine exactly what each job involves and who is required before specific staffing decisions can be made (Schneider and Konz, 1989).

Broadly speaking, job analysis refers to the process of getting detailed information about jobs (Brannick et al., 2007). Organisational conditions often change in response to new technology and machinery, as well as legislative and market requirements. Job analysis therefore becomes important in interpreting what the job currently involves. Having identified the objective of the job analysis, the HRM analyst must determine the type of information that needs to be collected, the source of the information, the method of data collection and how the data will be analysed.

environmental events, for example, means that it is frequently difficult to estimate internal labour demand. Indeed, Huselid (1993) established that environmental volatility had an important impact on the adoption of

The type of information that is collected is usually associated with the development of a job description, or the list of tasks, duties, and responsibilities of the job. Additionally, a job specification, or person specification, is derived that lists the knowledge, skills, abilities, and other characteristics that an individual must have to successfully perform the job. The most common source of information is the person already in the job. There are limits to the usefulness of this source, however, when the views of the present incumbents differ from those of their supervisors (O'Reilly, 1973). Employees may, for example, exaggerate their duties, especially if the process is associated with a review of remuneration, and it may become necessary to seek out additional information. When the job is a new position or when the incumbent has actually left the organisation, further input is usually sought. Under these conditions, for example, it becomes necessary to bring in the views of supervisors or co-workers.

Common methods of data collection include observation, interviews, questionnaires, diaries and critical incident approaches. The choice of the method depends largely on the purpose of the analysis and the nature of the job, and a number of methods are often used together:

- *Observation* is useful when the job involves standardised repetitive jobs and manual work: when jobs have actions, observation is a good way to track what needs to be done. More complex positions involving internal thought processing, such as the work of an accountant, are, however, difficult to measure through observation. Similarly, when a job involves irregular work, as, for example, with the role of a manager, observation becomes less useful.
- *Interviews* are more appropriate in these situations and overall are one of the most commonly used job analysis data collection methods.
- *Diaries* are also helpful when the responsibilities of a job do not form a regular pattern. If diaries are reliably maintained over an extended period, they are especially useful in tracking irregular and infrequent duties.
- Finally, critical incident approaches are employed to provide specific explanations for effective and ineffective job performance. This approach is usually used to track what is required and what is to be avoided for the success or failure of the job. The process can be onerous as it requires fairly detailed descriptions of what the employee did during a particular incident and explanations of why the performance was effective or ineffective; for this reason, it is not commonly used across routine tasks.

In addition to these qualitative approaches, quantitative questionnaires such as the position analysis questionnaire provide useful data that can be used to compare information across a range of jobs (Jeanneret and Strong, 2003). These quantitative surveys usually break jobs down into standardised dimensions that are rated; the information obtained can then be used to differentiate jobs with respect to levels of complexity, processing, and responsibility.

Class Activity

▸ When would quantitative approaches to job analysis be more suitable than qualitative approaches?

Despite the usefulness and importance of job analysis, a number of writers have explained that the rational approach described above – which breaks each job down and produces specific job descriptions and specifications – may no longer be viable. As the rate of technology changes and work becomes more knowledge based, task boundaries created by traditional job classifications are dissipating. Jobs have become more flexible, and their boundaries are vague and dynamic (Brannick et al., 2007).

Stewart and Carson (1997) have argued that, along with the move away from traditional hierarchical structure and control towards flexible, team-based designs, employees have become more than simple components that fit a series of static job descriptions. A key idea is the development of emerging relationships that may create new networks between employees. These emerging networks do not, however, always have a comfortable fit with traditional structures. The more fluid connections mean that what needs to be done and who does it become a product of what each person brings into the organisation and how he or she connects with existing staff. Therefore, rather than work roles being planned and fixed, they become indefinite. It is more likely that jobs will develop around individuals rather than the reverse. Therefore, as well as impacting on job content, environmental pressures have led to re-evaluations of who is employed and how the employer–employee relationship is managed.

The following section shifts our discussion away from a review of how HRP is approached to a broader discussion of managing the strategic issues associated with an over- or undersupply of labour and with attempts to maintain the employee–employer relationship during these periods.

THE STRATEGIC ROLE OF HRP

Restructuring and downsizing

Over the last two decades, technological and market changes have prompted major reviews of organisational processes and structure. During periods of economic uncertainty, firms struggle to find ways to cut costs and become more efficient and effective. Payroll expenses and employee downsizing are often targeted during periods of recession, for example, as a way to boost company profits (Cascio and Wynn, 2004).

The promise of workforce reduction is an immediate reduction of costs, coupled with increased levels of efficiency, productivity, and competitiveness (Farrell and Mavondo, 2004; Iverson and Zatzick, 2007). Unfortunately, the expectations of economic benefits following employee reductions are often not realised (Gandolfy, 2008). In an analysis of the financial impact of downsizing, Cascio and Wynn (2004) compared employers adopting a stable position with those who chose to downsize and found no consistent evidence to support the notion that employment downsizing led to an improvement in financial indicators such as return on assets.

The economic premise that profit is driven by either a reduction in costs or an increase in revenues is complicated by the human reactions associated with a reduction in the workforce. Organisations face problems with diminished productivity and loyalty and loss of critical organisational knowledge. The negative consequences of an organisational downsizing response can include heightened levels of stress, conflict, role ambiguity, and job dissatisfaction among employees (Appelbaum et al., 1999).

Downsizing survivors – those employees who remain in the organisation – generally find themselves with increased workloads and responsibilities without the necessary training and support. These stresses result in a range of mental and physical illness that impact on the quality of their work. Indeed, Gandolfy (2008), in a review of the research in the area, has shown that the 'victims', or those who are involuntarily downsized out of the job, report more positive outcomes than employees who stay. Victims commonly received transition packages and outplacement services and support, felt lower levels of stress in the job, and experienced fewer negative effects than survivors. Such conditions may also encourage talented employees who are already comfortable with mobility to leave organisations that do not offer the appropriate opportunities for development and advancement.

A primary reason given for the negative consequences associated with downsizing is the poor execution and management of these reduction initiatives (Appelbaum et al., 1999). It is possible, however, to strategically manage workforce reductions and tensions during periods of economic stress through effective HRM approaches. Cascio and Wynn (2004) similarly argue that downsizing remains a viable and sometimes necessary response to environmental pressure but reinforce that how the process is executed is critical. Specifically, employees' involvement and input are key in creating a sense of psychological control over events that have such major personal consequences. Avoiding rumours by honest, consistent, and regular communication from the executive group can also assist in reducing stress levels.

Ethical factors in downsizing

Wilcox and Lowry, in Chapter 5, point out that most, if not all, areas of HRM practice involve ethical considerations, and the following discussion highlights how the area of downsizing, as an HRP initiative, is not a morally neutral event.

The argument can be made that resource munificence, or abundance, may be grounds for judging whether a particular instance of downsizing is morally or socially responsible (Van Buren, 2000). In other words, an organisation's resource base can be used to evaluate the extent of its obligations to 'downsized' employees. Based on assumptions made about relationships within the psychological and social contracts between employers and their employees, the expectation is that employment should be stable and secure if firms are doing well. When organisations engage in downsizing merely to increase an already adequate rate of profit, however, they are likely to be held more culpable for such actions than when environmental forces such as technological change or competitive conditions constrain them. Consistent with this, when organisations are characterised by declining resource munificence, or abundance, downsizing is more ethically justifiable.

Zyglidopoulos (2003) empirically investigated the impact of downsizing on a firm's reputation for corporate social performance (RCSP) and found not only that downsizing had a negative impact on the firm's reputation but also that firms that experienced higher financial performance prior to downsizing suffered a greater negative impact on their RCSP. The research therefore indicated that, despite the apparent validity of downsizing as a structural response to economic stress, managers have implicit psychological and social contracts with and ethical responsibilities towards their employees, and these are carefully monitored by stakeholders. When these contracts are broken, the impact on the company's reputation can be such that companies that want to re-hire qualified employees after a downsizing cycle may find it more difficult to do so because of the damage done to their RCSP.

Later, Zyglidopoulos (2005) compared downsizing with 'downscoping', in which the structural response is to divest or sell off organisational divisions. Within downscoping, employees swap employers but do not necessarily lose their jobs. A comparison between these approaches revealed that although both restructuring attempts have negative impacts on corporate reputation, downsizing has more damaging ramifications within the market.

A further important ethical consideration within downsizing is how the process is carried out. Issues associated with procedural justice – the fairness and equity of the procedures that are used to make decisions – are critical and have important consequences for employees' behaviours and attitudes. Fair processes encourage organisational citizenship behaviour or discretionary behaviours lying outside the employees' formal roles that support and assist an organisation during a period of economic stress rather than work against it. These approaches provide survivors with a reason to stay and, importantly, give future prospective new hires a reason to join (Cascio and Wynn, 2004).

Zatzick and Iverson (2006) reinforce the on-going impact that careful HRM practices can make during a period of downsizing. They have established that firms that continue to invest in their employees through the use of HRM practices designed to provide employees with skills, information, motivation, and latitude can assist in maintaining workforce productivity during periods of reduction in the workforce. The argument is made that investment in these practices lessens perceived contract breaches as employees continue to receive opportunities for skill development as well as reassurance of their value in the workplace.

STOP AND REFLECT

HOW IMPORTANT IS PROCEDURAL JUSTICE IN DOWNSIZING?

In a study of the experience of workers in the European recession in France, Hungary, Sweden, and the United Kingdom, Brenner et al. (2014) established that downsizing has become highly common during the global recession of the late 2000s. The findings of the study revealed that affected employees were commonly impacted with depressive symptoms. What was interesting, however, was that where employees perceived that there had been attempts to ensure procedural justice, a socially responsible downsizing process, depressive symptoms were considerably mitigated.

Source: Brenner et al. (2014).

MEETING HUMAN RESOURCE PLANNING CHALLENGES THROUGH FLEXIBILITY

The preceding discussion has highlighted the HRP techniques that can be employed to match supply and demand. In reality, however, environmental factors such as economic uncertainty, technological change, demographic changes, and shifts in values often pose substantial difficulties that limit the success of the HRP process. HRP approaches that do not build in adaptive labour responses may therefore fail to meet environmental challenges. These realities have led to the emergence of flexible options within HRP as a way of managing fluctuations in the supply and demand of labour.

The concept of the flexible model of the firm was developed by Atkinson (1984) as an alternative to traditional hierarchical structures. The model redefines the organisation's workforce into two main segments: the *core* and the *periphery*. The core workforce is made up of permanent, highly skilled workers, and the peripheral workforce is made up of a range of temporary employment arrangements. Flexibility options underpin the management of these labour classifications:

- *Functional flexibility* involves opportunities for role and task variety and is normally associated with the core workforce. Higher levels of training and development in these core workers means that they tend to experience higher levels of job security (Burgess, 1997).
- *Numerical flexibility*, as the name suggests, refers to techniques to vary the quantity of labour on hand, rather than being related to investments in the range and scope of the employee skill base. Internal numerical flexibility refers to the amount and time of labour input required of existing employees; overtime and flex-time are examples of this type of flexibility (Rimmer and Zappala, 1988). Alternatively, external numerical flexibility involves changing the actual number of employees as well as the hours that they work. This latter type of numerical flexibility covers the arrangements made with casual or temporary workers who are called in when needed but do not benefit from a permanent contractual relationship with the employer.

Both functional and numerical flexibility are facilitated by financial and procedural flexibility:

- *Financial flexibility* refers to the compensation system that builds in variations in wages for different types of worker (Atkinson, 1984). These arrangements allow organisations to reward and therefore encourage skill development in the core workforce.
- Finally, *procedural flexibility* is critical in that it provides the consultative mechanisms for introducing the other forms of flexibility through changes in both legal and traditional practices covering employment (Boyer, 1988).

Mini Case Study Functional flexibility or work intensification?

Professor Francis Green, a labour economist, confirms that the emergent emphasis on multiskilling, or functional flexibility, has led to a more efficient use of labour but has also led to problems for employees who are managing a more diverse set of work expectations. The requirement to attend to a greater diversity of tasks, often supported by technological advances that allow multitasking, has meant that the worker has to deal with conflicting demands. Green argues that the British workforce has experienced a dramatic 'upskilling' over the last generation, as they have shifted the bulk of their work onto computers. At the same time as they have been mastering new technology, the demands on them have multiplied. The result of the increase in work demands is a more stressed workforce (Bunting, 2003).

Research conducted in the Philippines by Lu (2009) confirms the impact of work intensification (the workload for each worker), and work extensification (the reduction in work rest) on the ill health in women in manufacturing work. Globalisation has had a major impact in the Philippines where economic liberalisation has seen the deregulation of goods and services and the privatisation of government-owned companies. Presidential decrees in the Philippines have enforced a blanket on strikes and relieved employers of the obligation to pay overtime.

Consistent with trends elsewhere, global competition has induced downsizing in companies in the Philippines and promoted the need for multiskilled workers capable of multitasking. A key industry focus is in electronics and garment manufacturing in which there is a preference for female over male labourers. Lu's (2009) study documented various illnesses experienced by women workers as a result of work intensification and work extensification. Reproductive dysfunctions were reported by women who work at the soldering workstations in electronic establishments along with musculoskeletal stress. Women also reported that the need for upskilling and too much concentration in coping with the pace of the machines, the coordination between worker and the machine, as well as tiring visual strain in inspecting minute chips during the entire workshift, produced anxiety-related problems. According to the women, mental and psychological ill health were not uncommon in the workplace.

Questions

1 What are the negative outcomes of functional flexibility reported in the case?
2 What steps could be taken to reduce the impact of the flexibility response?

Sources: Bunting (2003); Lu (2009).

The promise of these forms of flexibility to help organisations respond more easily to environmental fluctuations and match labour resources more closely with variations in supply and demand have led to major shifts in the workforce profile. A trend has been the increase in the use of temporary workers or workers who are assigned by an employment agency to an employer for a set period of time. 'Temporary employment' is defined as a relationship among three players: the temporary employment agency, the employee who is on an assignment for a set period of time, and the employer. A 2014 study by *Page Personnel*, reported the global rise of temporary employment. Three in five professionals and one in three employers worldwide expect to see a rise in the need for temporary employment, with predictions of stronger growth in countries such as Portugal, Spain, and Italy.

Despite the benefits in terms of flexibility that are offered by alternative forms of work, the arrangements create numerous challenges for both employees and organisations. For the employee, casual work is closely associated with poor working conditions, including low hourly rates of pay, low and irregular earnings, reduced employment security, lack of access to notice and severance pay, reduced access to unfair dismissal rights, vulnerability to changes in schedules, loss of skill- and age-related pay increments, and lack of representational rights (Pocock et al., 2004). For the employer, although using this category of worker is associated with flexibility and often reduced costs, the arrangement does have potentially negative ramifications (Buultjens, 2001). For example, casual workers are, owing to the transient nature of their terms of employment, less likely to identify strongly with the organisation (Hall, 2006); as a result, they may not absorb and display appropriate organisational values and behaviours. The critical thinking Box 6.1 highlights some of the concerns about the work conditions of casual workers.

Critical Thinking 6.1 Casual workers: Are they ultimately hurting the economy?

The percentage of Australians who are estimated to be employed under casual or contract conditions is 35 per cent. The high level has raised concerns from a number of spokespeople, including AMP Capital economist Shane Oliver who has commented 'To have this situation where you are locked into part-time work for a long period can be debilitating.' The Australian Council of Trade Unions (ACTU) have also raised concerns. 'You lose sick leave and you lose annual leave,' President Ged Kearney says. 'You lose carers leave – you also lose things like superannuation and it becomes difficult to get a loan.' Indeed the growing level of employment uncertainty is a concern for many younger people who are entering the workforce, but the situation also impacts on older workers who are looking for work after retrenchments.

There are some advantages to casual and part-time work, as the hours allow for part-time study and flexibility when looking after a family. There is evidence that there are growing numbers of Australians who are choosing casual and part-time jobs, with job websites dedicated entirely to them. Recruitment specialist Don Robertson, for example, recently launched jobflex.com.au to tap into the demand and commented: 'What we've found is Generation Y job seekers are more inclined, are more interested to test a market if you will, in terms of potentially looking at different employment ideas before settling on one career.' Employer groups also argue that workplace flexibility is needed to achieve economic growth. For an employer, the option of being able to call on a ready workforce and then release workers when they are not required strengthens efficiency.

Mr Oliver believes, however, that the casualisation of the Australian workforce is not good for the economy. 'If we fully utilise the resources available to us in the labour market, then we could be having a higher level of economic activity and better living standards flowing from that.'

Source: Palan (2015)

Questions

1   What are the dangers to the Australian economy of a heavily casualised workforce?
2   Despite the proposed benefits to employers of a flexible workforce, what problems does a reliance on such a workforce profile present for organisations?

The limited organisational investment in casual workers also means that these employees may have less opportunity to develop the skills necessary for the job, and therefore the contribution that they make may be limited to generic industry tasks rather than adding real value in terms of the specialised tasks expected by some service providers. Lowry's (2001) investigation of the work arrangements for casual employees within the registered club industry in New South Wales indicated that casual workers are employed on a primarily transactional basis and that their employment conditions are characterised by an underinvestment in employee development (Buultjens, 2001; Lowry, 2001). The impact of an underinvestment in HRM activities such as training and feedback has ramifications for the quality of the service delivery provided by these workers. Lowry's (2001) findings, for example, indicated that some employees were so dissatisfied with the lack of feedback and recognition that they made a conscious decision not to improve the quality of their service. This finding is consistent with the previous research by Schneider et al. (1998), who established a relationship between HRM practices, including training and supportive supervision, and the quality of the service.

Despite the potentially negative ramifications for employees, there is evidence that the move to a greater reliance on non-standard types of worker – those without set hours or the expectation of continued employment – does have benefits for the organisation. Ghosh et al. (2009) have established that the greater use of non-standard workers is positively associated with increased financial performance on the part of the firm. As well as having cost-saving benefits, non-standard arrangements allow firms to give workers a trial of employment before assigning them permanent status.

Moreover, Ghosh et al.'s research indicates that non-standard forms of work are associated with a greater financial impact when firms are operating in less uncertain but more competitive environments. Once uncertainty rises, reliance on non-traditional workers becomes less effective, and when uncertainty is high, a permanent workforce becomes more valuable. Permanent staff's high level of task flexibility and knowledge and expertise specific to the firm help an organisation to sustain itself at a time when conditions are in flux. The argument is that, during periods of greater uncertainty, the core workforce assists the organisation in protecting its technical edge

What is the real impact of a temporary workforce?

In Canada, a study by the United Way and McMaster University in 2013 found only a little over half of the workforce, 50.3 per cent, had standard, full-time jobs. Across Canada, the category of self-employed workers increased almost 45 per cent between 1989 and 2007, according to the Statistics Canada labour survey. These workers include high-tech workers, accountants, social-service sector workers employed by temp agencies, and university lecturers hired on contract. The short-term employment prospects mean that there is a limited career path as workers lurch from one job to the next, get neither training nor benefits nor paid leave and are expected to save for their own pension. Lewchuck, who conducted the research, explained that 'Often they don't know their schedule until the day before, or their schedule changes at the last minute. They don't know where they have to be until just before their shift.' There are also financial issues, as those in insecure employment earned about 46 per cent less than workers in the same field who had standard jobs.

Source: Noakes (2015).

and consolidate activities that are considered important for organisational success (Ghosh et al., 2009). Although flexible forms of work allow companies to shed workers when they are not needed, the attraction and retention of a talented core workforce remains a priority.

Talent management

Vaiman and Vance (2008: 3–4) define talent as including 'all of the employed people within an organisation who may differ dramatically in levels of knowledge, skill and ability'. Although there will be a variation in the critical strategic nature of this talent within an organisation, these authors argue that all employees represent potential sources of valuable knowledge.

Ulrich (2006) provides a more specific definition and characterises 'talent' in two ways. The first is as competence, or an individual's knowledge, skills and values that are required for both the present and the future. Second, Ulrich specifies that such employees have commitment, as shown by their capacity to work hard, put the time in to do what they are asked to do, and give their discretionary energy to the firm's success. Finally, these employees make a real contribution and find meaning and purpose in their work.

The recognition of the value of talent comes at a time when, as indicated above, companies are adopting more flexible work practices and moving away from traditional commitments involving permanent work status. These shifts have been accompanied by a changing psychological contract within the employment relationship such that employees will increasingly look for employability rather than employment and will often want to change jobs (Losey, 2005). Indeed, these transitions often occur across borders as international employment markets offer advanced opportunities for development. Firms may

therefore need to refocus their HRM practices on what employees are looking for in order to attract and retain valuable staff.

Although HRM recognises the value of people as assets, this does not mean that HRM approaches always adopt an employee focus (Guest, 2002). The unitarist underpinnings of HRM assume that what is good for the organisation is also good for its employees (Legge, 2005). In times of economic stress, however, when organisations may constrict employees' conditions and benefits, it may become increasingly difficult for employees to see any evidence of employer and employee goal alignment. The view of people as a compliant organisational resource is further challenged by an increasingly well-educated workforce and generational shifts in the values of the workforce that now emphasise both challenging work and an acceptable work–life balance (Guest et al., 2003). Uncertain economic conditions may therefore heighten the need to become more employee-focused in order to retain existing talented employees.

Guest (2002) has previously provided some guidance on how to test for employee-focused HRM approaches by exploring the impact of various HRM approaches on employees' reports of work satisfaction. Results indicated that key HRM practices related to work satisfaction included those associated with the high-performance work systems approach discussed by Zatzick and Iverson (2006). Notably, these included efforts to make work more interesting and challenging, direct participation, and the extensive provision of information. Guest (2002) also identified the importance of a further set of more bureaucratic employee-oriented practices including family-friendly, equal opportunity, and anti-harassment initiatives. Pocock (2005) similarly makes the business case for a link between work–life balance and the attraction and retention of a firm's workers. The increase in the number of women in the workforce, coupled with an ageing population base that requires carers, increases the need for companies to support valued employees who have family responsibilities.

Along with these HRM practices, employees' expectations for personal growth, as reported by both Edgar and Geare (2005) and Boxall et al. (2003), are useful in designing employee-focused HRM. Boxall et al. (2003) identified training opportunities as a factor determining employees' decisions to leave their employer. This is consistent with the changing psychological contract that focuses individuals on their own personal development needs (Sheehan et al., 2006). Employees now tend to have a greater appreciation of opportunities to upgrade their knowledge, skills, and abilities so that they can remain in demand in the wider employment market (Holland et al., 2007).

Beechler and Woodward (2009) have identified a number of organisations that are implementing new practices to retain valuable employees. Within the accounting profession, where the supply of new talent is well below the anticipated demand and where professional service firms are finding it difficult to retain young associates who are focused on self-development, Deloitte, one of the 'Big Four'

global accounting and consulting firms, is engaging in what it calls 'mass career customisation'. This programme assists employees to map their careers through a series of interactive exercises and online resources. Other organisations have increased their emphasis on formal training. Goldman Sachs, for example, has set up the Goldman Sachs University. Australia's Macquarie Group, the international investment house, has similarly displayed a commitment to formal training, creating a partnership with INSEAD in 2006 in order to provide the first corporate-specific Master's degree from a top-tier business school. Despite the changing psychological contract and the current tendency for employees to move more freely between organisations, it is clear that many companies are taking quite specific steps to engage and retain talented employees.

One potential new labour source that has been on the rise involves company internships. While it is possible that businesses and other organisations may be motivated to accept interns as cheap labour, they are also a way to recruit and test new talent. Despite the possible benefits for both employees and prospective employers, however, these arrangements pose challenges for both parties as demonstrated in the critical thinking Box 6.2.

(?) **Critical Thinking 6.2 The value of internships**

New figures published in *The Australian Financial Review/GradConnection* list of *The top 50 most popular internship employers* show that thousands of undergraduate students are applying for vacation internships as a way to secure employment (Callaghan, 2015).

From the employers' perspective, such arrangements allow them to capture skilled employees before they are properly qualified to enter the labour market in their chosen area. Director of the *GradConnection* graduate job placement service Mike Casey has commented, 'What we see from our clients is that the majority use internship programs as a kind of "try before you buy" in preparation for their graduate programs.' At Deloitte, the firm looks for students with degree backgrounds and those who are able to bring diverse experiences or backgrounds to the consultancy. 'We try and offer a fun and engaging program that aims to support summer vacationers and interns to determine their future career direction and to experience all the elements that make Deloitte a great place to start their careers,' says Gemma Hudson, Deloitte talent graduate manager. 'There is the opportunity to be offered a graduate role for the future as a result of their placement with us.' (Callaghan, 2015).

Such graduate placements are popular in creative industries such as the media, advertising and public relations where it is important to see how a prospective employee applies the knowledge that he or she has learnt at university. There have, however, been reactions about the amount of work that is being expected of interns and the trend towards internships becoming a cheaper and easier substitute for paid work (Redrup, Han and Tadros, 2014). There are also dangers for employers who do not monitor the employment conditions of interns in the same way as permanent staff. Resultant intern experiences raise questions about the risks of reputation damage for the business or even loss of intellectual property or other secrets that could come from a disgruntled former intern. 'Employers need to be aware that there are risks and need to think about the steps they can take before interns come in, like what will the person be exposed to, what will they be doing?' says Middletons employment and industrial relations lawyer Lucy Shanahan. 'Have we defined anything we don't want them to be exposed to? And what can we do to limit that exposure?' (Bleby, 2012).

Many talented workers are willing to work for free in exchange for experience, but there are risks to companies who are not aware of their legal obligations before taking on unpaid interns. A partner of Middletons law firm's workplace relations and safety group, Seamus Burke, says that in its most simple form, an unpaid engagement (with the exception of accredited vocational placements) that exceeds simple observation and shadowing activities could be classified as employment and requires compensation. 'The rules are there really to deliver experience by osmosis.'

However, Burke says it's difficult to ascertain just who derives the benefit from an internship. 'Someone might say that they're willing to get experience, to do whatever jobs you ask them to do and then three months down the line, they then say it's a situation of employment and the employer is subject to compensation claims.' (Hutchinson, 2012).

Sources: Bleby (2012); Callaghan (2015); Hutchinson (2012); Redrup et al. (2014).

Questions

1 The companies that offer internships are providing students with a valuable opportunity to gain experience, so why should they go out of their way to make sure that students enjoy the experience?
2 How can companies ensure that interns have the same value alignment as permanent employees with the company? Is such value alignment actually necessary?

Class Activity

It could be argued that employee retention should not always be a priority – an important aspect of talent management may instead lie in acknowledging the fact that employees may at some point need to leave the organisation. Perhaps the focus should be on employees' engagement in their job while they are in the organisation rather than employee retention for its own sake.

▸ What situational factors are likely to promote this argument?

International considerations

As noted in the opening case, one of the developments resulting from new forms of work organisation as an HRP response has been an increase in the outsourcing of work and the resultant 'offshoring' of tasks to overseas providers. Offshoring refers to work that is not constrained by a need for actual customer contact or local knowledge, meaning that it can therefore be provided remotely or globally (Farrell et al., 2005). The key benefit from offshoring is the economic return of replacing high-wage labour costs with lower costs. Offshoring is also seen as a way of enabling organisations to focus their resources on their core business (Domberger, 1994).

The HRP decision to source labour from international sites is not without its complications. Often, the complexity or idiosyncratic nature of a particular set of tasks makes the move offshore difficult. A further issue is the lack of maturity in the newly developing offshoring market. Middle management

skills, for example, may still be under development in the target countries, and services may not meet the expectations of the companies that are choosing to relocate their operations overseas (Farrell et al., 2005). Connected with this is a generalised concern about the suitability of labour to fit with the quality of service demanded by customers. Key suitability factors include problems with language skills, an educational system that does not emphasise interpersonal skills and attitudes towards teamwork, and cultural fit. Tangible savings could be lost if these issues associated with quality and service are not managed (Nash et al., 2004).

These issues require additional monitoring to ensure that quality and service are being delivered in an appropriate manner. Shiu (2004) concludes that the aforementioned issues of culture, language, service integration, and maintenance will require time for clients and customers to adjust, and this may not always be an option for a firm that is trying to make strategic headway in a timely manner.

CONCLUSION

This chapter has provided an overview of technical approaches to HRP as well as a discussion of some of the strategic challenges that are now being incorporated into HRP thinking. As a strategic mechanism, HRP is not simply a matter of ensuring that a firm meets swings in the supply and demand of labour but rather that the process adds real value when addressing the strategic needs of the company. The strategic imperative has been heightened by environmental changes associated with increasing levels of uncertainty and competition.

These forces have alerted companies to the value of the people resource and have led to a rethink of traditional responses to an over- or undersupply or demand for labour. Downsizing to deal with a drop in labour demand, for example, has in the past been adopted as a necessary cost-cutting measure. Although this response is still used, the process is now more likely to factor in the impact on employees and ensure that workers are informed and have some sense of personal control. Such an approach assists in keeping employees engaged in the strategic goals of the company and also enhances the firm's corporate reputation.

Changes in the flexibility of work organisation have also been used to deal with variations in the supply and demand of labour and have resulted in a shift in the expectations of workers in terms of permanent work arrangements. Although this helps companies to deal with changes in demand patterns, it has also raised issues relating to employee loyalty and commitment. Revised expectations on the part of the workforce's employees have led companies to think more carefully about the relationships that they develop with their workers, especially those who provide critical talent resources. Even during periods of a slow-down in labour demand, firms have become more mindful of the importance of attracting and retaining talent. Overall, HRP has evolved considerably and has moved beyond a mere matching of labour needs with output requirements to incorporate a strategic view of the people resource and the impact that it can ultimately make on sustained competitive advantage.

End of Chapter Case Study Play Smart Toys

Five years ago Ken Williams gave up his job as a primary school teacher and founded the *Play Smart Toys Company*. It was clear to him at the time that there was a gap in the market for toys that challenged the thinking of children. As a teacher he had developed a number of games and puzzles for his students, and other teachers and parents wanted to use his ideas. With the help of a small management team, Ken developed a line of specialty toys that made a big impact on the market. Now *Play Smart Toys* has a large production site in Melbourne that employs over 100 staff with a product line that is sold in five specialty stores in Melbourne, Sydney, and Canberra as well as a steady line of sales in most of the major department stores. The products are also being sold in Singapore and Hong Kong and Ken hopes to break into the Chinese market in the next twelve months.

The growth of the company has been quite remarkable. At first the company employed about 20 staff, but as demand increased the business went from a small operation to a much larger concern, employing a permanent production staff. This group is supported by permanent staff working in support roles such as logistics, product design, personnel, sales and accounting, and finance.

Despite steady sales figures, profits during 2013 and into the first part of 2014 were down. At the time the accountant, Tom Boxall, explained to Ken that profit was falling because costs were increasing. The cost management figures showed increasing scrap and wastage rates and rising labour costs. Along with these cost increases there were further issues that were of a concern to Ken. First there were efficiency problems with the production staff: at times staff were hanging around not doing anything, yet at other times when the number of orders increased, people were stressed and working flat out. Variations in orders were the results of seasonal swings in toy demand associated with peak periods such as Christmas and Easter. Second, despite a record of good staff loyalty the company was having problems with staff retention. This was particularly an issue with the skilled staff on the floor but several key product design people had also left along with an IT specialist who had only been with the company for six months. The number of workplace accidents was also on the rise and Sandra, one of the machine operators, had approached the personnel officer, Jill Williams, to suggest that some of the workers failed to take enough care around the machinery. She also pointed out that at times the increasing cohort of workers from ethnic backgrounds felt uncomfortable with the way that existing staff spoke to them. Sandra suggested that if the issue was not dealt with appropriately the company could have a number of harassment cases to deal with.

By mid-2014 Ken had become so worried about declining performance and the staffing problems that he employed a consultant to find out what was going on. In September Ken met with the consultant, John Smith, and at the time John explained that most of the problems seem to be connected with the very quick growth of the company and, as is often the case with companies that grow at an accelerated rate, the HRM approach had not kept up with the expansion. With respect to workforce planning for example *Play Smart Toys* had not really planned its workforce around peak demand periods. Furthermore, whether Ken realised it or not, the workforce that he had in place was probably quite different from the workforce that he had had five years ago. John also observed that there was discontent within the skilled workforce who felt that they were not receiving enough professional development. This was exacerbated by the fact that all of the senior positions were taken up by the existing management group, and other employees could not see a career path for themselves in the organisation. John submitted his final report in late October 2014. Ken briefly read through the executive summary, and basically John seemed to be pushing for 'a more strategic approach to HRM'.

In 2015 sales began to fall and the economic situation really started to hit *Play Smart Toys*. During this time Tom Boxall reminded Ken that one of the major cost blowouts in 2014 had been associated with labour, and really if the company was going to survive it was going to have to cut its labour force – basically the company was going to have to downsize until conditions improved. Ken realised the practicality of this suggestion but was still concerned about the impact of such a message, especially in view of the comments that had been made by John Smith in late 2014. Ken decided to invite John Smith to come along to the next management meeting to discuss the company response to the downturn and provide some insights based on John's investigation from the previous year.

Ken rang John Smith to ask him if he would attend the management meeting, and John was pleased to be involved. Ken explained that *Play Smart Toys* were looking at downsizing the workforce, and John agreed that this was a reasonable and necessary response. John also made the observation, however, that in light of the staff problems from last year any downsizing approaches would have to be handled extremely carefully. John commented, 'Prior to the most recent downturn you already had problems with the workforce. The lack of an effective HRM approach that kept up with your expansion was becoming a major problem. You really needed at that time to look at your workflows and how your jobs were designed. You were also losing important staff. Now if you inform staff that they are going to lose their jobs, existing problems might be made worse. When I come to see you next week we need to re-think how you are managing some key HRM issues.'

As he rang off, Ken wondered whether getting John Smith involved was actually going to be a good idea – it might just complicate matters. He thought to himself that people either wanted to work for the company or they didn't. If they weren't happy at *Play Smart Toys* they would have to find work elsewhere – at least if they went, it would get rid of some of the labour cost problems.

Questions

1   What are the HRM problems and issues facing *Play Smart Toys*?
2   What sort of HRM approaches do you think need to be taken to ensure on-going strategic competitive advantage?

FOR DISCUSSION AND REVISION

1   What are the HRP implications associated with an increase in the services sector?
2   Do you agree that environmental changes render HRP so problematic that it becomes infeasible? Is there a way to approach HRP under volatile conditions that still adds value?
3   Discuss why some commentators argue that job descriptions have become redundant.
4   How can an organisation's resource munificence, or abundance, be used to assess whether downsizing is a morally or socially appropriate response?
5   If an organisation is committed to retaining talented workers, what sort of HRM initiatives may assist in the retention of valuable workers?

GLOSSARY

Human Resource Planning (HRP): the matching of projected human resource demand with its anticipated supply.

Labour demand forecasting in HRM: the determination of the quantity and quality of employees required to meet the organisation's goals.

Quantitative approaches to labour demand forecasting: statistical techniques and mathematical modelling used to predict changes in labour demand.

Qualitative approaches to labour demand forecasting: the use of expert opinions to determine possible changes in labour demand.

Labour trend projection: time series analysis that processes past and present information on the number of people hired in various departments, job categories or skills areas that, based on any observed increases or decreases, forms predictions about labour demand into the future.

Labour supply forecasting: the use of internal and external sources of HRM information that informs the supply of employees.

Job analysis: an analysis that determines what each job involves and who is required for the job before specific staffing decisions can be made.

Downsizing: a permanent reduction in the number of employees on the operating payroll.

Downsizing survivors: those employees who are retained in the organisation following a downsizing event.

Downscoping: a structural response in which an organisation divests or sells off organisational divisions. Employees may be transferred to other divisions and do not necessarily lose their jobs.

Functional flexibility: employee opportunities for role and task variety, normally associated with the core workforce.

Numerical flexibility: techniques to vary the quantity of labour on hand.

Financial flexibility: a compensation system that builds in variations in wages for different types of worker.

Procedural flexibility: consultative mechanisms for introducing the other forms of flexibility through changes in both legal and traditional practices covering employment.

Temporary workers: workers who are assigned by an employment agency to an employer for a set period of time.

Offshoring: the globally remote provision of work that is not constrained by a need for actual costumer contact or local knowledge.

FURTHER READING

BERGER, L. A. AND BERGER, D. R. (2011) *The Talent Management Handbook: Creating a Sustainable Competitive Advantage by Selecting, Developing, and Promoting the Best People* (2nd edn). New York: McGraw-Hill.

BOXALL, P. AND PURCELL, J. (2015) *Strategy and Human Resource Management*. Basingstoke: Palgrave Macmillan.

CAPLAN, J. (2011) *The Value of Talent: Promoting Talent Management across the Organization*. London: Kogan Page.

CASCIO, W. (2010) *Managing Human Resources: Productivity, Quality of Work Life, Profits*. Boston: McGraw-Hill/Irwin.

DELAHAYE, B. (2011) *Human Resource Development: Managing Learning and Knowledge Capital*. Prahran: Tilde University Press.

GUEST, D. (2004) Flexible employment contracts, the psychological contract and employment outcomes: An analysis and review of the evidence. *International Journal of Management Reviews*, 5/6(1): 1–19.

GRANT, R. (2003) Strategic planning in a turbulent environment: evidence from the oil majors. *Strategic Management Journal*, 24(6): 491–517.

HARTEL, C. E. J., FUJIMOTO, Y., STRYBOSCH, V. E. AND FITZPATRICK, K. (2007) *Human Resource Management. Transforming Theory into Innovative Practice*. French's Forest, NSW: Pearson.

KRAMAR, R., BARTRAM, T., DE CIERI, H., NOE, R., HOLLENBECK, J., GERHART, B. AND WRIGHT, P. (2010) *Human Resource Management in Australia* (4th edn). Sydney: McGraw-Hill.

LEPAK, D. AND SNELL, S. (2002) Examining the human resource architecture: The relationships among human capital, employment and human resource configurations. *Journal of Management*, 28(4): 517–543.

TEICHER, J., HOLLAND, P. AND GOUGH, R. (eds) (2006) *Employee Relations Management: Australia in a Global Context* (2nd edn). Frenchs Forest, NSW: Prentice Hall.

TSUI, A., PEARCE, J., PORTER, L. AND HITE, J. (1995) Alternative approaches to the employee-organizational relationship: Does investment in employees pay off? *Academy of Management Journal*, 44: 1089–10121.

WITHERS, M., WILLIAMSON, M. AND REDDINGTON, M. (2010) *Transforming HR: Creating Value Through People* (2nd edn). Amsterdam: Butterworth-Heinemann.ENDFR

WEB RESOURCES

Lessons from GM Holden on how to manage a reduction in production. Available at: http://www.hrmonline.com.au/section/profiles/hrm-tv-holden-restructure-lessons-learnt/.

Diverted to Delhi – Commentary on the outsourcing of jobs overseas. Available at: http://www.youtube.com/watch?v=2vvCKoETTF0.

Is a bad job better than no job at all? Dr Liana Leach. Available at: http://www.youtube.com/watch?v=TpcHlVSQV3s.

REFERENCES

APPELBAUM, S., EVERARD, A. AND HUNG, L. T. S. (1999) Strategic downsizing: Critical success factors. *Management Decisions*, 37(7): 535–552.

ATKINSON, J. (1984) Manpower strategies for flexible organisations. *Personnel Management*, (August): 28–31.

Australian, The (2009a) Others to follow bank's executive pay cuts. Available at: http://www.theaustralian.com.au/business/news/bank-pay-cuts-set-trend/story-e6frg906-1225700359387. Accessed 20 January 2016.

Australian, The (2009b) Holden trims shifts to avoid layoffs. Available at: http://theage.drive.com.au/motor-news/holden-axes-600-jobs-in-adelaide-20070305-140fo.html. Accessed 20 January 2016.

Australian Bureau of Statistics (2006) *Yearbook Australia 2006*. Cat. No. 1301.0. Canberra: Australian Bureau of Statistics.

BARNEY, J. B. AND WRIGHT, P. M. (1998) On becoming a strategic partner: The role of human resources in gaining competitive advantage. *Human Resource Management*, 37(1): 31–46.

BEECHLER, S. AND WOODWARD, I. C. (2009) The global 'war for talent'. *Journal of International Management*, 15(3): 273–285.

BLEBY, M. (2012) Can you trust interns? *BRW*. Available at: http://www.brw.com.au/p/sections/fyi/can_you_trust_interns_xZrnoPNz7rIx4tlMHP6bbL. Accessed 21 July 2015.

BLYTON, P. (1989) Working population and employment. In Bean, R. (ed.), *International Labour Statistics*. London: Routledge, pp. 18–51.

BOXALL, P., MACKY, K. AND RASMUSSEN, E. (2003) Labour turnover and retention in New Zealand: The causes and consequences of leaving and staying with employers. *Asia Pacific Journal of Human Resources*, 41(2): 195–214.

BOYER, R. (1988) *The Search for Labour Market Flexibility: The European Economies in Transition*. Oxford: Clarendon Press.

BRANNICK, M. T., LEVINE, E. L. AND MORGESON, F. P. (2007) *Job and Work Analysis: Methods, Research, and Applications for Human Resource Management* (2nd edn). Los Angeles: Sage.

BRENNER, H., ANDREEVA, E., THEORELL, T. , GOLDBERG, M., WESTERLUND, H. , LEINEWEBER, C., HANSON, L., IMBERNON, E. AND BONNAUD, S. (2014) Organisational downsizing and depressive symptoms in the European recession: The experience of workers in France, Hungary, Sweden and the United Kingdom. *PLoS One*, 19:9(5): e97063. Available at: http://www.ncbi.nlm.nih.gov/pubmed/24841779.

BUNTING, M. (2003) Hard work is getting harder. Available at: http://www.theguardian.com/money/2003/mar/26/madeleinebunting.

BURGESS, J. (1997) The flexible firm and growth of non-standard employment. *Labour and Industry*, 7(3): 85–102.

BURGESS, J. AND CAMPBELL, I. (1998) Casual employment in Australia: Growth, characteristics, a bridge or trap? *Economic and Labour Relations Review*, 9(1): 31–54.

BUULTJENS, J. (2001) Casual employment: A problematic strategy for the registered clubs sector in New South Wales. *Journal of Industrial Relations*, 43(4): 470–477.

CALLAGHAN, R. (2015) Students choose internships as fast track to jobs. *Financial Review*. Available at: http://www.afr.com/leadership/management/business-education/students-choose-internships-as-fast-track-to-jobs-20150719-gidaao. Accessed 21 July 2015.

CAMPBELL, I. AND BURGESS, J. (2001) Casual employment in Australia and temporary employment in Europe: Developing a cross-national comparison. *Work, Employment and Society*, 15(1): 171–184.

CASCIO, W. AND WYNN, P. (2004) Managing a downsizing process. *Human Resource Management*, 43(4): 425–436.

Corporate Leadership Council (2008) *HR Quarterly Trends Report*. Q4 – 2008, Catalogue Number CLC2456755.

DOMBERGER, S. (1994) Public sector contracting: Does it work? *Australian Economic Review*, (Third quarter): 91–96.

DORNIN, T. (2007) Holden axes 600 jobs in Adelaide. Available at: http://www.drive.com.au/motor-news/holden-axes-600-jobs-in-adelaide-20070305-140fo.html. Accessed 20 January 2016.

EDGAR, F. AND GEARE, A. (2005) Employee voice on human resource management. *Asia Pacific Journal of Human Resources*, 43(3): 361–380.

FARRELL, D., LABOISSEIRE, M., PASCAL, R., ROSENFELD, J., DE SEGUNDO, C., STURZE, S. AND UMEZAWA, F. (2005) *The Emerging Global Labour Market*. McKinsey Global Institute. Available at: http://www.mckinsey.com/insights/employment_and_growth/the_emerging_global_labor_market. Accessed 21 January 2016.

FARRELL, M. AND MAVONDO, F. (2004) The effect of downsizing strategy and reorientation strategy on a learning orientation. *Personnel Review*, 33(4): 383–402.

GANDOLFY, F. (2008) Learning from the past – downsizing lessons for managers. *Journal of Management Research*, 8(1): 3–17.

GHOSH, D., WILLINGER, G. L. AND GHOSH, S. (2009) A firm's external environment and the hiring of a non-standard workforce: implications for organisations. *Human Resource Management Journal*, 19(4): 433–451.

GRAHAM, D. (2012) The case for 'offshoring' is quite clear: It works. *The Age Business Day*. Available at: http://www.smh.com.au/business/the-case-for-offshoring-is-quite-clear-it-works-20120419-1x9yd.html#ixzz3gTcKhY6o. Accessed 21 July 2015.

GRIFFITHS, E. (2014) Holden to cease manufacturing operations in Australia in 2017. Available at: http://www.abc.net.au/news/2013-12-11/holden-to-cease-manufacturing-operations-in-australia-by-2017/5150034. Accessed 22 July 2015.

GUEST, D. (2002) Human resource management, corporate performance and employee wellbeing: building the worker into HRM. *Journal of Industrial Relations*, 44(3): 335–358.

GUEST, D., MICHIE, J., CONWAY, N. AND SHEEHAN, M. (2003) Human resource management and corporate performance in the UK. *British Journal of Industrial Relations*, 41(2): 291–314.

HALL, R. (2006) Temporary agency work and HRM in Australia: 'Cooperation, specialization and satisfaction for the good of all'? *Personnel Review*, 35(2): 158–174.

HOCHSCHILD, A. R. (1983) *The Managed Heart: Commercialization of Human Feeling*. Berkeley, CA: University of California Press.

HOLLAND, P., SHEEHAN, C. AND DE CIERI, H. (2007) Attracting and retaining talent: Exploring human resources development trends in Australia. *Human Resource Development International*, 10(3): 247–262.

HUSELID, M. A. (1993) The impact of environmental volatility on human resource planning and strategic human resource management. *Human Resource Planning*, 16(3): 35–51.

HUSELID, M. A. (1995) The impact of human resource management practices on turnover, productivity and corporate financial performance. *Academy of Management Journal*, 38: 635–672.

HUTCHINSON, S. (2012) The intern fights back. *BRW*. Available at: http://www.brw.com.au/p/sections/the_business_end/the_intern_fights_back_Y7ZQciA4jswo23sUOyXvAP?hl. Accessed 21 July 2015.

IVERSON, R. D. AND ZATZICK, D. (2007) High commitment work practices and downsizing harshness in Australian workplaces. *Industrial Relations*, 46(3): 456–480.

JEANNERET, P. R. AND STRONG, M. H. (2003) Linking O*NET job analysis information to job requirement predictors: An O*NET application. *Personnel Psychology*, 56: 465–492.

KALLEBERG, A. (2000) Nonstandard employment relations: Part-time, temporary and contract work. *Annual Review of Sociology*, 26: 341–365.

KRYGER, T. (2004) Casual employment: Trends and characteristics. Research Note No. 53, 2003–4. Canberra: Statistics Section, Australian Parliamentary Library.

KULIK, C., AND BAINBRIDGE, H. T. J. (2006) HR and the Line: The distribution of HR activities in Australian organisations. *The Asia Pacific Journal of Human Resources*, 44(2): 240–256.

LAM, S. S. AND SCHAUBROECK, J. (1998) Integrating HR planning and organisational strategy. *Human Resource Management Journal*, 8(3): 5–19.

LEGGE, K. (2005) *Human Resource Management: Rhetorics and Reality*. Basingstoke: Palgrave Macmillan.

LOSEY, M. (2005) Anticipating change: Will there really be a labor shortage? In Losey, M., Meisinger, S. and Ulrich, D. (eds), *The Future of Human Resource Management*. Virginia: John Wiley and Sons, pp. 23–37.

LOWRY, D. (2001) The casual management of casual work: Casual workers' perceptions of HRM practices in the highly casualised firm. *Asia Pacific Journal of Human Resources*, 39(1): 42–62.

LU, J. (2009) Effect of work intensification and work extensification on women's health in the globalised labour market. *Journal of International Women's Studies* 10(4): 111–126.

MACDONALD, C. L. AND SIRIANNI, C. (eds) (1996) *Working in the Service Society*. Philadelphia: Temple University Press.

NASH, B., HOLLAND, P. J. AND PYMAN, A. (2004) The role and influence of stakeholders in off-shoring: Developing a framework for analysis. *International Employment Relations Review*, 10(2): 20–49.

NOAKES, S. (2015) Secure jobs in short supply in Canada's new tough labour market. Available at: http://www.cbc.ca/news/business/secure-jobs-in-short-supply-in-canada-s-new-tough-labour-market-1.3050449.

O'REILLY, A. (1973) Skill requirements: Supervisor–subordinate conflict. *Personnel Psychology*, 26: 75–80.

Page Personnel (2014) Global insights: How the world views temporary employment and interim management report. Available at: http://www.pagepersonnel.be/media/ppbe/GlobalTempSurvey2014/report/PP_CEA_REPORT_HOW%20THE%20WORLD%20VIEWS%20TEMPORARY%20EMPLOYMENT_EN.pdf. Accessed 15 October 2015.

PALAN, S. (2015) Australia's large casual workforce masking real unemployment rate. Available at: http://www.abc.net.au/news/2013-06-12/australia-casual-workforce-masking-unemployment-figures/4749900. Accessed 22 July 2015.

POCOCK, B. (2005) Work–life 'balance' in Australia: Limited progress, dim prospects. *Asia Pacific Journal of Human Resources*, 43(2): 198–209.

POCOCK, B., BUCHANAN, J. AND CAMPBELL, I. (2004) Meeting the challenge of casual work in Australia: Evidence, past treatment and future policy. *Australian Bulletin of Labour*, 30(1): 16–32.

REDRUP, Y., HAN, M. AND TADROS, E. (2014) Unpaid internships rife in media and marketing industries. *BRW*. Available at: http://www.brw.com.au/p/leadership/unpaid_internships_rife_in_media_glmepoF2RsiE4Lv3wCpjAL. Accessed 21 July 2015.

RIMMER, M. AND ZAPPALA, J. (1988) Labour market flexibility and the second tier. *Australian Bulletin of Labour*, 14(4): 564–591.

ROTHWELL, S. (1995) Human resource planning. In Storey, J. (ed.), *Human Resource Management: A Critical Text*. London: Routledge, pp. 167–201.

RUDD, K., SWAN, W., SMITH, S. AND WONG, P. (2007) *Skilling Australia for the Future: Election 2007 Policy Document.* Canberra: T. Gartrell.

SCHNEIDER, B. AND KONZ, A. M. (1989) Strategic job analysis. *Human Resource Management*, 28(1): 51–63.

SCHNEIDER, B., WHITE, S. AND PAUL, M. (1998) Linking service climate and customer perceptions of service quality: Test of a causal model. *Journal of Applied Psychology*, 8(2): 150–163.

SHEEHAN, C., HOLLAND, P. AND DE CIERI, H. (2006) Current developments in HRM in Australian organisations. *Asia Pacific Journal of Human Resources*, 44(2): 2–22.

SHIU, K. (2004) Outsourcing: Are you sure or offshore? Identifying legal risks in offshoring. *NSW Society for Computers and the Law*, 37(3): 7–10.

SMITH, M. (2005) The incidence of new forms of employment in service activities. In Macdonald, C. and Sirianni, C. (eds), *Working in the Service Society*. Philadelphia: The University Press, pp. 54–73.

STEWART, G. L. AND CARSON, K. P. (1997) Moving beyond the mechanistic model: An alternative approach to staffing for contemporary organizations. *Human Resource Management Review*, 7(2): 157–184.

ULRICH, D. (1987) Strategic human resource planning: Why and how? *Human Resource Planning*, 10(1): 37–56.

ULRICH, D. (2006) The talent trifecta. *Workforce Management*, September: 32–33.

VAIMAN, V. AND VANCE, C. M. (eds) (2008) *Smart Talent Management*. Cheltenham: Edward Elgar.

VAN BUREN, H. J. III (2000) The bindingness of social and psychological contracts: Toward a theory of social responsibility in downsizing. *Journal of Business Ethics*, 25(3): 205–219.

VAN DEN HEUVEL, A. AND WOODEN, M. (1997) Self-employed contractors and job satisfaction. *Journal of Small Business Management*, 35(3): 11–20.

WADE, M. AND HAWTHORNE, M. (2012) Offshoring: High price of low cost. *The Age*. Available at: http://www.smh.com.au/business/offshoring-high-price-of-low-cost-20120127-1qlot.html#ixzz3gTeZblZk. Accessed 21 July 2015.

WRIGHT, P., MCMAHAN, G. AND MCWILLIAMS, A. (1994) Human resources as a source of sustained competitive advantage. *International Journal of Human Resource Management*, 5: 299–324.

YEATES, C., (2012) Bank 'offshoring' risks customers' privacy. *The Age*. Available at: http://www.smh.com.au/business/bank-offshoring-risks-customers-privacy-20121211-2b7gb.html#ixzz3gTbCAh4o. Accessed 21 July 2015.

ZATZICK, C. AND IVERSON, R. D. (2006) High-involvement management and workforce reduction: Competitive advantage or disadvantage? *Academy of Management Journal*, 49: 281–303.

ZULA, K. J. AND CHERMACK, T. J. (2007) Human capital planning: A review of literature and implications for human resource development. *Human Resource Development Review*, 6(3): 245–262.

ZYGLIDOPOULOS, S. C. (2003) The impact of downsizing on the corporate reputation for social performance. *Journal of Public Affairs*, 4(1): 11–25.

ZYGLIDOPOULOS, S. C. (2005) The impact of downsizing on corporate reputation. *British Academy of Management*, 16: 253–259.

JOB AND WORK DESIGN

Peter Holland

LEARNING OUTCOMES

After reading this chapter, you should be able to:

➤ Explain the origins of contemporary job and work design
➤ Outline the different theoretical perspectives involved
➤ Describe and analyse the different practical approaches to job and work design
➤ Describe and analyse the job characteristic model
➤ Discuss the changing dynamics of the workplace in the twenty-first century, exploring contemporary developments in job and work design.

SUMMARY OF CHAPTER CONTENTS

➤ **Opening Case Study**: Work is anything but blue!
➤ Introduction
➤ The classical theory of job and work design – the mechanistic era
➤ The foundations of contemporary theory of job design – the sociotechnical era
➤ Contemporary theory of job and work design – the human relations school
➤ Contemporary theory of job design – the neo-human relations or motivational theorists
➤ Contemporary theory of job and work design – the concertive era
➤ Conclusion
➤ **End of chapter Case Study**: Job design at TechCo
➤ For discussion and revision
➤ Glossary
➤ Further reading
➤ Web resources
➤ References

The impact of technology in the twenty-first century is increasingly being seen in jobs that were considered standard positions that required an office; for example, an airline booking office where the traditional call centre undertaking standardised calls would be the norm. However, through technology the way jobs and work are designed has fundamentally changed. As JetBlue have found, not only can they save on cost by redesigning work but they have increased retention and productivity. JetBlue is a US-based airline carrier that employs 800 reservation agents – nothing special in that except where they work. All of the agents work from home, and there is no physical booking office. Employees log on from home.to undertake their work. The original reasons for this were to reduce turnover associated with commuting to work and then working in a call centre–type environment. Not only has this change in time, place, and space of work reduced turnover, it has increased productivity by 25 per cent. The reason behind this success is a change in mind-set in terms of the way the organisation views how it designs work and jobs.

Question

1 Consider your workplace or university class. How could work and job design be used to increase your productivity?

INTRODUCTION

In this chapter, we will explore the development of job and work design. First, we will examine and review the literature on work organisation and design from classical to contemporary perspectives. This will provide a contextual analysis for the development of 'modern' job and work design and explain how it has evolved, and continues to evolve. It will also discuss, from a human resource perspective, how it plays a critical role in the development of sustained competitive advantage within organisations.

Writing in 1998, Parker and Wall noted that:

These are exciting times for those concerned with job and work design. More than ever before, companies are introducing new forms of work organisation, often involving major changes in the nature of people's jobs. The opportunity to create more fulfilling and effective work is considerable; but so too is the danger of making it worse. (Parker and Wall, 1998: ix)

This quote illustrates the dynamic, complex, and changing times we live in, which are reflected in the changing nature of job and work organisation. In an increasingly deregulated and global work environment, there is immense scope to introduce new patterns of work organisation. However, as Parker and Wall note, the danger of making work worse is also a potential outcome.

As advanced market economies (AMEs) move from a manufacturing to a knowledge- and service-based economy, the need to attract and retain employees has attained critical importance. This is because, in this new work environment, the workers own the means of production – knowledge – and have the ability to move their

valued skills in the external labour market as they focus their knowledge and skill development on employability rather than employment (Drucker, 1998; Holland et al., 2007). Research shows that what attracts and retains skilled workers is exciting and challenging work that has significant development opportunities (Michaels et al., 2001; Newell et al., 2002). These findings are supported by PricewaterhouseCoopers' (2009: 30) 12th Annual Survey of CEOs (involving 1,124 CEOs from more than 50 countries), which shows that 'ninety-seven per cent of CEOs believe that the access to and retention of key talent is critical or important to sustaining growth over the long term'. Therefore, the need for talent management underpinned by quality work has seen a re-emergence of job and work design as critical factors for talent management.

However, in the midst of these new developments, advances in technology have also seen the return of the worst aspects of work organisation. Arguably the most significant sector to develop in the past decade has been that of call centres. This sector has gained a mixed reputation, mainly through how jobs have been designed. Call centres have been variously described as the 'workhouses of the twenty-first century', 'electronic sweatshops', 'dungeons with telephones', and 'assembly lines of the head' (Deery and Kinnie, 2002; Kinnie et al., 2000; Taylor and Bain, 1999), on account of work that is characterised as a narrow range of routine telephone operations underpinned by close monitoring and surveillance (Barnes, 2004; Connell and Harvey, 2004). In the midst of this, however, Salesforce, a Melbourne-based call centre, was awarded the 2004 Australian Employer of Choice Award by the Australian Financial Review and Hewitt and Associates, emphasising the fact that new forms of work do not have to be the same but reflect the dynamic nature of job design.

Before exploring contemporary aspects of job design, it is, however, important to examine the development of modern job and work design so that we can better understand the contemporary nature of work organisation.

THE CLASSICAL THEORY OF JOB AND WORK DESIGN – THE MECHANISTIC ERA

The foundations of modern job and work design can be traced to the economic expansion associated with the Industrial Revolution in the eighteenth century. The increasing scale of production during this period put the traditional craft-based mode of production under pressure to maintain pace. This increasing demand became the catalyst for the development of more efficient and effective work practices (Berg, 1985; Thompson and McHugh, 1995). It was Adam Smith in 1776 (Smith, 1979) who identified that the restructuring of work patterns and practices would be a central factor in increasing organisational efficiency and production. The key features included increased dexterity achieved by one person doing a narrow range of tasks and the application of simple machinery. Through this process of work (re)organisation, the monopoly of skilled workers over production was gradually eroded, allowing for the dual effect of falling labour costs and increased productivity.

The deconstructing of work processes and the development of simple machinery continued to reform work patterns and practices (Mathias, 1969). This facilitated the shift from cottage industries to factories in major urban areas, close to markets, sources of power and cheap unskilled and semi-skilled labour (Berg, 1985; Grint, 1991). Significantly, during this period of rapid industrialisation, the major changes in work occurred in the organisation of the patterns and practices of work, rather than in technology (Hobsbawm, 1968).

Through the nineteenth century, factories developed in both size and complexity, becoming the dominant mode of production (Grint, 1991; Hobsbawm, 1968). The increased complexity of the machines and organisations that emerged during this period was associated with an almost direct correlation with the reduction in the human skills required (Thompson, 1983). However, in terms of efficiency, effectiveness and organisational performance, the organisation of work was still based upon arbitrary decision-making (Merkle, 1980). From this period (and perspective) emerged F. W. Taylor and his concept of scientific management, as described in his seminal books, *Shop Management* (1903) and *The Principles of Scientific Management* (1911).

The techniques of scientific management focused on the elimination of 'rule of thumb' approaches to work organisation and on increasing productivity and efficiency by scientific methodology. As Merkle (1980: 15) notes:

> the core of Taylorism was clearly an explicit call for reconciliation between capital and labour, on the neutral ground of science and rationality.... Science would replace the old tyranny and resistance in industrial society.

The increase in productivity that Taylor described (and demonstrated – see Question 1 in Critical Thinking 7.1, below) during this period of rapid industrialisation ensured that these developments in work organisation would attract attention. Taylor focused on identifying the optimal relationship between the method of production, the time taken, the tools used, and the fatigue generated by the task (Rose, 1988). Although job reconstruction was not a new concept in itself, what was significant with Taylor's methods was the rigorous deconstruction and reconstruction of jobs (eliminating all superfluous actions), 'scientifically – in the one best way', as Nyland (1987) described it.

Despite criticism and resistance (Rose, 1988), scientific management–based job design permeated a wide variety of industries in the first two decades of the 20th century (Chandler, 1977). The significance of scientific management in developing new patterns and practices of work was illustrated by Braverman (1974: 120–122), who stated:

> Modern management came into being on the basis of these principles. It arose as a theoretical construct and as systematic practice, in the very period during which the transformation of labor from processes based on skill to processes based upon science was attaining its most rapid tempo ... It was to ensure that as craft declined, the worker would sink to the level of general and undifferentiated labor power, adaptable to a large range of simple tasks.

In the context of working patterns and practices, the development of scientific management varied across industries. However, the underlying theme of 'science' as the neutral arbitrator of work design provided the framework for it to become the dominant paradigm of work organisation in the twentieth century. The overall effect of scientific management on work organisation was the separation of the conception and execution and the 'systemisation' of work through the reduction of jobs into narrowly defined, repetitive tasks under strict conditions of (management) decision-making and time (Thompson,

1983; Rose, 1988). As Cole (1988) notes, the key features of job design under this system included:

- minimum degrees of job specialisation;
- minimum levels of skill;
- minimum time for completion of the tasks;
- minimum learning time;
- maximum use of machines;
- minimum degree of flexibility or discretion in the job;
- minimum number of job tasks.

In appraising the development and prospects of the scientific management system, Taylor concluded that it would require a revolution for it to become accepted (Rose, 1988). This revolution was to come when the principles of scientific management and the process of mass production were combined. Although Taylor provided the framework, it was the American industrialist Henry Ford who realised the true potential of combining these work patterns and processes (Littler and Salamon, 1982).

The combination of scientific management and mass production allowed for standardisation, continuity and simplification of the production process and, by implication, of work patterns and practices. The success of this mode of production and its associated patterns of work (through the reduction of labour and production costs, and the pace of production being controlled by the speed of the line) gave competitors the option of adopting these patterns of work organisation or surrendering their market share. This allowed Fordism (as it became known) to emerge as the dominant mode of production and work organisation through eliminating alternative patterns of work (Lipietz, 1987; Thompson, 1983).

The key feature that distinguished Fordism from scientific management was the control (of pace and intensity) of production. The determinant of this was the technology rather than the 'scientific manager'. As Kelly (1982: 29) notes: 'the degree of the division of labour was taken much further than under Taylorism'. Fordism also had the effect of reversing the dominant relationship between labour and technology (Edwards, 1979; Gorz, 1976). As Littler and Salamon (1982: 75), highlight: 'The model of production worked out by Ford to serve the mass market presupposed the major principles of Taylorism, but went further in the transfer of traditional skills to specialist machines.'

Thus, Fordism provided a more intensive form of Taylorist work organisation and job design at a time of an expanding (international) market, leading to its dominance as the leading form of work organisation in the 20th century (Lipietz, 1987).

Critical Thinking 7.1 The case of Schmidt

In Taylor's most famous experiment, he studied men shovelling pig iron. He noted that one particular man – Schmidt – finished the day's work and jogged home to finish building his own house. Taylor therefore picked Schmidt for his experiment. After restructuring the shovel and how the work was to be undertaken (eliminating all superfluous activity), Taylor told Schmidt when to shovel and when to rest. From this experiment, Taylor was able to demonstrate an increase in production per man from 12 tons to 48 tons a day – a 300 per cent increase in productivity. For this achievement, Schmidt's wages were increased from $1.15 a day to $1.85 a day – a 60 per cent increase.

Questions

1 Identify the ethical issues associated with the choice of Schmidt for this study.
2 Do you agree with Schmidt's wage increasing by 60 per cent compared with the productivity gain of 300 per cent?

THE FOUNDATIONS OF CONTEMPORARY THEORY OF JOB DESIGN – THE SOCIOTECHNICAL ERA

The foundation underpinning scientific management-based job design was the concept of rational-economic man (Schein, 1965). The concept is based upon a belief that man will calculate actions that will result in maximum self-benefit (Birchall, 1975). As such, man will be primarily motivated by the economic incentives that provide the greatest gain. In a work context, issues such as working conditions, the environment, and relationships are subsidiary to the economic rewards – see Critical Thinking 7.1.

However, a series of British studies into the issues of monotony and the work cycle in the mid-1920s by the Industrial Fatigue Research Board identified a link between social conditions and workers' mental health, productivity, and autonomy (Buchanan and Huczynski, 1985; Rose, 1988). Further studies revealed that workers consistently prioritised working conditions and relationships above pay and there was a relationship between group dynamics and monotony (Brown, 1986). The emerging evidence led this British research group, under the leadership of C. S. Myers, to be increasingly critical of the neglect of human factors in the workplace.

These studies provided the first connection between the human aspects of work and productivity, creating foundations for the ground-breaking work of Elton Mayo's group at the Harvard Business School. In the UK, Myers (1926) had noted the hostility generated among workers by scientific management work practices through their attack on skills and the effects of time and motion studies and speed-ups (Thompson and McHugh, 2002). In the USA, Sward (cited in Braverman, 1974: 148–149) notes on the introduction of these work practices at the Ford car plant that:

> They proved to be increasingly unpopular, more and more it went against the grain. And the men exposed to it began to rebel. They registered their dissatisfaction by walking out in droves…. Ford admitted later that his startling factory innovations had ushered in an outstanding labor crisis.

Rose (1988) highlights two strikes in 1911, one by bricklayers and the second at the federal munitions factory – the Watertown Arsenal – which led to a Special House Committee set up by the American House of Representatives to investigate these (scientific management) work practices in 1912, for which Taylor was a witness. As Parker and Wall (1998: 5), describe: 'The committee failed to completely condemn scientific management, concluding that it was a useful tool, but also noted that it could give managers too much power.'

STOP AND REFLECT

Does money motivate you?

If you answered yes, considered this situation.

Your current job or a job you want and the wages, terms and conditions – write the value of the total package down. Now you have just been offered a job with an increase in wages, terms and conditions of 50 per cent on your estimated total package value above. Would you take it – the job is cleaning clogged drain in your city.

Consider the argument you make as to whether you take the job or not; then read the following sections.

The Hawthorne studies

The Hawthorne studies provided a paradigm shift in the theory of work design and organisation. As Thompson and McHugh (2002) note, the significance of the Hawthorne studies lies in the engagement of social science with industry, with the studies providing the foundations

of the *human relations school* of thought and management practice.

The human relations school of management emphasised the sociological and psychological aspects of work and work organisation. The Hawthorne studies took place between 1924 and 1932 at the Hawthorne plant of the Western Electric Company in Chicago (Boxes 7.1 and 7.2). The company was seen as an enlightened employer paying high wages and providing welfare facilities for its workers. However, it should be noted that the Hawthorne studies were conducted in a period when scientific management was the central focus of work organisation and industrial efficiency, and they were initially run through this frame of reference exploring optimum working conditions and performance (Pratt and Bennett, 1985).

Box 7.1 The telephone relay study

The telephone relay study was conducted over a five-year period and explored the effect of a variety of working conditions on a group of six women whose job it was to assemble telephone relays. Each relay consisted of around 40 parts, and the employees were paid on a group incentive basis. Changes in working conditions included the incentive scheme, rest breaks, hours of work and refreshments, as well as the withdrawal of the changes (Watson, 1995). In most cases, the employees were consulted before the changes were implemented. As Cole (1988) notes, the focus was on the differing conditions on productivity. There was no deliberate attempt at this stage to examine social relationships or employee attitudes.

Productivity rose throughout the study. On the basis of this study, Mayo identified that, rather than the physical environment being the key variable in productivity, it was in fact the social aspects of the workplace. The close interest taken in the employees and their work by the researchers, the high levels of communication and high social cohesion within the group, the freedom to control and organise their own work, and the more democratic style of management/supervision were seen as the critical factors in improving productivity (Pratt and Bennett, 1985; Watson, 1995). From this work, the concept of the 'Hawthorne effect' emerged.

The purpose of the research originally conducted by the company's own research group was to identify optimum working conditions. The first studies were based on artificial light and productivity. Two groups of workers were set up, one a control group and the second to test the effect of lighting conditions on productivity. Despite varying the light in the test group, productivity increased at a similar rate in both groups (Rose, 1988). Follow-up studies revealed an increase in productivity in both groups even when the lighting level was reduced. At the time, these results greatly puzzled the researchers at Western Electric (Thompson and McHugh, 2002). What the researchers realised was that unidentified factors were at work in determining productivity (Cole, 1988). This led to a request for assistance from Australian Elton Mayo and his colleagues at the Harvard Business School, who led the research from 1927 onwards.

Box 7.2 The bank wiring room

The bank wiring room was the site of the second major investigation associated with the Hawthorne studies; this focused on a group of 14 metal workers separated from the main work group. The most important observation that came from this study was how the group developed its own cohesive rules, value system and dynamics, separate from those of the organisation. This value system included restricting production, effectively negating the organisation's wage-incentive system and informally sanctioning workers who did not adopt these values (Cole, 1988).

The key outcomes for management from this study were to see individuals and the organisations of work in the context of the work groups, and not in isolation. This reinforced the increasing importance of Schein's social man over economic man in terms of reward systems. As Cole (1988) points out, intrinsic factors such as group membership are more important than extrinsic rewards, and, as such, groups in the workplace exercise a strong influence over employees. These findings reinforced the significance of social aspects of work and, more importantly, the need for management to account for social relationships and to consider these issues when developing work design and organisational practices congruent with organisational goals.

The impact of the Hawthorne studies

Although the Hawthorne studies have been criticised at a variety of levels in terms of their methodology, assumptions, and interpretations, these studies, as Thompson and McHugh (2002) identify, occupy a pivotal place in organisational and management theory. The studies recognised the relationship between the social and technical aspects of work organisation and provided the first evidence that productivity was to

a large extent dependent on social relationships. They also provided a counter-critique of scientific management and economic man and their neglect of human factors in the workplace (Rose, 1988; Thompson and McHugh, 2002). The studies laid the foundations for the human relations school of management and further research on the social and psychological aspects of work (Pratt and Bennett, 1985). In addition, they introduced the concept of social man into the mainstream context of the work relationship, highlighting the power that social relationships had over workers through the development of informal groups establishing their own values and norms outside the formal organisation.

These findings provided the basis for management to recognise the importance of these informal groups and look to work with them, by integrating them into organisational goals and strategies. As Thompson and McHugh (2002) argue, this laid the foundations for engaging in participation and communication with employees on workplace issues and acted as a catalyst for the development of managers with the appropriate skills to manage in such an environment.

CONTEMPORARY THEORY OF JOB AND WORK DESIGN – THE HUMAN RELATIONS SCHOOL

The human relations school began what Parker and Wall (1998) describe as the heyday of job and work design (spanning the 1940s through to the 1980s), in terms of both theory and practice. Building on the work of Mayo and his colleagues, the first of these advances came with the development of the sociotechnical systems approach. The sociotechnical approach originated at the Tavistock Institute of Human Relations in London. The Institute was founded in 1947 as an agency for psychologists to disseminate to industry the expertise they had accumulated during the war (Rose, 1988).

The key features of the sociotechnical approach were that organisations should be viewed as a combination of technical elements and social networks (Warr, 1987). From this perspective, the sociotechnical system approach acts to find the optimum relationship, or what we would term today the 'best fit', between the social and technical components of the organisation. This therefore requires both systems to be designed in parallel to take account of each other (Watson, 1995; Parker and Wall, 1998). The importance of this approach lies therefore in its comprehensive overview and joint optimisation of the two systems to best attain the organisation's goals (Warr, 1987).

It is important to note that, because of the wide range of factors to consider, the sociotechnical approach provides a framework of values to understand the organisation, rather than a prescriptive map of how to undertake the organisation of these systems (Buchanan and Huczynski, 1985; Warr, 1987). A further critical legacy of the sociotechnical approach is that, in contrast to the previous research on the organisation of work and job design, the focus was on teamwork (Parker and Wall, 1998). From this frame of reference, the key innovation was the development of work organisation around autonomous and semi-autonomous work groups (Passmore, 1998). This meant that work groups could decide their own methods of work (minimal specification) and handle as many of the operational issues encountered as possible (Parker and Wall, 1998).

Watson (1995) states that the impact of the Tavistock studies into job design were among the most theoretically sophisticated. The two most famous studies of the Tavistock Institute of Human Relations were the Durham mining studies of longwall coal mining in north-east England, and that of the Ahmedabad knitting mills in north-west India (Boxes 7.3 and 7.4).

Box 7.3 The longwall studies

In post–World War II Britain, a nationalisation of major industries, including the coal mining sector, was taking place. A major feature of this process was the modernisation of these industries. In coal mining, the focus was on implementing modern technological processes to improve productivity. The actual result of the introduction of new technology was decreased productivity and increased disputation, absenteeism, and accidents. This was the catalyst for researchers from the Tavistock Institute – Trist and Bamforth – to be invited to help.

Traditional work practices in the coal mine revolved around small (self-selected) teams of up to eight men working a small section of the coal face. The nature of the work required these teams to have a multitude of skills to cut and load the coal and prop the roof (Pratt and Bennett, 1985). This system of work was known as the 'shortwall' method (Cole, 1988). Because of the dangerous conditions, the miners relied extensively on the skills of each group member. Group bonds extended to families: should a group member be injured or killed, his family was often supported (financially and socially) by the group (Pratt and Bennett, 1985). The team also regulated the pace of work, and rewards were group-based (Buchanan and Huczynski, 1985; Cole, 1988).

With technological modernisation, the organisation of the work in the mine moved from the 'shortwall' to 'longwall' method. In the longwall model of work organisation, small groups were replaced by three shifts of miners of between 40 and 80 men working along a coalface up to 150 m in length (Pratt and Bennett, 1985). Each shift concentrated on one specialist task in the production cycle (Buchanan and Huczynski, 1985). As Cole (1988) and Rose (1988), note, the new system was effectively a mass-production system requiring a high degree of job specialisation and simplification. The consequences of the new system were the physical, social, and psychological isolation of the miners and the breakdown of the highly integrated social structures (developed by the small groups). These changes resulted in a decrease in productivity, an increase in industrial conflict, pay disputes, absenteeism, accidents, and the emergence of previously unknown pilfering (Pratt and Bennett, 1985; Cole, 1988).

Trist and Bamforth identified the changes in work organisation and job design as the source of the problem (Buchanan and Huczynski, 1985). A 'composite longwall' method was adopted, which maintained the new technology but organised the work around self-selected teams responsible for all the tasks (Pratt and Bennett, 1985). Immediate outcomes included increased productivity, decreased absenteeism, and fewer accidents (Argyle, 1989).

Box 7.4 The Ahmedabad knitting mills

The second major study was carried out by A. K. Rice in the Calico knitting mills of Ahmedabad in northern India, where the introduction of automated looms had not increased production. Rice suggested the introduction of small work groups that would be responsible for the productivity of a cluster of looms as well as their maintenance (Sofer, 1972). The workers took up the idea, developing their own scheme based around self-selected groups of seven men responsible for 64 looms.

Results from the study indicated that, as a result of the new work organisation, productivity rose by 21 per cent, and the amount of damaged cloth (wastage) was reduced by 59 per cent – both outcomes were reflected in the workers' wages (Argyle, 1989). The reasons put forward for the success of this case study were the development of small cohesive work groups and the increased complexity of the work (Argyle, 1989). As Rice's colleague noted in regard to outside pressure for the workers to conform to the traditional model of work organisation:

> The workers stuck to a system that was very largely their own creation and that enabled them to enjoy a quality of work–life as well as a level of income that they had not previously known. (Trist, 1973: 59)

The impact of the sociotechnical research

The Tavistock research demonstrated the importance of the relationship between the social and psychological aspects of work and the technical side, in particular that changes in the organisation of work cannot be undertaken without consideration of the social-technical balance. The acceptance of this principle occasioned a paradigm shift in how work organisation and job design should be undertaken at both the individual and the group level (Pratt and Bennett, 1985; Watson, 1995). The key sociotechnical findings were summarised by Buchanan as in Figure 7.1.

CONTEMPORARY THEORY OF JOB DESIGN – THE NEO-HUMAN RELATIONS OR MOTIVATIONAL THEORISTS

The sociotechnical research primarily developing out of the Tavistock Institute provided the foundation for behavioural psychology research in the workplace (also known as the *neo-human relations school*), particularly in the field of motivation (Bendix, 1963; Thompson and McHugh, 2002). The motivational theorists developed the concept of social man, further advocating the model of 'self-actualising' man (Schein, 1965). In other words, work has to fulfil individuals' inherent needs to use their skills and capacity to realise their own potential (Birchall, 1975).

From a job and work design perspective, the notion of organising work to release employees' potential became a powerful concept and continued to challenge the mechanistic perspective of designing jobs (Thompson and McHugh, 2002; Watson, 1995). The origin and essence of the 'motivational' perspective can be found in the work of Fredrick Herzberg, Douglas McGregor, and Abraham Maslow.

Maslow's hierarchy of needs

Abraham Maslow, an American psychologist, proposed that people need to satisfy a hierarchy of five sets of genetic or instinctive needs (Box 7.5). Maslow argued that when a person satisfies most of one need, he or she moves to seek satisfaction at the next level up. In striving for these needs, the goals are seen as attainable and

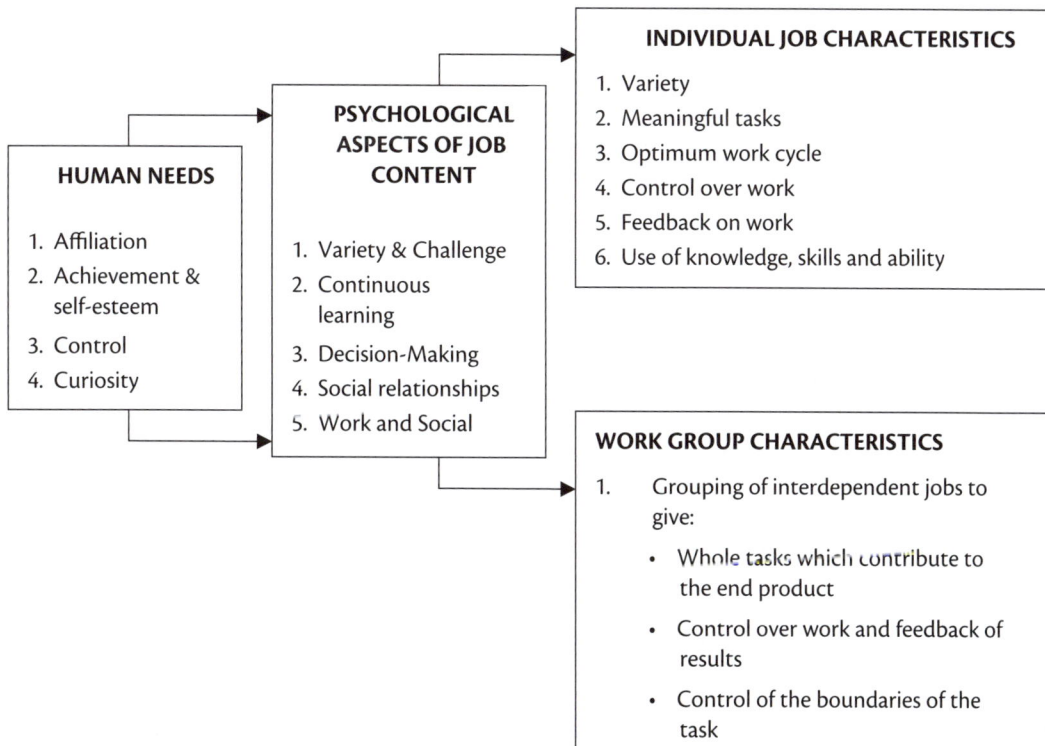

Figure 7.1 The work organisation approach to job design
Source: Adapted from Buchanan (1979: 112)

can therefore prove to be powerful motivators, eventually leading to self-actualisation. However, a failure to achieve the next level in the set of needs can result in frustration and pathological symptoms (Rose, 1988).

Box 7.5 Abraham Maslow – the hierarchy of needs

▸ Physiological needs – for survival, such as food and water
▸ Safety needs – shelter and security
▸ Love needs – relationships and affection
▸ Esteem needs – achievement, recognition, reputation, and appreciation, based on capability and respect
▸ Self-actualisation needs – the development of capabilities to their fullest potential.

In addition, Maslow also identified two further criteria to enhance and maintain self-actualisation:

▸ Freedom of inquiry and expression needs – for social conditions that permit free speech and encourage justice and fairness
▸ The need to know and to understand – to gain insight and knowledge to satisfy curiosity and enable continued learning.

Source: Adapted from Buchanan and Huczynski (1985: 52)

Obviously, the first two needs – physiological and safety – are required to live, with the second two – love and esteem – providing a sense of usefulness and belonging (Buchanan and Huczynski, 1985). The ultimate step is to reach self-actualisation where one achieves one's potential.

Maslow's theory provided an important platform for understanding the motivational drives of individuals. This general theory was adopted by researchers of work organisations and managers, although it was not specifically developed for the workplace, as is often assumed. Maslow qualified this general theory by acknowledging the role and impact of external factors such as the organisation and its culture on the individual (Rose, 1988). In addition, Maslow argued that the hierarchy was true for most people but could vary (Pratt and Bennett, 1985).

Subsequent research has been inconclusive regarding the hierarchy. Issues associated with the measurement of satisfaction and the 'tipping point' at which an individual moves to the next stage are unique to each person. In addition, some have suggested that individual needs are so complex and different that the issues of motivation and job satisfaction may be too varied to be generalised

(Parker and Wall, 1998). This said, Buchanan and Huczynski (1985) argue that Maslow's theory is a social philosophy in which we can find enough evidence that some individuals pursue this hierarchy of needs. Importantly, the theory draws attention to the different motivations that influence people.

Herzberg's motivation–hygiene theory

Fredrick Herzberg's motivation–hygiene or two-factor theory builds on Maslow's research on intrinsic motivation and, importantly, views this from a workplace perspective. Based on what employees found enjoyable or made them feel good at work and what was bad about work, Herzberg identified two groups of factors, for which he coined the terms satisfiers or motivation factors, and hygiene factors. He further refined these paradigms into content- and context-based work issues. The *content-based or motivator* factors were intrinsic job satisfaction issues that gave the employee a sense of well-being; these were:

● achievement
● autonomy
● recognition
● responsibility
● the work itself.

The *context-based or hygiene factors* were extrinsic issues that could be neutral or cause job dissatisfaction, and included:

● company policies and administration
● supervision
● salary
● interpersonal relationships
● working conditions.

The motivation (intrinsic) factors relate closely to Maslow's higher levels needs, whereas the hygiene factors satisfy only Maslow's lower level needs. From a work perspective, Herzberg's research focused on building facets of motivation into job and work design in order to increase performance. From a practical perspective, this meant that jobs needed to be enlarged and more challenging, as well as to provide a degree of autonomous decision-making (Watson, 1995). Herzberg advocated this as *job enrichment*, in which work and job design deliberately included more complex and more responsible tasks, as a way to engage employees' knowledge, skill and abilities (Brown, 1986). This also provided further arguments against the development of scientific management–based job design. Herzberg developed six applications of *vertical* loading factors, as these job enrichment features became known:

- Remove control.
- Increase accountability.
- Create natural work units.
- Provide direct feedback.
- Introduce new tasks.
- Allocate special assignments.
  (Buchanan and Huczynski, 1985).

Initially, Herzberg's theory had a positive impact on management thinking and enlightened managers (Brown, 1986). However, the study upon which the research was based has been the focus of criticism. The original study was based on the responses of 203 professional engineers and accountants in Pittsburgh, which reflected a very narrow (and privileged) section of US society in the 1950s. Research replicating Herzberg's study using alternate methodologies has failed to confirm the findings of the study, suggesting that the theory is 'method-bound' (Pratt and Bennett, 1985). The main criticism, however, is concerned with Herzberg's assertion that motivation and hygiene factors are mutually exclusive. The situation is today generally seen as being more complex and less clearly delineated. But despite these criticisms, Herzberg's theory is widely credited with directing the focus of research and management practice towards the importance of intrinsic motivation (Pratt and Bennett, 1985).

McGregor's theory X and theory Y

Douglas McGregor's theory X and theory Y are useful to draw together research on the organisation of work in the first half of the 20th century. The two assumptions about work reflect the dominant paradigms of the time: the mechanistic system, theory X, and the sociotechnical system, theory Y (Box 7.6).

The assumptions of theory X about employees and how they should be managed reflects the scientific management paradigm that workers need controlling and are focused on extrinsic rewards (Schein's rational-economic man). As Watson (1995) notes, this approach in effect creates the culture and behaviour that management seeks to avoid. In contrast, theory Y was more consistent with the sociological and psychological research of the time, in which employees preferred discretion and autonomy in work that provided more opportunities to be creative (Schein's self-actualising man).

Although McGregor's theory was, like many of the theories of the sociotechnical period, influential among managers, he and others have been criticised from a labour process perspective for not challenging the inherent

> ### Box 7.6 The key features of McGregor's theory X and theory Y
>
> **Theory X**
>
> - Employees have an inherent dislike for work and will avoid it wherever possible.
> - Employees must be coerced, directed and threatened with sanctions in order to get them to cooperate.
> - Employees are passive, lack initiative, and require direction.
>
> **Theory Y**
>
> - Work is a natural aspect of life.
> - Employees seek opportunities to be creative and assume responsibility.
> - Commitment and the achievement of objectives are a function of the intrinsic rewards associated with achievement.

power relationships in the workplace and the inbuilt conflicts between the interests of management and employees. The focus of research from the neo-human relations school was the improvement of work organisation and satisfaction only where it enhanced productivity (Brown, 1986). However, the key conclusions that can be drawn from the motivational research is that work needs to be psychologically empowering in order to achieve intrinsic motivation leading to enhanced performance at work and increased productivity (Cordery and Parker, 2007). Underpinning this is work organisation designed to satisfy the psychological needs of autonomy, competence, and relatedness (Ryan and Deci, 2000).

Parker and Wall (1998) distilled a set of work design criteria from the work of motivational systems research and sociotechnical research, which included the ability to:

- arrange work in a way that allows individual employees to influence their own work method and pace;
- where possible combine independent tasks into jobs;
- group tasks into meaningful jobs that allow for an overview and understanding of the work process as a whole and as part of the wider organisational objectives;
- provide a sufficient variety of tasks within a job, including tasks that offer a degree of employee responsibility, which makes use of the skills and knowledge valued by the individual;
- arrange work to enable it to be undertaken in the normal work time allotted, so as not to create work–life balance tensions;
- provide opportunities for employees to achieve the (extrinsic or intrinsic) outcomes they value;

- ensure that feedback is communicated promptly and efficiently to employees on their performance from both a supervisor and a task perspective;
- provide internal and external customer feedback directly to employees;
- provide employees with the information they need to make decisions.

Hackman and Oldham's job characteristic model

The development of psychological perspectives of work organisation, the understanding of group dynamics and the development of job enrichment by the neo- and human relations school were combined in the theory and framework of Hackman and Oldham's job characteristic model (JCM) and its accompanying measurement instrument – the Job Diagnosis Survey. The model defined five core job characteristics that relate to employee motivation and satisfaction (Parker and Wall, 1998):

1 *Skill variety* – the degree to which the job requires different skills.
2 *Task identity* – the degree to which the job involves completing a whole identifiable piece of work rather than simply a part of it.
3 *Task significance* – the extent to which the job has an impact on other people, either inside or outside the organisation.
4 *Autonomy* – the extent to which the job allows job-holders to exercise choice and discretion in their work.
5 *Feedback from the job* – the extent to which the job itself (as opposed to other people) – provides job-holders with information on their performance.

The JCM has proved to be the most enduring of the theoretical approaches to job and work design, drawing on key aspects of earlier research (Figure 7.2). However, it is not without its critics. Findings using the JCM have been inconsistent, with the relationship between the core

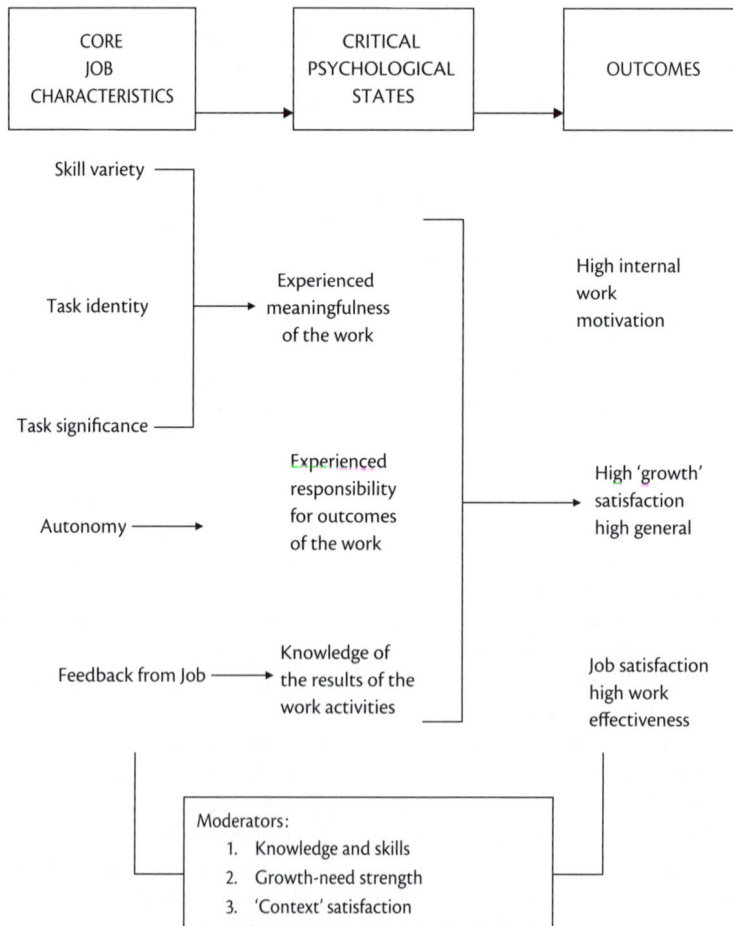

Figure 7.2 The job characteristic model
Source: Oldham (1996)

characteristics and the outcome variables often being cited as difficult to replicate (Parker and Wall, 1998). But, in acknowledging this, Parker and Wall (1998: 14–15) do make the important point that:

> Given the problems, it is clear that all the detailed predictions of the job characteristic model have not stood up to empirical test. Nonetheless, this does not undermine its usefulness…. On the whole, the job characteristic model clearly has some concurrent and predictive value, even though it is incorrect in its finer detail.

Theory to practice: Job design in the 'long boom'

With the end of World War II and the development of a period of stable economic growth (which became known as the 'long boom'), the developments in understanding employees in the workplace became more important in increasingly 'tight' labour markets. This lack of labour forced employers to seriously address issues of dissatisfaction and alienation in the workplace – in other words, employees' lack of relationship with, and the attachment and self-fulfilment being demanded from, their work.

The first practical attempts at addressing the more oppressive aspects of scientific management work patterns were through job rotation and job enlargement. Job rotation involves moving employees from one job to another at regular intervals. The benefits were seen as increasing the variety of tasks, reducing boredom, and increasing the flexibility of the workforce (Parker and Wall, 1998). As with scientific management, the automobile industry was at the vanguard of these new work practices: at Renault's Le Mans factory, employees moved from job to job every hour (Pratt and Bennett, 1985).

Job enlargement involves widening the duties of employees by adding new tasks that broaden the skills required and reduce overspecialisation and monotony. In some situations, this can mean the enlargement of tasks to enable the employee to complete the whole job (Parker and Wall, 1998). An example of this was the Philips factory in Scotland, which built heaters on a traditional production line. After major disputes and industrial unrest, and in consultation with the trade unions, work was reorganised to allow employees to build complete heaters. Research identified increased job satisfaction, productivity increases of 10 per cent and a reduction in defect rates of 50 per cent (Thornley and Valantine, 1975).

Although both job rotation and job enlargement can be seen to alleviate the worst excesses of mechanistic job design, they have been criticised for the lack of vertical task integration and decision-making, which remains solely in the hands of management. As such, job rotation and job enlargement do not increase the quality or discretion of the work. Indeed, this 'horizontal' loading approach to job design can at best be seen as a short-term measure. As Child (1984: 34) notes:

> To paraphrase Herzberg, adding one Mickey Mouse job to another does not make any more than two Mickey Mouse jobs. In other words, simply adding specialised, repetitive, routine and dreary tasks to one another, or rotating around these, is not likely to create a job that is satisfying or motivating.

Job enrichment developed out of the neo-human relations school of research. In contrast to both job rotation and job enlargement, job enrichment introduces vertical integration into the organisation of work. The key aspects of job enrichment are to increase control and discretion into the work environment. This can include how the work is undertaken, quality inspection, and maintenance, processes formerly undertaken by front-line supervisors (Child, 1984). Job enrichment emphasises the redesign of work to increase the individual's satisfaction by focusing on intrinsic needs such as responsibility, recognition, and personal growth (Cole, 1988). These critical psychological criteria clearly correlate with Hackman and Oldham's JCM, with its emphasis on meaningful, responsible work with knowledge of its results.

The many examples of job enrichment (both blue collar and white collar) have all emphasised the role of intrinsic satisfaction as a key to job satisfaction (Birchall, 1975; Buchanan and Huczynski, 1985). However, as Child (1984) points out, the focus on the individual needs to be put into the context of the workplace, where jobs are increasingly part of an interdependent cluster forming work groups. As the work of the human relations school has highlighted, the work group can be critical in the determination of successful work design. As such, the design of work needs to be seen in relation to the work group as the platform of work design. Therefore, restructuring work at the group level increasingly becomes the level at which potentially the most effective work redesign will take place.

The work group is also seen as the natural focus for work redesign due to the increased complexity and integration of work. A group approach also offers more scope for individual differences and skills, as well as a natural platform for disseminating knowledge (Wall et al., 1986). In a group context, discretion over a variety of work decisions can fall within the realms of the group – from, for example, decisions about the day-to-day organisation of the work to dealing with buyers and suppliers (Mathews, 1989; Parker and Wall, 1998). This approach also fits with Schein's final development of the individual's motivation – complex man – a person in whom motivation is complex and variable and changes over time owing to shifting needs, experiences, and relationships (Birchall, 1975). The group work environment thus has the potential to provide for these changing needs and the social context in which to achieve individual goals.

Some of the most significant and well-documented studies of work design have emerged out of group-based job design. Of these, the job design carried out by Volvo in the mid-1970s at its then new car manufacturing plant is probably the most famous. Work in the Kalmar plant was designed for groups of 15–20 employees to assemble major car components. Although management determined the output, how the work was conducted was at the discretion of the group (Pratt and Bennett, 1985). Despite initial problems, research by the Swedish government found productivity, quality, and job satisfaction to be higher than in traditionally laid out plants (Mathews, 1989).

Similarly, at Air Canada, teams were given the responsibility of determining when and how to replace aircraft windows. Productivity doubled, and supervisory time dropped by 75 per cent (Child, 1984). Other well-documented case studies included Saab, Philips, Shell, ICL, AT&T Xerox, and Levi Strauss. However, as noted in the Volvo case, management discretion over work outputs remained.

As Kelly and Clegg (1981) have noted, by the late 1970s and despite the high-profile case studies of Volvo and Saab, the scale, scope and impact of job design had been limited. The lack of impact of job and work design can be linked to a variety of issues including a resistant organisational culture and the development of job design being limited to a particular department or sector of the organisation but not translated to other areas of the organisation. This is an important point to note as, for example, Volvo's approach at Kalmar was undertaken at a 'greenfield' site location where no previous culture or work practices existed, so new patterns of work could be far more effectively implemented.

Other factors can be a lack of understanding of the problem, including misdiagnosis, which may lead to the failure of job design. This can be linked to the lack of management skills in understanding, diagnosing and developing appropriate strategies for change management and integrative job design. In addition, the impact of job design may, by its very nature, result in redundancies or redeployment, causing workplace stress and potential trade union resistance. In addition, the simple fact is that job design or redesign is not for all workers. Many workers may simply see work through Schein's lens of rational-economic man and view work as an instrument for other needs. Indeed, Goldthorpe's classic study of affluent workers in the British car industry in the 1950s illustrates exactly this point (see Goldthorpe, 1966).

Possibly the most important factor underpinning all of these points was, however, the continuation of the 'long boom', which provided little incentive to alter practices. But this factor was about to change.

CONTEMPORARY THEORY OF JOB AND WORK DESIGN – THE CONCERTIVE ERA

Concertive work systems are team patterns of work organisation that are designed to maximise the employee's effectiveness in pursuing organisational goals (Cordery and Parker, 2007). It was not until the early 1980s that management thinking and commitment to the organisation of work significantly changed. As with the implementation of the Fordist mode of work organisation, these changes were driven by the issues of sustained competitive advantage (Boxall and Purcell, 2015), as the 'oil shocks' of the 1970s brought to an end the era of the long boom, which was underpinned by certainty in markets and employment.

The emergence of quality as an issue in the late 1970s can be seen as one catalyst for change in the early 1980s, with its links to the success and increasing dominance of Japanese organisations in all the major world markets. Underpinning the competitiveness of these organisations was the high value placed on the management of quality (via quality circles teams) as a key feature of the production process. The irony in the increasing attention given in Anglo-American countries to quality as a means of competitive advantage was the fact that the concept of quality had had its origins in the USA in the 1920s and was imported to Japan from the USA after World War II, under the guidance of luminaries such as Dr E. W. Deming and, later, Dr Joseph M. Juran (Brewster et al., 2003). Through the concept of total quality management (TQM), quality became an issue for all members of the organisation. Echoing the arguments of the sociotechnical and psychological perspectives of work organisation, Hill (1991: 197) states:

> [TQM] seeks to involve employees from shopfloor to senior management in a quality improvement culture. It is not just tacked on, so the argument runs, but promises a fundamental overhaul of the labour process.

The fundamental change that TQM brings to organisations is cultural, which Tuckman (1995) asserts can only be achieved with a fundamental review of work patterns and practices. Legge (1995) takes this further by arguing that TQM requires the development of interdepartmental and cross-functional project teams and enlisting of the commitment of 'empowered' workers, organised into teams and participating in decision-making.

TQM therefore focuses on the organisational culture, structure, and management of human resources to develop team-based work design. At an organisational level, management's focus is on delayering and simplifying the organisational processes, so that decision-making can be pushed down the organisation in order to facilitate team-based work and more open communication (Hill, 1995). These tenets are central to empowering employees collectively to become responsible for the quality of their work. Supporting these changes is the need to develop a participative management style based on a relationship of consensus and trust through increased autonomy and self-direction, if employees are to embrace these organisational goals (Legge, 1995; Tuckman, 1995; Wilkinson et al., 1998).

With the increasing complexity and pace of work, and the growing volatility in markets since the 'long boom', the focus has continued on developing work organisation around highly integrated work teams. Reflecting the underlying philosophy of the sociotechnical theorists, as well as the work of Hackman and Oldham (1976, 1980) and Oldham (1996), at the core of these teams lie the semi-autonomous work groups or 'high-involvement work systems' (HIWSs); advanced developments in work design see these teams becoming 'self-designing' (Hackman, 1987) or 'self-leading' (Manz, 1992).

What is significant about this is that these self-managed teams encompass (vertical) work tasks that would traditionally be seen as functions of supervisors and middle management (Cordery and Parker, 2007). These teams are increasingly having an influence over strategic decisions in terms of what the group actually does and why, rather than just how they undertake the work (Parker and Wall, 1998). Within the team, work is allocated to multiskilled team members as whole tasks. These team members have substantial discretion over how the work is organised (Cordery and Parker, 2007). The components of HIWSs of work design has been articulated by Vanderberg et al. (1999) – see Figure 7.3 – whose work builds on Lawler's (1986) model of high involvement. This in turn is underpinned by issues associated with the dissemination of power, information, reward, and knowledge in the workplace (Boxall and Purcell, 2015).

Although evidence of the success of HIWSs has been found in studies of the steelmaking, electronics and automobile industries (Boxall and Purcell, 2015), the development of these work patterns and practices brings with it its own demands. For example, research identifies that the human resource implications of these initiatives are also a critical dimension for success. As Lepak and Snell (1997, 2007) note, human resource systems need to reflect a high-commitment philosophy. In an environment characterised by continuous change and increased competition, where downsizing and offshoring are always options, there needs to be a fit between human resource policies and practices to ensure the development of a relationship of high trust and commitment between employees and management (Brewster et al., 2003).

Middle management can potentially become the strongest advocate of HIWSs. However, the changes that these work practices bring require significant resources

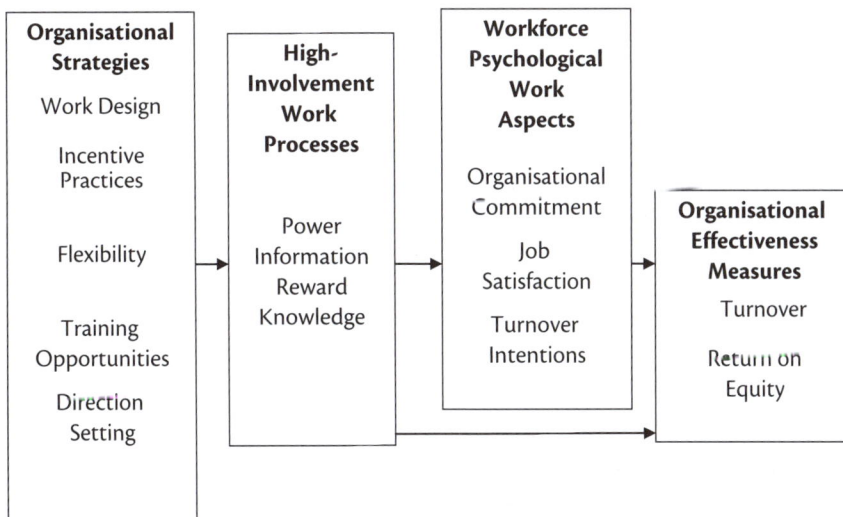

Figure 7.3 Conceptual model of high-involvement work systems
Source: Adapted from Vanderberg et al. (1999: 307)

to be focused on management training and development in order to ensure a successful transition for these leaders from a role as controller to one as coach or facilitator. Without this, management may resist these changes as they can be seen as a threat associated with a loss of expert power (Marchington, 1995; Wilkinson et al., 1997). Klein (1984) identifies the issues of job security and loss of status as being central to opposition on the part of supervisors to change, as well as, to a lesser extent, a lack of training, resources and belief in their own ability to undertake such a change programme. These findings are also supported by research by Marchington (1995).

In an environment where job insecurity is increasing while promotion opportunities are decreasing, the development of empowerment can lead to increased stress (Delbridge, 2005) and to what Jackson et al. (1996) describe as 'career defence' on the part of lower and middle management. These and industry-specific issues can result in significant variations across industries implementing HIWSs (Appleyard and Brown, 2001; Kalleberg et al., 2006). These points are reflected in research indicating that the effects of HIWSs on organisational profitability are still unclear (Cappelli and Neumark, 2001; Way, 2002).

📖
In the News Telecommuting Is the Future

Telecommuting is a term that generally refers to working from home such as a mother with small children, or employees in their twenties. However, in fact, the typical telecommuter is a 49-year-old college graduate – who earns about US $58,000 per annum and usually works in a company with more than 100 employees.

And the phenomenon seems to be on the rise. An annual survey the Society for Human Resource Management (SHRM) found a greater increase in the number of companies planning to offer telecommuting as part of their flexibility and benefits policies.

There is also a business case. Federal employees in Washington who worked from home during four official snow days saved the government an estimated $32 million.

This means that companies will have to build workplaces and design work practices and make decision about appropriate technical support.

It is widely known that those who work at home tend to put in longer hours and are usually more productive. However, there is also social cost and telecommuting can hurt an employee's promotion chances, and may not work in certain work situations at all.

Source: Tugend (2014).

'NEW' NEW TECHNOLOGY AND JOB AND WORK DESIGN

Whilst technology has been a key driver of work and work patterns for centuries, it can be argued that the advancement we have seen in the twenty-first century are the most ground-breaking since the industrial revolution. Advancements in information communication technologies (ICT) combined with diminished costs, have created a significant shift in the type and availability of work practices in the workplace of the twenty-first century. This has occurred at the same time as the paradigm shift of work into cyber-space, which has created a further dimension of work both inside and outside the conventional workplace (see JetBlue case above). As Howcroft and Taylor (2014: 3), point out, innovation in labour utilisations and scheduling the temporal dimensions of work have an impact on how work is done, as the boundaries of the organisation 'melt' away. Indeed, they argue that society is seeing a new wave of revolutionary technological that provides the platform for significant change in the way we work. These changes are creating renewed interest in how work is conceptualised. In this context Holtgrewe (2014: 12), notes the key technological trends appear to be:

- The convergence of telecommunications and IT;
- the increasing omnipresence, not just of 'chips' but of internet connectivity and consequently, the diffusion of web-based services and functionalities into increasingly diverse spaces and spheres of activity;
- the increasing independence of computing capacity from local hardware equipment and software ('cloud computing');
- the utilisation of the resulting amounts of data and meta-data for various commercial and public purposes and business models ('big data').

All these are closely interrelated because of the ubiquitous connectivity which enables remote access to data and computing capacity and data flows. As such this diffusion of mobile devices and the convergence of telecommunications and IT will no longer just focus on computers and smart phones but data, multimedia content, social networks, and computer-processing power that can be accessed from ever more places and situations (Holtgrewe, 2014: 12). As an example of this, in 2012 IBM developed an internal (crowdsourcing) platform, using a globally standardised skill databases which combines with ICT to enable project teams to be put together regardless of location – dubbed the 'talent cloud'. (Holtgrewe, 2014: 18). This approach to the virtual 'flexible firm' would see employees employed brought together 'virtually' based on their knowledge, skills, and ability to work together through this global platform. Whilst these technologies are going to have a significant impact on the future of work and work and job design, there are two sides to the these technologies – the smart and dark sides. Whilst the positives aspects of these new patterns are often emphasised, for example managing work–life boundaries and bringing together the best people globally, there is also evidence to suggest that without checks and balances, burnout and role exhaustion can occur due to the role ambiguity, time pressures, and reduced support and feedback of working in these non-standard environments (Sardeshmukh, Sharma and Golden, 2012).

Using the 'Job-Demand Resource Model (JD-R), Sardeshmukh et al. (2012), analysed these issues. The JD-R is a useful and increasingly popular frame of reference highlighting the impact and balance (imbalance) of the job demands and job resources (which refer to physical, psychological, social, and organisational aspects of the job). As Sardeshmukh et al. (2012) note, whilst the demands of a job are not necessarily inherently negative, the on-going and sustained effort associated with the tasks may lead to exhaustion. This can also impact on job engagement, often a key reason for developing such work practices (Sardeshmukh et al., 2012). As such, Collins and Cartwright (2013) argue employee's psychological contract is an important aspect of the ability to deal with these new flexible patterns of work. As they note, little research has been undertaken on the impact of these types of working practices, including what employees expect from the organisation or how the move to virtual teams or teleworking is negotiated. Negotiation and culture are particularly important, because managers or supervisor support for these working arrangement influences both implementation and practice. As Collins and Cartwright (2013) note, the psychological contract deals with the unwritten and implied reciprocal obligations (and expectations) between employee and employer (as represented by the line manager or supervisor). From their research, two keys themes of temporal flexibility and fairness emerged as key in adopting these patterns of work. However, what was of more significance was the inconsistency of policy implementation from the supervisor (representing the organisation). Collins and Cartwright (2013) also found of interest that, despite these inconsistencies, virtual or teleworkers were still appreciative of the level of flexibility they were allowed.

In this context the concept of teleworking has gained increasing prominence as a way to make work more flexible, particularly for high-skilled workers, to attract and retain these key human resources as discussed below.

Teleworking

With the advent of high quality ICTs, teleworking has become an increasing viable form of flexible work organisation from a cost benefit perspective to both sides of the employment relationship (Neirotti, Paoluccis and Raguseo, 2013). For employees these flexible work patterns allow them to blend, blur, and balance a variety of life issues with work time. In terms of a definition, telework refers to work arrangements in which employees perform their regular work outside of the normal place of work – at home, but also at client sites and/or on the move supported by ICT (Wheatley, 2012). Increasingly in countries such as the UK this type of work has been facilitated by government regulations allowing employees to request this type of working arrangement – The Flexible Working Regulations introduced in 2003 and extended in 2007 and 2009 (Wheatley, 2012). It is worth noting that these types of work patterns are more prevalent in the public sector in the UK than the private sector, with arrangement in the private sector being more informal and ad hoc (Wheatley, 2012). As a result, figures indicate that there has been a steady increase in teleworking in the European Union and USA (Beham et al, 2014). Teleworking in US grew by 61 per cent between 2005 and 2009 and is projected to grow at 69 per cent until 2016 (Lister and Harmish, 2011).

From the employers' perspective, teleworking provides innovative ways to allow the workforce to be developed and retained over significant geographical distances, and as these are increasingly skilled knowledge workers, from a human capital and talent management context it can be a significant strategy in retaining high quality human resources; this is in line with the move of major advanced market economies (AMEs) to knowledge- and service-based based structures (Holland et al., 2015). As Maruyama and Tietzs (2012) point out, the development of flexible and teleworking practices poses testing and exciting times in particular for those tasked with developing appropriate system and structures to ensure the initial and sustained integration of these workers into the strategic focus of the organisation – often this falls on the human resources department. These changes require a review of managerial style, human resource development and performance management as well as softer issues such as culture and communications.

Fortune Magazine (2013) notes that up to 85 per cent of the '100 Best Companies to Work For' in the USA offered teleworking in 2012, with the Netherlands and Nordic countries having up to 40 per cent of employees in some form of telework. In Germany the figures show teleworking increasing threefold to 21 per cent in the period between 2003 to 2012 (EuroFound, 2012). Equally, in the current dynamic environment, the demand increasingly from skilled knowledge workers for these forms of work will likely see firms investing in telework and other flexible work arrangements (Neirotti et al, 2013). Research by Wheatley (2012) indicates that satisfaction with this form of work is higher amongst skilled occupations, with those working in the public sector indicating greatest satisfaction. This, he suggests, is because of the greater access to these flexible working arrangements.

POSSIBILITIES AND CHALLENGES

One of the key challenges often overlooked in the context of teleworking is the role and support of managers. As Beham, Baierl and Poelmans (2014), argue, managers play a critical role in policy development and implementation as well as the management of the 'virtual' relationship. In their research they found that formal policies were central to a successful management relationship supported by organisational resources. Other cost/benefits they identified for management and the organisation as a whole were the reduction of costly fixed office space; in addition, the potential for increased job satisfaction through the employee having more control over work-family boundaries. However, the implementation of policies does not necessarily mean usage or success. An unsupportive culture or management concerned by a lack of control (and trust) over the process with employees being out of sight can be a significant barrier. As Wheatley (2012) notes, research continually indicates that control and governance (trust) remain a restricting barrier to telework despite the increasing use and demand for it from professional (high-skilled talent) in the workforce.

Alternatively, the perception of not being a committed member of the team or of being out-of–mind for potential opportunities and promotions are other factors in the success or otherwise of these policies and practices. As Wheatley (2012) notes, invisibility to management and career stagnation due to a current perception by managers about an association between long hours and 'presenteeism' creates a potential second-class employee perception of teleworkers. Equally for the manager these are not one-size-fits-all solutions, and often work will have to be undertaken (and resources provided) to tailor the arrangement to suit all parties (Beham et al., 2014). A further issue managers needs to handle is the perception of fairness amongst a team of 'blended' workers, i.e. that non-teleworkers do not believe they are missing out or shouldering more of the burden of the work because of perceived 'absent' colleagues. Holtgrewe (2014) therefore argues that such hybrid teams of virtual and non-virtual workers need time and resources invested in them in order to set up and maintain the team structure and

dynamics. When this doesn't occur, teams can quickly break down; the manager or project manager needs to have the skills and ability to manage these teams and systems. These findings are supported by Taskin and Bridoux (2010), who argue that teleworking could also be a significant issue in the management of knowledge and knowledge transfer. Taskin and Bridoux (2010) note that whilst teleworking has been shown to have positive outcomes for both employers and employees, the nature of the work may endanger an organisation's knowledge base and competitive advantage, as knowledge transfer breaks down between teleworkers and non-teleworkers. They argue that the decreased visibility of teleworkers in the workplace creates less direct or spontaneous interaction. As such they argue that telework has the potential to disrupt or degrade interaction and thus disrupt the social fabric of the workplace and is an area in which again management needs to invest significant and on-going resources.

A solution to this can be a compromise situation where a hybrid approach has the teleworkers periodically coming in to the workplace. In this context, Bosch-Sijtsema, Ruohomaki and Vartianen (2010) have researched this option also known as 'drop-in desks'. A key issue with teleworkers they found was that they can and are (because of smart technology) increasingly multilocational. In this context the opportunity to work occasionally in the office therefore appears to be a logical progression of these virtual work team relationships. The focus of Bosch-Sijtsema et al.'s (2010) research was to determine how organisations have adapted to these issues. Their survey found that there was a negative impact upon employee productivity, especially in an open plan office environment. They indicate that managers need to be aware of these factors and, as noted, provide time and resources to develop and continually reflect on the management of virtual/non-virtual teams. Bosch-Sijtsema et al. (20120: 194) sum up:

> The prevalence of new types of workplaces, such as, for example mobile desks has increased rapidly during the last 10 years and will continue to do so. Telework and mobile work have increased dramatically in the last couple of years in Europe and America. Therefore, it becomes more important to continue to study mobile desk workers in relation to their workspaces (physical, virtual and social effectiveness) to understand the impact of multilocationality on their work and effectiveness.

This point is supported by Collins and Cartwright (2013), who argue that it is likely that negotiations between employers and employees across all employment levels is going to intensify, because increasingly employees are looking for flexible working arrangements for a variety of reasons. A key element in this is how these practices are managed, and summing up this issue Collins and Cartwright (2013) make the point that whilst organisations introduce policies on flexible work arrangements, these are interpreted by line managers or supervisor in practice in different ways, depending on the manager's level of comfort with these patterns of work (as noted). The danger arises here that if the policies are managed inconsistently across the same work group, tensions can arise. It may be an area that should therefore be negotiated in conjunction with the HRM department. Managers also need to be aware of the concerns and anxieties of workers moving into these flexible patterns of work.

CONCLUSION

Job and work design in the twenty-first century – back to the future or forward to the past?

With the emergence of an increasingly complex and competitive global economy, many organisations have embraced new work patterns and practices to sustain their competitiveness. Underpinning these work patterns are the development of sophisticated human resource management strategies. These strategies have the potential to develop high-quality, high-involvement work environments. Conversely, the increasingly deregulated nature of work in AMEs can result in a negative work environment with little opportunity for employees to have a say in the work they do or how they do it. This can create a climate of oppression and control, a situation identified by Guest (1995) as the 'black hole human resource management scenario'.

For example, the archetypal workplaces of the twenty-first century – call centres – have been variously been described as electronic sweatshops and dungeons with telephones (Kinnie et al., 2000; Deery and Kinnie, 2002).

Equally, SalesForce, a call centre based in Melbourne, has been awarded best employer in Australia, which suggests that there is scope for significant opportunities to develop work design policies and practices even in highly structured work environments.

In manufacturing, where traditional scientific management practices of standardisation and cost minimisation remain highly favoured, industrialists such as Ricardo Semler and his ship component company, Semco, have led the way in job and work design strategies, with high-involvement teams becoming 'self-designing' and 'self-leading'. These teams have the ability to hire and fire their own bosses and peers, set their own budgets and determine how they organise their work and when they do it. These examples and contemporary research reflect the fact that well-thought-out job design strategies can increase employee involvement. As such, it can have a positive impact on organisational performance from an attraction and retention perspective, where highly skilled employees are likely to remain engaged with and committed to the organisation for a longer period of time. This will, in turn, be likely to result in enhanced productivity of the organisation's key assets – its people.

Returning to the quote at the start of this chapter by Parker and Wall (1998) on the excitement and dangers of developing work organisation in a highly deregulated knowledge-based global market, it is worth reflecting, as we acknowledge the 100th anniversary of the first Model T Ford rolling off the first production line in 1908, that although people working in call centres might not see a significant difference in work, the production line has now become mental rather than physical. On the other hand, people working in environments such as that developed by Riccardo Semler at Semco appear to have taken on the ideas of the sociotechnical, motivational, and concertive theorists and developed a truly post-Fordist work environment. The next 100 years may provide an increasing number of paradoxical situations in the way work systems are organised.

End of Chapter Case Study Job design at TechCo

The rapid development of the information technology industry has resulted in significant skill shortages in many AMEs. In Australia, the ability to develop and retain key IT staff is a major human resource management issue. The alternative for many organisations is the loss of key staff, intellectual capital, and market share. This case study examines human resources policies and practices developed around strategies of innovative work organisation and job design to first retain and second attract key IT staff.

TechCo is a leading supplier of networking IT, providing support applications for the development of e-business and employing over 200 staff in offices in all Australia's major cities. TechCo identified the issue of attracting and retaining its IT staff as a major problem. Whereas the average turnover was high in this sector – at around 10 per cent – TechCo was experiencing a turnover of over 15 per cent. After surveying their staff, the major finding linked to developing and retaining the company's key talent was the understanding that employees required a challenging and stimulating work environment in which to develop their skills.

A clear division emerged from a survey of the requirements of TechCo's IT staff. They were looking to develop their skills as either (internal) project managers or (external) self-employed contractors. The key challenge for TechCo was that, as a small to medium-sized company, it was not able to provide a continuous range of project management roles in-house and could not afford to lose employees who wanted to move into contracting. The key paradigm shift for TechCo to address the critical issue was to see itself as part of a network with its customers and suppliers. In doing so, it increased its opportunities to provide its workforce with a variety of work design opportunities.

In response to the project management problem, TechCo developed a partnering programme with its network of distributors and customers. This approach had the dual effect of providing partners with the appropriately skilled staff to project-manage on-site, at the same time providing these staff with on-going (higher order) career and skill development. From an organisational perspective, it also allowed for the growth and retention of knowledge on the part of these core knowledge workers, while enhancing the skills and ability of this critical human resource.

For those employees wanting to become independent contractors, TechCo embraced this by helping them set up autonomously as contractors and then contracting their services back to the organisation. The employee is thus guaranteed work, and TechCo enables these employees to remain working for the organisation without the on-costs associated with full-time employees. As noted above, the organisation restructured its approach to the organisation of work in order to facilitate the development of these new work patterns and practices. The success of these work design strategies is reflected in the turnover of IT staff – down from 15 per cent to around 5 per cent.

The achievements of this programme have resulted in the organisation including it as a strategy in its recruitment and selection process. Specifically, TechCo identifies people with the appropriate skills in business and management who are looking for knowledge and skill development to enhance their careers. In particular, TechCo has identified a series of high-performance competencies that can deliver success at entry-level positions. These include customer service, problem-solving, communication skills, teamworking, and project management. In terms of the developmental side of this approach, TechCo has initiated management learning and development programmes that provide more senior IT staff with the skills to advance their career paths into middle- and senior-level management. As one manager noted:

IT professionals need to have business, communication and leadership skills in order to fully understand their clients' mission statements and the role technology plays in meeting corporate goals and objectives. As an industry, we need to do a better job of teaching our people these skills because they are the fundamental building blocks for successful organisations. Those who ignore them are likely to fail.

Source: Adapted from Holland et al. (2002)

Questions

1   Identify the key job and work design features of this case.
2   What are the seemingly paradoxical issues associated with this job and work design when management received the feedback for the workforce?
3   Why did this approach become so successful?

FOR DISCUSSION AND REVISION

Questions

1   Why has the concept of job design proved to be attractive to both employers and employees?
2   Explain the 'Hawthorne effect'.
3   Despite the criticisms and research, why does the mechanistic approach remain a dominant force in work design today?

4   What are the potential issues that organisations have to deal with when developing HIWSs?
5   How is work design evolving in the early twenty-first century? Explain some of the key features?
6   Considering what we know today about job satisfaction and work design, do you think it is ethical for employers to continue to develop work patterns and practices along Taylorist/Fordist lines?

GLOSSARY

Flexibility: the ability to adjust to changing conditions. During absences caused by illness or vacation, it is easier to cover a job if the population capable of performing it has not been limited too severely by the job design. Management has more options and, therefore, more flexibility if more people have the needed skills or capacities.

Flextime: a work schedule, usually on the day shift, that requires employees to be at work for the core hours, usually between 10 a.m. and 3 p.m., with the remaining work hours being chosen according to individual needs or work preferences. Each person is expected to work 40 hours per week. The schedule has been successfully applied in white-collar jobs in Europe and the United States.

Hawthorne Effect: refers to a study at the Hawthorne plant of Western Electric Company that illustrated a confounding factor in work studies in which the attention paid to the workers was considered to have a profound effect on the success of the workplace intervention.

Job Analysis: a study to determine and identify duties, tasks, and functions in a job, together with the skills, knowledge, and responsibilities required of the worker. It is accomplished through measurement, observation, and interviews.

Job Demands: the physiological, psychological, and perceptual requirements of a job that determines the suitability of a given workload for the potential workforce.

Job Design: the arrangement of tasks over a work shift, whether in terms of the distribution of light and heavy physical work or the arrangement of rest breaks in a mentally or perceptually demanding task. Good job design reduces the dangers of fatigue and human error.

Job Rotation: the movement of a worker from one defined task to another, particularly when more than one workstation is involved.

Job Satisfaction: a multidimensional psychophysical measure that compares and rates a person's opinions about job requirements to individual goals for meaningful work.

Work Study: the analysis of work methods, techniques, and procedures.

FURTHER READING

Books

BOXALL, P., PURCELL, J. AND WRIGHT, P. (2015) *The Oxford Handbook of Human Resource Management: A Critical Text.* Oxford: Oxford University Press.

This book provides an analysis of HIWSs within the context of human resource management policies and practices.

HOLMAN, D., WALL, T., CLEGG, C., SPARROW, P. AND HOWARD, A. (2004) *Essentials of the New Workplace.* New York: Wiley.
This book provides a variety of perspectives from which to explore the development of work design.

PARKER, S. AND WALL, T. (1998) *Job and Work Design: Organizing Work to Promote Well-Being and Effectiveness.* Thousand Oaks, CA: Sage.
A definitive review of the area of work design by two leading experts.

THOMPSON, P. AND MCHUGH, D. (2002) *Work Organisation: A Critical Introduction* (3rd edn). London: Macmillan Business.
A critical text exploring a variety of issues in the organisation of work.

Journals

The following are articles illustrating contemporary aspects of work organisation.
Campion, M. A., Mumford, M. M., Morgeson, P. and Nahrgang, D. (2005) Work design, eight obstacles and opportunities. *Human Resource Management,* 44(4): 367–390.
FOSS, N. J., MINBAEVA, T. P, AND REINHOLT, M. (2009) Encouraging knowledge sharing among employees: How job design matters. *Human Resource Management,* 48(6): 871–893.
LANTZ, A. AND BRAV, A. (2007) Job design for learning in work groups. *Journal of Workplace Learning,* 19(5): 269–285.
TORRACO, R. J. (2005) Work design theory: A review and critique with implications for human resource development. *Human Resource Development Quarterly,* 16(1): 85–109.

WEB RESOURCES

Channel 4: Show Me Your Money (2015)
  In a groundbreaking experiment, the managing director of Pimlico Plumbers challenges his staff to tell each other how much they earn and to help establish a fairer system of pay. This can be related to the stop and reflect activity www.channel4.com/programmes/show-me-your-money.

Ford and Taylor Scientific Management (Edited) – YouTube (2008). This is a seven-minute video on Scientific Management.   https://www.youtube.com/watch?v=8PdmNbqtDdI.

A brief view on The Hawthorne Effect. YouTube 2013 www.youtube.com/watch?v=IxZoxN5IjFE.

Tour of Semco and interview with Ricardo Semler. This is contemporary work and job design in action. YouTube 2012. https://www.youtube.com/watch?v=vLtpdtGJ3Dw.

REFERENCES

APPLEYARD, M. AND BROWN, C. (2001) Employment practices and semiconductor manufacturing performance. *Industrial Relations*, 40(3): 436–471.

ARGYLE, M. (1989) *The Social Psychology of Work*. London: Penguin.

BARNES, A. (2004) Dairies, dunnies and disciple: Resistance and accommodation to monitoring in call centres. *Labour and Industry*, 13(3): 127–138.

BEHAM, B., BAIERL, A. AND POELMANS, S. (2014). Managerial telework allowance decisions – a vignette study among German managers. *International Journal of Human Resource Management*, 26 (11, 2015). Published online: 16 July 2014.

BENDIX, R. (1963) *Work and Authority in Industry*. New York: Harper Row.

BERG, M. (1985) *The Age of Manufactures 1700–1820*. London: Fontana.

BIRCHALL, D. (1975) *Job Design*. Essex: Gower Press.

BOSCH-SIJTSEMA, PETRA M., RUOHOMÄKI, V. AND VARTIAINEN, M. (2010) Multi-locational knowledge workers in the office: Navigation, disturbances and effectiveness. *New Technology, Work and Employment*, 25(3): 183–195.

BOXALL, P. AND PURCELL, J. (2015) *Strategy and Human Resource Management* (4th edn). Basingstoke: Palgrave Macmillan.

BRAVERMAN, H. (1974) *Labor and Monopoly Capital*. New York: Monthly Review Press.

BREWSTER, C., CAREY, L., DOWLING, P., GROBLER, P., HOLLAND, P. AND WARNICH, S. (2003) *Contemporary Issues in Human Resource Management: Gaining a Competitive Advantage*. Oxford: Oxford University Press.

BROWN, J. A. C. (1986) *The Social Psychology of Industry*. London: Penguin.

BUCHANAN, D. A. (1979) *The Development of Job Design: Theories and Techniques*. Farnborough: Saxon House.

BUCHANAN, D. A. AND HUCZYNSKI, A. A. (1985) *Organizational Behaviour*. Upper Saddle River, NJ: Prentice Hall.

CAPPELLI, P. AND NEUMARK, D. (2001) Do 'high performance' work practices improve established level outcomes? *Industrial and Labor Relations Review*, 54(4): 737–776.

CHANDLER, A. (1977) *The Visible Hand*. Cambridge, MA: Harvard University Press.

CHILD, J. (1984) *Organization: A Guide to Problems and Practice* (2nd edn). London: Harper and Row.

COLE, G. A. (1988) *Personnel Management: Theory and Practice*. London: DP Publications.

COLLINS, A. M., CARTWRIGHT, S. AND HISLOP, D. (2013) Homeworking: Negotiating the psychological contract. *Human Resource Management Journal*, 23(2): 211–225.

CONNELL, J. AND HARVEY, H. (2004) Call centres and labour turnover: Do HRM practices make a difference? *International Employment Relations Review*, 10(2): 49–66.

CORDERY, J. AND PARKER, S. (2015) Work organisation. In Boxall, P., Purcell, J. and Wright, P. (eds), *The Oxford Handbook of Human Resource Management: A Critical Text*. Oxford: Oxford University Press, pp. 187–209.

DEERY, S. AND KINNIE, N. (2002) Call centres and beyond: A thematic evaluation. *Human Resource Management Journal*, 12(2): 2–13.

DELBRIDGE, R. (2005) Workers under lean manufacturing. In Holman, D., Wall, T., Clegg, C., Sparrow, P. and Howard, A. (eds), *Essentials of the New Workplace*. New York: Wiley, pp. 15–32.

DRUCKER, P. (1998) *Knowledge Management*. Boston: Harvard Business School Press.

EDWARDS, P. K. (1979) *Contested Terrain*. London: Heinemann.

EuroFound (2012) *Telework in the European Union*. Dublin: European Foundation for the Improvement of Living and Working Conditions.

GOLDTHORPE, J. D. (1966) Attitudes and behaviour of car assembly workers: A deviant case and theoretical critique. *British Journal of Sociology*, 17: 227–244.

GORZ, A. (ed.) (1976) *The Division of Labour: The Labour Process and Class-Struggle in Modern Capitalism*. Brighton: Harvester Press.

GRINT, K. (1991) *The Sociology of Work*. Cambridge: Polity Press.

GUEST, D. (1995) Human resource management, trade unions and industrial relations. In Storey, J. (ed.), *Human Resource Management: A Critical Text*. London: Routledge, pp. 110–141.

HACKMAN, J. R. (1987) The design of work teams. In Lorsch, J. (ed.), *The Handbook of Organizational Behavior*. Upper Saddle River, NJ: Prentice Hall, pp. 315–342.

HACKMAN, J. R. AND OLDHAM. G. (1976) Motivation through the design of work: Test of a theory. *Organizational Behavior and Human Performance*, 16: 250–279.

HACKMAN, J. R AND OLDHAM, G. (1980) *Work Design*. MA: Addison-Wesley.

HILL, S. (1991) Why quality circles failed but total quality might succeed. *British Journal of Industrial Relations*, 29(4): 541–569.

HILL, S. (1995) From quality circles to total quality management. In Wilkinson, A. and Wilmott, H. (eds), *Making Quality Critical: Studies in Organisational Change*. London: Routledge, pp. 33–53.

HOBSBAWM, E. J. (1968) *Industry and Empire*. Harmondsworth: Pelican.

HOLLAND, P. J., HECKER, R. AND STEEN, J. (2002) Human resource strategies and organisational structures for managing gold collar workers. *Journal of European Industrial Training*, 26(2): 72–80.

HOLLAND, P. J., SHEEHAN, C. AND DECIERI, H. (2007) Attracting and retaining talent: Exploring human resource development trends in Australia. *Human Resources Development International*, 10(3): 247–261.

HOLLAND, P., SHEEHAN, C., DONOHUE, R., PYMAN, A. AND ALLEN, B. (2015) *Contemporary Issues and Challenges in HRM* (3rd edn). Melbourne, Australia: Tilde Press.

HOLTGREWE, U. (2014) 'New' new technologies: The future and the present of work in information and communication technology. *New Technology, Work and Employment*, 29(1): 9–24.

HOWCROFT, D. AND TAYLOR, P. (2014) Plus ça change, plus la meme chose? Researching and theorising 'new' new technologies. *New Technology, Work and Employment*, 29(1): 1–8.

JACKSON, C., ARNOLD, A., NICHOLSON, N. AND WATTS, T. (1996) *Managing Careers in the Year 2000 and Beyond*. Report No. 304. London: Institute of Employment Studies.

KALLEBERG, A., MARSDEN, P., REYNOLDS, J. AND KOOKE, D. (2006) Beyond profit? Sectorial differences in high-performance work practices. *Work and Organisation*, 33(3): 271–302.

KELLY, J. AND CLEGG, C. (1981) *Autonomy and Control at the Workplace*. London: Croom Helm.

KELLY, P. (1982) *Scientific Management, Job Redesign and Work Performance*. London: Academic Press.

KINNIE, N., HUTCHINSON, S. AND PURCELL, J. (2000) Fun and surveillance: The paradox of high commitment management in call centres. *Human Resource Management Journal*, 11(5): 967–985.

KLEIN, J. A. (1984) Why supervisors resist employee involvement. *Harvard Business Review*, September–October: 87–95.

KODAK (2004) *Kodak's Ergonomic Design for People at Work* (2nd edn). The Eastman Kodak Company. Available at: http://onlinelibrary.wiley.com/store/10.1002/978047 0172469.gloss/asset/gloss.pdf?v=1&t=ifruini5&s=513bba91 51e4ddfb01a77411cbf68528d1f37b4e.

LAUTSCH, B. AND KOSSEK, E. (2011). Managing a Blended Workforce: Telecommuters and Non-Telecommuters. *Organizational Dynamics*, 40:10–17.

LAWLER, E. E. (1986) *High Involvement Management*. San Francisco: Jossey-Bass.

LEGGE, K. (1995) *Human Resource Management: Rhetorics and Realities*. London: Macmillan.

LEPAK, D. AND SNELL, S. (1999) The human resource architecture: Towards a theory of human capital allocation and development. *Academy of Management Review*, 24(1): 31–48.

LEPAK, D. AND SNELL, S. (2007) Employment subsystems and the 'HR architecture'. In Boxall, P., Purcell, J. and Wright, P. (eds), *The Oxford Handbook of Human Resource Management: A Critical Text*. Oxford: Oxford University Press, pp. 210–230.

LIPIETZ. A. (1987) *Mirages and Miracles: The Crises of Global Fordism*. Verso: London.

LISTER, K. AND HARMISH, T. (2011) *The State of Telework in the US*. San Diego: Telework Research Network.

LITTLER, C. R. AND SALAMAN, G. (1982) Bravermania and beyond: Recent theories of the labour process. *Sociology*, 16(2): 251–269.

MANZ, C. (1992) Self-leading work teams: Moving beyond self-managed myths. *Human Relations*, 45: 1119–1140.

MARCHINGTON, M. (1995) Fairy tales and magic wands: New employment practices in perspective. *Employee Relations*, 17(1): 51–66.

MARUYAMA, T. AND TIETZS, A. (2012). From anxiety to assurance: Concerns and outcomes of telework. *Personnel Review*, 41(94): 450–469.

MATHEWS, J. (1989) *Tools of Change: New Technology and the Democratisations of Work*. Sydney: Pluto Press.

MATHIAS, P. (1969) *The First Industrial Nation: An Economic History of Britain 1700–1914*. London: Methuen.

MERKLE, J. (1980) *Management and Ideology: The Legacy of the International Scientific Management Movement*. Los Angeles: University of California Press.

MICHAELS, E., HANDFIELD-JONES, H. AND AXELROD, E. (2001) *The War for Talent*. Boston, MA: Harvard Business School Press.

MYERS, C. S. (1926) *Industrial Psychology in Great Britain*. London: Jonathan Cape.

NEIROTTI, P., PAOLUCCIS. E. AND RAGUSEO, E. (2013) Mapping the antecedents of telework diffusion. *New Technology, Work and Employment*, 28(1): 16–35.

NEWELL, S., ROBERTSON, M., SCARBROUGH, H. AND SWAN, J. (2002) *Managing Knowledge Work*. Hampshire: Palgrave.

NYLAND, C. (1987) Scientific planning and management. *Capital and Class*, 33: 55–83.

OLDHAM, G. (1996) JOB DESIGN. IN COOPER, C. L. AND ROBERTSON, I. T. (eds), *International Review of Industrial and Organisational Psychology*. New York: John Wiley, 11: 33–60.

PARKER, S. AND WALL, T. (1998) *Job and Work Design: Organizing Work to Promote Well-being and Effectiveness*. Thousand Oaks, CA: Sage.

PASSMORE, W. A. (1998) *Designing Effective Organisations: The Sociotechnical Systems Perspective*. New York: Wiley.

PRATT, K. J. AND BENNETT, S. G. (1985) *Elements of Personnel Management* (2nd edn). London: Van Nostrand Reinhold.

PricewaterhouseCoopers (2009) 12th Annual Global CEO Survey – Future Proof Plans. Available at: http://www. pwc.com/ceosurvey. Accessed 27 July 2009.

ROSE, M. (1988) *Industrial Behaviour* (2nd edn). London: Penguin.

RYAN, R. M. AND DECI, E. L. (2000) Self-determination theory and the facilitation of intrinsic motivation, social development and well-being. *American Psychologist*, 55: 68–78.

SARDESHMUKH, S. R., SHARMA, D. AND GOLDEN, T. D. (2012) Impact of telework on exhaustion and job engagement: A job demand and job resource model. *New Technology, Work and Employment*, 27(3): 193–207.

SCHEIN, E. H. (1965) *Organisational Psychology*. New Jersey: Prentice Hall.

SMITH, A. (1979) *The Wealth of Nations*. New York: Penguin Books. (First published 1776.)

SOFER, C. (1972) *Organizations in Theory and Practice*. London: Heinemann Education.

TASKIN, L. AND BRIDOUX, F. (2010). Telework: A challenge to knowledge transfer in organisations. *International Journal of Human Resource Management*, 21(13): 2503–2520.

TAYLOR, F. (1903) *Shop Management*. New York: Harper.

TAYLOR, F. (1911) *The Principles of Scientific Management*. New York: Harper.

TAYLOR, P. AND BAIN, P. (1999) An assembly line in the head: The call centre labour process. *Industrial Relations Journal*, 30(2): 101–117.

THOMPSON, P. (1983) *The Nature of Work*. London: Macmillan Business.

THOMPSON, P. AND MCHUGH, D. (1995) *Work Organisation: A Critical Introduction* (2nd edn). London: Macmillan Business.

THOMPSON, P. AND MCHUGH, D. (2002) *Work Organisation: A Critical Introduction* (3rd edn). London: Macmillan Business.

THORNLEY, D. AND VALANTINE, G. (1975) *Job Enlargement: Some Implications of Longer Cycle Jobs in Fan Heater Production in Making Work More Satisfying*. London: HMSO.

TRIST, E. (1973) A socio-technical critique of scientific management. In Lockett, M. and Spear, R. (eds), *Organisations as Systems*. Milton Keynes: Open University Press, pp. 58–65.

TUCKMAN, A. (1995) Ideology, quality and TQM. In Wilkinson, A. and Wilmott, H. (eds), *Making Quality Critical: Studies in Organisational Change*. London: Routledge, pp. 54–81.

TUGEND, A. (2014) It's unclearly defined, but telecommuting is fast on the rise. *The New York Times*, March 7. Available at: http://www.nytimes.com/2014/03/08/your-money/when-working-in-your-pajamas-is-more-productive.html.

VANDERBERG, R. J., RICHARDSON, H. A. AND EASTMAN, L. J. (1999) The impact of high involvement work process on organizational effectiveness: A second-order latent variable approach. *Group and Organizational Management*, 24(3): 300–339.

WALL, T., KEMP, N., JACKSON, P. AND CLEGG, C. (1986) An outcome evaluation of autonomous work groups: A longitudinal field experiment. *Academy of Management Journal*, 29: 280–304.

WARR, P. (1987) *Psychology at Work*. (3rd edn). London: Penguin.

WATSON, T. J. (1995) *Sociology, Work and Industry* (3rd edn). London: Routledge Press.

WAY, S. (2002) High performance work systems and intermediate indicators of firm performance with the US small business sector. *Journal of Management*, 28(6): 762–785.

WHEATLEY, D. (2012) Good to be home? Time use and satisfaction levels among home-based teleworkers. *New Technology, Work and Employment*, 27(3): 224–241.

WILKINSON, A., GOFFREY, G. AND MARCHINGTON, M. (1997) Bouquets, brickbats and blinkers: Total quality management and employee involvement in practice. *Organizational Studies*, 18(5): 799–819.

WILKINSON, A., REDMAN, T., SNAPE, E. AND MARCHINGTON, M. (1998) *Managing with Total Quality Management: Theory and Practice*. London: Macmillan Business.

8

RECRUITMENT AND SELECTION

Olivia Kyriakidou

LEARNING OUTCOMES

After reading this chapter, you should be able to:

➤ Describe the personnel selection system and its component parts
➤ Understand the role played by the rational and objective staffing technologies, including job analysis and recruitment and selection methods
➤ Critically assess the concern with the selection–performance relationship that underlines the personnel staffing agenda
➤ Come to terms with the fact that employees are not simple 'human resources' that can be selected, recruited, controlled, and processed, but are human beings characterised by agency, subjectivity, and reflexivity
➤ Consider the international implications of recruitment and selection, analyse the different selection methods for expatriates, and develop effective methods for selecting expatriate managers
➤ Understand the necessity of studying recruitment and selection from a critical perspective, exploring, in particular, the ethical dimensions
➤ Identify future theoretical and practical challenges in the field of research into recruitment and selection.

SUMMARY OF CHAPTER CONTENTS

➤ **Opening Case Study**: Structuring interviews
➤ Introduction
➤ Stages of recruitment and selection
➤ Critical analysis and discussion
➤ Benefits of studying HRM from a critical perspective
➤ Conclusion
➤ **End of Chapter Case Study**: The design of a new multinational personnel selection system at MobilCom
➤ For discussion and revision
➤ Glossary
➤ Further reading
➤ Web resources
➤ References

INTRODUCTION

Recruitment and selection are seminal topics within human resource management (HRM), ensuring that organisations have the necessary human skills, knowledge, and capabilities to enable the organisation to continue into the future. Because of this, the contest for qualified candidates has intensified over the last several years (Chapman et al., 2005). This phenomenon is referred as the 'war for talent' (Michaels et al., 2001). Although competition for talent diminished during the recent recession, qualified employees still provide a competitive advantage in many industrial sectors (e.g. the automotive sector). As the economy recovers from the recent recession, this so-called war for talent has begun to intensify once again (Beechler and Woodward, 2009), and companies with high levels of applicant attraction secure the best employees (Ployhart, 2011). The 'war for talent' has placed great emphasis on getting the 'right person' for a post (see also Chapters 2 and 12). Selecting the 'right person' means that the personnel recruitment and selection agenda should be dominated by a concern with formalisation, enshrined in its language of 'objectivity', 'reliability', and 'validity', with a technology and method that attempt to maximise 'decision-making accuracy' and with the selection–performance relationship.

In most HRM practice, performance is conceptualised in strict economic terms, excluding any consideration of issues of fairness and acceptability for whichever individuals, groups, or authorities might take an interest in the selection decisions. Moreover, formalisation refers to the use of formal methods that are supposed to aid an objective, fair, and rational selection decision, guarding at the same time against inefficiency and discrimination through the use of scientifically validated techniques. This agenda prescribes practices that, if followed properly, should guarantee the 'truth' of selection decisions, producing a better match between the individual and the organisation at the point of selection. These practices should also remove any ethical uneasiness from personnel decision-making (see also Chapters 5 and 8).

Underpinning this assumption is the idea that the information identified as being central or critical to good selection decisions can be understood as being relatively neutral. 'Neutral' means here that the content of knowledge, skills, and ability profiles is treated as largely reflecting the reality of the person's role. However, there is a considerable danger of managers having too much faith in the neutrality and predictive powers of selection techniques and procedures that tend to ignore the amount of human interpretation and intuition involved in all staffing activities. A more critical way of thinking indicates that selection processes should not exclude the broader moral, social, and political considerations (Janssens and Steyaert, 2009) that are embedded in a pluralist approach – an approach that stresses the existence of divergent interests within organisations – or the roles of the following in enacting certain types of personnel selection technology:

- *human agency* – in other words, employees' capacity to make choices and to impose those choices on their world of work;

- *subjectivity* – defined as the ability of the employees to have consciousness and relationships with other entities;
- *reflexivity* – the capacity of employees to recognise the impact of forces of organisational socialisation on them and to alter their places in the organisation's social structure.

Such a critical way of thinking is further strengthened by research studies exploring the international dimensions of personnel selection. For instance, it has been reported that, consistent with the national culture, organisations in the USA typically have cultures that emphasise individual achievement, competition, and rationality (Stone and Stone-Romero, 2004). As a result, the ideal job applicant is one who is individualistic and achievement-oriented (Syed, 2008). In such situations, individuals who come from collectivist societies could be disadvantaged during the processes of recruitment and selection. Similarly, Bevelander (1999) highlights the fact that, in many countries, many monotonous jobs that used to involve low or unskilled labour are increasingly being replaced by jobs that require higher communicative and social abilities, as well as culture-specific social competence and language skills. Such an orientation towards specific social skills that are mainly possessed by those who are native born may, however, lead to personnel recruitment and selection practices that are not sensitive to the cultural diversity of the labour force.

The structure of this chapter is as follows. In the first section, we will explore the classical theories and current research that underpin the three basic elements of a personnel selection system:

- studying the job to be performed;
- recruiting a pool of applicants for the job;
- selecting the 'best' from the applicant pool.

Such an exploration will be enriched by international considerations and implications for recruitment and selection, with a special focus on expatriate managers.

Finally, we will adopt a critical perspective that tries to reveal the ethical issues underpinning personnel staffing and problematise the currently strong relationship between selection practices and performance.

STAGES OF RECRUITMENT AND SELECTION

Most recruitment and selection procedures involve several stages that occur over a period of time. The process usually first includes a job analysis (see Chapter 7) that

results in a job description and personnel specification in order to uncover all the qualities that are necessary to perform the job successfully. This analysis also incorporates an initial recognition of the need for new staff (see Chapter 6) and recruitment advertising, followed by pre-screening applicants, and finally the selection decisions and induction of new employees into the organisation. The system's view is generally based on the traditional 'predictivist' perspective on selection, which views the job as a given and stable entity into which the most suitable candidate needs to be recruited. Person–job fit is therefore of primary importance. Figure 8.1 illustrates the process and is reasonably self-explanatory in terms of the critical objectives and key activities that are involved at each phase.

The advantage of taking such a 'systems view' of selection is that it provides a holistic overview of the entire process underlying two pertinent issues: bilateral decision-making and validation feedback loops. First, decisions are made by both the recruiter and the candidate at several points in the process, supporting the constructivist perspective that both parties consider possible employment options and make decisions over whether to accept a working relationship with each other. Selection therefore serves as an opportunity to exchange information and develop mutual expectations and obligations. Hence, from this perspective, selection aims to ensure not only a person–job fit but also a person–organisation fit (that is, a fit between the applicant's values and the organisational culture) and a person–team fit (that is, a fit between the applicant's skills and attitudes and the climate of the immediate working group).

Second, the systems view highlights the importance of the validation feedback loop. In larger-scale selection processes, where numerous recruitment decisions are reached over a period of time, the crucial question from the organisation's perspective is: 'How accurate are these decisions in selecting individuals who subsequently turn out to be effective job performers?' This question has driven much of the research from the psychometric perspective. Validation feedback loops recycle information on the effectiveness of selection decisions into the selection process at different stages in order to modify and improve the procedure.

Job analysis

The traditional role of job analysis is to provide a fixed starting point for all subsequent steps in the selection process. Job analysis refers to one or more procedures designed to collect information about the tasks people perform and the skills they require to do those jobs effectively. It is a process for describing what is done in any job – not the best way to do it, nor what it is worth to have the

	Critical objectives	Key activities
Phase I Recruitment	To attract a suitable quality and quantity of applicants	Recognition of the need for new HRs ↓ Job analysis: Job description, person specification ↓ Recruitment of applicants: advertisements, agencies ↓ Candidate decision-making ↓
Phase II Pre-screening	To reduce applicant numbers to manageable proportions	Pre-screening techniques ↓ Organisational and candidate decision-making ↓
Phase III Assessment	To conduct in-depth assessments and reach suitability decisions	Candidate assessment techniques: interview, Work sample, psychometric tests, assessment centre ↓ Organisational and candidate decision-making ↓ Offer of employment: Reference/testimonial, terms and conditions ↓
Phase IV Induction	To facilitate transition into new work role	Candidate decision-making ↓ Induction procedures: placement, training needs analysis, review and appraisal ↓ Validation

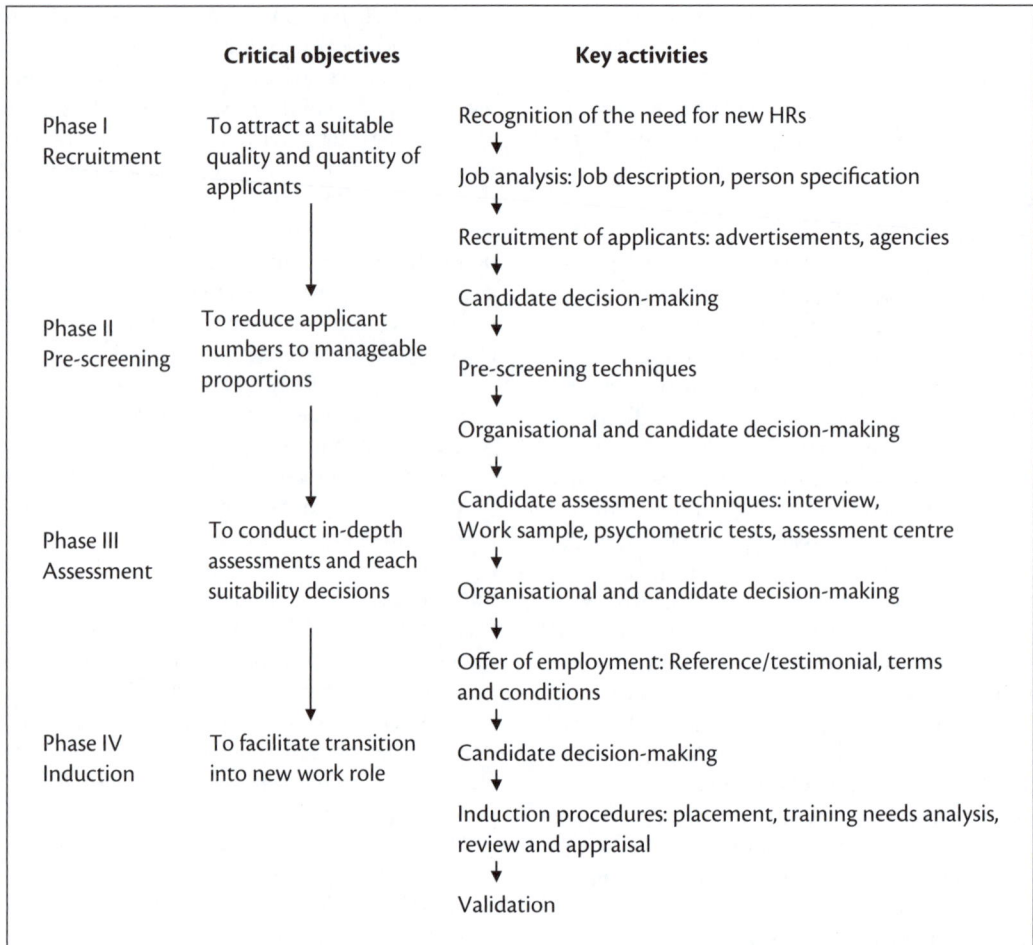

Figure 8.1 The recruitment and selection process

job done. Job analysis traditionally seeks the information on the following:

- work activities, including both individual behaviours and job outcomes;
- the machines, tools, equipment and work aids used;
- job-related tangibles and intangibles, such as materials processed and knowledge applied, respectively;
- standards of work performance;
- job context;
- personnel requirements, such as education, experience, aptitudes, and so forth.

The end product of job analysis is often a job description, which is a factual statement of the tasks, responsibilities, and working conditions involved in a particular job. Box 8.1 presents an example of a job description for a first-level supervisor post. The job description should also include

elements of contextual performance, as there is still a tendency to focus upon specific, discrete tasks and ignore contextual aspects such as maintaining morale, courtesy, and other citizenship behaviours (Viswesvaran and Ones, 2000). There may also be a person specification, which details the knowledge, skills, abilities, experiences, and attributes or attitudes required to perform the job effectively.

However, Hough and Oswald (2000) indicate that, in recognition of the increasingly rapid changes that are taking place in the workplace, job analysis should focus on tasks and on the cross-functional skills of workers, including information on personality, cognitive, behavioural, and situational variables, rather than on more static aspects of jobs. Moreover, in many selection situations, the need to understand the job is made particularly complex and difficult because the job in question is likely to be radically different, in ways that are very difficult to predict, within as little as five or maybe ten years. Finally, at the managerial/

professional level, someone may be employed to fulfil objectives or agendas as opposed to specific tasks. In such instances, Cascio (1995) says that what can often remain is something more 'person-like' than 'job-like' insofar as the job (as a set of objectives or agendas) is defined and enacted in a highly individualised manner.

The recruitment process

In most reviews of recruitment research, authors have offered organising models of the recruitment process (see, for example, Rynes and Cable, 2003). Figure 8.2 presents a model developed by Breaugh et al. (2008). Given the detailed nature of the model, we will not provide a thorough discussion of all of its contents. However, a key part of Figure 8.2, the box labelled 'Intervening job applicant variables' does merit elaboration. Although some of these variables (for example, what makes a position attractive) have received attention, many other variables (such as attracting applicants' attention and applicant self-insight) have received almost no attention from recruitment researchers (Breaugh et al., 2008).

A consideration of the job applicant variables portrayed in Figure 8.2 should play a central role in how an employer plans its recruitment process. For example, if an employer is interested in attracting the attention of individuals who are not currently looking for jobs, many commonly used (and commonly studied) recruitment methods (for example, newspaper advertisements or job fairs) may not be particularly effective. Similarly, if an organisation hopes to improve person–job/organisation fit by providing realistic information during the recruitment process, applicant self-insight is important to consider – even having received the information, applicants without such insight may not be able to evaluate whether the position described represents a good fit for them. Research (see Rynes and Cable, 2003; Breaugh et al., 2008) has found that many job applicants:

- have an incomplete and/or inaccurate understanding of what a job opening involves;
- are not sure what they want from a position;
- do not have a self-insight with regard to their knowledge, skills, and abilities;
- cannot accurately predict how they will react to the demands of a new position.

At the same time, Walker and his colleagues (2013) indicate that organisations provide signals through recruiting activities. It appears that the correspondence delivered to prospective applicants convey justice signals, which are interpreted and integrated into applicants' personal narratives of fit (Shipp and Jansen, 2011). These personal

---

Box 8.1 Job analysis: Financial Planning Sales

Job requirements

A. Summary of position

Researches and identifies target client sectors for financial product services. Develops and implements a sales process to include initial contact, follow up, presentation and closing procedures. Maintain records of contacts and sales status including contact reports, sales projections, and quota rations

B. Job duties

1) Researches and creates targeted new client lists within his or her territory.
2) Makes initial contact with potential clients.
3) Performs routine and regular follow up with potential clients.
4) Performs routine and regular follow up with former clients.
5) Visits potential clients and makes sales presentations.
6) Closes sales.
7) Maintains regular record reporting sales activity.

C. Computer skills and software used

1) Windows operating system;
2) MS Office including Word, Excel, and PowerPoint;
3) Constant contact or other customer relations management.

D. Reporting Structure

1) Reports to regional sales manager.
2) Has nobody directly reporting to this position.
3) Required to participate in annual sales meeting.

Employee requirements

A. Education and training

1) Bachelor Degree in business, finance or accounting or five years experience and High School Diploma. Bachelors Degree preferred.
2) ABC Financial Planning – Level 3 or higher.

B. Skills and aptitudes

1) Fearless cold caller, 250+ outbound calls per week;
2) Ability to close a sale;
3) Adapts to changing financial conditions and meet customer expectations.

C. Environment and physical

1) Works in high volume sales office.
2) Is able to sit for prolonged periods of time.
3) Is able to travel to client locations 25 per cent of time.

D. Licenses/certificates

1) CFP – Certified Financial Planner;
2) UK Drivers License.

Recruitment Objectives	Strategy Development	Recruitment Activities
Filling 'X' number of positions Type of applicant sought: • education • knowledge, skills, ability • work experience • interests • diversity Time frame Number of applicants Job performance of new hires New hire retentions rate Job satisfaction of new hires	Whom to recruit? Where to recruit? Timing of activities? How to reach targeted individuals What message to communicate? Whom to use as recruiters? Nature of site visit? Nature of job offer? Budget considerations?	Methods used Information conveyed: • completeness • realism • timeliness Recruiters used Hosting the site visit Extending the job offer

Intervening Job Applicant Variables

Applicant attention
Message credibility
Applicant interest:
• position attractiveness
• expectancy of job offer
• alternative opportunities
• person-job /organisation fit
Accuracy of expectations
Applicant self-insight
Applicant decision-making
   process

Recruitment Results

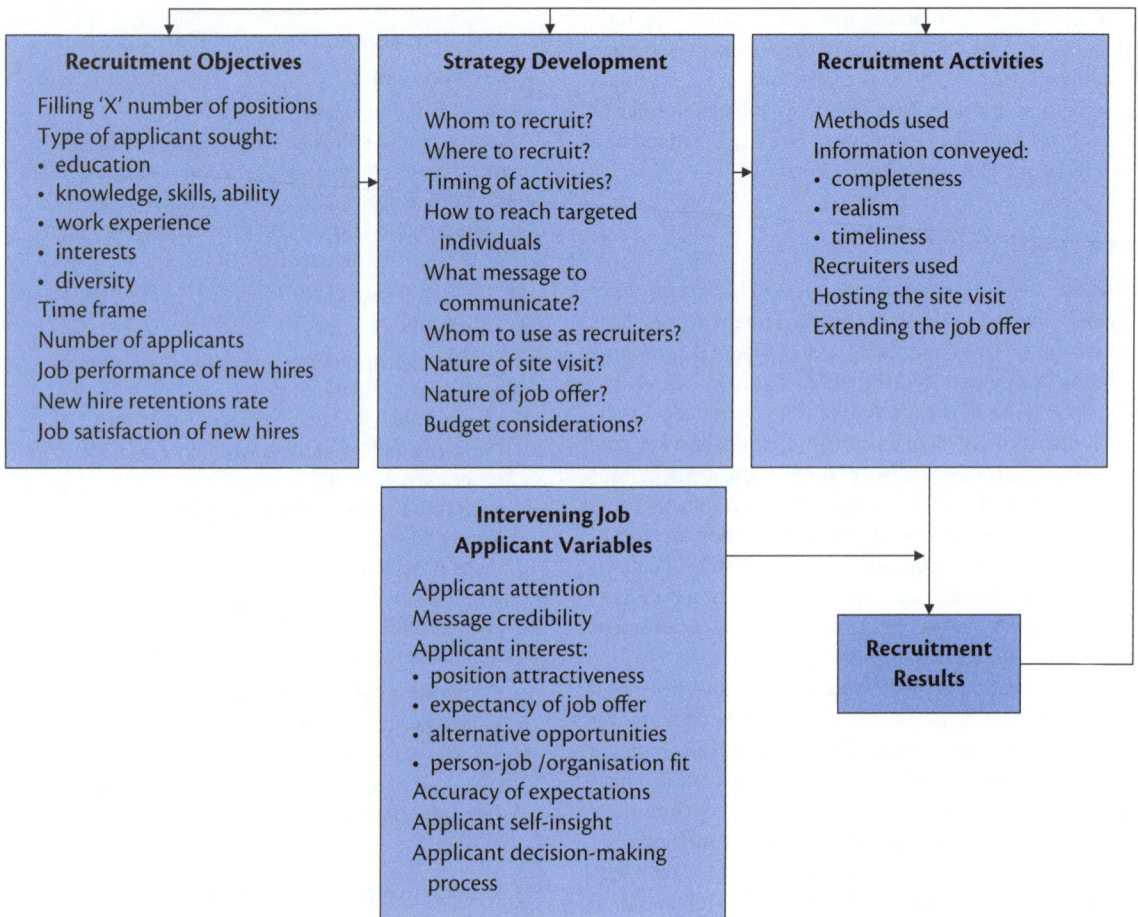

Figure 8.2 A model of the recruitment process

narratives of fit provide applicants with answers to questions such as 'Why should I want to work here?' and 'Would I fit in here?' Therefore, it is important for organisations to carefully consider the quality of interactions because they can influence organisational attitudes during the maintenance phase of recruitment. One way to accomplish this task and encourage the development of positive relationships early in the recruitment process is through the correspondence provided to applicants immediately following application submission (Truxillo et al., 2009). Even initial correspondence sent to applicants, which is often an automatic reply following application receipt, appears to influence applicants' reactions to hiring organisations.

Recruiting methods

External recruitment

Having done a thorough job analysis and produced an accurate job description, including a realistic person specification, the organisation is now ready to start recruiting potential applicants. With regard to the term 'external recruitment', this could be defined as encompassing an employer's actions that are intended to:

• bring a job opening to the attention of potential job candidates who do not currently work for the organisation;
• influence whether these individuals apply for the opening;
• affect whether they maintain interest in the position until a job offer is extended;
• influence whether a job offer is accepted.

External recruitment sources

The types of recruitment method (Table 8.1) that an employer uses may make a difference to the process here. The two most common explanations for why this might happen (Zottoli and Wanous, 2000) have been labelled

Table 8.1 External recruitment sources

Employee referrals	Advantages: low-cost, high-quality hires, decreased hiring time, opportunities to strengthen the bond with current employees. Employees carefully pre-screen applicants due to the activation of a mechanism to protect their reputation: they provide difficult-to-obtain information and coaching and press their referrals to perform.
Job advertisements	Advertisements with more information result in job openings being viewed as more attractive and more credible, increasing applicants' interest and resulting in a better person–organisation fit. The inclusion of pictures of minority groups seems to increase the attraction of diverse applicants to the organisation.
Internet/employer's website	Organisations can significantly reduce costs of advertising positions by using third-party job boards (e.g. Monster.com) or company websites. The inexpensive nature of online recruiting permits the conveyance of large amounts of information to potential applicants at a minimal cost relative to traditional advertising venues such as newspapers. Media content can be substantially richer, including graphics, photos, interactive text, and video. Recruitment websites have been shown to increase applicants' employer knowledge, in terms of familiarity, reputation, and job information (Baum and Kabst, 2015). The potential also exists for the immediate tailoring of recruiting information to target the needs of prospective applicants (Dineen et al., 2007). For example, after completing a needs questionnaire online, a prospective applicant could be provided with targeted information about the organisation, its benefit programmes, and opportunities that addresses their individual needs. The effectiveness of these sources depends upon the employer's visibility and reputation, as well as the aesthetics, content and function of the website. A potential limitation is that a firm may be inundated with applications from individuals who are not good candidates for the positions. As a way to address this issue and given its interactive capability, a website could provide potential applicants with feedback concerning person–job/organisational fit.
Universities, colleges, and placement offices	These are a source of people with specialised skills for professional positions. The choice of colleges and universities might depend on past experiences with students at the school, the quality of recent hires, offer acceptance rates, and skills, experience, and training in the desired areas, ranking of school quality, and the costs of recruiting at a particular school.
Cooperatives, internships, and job fairs	These are part-time working arrangements that allow the organisation to obtain services from a part-time employee for a short period of time; they also give the organisation an opportunity to assess the person for a full-time position after graduation.
Employment agencies and executive search firms	One source of lower-level, non-managerial employees is employment agencies. For higher-level positions, executive search firms ('headhunters') may be used. Care must be exercised in selecting an employment agency for two reasons. First, many agencies may flood the organisation with CVs without careful screening. Second, they may misrepresent the organisation to the candidate and the candidate to the organisation if they are concerned only with a quick placement and pay no regard to the costs of poor future relationships with clients.

the *realistic information hypothesis* and the *individual difference hypothesis*. Simply stated, the realistic information hypothesis suggests that individuals recruited via certain methods such as employee referrals have a more accurate understanding of what a position involves. The individual difference hypothesis posits that different recruitment methods may bring a job opening to the attention of different types of individual who vary in terms of important attributes (for example, their ability or work ethic).

Organisational image and employer branding

Applicants consider the image of an organisation as an important factor for evaluating employers (Chapman et al., 2005). Beyond brand recognition, Lievens and Highhouse (2003) suggest that in forming images of organisations, individuals draw symbolic associations between the organisation and themselves. This anthropomorphic approach to conceptualising organisational image demonstrates that applicants ascribe human personality traits such as sincerity, excitement, competence, and sophistication to organisations. Along these lines, organisational corporate social responsibility (CSR) appears to influence the attractiveness of a company to applicants (Jones et al., 2014), sometimes over and above pay and promotional opportunities (Slack et al., 2015). Applicants take note of CSR information such as an organisation's environmental practices, known as green recruitment practices (Guerci et al., 2016), community relations, sponsorship activities, and treatment of women and minorities (e.g. Almeida et al., 2015; Stewart et al., 2011). These authors suggest that attraction stems from interpreting company image information as a signal of working conditions – a proxy of 'organisational values' – and applicants develop an affective reaction to these signals, which may manifest in being attracted to that organisation.

At a practical level, this increased interest in organisational image is paralleled by the approach of employer branding (Avery and McKay, 2006). The employer brand is the package of psychological, economic, and functional benefits provided by employment and identified with an employer (Thorne, 2004). Managing these benefits to position the organisation in the minds of potential employees as a great place to work (an employer of choice) is the role of employer branding (Wilden et al. 2010). A strong employer brand has the potential to affect the pride that individuals expect from organisational membership (Cable and Turban, 2003) as well as applicant pool quantity and quality (Collins and Han, 2004). According to Backhaus and Tikoo (2004), employer branding is essentially a three-step process. First, a firm develops a concept of what particular value ('brand equity') it offers to prospective and current employees. The second step consists of externally marketing this value proposition to attract the targeted applicant population. The third step of employer branding involves carrying the brand 'promise' made to recruits into the firm and incorporating it as part of the organisational culture. Wilden et al. (2010) suggest that the effectiveness of a brand signal to potential employees is dependent on the consistency, clarity, credibility, and associated investments in the employer brand. They also indicate that word of mouth through referrals appears to be the most credible source of employer brand information.

Addressing aging populations

Whereas traditional recruiting research has predominantly examined attracting young employees from universities and colleges, looming demographic realities involving a major shift in the age of employees are forcing employers to learn more about attracting and retaining older workers. Rau and Adams (2004) examined the growing area of offering semi-retirement opportunities to older workers. This typically involved part-time employment that can serve to supplement retirement income as well as to serve a variety of social and esteem needs in older workers. Emphasising equal opportunity for older workers, flexible schedules, and pro–older worker policies have been shown to interact to improve attraction of older workers (Rau and Adams, 2005). Other suggestions for appealing to older workers include flexible compensation and benefits programmes, and job redesign to accommodate and appeal to older workers (Hedge et al., 2006).

Recruiter effect

Chapman et al. (2005) found that individuals who viewed a recruiter as having been personable, trustworthy, informative and/or competent were more attracted to a position with the recruiter's organisation. Recruiters' behaviour can be very important as the way they treat an applicant may be viewed as a signal of how the person would be treated if hired.

Rynes et al. (1991: 59) found that recruiters were:

> associated with changes in many job seekers' assessment of fit over time – 16 of 41 individuals mentioned recruiters or other corporate representatives as reasons for deciding that an initially favored company was no longer a good fit, whereas an identical number mentioned recruiters as a reason for changing an initial impression of poor fit into a positive one.

Breaugh et al. (2008) underline the importance of different types of recruiters because:

- They vary in the amount of job-related information they possess.
- They differ in terms of their credibility in the eyes of recruits.
- They signal different things to job candidates.

Finally, with regard to the relative importance of recruitment with respect to characteristics associated with the position being offered, conventional wisdom is that position attributes such as pay, job tasks and working hours are more important to job applicants than such recruitment variables as the content of a job advertisement, the design of a company's employment website, or a recruiter's behaviour. Comparisons of the relative impact of recruitment variables and position attributes have resulted in some individuals questioning whether the manner in which an employer recruits is important.

In this context, two factors should be considered. First, if an employer does a poor job of recruiting, it may not bring job openings to the attention of the types of people it is seeking to recruit. Second, even if a position is brought to the attention of targeted individuals, poor treatment during the recruitment process may result in individuals withdrawing as job candidates before an employer has even had a chance to present a job offer (Boswell et al., 2003).

Internal recruitment

The objective of the internal recruitment process is to identify and attract applicants from among individuals already

In the News **DiversityInc: Innovative tactics to recruit women in tech – Amy Brady from KeyCorp**

The number of women in key roles in the technology industry has remained roughly unchanged for 10 years. Amy Brady from KeyCorp presents some innovative tactics from the field of recruitment in order to enhance the low numbers of women in technology.

1 Gender neutral job description
   ✓ Edit job ads and recruiting materials so that they appeal to highly qualified candidates of both sexes.
2 Check your digital profile
   ✓ Make sure that the language and the look and feel of the digital space of the company are inclusive
3 Introduce female recruits to other women
   ✓ Put your best and brightest women and have a diverse group of people in the interview panel so that the prospective candidates could see themselves in your environment.
4 Build a recruiting pipeline
   ✓ Attend and support events that recognise young women for their contributions in the tech space.
   ✓ Proactively work with high school and middle school students
   ✓ Invite high school students to take part in summer internship programmes
5 Partner with professional organisations
   ✓ Professional organisations, such as the National Center for Women in Technology, Women in Technology International, Black Data Programmers Association
6 Recruit across the ages
   ✓ Structure roles in technology that allow for diversity of experience and tenure of experience to fit those roles.

Source: Adapted from Cody, 2015.

holding jobs within the organisation (Table 8.2). Many organisations have recognised that careful management of their existing employee base may be a cost-effective way to fill upper-level managerial and professional vacancies.

Realistic job previews

A realistic job preview (RJP; provided through work simulations and work tours among other things) requires that employers should provide recruits with candid information

Table 8.2 Internal recruitment sources

Job postings	These spell out the duties and requirements of the job and show how applicants can apply. Their content should be based on the job description and should clearly define the knowledge, skills, abilities and other characteristics (KSAOs) needed to perform the job. The main characteristics that lead to high satisfaction on the part of users include the adequacy of job descriptions and job notification procedures, the treatment received during the interview, the helpfulness of counselling and the provision of constructive feedback, and the fairness of the job-posting system.
Intranet and intraplacement	These inform employees quickly about job postings and prospects inside the organisation. Some companies include an online career centre where employees can also gain access to information about the KSAOs needed for positions that might interest them.
Talent management system	This monitors and tracks the utilisation of employees' skills and abilities throughout the organisation.
Career development centres	These provide employees with opportunities to take interest inventories – self-assessment tools that assess employees' likes and dislikes related to a variety of activities, objects, and types of person – assess their personal career goals, and have discussions with representatives across the organisation. In this way, employees learn about themselves, have a chance to hear about the career options within the organisation, and develop methods to structure internal career paths that match their interests.
Replacement and succession plans	Succession plans are organised by position and list the skills needed for the prospective position.

concerning the pleasant, and also the unpleasant, aspects of the job as a way to address inaccurate job expectations and decrease turnover.

Three important job applicant–related variables – anchoring and adjustment, the inability to predict how one will react to events in the future, and a lack of self-insight – need to be highlighted in the context of RJPs. Concerning anchoring and adjustment, research in social psychology (Kruglanski and Sleeth-Keppler, 2007) has found that, having formed an initial attitude concerning a topic, individuals typically do not adjust this attitude sufficiently after receiving additional relevant information. This suggests that providing an RJP to an applicant who already has an opinion of what a position with an employer involves may not result in an adequate adjustment of their initial opinion.

Moreover, Dunning (2007) has shown that people who are asked to predict how they will react to a future state of events they have little experience of are typically unable to make accurate predictions. This inability to predict one's reactions means that, even if an organisation provides descriptive information about what a job involves, the recipient of an RJP may have difficulty anticipating how he or she will react to various aspects of the new job. This inability to predict one's reactions can be at least partially overcome if an RJP includes information that is both descriptive (that is, factual) and judgemental (that is, addresses the reactions other employees have to the job attributes) (Breaugh et al., 2008).

The effectiveness of an RJP can also be limited by a lack of self-insight on the part of applicants concerning their abilities or what they want in a job. Schmeichel and Vohs (2009) indicate that individuals frequently lack self-insight and typically have an inflated view of their abilities.

Finally, RJPs could be used not only for entry-level hiring but also for internal recruitment. For example, a study by Caligiuri and Phillips (2003) described how one employer successfully used an RJP to help its current employees make decisions concerning overseas assignments. Templer et al. (2006) also documented the effectiveness of an RJP in facilitating the cross-cultural adjustment of employees transferred to non-US assignments.

Personnel selection methods

Application forms, CVs, and references

CVs and application forms are used as a straightforward way of giving a standardised synopsis of the applicant's history in order to pre-screen applicants and generate a shortlist of candidates to be invited to the next stage. To facilitate effective pre-screening decision-making, an application form should ideally be designed according to the selection criteria, and a systematic screening process should be adhered to. However, research into graduate recruitment suggests that the typical process is far from systematic (Knights and Raffo, 1990), and this can clearly impact negatively on the selection process in the longer term. Moreover, there is evidence suggesting that the inclusion of competency statements in CVs (for example, 'I am highly motivated with a proven track record in achieving goals and targets') increases the probability of producing an invitation to an interview (Earl et al., 1998). Although application forms are very popular in the UK, there are cultural differences across Europe, with standard application documents being more popular in Germany and CVs being more widely used in Denmark (Shackleton and Newell, 1997).

References involve the assessment of an individual by a third party, for example the applicant's previous employer. The use of references is more common in the UK, Ireland, and Belgium than in France, Sweden, the Netherlands, and Portugal (Shackleton and Newell, 1997). References may involve either an open-ended format or a structured format with questions developed from selection criteria. References may serve at least two purposes: first, to confirm the accuracy of information provided by the applicant, and second, to obtain information about the applicant's previous work experience and performance.

However, references suffer from problems of restriction of range (as they may provide limited information regarding the areas of interest), low predictive validity, low inter-rater reliability, low criterion-relatedness (as they are not linked to specific performance areas), and leniency (a bias that occurs when a manager rates an employee too positively), with few applicants being given negative evaluations; this suggests that not too much reliance should be placed upon their content (Shackleton and Newell, 1997). Their validity can be improved when references are sought on a criterion-specific basis (Smith and George, 1992) or by structuring references in the form of systematic ratings of 'personality' (Mount et al., 1994). References are therefore rarely used in the decision-making process, being more likely to be used merely as a final check before any job offer is made.

Selection interviews

The use of interviews as a selection technique continues unabated. In organisations around the world, selection interviews continue to be one of the most frequently used methods to assess candidates for employment (Wilk and Cappelli, 2003). McDaniel et al. (1994: 599) define the interview as a 'procedure designed to predict future job performance on the basis of applicants' oral responses to oral enquiries'. Guion (1998), however, cautions against this generic definition because it assumes that interviews are monolithic entities, like tests. Beyond everything else, we should keep in mind that the selection interview is a social interaction where the interviewer and applicant exchange and process information gathered from each other.

The clearest boundary can be drawn between the traditional unstructured interview (measuring, for example, social skills and aspects of personality) and more structured forms of interview (measuring, for example, cognitive ability and tacit or job knowledge). Traditionally, interviews are used merely to form a global impression about applicants' job suitability, including whether they would 'fit in', rather than asking them job-related questions. By contrast, structured interviews involve a series of job-related questions with predetermined answers consistently applied across all interviews for a particular job (that is, there is a standardisation of questions, question sequence, interview length, evaluation and so on). Probably the most consistent finding in interview research is that interviewers' judgements are more predictive of job performance when based on structured rather than unstructured interviews (Dipboye et al., 2004).

The two main ways of structuring interviews are situational interviewing and behaviour description interviewing. The *situational interview* (Latham and Saari, 1984), which assumes that intentions and behaviours are related, tries to elicit from candidates how they would respond to particular work situations. The situational questions can be developed using the critical incident technique of job analysis, which tries to identify the behaviours critical to effective performance on the job. This is then translated into a question about a hypothetical but job-relevant situation. A scoring guide is developed for evaluating an interviewee's response to each question by providing examples of behavioural responses to that question. One such example of a situational interview taken from Latham and Saari (1984) is shown in Box 8.2.

The *behavioural description interview* is a variant of the situational interview (Janz, 1982). But where the situational interview invites applicants to respond to questions in light of how they might behave, the behavioural interview requires an examination of how the applicant has actually behaved in the past when encountering similar incidents (with the assumption that past behaviour predicts future behaviour).

Interestingly, *panel interviews*, also referred to as board interviews or team interviews, involving multiple raters for the same set of applicants, are another means of adding structure. Despite their considerably higher administrative costs, they are expected to result in increased reliability and validity over comparably structured one-to-one interviews (Conway et al., 1995). However, the relational demography, which refers to similarity in terms of demographic attributes, and the racial composition of

---

Box 8.2 Example of a situational interview

For the past week you have been consistently getting the jobs that are the most time-consuming (for example, poor handwriting, complex statistical work). You know it's nobody's fault because you have been taking the jobs in priority order. You have just picked your fourth job of the day and it's another 'loser'. What would you do?

Interviewees offer unstructured responses that are then scored against benchmark answers. The benchmark answers for the example question are 1 = Thumb through the pile and take another job (poor); 3 = Complain but do the job anyway (average); 5 = Take the job without complaining and do it (good).

Source: Adapted from Latham and Saari (1984: 571).

---

the interview panel may affect judgements in ways that are consistent with similarity–attraction and social identity theories showing same-race biases (McFarland et al., 2004; Buckley et al., 2007). Moreover, Herriott (2003) has suggested that the process of discussion among individual raters can substantially distort the consensual score through conformity and polarisation effects, implying that it is perhaps better to obtain individual ratings from panel members before they have a chance to discuss them.

Despite the evidence showing that interviews containing high levels of structure can be valid predictors, surveys show that managers, human resources professionals and organisations use them only infrequently. Most human resources professionals report using interviews with a moderate degree of structure as this affords them more autonomy and ownership over the process (Lievens and De Paepe, 2004). The use of less structured interviews is related to interviewers' concerns about:

- having discretion in terms of how the interview is conducted;
- losing informal, personal contact with the applicant;
- the time demands of developing structured interviews (Lievens and De Paepe, 2004).

There is also a tendency for operational and human resources personnel to use 'satisficing' as opposed to maximising selection practices. This means that human resources personnel mainly ask themselves 'What must I do at the very minimum to get the best applicants?' instead of asking 'What can I do to most maximise the possibility of getting the best applicants?' Finally, when interviewers are required to justify the procedures they followed in making their ratings – procedure account-ability – they are more likely to use structured interview procedures and make better judgements (Brtek and Motowidlo, 2002).

In practice, there is tension between increasing the structure of the interview (to enhance its validity) and avoiding adverse reactions on the part of the applicant. Although the unstructured interview may be charged with being overly personal, the highly structured interview may create an adverse reaction because it is perceived as 'dep-ersonalising'. Overall, applicants demonstrate a distinct preference for unstructured over structured interviews (Hough and Oswald, 2000). Also, the less structured the interview, the more symbolic opportunity there is for the applicant to get a feel for the organisation and its culture (via the interviewer), enabling a more realistic decision to be made on whether to accept any job offer (Ander-son, 2001). Mini Case Study 8.1 highlights the dilemmas behind the use of highly structured interview formats.

Applicant factors and characteristics

Recent research has found evidence for the existence of subtle discrimination in interviews. Frazer and Wiersma (2001) found that, one week after conducting interviews, interviewers recalled African-American applicants as hav-ing given less intelligent answers compared with white applicants. Similarly, Purkiss et al. (2006) observed that those applicants with both an ethnic name and a corre-sponding accent received the least favourable interviewer ratings, whereas applicants with a Hispanic name but no accent were evaluated most favourably. This result provides support for 'expectancy violation theory' (Jussim et al., 1987): the applicants with Hispanic names were likely to be expected to speak with an accent; when they did not, thus violating expectations, they were viewed more positively.

Finally, there is evidence suggesting an existence of selection bias against overweight applicants, especially when the interviewers perceive the applicants' obesity as being controllable (Kutcher and Bragger, 2004). In addi-tion, Bragger et al. (2002) indicate that pregnancy discrim-ination claims are the fastest growing type of employment discrimination charge.

Biodata

The use of biodata for employee selection has a long his-tory, and many researchers (for example, Ployhart et al., 2006) have concluded that biodata constitute one of the best selection devices for predicting employees' perfor-mance and turnover.

Biodata forms typically assess factual and sometimes also attitudinal factors; they seek biographical informa-tion or assess descriptions of individuals' life histories using a retrospective, quasi-longitudinal, self-report for-mat; they should be defined only in terms of an applicant's past behaviour and experience (Mael, 1991). These past behaviours and experiences can reflect events that have occurred in various contexts:

- a work setting (for example, quitting a job without giv-ing notice);
- an educational setting (for example, graduating from college);
- a family environment (for example, travelling widely while growing up);
- community activities (for example, volunteering for a not-for-profit organisation);
- other domains (for example, activity in local politics and religious activities, or whether the applicant knows people who work for the organisation).

Biodata items are often referred to as 'hard' and 'soft' items respectively, in that the former are potentially verifi-able whereas the latter are not. Among the factors that biodata have been viewed as encompassing are: (a) per-sonality traits, (b) attitudes, (c) preferences, (d) future expectations, (e) self-assessed skills, (f) values, and (g) interests (Sisco and Reilly, 2007). Finally, research suggests that biodata scales can be developed so as to be use-ful in different organisations since the biodata items are relevant to a given job (for example, insurance agent or supervisor) regardless of the organisation. Indeed, Dales-sio et al. (1996) argue that a biodata scale that has been found to be valid in one country will have value if used in other countries.

A concern that has been raised with using biodata is their adverse impact on members of protected groups (Breaugh, 2009). Drakeley (1989) also criticises the model for being derived from work primarily involving a 'classi-fication' of North American university students and thus not being generalisable to other populations. Given some of the items that have been used (for example, age and educational level), this concern seems appropriate. In par-ticular, biodata items that reflect cognitive ability (such as college grade point average) are likely to result in a negative effect. As there is not a lot of research regarding adverse impact, it seems prudent for an organisation to examine each biodata item it is considering using. Appli-cants might also be likely to react negatively to items that are perceived as lacking job-relatedness, are perceived as fakable, or are perceived as overly personal in nature.

Psychometric tests

A test can be defined as a standardised measure of aptitude, knowledge, ability or performance that is administered and scored using fixed rules – most of them statistical – and procedures. All psychometric tests are scaled using a finely graded numerical system and a set of statistical formulae to ensure their reliability and validity. Most psychometric tests are also norm-referenced such that the range and distribution of scores obtained from many different types of sample provide group-specific norms against which to compare an individual's score. The scores for a managerial applicant, for example, will be examined with reference to the most closely matching set of norms (that is, managerial).

Reference to norms can also demonstrate whether the test is 'transportable' from one context to another. For example, it has only been fairly recently that UK norms for the well-known and much-used US-developed 16 Personality Factors Test (16PF) have become available. Finally, there is a variation across Europe in relation to the use of psychometrics, with Britain, Belgium, and Portugal making more substantial use of the technique than Germany or Italy (Shackleton and Newell, 1997). Psychometric tests can be divided into two main categories: cognitive ability tests (CATs) and personality tests.

Cognitive ability tests

Since the very earliest research on personnel selection, cognitive ability has been one of the major methods used to attempt to discriminate between candidates and to predict their subsequent performance. CATs can be classified somewhat arbitrarily into:

- achievement tests;
- specific aptitude tests;
- general mental ability (GMA) tests.

Achievement tests measure skills that have already been acquired and tap current knowledge or ability in a particular ability domain, usually as a function of education or training. *Aptitude tests* look at what one is capable of doing in the future, usually in specific domains such as mechanical aptitude, spatial and perceptual ability, verbal and numerical aptitude, and psychomotor ability. *GMA tests* are designed to give an overview of mental capacity indicative of the individual's overall capability for acquiring and using knowledge, passing examinations and succeeding at work.

A variety of questions are included in such tests, including ones relating to vocabulary, analogies, similarities, opposites, arithmetic, number extension, and general information. Many meta-analytic studies (see, for example, Salgado et al., 2003; Schmidt and Hunter, 1998;) have produced conclusive results not only concerning the validity of cognitive validity but also showing that the core dimension of cognitive ability (GMA, or 'g') is the key component in providing predictions of subsequent job performance.

The idea of using only an ability test score to select someone is nonetheless highly controversial, surrounded by moral as well as legal debate. For years, it has been consistently argued that ability-testing does not produce differentially unfair predictions for different groups of people. Recently, however, there have been findings suggesting that ability-testing is unfair to minority groups, with over 60 per cent of black individuals likely to be incorrectly rejected for a job (Chung-Yan and Cranshaw, 2002). This finding is set to cast the legal and moral debate into a completely different landscape and has prompted some to develop latent intelligence tests presented as work samples (Klingner and Schuler, 2004). These are, however, potentially costly to develop because they 'sample' work pertinent to particular occupational groups or job, but they may signal one constructive way forward on the issue of how to balance efficiency needs against legal imperatives and psychological concerns.

Moreover, some maintain that many jobs, especially managerial jobs, presuppose 'tacit' knowledge or action-oriented 'know how' rather than ability per se (Sternberg and Wagner, 1995), 'emotional intelligence' (the ability to perceive, understand, and manage emotion; Goleman, 1996), and at least some level of commitment (Meyer and Allen, 1997). Reviews, however, show that tests of tacit knowledge, emotional intelligence, and 'practical' intelligence do not produce better predictive or incremental validities than CATs (Salgado, 1999), indicating that they are just different ways of referring to 'job knowledge' (Schmidt and Hunter, 1993). Finally, the increased cognitive demands of today's technologically complex, fast-paced, consumer-oriented economic environment underline the fact that GMA might seriously matter to performance.

Personality inventories

Personality measures are increasingly being used by managers and human resource professionals to evaluate the suitability of job applicants for positions across many levels in an organisation. There are many different types of personality measure, each assuming a certain number of traits and trait structures. Cattell's (1965) work led to the development of the now-renowned 16PF, one of the most widely used measure of personality in the occupational context. A contrary view is provided by the Eysenck Personality Questionnaire (Eysenck, 1982), which assumes a three-factor personality model: extroversion/introversion, neuroticism/stability, and psychoticism.

The contemporary view is that there are five superordinate trait dimensions (the so-called 'big five', or FFM) by which all people can be described (Costa and McCrae, 1990):

- *Extroversion*: the degree to which someone is talkative, sociable, active, aggressive, and excitable.
- *Agreeableness*: the degree to which someone is trusting, amiable, generous, tolerant, honest, cooperative, and flexible.
- *Conscientiousness*: the degree to which someone is dependable and organised and conforms and perseveres on tasks.
- *Emotional stability*: the degree to which someone is secure, calm, independent, and autonomous.
- *Openness to experience*: the degree to which someone is intellectual, philosophical, insightful, creative, artistic, and curious.

Box 8.3 provides some sample items from a personality characteristics inventory.

Box 8.3 Sample items from a personality characteristics inventory

Conscientiousness

I can always be counted on to get the job done.
I am a very persistent worker.
I almost always plan things in advance of work.

Extraversion

Meeting new people is enjoyable to me.
I like to stir up excitement if things get boring.
I am a 'take-charge' type of person.

Agreeableness

I like to help others who are down on their luck.
I usually see the good side of people.
I forgive others easily.

Emotional stability

I can become annoyed at people quite easily (reverse-scored).
At times, I don't care about much of anything (reverse-scored).
My feelings tend to be easily hurt (reverse-scored).

Openness to experience

I like to work with difficult concepts and ideas.
I enjoy trying new and different things.
I tend to enjoy art, music, or literature.

Source: Adapted from Mount and Barrick (1995: 43).

Until quite recently, personality was not a popular method on which to base the selection of personnel. Schmitt et al. (1984) reported very low validities for the relationship between personality and job performance, and Blinkhorn and Johnson (1990) have argued that using personality tests can delude people into assuming that these offer a comprehensive picture of a person, as well as 'overly objectifying' the person. Moreover, few would dispute the conclusion that non-work-related selection tools are relatively poor predictors of job success relative to structured interviews and ability tests and should thus be treated with caution (Robertson and Smith, 2001). However, renewed interest in personality testing and the acceptance of the FFM personality structure has led to a widespread belief and confidence that personality can play a significant role in effective personnel selection.

Conscientiousness is considered to be the best predictor of job performance across various performance criteria such as team performance, leadership emergence, task role behaviour, and occupational groups (Schmidt and Hunter, 1998). Ones and Viswesvaran (1998) argue that this finding is not surprising really in that a conscientious person is more likely to spend time on assigned tasks, acquire greater job knowledge, set goals autonomously and persist in achieving them, go beyond role requirements and avoid being counterproductive; however, they advocate the use of some kind of 'social desirability' screening measure in order to minimise the likelihood of distortion.

Apart from conscientiousness, the other FFM dimensions vary in their predictive effects depending on the nature of the performance criterion and the occupational group. For example, agreeableness and openness to experience are related to performance involving interpersonal skills (Nikolaou, 2003), whereas conscientiousness and extraversion predict managerial performance significantly better in jobs categorised as being high in autonomy (Barrick and Mount, 1993). Witt (2002) reported that extraversion was related to job performance when employees were also high in conscientiousness, but with employees low in conscientiousness, extraversion was negatively related to performance. Mol et al. (2005) investigated the relations between expatriate job performance and the FFM personality dimensions and found that extraversion, emotional stability, agreeableness, and conscientiousness predicted job performance.

Finally, regarding the relationship between FFM and non-standard performance criteria, Williams (2004) found that openness to experience was significantly related to individual creativity, whereas O'Connell et al. (2001) reported a significant correlation between conscientiousness and organisational citizenship behaviours. Lin et al. (2001), investigating the relation between the FFM and customers' ratings of service quality, reported significant relationships between openness to experience and assurance behaviours, conscientiousness and reliability, extraversion and responsiveness, and agreeableness and both empathy and assurance behaviours. In addition, LePine and Van Dyne (2001) found that conscientiousness, extraversion and agreeableness were related more strongly to change-oriented communications and cooperative behaviour than to task performance. Finally, Lievens et al. (2003) found that openness to experience was significantly related to performance during cross-cultural training in a sample of European expatriate managers.

The study of the impact of personality on team behaviour and performance is another area that has seen renewed activity in recent years. Overall, extraversion appears to be the best predictor of team performance (Morgeson et al., 2005), group interaction styles (Balthazard et al., 2004), oral communication (Mohammed and Angell, 2003), emerging leadership behaviour (Kickul and Neuman, 2000), task role behaviour (Stewart et al., 2005), and performance in leadership tasks (Mohammed et al.,

2002). Moreover, conscientiousness and emotional stability are the two other FFM constructs found to be generally good predictors of team-related behaviour and performance (Halfhill et al., 2005).

Faking and personality assessment

The most pervasive concern that human resources practitioners have regarding the use of personality testing in personnel selection is that applicants may strategically 'fake' their responses and thereby gravely reduce the usefulness of the personality scores. However, most of the research concerning the effects of impression management or intentional or unintentional distortion on the validity of personality assessment has provided results indicating that, in practical terms, there are relatively few problems (see, for example, Barrick and Mount, 1996). Intentional distortion could be minimised if applicants were warned of the consequences of such distortion. Moreover, human resources professionals should also consider incorporating the 'threat of verification' into the faking warning, as applicants may respond more honestly when they believe that their responses will be subject to verification. The threat of verification becomes even more real when accompanied by carefully developed letters of reference that may provide a valid assessment of the applicant's personality.

Finally, it may still be valuable to include 'social desirability' scales in personality instruments, even though there is now considerable evidence that they generally do not improve validity and that elevated scores on typical social desirability scales may be more a function of valid personality differences than of the motivation to fake the results (Ellingson et al., 1999).

Assessment centres

The assessment centre method has been used for many purposes in human resource management, including selection, diagnosis, and development since its introduction over 50 years ago (Thornton and Rupp, 2006). It is

---

(?) Critical Thinking 8.1 Adverse impact in selection

A large organisation was found to have discriminated against ethnic minority applicants after an employment tribunal. Following a restructuring of the organisation, 100 new middle management posts were created. Approximately 30 per cent of employees are of ethnic minority origin, and currently 3 per cent of management are of ethnic origin. The personnel department decided to use a structured interview and two cognitive ability tests (a measure of verbal reasoning and a measure of numerical reasoning). Six hundred employees applied for management posts, of whom 30 per cent were of ethnic origin. However, only 10 per cent of the job offers were made to ethnic candidates. The tribunal ruled that the tests were inappropriate in terms of the time allowed, the level of difficulty, the skills tested, and the content covered. There was evidence of adverse impact and unlawful discrimination. The organisation conceded there was unintentional and indirect discriminatory impact on ethnic minority candidates and suggested compensation.

Questions

1 What's the difference between fair and unfair selection testing?
2 How can unfair discrimination be recognised?
3 What needs to be considered in evaluating the test?

✐ Class Activity

You work for a medium-sized, high-tech firm that faces intense competition on a daily basis. Change seems to be the only constant in your workplace, and each worker's responsibilities shift from project to project. Suppose you have the major responsibility for filling the job openings at your company.

▸ How would you go about recruiting and selecting the best people?
▸ How would you identify the best people to work in this environment?

meant to assess suitability across a whole range of jobs and simulate the jobs realistically. The term 'assessment centre' refers to a method involving a unique combination of essential elements codified in the *Guidelines and Ethical Considerations of Assessment Center Operations* (International Task Force on Assessment Center Guidelines, 2008):

- Multiple trained assessors observe overt behaviour displayed by assessees in complex organisational simulations and make ratings of performance on dimensions deemed important for effective performance in target positions.
- Dimensions of performance are identified by various methods of job analysis (e.g. the analysis of tasks and responsibilities in a particular job or job group) and/or competency modelling (e.g. identification of competencies needed to achieve the organisation's strategic goals).
- Any dimension that can be defined in terms of observable behaviours has potential for assessment. Examples of typical dimensions include managerial skills, interpersonal effectiveness in teams, leadership, and sales abilities.
- Behavioural observations can also be summarised in terms of tasks or responsibilities in the target job.
- Assessors can be operational managers above the target positions, human resource managers, psychologists, and external consultants.
- Assessors follow a systematic process of recording behavioural observations and making independent evaluations.
- Other information from objective performance indices, background interviews, scores on cognitive ability and personality tests, performance evaluations from supervisors, and descriptions from multisource (360°) rating systems may also be considered.
- Methods of integrating information can include the classic process of sharing and discussion behavioural observations and evaluations to achieve consensus, statistical processes of combining ratings, or some combination of these.

When used for selection, the objective is to provide an overall evaluation of a candidate's ability to be successful in the future in a new assignment. Thus, ratings are typically combined into a single overall assessment rating, which is used for decision-making.

The types of activity involved vary considerably from one assessment centre to another. Individual activities may include psychological tests, biodata inventories, and personality tests. Candidates may be asked to perform written and oral communication exercises (such as preparing written and oral reports) and undertake an in-basket exercise. An in-basket exercise requires the candidate to deal with the kind of correspondence that usually accumulates while an executive is on vacation. It contains requests, questions, directives and various pieces of information that must be handled within a specified period of time. Dyadic activities include role-playing exercises, such as how to deal with a troublesome employee or how to interview an applicant for a job, as well as group exercises including the leaderless group discussion, in which candidates work together without any assigned roles on some organisational problem.

However, Zedeck and Cascio (1984) suggest that we should question the assessment centre as a valid selection procedure, as many questions have arisen over the validity and reliability of assessing specific competencies. In addition, Lievens and Klimoski (2001) argue for a need to establish the utility and cost-effectiveness of assessment centres. Finally, assessment centres may operate to maintain the status quo in managerial jobs. Individuals who might be successful on the job yet do not resemble the present employees can be neglected. Organisational policies and traditions in hiring and promotion may influence who is successful in the organisation. If this is the case, basing assessment centres on current employees will amplify these effects.

Situational judgement tests

Situational judgement tests (SJTs) are designed to assess an applicant's judgement regarding a situation encountered in the workplace (Weekley and Ployhart, 2006). SJT items present respondents with work-related situations and a list of plausible courses of action. Respondents are asked to evaluate each course of action for either the likelihood that they would perform the action or the effectiveness of the action. Motowildo and his colleagues (2006) noted that SJTs emanate from the tenet of behavioural consistency (i.e. that past behaviour is the best predictor of future behaviour. That is, by eliciting a sample of current behaviour, one can predict how someone will behave in the future. The second major contribution to SJT theory is the concept of implicit trait policy (Motowildo et al., 2006). Implicit trait policies are inherent beliefs about causal relationships between personality traits and behavioural effectiveness. Motowildo et al. (2006) argue that individual differences in personality traits affect judgement of the effectiveness of behavioural episodes that express those personality traits. For example, if actions in SJT response options that express high agreeableness are truly more effective than actions that express low agreeableness, more agreeable people will weigh those response options more heavily than those low in agreeableness. SJTs can measure cognitive ability

Box 8.4 Example of an SJT item

You are facing a project deadline and are concerned that you may not complete the project by the time it is due. It is very important to your supervisor that you complete the project by the deadline. It is not possible to get anyone to help you with the work.

A. Ask for an extension of the deadline.

B. Let your supervisor know that you may not meet the deadline.

C. Work as many hours as it takes to get the job done by the deadline.

D. Explore different ways to do the work so it can be completed by the deadline.

E. On the day it is due, hand in what you have done so far.

F. Do the most critical parts of the project by the deadline and complete the remaining parts after the deadline.

G. Tell your supervisor that the deadline is unreasonable.

H. Give your supervisor an update and express your concern about your ability to complete the project by the deadline.

and personality, cross-cultural social intelligence (Ascalon, 2005), employee integrity (Becker, 2005), and teamwork (Mumford et al., 2008) among other constructs.

Work samples

Work samples are said to be one of the most appropriate means of selection because of the 'point-to-point correspondence' between the job and the assessment scenario (Smith and George, 1992). It is an analogous test (as opposed to an analytical test) designed to replicate the key activities of a job. Work samples are relatively easy to construct for manual jobs, clerical jobs (for example, typing), or those involving contact with clients (for example, role-play dealing with a complaint). For more managerial/intellectual jobs, work samples may be built around specific and identifiable concrete tasks (such as writing a report or dealing with the in-basket). These can then be used to assess both performance and 'trainability' potential.

A prime example of a work sample test is the 'in-basket' exercise. One potential problem with the use of in-basket exercises, however, is the organisations' heavy reliance on 'off-the-shelf' packages. Moreover, just like any other test, a work sample needs to be carefully constructed and validated. The most valid work samples not only correspond with a particular task but also capture some of its contextual features (Robertson and Kandola, 1982). A basic rule

of thumb is to ensure that the work sample is as 'complex' and 'ambiguous' as the task itself; however, the downside here is that the 'sample' cannot be 'transferred' across jobs (unless jobs are similar). On the other hand, the approach provides a good source of RJP for the applicant. Porteous (1997) says that because reliable and valid work samples are time-consuming and costly to construct, administer and score, they are of most value when used in the final stages of a selection process.

Integrity and honesty tests

Integrity and honesty tests are used to predict the likelihood that the individual will engage in counterproductive behaviour such as theft, violence, excessive absenteeism, and dishonesty (Hogan and Brinkmeyer, 1997). Integrity tests are more popular in the USA than in most European countries, although both US and French applicants have been found to react somewhat negatively to these tests (Steiner and Gilliland, 1996). There are three types of integrity testing:

- overt measures of integrity dealing with attitudes towards theft and other forms of dishonesty, including admissions of theft and other illegal activity;
- personality-oriented methods, which include questions on various dimensions, such as dependability, conscientiousness, and social conformity;
- clinical measures such as the 'galvanic skin response', an indicator of increased physiological arousal.

There are many disagreements about the value of integrity testing, as well as about its ethical status since the construct of integrity is vague and ill-defined and there is no compelling evidence for its criterion-related validity (Camara and Schneider, 1995). Other concerns include misclassification, high selection thresholds, and the adverse impact on applicants screened out by integrity test results, coupled with the fact that anyone can use them. By contrast, Ones et al. (1995) point to good construct and criterion validities, suggesting that promising results that should not be ignored.

Social media and personnel selection

New technology has the capacity to change how we work. One of the more salient new technologies is the use of social media, and an emerging application of this technology is its use in personnel decisions, such as the selection of job applicants. Research suggests about half of US organisations are using Google searches in the hiring process (Kluemper and Rosen, 2009; Slovensky and Ross, 2012) and there are reports that organisational use of social media assessment increased approximately 20 per cent from 2010 to 2012 (Preston, 2011). Senior managers for the Equal Employment Opportunity Commission in the United States note that approximately 75 per cent of recruiters are required to do online research of applicants, and 60 per cent of recruiters surveyed reported rejecting individuals as a result (Seibert et al., 2012; Sinar and Winter, 2012). Social media assessments represent the review of online information from websites/platforms designed to connect individuals (e.g. Facebook, LinkedIn, Pinterest) and involve one or more judgements of how various pieces of information might predict job performance, withdrawal, or related variables.

However, the purpose of social media websites is often social interaction, though there are exceptions (e.g. LinkedIn). As a result, there is likely a wide variety of personal information available to organisations such as gender, race, age, religion, and disability status (Braun and Vaughn, 2011). Furthermore, social media websites may provide information about political party membership, social causes an individual is associated with, involvement in union activity, marital status, or domestic responsibilities. One concern is that stereotypes might influence judgements made from social media information (Madera et al., 2009). In short, it appears that almost every

In the News Claire Cain Miller, *The New York Times*, June 25, 2015

Can an algorithm hire better than a human?

A new wave of start-ups, including Gild, Entelo, Textion, Doxa, and GapJumpers, is trying various ways to automate hiring. They say that software can do the job more effectively than people can. Established headhunters are incorporating algorithms into their work, too. So where do humans fit if recruitment and hiring become automated? Data are just one tool for recruiters to use. Human expertise is still necessary. And data is creating a need for new roles, like diversity consultants who analyse where the data show a company is lacking and figure out how to fix it.

Source: Miller, 2015.

category of biographically relevant information can be found on social media websites, although the influence of this information on assessments is ultimately an empirical question that deserves attention. For example, non-work-related variables such as political affiliation, views on social issues (e.g. statements about drug legalisation), or

---

? Critical Thinking 8.2 Social media and personnel selection

Kevin Gardner, the Chief Executive Officer of a New York–based luxury goods company, was planning to expand the company into China. As a consequence, they were looking for someone to lead the establishment of the company in China. The most promising candidate was Pam, a Harvard MBA and the daughter of Kevin's best friend, a US citizen who ran a number of newspapers in China. Pam was born in Shanghai. She had grown up in China, she spoke both Mandarin and a local dialect, and she had majored in modern Chinese history. After graduating she held a position in a major management consultancy firm and after her MBA graduation she held a post in a major luxury goods company in the USA. When Kevin met Pam, he was impressed by her insights and her ideas about expanding the company into China. After the meeting, Kevin forwarded her file to Clara.

Clara Yeow, Vice President of Human Resources, did not approve of the way Kevin brought together his top team. He ignored internal talent and downplayed the value of HR, relying overmuch on his 'sixth sense' about who were the right people to bring on board. As she put together a file on Pam for the staff, Clara had to concede that the candidate's letters of recommendation were impressive. Employers described her as aggressively creative, original, opinionated, and a risk-taker. She rounded out the file by running a routing Google search on Pam and on page three she glimpsed something that might cause concern. A story in the local free press identified Pam, fresh out of college, as the leader of a nonviolent but vocal protest group that had helped mobilise campaigns against the World Trade Organisation. On another instance, she found a story featuring Pam protesting outside the China's consulate about on China's treatment of an activist Chinese professor. Clara immediately informed Kevin that they might have a situation on their hands, something that they might need to worry about. She pointed out that Pam could be the kind of person who could get the company into trouble in China.

Questions

1 Should Kevin hire Pam despite her online history?
2 What type of selection system could be used in this case?

other behaviours (e.g. posts about Friday night drinking) may have cumulative negative influences on assessments. Consequently, various types of social media information could affect perceptions of similarity between a rater and a ratee and, in turn, influence processes that involve subjective evaluations.

In this sense, decisions to use social media assessments should be made with considerable caution. Social media assessments have little or no track record of predicting any outcome variables (e.g. job performance, training performance, turnover). It is thus somewhat difficult to argue that inferences based on social media information are empirically valid. Moreover, it may be difficult to establish the content validity of those assessments that assess social media websites that reflect job content in a systematic manner. It would appear that socially purposed websites such as Facebook would be particularly troublesome in this regard. Organisations should not engage in social media assessments unless there is job analytic information available and should consider avoiding the use of social media assessments that are unstructured (Roth et al., 2016).

Recruiting and selecting for international assignments

For effective performance in international assignments (see also Chapter 3), many researchers have concentrated on how to recruit and select individuals for such assignments. Finding and selecting the best possible international assignees is a complicated process but absolutely critical to future success of multinational organisations (Scullion and Collings, 2006). Selecting individuals for international assignments is unique given that the selection systems involve a primary focus on predicting to a job context (working internationally) rather than job content (i.e. tasks, duties, position, or title). In reality, selection for international assignments starts where other systems stop, in that only those individuals who have a demonstrated competence for the tasks and duties of the job are considered. In essence, international assignment selection attempts to take a group of 'qualified individuals' and determine who can effectively deal with the challenges inherent in working with individuals, groups, and organisations that may approach work in a very different way. Not everyone with a proven record of professional success in a domestic context for a given job title will have what it takes to be successful in an international context, even doing the same job with the same job title.

Past research has found that many psychological and biodata-type factors, including personality characteristics, language skills, and international experience, are important for international assignee adjustment and performance (e.g. Bhaskar-Shrinivas et al., 2005) and should be included in an international assignee selection system. Specific personality characteristics have been shown to enable international assignees a) to be open and receptive to learning the norms of new cultures, b) to initiate contact with host nationals, c) to gather cultural information, and d) to handle the higher amounts of stress associated with the ambiguity of their new environments (Shaffer et al., 2006), all important for international assignee success. A meta-analysis examining personality characteristics as predictors of expatriate performance found that extroversion, emotional stability, agreeableness, and conscientiousness were predictive of expatriate performance (Mol et al., 2005). This same meta-analysis also found cultural sensitivity and local language ability to be predictive.

Moreover, there are three important 'best' practices in the literature regarding international assignee selection (Caliguiri and Tarique, 2006). The first is the application of realistic previews to international assignments to help create realistic expectations during selection. Moderately accurate expectations prior to an international assignment have been shown to facilitate international assignees' cross-cultural adjustment and increase their self-efficacy for an international assignment. In this sense, in the selection phase, it is useful for firms to provide some information to assist candidates in making realistic decisions on whether an assignment is right for them and to help them with realistic expectations. Many firms have pre-selection programmes that pair repatriates with international assignee candidates to give international assignees the opportunity to find out how others, who were similarly situated, found the experience (Tung, 1998).

The second is the concept of self-selection, which enables international assignee candidates to determine whether the assignment is right for his or her personal situation, family situation, career stage, and more. Self-assessment has been found to be useful because global assignment candidates actively self-assess their fit with the personality and lifestyle requirements of the assignment (Caligiuri and Phillips, 2003). Many firms have found that this self-assessment stage fosters the creation of a candidate pool of potential international assignees with high probabilities of success. This stage should include the following pieces of information: the availability of the employee (when and to what countries), languages that the employee speaks, countries preferred, technical knowledge, skills, and abilities, along with personality characteristics and employee biodata.

The third is traditional candidate assessment, which would include appropriate personality characteristics, language skills, and past experience in a structured organisational selection programme. Two aspects of international assignee selection process have shown promise. The first is to better understand ways to engage employees early, even before an international assignment is available. The best candidates can build their efficacy for the assignment when their decision-making processes are engaged well before a position becomes available (Caliguiri and Phillips, 2003). The second is to better understand ways to effectively involve the family as early as possible in the selection process. Research has concluded that each family member will influence the assignment positively or negatively (Caligiuiri et al., 1998), so their influence should not be disregarded in the assessment phase.

Class Activity

The company in this exercise is one of the leading pharmaceutical manufacturers in the UK. Because of the intense competition in the industry and the heightened competition for highly skilled personnel, the company believes that quality of work–life balance is a key factor in achieving competitive advantage. In support of this belief, the company is considering adopting a telecommuting work arrangement for selected jobs.

The job of Public Relations (PR) Specialist has been identified as an appropriate position for telecommuting, owing to the fact that its responsibilities are mostly information-related activities that require independent mental effort with no supervisory responsibilities. The current job description for the PR Specialist is shown below; this reflects the primary job activities and qualifications for a full-time, in-office PR Specialist. There is currently only one job incumbent, and that person has just resigned. You have been asked to develop a plan for recruiting and hiring a replacement who will telecommute from home.

▸ What method of job analysis would you recommend to determine the job requirements and job specifications for a telecommuting job? Is the method you are recommending different from the method you would use if the job were being performed in a traditional office environment?
▸ What procedures do you recommend for recruiting and hiring a telecommuter? Are the procedures you are recommending different from the procedures you would use if the job were being performed in a traditional office environment?
▸ What changes would you make to the job description below in order to reflect the telecommuting nature of the job?
▸ What other recommendations would you make in order to ensure the successful implementation of a telecommuting work arrangement?

Job description

Job title: Public Relations Specialist

Department: Public Relations

Reports to: Director of Public Relations

General summary: Serves as a writer on numerous publications for the firm; coordinates materials; writes, edits, and proofs articles, public relations publications and advertising copy using WordPerfect software.

Essential job functions:

▸ Writes, edits, and proofs public relations articles, newspaper copy and human interest stories.
▸ Writes advertising copy in conjunction with the marketing department.
▸ Writes, edits and coordinates the printing and layout of the company newsletter.
▸ Meets with executives to determine PR needs.
▸ Meets with media officials and the public to publicise the firm's accomplishments.
▸ Attends information meetings at the main office on an as-needed basis.
▸ Gives presentations at meetings and other public events.
▸ Performs other related duties as assigned by management.

Education and experience required: Degree in Art/Graphic Design; demonstrated ability to use Windows computer hardware/software; some experience in television or public speaking; considerable knowledge of journalism principles, English grammar and usage; demonstrated ability to write newspaper, news and human interest articles, reports, brochures, and advertising copy; demonstrated ability to work and communicate effectively with others.

Critical summary of theories

The above literature review shows an increasing homogenisation in the approaches employed to account for the phenomena currently seen in personnel recruitment and selection; these are mainly dominated by a generic focus on improving the efficiency, effectiveness, and fairness of personnel management practice and by a concern with the selection–performance relationship. Performance is conceptualised in strictly economic terms, thus excluding any broader moral, social, and political considerations of selection practice and policy.

Moreover, such approaches (for example, those that try to achieve a person–organisation fit) assume that all members of an organisation have mutual interests and are assimilated into the prevailing socioeconomic order of capitalism. This means that organisations will try to govern the souls of employees and regulate their social behaviour by attempting to persuade them to identify with managerial objectives and the philosophy of individualism as a fundamental way of thinking and behaving in the social and organisational world. The unreflecting adoption of the scientific and rational discourse of 'objectivity', 'validity', and 'reliability' that characterises recruitment and selection practices reinforces the use of 'scientific' discourse and plays a decisive role in the effective management of employees' performance by persuading them of the objective and rational character of these practices. Such an approach, however, mainly ignores the fact that personnel practices are the outcome of human interpretations, conflicts, and generalisations (Watson, 2004) and that employee agency, subjectivity, and reflexivity lead employees to many different types of engagement with HRM practices (Zanoni and Janssens, 2007).

Finally, there has been a standardisation of employee selection practices and a treatment of certain individual competencies and job characteristics as neutral (that is, as reflecting the reality of the person or the role) rather than as socially constructed or situated. Instead of limiting inequalities, this has paradoxically legitimised gendered employment practices by cloaking them in false objectivity (Özbilgin and Woodward, 2004).

Personnel selection and ethics

Legge (2007) has argued that we need to consider 'moral economy', that is, what moral norms concerning the good and the just should be embodied in and guide choices and action in organisations (see also Chapter 5). Moral economy implies that, instead of being preoccupied with issues of efficiency and performance in strict economic terms, we should include broader moral, social, and political considerations related to the practice and policy of recruitment and selection.

First of all, personnel selection should refocus its attention on the employees themselves by considering not only individual variables, such as abilities, skills and competencies, but also the political nature of the employment relationship (Janssens and Steyaert, 2009), adopting a pluralist approach to managing the employment relationship. Such an approach criticises the belief that staffing techniques that lead to high performance are beneficial for employees and for unions that accept them, draws attention to the negative effects of such techniques (such as work intensification), and highlights the existence of continued discrimination against marginalised groups (Knights and McCabe, 1998). Moreover, the complexity of the employment relationship demands an exploration of the impact of a number of issues, such as fear of lay-offs, perceptions of job opportunities, unemployment, and labour market positions, on personnel recruitment and selection; however, the interests and perspectives of multiple stakeholders (including employees) must not be ignored.

Furthermore, the quantitative techniques involved in recruitment and selection procedures are methods that create a technical-scientific order in which the technical is superimposed on the moral and constructs a rational, goal-directed image of organisational effectiveness. Consequently, the management of personnel staffing concerns itself with the technical application of techniques even where circumstances may indicate that these might not be the most appropriate responses.

Finally, we need to ensure that the voices of those who tend to be excluded from mainstream analyses are better represented in the theory and practice of recruitment and selection (see also Chapter 4). This includes, but is not limited to, those in non-standard forms of employment, minority workers, and those working outside Western industrialised economies.

CRITICAL ANALYSIS AND DISCUSSION

The formalisation part of the personnel selection agenda reinforces an image of the work organisation as a black-box system that functions more or less well in performance terms according to the neutral, scientific, and formal, rational procedures that convert human resource 'inputs' into outputs. Consequently, the objectives pursued by the implementation of such procedures (that is, a maximisation of efficiency and effectiveness) should be of benefit to all concerned – managers, employees, government, and 'the public' alike. However, it is rare for such 'best practices' to be subjected to any critical analysis of the potential 'operating' costs, the 'unintended consequences' or – more graphically – the 'collateral damage' resulting from their introduction. What is 'good' for business is not necessarily 'best practice' for employees. In this respect, it is important to note that such procedures are never neutral: they always implicate and privilege particular social values, if not also specific socioeconomic interests.

Moreover, the mainstream analysis of personnel selection processes and procedures is based on a unitarist approach – one in which all members of an organisation are assumed to have mutual interests. In practice, however, recruitment and selection practices seem to be enacted by both candidates and selectors within organisations. If we take into account concepts such as agency and subjectivity and recognise employees as human beings capable of reflexive thought and action (Giddens, 1993), there is a possibility that different employees actively engage in different ways with recruitment and selection practices, undermining, delaying, or supporting their implementation. On the other hand, selectors do not simply adopt the 'scientific' and rational principles of the practices but appear to manipulate them according to pre-existing local power relations, since the design of such practices is 'mediated' by managerial interpretation and political manoeuvring (Watson, 2004). One should not ignore the fact that human resources strategies are the outcomes of human interpretations, conflicts, guesses and rationalisations, albeit those of human agency operating within a context of social and political-economic circumstances.

Finally, a significant consequence of the ever-increasing emphasis on the human resources–performance link has been the progressive exclusion of more and more alternative voices, as well as practices that do not necessary promote high commitment and high performance (MacDuffie, 1995). Hence, the problems and issues of personnel selection have largely been ignored in small and medium-sized organisations (see, for example, Taylor, 2004), in various forms of subcontracting designed to increase 'flexibility' through the creation of 'dependent self-employment' (Muehlberger, 2007); there is little specific reference to unionised workplaces or to the increasing problems associated with (and for) immigrant labour, as well as employees in non-Western and so-called developing economies. Similarly, the increasing resort to outsourcing work to countries where labour is cheaper is excluded from the mainstream 'recruitment and selection agenda'. The irony here, of course, is that most of these social practices can be seen as reflecting the 'success' of the globalisation project, as they can all be seen to be symptoms of the successful deregulation of labour markets, which is a central element of the neoliberal policy agenda.

BENEFITS OF STUDYING HRM FROM A CRITICAL PERSPECTIVE

A critical perspective is advanced here in order for personnel recruitment and selection practices to be better contextualised within the prevailing socioeconomic, political, and cultural factors that shape those practices. In addition, the aim is that the scientific, objective, and rational assumptions and language of recruitment and selection may be challenged and that voices excluded from mainstream personnel selection may be heard. The adoption of a pluralist frame of reference, in which the employment relationship is understood to involve and articulate different interests, has the potential to reintroduce the possible contribution of those 'external' to the organisation, such as the state or trade unions, as significant actors in devising selection policies and practices. Such an approach will force selection specialists to consider possible ways of managing the endemic potential conflicts associated with such differential interests.

Moreover, the deconstruction of the natural and neutral language of science, rationality, and objectivity that is used to legitimise 'reliable' and 'valid' recruitment and selection procedures might expose the institutionalised power inequalities, as well as the local power relations within organisations that reinforce, but also impede, the implementation of these procedures in practice. A critical perspective directs us towards an analysis of the contextual circumstances in which certain practices are, or are not, adopted by management.

This is perhaps most clearly evident in another aspect of denaturalisation: the concern of critical approaches to reveal how the content of knowledge and the individual skills and ability profiles identified as central or critical to making good selection decisions are understood as relatively neutral and are treated as largely reflecting the reality of the role or the person. Viewing competencies as individual-level attributes deflects attention away from how their meaning is socially constructed in specific contexts. By treating individual skills and job characteristics as neutral rather than as socially constructed or situated, we are in danger of either privileging certain modes of performance or reproducing the idea that different groups are naturally suited to some roles rather than others; this then undermines the chances of achieving equal opportunities. Consequently, recruitment and selection would benefit from the adoption of a critical perspective as it can offer additional insights into how roles, identities, and individual competencies are socially constructed and identify the implications of these processes for selection and recruitment.

Finally, a critical perspective will provide a voice for all those marginalised from mainstream personnel recruitment and from research into and the practice of selection. These include, for example, employees of the following: large multinational corporations; non-Western and so-called developing economies; small and medium-sized enterprises; public and third-sector organisations; alternative forms of organisation (for example, cooperatives; and non-standard forms of employment. It will also encompass those who are self-employed, subcontractors, part-time and agency workers, and immigrant labour, among others. Such a focus will enhance our understanding of what is happening to employment regulation outside large and multinational corporations.

In short, Boxall et al. (2015) argue that a critical perspective on HRM should be concerned with why management does what it does; with how contextualised processes of HRM work in practice; and with questions of 'for whom and how well' when assessing the outcomes of HRM, taking account of both employee and managerial interests and laying a basis for theories of wider social consequence.

CONCLUSION

Employee staffing decisions involving the recruitment and selection of individuals are made every day in work organisations. There has been a tendency for a rational and scientific technology to be applied to these personnel choices. This involves strongly formalised procedures and the heavy use of such devices as psychological tests. Such technology is intended to help select individuals in a way that will be deemed efficient, acceptable, and fair.

However, this approach tends to become restrictive and counterproductive. Its use can be associated with a controlling way of thinking about work organisations and people. A more realistic and critical way of thinking indicates that selection processes are highly ambiguous and are dependent on basic human processes of judgement, guesswork, chance-taking, debate, and negotiation. Selection processes in general are better seen as parts of broader and more continuous processes of bargaining and adjustment in which both organisational arrangements and human beings themselves change and adapt within the on-going negotiated order of the organisation.

End of Chapter Case Study The design of a new multinational personnel selection system at MobilCom

On Monday morning at 7.30 a.m., Dr Hans was leaving his apartment, one specifically rented to expatriates, and was heading towards his office in Kuala Lumpur's central business district. On the way, he listened to the voice messages on his mobile phone, one of which was from the assistant of the firm's owner, Frank. The message stated that Hans was expected to call back before his meeting with the human resources (HR) team that he was leading. The team meeting was scheduled in order to bring together Hans and Chinese HR experts to form a cross-functional project team responsible for the development and implementation of a new personnel process within the context of global restructuring, in order to fill 25 middle management positions in the Australasia region.

According to the in-house global localisation policy of the company, MobilCom, 90 per cent of the new management positions were to be filled by individuals originating from the country they would be working in. The affected areas included sales and marketing, purchasing, supply chain management, and finance and accounting, at locations in Hong Kong, Kuala Lumpur, Bangkok, Jakarta, Singapore, Sydney, Oakland and Port Moresby (Papua New Guinea). The new personnel selection system was part of the company's new objective to standardise all HR instruments for selection purposes around the globe. This new personnel selection system had to be developed internally.

When Hans first heard about the above changes, it immediately occurred to him that this would not be easy as personnel selection procedures varied significantly between countries. He also knew that the existing selection instruments were by no means flawless in any specific country. After the application documents had been analysed, structured interviews with the candidates were conducted by a department representative and an HR specialist. If both interviewers came to a positive conclusion on the candidate's qualifications, the top candidates were sent to an individual assessment centre in order to highlight their interpersonal competencies rather than their professional competencies. The approach of the individual assessment centres consisted of biographical questions, case studies on leadership in an international context, and participation in a leaderless group discussion. Ultimately, additional references were obtained for each candidate, although different procedures existed in different countries. After the reference checks had been completed, each candidate received written feedback, and a report was generated and added to the successful candidate's personnel file.

For several years now, Hans had been finding faults in the design of the procedures used at the individual assessment centres, but he could not influence possible modifications because the individual assessment centres were run by external consulting firms. In addition, he had been questioning the validity of the information obtained from the centres, as well as the selection system as a whole. He felt there was a need to improve the contents of the structured interviews that were based on the candidate's current situation, as opposed to the candidate's previous work experience. Overall, efforts to improve the current selection systems had only rarely been undertaken owing to limited time and a limited budget allotted for personnel affairs – a fact that Hans had already pointed out to management several times.

The development of a new multinational personnel selection system now posed a huge challenge for Hans and his project team. His team, comprising Australian and Chinese members with HR knowledge as well as HR managers from headquarters, had already been working on the development of the new personnel selection system for four months. Over the past few weeks, numerous meetings had been held, yet no significant progress had been made. One reason could be the fact that there was obvious heterogeneity between the opinions of the Australian and Asian team members regarding the new personnel selection system. This created a tense atmosphere and dissent with respect to sharing the workload. The goal of today's meeting was to come to a consensus on several important issues:

- what individual modules the new personnel selection system should contain;
- whether country-specific adaptations were necessary and feasible for each module;
- the implementation process of the new personnel instrument at each location.

When Hans arrived at his office, one of the three Chinese secretaries reminded him that Frank was waiting for him to return his call. She avoided eye contact by looking down to the floor, but with a big smile and gestures that appeared submissive as she perpetually nodded her head. Hans rang Frank, and Frank began speaking:

> Dr Hans, you know how much I appreciate your dedication to the company, but I have concerns about the current international selection procedures. We need something that is going to work, and work immediately! And don't you dare try to offer me this empirical or validity stuff. I don't give a damn. You have a whole department with highly qualified people. I assume you are capable of filling these vacant management positions. We also need a selection system that works everywhere. We cannot afford to apply different procedures in every country. What we need are consistent procedures, something applicable cross-nationally and cross-regionally. You, as a cosmopolitan man, should know exactly what I mean. I also expect everything to be documented in complete detail.

Although Hans shared Frank's enthusiasm for an improved personnel selection system, there were many complications that could arise; Frank seemed completely unaware of these, and Hans tried to inform him about the possible problems. Hans argued that although a multinational selection system would have its advantages, these advantages might become costly if they could not easily be implemented in each region. Each country has its own unique economic and education situations, which would undoubtedly cause difficulties when creating a universal personnel selection system. With respect to cultural difference, he argued that a standardised personnel selection system would also ignore cultural differences and culture-specific circumstances. This would affect not only individual modules in the system but also the basic job requirements, the adaptation of modules to specific countries, and the use of specific selection methods. Hans also expressed his concern with Frank's lack of interest in testing the validity of the new selection procedures.

Of course, that wasn't exactly what Frank wanted to hear:

> Don't tell me about problems; I want solutions. And you should not forget that this is what I pay you and your team to do. You have until the end of this week to deliver the final and written conclusions on this matter. If not, I will reduce your team in Kuala Lumpur by half, and I will delegate the development of this new system to global headquarters. Either you come up with something useful by the end of this week, or central headquarters will do the job. End of discussion.

The team meeting

At the meeting, Hans informed everyone about the current situation with Frank, set the objectives of the meeting, and asked for the detailed recording of everything they discussed. The Chinese colleagues agreed by nodding their heads uniformly, a behaviour that was always expected when there was an order from a member with higher hierarchical status, whereas the Australian colleagues openly disapproved of the detailed recording of the discussions.

During the meeting, there was an apparent disagreement between a Chinese HR employee and the Australian economist regarding the definitions of the job requirements and their profiles. Yu wanted to include 15 dimensions – 5 components that tested the candidate's professional competencies and 10 dimensions that evaluated social competencies. However, Andreas openly disagreed with this proposition: 'I have told you many times that the acquisition of 15 dimensions is simply impossible. It is important to define clearly distinguishable job requirements that are measurable, describable, and equally relevant in all countries in the region'.

Yu, intimidated by her Australian colleague's manner, blushed and looked down towards the floor, signalling that she did not dare to say anything further. She often found it difficult to cope with negative feedback, particularly when it occurred in front of her colleagues. There had been several times already when she had not been able to stand up to Andreas, which seemed to affect her more and more each time. She had once spoken to Hans about her difficulties communicating with Andreas; however, Hans quickly grew irritated by the complaint and asked her to wait and hope for an improvement in the situation. Yu never discussed the situation with Hans again.

The German in-house psychologist intervened in the discussion and proposed the inclusion of six competencies – technical and vocational skills, social competencies, leadership competencies, communicative competencies, flexibility, and adaptability – that showed great validity and reliability. There was disagreement from some Chinese members, who proposed the inclusion of several more and different competencies, which ended with them feeling irritated and intimidated. Andreas proposed that, due to the time pressure, they should bring a majority vote with respect to the skills, but the Chinese HR member argued: 'No, a majority vote is not the solution. It may lead to good decisions not succeeding because certain team members follow the uniform opinion of the majority. We should try to reach a consensus on this issue.' The dispute was solved by Hans, who decided which would be the final job requirements for selecting the managers and adopted the six dimensions proposed by the German team members.

The next important issue on the agenda was to define the modules and the job requirements for each module. For this issue, there was agreement that a multinational selection system should be two-tiered. The first tier would consist of three modules: viewing the candidates' application documents, a telephone conference with the applicants that should be conducted in an unstructured manner, and obtaining three references from former employers. Unlike the current procedures, references should not only be used to verify the past employment and duration of employment but also include a statement regarding the candidate's personality. Four modules would follow in the second tier – a panel interview, a biography-oriented in-depth interview, a simulated group exercise and testing procedures. All the modules were described in great detail, and emphasis was placed on including standardised tests in order to increase the validity of the entire process, even though there is evidence that intelligence and personality tests are not generally highly accepted and that cultural problems exist.

Towards the end of the long and detailed presentation of the modules, Hans's colleague Anne, who held a MBA degree from one of the major Australian business schools, interrupted: 'I don't want to be rude, but isn't it important to take the candidate's perspective into consideration, as well?' But Andreas countered: 'Unfortunately, nobody cares about the candidate's perspective. We are interested in choosing the right person, certainly not in satisfying the applicants – these never-ending discussions on fairness and acceptance. Reality differs significantly from the ideal procedures we are taught in university.'

Now, Angela jumped into the discussion:

> But let's not forget that management is not just a technical matter, and sometimes, if you find someone generally useful, then you could adapt the job to fit the person. The selection process is always a sort of negotiation between the potential employee and the potential employer. We, as recruiters, cannot really know what any of these people are really going to be like if you take them on. Therefore, we need to deploy the basic human skills of eliciting helpful responses from people and judging the likelihood of one person being a better bet for the organisation than another. In this sense, there is no 'right person', there is only 'the better bet'. Some of the most important determinants of how well someone does the job are ones that arise after the appointment of the individual.

Hans could not stand any further disputes at the time and took the initiative to terminate the long meeting, which had at least achieved the first step towards specifying the modules in terms of content and procedures.

However, they had not been able to specify the adaptations for each target country and the ways of implementing those modules. Hans thought that he should make the decisions himself and then include them in the report to be handed to Frank.

Right after the meeting, Hans went straight to his office and did not come out again for the rest of the afternoon. As soon as he had received the minutes of the meeting, he wrote his final report for Frank. He later received a short notice sent by Frank, informing him that important basic conditions and necessary adaptations had not sufficiently been taken into consideration in the new multinational personnel selection system; therefore, he had handed the case over to global headquarters. Finally, he stated that there would be staff-related consequences for Hans's department in Kuala Lumpur.

Questions

1 Describe in detail all the modules included in the two-tiered selection system proposed by the team.
2 What is the critical analysis of the case study?

FOR DISCUSSION AND REVISION

1 If you had entered into a joint venture with a foreign company but knew that women were not treated fairly in that culture, would you consider sending a female expatriate to handle the start-up? Why or why not?

2 Evaluation hiring is a procedure in which a job candidate is hired by a staffing company but put to work at another company. After a set period of time (usually 90 days), the company decides whether to hire the person as a permanent employee. Analyse the benefits for the company that arise from using such a procedure. What ethical issues are involved in evaluation hiring?

3 Should applicants be selected primarily on the basis of their ability or on personality/fit? How can fit be assessed?

4 In many organisations that have worked to a team structure, the team is the principal unit where the work gets done. However, most organisations recruit and hire as though there were one job description and the team did not exist. If there are distinct roles to be played within a team, how would you go about recruiting and hiring for them? The characteristics needed by individual team members depend on the team and the strengths and weaknesses of other team members. How could you include this dynamic and interactive nature in the recruitment and hiring process?

5 One of the strategic staffing choices is whether to pursue workforce diversity actively or passively. First suggest some ethical reasons for an active pursuit of diversity, and then suggest some ethical reasons for a more passive approach. Assume that the type of diversity in question is an increasing representation of women and ethnic minorities in the workforce.

6 Why is it important for the organisation to view all components of staffing from the perspective of the job applicant?

7 Assume that the organisation you work for practices strict adherence to the rules of objective, scientific, and rational recruitment and selection. But beyond that, it seems that 'anything goes' in terms of tolerated staffing practices. What is your assessment of this approach?

8 Do you think that targeted recruitment systems, for example those targeting older workers, women, minority groups, or people with the desired skills, are fair? Why or why not?

9 Cognitive ability tests are one of the best predictors of job performance, yet they have a substantial adverse impact on minority groups. Do you think it is fair to use such tests? Why or why not?

10 Do you think it is ethical for employers to select applicants on the basis of questions such as 'Dislike loud music' and 'Enjoy travelling around the world with a backpack', even if the scales that such items measure have been shown to predict job performance? Explain your answer.

11 Given recent changes in the nature of work, especially during the period of economic turbulence, discuss the relative effectiveness of job analysis techniques and suggest how they might be improved.

12 Suppose that you are asked to write a recommendation letter for a friend you like but consider unreliable. Would it be ethical for you to write a positive reference even though you anticipate that your friend will not be a good employee? If not, would it be ethical for you to agree to write the letter knowing that you will not be very positive in your assessment of your friend's abilities?

GLOSSARY

Assessment Centre: A technique for selecting individuals with high managerial potential based on their performance on a series of simulated managerial tasks.

Big Five Personality factors: Dimensions that describe an individual's extroversion, agreeableness, conscientiousness, emotional stability, and openness to experience.

Job analysis: The systematic process of gathering and interpreting information about the essential duties, tasks, and responsibilities of a job.

Person-job fit: The extent to which a person's ability and personality match the requirements of a job.

Personality: The set of characteristics that underlie a relatively stable pattern of behaviour in response to ideas, objects, or people in the environment.

Realistic job preview: A recruiting approach that gives applicants all pertinent and realistic information about the job and the organisation.

Recruiting: The activities or practices that define the desired characteristics of applicants for specific jobs.

Selection: The process of determining the skills, abilities and other attributes a person needs to perform a particular job.

Stereotyping: Placing an employee into a class category based on one or a few traits or characteristics.

Validity: The relationship between an applicant's score on a selection device and his or her future job performance.

FURTHER READING

Books

BOLTON, S. C. AND HOULIHAN, M. (2007) *Searching for the Human in Human Resource Management*. London: Palgrave Macmillan.

BOXALL, P., PURCELL, J. AND WRIGHT, P. (2015) *The Oxford Handbook of Human Resource Management*. Oxford: Oxford University Press.

GREY, C. AND WILLMOTT, H. (2005) *Critical Management Studies: A Reader*. Oxford: Oxford University Press.

LEGGE, K. (1995) *Human Resource Management: Rhetorics and Realities*. London: Palgrave Macmillan.

LEOPOLD, J., HARRIS, L. AND WATSON, T. J. (2005) *The Strategic Management of Human Resources*. London: FT Prentice Hall.

PINNINGTON, A., MACKLIN, R. AND CAMPBELL, T. (2007) *Human Resource Management: Ethics and Employment*. Oxford: Oxford University Press.

WEB RESOURCES

American Psychological Association http://www.apa.org.

Chartered Institute of Personnel and Development http://www.cipd.co.uk.

DiversityInc http://www.diversityinc.com/.

European Association of Work and Organizational Psychology http://www.eawop.org.

Office of Personnel Management, Assessment and Selection https://www.opm.gov/policy-data-oversight/assessment-and-selection/.

Personnel Today www.**personnel**today.com.

Recruitment and Employment Federation https://www.rec.uk.com/.

Society for Strategic Human Resource Management http://shrm.org.

Society for Industrial and Organizational Psychology www.siop.org.

Workforce http://www.workforce.com.

REFERENCES

ALMEIDA, S., FERNANDO, M., HANNIF, Z. AND DHARMAGE, S. (2015). Fitting the mould: The role of employer perceptions in immigrant recruitment decision-making. *International Journal of Human Resource Management*, 26(22): 2811–2832.

ANDERSON, N. (2001) Towards a theory of socialization impact: Selection as pre-entry socialization. *International Journal of Selection and Assessment*, 9(1/2): 84–91.

ASCALON, E. M. (2005) Improving expatriate selection: Development of a situational judgement test to measure cross-cultural social intelligence. *Dissertation Abstracts International*, 65, 4880.

AVERY, D. R. AND MCKAY, P. F. (2006) Target practice: An organizational impression management approach to attracting minority and female job applicants. *Personnel Psychology*, 59: 157–187.

BACKHAUS, K. AND TIKOO, S. (2004) Conceptualizing and researching employer branding. *Career Development International*, 9: 501–517.

BALTHAZARD, P., POTTER, R. E. AND WARREN, J. (2004) Expertise, extraversion and group interaction styles as performance indicators in virtual teams. *Database for Advances in Information Systems*, 35(1): 41–64.

BARRICK, M. R. AND MOUNT, M. K. (1993) Autonomy as a moderator of the relationship between the Big Five personality dimensions and job performance. *Journal of Applied Psychology*, 78(1): 111–118.

BARRICK, M. R. AND MOUNT, M. K. (1996) Effects of impression management and self-deception on the predictive validity of personality constructs. *Journal of Applied Psychology*, 81: 261–272.

BAUM, M. AND KABST, R. (2014) The effectiveness of recruitment advertisements and recruitment websites: Indirect and interactive effects on applicant attraction. *Human Resource Management*, 53(3): 353–378.

BECKER, T. E. (2005) Development and validation of a situational judgement test of employee integrity. *International Journal of Selection and Assessment*, 13: 225–232.

BEECHLER, S. AND WOODWARD, I.C. (2009) The global 'war for talent'. *Journal of International Management*, 15: 273–285.

BEVELANDER, P. (1999) The employment integration of migrants in Sweden. *Journal of Ethnic and Migration Studies*, 25(3): 445–468.

BHASKAR-SHRINIVAS, P., HARRISON, D., SHAFFER, M. AND LUK, D. (2005) Input-based and time-based modes of international adjustment: Meta-analytic evidence and theoretical extensions. *Academy of Management Journal*, 8: 257–281.

BLINKHORN, S. AND JOHNSON, C. (1990) The insignificance of personality testing. *Nature*, 348: 671–672.

BOSWELL, W. R., ROEHLING, M. V., LEPINE, M. A. AND MOYNIHAN, L. M (2003) Individual job-choice decisions and the impact of job attributes and recruitment practices: A longitudinal field study. *Human Resource Management*, 42: 23–37.

BOXALL, P., PURCELL, J. AND WRIGHT, P. (2015) Human resource management: Scope, analysis, and significance. In Boxall, P., Purcell, J. and Wright, P. (eds), *The Oxford Handbook of Human Resource Management*. Oxford: Oxford University Press, pp. 1–16.

BRAGGER, J. D., KUTCHER, E., MORGAN, J. AND FIRTH, P. (2002) The effects of the structured interview on reducing biases against pregnant job applicants. *Sex Roles*, 46: 215–226.

BRAUN, V. R. AND VAUGHN, E. D. (2011) The writing on the (Facebook) wall: The use of social networking sites in hiring decisions. *Journal of Business and Psychology*, 26: 219–225.

BREAUGH, J. A. (2009) The use of biodata for employee selection: Past research and future directions. *Human Resource Management Review*, 19: 219–231.

BREAUGH, J. A., MACAN, T. H. AND GRAMBOW, D. M. (2008) Employee recruitment: Current knowledge and directions for future research. In Hodgkinson, G. P. and Ford, J. K. (eds), *International Review of Industrial and Organizational Psychology*, vol. 23. New York: John Wiley and Sons, pp. 45–82.

BRTEK, M. D. AND MOTOWIDLO, S. J. (2002) Effects of procedure and outcome accountability on interview validity. *Journal of Applied Psychology*, 87(1): 185–191.

BUCKLEY, M. R., JACKSON, K. A., BOLINO, M. C., VERES, J. G. III AND FIELD, H. S. (2007) The influence of relational demography on panel interview ratings: A field experiment. *Personnel Psychology*, 60: 627–646.

CABLE, D. M. AND TURBAN, D. B. (2003) The value of organizational reputation in the recruitment context: A brand-equity perspective. *Journal of Applied Social Psychology*, 33: 2244–2266.

CALIGIURI, P., HYLAND, M., JOSHI, A. AND BROSS, A. (1998) Testing a theoretical model for examining the relationship between family adjustment and expatriates' work adjustment. *Journal of Applied Psychology*, 83: 598–614.

CALIGIURI, P. M. AND PHILLIPS, J. M. (2003) An application of self-assessment realistic job previews to expatriate assignments. *International Journal of Human Resource Management*, 14: 1102–1116.

CALIGUIRI, P. AND TARIQUE, I. (2006) International assignee selection and cross-cultural training and development. In Bjorkman, I. and Stahl, G. (eds), *Handbook of Research in International Human Resource Management*. London: Edward Elgar Publishing, pp. 302–322.

CAMARA, W. J. AND SCHNEIDER, D. L. (1995) Questions of construct breadth and openness of research in integrity testing. *American Psychologist*, 50: 459–460.

CASCIO, W. F. (1995) Whither industrial and organizational psychology in a changing world of work. *American Psychologist*, 50(11): 928–939.

CATTELL, R. B. (1965) *The Scientific Analysis of Personality*. Harmondsworth: Penguin.

CHAPMAN, D. S., UGGERSLEV, K. L., CARROLL, S. A., PIASENTIN, K. A. AND JONES, D. A. (2005) Applicant attraction to organizations and job choice: A meta-analytic review of the correlates of recruiting outcomes. *Journal of Applied Psychology*, 90: 928–944.

CHUNG-YAN, G. A. AND CRANSHAW, S. F. (2002) A critical re-examination and analysis of cognitive ability tests using the Thorndike model of fairness. *Journal of Occupational and Organisational Psychology*, 75(4): 489–509.

CODY, T. (2015) Innovative tactics to recruit women in tech. DiversityInc, December 1. Available at: http://bestpractices.diversityinc.com/workforce/workforce-recruiters/how-to-recruit-women-in-tech/.

COLLINS, C. J. AND HAN, J. (2004) Exploring applicant pool quantity and quality: The effects of early recruitment practices, corporate advertising, and firm reputation. *Personnel Psychology*, 57: 685–717.

CONWAY, J. M., JAKO, R. A. AND GOODMAN, D. F. (1995) A meta-analysis of interrater and internal consistency reliability of selection interviews. *Journal of Applied Psychology*, 80: 565–579.

COSTA, P. T. JR AND MCCRAE, R. R. (1990) *The NEO Personality Inventory Manual*. Odessa, FL: Psychological Assessment Resources.

DALESSIO, A. T., CROSBY, M. AND MCMANUS, M. A. (1996) Stability of biodata keys and dimensions across English-speaking countries: A test of the cross-situational hypothesis. *Journal of Business and Psychology*, 10: 289–296.

DINEEN, B. R., LING, J., ASH, S. R. AND DELVECCHIO, D. (2007) Aesthetic properties and message customization: Navigating the dark side of Web recruitment. *Journal of Applied Psychology*, 92: 356–372.

DIPBOYE, R. L., WOOTEN, K. AND HALVERSON, S. K. (2004) Behavioral and situational interviews. In Thomas, J. C. (ed.), *Comprehensive Handbook of Psychological Assessment, vol. 4, Industrial and Organizational Assessment.* Hoboken, NJ: John Wiley and Sons, pp. 297–316.

DRAKELEY, R. J. (1989) Biographical data. In Herriot, P. (ed.) *Handbook of Assessment in Organizations.* Chichester: Wiley, pp. 439–453.

DUNNING, D. (2007) Prediction: The inside view. In Kruglanski, A.W. and Higgings, E. T. (eds), *Social Psychology: A Handbook of Basic Principles.* New York: Guilford Press, pp. 69–90.

EARL, J., BRIGHT, J. E. AND ADAMS, A. (1998) 'In my opinion': What gets graduates resumes short-listed? *Australian Journal of Career Development*, 7: 15–19.

ELLINGSON, J. E., SACKETT, P. R. AND HOUGH, L. M. (1999) Social desirability corrections in personality measurement: Issues of applicant comparison and construct validity. *Journal of Applied Psychology*, 84: 155–166.

EYSENCK, M. W. (1982) *Attention and Arousal.* New York: Springer-Verlag.

FRAZER, R. A. AND WIERSMA, U. J. (2001) Prejudice versus discrimination in the employment interview: We may hire equally, but our memories harbour prejudices. *Human Relations*, 54: 173–191.

GIDDENS, A. (1993) *The Constitution of Society: Outline of the Theory of Structuration.* Cambridge: Polity Press.

GOLEMAN, D. (1996) *Emotional Intelligence.* New York: Bantam Books.

GUERCI, M., MONTANARI, F., SCAPOLAN, A. AND EPIFANIO, A. (2016) Green and nongreen recruitment practices for attracting job applicants: Exploring independent and interactive effects. *International Journal of Human Resource Management*, 27(2): 129–150.

GUION, R. M. (1998) *Assessment, Measurement and Prediction for Personnel Decisions.* Mahwah, NJ: Lawrence Erlbaum.

HAILEY, J. (1996) The expatriate myth: Cross-cultural perceptions of expatriate managers. *International Executive*, 38(2): 255–271.

HALFHILL, T., NIELSEN, T. M., SUNDSTROM, E. AND WEILBAECHER, A. (2005) Group personality composition and performance in military service teams. *Military Psychology*, 17(1): 41–54.

HEDGE, J. W., BORMAN, W. C. AND LAMMLEIN, S. E. (2006) *The Aging Workforce: Realities, Myths, and Implications for Organizations.* Washington, DC: American Psychological Association.

HERRIOTT, P. (2003) Assessment by groups: Can value be added? *European Journal of Work and Organizational Psychology*, 12(2): 131–145.

HOGAN, J. AND BRINKMEYER, K. (1997) Bridging the gap between overt and personality-based integrity tests. *Personnel Psychology*, 50: 587–600.

HOUGH, L. A. AND OSWALD, F. L. (2000) Personnel selection: Looking toward the future – remembering the past. *Annual Review of Psychology*, 51: 631–664.

International Task Force on Assessment Center Guidelines (2008) *Guidelines and Ethical Considerations for Assessment Center Operations.* Available at: www.assessment-centers.org.

JANSSENS, M. AND STEYAERT, C. (2009) HRM and performance: A plea for reflexivity in HRM studies. *Journal of Management Studies*, 46(1): 143–155.

JANZ, T. (1982) Initial comparisons of patterned behaviour description interviews versus unstructured interviews. *Journal of Applied Psychology*, 67: 577–580.

JONES, D. A., WILLNESS, C. R. AND MADEY, S. (2014) Why are job seekers attracted by corporate social performance? Experimental and field tests of three signal-based mechanisms. *Academy of Management Journal*, 57(2): 383–404.

JUSSIM, L., COLEMAN, L. M. AND LEARCH, L. (1987) The nature of stereotypes: A comparison and integration of three theories. *Journal of Personality and Social Psychology*, 52: 536–546.

KICKUL, J. AND NEUMAN, G. (2000) Emergent leadership behaviors: The function of personality and cognitive ability in determining teamwork performance and KSAs. *Journal of Business and Psychology*, 15(1): 27–51.

KLINGNER, Y. AND SCHULER, H. (2004) Improving participants' evaluations while maintaining validity by a work sample-intelligence test hybrid. *International Journal of Selection and Assessment*, 12(1–2): 120–134.

KLUEMPER, D. H. AND ROSEN, P. A. (2009) Future employment selection methods: Evaluating social networking websites. *Journal of Managerial Psychology*, 24: 567–580.

KNIGHTS, D. AND MCCABE, D. (1998) The times they are a changin'? Transformative organizational innovations in financial services in the UK. *International Journal of Human Resource Management*, 9: 168–184.

KNIGHTS, D. AND RAFFO, C. (1990) Milk round professionalism in personnel recruitment: Myth or reality? *Personnel Review*, 19: 28–37.

KRUGLANSKI, A. W. AND SLEETH-KEPPLER, D. (2007) The principles of social judgement. In Kruglanski, A. W. and Higgings, E. T. (eds), *Social Psychology: A Handbook of Basic Principles.* New York: Guilford Press, pp. 116–137.

KUTCHER, E. J. AND BRAGGER, J. D. (2004) Selection interviews of overweight job applicants: Can structure reduce the bias? *Journal of Applied Social Psychology*, 34: 1993–2022.

LATHAM, G. P. AND SAARI, L. M. (1984) Do people do what they say? Further studies on the situational interview. *Journal of Applied Psychology*, 69: 569–573.

LEGGE, K. (2007) Putting the missing H into HRM: The case of the flexible organisation. In Bolton, S. C. and Houlihan, M. (eds), *Searching for the Human in Human Resource Management*. London: Palgrave Macmillan, pp. 115–136.

LEPINE, J. A. AND VAN DYNE, L. (2001) Voice and cooperative behavior as contrasting forms of contextual performance: Evidence of differential relationships with big five personality characteristics and cognitive ability. *Journal of Applied Psychology*, 86(2): 326–336.

LIEVENS, F. AND DE PAEPE, A. (2004) An empirical investigation of interviewer-related factors that discourage the use of high structure interviews. *Journal of Organizational Behavior*, 25: 29–46.

LIEVENS, F., HARRIS, M. M., VAN KEER, E. AND BISQUERET, C. (2003) Predicting cross-cultural training performance: The validity of personality, cognitive ability, and dimensions measured by an assessment center and a behavior description interview. *Journal of Applied Psychology*, 88(3): 476–486.

LIEVENS, F. AND HIGHHOUSE, S. (2003) The relation of instrumental and symbolic attributes to a company's attractiveness as an employer. *Personnel Psychology*, 56: 75–102.

LIEVENS, F. AND KLIMOSKI, R. J. (2001) Understanding the assessment centre process: Where are we now? *International Review of Industrial and Organizational Psychology*, 16: 245–286.

LIN, N.-P., CHIU, H.-C. AND HSIEH, Y.-C. (2001) Investigating the relationship between service providers' personality and customers' perceptions of service quality across gender. *Total Quality Management*, 12(1): 57–67.

MACDUFFIE, J. P. (1995) Human resource bundles and manufacturing performance: Organizational logic and flexible production systems in the world auto industry. *Industrial and Labor Relations Review*, 48(2): 197–221.

MADERA, J. M., HEBL, M. R. AND MARTIN, R. C. (2009) Gender and letters of recommendation for academia: Agentic and communal differences. *Journal of Applied Psychology*, 94: 1591–1599.

MAEL, F. A. (1991) A conceptual rationale for the domain and attributes of biodata items. *Personnel Psychology*, 44: 763–792.

MCDANIEL, M. A., WHETZEL, D. L., SCHMIDT, F. L. AND MAURER, S. (1994) The validity of employment interviews: A comprehensive review and meta-analysis. *Journal of Applied Psychology*, 79: 599–616.

MCFARLAND, L. A., RYAN, A. M., SACCO, J. M. AND KRISTA, S. D. (2004) Examination of structured interview ratings across time: The effects of applicant race, rater race, and panel composition. *Journal of Management*, 30: 435–452.

MEYER, J. P. AND ALLEN, N. J. (1997) *Commitment in the Workplace: Theory, Research and Application*. Thousand Oaks, CA: Sage.

MICHAELS, E., HANDFIELD-JONES, H. AND AXELROD, B. (2001) *The War for Talent*. Boston, MA: Harvard Business School Press.

MILLER, C. C. (2015) Can an algorithm hire better than a human? *New York Times*, June 25. Available at: http://www.nytimes.com/2015/06/26/upshot/can-an-algorithm-hire-better-than-a-human.html?_r=0.

MOHAMMED, S. AND ANGELL, L. C. (2003) Personality heterogeneity in teams: Which differences make a difference for team performance? *Small Group Research*, 34(6): 651–677.

MOHAMMED, S., MATHIEU, J. E. AND BARTLETT, A. L. (2002) Technical–administrative task performance, leadership task performance, and contextual performance: Considering the influence of team- and task-related composition variables. *Journal of Organizational Behavior*, 23(7): 795–814.

MOL, S. T., BORN, M. P., WILLEMSEN, M. E. AND VAN DER MOLEN, H. T. (2005) Predicting expatriate job performance for selection purposes: A quantitative review. *Journal of Cross-Cultural Psychology*, 36(5): 590–620.

MORGESON, F. P., REIDER, M. H. AND CAMPION, M. A. (2005) Selecting individuals in team settings: The importance of social skills, personality characteristics, and team work knowledge. *Personnel Psychology*, 58(3): 583–611.

MOTOWILDO, S. J., HOOPER, A. C. AND JACKSON, H. L. (2006) Implicit policies about relations between personality traits and behavioral effectiveness in situational judgment items. *Journal of Applied Psychology*, 91: 749–761.

MOUNT, M. K. AND BARRICK, M. R. (1995) *Manual for Personal Characteristics Inventory*. Livertyvill: Wonderlic Personnel Test.

MOUNT, M. K., BARRICK, M. R. AND STRAUSS, J. P. (1994) The joint relationship of conscientiousness and ability with performance: Test of the interaction hypothesis. *Journal of Management*, 25: 707–721.

MUEHLBERGER, U. (2007) *Dependent Self-employment: Workers on the Border between Employment and Self-employment*. Basingstoke: Palgrave Macmillan.

MUMFORD, T. V., MORGESON, F. P., VAN IDDEKINGE, C. H. AND CAMPION, M. A. (2008) The team role test: Development and validation of a team role knowledge situational judgment test. *Journal of Applied Psychology*, 93: 250–267.

NIKOLAOU, I. (2003) Fitting the person to the organisation: Examining the personality – job performance relationship from a new perspective. *Journal of Managerial Psychology*, 18(7/8): 639–648.

O'CONNELL, M. S., DOVERSPIKE, D., NORRIS-WATTS, C. AND HATTRUP, K. (2001) Predictors of organizational citizenship behavior among Mexican retail salespeople. *International Journal of Organizational Analysis*, 9(3): 272–280.

ONES, D. S. AND VISWESVARAN, C. (1998) The effects of social desirability and faking on personality and integrity assessment for personnel selection. *Human Performance*, 11: 245–269.

ONES, D. S., VISWESVARAN, C. AND SCHMIDT, F. L. (1995) Integrity tests: Overlooked facts, resolved issues, and remaining questions. *American Psychologist*, 50(6): 456–457.

ÖZBILGIN, M. AND WOODWARD, D. (2004) Belonging and otherness: Sex equality in banking in Turkey and Britain. *Gender, Work and Organization*, 11(6): 668–688.

PLOYHART, R. E. (2011) Emergence of the human capital resource: A multilevel model. *Academy of Management Review*, 36: 127–150.

PLOYHART, R. E., SCHNEIDER, B. AND SCHMITT, N. (2006) *Staffing Organizations: Contemporary Practice and Theory* (3rd edn). Mahwah, NJ: Lawrence Erlbaum.

PORTEOUS, M. (1997) *Occupational Psychology*. London: Prentice Hall.

PRESTON, J. (2011) Social media becomes a new job hurdle. *New York Times*, July 20, 1.

PURKISS, S. L., SEGREST, W. L., PERREWE, P. L., GILLESPIE, T. L., MAYES, B. T. AND FERRIS, G. R. (2006) Implicit sources of bias in employment interview judgments and decisions. *Organizational Behavior and Human Decision Processes*, 101: 152–167.

RAU, B. L. AND ADAMS, G. (2004) Job seeking among retirees seeking bridge employment. *Personnel Psychology*, 57: 719–744.

RAU, B. L. AND ADAMS, G. (2005) Organizational attraction of retirees for bridge employment. *Journal of Organizational Behavior*, 26: 649–660.

ROBERTSON, I. T. AND KANDOLA, R. S. (1982). Work sample tests: Validity, adverse impact, and applicant reaction. *Journal of Occupational Psychology*, 55: 171–183.

ROBERTSON, I. T. AND SMITH, M. (2001) Personnel selection. *Journal of Occupational and Organizational Psychology*, 74: 441–472.

ROTH, P. L., BOBKO, P., VAN IDDEKINGE, C. H. AND THATCHER, J. B. (2016) Social media in employee selection-related decisions: A research agenda for uncharted territory. *Journal of Management*, 42(1): 269–298.

RYNES, S. L., BRETZ, R. D. JR AND GERHART, B. (1991) The importance of recruitment in job choice: A different way of looking. *Personnel Psychology*, 44: 487–521.

RYNES, S. L. AND CABLE, D. M. (2003) Recruitment research in the twenty-first century. In Borman, W. C., Ilgen, D. R.

and Klimoski, R. J. (eds), *Handbook of Psychology: Industrial and Organizational Psychology*, vol. 12. Hoboken, NJ: John Wiley and Sons, pp. 55–76.

SALGADO, J. F. (1999) Personnel selection methods. In Cooper, C. L. and Robertson, I. T. (eds), *International Review of Industrial and Organizational Psychology*, vol. 14. Chichester: Wiley, pp. 1–54.

SALGADO, J. F., ANDERSON, N., MOSCOSO, S., BERTUA, C., DE FRUYT, F. AND ROLLAND, J. P. (2003) A meta-analytic study of general mental ability validity for different occupations in the European Community. *Journal of Applied Psychology*, 88(6): 176–184.

SHACKLETON, V. AND NEWELL, S. (1997) International assessment and selection. In Anderson, N. and Herriot, P. (eds), *International Handbook of Selection and Assessment*. New York: Wiley.

SCHMEICHEL, B. J. AND VOHS, K. D. (2009) Self-affirmation and self-control: Affirming core values counteracts ego depletion. *Journal of Personality and Social Psychology*, 96(4): 770–782.

SCHMIDT, F.L. AND HUNTER, J. E. (1993) Development of causal models of processes determining job performance. *Current Directions in Psychological Science*, 1: 89–92.

SCHMIDT, F. L. AND HUNTER, J. E. (1998) The validity and utility of selection methods in personnel psychology: Practice and theoretical implications of 85 years of research findings. *Psychological Bulletin*, 124(2): 262–274.

SCHMITT, N., GOODING, R. Z., NOE, R. A. AND KIRSCH, M. (1984) Meta-analyses of validity studies. *Journal of Applied Psychology*, 70: 280–289.

SCULLION, H. AND COLLINGS, D. (2006) *Global Staffing*. London: Routledge.

SEIBERT, S., DOWNES, P. E. AND CHRISTOPHER, J. (2012) Applicant reactions to online background checks: Welcome to a brave new world. Paper presented at the annual meeting of the Academy of Management, Boston.

SHAFFER, M. A., HARRISON, D. A., GREGERSEN, H., BLACK, J. S. AND FERZANDI, L. A. (2006) You can take it with you: Individual differences and expatriate effectiveness. *Journal of Applied Psychology*, 91: 109–125.

SHIPP, A. J. AND JANSEN, K. J. (2011) Reinterpreting time in fit theory: Crafting and recrafting narratives of fit in medias res. *Academy of Management Review*, 36: 76–101.

SINAR, E. F. AND WINTER, J. 2012 Social media and selection: How on-line information helps and hurts your hiring process. *DDIDirections*, 1–9.

SISCO, H. AND REILLY, R.R. (2007) Development and validation of a Biodata Inventory as an alternative method to measurement of the five factor model of personality. *Social Science Journal*, 44: 383–389.

SLACK, R., CORLETT, S. AND MORRIS, R. (2015) Exploring employee engagement with corporate social responsibility: A social exchange perspective on organizational participation. *Journal of Business Ethics*, 127(3): 537–548.

SLOVENSKY, R. AND ROSS, W. H. (2012) Should human resource managers use social media to screen job applicants? Managerial and legal issues in the USA. *Info*, 14: 55–69.

SMITH, M. AND GEORGE, D. (1992) Selection methods. In Cooper, C. L. and Robertson, I. T. (eds), *International Review of Industrial and Organizational Psychology*, vol. 7. Chichester: Wiley, pp. 55–97.

STEINER, D. D. AND GILLILAND, S. W. (1996) Fairness reactions to personnel selection techniques in France and the United States. *Journal of Applied Psychology*, 81: 134–141.

STERNBERG, R. J. AND WAGNER, R. K. (1995) *Practical Intelligence in Everyday Life*. Cambridge: Cambridge University Press.

STEWART, G. L., FULMER, I. S. AND BARRICK, M. R. (2005) An exploration of member roles as a multilevel linking mechanism for individual traits and team outcomes. *Personnel Psychology*, 58(2): 343–365.

STEWART, R., VOLPONE, S., AVERY, D. AND MCKAY, P. (2011) You support diversity, but are you ethical? Examining the interactive effects of diversity and ethical climate perceptions on turnover intentions. *Journal of Business Ethics*, 100(4): 581–593.

STONE, D. L. AND STONE-ROMERO, E. F. (2004) The influence of culture on role-taking in culturally diverse organizations. In Stockdale, M. S. and Crosby, F. J. (eds), *The Psychology and Management of Workplace Diversity*. Malden, MA: Blackwell Publishing, pp. 78–99.

SYED, J. (2008) Employment prospects for skilled immigrants: A relational perspective. *Human Resource Management Review*, 18: 28–45.

TAYLOR, S. (2004) Hunting the Snark: A critical analysis of human resource management discourses in relation to managing labour in smaller organizations. In Marlow, S., Patton, D. and Ram, M. (eds), *Managing Labour in Small Firms*. London: Routledge, pp. 18–42.

TEMPLER, K. J., TAY, C. AND CHANDRASEKAR, N. A. (2006) Motivational cultural intelligence, realistic job preview, realistic living condition preview, and cross-cultural adjustment. *Group and Organization Management*, 31: 154–173.

THORNE, K. (2004) *One-Stop Guide: Employer Branding*. Sutton: Personnel Today.

THORNTON, G. C. III AND RUPP, D. R. (2006) *Assessment Centers in Human Resource Management: Strategies for Prediction, Diagnosis and Development*. Mahwah, NJ: Lawrence Erlbaum.

TRUXILLO, D. M., BODNER, T. E., BERTOLINO, M., BAUER, T. N. AND YONCE, C. A. (2009) Effects of explanations on applicant reactions: A meta-analytic review. *International Journal of Selection and Assessment*, 17: 346–361.

TUNG, R. (1998). American expatriates abroad: From neophytes to cosmopolitans. *Columbia Journal of World Business*, 33: 125–144.

VISWESVARAN, C. AND ONES, D. S. (2000) Perspectives of models of job performance. *International Journal of Selection and Assessment*, 8: 216–225.

WALKER, H. J., BAUER, T. N., COLE, M. S., BERNERTH, J. B., FIELD, H. S. AND SHORT, J. (2013) Is this how I will be treated? Reducing uncertainty through recruitment interactions. *Academy of Management Journal*, 56(5): 1325–1347.

WATSON, T. (2004) HRM and critical social science analysis. *Journal of Management Studies*, 41: 447–467.

WEEKLEY, J. A. AND PLOYHART, R. E. (2006) An Introduction to situational judgment testing. In Weekley, J. A. and Ployhart, R.E. (eds), *Situational Judgment Tests*. Mahwah, NJ: Lawrence Erlbaum Associates, pp. 1–12.

WILDEN, R., GUDERGAN, S. AND LINGS, I. (2010) Employer branding: Strategic implications for staff recruitment. *Journal of Marketing Management*, 26(1–2): 56–73.

WILK, S. L. AND CAPPELLI, P. (2003) Understanding the determinants of employer use of selection methods. *Personnel Psychology*, 56: 103–124.

WILLIAMS, S. D. (2004) Personality, attitude, and leader influences on divergent thinking and creativity in organizations. *European Journal of Innovation Management*, 7(3): 187–204.

WITT, L. A. (2002) The interactive effects of extraversion and conscientiousness on performance. *Journal of Management*, 28(6): 835–851.

ZANONI, P. AND JANSSENS, M. (2007) Minority employees engaging with (diversity) management: An analysis of control, agency and micro-emancipation. *Journal of Management Studies*, 44: 1371–1397.

ZEDECK, S. AND CASCIO, W. F. (1984) Psychological issues in personnel decisions. *Annual Review of Psychology*, 35: 461–518.

ZOTTOLI, M. A. AND WANOUS, J. P. (2000) Recruitment source research: Current status and future directions. *Human Resource Management Review*, 10: 353–383.

9

PERFORMANCE MANAGEMENT

Jane Maley

LEARNING OUTCOMES

After reading this chapter, you should be able to:

➤ Understand the strategic importance of the performance management system in a global context
➤ Explain the purpose, criteria, and ethics of an effective global performance management system
➤ Identify the main approaches to performance appraisals
➤ Critically reflect on the most effective sources for performance management
➤ Recognise strategies to improve performance
➤ Manage performance in uncertainty
➤ Consider alternatives to performance appraisal.

SUMMARY OF CHAPTER CONTENTS

➤ **Opening Case Study**: Performance management in Brazilian bureaucracy
➤ Introduction
➤ The strategic importance of performance management in a global context
➤ Characteristics of performance management
➤ The criteria of an effective performance management system
➤ Ethics in performance management
➤ Multisource feedback
➤ Strategies to improve global performance
➤ Performance management in a global context
➤ The cultural impact of performance management
➤ Managing performance in uncertainty
➤ Alternatives to performance appraisal
➤ Conclusion
➤ **End of Chapter Case Study**: Feedback in politics and government
➤ For discussion and revision
➤ Glossary
➤ Further reading
➤ Web resources
➤ References

This chapter defines performance management processes and provides an overview of its western origins. The strategic importance of performance management in a global context is considered, and the benefits and problems associated with typical approaches to performance management are examined. Subsequently, the factors that impact on performance management in different cultural contexts are considered. Throughout the chapter regular face-to-face contact, repeated opportunity for feedback, and performance follow-up are stressed as key factors that help contribute to a positive global performance management culture.

Performance management in Brazilian bureaucracy

The beginning of post-dictatorial periods in Latin American countries was characterised by the creation of a new democratic era. In the case of Brazil, it meant the creation of a whole new legal system under the 1988 Constitution. The country re-embraced democracy and started a new era of social and economic development. Another aspect of the 1988 Constitution, however, had a tremendous importance for the country: it shaped the Brazilian merit-based bureaucratic public sector system in an effort to overcome clientelism.

Clientelism is the exchange of goods and services for political support, often involving explicit or implicit quid pro quo. Clientelism is the reverse version of a merit-based system. It has been one of the biggest obstacles to economic growth and public sector efficiency in Latin America. Under the regime of a clientelist state, government bureaucrats are not hired based on knowledge, personal qualifications, or organisational skills, but merely on network and political connections. Architects of the 1988 Constitution chose to address the problem of clientelism by implementing a regime where the majority of government jobs would be filled based on a competitive entry examination called the *concurso*. Under this regime, only the top qualifiers of government exams, i.e. the ones with highest scores, would be hired (the rule applies to all three government branches). This constitutional requirement intended to avoid clientelism and nepotism (hiring based on kinship) in government.

There is, however, an inherent collateral effect to the merit-based bureaucratic public sector system. Tenured public employees have very little chance of being dismissed by public organisations in which they work. Most future bureaucrats face an average directed study period of two to six years before passing the entry-level examination for a public sector life-time position. They dedicate time and money into an effort that will eventually secure a job for the rest of their lives. As mentioned above, the overwhelming majority of positions require this examination – including paid internships. After passing the exam, a three-year period will give them tenure. Because of such privilege, public employees get easily accommodated over time and tend to perform below expectations.

As a consequence, the implementation of performance management in Brazil could face several challenges. Brazilian bureaucracy is yet far from the requirements advocated by the performance management doctrine, which calls for more focus on results and increased managerial authority, as previously implemented in countries such as Australia, New Zealand, and the United Kingdom. The current system has a low focus on results and low managerial authority as a result of administrative restrictions over human resources. Recently, initiatives at the state and local levels have attempted to address this issue.

Questions

1 'Given the facts and challenges outlined above, it is futile for the Brazilians to attempt to introduce performance measurement in their public sector system.' How would you argue against this assertion?

2 What do you foresee as the key difficulties in implementing a performance management system and how would you set about reducing them?

Adapted from an article by Gomes, 2010.

INTRODUCTION

This chapter looks at one of a multinational organisation's (MNCs) most critical procedures. Specifically, it reviews the global performance management system. Performance management is the process by which organisations set goals, determine standards, assign and evaluate work, and distribute rewards. These systems are now widely and routinely used for many employees. Their use increased through the 1990s as a result of the pressures of globalisation, increased competition, and greater analysis of all characteristics of employee performance (Varma, Budhwar and De Nisi, 2008).

Performance management systems were originally used for managers, professionals and technical employees, but today they are frequently used to appraise staff at all levels in many parts of the world.

Measuring the performance of individuals and teams has become an important tool to ensure organisational performance and is critical to identify possible gaps between job expectations and the strategic intent of the organisation. Hence performance management is considered to be a central element of strategic human resource management, and a successful performance management system is argued to be vital if an organisation wants to implement strategy into employee action. If the process is conducted appropriately, it can provide a huge benefit to a firm, the supervisor and the employee. An effective performance management system can help create a sustainable competitive advantage to the firm that is not easy to replicate (Maley and Kramar, 2014).

Nonetheless, performance management is often viewed by many managers around the world as a pointless annual ritual, and the use of, and satisfaction with, performance appraisal systems has a history of being problematic (Nankervis and Compton, 2006). More recently the process of evaluating and managing people with a performance management framework has come under scrutiny and some well recognised multinational corporations have cancelled them (Baker, 2014). As with everything else in the global arena, managing performance in a global context is a lot more complex than is the case with a one-dimensional national structure. The issue of performance management and its counterpart performance appraisal has occupied much debate amongst both scholars and practitioners. For example, a recent review of the literature finds no less than 67 articles published on global performance management (Festing et al., 2010). GPM has been the subject of numerous chapters in edited books and the topic has also been covered by special workshops and dedicated sessions in academic conferences (Cascio, 2014).

There are a number of reasons for the complications in the cross-border context. First, culture profoundly influences management practices. For example the purpose, employee acceptance of the system, and the cultural value dimensions that affect performance management vary immensely across borders (Claus and Briscoe, 2009). The unique norms, values and beliefs inherent in different cultures affect the way employees are controlled as well as their equity, expectancy, and justice perceptions. Consequently, a performance management system developed in one country may not be suitable in another country (Chiang and Birtch, 2010; Engle, Festing and Dowling, 2014).

Second, organisations must be cognisant of the potential influence of other institutional and economic factors that may influence the performance management (Chiang and Birtch, 2010). Thirdly, global human resource managers in MNCs face a major dilemma in terms of reconciling whether performance management should be a single, standard practice throughout the organisation or a divergent system that can be used to reflect local culture and local management practices (Engle et al., 2014). Finally the performance management of global employees presents particular challenges. In addition to the special case of the expatriate manager, who has received a lot of research awareness over the past two decades, other global employees need attention. For instance, employees in a MNC subsidiary who are nationals of the country in which they work have been found to be neglected in global performance management studies (Maley and Moeller, 2014). For example, the manager of the subsidiary has been found to require particular reflection. These managers are usually isolated from their supervisors, and it has been found (Maley and Kramar, 2007) that they may experience difficulties in the conduct of their performance appraisal. In other words, the dilemma of both geographical distance and cultural distance must be considered when a company operates across different countries and continents (Harzing and Noordhaven, 2005). The performance management system cannot be one-dimensional, and human resource managers need systems that can be applied to a range of cultural values.

The structure of this chapter is as follows. The chapter begins with a review of the strategic importance of the performance management system in a global context. This is followed by an examination of the various characteristics that underpin a performance management system which includes the purpose, criteria and ethics of performance management. Subsequently, the key approaches and the value of multiple sources in a cross-cultural setting are considered. This section includes various suggestions to help improve the performance management process. Next there is an overview of performance management in a global context. Following this there is a review of managing performance in uncertain times and a discussion of alternatives to performance appraisal. Finally there is a summary of the chapter which incorporates a critical evaluation and future direction of performance management and outlines the benefits of studying performance management from a critical perspective.

THE STRATEGIC IMPORTANCE OF PERFORMANCE MANAGEMENT IN A GLOBAL CONTEXT

In order to understand the strategic significance of performance management in a global setting, it is important to recognise that the purpose and approach of performance management changes as the MNC expands and subsidiaries develop. These changes have been attributed to the human resource staffing structures and strategies (Birkinshaw and Morrison, 1995). Evidence suggests that it is these structures and strategies that determine the types of employees that will be employed in a global setting (Dowling et al., 2008) and the importance placed on the purpose and approach of performance management (Maley, 2011).

There are three key types of global employees that have been identified:

- Parent-country nationals (PCNs). These employees are from the parent country, expatriates are always PCN.
- Host-country nationals (HCNs). These employees work in their host subsidiary.
- Third-country nationals (TCNs). These employees are not from the parent office and do not work in their host country.

For example, the US MNC General Electric employs Australian citizens in its Australian operations (HCNs), often sends US citizens (PCNs) to Asia Pacific countries on assignment, and may send some of its UK employees on an assignment to its Japanese subsidiary (TCNs). The nationality of the employee has been found to be a major factor in determining the person's category. However, more recently other types of global employees have emerged in the global marketplace. These include transfers from subsidiary operations to the corporate HQ (inpatriates) (Moeller et al., 2016; Reiche, 2012) and temporary employees (flexipatriates) (McPhail et al., 2012).

The employees in the subsidiaries (HCNs, TCNs) become increasingly important to the success of the MNC as the globalisation strategy advances and the subsidiary takes a central role in the success of MNC. For that reason, the global performance management process must consider not only the employees from the parent (HCNs) but also these new forms of employees (Milliman et al., 2002). In this chapter, the concept of global professional is extended to illustrate three distinct categories of global employees. What is more, as the MNC continues to expand there will be an increasingly larger percentage of the organisation that is both geographical and culturally distant from the parent MNC (Harzing and Noordhaven, 2005). The widening cultural distance has been found to have a major effect on the purpose, criteria, acceptance and ethics of performance management (Chiang and Birtch, 2010; Fenwick, 2005). Consequently, the global performance management process needs to adopt a broader cultural perspective with an appreciation for cultural diversity.

CHARACTERISTICS OF PERFORMANCE MANAGEMENT

Performance management and performance appraisal

Performance management is the general term for a number of human resource functions that are concerned with managing performance. It is the systematic process that involves employees, as individuals and members of a group, in improving organisational effectiveness in the accomplishment of the firm's mission and goals. Employee performance management includes: planning work and setting expectations, continually monitoring performance, developing the capacity to perform, periodically appraising performance, and rewarding good performance. It is important to reiterate here that these numerous functions are much more complex to administer in a global setting.

The aspects of the performance management cycle are magnified and become more complex when a firm globalises. When a company does globalise its operations, the human resource manager needs to become familiar with the aspects of performance management that may be influenced by the political, economic, legal and cultural feature of the countries in which the MNCs is operating. In addition the human resource manager must be aware of the various stages of evolution of the subsidiary and how these stages may impact on the individual functions of the performance management system. The appraisal is therefore a component of the performance management system, albeit a major component. It forms part of the umbrella of performance management along with the other important functions. The cycle can form a structure for the design of a performance management system in diverse cultures. However its particular form and method of implementation may vary in different cultures.

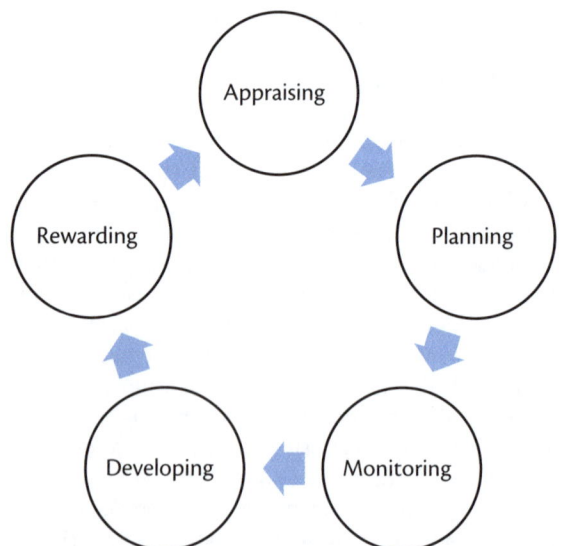

Figure 9.1 The performance management cycle

The purpose

The purpose of the global performance management system and in particular the performance appraisal has been the focus of recent debate and discussion by academic scholars and practitioners and has indicated that the employees often have little idea why their supervisor is conducting the performance appraisal (Chiang and Birtch, 2010). Because the purposes are not always well understood, the performance management systems tend to be poorly implemented in many countries (Claus and Briscoe, 2009). Three key aspects of purpose in the global context have been considered in this chapter: firstly, what influences the purpose, secondly the implications of the purpose, and thirdly the actual purposes. Each element will now be considered.

What influences the purpose?

The strategic human resource literature (Delery and Doty, 1996; Ulrich, 1997; Wright and McMahan 1992) and global human resource management literature (De Cieri and Dowling, 1998; Ghoshal and Bartlett, 1998; Harvey, Speier and Novicevic, 2002) establish that strategic alignment and globalisation have an enormous influence on the purpose of performance management. Claus and Briscoe (2009) argue that context-specific issues need to be taken into account when executing performance management activities and multiple contextual elements are critical to understanding the universality and purpose of performance management practices. Similarly, Milliman et al. (2002) propose that contextual factors direct the purpose of the performance appraisal, for example the firm's strategy, structure, industry, culture (both national and organisational), and local regulations may influence the type and selection of performance management purposes (see Figure 9.2).

Implications of the purpose

In turn, the purpose of the performance management has been found to affect the level of accountability (Maley and Kramar, 2014), the feedback (Aguinis, 2008), the relationship with the supervisor (Maley and Kramar, 2007), and the level and accuracy of observation and recall (Cleveland and Murphy, 1995; Farr and Jacobs, 2006).

The purpose of performance management in multinational corporations

Milliman, et al. (2002) contend that the purpose of performance management is based on a similar fundamental premise in most countries; that is to control individuals in firms to maximise the MNCs financial performance. This view is shared by Cardy and Dobbins (1994) and Maley and Kramar (2014). Milliman et al., (2002) add that, while performance management is based on similar fundamental notions in many countries, their specific purpose and practice may vary slightly between nations. International performance management is also seen as an important way to identify employee strengths and weaknesses, evaluate training needs, set plans for further development, and provide motivation by ascertaining rewards and career advancement (Maley and Moeller, 2014).

A pragmatic depiction of performance management purpose is offered by Kramar, and Bartram, (2015), who

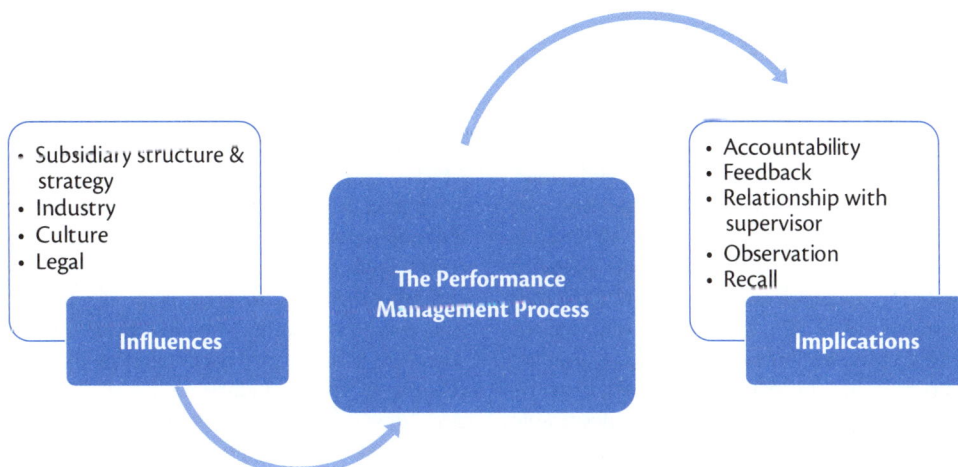

Figure 9.2 The purpose of performance management: The influences and implications

Box 9.1

Chiang and Birtch (2010) recently investigated culture's consequences on the purposes of performance appraisal from the banking industry in seven countries across Europe, Asia, and North America. They found that the effects of power distance, collectivism, masculinity, and uncertainty avoidance should not be overstated nor are they straightforward. Multinational organisations must be cognisant of the potential influence that a range of other organisational, institutional, and economic factors may wield on appraisal. These findings hold significant implications for the theoretical underpinnings of appraisal, a management tool largely rooted in US equity, expectancy, and procedural justice values and traditions. They conclude that not only is the transferability of appraisal and its operationalisation affected by interactions with divergent cultures and contextual settings, but new hybrid appraisal architectures are emerging that necessitate further research.

two purposes tend to dominate and cancel out the others. The above argument was also advanced by Milliman et al. (2002), who propose that expectations may be high in relation to what can be realistically achieved and that firms need to devote more time and effort to the appraisal process. Furthermore they concluded that the purpose of appraisal has fallen short not only in the US but in ten other countries they sampled. A simple definition of the purpose of performance management has been proposed by DeNisi and Pritchard (2006). They propose that the purpose is to accurately diagnose individual and group performance so as to be able to reward good performance and remedy poor performance such that overall organisational performance will be enhanced.

In sum, the evidence in the literature points to a MNC's purpose for conducting appraisals is shaped by several contextual factors. In addition, the purpose may influence various aspects of the appraisal process and outcome. It is for these reasons that the purpose needs to be clearly verbalised by the firm or at least understood by all global employees. In other words, not only should the subordinate's and supervisor's expectations be aligned, both need to be in congruence with the MNC's rationale for conducting a performance management system (Maley and Kramar, 2014). The literature on the purpose of performance management indicates that the purpose is vitally important and has widespread and pervasive implications that impinge on many aspects of the MNCs operations.

describe the purpose as three-fold: firstly, as a strategic link to the firm's goals; secondly, to supply data for administrative use; and thirdly for developmental purposes. Milliman et al. (2002) expand this viewpoint by describing five foremost purposes, which include documentation, development, administrative purposes involving pay and promotion, and subordinate expression.

Moreover, subordinate expression is an important addition and highlights the significance of feedback in the appraisal (Bouskila-Yam and Kluger, 2011; Cascio, 2003; 2000; DeNisi and Pritchard, 2006). Milliman et al. (2002) found that high individualistic cultures (Hofstede, 1980) and, in particular Australians, place an enormous emphasis on subordinate expression and feedback and view this as a crucial part of the appraisal purpose.

It appears that the purpose of the performance appraisal may vary between cultures and change as the subsidiary evolves through various structures and strategies. Murphy and Cleveland (1995) claim that while over 85 per cent of US MNCs use appraisals for administrative purposes, in particular salary decisions, performance management is less frequently used for training and development purposes. They also expressed a key concern that information from performance appraisals is used by raters, ratees, and firms for many purposes and that the goals pursued by the rater and ratees are not necessarily the same as those pursued by the firm. However, Murphy and Cleveland (1991) suggested in an earlier study that too many purposes could be conflicting and that one or

THE CRITERIA OF AN EFFECTIVE PERFORMANCE MANAGEMENT SYSTEM

Just as it is important to have a clearly defined purpose for conducting the performance management process, particularly in a global context, it is also fundamental to have a set of clear criteria by which to measure the performance of employees. All too often employees do not fully understand the particular criterion according to which they are being measured. Research has focused on whether culture affects performance criteria used in performance appraisal. Lam, Hui and Law (1999) found that criteria were treated differently across different cultures, indicating that there are emic (culturally specific) and etic (universal) dimensions in the perceptions of performance criteria. In addition national differences in power distance also played an important role in defining criteria (Lam et al., 1999). Another study found that there are cultural-related and cultural-neutral performance dimensions for retail managers in Singapore and Australia and that the importance attached to the criteria varied significantly, showing the mediating effect of culture (Campbell and Zarkada-Fraser, 2000).

A effective global performance management system in particular needs to identify performance criteria that are important to the MNC and related to the job at hand (Avery and Murphy, 1998). There are several different opinions on which external criteria to use to evaluate performance. A recent standpoint (Kramar and Bartram, 2015) advocates five clear criteria: strategic alignment, validity, reliability, specificity and acceptability. These recommendations are unequivocal and importantly encompass all the important areas including strategic congruence and acceptability. As a consequence, a modified version of their representation has been suggested. Each criterion will now be discussed in relation to the performance appraisal.

Strategic alignment

Strategic alignment is the degree to which the employee's individual performance management system matches or fits with the organisation's global business plan. In other words, the employee's performance objectives should be aligned with those of his or her supervisor and the supervisor's plan aligned with the manager's performance objectives and so forth up to the objectives of the CEO and the board of directors. It has been proposed that performance criteria include the aspirations of the individual and that the individual's best possible performance criteria need to be identified and fitted with the firm's conceptual criteria.

Validity

Validity and reliability are statistical terms (and concepts) that are at the centre of most research on various aspects of performance appraisals. They get at the heart of concerns over biases inherent to the performance appraisal process. Reducing these biases increases the effectiveness of the performance management system.

Validity refers to fact that people are being measured on areas that are truly important to the firm's objectives and refers to the extent to which a performance measure assesses all the relevant aspects of the job (Kramar and Bartram, 2015). If a performance management process lacks validity, it does not measure all aspects of the performance of the employee. Validity failure is a very common phenomenon in performance management. A recent study of the performance management systems of national managers from MNCs of British, European, and US origin found that 80 per cent of performance appraisal lacked validity and did not measure important aspects of the national manager's job (Maley and Moeller, 20014). Validity has been found to be particularly important to

many employees and has been found to be a major contributor in the poor acceptance uptake of the system. Both validity and reliability are also important in recruitment and selection, and it is therefore well worth understanding these scientific terms and their relevance in global human resource management.

Reliability

Reliability refers to the uniformity of performance and autonomy from Random error. There are several types of reliability that are pertinent to the performance appraisal. The most important is inter-rater reliability and refers to the level of consistency amongst the supervisors who are appraising employees. Evidence indicates that many supervisors are subjective and, therefore, that their appraisal of employees will be low in reliability. Another important and relevant form of reliability in performance measurement is the reliability and constancy of measures over time. This is particularly important in a seasonal business. Take, for example, sales people who work in real estate. The real estate market in most Western countries typically picks up in late winter and reaches a peak in late summer. Louis Evangelidis, a real estate proprietor in Sydney, Australia, has stated that to accurately assess a new salesperson, his or her sales performance needs to be assessed over a complete year. If, for example, a salesperson starts with the firm in early autumn and is first reviewed at the end of their first six months in late winter, their sales will be evaluated over a period when sales are predictably slow. This will most likely compare unfavourably with the results of another salesperson who worked the previous six months (over the high season). Many businesses exhibit such seasonal fluctuations and these must be considered in order to improve appraisal reliability. It is extremely challenging in the workplace to obtain good reliability in performance appraisal but it is a challenge that human resource managers and supervisors must strive to achieve. Scholars have researched and produced copious amounts of data on performance appraisal reliability, but there is little evidence of a quick fix. The whole culture of a firm often needs to change in order to achieve high reliability in performance appraisals.

Acceptability

The behavioural criterion of 'acceptability' of the performance appraisal is a fairly recent addition to the field, and research literature on acceptability from the perspective of the employee is limited. An exception is a recent study conducted in China (Taormina and Gao, 2009) that found performance appraisal acceptability to be paramount and that it related to the way the performance appraisal process was executed. In the same way, ratee appraisal acceptability in a global context has been found to increase when the ratee has regular communication and a positive relationship with the rater (Milliman et al., 2002). From the perspective of the appraisees, acceptability is more likely to occur when they perceive the appraisal to be fair (Bradley and Ashkanasy, 2001) and when the feedback they receive from the appraiser is timely and accurate (Milliman, et al., 2002; Sully De Luque and Sommer, 2007). Moreover, where a subordinate and supervisor are geographically distant, regular feedback has been found to be particularly important (Cascio, 2000; Harzing and Noordhaven, 2005; Milliman, et al., 2002; Sully De Luque and Sommer, 2007). Hedge and Teachout (2000) have claimed that acceptability may be the critical criterion for determining the success of the performance management process.

In the global setting, a vital aspect of the acceptability of the performance appraisal process by both the supervisor and the employee has been found to be attributed back to the clarity of purpose of the appraisal (Maley 2009; Milliman et al., 2002;). Performance management acceptability and purpose emerge from the literature as both paramount and interdependent. Evidence suggests that, from an employee perspective, in order to be acceptable the performance management process needs to have a clear purpose and the purpose has to be acceptable. The relationship between purpose and acceptability reinforce the need for the performance appraisal to be embedded in a performance management system rather than to stand alone as a human resource event. For example, if appraisal is part of a fully fledged performance management system, it is more likely that the appraisal will be linked to the organisation's strategy and that both compensation and training and development needs will be achieved. Under these conditions the appraisal is more likely to be acceptable to the ratee.

Construct theories and acceptability

Construct theories may help to explain the phenomenon of acceptability of performance management. For example, a psychological explanation for people's resistance to performance evaluation could be that a negative evaluation can represent a threat to one's self-efficacy. Consequently it might be expected that these feelings might be reduced to some extent if the appraisal criteria were acceptable and the purpose clear to the person receiving the appraisal. The threat to self-efficacy that may occur in a dysfunctional appraisal could have a flow-on effect on many psychological aspects of the employee-employer relationship. Cognitive dissonance theory (Festinger, 1957) is a theory on the basis of which aspects of performance appraisal may be interpreted. From the perspective

of cognitive dissonance theory, a negative evaluation from another person would be inconsistent with the individual's general upbeat perception of her/himself as a capable person. Such conflicting cognitions would possibly affect the spirit of the individual's relationship with the MNC, that is, her/his psychological contract with the organisation.

Organisational justice (Colquitt, Kossek and Raymond, 2001) is another theoretical construct with which performance appraisal acceptability may be viewed. A dysfunctional performance appraisal system may affect the employee's perception of organisational justice. This construct may help to explain employees' attitudinal and behavioural reactions to both performance appraisal and organisational commitment. Because the appraisal has implications for individual reward, employee perceptions of justice are especially significant. Erdogan (2002) claims that organisational justice has two subjective perceptions: procedural justice (the fairness of procedures) and distributive justice (the fairness of outcome). For example, when employees feel unfairly treated in their appraisal, they are likely to react negatively. Distributive justice is concerned with the perceived fairness of the outcomes or allocations received. In appraisal, to reach a perception of distributive justice, individuals compare their efforts with the rating they receive and the fairness of that rating (Erdogan, 2002).

On the basis of the two construct theories above, an appraisal is unlikely to be perceived as acceptable unless those involved in the process perceive it as unbiased (i.e. from the perspective of cognitive dissonance theory) and fair (i.e. from the perspective of MNC justice theory). It is reasonable to expect that, if an employee believes that she/he is being treated unfairly by the organisation, this will in turn impact on her/his perception of her/his relationship with the organisation. Thus, cognitive dissonance theory and organisational justice theory assist in understanding the acceptability of the performance management process. The important point here is that the additional complexity of geographical distance and cultural distance in the global setting makes achieving the criterion of acceptability of the performance management system increasingly challenging to achieve. It is therefore essential that global human resources managers be mindful of the various contrasts that influence the acceptability of a performance management system in the MNC.

ETHICS IN PERFORMANCE MANAGEMENT

For a performance appraisal to be acceptable it must be ethical. One of the key intentions of an ethical performance appraisal should be to provide an honest assessment of performance. While some supervisors are competent and lawful in reviewing an employee's performance, evidence suggests that when a firm goes global there is an inconsistency in the approach to ethics of performance management which may cause employees to become frustrated, cynical, and withdrawn (Murphy, 1993). Survey results in one large study (Aydinlik, Arzu and Ulgen, 2008) examined the ways that the largest private sector organisations in Sweden and Turkey communicate the intent of their codes of ethics to their employees. The research identified some interesting findings that showed that the small group of companies in Turkey that have a code may appear to be more 'advanced' in ethics artefacts usage than Sweden. Such a conclusion is counterintuitive as one would have expected a developed nation such as Sweden to be more advanced in these measures than a developing nation such as Turkey. Culture may play a large role in the implementation of ethics artefacts in corporations and could be a major reason for this difference. Moreover, it has been reported that in performance appraisals, non-performing factors (for example race) are one of the top ten serious ethical considerations for human resource managers in MNCs. It is, therefore, paramount that firms ensure that their performance management processes are conducted to a high ethical standard.

The climate in some organisations does not encourage people to think through ethical considerations because of the overwhelming focus on the bottom line (Maley and Kramar, 2007). The pressure from the parent company to meet unrealistic performance objectives may encourage managers to cut corners or act in an unethical manner. A case in point can be found in the Enron chronicle (see page xxx). Managers at Enron were given unrealistic performance objectives that resulted in dysfunctional and unethical behaviour.

In a cross cultural setting, the supervisor must take extra precautions to ensure that the performance management process maintains equality, equity, and justice. Stakeholder theory states that 'the MNC and its managers are responsible for the effects of activities on others' and that 'the MNC should be managed for the benefit of the stakeholders'. This theory supports utilitarian ethics. In performance management this relates to equity, procedural and distributive justice, autonomy, respect, and safety in the workplace. As a rule, these principles to some degree are understood by many cultures. Nevertheless, basic rights in a performance management process also include principles which are not easily translated across all cultures. These principles include: feedback, openness, and consultation, which are not the usual traits of collectivist, high-power distance cultures. The global human resource manager must be alert to sensitivities of these ideals within the four key dimensions of cultures (Hofstede, 1980). Global research evidence indicates that, if the firm's purpose for doing the performance appraisal is clearly communicated throughout the organisation, and the criteria of strategic congruence, validity, reliability, and acceptability are upheld to a high ethical standard, the performance management is more likely to be successful.

STOP AND REFLECT

Performance evaluations are by nature rather subjective. This may leave employee reviews open to potential ethical complications. Managers may intentionally or unintentionally evaluate staffers using different criteria, which can elevate or devalue individual scores in an unethical manner. Managers may also base decisions on their personal attitudes when issuing performance judgment, which can bias their assessment, take the focus away from the professional elements of an evaluation, and skew the results.

Question

1 How can managers reduce some of the potential for ethical missteps in performance evaluations?

Informal

Performance appraisal may be informal or formal. An informal approach to performance appraisal was once commonplace and still occurs in some small to medium-sized organisations. An informal approach usually involves giving an employee some degree of guidance and feedback. Bernadette Harris is owner and manager of a small estate agency in North Yorkshire, England, and manages her employees with an informal performance appraisal process. Bernadette has five staff members, three salespeople, a receptionist, and a customer service assistant, and she considers that she gives her staff regular feedback and guidance but does not formally document the process. Bernadette believes that her company is small enough to manage with an informal performance appraisal system. While this method may be satisfactory for small businesses, it can become cumbersome and unmanageable in larger organisations. Once a firm has more than about a dozen employees it is recommended that a more formal system be introduced. According to Chiang and Birtch (2010), informal performance appraisal will more commonly be found in individualistic cultures.

Formal

A formal system of performance appraisal involves a formal documented interview with the employee and is typically found in a MNC. There are several types of formal appraisal systems. When choosing the type of performance appraisal system that the company should use, the human resource manager needs to consider the compatibility of the system with the strategic business objectives of the organisation as well as specific performance evaluation purposes. The major types of appraisal methods will now be reviewed.

Major types of performance appraisal systems

In this section we will explore the various approaches to measuring and managing performance. Today, most firms, and certainly most MNCs, use a behavioural type of performance appraisal combined with an objective goal-based method such as management by objectives (MBO) or key performance indicators (KPI). Essays and critical incidents are rarely used these days, except perhaps in a very small number of small to medium-sized enterprises. In the past, some firms conducted closed or blind performance appraisal systems. In a closed system, the employees did not participate in the process and were unaware of what was written about them (see box 9.2).

Major types of performance appraisal (illustrated in Table 9.1) will be discussed below.

Ranking

Ranking compares each person's performance, with the manager ran all subordinates from 'best' to 'worst'. Typically, 10 per cent of ratings are required to be poor or excellent. Ranking forces the rater to evenly distribute the ratings across a broader range of results. This is similar to scaling requirements in university exams. Ranking can occur independently without any other system, but the

> **Box 9.2**
>
> The former UK atomic energy organisation was one of the first government agencies to be privatised by Margaret Thatcher in 1981. The newly formed company was named Amersham International. This new organisation continued with the old system of performance appraisal, which utilised a closed appraisal method for all employees. Not surprisingly, this process resulted in a degree of mistrust between the management and employees. A more transparent process that involved employee participation was introduced in the mid 1980s. Following the introduction of an open transparent performance management system the company's profits started to increased dramatically following a five-year decline.
>
> *Source*: Interview with COO Amersham International, May 2000.

raw ranking method is rarely used these days. On the one hand, the General Electric Company gave forced ranking a degree of respectability. Forced ranking is argued to avoid problems of manager bias and, in particular, leniency. On the other hand, forced ranking was believed to be one of the major contributing factors to the dysfunctional behaviour of employees that triggered the downfall of Enron (see box 9.3).

Behaviour observation scales (BOS)

Behaviour observation scales (BOS) use critical incidents to develop a list of the desired behaviours needed to successfully perform a specific job. This method has recently gained in popularity and is used by many large MNCs. Medtronic Incorporated is a Fortune 500 company that makes medical and surgical devices. Their US headquarters are in Minneapolis, but the company operates in 120 countries around the world. Medtronic uses a BOS

Table 9.1 Summary of performance appraisal approaches

Method	Description	Positive features	Drawbacks
Ranking	Employees ranked from best to worst.	Reduces bias	Disliked by both individualistic and collectivist cultures.
BOS	Uses critical incidents to develop a list of the desired behaviours.	High acceptability Reliable Validity	Can be complicated and costly to set up, particularly for global operations.
MBO/KPI	Manager and employee set goals.	High acceptability	May not fit collective culture. Destroys teamwork. Lacks comparability.

Box 9.3

One of the leading practitioners of forced ranking was Enron Corporation, the Texas energy and trading giant that collapsed in late 2001 under a tidal wave of debt and scandal. It is sobering to reflect that commentators had, in the months preceding its demise, held up the once highly profitable company as proof that 'rank and yank' was the way of the future for all performance appraisals. It was said that rank and yank had produced in Enron 'a hotbed of overachievers' – bold rhetoric that now seems a little embarrassing, to say the least.

Adapted from article in TIME, June 11, 2001.

appraisal based system for its 38,000 employees. A study performed by Tziner and Kopelman (2002) collected in four separate studies and with samples in two nations (Israel and Canada) lends credence to the proposition that a BOS-based performance appraisal and review may be superior to other appraisal methods in terms of yielding more favourable attitudinal effects.

Goal setting

Employee motivation and performance are improved if the employee clearly understands and is challenged by what is to be achieved. If performance management is to have a developmental purpose, it ought to focus on the process of getting results, and that process must be considered in terms of the job-related behaviours over which the individual employee has control. There has been much support amongst human resource management scholars for MBOs; for example, Maley and Kramar (2014) consider that MBO is a flexible process and its flexibility allows for its use across a large number of jobs. Although MBOs were originally intended to be used as a stand-alone process, in practice they have been found to be used alongside traditional methods of appraisal such as behavioural methods in a belt-and-braces style of approach. MBOs have been found to be an acceptable method of appraisal in individualistic cultures. This could be owing to the emphasis on goal and measurement, and employee's involvement and collaborative efforts, which are integrated into the philosophy of MBO. Performance management system that incorporates MBOs appears to offer significant advantages such as good validity, reliability, strong specificity in results, high acceptability, and very good opportunity for strategic congruence.

In contrast, some scholars are not in favour of MBOs. For example, it has been argued that MBOs may destroy

teamwork (Deming, 1982) and conflict with total quality management (TQM) initiatives (Levinson, 1991). Furthermore, they can lack comparability and, therefore, have limitations in regards to administration, particularly if the administration requires valid comparisons, such as promotion and salary awards. Importantly, the concept of individual objectives does not fit with the ideals of teamwork found in a collectivist society (Hofstede and Hofstede, 2005) and therefore MBOs type objectives may have cross-cultural limitations.

The balanced scorecard (BSC) is a performance management framework that became popular during the early 1990s. Kaplan and Norton (1992) presented the BSC as an integrative device that would encourage and facilitate the use of non-financial information by senior managers of organisations, with the choice of non-financial measure being driven primarily by 'strategic' considerations. They argued that when equipped with this better information, managers would be able to deliver improved strategic performance. As a consequence BSC attracted considerable interest among organisations seeking to improve the implementation of their strategy (Lawrie, 2004). On the other hand, Othman et al. (2006) raise questions about BSC's effectiveness and argue that the effective implementation of the BSC requires the presence of human relations norms; they found that studies on Malaysian culture indicate that this may be more difficult to develop in Malaysian organisations. Certain characteristics of cultures may impede the development of human relations norms. Other researchers argue that there are inherent weaknesses in the BSC concept itself. These weaknesses will limit the usefulness of the BSC.

MULTISOURCE FEEDBACK

The supervisor as a source

So far, this chapter has assumed that the sole arbiter of performance is the supervisor and that information from other sources is indirect and filtered through the supervisor. In many MNCs this is the case, yet there is evidence that this may not always be the best practice. It is apparent from human resources research that one of the key problems for the supervisors in evaluating the performance of their subordinates is that it is extremely difficult to directly observe their behaviour. Supervisors often complain that they do not always have time to fully observe the performance of their employees.

This is particularly evident in MNCs where supervisors may be managing employees across national borders. Murphy and Cleveland (1995) argue that supervisors are one of the least able assessors of behaviour and contend that much of what the supervisor knows about the employee is probably the result of secondary data or indirect data, rather than direct observation. For this reason, people other than the supervisor may be better placed to evaluate the employee performance, as they may have more opportunity to directly observe her/him. As a result, direct supervisors, peers, customers, and employees themselves can all provide information on the employee's performance. Moreover, the requirement for superior objectivity, the increased use of teams, and the accent on customer service and quality have created awareness about using multiple sources to evaluate employee performance (Eichinger and Lombardo, 2003; Levy and Williams, 2004). A study conducted by the Corporate Leadership Council (2006) revealed that 90 per cent of Fortune 1000 firms had implemented some of multisource feedback. The same study revealed that the presence of multisource feedback increases individual performance by 8.1 per cent.

Subordinates as sources

Murphy and Cleveland (1995) argue that the subordinate may be a strong source of information for the employee, especially in relation to interpersonal behaviours and results. The subordinate may not fully understand aspects of the manager's job, but she/he will directly witness interpersonal behaviours that the supervisor or peer assessor may miss. The subordinate usually has day-to-day contact with the employee and would usually, therefore, have a reasonable view of her/his behaviours. Feedback from a subordinate is a valuable resource for the employee, as one of the keys to effective performance as a manager is the ability to get good work from one's subordinate (Maley and Moeller, 2014). Even though the subordinates may be the optimal source for behavioural information,

they usually cannot assess all tasks or technical skills (Murphy and Cleveland, 1995), and subordinate assessment, which turns normal hierarchy on its head, may be uncomfortable for both the subordinate and the boss. This has been suggested as the principle reason that all MNCs have not adopted this system, despite the merits it has to offer for assessment of behaviours (Eichinger and Lombardo, 2003). The idea of reversing hierarchy does not translate well into a collectivist society with a low individuality or a high power-distance dimension. These cultures acknowledge a leader's power and do not like to reveal or ask too much personal information.

Self as source

Self-assessment, the facility of the employee to assess her/his own performance has become routine over the last decade. Ashford, Blatt and Vande Walle (2003) found that self-assessment offered the qualities of self-trust, reliability, availability, and trustworthiness. They found that, in order to perform self-assessment, an individual must perform three tasks: establish a standard, decide which feedback cues to use, and correctly interpret those cues. She also stressed that decoding cues was the most vital aspect and the most neglected. Many of the employee's cues from supervisors may come indirectly by email, or by telephone and, according to Cascio (2000), these indirect cues could be more susceptible to encoding problems. According to Ashford et al. (2003), when decoding cues the individual needs to maintain self-preservation as a self-confident performer. There is evidence from the USA that self-rating is more lenient than ratings obtained from supervisors (Eichinger and Lombardo, 2003). In contrast, self-ratings in Asia show that workers typically self-rate themselves lower than their peers or supervisors (Barron and Sackett, 2008).

Evidence, therefore, points to self-appraisal offering a degree of reliability, validity, and acceptability to the employee. Moreover, in turbulent times, when such events as mergers and restructuring occur with increasing frequency, the pressing reality of having to survive in such a setting makes the self-assessment process an important area of inquiry for the employee.

Peers as sources

It is reasonable to assume that peers are in closer proximity to ratees than supervisors and are, therefore, more able to give accurate assessments. This is particularly evident in teams. However, research indicates that effective peer appraisals require a lot of trust among team workers, a non-competitive reward system, and frequent opportunities for colleagues to observe each other. There is evidence

---

Box 9.4

The Peace Corps, a government initiative created by President John F. Kennedy, implemented the use of self appraisal tests, based on the premise that a better understanding of themselves would help individuals adapt to cultural change.

In 1970 Robert Dorn, who worked in the Peace Corps leadership training, joined the Centre for Creative Leadership and introduced the practice of self appraisal. Years later, Robert Bailey, an economist who worked for Dorn, had the idea of including others in the assessment process and initiated the multisource assessment process.

Vandy Massey www.engauge.co.uk/ask

that peers tended to give harsh evaluations (Saavedra and Kwun, 1993). Peer evaluations are often not acceptable in collectivist cultures and have been found to be unacceptable in China, Korea, and Japan (Gillespie, 2006).

Multisource feedback (360-degree appraisal)

The process of multisource feedback (360-degree appraisal) involves obtaining feedback from subordinates, peers, supervisor, self, and customers. This gives everyone more information about a ratee's behaviours, thus enhancing the potential for improvement. In recent years, multisource feedback has received a deal of research and management attention, and the general findings suggest that multisource feedback results in more accurate ratings (Palmer and Loveland, 2008). There is sometimes disagreement among the various sources (Eichinger and Lombardo, 2003) yet, if all the ratings produced the same findings, there would probably be little value in obtaining information from all sources. Each of the rating sources appears to have inherent advantages and disadvantages.

On the one hand, experienced supervisors usually have good norms because they have seen several employees working on the job, which can result in well-calibrated views of different performance levels, and supervisor rating is acceptable across most cultures. Peers are often in closer proximity to the work being performed. Self-ratings have the advantage that there is a great amount of information conveniently available, and they have been found to be useful in cross-cultural settings. For example, the organisation Peace Corps found self-appraisal to be particularly useful for increasing one's personal cultural awareness (see Box 9.4). In addition, other forms of feedback have been found to be invaluable when managing employees who are geographically distant so that the supervisor may not witness the majority of subordinates behaviours. Evidence does suggest that multiple sources are necessary if an accurate and comprehensive assessment is to be achieved.

On the other hand, peers and subordinates are often inexperienced in making rater and task judgments and may only be aware of a small portion of a manager's performance, and self-ratings can be distorted because of an inflated perception of one's own performance. In a global context, multisource feedback has been found to be particularly challenging, and recent evidence suggests that multisource feedback is not transferable across all cultures. For example, Varela and Premeaux (2008) investigated the effect of cross-cultural values on multisource feedback with managers from Venezuela and Colombia, two collectivistic and high-power distance countries, and results of the study indicate that cultural values distort

the evaluations involved in multisource systems. Specifically, unlike reports of studies conducted in individualistic and low-power distance environments, they found that peers are the least discrepant source of information, subordinates tend to provide the highest evaluations across feedback sources, and there is an excessive emphasis on people-oriented behaviours. Likewise, Gillespie (2006) addressed whether multisource feedback ratings made by subordinates are equivalent across national cultures in Great Britain, Hong Kong, Japan, and the USA. The results emphasise the need for MNCs to use caution when transporting multisource feedback, to global locations.

STRATEGIES TO IMPROVE GLOBAL PERFORMANCE

In many cases the appraisal interview will provide the foundation for noting inadequacies in employee performance and for making improvement. Unless these inadequacies are brought to the employee's notice, they are likely to become critical. Poor employee performance is most likely due to one or more of three conditions. For example, if an employee's performance is not up to standard, it could be caused by either a lack of skill, a lack of knowledge, or a lack of motivation. For satisfactory performance to occur, an employee usually requires certain skills, knowledge, and motivation. In addition, the supervisor needs to be able to detect these three important traits, which can be challenging when the supervisor and employee are from different cultures.

The first step in managing unsatisfactory performance is to detect and determine the reason for the inadequate performance. This almost certainly requires the supervisor to be trained to conduct a professional performance appraisal interview. Once the source of the problem is known, a course of action can be planned. For instance, if the performance issues are due to a lack of skills or knowledge, the solution may lie in providing training and development in an effort to improve the employee's deficiency in skills and knowledge. Poor motivation may have a devastating effect on performance, but it is often difficult to diagnose and is frequently a multifaceted, complex matter and may be particularly difficult to detect in another culture. Nonetheless, it is essential that employees with low levels of motivation are identified during the appraisal interview. These employees in particular, need to be given enough time to express their views through an adequate feedback session.

Politics

It has also been found that politics combined with power play a fundamental role in the appraisal process. Adonis

(2015) found that increased power of the rater may make the rater more critical and more likely to rate the employee harshly. It is therefore necessary for the human resource manager to carefully monitor the performance appraisal process and ensure that the appraisal system is fair and that politics are kept to a minimum.

Trust

A low level of trust between either the employee and the company or the employee and the supervisor has been found to have a detrimental effect on the outcome of the appraisal (Maley and Moeller, 2014). Murphy and Cleveland (1995) noted that trust between an individual and the organisation reduces the necessity for appraisal to be used as a control mechanism and, as trust increases, it is likely that the appraisal will be future oriented, focused on developmental processes, generally used in a productive manner and, above all, fair. It is essential, therefore, that the supervisor and employee meet regularly in an attempt to build trust. The performance appraisal also needs to be transparent and open in order to built trust. The Amersham case shows problems encountered by a closed performance management system (see box 9.2).

Fairness

The employee's perception of the supervisor's trustworthiness has been found to be related to the interpersonal atmosphere, helpfulness, and perceived fairness of the session (Bradley and Ashkanasy, 2001). Kramar and Bartam (2015) contend that, for a performance appraisal system to be fair, the employee must have adequate notice; fully understand the purpose, criteria, and standards of the system; be given a fair hearing; and the rater must apply performance standards with consistency across all employees. A fair appraisal system has been found to increase the level of trust and acceptability (Juncaj, 2002), which makes fairness a crucial component of the appraisal system.

Feedback

It has been identified that feedback is essential for a satisfactory performance appraisal. In spite of that, most employees do not get adequate feedback from their supervisors (Cascio, 2003; Juncaj, 2002; Maley, 2009; Milliman et al., 2002). It is necessary, therefore, that during the appraisal interview the supervisor must ensure that there is adequate time for feedback and employee expression. Maley and Kramar (2007) established that employees preferred receiving formal appraisals at least twice per year and on-going informal feedback throughout the year. A study conducted by the Corporate Leadership Council

? Critical Thinking 9.1 Supervisor feedback

In an ideal corporate setting, the manager's feedback is supposed to help your employees realise the reasons for inconsistencies in their performance. Thus, feedback should facilitate employees' career growth. However, in most situations, the opposite happens. There are varied reasons. Most of the time, knowingly or unknowingly, managers make certain mistakes while passing on feedback to their employees. These mistakes negate the very purpose of giving feedback and jeopardise the relationship between managers and their subordinates.

Questions

1   Think about the mistakes that your managers may have made when giving you feedback?
2   How could the environment surrounding feedback have been improved?

(2006) revealed that feedback and fairness and accuracy of informal feedback increase staff performance by 39.1 per cent.

PERFORMANCE MANAGEMENT IN A GLOBAL CONTEXT

It has been identified that the performance management is susceptible to many problems when a firm globalised its operations. All human resource management processes have been identified as becoming more complex due to geographical and cultural distance between the subsidiary and head office. (Harzing and Noordhaven, 2005; Shen, 2004 Sully De Luque and Sommer, 2007; Taormina and Gao, 2009). The end result is that global employees are often found to be predominantly despondent about their performance management (Fenwick 2004; Maley and Kramar, 2014; Taormina and Goa, 2009).

THE CULTURAL IMPACT OF PERFORMANCE MANAGEMENT

A recent study identified that the purpose of performance management could be easily categorised into three broad groups by their different purposes, namely: 1) bottom-line profit incorporating pay for performance; 2) communication, training, and development; and 3) control, increasing performance and deciding on promotion. When these categories were tabled, it become obvious that there was a noticeable difference between Western and Eastern countries. The inference is that the purpose and practice of the performance management differs between individualistic and collectivist societies (see Hofstede, 1980). These findings will now be discussed.

Bottom-line profit

A bottom-line profit and pay for performance was used as the key purpose of the performance management in Australia (Maley and Kramar, 2014) and the UK and the USA (Milliman et al., 2002). It was plain in some cases that an intense focus on profit can contribute to employee disappointment with the performance appraisal process and may results in poor acceptability of the performance management process.

Communication and career development

Communication and career development were found to be the key purpose in Sweden. (Chiang and Birtch, 2010). This finding reflects the emphasis on egalitarianism and more collective distribution of rewards inherent in Nordic society (Gupta and Hanges, 2004). In France, training is the principal purpose, and performance management is used as basis for training employees to correct for performance errors (Groeschl, 2003). German MNCs use performance management chiefly for long-term career development (Festing and Barzantny, 2008).

Control, increased performance, and promotion

Control, increased performance, and promotion were found to be evident in Eastern countries. In China the performance management's purpose has been found to be restricted to control and relationship building and to be less transparent and limited in communication and feedback (Shen, 2004). However (Shibata, 2000) found that difficult economic conditions and increasing labour costs have induced many Japanese firms to transform their human resource management systems, and in an effort to imitate the performance-based pay in US MNCs, Japanese firms are changing the purpose of their performance management systems towards using the process for assessing and rewarding performance.

The findings in Greece appeared to be something of a contradiction. Nonetheless, Myloni, Harzing and Mirza (2004) contend that the purpose of the performance management in Greek subsidiaries often reflects the Greek national culture. They also assert that due to a combination of high levels of family/in-group orientation and low levels of performance and future orientation, the purpose of performance management is frequently underdeveloped in Greek subsidiaries and is often based on subjective criteria. Papalexandris, Chalikias and Panayotopoulou (2002), also studied the performance management in several MNCs' Greek subsidiaries and found that performance management is used to justify promotion decisions that had already been taken. Moreover, they argue that high levels of power distance (Hofstede, 1980) lead to less direct communication between supervisor and employee and that the supervisor's opinion will be more important in performance management than that of the employee, peers, or subordinates compared to other MNC subsidiaries. Galang (2004) explored the purpose of performance management in Singaporean firms and found the process was used for decisions about promotion.

Western countries that rank high on individualism tend to use the performance management for pay linked to performance and they tend to focus on bottom-line profit (USA 1st, Australia 2nd, and UK 3rd when ranked on individualism). However, European and Scandinavian countries with a moderate rank for individualism (Sweden 10th, France 10th and Germany 15th) tend to use the performance management for communication, training, and development. Whereas the largely Eastern countries that are clearly collectivist (Asia: China, India, the Philippines, Thailand, Singapore – plus Greece and the Middle East) used the process to increase performance, control, and promotion. This finding is in agreement with Peretz and Fried (2008) who examined national values and performance management practices across 21 countries.

Dowling et al. (2008) state that culture is one of the most significant constraints that must be considered when evaluating foreign subsidiary employees. They argue that variations in work practices between the parent multinational corporation and the subsidiary need to be recognised. For example, one does not fire a Mexican manager because worker productivity is half the US average. In Mexico that would mean the manager is working at a level three or four times as high as the average Mexican manager. They argue that global appraisals require relevant comparative data, not absolute numbers; the harassed Mexican manager in the above example has to live with Mexican constraints, not European or US ones, which can be very different. Additionally, Harvey et al. (2002) and Milliman et al. (2002) found that the way MNCs measure worker productivity is often similar but the results appear differently because of cultural nuances.

Interpretation of the performance appraisal confronts the issue of cultural applicability (Milliman et al., 2002). For example, in different cultures the performance appraisal can be interpreted as a signal of distrust or

? Critical Thinking 9.2 Point of view: Unfair performance management in schools in England

? Critical Thinking 9.2 Point of view: Unfair performance management in schools in England

Tim O'Malley Geography Teacher in Southern England

When performance management first came in, it was seen as an initiative aimed at tightening control on the profession. Performance management would ensure teachers set annual targets that were deemed appropriate by the establishment, agreed by the schools, and overseen by local authority inspectors and OFSTED (Office for Standards in Education). Targets were to be agreed between the individual being assessed and an assigned performance management mentor. Targets were usually, though not always, at least in part tied closely to measurable academic standards. Teachers who were deemed to have successfully completed set targets by their line managers and performance management mentors, and the Head teacher, were often eligible for rewards in the way of promotion and salary increase. The whole system is hampered by the practical difficulties of finding the time for meetings between key staff to complete the process and verification of progress through lesson observation etc., not to mention agreeing recorded outcomes. Establishing what constitutes 'progress' in the world of education and understanding what this looks like for any given child or class or cohort, and then agreeing how best this can be measured, are fraught with difficulty. In practice, a successful annual performance management depends as much or more on a positive relationship with a teacher's assessor than any real 'progress' in relation to the actual or perceived needs and progress of the children being educated. Consequently performance management is becoming increasingly viewed as an unfair game one needs to play, and in terms of improving schools, it is gradually diminishing.

Question

1　Is this another disgruntled teacher or is there evidence that there are more widespread performance management problems in the English school system?

even an insult. In Japan, for instance, it is important to enable one to 'save face' by avoiding direct confrontation and, according to Dowling et al. (1999), this influences the way performance appraisal is conducted. A Japanese manager cannot point out a work-related problem or error committed by a subordinate. He would explain the consequences of a mistake without pointing out the actual mistake. A study involving ten leading Chinese multinational corporations (Shen, 2004) found that there are commonalities in global performance appraisal procedures and criteria between Chinese and Western multinational corporations (see box 9.5). However, Shen (2004) found that the purpose of performance appraisal in Chinese MNCs was largely to decide how much to pay rather than organisational development by being more concerned with short-term business achievement. He also found performance appraisals in Chinese MNCs to be short in feedback and less transparent. In addition, it has been established that different forms of multisource assessments other than the traditional supervisory appraisal are virtually nonexistent in China and Hong Kong (Entrekin and Chung, 2001; Shen, 2004). Research from Hong Kong (Snape et al., 1998) revealed that Hong Kong respondents had a preference for group-based appraisal and that appraisals were more directive and less participative. The appraisals in Hong Kong companies were found to have been modified to suit the cultural collectivist characteristics of the society.

In Indian firms, Varma, Pichler and Ekkirala (2005) found that interpersonal relations and performance levels had a significant effect on performance ratings and that supervisors inflated ratings of low performers, suggesting that local cultural norms may be operating as a moderator.

Acceptance of the performance appraisal by both the rater and ratee have been argued as being essential for a successful appraisal (Bradley and Ashkanasy, 2001). In the global setting, performance appraisal acceptance has been found to vary widely across different cultures (Milliman et al., 2002). For instance, Japanese employees have been found to be less accepting of the appraisal process than US employees.

This concise summary of the purpose and practice of performance management is by no means conclusive, but it does give some indication of the different trends of the purpose and practice of global performance management process. It also suggests that national culture may affect the HRM purpose and practices that the MNCs' subsidiaries and global managers are likely to more eagerly adopt (Aycan, 2005; Maley, Moeller, and Harvey, in press; Peretz and Rosenblatt, 2006).

Box 9.5 Performance appraisals at Chinese multinationals

In a recent large study, Chinese multinationals were found to adopt different approaches towards different groups, particularly different nationalities and managerial status. The Chinese global performance appraisals were found to be a mix of home and local appraisal systems and a mix of traditional Chinese personnel management and modern Western human resource concepts. Moreover, Chinese global performance appraisal policies and practices were found to be affected by various host-contextual and firm-specific factors, and there was also an interplay between global performance and other global human resource management activities.

Shen (2004).

Divergence–convergence question

Moreover, one of the most perplexing questions on the cultural impact of appraisal is whether performance appraisal systems designed in the parent MNCs should be transferred to other countries (Harvey, 1997). On the one hand, Dowling et al. (2008) espouse that this is possible, providing the manager conducting the performance appraisal has sensitivity to foreign values. On the other hand, Hempel, (2001) and Vance (2006) argue that it is doubtful that the traditional principles that guide the design and management of appraisal in Western countries can be successfully transferred to other countries. Vance (2006) found that cultural management styles may translate into distinct differences in the optimal management of performance, thus suggesting important reservations about the transferability of traditional performance appraisal principles across boundaries. Hempel (2001) presented both theoretical arguments and exploratory results that suggest that Western-style performance appraisals would need to be modified extensively in order to work with Chinese employees. He argues that until more is known in this area, strong reservations need to be expressed about the direct applicability of the performance appraisal practices typically implemented by US and European MNCs. All foreign multinational corporations need to consider the cultural implications of their performance management system and to listen to feedback from global employees, as shown by the Korean case (see box 6).

Global legislation

It is important for the global human resource manager to understand that industrial relations governing performance management will most likely differ across national boundaries (Harzing and Ruysseveldt, 2005). It is essential to acknowledge that in the industrial relations field no industrial relations system can be understood without an appreciation of the way in which rules are established and implemented and decisions are made in the society

Box 9.6 Korean boss to take on Twitter attack on performance appraisal

Unhappy staff at Hyundai Australia have vented their frustration with management about their performance appraisal on Twitter. The boss of Hyundai Australia plans to confront staff and conduct 'an open discussion' about a barrage of negative comments on the social networking site Twitter. Hyundai Australia staff members have attacked the company's local boss on Twitter, complaining of unfair redundancies and stressful working conditions. In a year when the market contracted due to the global financial crisis, Hyundai bucked the trend, increasing sales almost 40 per cent. The Twitter comments claim morale is at a low ebb and that staff are overworked and underappreciated, with Korean employees favoured over locals. One comment says: *I can tell you there are a lot of stressed employees who take their frustrations home with them. There are sleepless nights, health problems.'* Another asks: *'How do you expect them to be productive, motivated and perform well under the current conditions?'*

Mr Lee, the Managing Director admits *' I am very surprised'* by the negative comments and *will meet with staff to discuss their concerns. We are a growing company and we are doing very well. Most of all people are very happy.'* He goes on to say *'I will meet our employees next Monday and I will have an open discussion about what is wrong and what is the concern. You could say I am a little concerned about this situation, but we are going forward so if there is any concern we can discuss. I am open minded, and this our open policy.* He says *'staff concerns appear to be centred on a new performance appraisal system,'* and he rejected claims that bonuses had not been properly paid.

Source: http://theage.drive.com.au/motor-news/hyundai-boss-to-take-on-twitter-attack-20100212-nwvv.ht.

Box 9.7 Note from an Australian expatriate manager in China

I'd be happy to share some of my experiences managing Chinese staff. The staff in my office are probably quite different from staff in Chinese companies or government agencies, but I presume that the general themes are consistent.

A few points below:

▸ The majority of our Chinese locally engaged staff are university educated with a very high level of written and spoken English. While some of the staff have considerable experience in the office (between 10 and 20 years' experience in the same office), some of the younger staff have lived and studied in English-speaking countries (Australia, UK, USA) or have previous work experience in other English-speaking environments (embassies or the private sector in business or hospitality).

▸ Hierarchy within the office is important – staff report to their team leaders, who in turn report to the office manager and then the expatriate managers. Unlike the Australian management style which can be quite egalitarian, Chinese offices generally have a strict hierarchical structure – there is an overarching hierarchy in the office, and smaller team hierarchies, which align with work roles and responsibilities.

▸ There are often challenges with staff not using their initiative to solve problems or complete challenging tasks. This is partly cultural, with some of the older staff preferring to be specifically tasked and diligently completing assigned tasks without question. Younger staff, particularly those with overseas experience, are generally more proactive in using their initiative or suggesting solutions to management. One strategy that has been developed in our office over many years by expatriate managers is encouraging staff to think about solutions to problems/challenges as they arise (taking responsibility for mistakes made) and encouraging self-initiative.

▸ Staff performance in our office is managed using Australian standard tools (performance agreements and regular discussions between staff and managers). Staff are accustomed to formal and informal discussions with their team leaders and the expatriate managers – these discussions are an opportunity for staff and managers to comment on performance and discuss development opportunities and determine a performance rating which is linked to an annual performance bonus.

Questions

1 How would you describe the management of human resource function in this office?
2 Who is the best person to manage the performance appraisals of the Chinese staff?
3 What challenges may the Australian expatriate manager experience in conducting performance appraisal with Chinese employees?
4 Who is the ideal person to perform the Australian manager's appraisal?
5 What do you consider are the challenges in setting up a 360-degree feedback process in the office?

Based on a personal note from author to the informant, 2 October 2015

concerned. It is usually necessary to have some appreciation of the historical origin of the performance appraisal legislation.

MANAGING PERFORMANCE IN UNCERTAINTY

Global uncertainty has been found to directly or indirectly have an adverse impact on performance management (Maley and Kramar, 2014). Moreover, it has been found to impact on a firm's ability to meet financial performance indicators (Engle, Dowling and Festing, 2008). This predictably will mean that there will be upward pressure on revenue growth and a downward squeeze

on costs and the firm will be focused on improving the bottom line (Bhattacharya, Gibson and Doty, 2005). This change in focus often means that the employee performance management is given less attention. Senior managers have less time to effectively conduct performance management for their subordinates, appraisals may be rushed or omitted completely, and there is less time for communication and feedback. In addition there may be added pressure on employees to work longer hours, and objectives and performance targets will almost certainly be more challenging. These cost-cutting decisions are important and can have a short-term positive effect on the bottom line, but they can also have enduring negative repercussions on the performance management process (Carpenter and Fredrickson, 2002; Maley and Kramar,

2014). Accordingly, evidence suggests that global uncertainty may wield a powerful influence on global performance management.

ALTERNATIVES TO PERFORMANCE APPRAISAL

The performance review has been under constant scrutiny, and whilst scholars and practitioners alike have recognised that the process of assessing people under the guise of performance management and performance appraisal has many flaws, they have acknowledged that a process is needed and a performance review even with its faults is better than nothing. However, more recently there has been mounting evidence that the process of the performance review is irretrievably defective and does more damage than good. The popular press has started to publish articles such as: 'Deloitte dumps bi-annual performance reviews, opts for weekly updates' (King, 2015); 'Prepare to fire the

annual performance review' (Nickless, 2015); 'A blast of common sense frees staff from appraisals' (Kellaway, 2015); 'No please not the performance review' (Delves-Broughton, 2015); and 'In big move, Accenture will get rid of annual performance reviews and rankings (Cunningham, 2015).

Based on a study of 1, 2000 HR managers across 21 industries, Baker (2014) contends that there are eight major pitfalls that we need to reappraise in regard to the formal performance appraisal as part of the performance management process. These are (1) appraisals are a costly exercise; (2) appraisals can be destructive; (3) appraisals are often a monologue rather than a dialogue; (4) the formality of the appraisal stifles discussion; (5) appraisals are too infrequent; (6) appraisals are an exercise in form-filling; (7) appraisals are rarely followed up; (8) most people find appraisals stressful.

Certainly, there is recent evidence that several well-known multinational corporations are abandoning their formal performance review process. First Deloitte and now Accenture, two giant consultancies that have

---

In the News Why discontinuing performance reviews may be damaging for your career

In the business world, performance management evaluation is an annual ceremony that few employees relish. However, a growing number of senior managers are ceasing this custom. In Australia, for example, a major bank (NAB), and the subsidiary of a large consulting firm (Deloitte) announced the end of their formal performance management reviews. In both firms, the reviews and forced rankings will be superseded by weekly or fortnightly informal and dynamic meetings, which the firms guarantee will be less formal and threatening. Then does this mark the end of the dreaded performance review season? Or are they turning an annual event into a stack of diary invites and a meaningless meeting?

Some commentators have suggested completely abandoning all categories of review meetings (Kelley, 2015). While others, such as the major job search company SEEK, have substituted their performance evaluations with criteria that include classifications such as: exceeds, meets expectations and needs improvement. This technique is combined with a comprehensive 360-degree feedback where the employee's work is analysed by a variety of peers, non-line managers, subordinates, and in some cases even customers. The Melbourne-based software company Brownie Points has introduced a novel 360 appraisal system, while LinkedIn, has publicised that they will keep a mix of formal and informal management reviews.

Some may be encouraging the end of the formal review process with rankings and ratings, but overall the performance appraisal as part of a performance management process is also a great safety net. It provides evidence of an employee's performance. Should the tumultuous tides of office politics inevitably turn, it is tangible evidence that an employee can prove that her/his performance is satisfactory.

Having an informal process has merit, however, according to Rhonda Brighton-Hall (former HR executive, Commonwealth Bank of Australia). If a manager can't offer suitable feedback once a year, things won't get any better just because the conversation turns weekly. Perhaps, before firms rush to change their appraisal process, they should consider that they may be abandoning one of few occasions where their employees can get a tangible report card and have a face-to-face meeting with their boss.

Adapted from:

Han, M. (2015) Why scrapping performance reviews is bad news for your career. *Australian Financial Review*, July 31.
Kelley, L. (2010) It's time to sack job appraisals. *Financial Times*, July, 26.

implemented and advised on such systems, have recently acknowledged they cause more pain than gain (Delves-Broughton, 2015). The Melbourne-based firm that supplies concierge and reception staff to some of Australia's biggest companies and luxury properties has also announced that it is stopping a formal review process. Its chief executive James Armstrong contends, 'our business is all about our people. That is why we have replaced formal appraisals with something more meaningful'. He is expecting the change to boost staff engagement levels with frequent feedback sessions. In the USA, Netflix abandoned reviews years ago. Former chief talent officer Patty McCord says the company has never looked back (Kellaway, 2015).

The overall response from these companies suggests that performance reviews are failing to improve performance, and is the product of a profession that is 'too inward looking' and process-driven. They contend that managers and employees consider performance reviews to be an awkward conversations filled with form-filling duties. Nonetheless, evidence is emerging that many of the companies changing from performance review are not actually abandoning them, they are changing from a stilted review to a process involving regular feedback, which according to Maley and Kramar (2007) has to be a positive change.

BENEFITS OF STUDYING PERFORMANCE MANAGEMENT FROM A CRITICAL PERSPECTIVE

Critical thinking in global performance management, in short, encourages self-directed, self-disciplined, self-monitored, and self-corrective thinking. It presupposes assent to rigorous standards of excellence and mindful command of their use. It entails effective communication and problem-solving abilities and a commitment to overcome tendencies to native egocentrism and sociocentrism (Paul and Elder, 2008).

Thus, studying performance management in organisations from a critical outlook permits future global managers to acquire an enhanced perception of the numerous perspectives of different employees. This involves cultural divergence and human resource structural and strategic inconsistency. Interpreting both cultural and structural differences and their effect on performance management will permit future global managers to weigh up situations, identify problems, and determine suitable solutions to the multifaceted issue of global performance management.

Global performance management, while not new, has not yet matured. Some significant studies have been done, but there are conflicting results, and a complete body of knowledge is some time away. Nevertheless, there is little doubt that in some form performance management and its main activity, performance appraisal, are preferred to the alternative of doing nothing. It is, therefore, critical that we not only continue to refine and perfect the process but that we gain a better insight to the process in the global context. It is only by studying the process that we can redefine and improve it.

Finally, global performance management research will be substantially strengthened by effective collaboration between university scholars and industry practitioners (Perkmann and Walsh, 2007). As the complexity of global management issues and velocity of change in global business increase, such collaborations may become essential if research is to make any real difference in academic understanding of the issues surrounding global performance management.

CONCLUSION

This chapter has addressed the crucial issue of performance evaluation. It has discussed the contentious nature of performance management and its implications for the organisation and its employees. Recommendations to improve performance management are nothing new. Improvements to the system have been recommended since the inception of performance appraisal over 50 years ago. There has been a plethora of ideas to improve the basic concept of managing employee performance. Fifty years later, the area is still controversial and, if we make predictions about the future based on the past, we can expect more change.

Further use and refinement of behavioural methods (BOS) will be a major step in the development of a performance appraisal system. The behavioural methods have good validity and reliability and are presently used widely in multinational corporations. BOS will become cost effective and accessible for smaller and medium-sized enterprises.

A weakness in many performance appraisals programmes is that managers and supervisors are not trained to give appraisals. This means that these managers may give inadequate appraisals; they particularly make rater errors and are less likely to give sufficient feedback to their subordinates. Avery and Murphy (1998) proposed that rater training showed some promise in improving the effectiveness of performance ratings and that the systematic errors, particularly leniency and halo, were found to be reduced with rater training. It is envisaged that there will be more emphasis on training managers to give effective performance appraisal and manage the overall performance management process.

The area of culture in the MNC presents many challenges, and firms will need to consider the acceptability of performance appraisal and performance management in different cultures and recognise that 'one performance management system may not fit all' (Chong, 2007). Research has revealed that only scant attention has been paid to the performance management of global employees (Claus and Briscoe, 2009; Harvey, 1997; Maley and Kramar, 2014). Multinational corporations, therefore, should consider their global employees and need to think about tailoring the performance management system to fit the norms and beliefs of local national cultures.

The virtual office presents difficulties for performance management. Online performance management systems are now widespread. Firms often introduce elaborate and expensive performance management systems but fail to ensure that employees know how to use them adequately. It has even been suggested that managers tend to give more negative ratings with online appraisals compared to those given on an old-fashioned paper form (Kurzberg, Naquin and Belkin, 2005). There is little doubt that technology has impacted the way firms manage performance management. It is an area that will continue to witness enormous change. For example, the impact of the speed of communication and social network sites could have a major influence on the politics of performance management.

Performance management is a human relations process and needs trust between the supervisor and the employee to work well. Although progressive contemporary technology has removed the burden of many tedious administrative tasks in the office, it must be considered that for a performance management process to work effectively across a diversity of cultures, there need to be three vital activities between the supervisor and the subordinate that cannot be replaced by a computer. These activities are regular face-to-face contact, repeated opportunity for feedback, and performance appraisal follow-up. In other words, looking towards the future, the MNCs' performance appraisal must be embedded in a performance management system that transcends all cultures.

End of Chapter Case Study Feedback in politics and government

When Joshua secured a job as a junior staffer with a senior Australian government minister, he was delighted. The industrious 27-year-old had studied economics, prior to gaining experience in marketing and working for a NSW State Government electoral office. Moving to Canberra was a great adventure for Joshua, and he looked forward to gaining experience working with this prestigious politician. He was familiar with the long hours and travel customary in politics, and this did not faze him.

The ministerial office had approximately 20 staff, divided into policy, admin, media, and political teams. The office was led by a Chief of Staff (the equivalent of the CEO) and a Deputy-Chief of Staff.

However, from day one Joshua's experience was extraordinary. After being approached via political contacts, Joshua submitted a resume and had interviews with the politician and approximately three other senior staff. Aside from this, there were no other selection criteria or process around the appointment.

There was no job specification, no job description, and no induction. Upon entering the office, Joshua was shown his desk and not introduced to any other staff. His direct supervisor, the Chief of Staff, hardly spoke to him. There wasn't even an introduction during that day's staff meeting.

Over time, through taking the initiative and speaking to fellow staff, Joshua was able to create a role. Unfortunately, the seemingly disorganised entry into the office was symbolic of its general organisation and leadership.

Performance reviews were quarterly meetings with the Chief of Staff. The hectic nature of politics meant that they were often very short or cancelled altogether. Additionally, it was not a formal process, with no agenda to begin with and no follow up.

Joshua found in his first year that he was required to travel to all domestic locations with the politician, working 40 weekends out of 52 on over 150 trips. Whilst the travel was a privilege, the lack of staff rotation or coherent office strategy began to drain and distress Joshua.

Moreover, he rarely had constructive feedback from his supervisor. Formal performance review systems are entirely organised by the Chief of Staff in political offices – there was no accountability more broadly within the Government.

As time progressed, the chaos and negative atmosphere appeared to become evident even to the general public. The job of the Chief of Staff is to give feedback and advice not only to subordinates but also to the politician. This particular chief of staff did neither.

Joshua began to worry that the politician might lose his job and as a consequence the whole office would lose their jobs. He started to look for other opportunities and was quickly offered a job back in Sydney working for another senior minister.

Five months later, the Minister was dumped in reshuffle and the entire office lost their jobs.

Questions

1   Describe the major human resource management issues in this office?
2   If you were responsible for human resources in this office, how would you have handled this situation?
3   Define the role of objectives and feedback in this case?
4   Discuss the process you might implement to strengthen the performance management process in the office?

This case is based on a personal interview with the informant. The name of the organisation and employee have been changed for confidentiality.

APPENDIX TO CASE

Emailed Feedback from Joshua to Minister's office after departing for one month.

Dear Janet,

As discussed on the phone, below are a few of my suggestions for the office. Thank you again for the opportunity allowing me to do so.

Diary meeting

A twice-weekly diary meeting, on Monday and Thursday, where diary requests are actioned (re-active) and suggestions for events for Fred to do (pro-active) are decided.
Somebody (i.e. you) has the power to say NO and reject and accept event invitations.
A regular meeting between the politician and yourself is arranged to advise the politician of upcoming travel and his events

In my experience:

• The politician likes to review travel arrangements. The regular meeting with the politician where you advise him of the events needs to be different to the politician reviewing virtually every request (and saying yes to every request, putting the office under enormous pressure).

Traveling roster

Who is going on which trip, who is responsible (includes speech writing, stakeholder meetings) weeks in advance.

In my experience:

• The adviser responsible doesn't coordinate between teams, and trips are rushed and last-minute as a result.
• Someone needs to constantly chase the person responsible and keep them accountable in advance of the trip.

Sitting roster

A roster indicating which staff (two at most) are required to stay back till the end of Government Business in the House, or after the politician's last event. Ideally, this would be one political/policy person and one media person.

In my experience:

• Previous attempts have failed because the Chief of Staff derided those who left before 7:00 p.m.
• The CoS may have no family commitments when they visit Parliament House, but Canberra-based staff do.

Email culture

Fewer office-wide emails. 'All staff emails' should be reserved for items that directly affect each team (admin, policy, politics, media).
Staff are directed to reply to emails from colleagues – Task management is not possible when staff do not respond to emails.

In my experience:

• Staff need to heed Email Etiquette 101:

1 Understand the difference between 'To' and 'CC'. As a rule of thumb, the more people you send an email to, the less likely any single person will respond to it, much less perform any action that you requested. The people you include in the 'To' field should be the people you expect to read and respond to the message. The 'CC' field should be used sparingly. You should only CC people who have a need to stay in the know.

Morning Parliament meetings

The media team brief on relevant articles.
The politician's diary for that day is discussed.

In my experience:

- There is no point reading out word-for-word key paragraphs of articles – everyone has done that already. Individual teams need to know the impact of the articles.

Staff meeting

1 Melbourne and Canberra offices do the joint staff meeting via video-link.
2 A set time, with a set agenda (which is circulated a day in advance).

In my experience:
The staff meeting was pushed back 30 mins then 1 hour and/or finally cancelled nearly every week. This has very negative effects on morale.

My suggestions:
When the meeting was cancelled, a discussion about how bad things would take place.
Video-link between each will stop the eye-rolling.
Ideally, action items are sent after the meeting to relevant staff.
In a perfect world, the meeting isn't on a Friday (write-off after a week of Parliament).

Regular one-on-ones

- occur quarterly, with personalised items to discuss;
- two-way feedback.

In my experience:
A scheduled one-on-one would change time-slots a dozen times and would occur a month or two after being originally planned.

In my experience:
The Chief of Staff needs to physically sit at the meeting table, not at his desk (he would often get distracted by emails).
Meetings should run for half an hour, not five minutes.
Follow up with action items.

Staff arrivals

- Incoming staff are announced at a staff meeting, then welcomed with a morning tea, etc.
- The politician formally meets the new staff member.

In my experience:
Staff introductions were extremely poor, to nonexistent. You need to carve out the time for this to occur.

The above, along with any suggestions other staff may have, will make life a little easier for the over-worked and very stressed staff.

Finally, (and I know you didn't ask for this) but a month out of that office has given me clarity about one thing:

If the politician's fortunes are to improve, he needs someone who can:

act a shock absorber for the other staff and Fred;
make decisions and direct traffic in the office;
deliver the bad news.

In my experience, the politician's current Chief of Staff does not perform any of the above duties to any effect.

If the process doesn't change, the outcome won't change – the Chief of Staff needs to resign or take a secondary role immediately, if the politician is to remain a minister.

Again, I know you didn't ask for personnel advice, but I think it is important to recognise that some change will help staff, but Chief of Staff change will help the politician (and in effect the Government/country). Thank you for giving me the chance to provide process suggestions.

Regards,
Joshua

FOR DISCUSSION AND REVISION

- You are the human resource managers of a major multinational corporation. What reasons would you give to argue for maintaining a global performance management system? What reasons would you use against establishing a global performance management system?
- How has globalisation changed the nature of the performance appraisals in multinational corporations?
- Explain the key differences between performance appraisal and performance management. Why do you consider that these terms are often confused in business, and what are the implications in practical terms of this confusion?

- What are the challenges for giving feedback to employees from a different culture? How can you moderate these challenges?
- If you were developing a performance management system for expatriate managers, what types of features and behaviours would you measure and what sorts of results would you look for?
- 'Performance appraisals are better than nothing.' Clarify what is meant by this statement.
- Go to the University of Massachusetts,(UMASS) web site: http://www.umass.edu/humres/library/PMPGuide.pdf, and review the information about the performance management process for academic staff.
- Assess the procedure and criteria used at UMASS and suggest the strengths and weaknesses of the system?
- Compare and contrast the performance management at UMASS with the multinational healthcare company Medtronic. Website: http://www.medtronic.com/2010CitizenshipReport/total-employee/global-learning.html.

GLOSSARY

Performance management: A general term for a number of human resource functions that are concerned with managing performance.

Performance appraisal: A component of the performance management system that involves an interview.

Appraisal purpose: The motive/s for performing the performance appraisal.

Appraisal criteria: A set of clear standards by which to measure the performance of employees.

Appraisal acceptability: Employee and manager satisfaction with the purpose and method of the performance appraisal process.

Multisource feedback: The activity of multisource feedback that involves obtaining feedback from subordinates, peers, supervisor, self, and customers. Also known as 360-degree appraisal.

Global professional: An international manager, such as PCNs, HCNs or TCNs.

Parent-country national (PCNs): PCNs are global employees from the parent-country headquarters of the multinational corporation. Also termed 'expatriates'.

Host-country national (HCNs): HCNs are global employees who work in their host subsidiary.

Third-country national (TCNs): TCNs are global employees who are not from the multinational parent headquarter office and do not work in their host-country subsidiary.

Inpatriate manager: HCNs or TCNs global employees who are transferred to the multinational corporations headquarter office.

The performance management cycle: The sequence of performance management, i.e. planning, monitoring, developing, rewarding, and appraising.

Cultural competence: A set of congruent behaviours, attitudes, and policies that come together in a system, agency, or among professionals and enable that system or agency or those professions to work effectively in cross-cultural situations.

Cultural distance: A function of differences in values and communication styles that are rooted in culture (demographic or organisational).

Subsidiary: A company that is owned or controlled by a multinational corporation, usually located in another country.

Subsidiary structure: The way an MNC chooses to configure its human resource staffing in subsidiaries.

Subsidiary strategy: The way an MNC chooses to configure its human resource plan in its subsidiaries.

FURTHER READING

BREWSTER, C., CAREY, L., DOWLING, P., GROBBLER, P., HOLLAND, P. AND WARNICH, S. (2007) *Contemporary Issues in Human Resource Management* (2nd edn). Southern Africa: Oxford University Press.

BUDHWAR, P. S. AND DEBRAH, Y. A. (eds) (2013) *Human Resource Management in Developing Countries*. Routledge.

BRISCOE, D., RANDALL, S. AND CLAUSS, L. (2009) *Global Human Resource Management: Policies and Practice for Multinational Enterprises* (3rd ed.). London: Routledge.

KRAMAR, R. AND BARTAM, T. (2015) *Human Resource Management in Australia: Strategy, People and Performance*, 5th edn. McGraw Hill

TARIQUE, I., BRISCOE, D. R. AND SCHULER, R. S. (2015) *International Human Resource Management: Policies and Practices for Multinational Enterprises*. London: Routledge.

WEB RESOURCES

NWS Performance Management - Performance ...https://verification.nws.noaa.gov/.

http://www.medtronic.com/2011CitizenshipUpdate/total-employee/.

Australian Public Service Commission (APSC) website (www.apsc.gov.au), type in 'performance management'.

REFERENCES

ADONIS, J. (2015) Are performance appraisals worth it? *Sydney Morning Herald*, February 20th. Available at: ww.smh.com.au/small-business/managing/work-in-progress/are-performance-appraisals-worth-it-20150219-13jvez.html. Accessed September 2015.

ARVEY, R. D. AND MURPHY, K. R. (1998) Performance evaluation in work settings. *Annual review of psychology*, 49(1), 141–168.

AGUINIS, H. (2008) Enhancing the relevance of organizational behavior by embracing performance management research. *Journal of Organizational Behavior*,9: 139–145.

ASHFORD, S. J., BLATT, R. AND VANDE WALLE, D. (2003) Reflections on the looking glass: A review of search on feedback-seeking behavior in organizations. *Journal of Management*, 29(6):773–790.

AYCAN, Z. (2005) The interplay between cultural and institutional/structural contingencies in human resource management practices. *International Journal of Management*, 16(7): 983–1119.

AYDINLIK, D., ARZU, D. AND ULGEN, G. (2008) Communicating the ethos of codes of ethics within the organization: A comparison of the largest private sector organizations in Sweden and Turkey. *Journal of Management Development*, 27(7): 778–795.

BARRON, L. G. AND SACKETT, P. R. (2008) Asian variability in performance rating modesty and leniency bias. *Human Performance*, 21(3): 277–290.

BHATTACHARYA, M., GIBSON, D. AND DOTY, H. (2005) The effects of flexibility in employee skills, employee behaviors, and human resource practice on firm performance. *Journal of Management*, 31(4): 1–9.

BIRKINSHAW, J. AND MORRISON, A. (1995) Configurations of strategy and structure in subsidiaries of MNCs. *Global Business Studies*, 26(4): 729–740.

BOUSKILA-YAM, O. AND KLUGER, A. N. (2011) Strength-based performance appraisal and goal setting. *Human Resource Management Review*, 21(2): 137–147.

BRADLEY, L. AND ASHKANASY, N. (2001) Performance appraisal interview: Can they really be objective and are they useful anyway? *Asian Pacific Journal of Human Resources*, 39(2): 83–94.

CAMPBELL F. AND ZARKADA-FRASER, A. (2000) Measuring the performance of retail managers in Australia and Singapore. *Global Journal of Retail and Distribution Management*, 28(6).228–243.

CARDY, R. L. AND DOBBINS, G. H. (1994) *PA: Alternative Perspectives*. Cincinnati, OH: Southwest.

CARPENTER, M. AND FREDRICKSON, J. (2002) Top management teams, global strategic posture, and the moderating role of uncertainty. *Academy of Management Journal*, 44(93): 533–546.

CASCIO, W. F. (2000) Managing a virtual work place. *Academy of Management Executive*, 12(3): 81–91.

CASCIO, W.F. (2003) *Managing Human Resources: Productivity, Quality of Work Life, Profits* (8th edn). New York: McGraw-Hill.

CASCIO, W. F. (2014) Leveraging employer branding, performance management and human resource development to enhance employee retention. *Human Resource Development Global*, 17(2): 121–128.

CHIANG, F. T. AND BIRTCH, T. (2010) Appraising performance across borders: An empirical examination of the purpose and practices of performance appraisal in a multi-country context. *Journal of Management Studies*, 47(7): 1365–1392.

CHONG, E. (2008). Managerial competency appraisal: A cross-cultural study of American and East Asian Managers. *Journal of Business Research*, 61(3): 191–200.

CLAUS, L. AND BRISCOE, D. (2009) Employee performance management across borders: A review of the relevant literature. *Global Journal of Management Reviews*, (11(2): 175–196.

COLQUITT, J. A., KOSSEK, E. E. AND RAYMOND, A. (2001) Care giving decisions, well-beings, and performance: The effects of place and provider as a function of dependent type and work-family climates. *Academy of Management Journal*, 44(1): 29–44.

Corporate Leadership Council (2006) *Considerations for Implementing 360-degree Reviews: Secondary Research Findings*. Washington, DC: Corporate Executive Board.

CUNNINGHAM, L. (2015) In big move, Accenture will get rid of annual performance reviews and rankings. *Washington Post*, July 21. Available at: https://www.washingtonpost.com/news/on-leadership/wp/2015/07/21/in-big-move-accenture-will-get-rid-of-annual-performance-reviews-and-rankings/.

DE CIERI, H. AND DOWLING, P. (1998) The tortuous evolution of strategic human resources in multinational enterprises. Department of Management Working Paper in *HRM and Industrial Relations*, 5.

DELERY, J. AND DOTY, D. H. (1996) Modes of theorising in strategic human resource management: Tests of universalistic, contingency and configurational performance predictions. *Academy of Management Journal*, 39(4): 802–822.

DELVES-BROUGHTON, P. (2015) No please not the performance review. *London Times*. 12:01 a.m. July 30 2015. Available at: 20http://www.thetimes.co.uk/tto/life/article4512018.ece. Accessed July 30 2015.

DEMING, W. E. (1982). *Quality Productivity and Competitive Position*. Cambridge, MA: Massachusetts Institute of Technology Press.

DENISI, A. S. AND PRITCHARD, R. D. (2006) Performance appraisal, performance management and improving individual performance: A motivational framework. *Management and Organization Review*, 2: 253–277.

DOWLING, P., FESTING, M. AND ENGLE, S. (2008) *Global Human Resource Management* (5th edn). Melbourne, Australia: Cengage Learning.

DOWLING, P., WELCH, D. AND SCHULER, R. (1999) *International Human Resource Management: Managing People in a Multinational Context. (3rd ed.).* Wadsworth Publishing: Belmont, CA.

EICHINGER, R. AND LOMBARDO, M. (2003) Knowledge 360-degree theory. *Human Resource Planning*, 26(4): 34–45.

ENGLE, A. D., FESTING, M. AND J. DOWLING, P. (2014) Proposing processes of global performance management: an analysis of the literature. *Journal of Global Mobility*, 2(1): 5–25.

ENGLE, A. D., DOWLING, P. AND FESTING, M. (2008) State of origin: Research in global performance management, a proposed research domain and emerging implications. *European Journal of Management*, 2(92): 153–169.

ENTREKIN, L. V. AND J. K. Chung (2001) The attitudes toward different sources of executive appraisal: A comparison of Hong Kong Chinese and American managers in Hong Kong. *Global Journal of Human Resource Management. Routledge Journals*, 12(6): 965–987.

ERDOGAN, B. (2002) Antecedents and consequences of justice perceptions in performance appraisals. *Human Resource Management Review*, (12): 555–578.

FARR, J. AND JACOBS, R. (2006) The criterion problem today and into the 21st century. In BENNETT, W., LANCE, C. E. AND WOEHR, D. J. (eds), *Performance Measurement: Current Perspectives and Future Challenges.* Mahwah, NJ: Lawrence Erlbaum Associates.

FENWICK, M. (2004) On International Assignment: Is expatriation the only way to go?, *Asia Pacific Journal of Human Resources*, 42, 365–377.

FENWICK, M. (2005) International compensation and performance management. In Harzing, A.W. and Ruysseveldt, J. (eds), *Global Human Resource Management.* London: Sage.

FESTING, M., KNAPPERT, L., DOWLING, P. AND ENGLE, A. (2010) Country-specific profiles in global performance management: A contribution to balancing global standardisation and local adaptions in MNEs. *11th Conference on International Human Resource Management*, Aston Business School, Birmingham June 2010.

FESTING, M. AND BARZANTNY, C. (2008) A comparative approach to performance management in France and Germany: The impact of the European and the country-specific environment. *European Journal of International Management*, 2(2): 208–227.

FESTINGER, L. (1957) *A Theory of Cognitive Dissonance.* Stanford, CA: Stanford University Press.

GALANG, M. (2004) The transferability question: Comparing HRM practices in the Philippines with the US and Canada. *International Journal of Human Resource Management* 15(7): 1207–1233.

GHOSHAL, S. AND BARTLETT, C. (1998) *Managing across Borders: The Transnational Solution.* London: Random House Business Books.

GILLESPIE, T. (2006) Globalizing 360-degree feedback: Are subordinate ratings comparable? *Journal of Business and Psychology*, 19(3): 361–382.

GOMES, R. (2010) The need for real performance management in Brazil. Available at: www.academia.edu/225425/The_Need_for_Real_Performance_Management_in_Brazil. Accessed 15 October 2015.

GROESCHL, S. (2003) Cultural implications for the appraisal process. *Cross-Cultural Management*, 10: 67–79.

GUPTA, V. AND HANGES, P. J. (2004) Regional and Climate Clustering of Societal Cultures. In House, R. J., HANGES, P. J., JAVIDAN, M., DORFMAN, P. W. AND GUPTA, V. (eds), *Culture, Leadership, and Organizations: The GLOBE Study of 62 Societies.* Thousand Oaks, CA: Sage, pp. 178–218.

HANSON, D., DOWLING, P. J., HITT, M. A, IRELAND, D. R. AND HOSKISSON, R. E. (2005) *Strategic Management: Competitiveness and Globalisation* (2nd ed.). Victoria, Australia: Thomson Learning Australia.

HARVEY, M. 1997) Focusing on global performance appraisal process. *Human Resources Development*, 8(1): 41–62.

HARVEY, M., NOVICEVIC, M. AND SPEIER, C. (2000) Strategic global human resource management: The role of the inpatriate managers. *Human Resource Management Review*, 10(2): 153–175.

HARVEY, M., SPEIER, C. AND NOVICEVIC, M. (2002) The evolution of SHRM systems and their application in a foreign subsidiary context. *Asian Pacific Journal of Human Resources*, 40(3): 284–300.

HARZING, A. W. AND NOORDHAVEN, N. (2005) Geographical distance and the role of management of the subsidiaries: The case of subsidiaries down under. *Asian Pacific Journal of Management*, 23: 167–185.

HARZING, A. W. AND RUYSSEVELDT, J. (2005) *Global Human Resource Management.* London: Sage.

HEDGE, J. W. AND TEACHOUT, M.S. (2000) Exploring the concepts of acceptability as a criterion for evaluating performance measures. *Group and Organisation Management*, 25(1): 22–44.

HEMPEL, P. (2001) Differences between Chinese and western managerial views of performance. *Personnel review*, 30(2): 203–226.

HOFSTEDE, G. (1980) *Culture's Consequences: Global Differences in Work-Related Values.* Beverly Hills, CA: Sage.

HOFSTEDE, G., AND G. J. HOFSTEDE (2005) *Cultures and Organisations: Software of the Mind*. London: McGraw-Hill.

JUNCAJ, T. (2002). Do performance appraisals work? *Quality Progress*, 35(11): 45–49.

KAPLAN, R. S. AND NORTON, P. (1992) The balanced scorecard – measures that drive performance. *Harvard Business Review*, 70(1):71–75.

KAVANAGH, P., BENSON, J. AND BROWN, M. (2007) Understanding performance appraisal fairness. *Asia Pacific Journal of Human Resource Management*, 45(2): 132–150.

KELLAWAY, L. (2015) A blast of common sense frees staff from appraisals. *Australian Financial Review*. July 27, 2015, at 11:11 a.m., updated July 28, 2015, at 10:59 a.m. Available at: http://www.afr.com/leadership/management/a-blast-of-common-sense-frees-staff-from-appraisals-20150726. Accessed 15 September 2015.

KING, A. (2015). Deloitte dumps bi-annual performance reviews, opts for weekly updates. Financial Review, July 28. Available at: http://www.afr.com/business/accounting/afr23accdeloitte-20150617-ghq5wu

KRAMAR, R. AND BARTRAM, T. (2015) *Human Resource Management in Australia* (5th edn). Australia: McGraw-Hill.

KURZBERG, T., NAQUIN, C. AND BELKIN, Y. (2005) The effects of e-mail communication on peer ratings in actual and simulated environments. 98, 216–226.

LAM, S., HUI C. AND LAW, K. (1999) Job-analysis; organizational-behavior; supervision-of-employees; cultural-differences. *Journal of Applied Psychology*, 84(4): 594–601.

LAWRIE, G. (2004) Third-generation balanced scorecard: Evolution of an effective strategic control tool. *Global Journal of Productivity and Performance Management*, 53(7): 611–630.

LEVEY, P. AND WILLIAMS, J. (2004) The social context of performance appraisal: A review and framework for the future. *Journal of Global Management*, 30(6): 881–905.

LEVINSON, H. (1991) Management by whose objectives. *Harvard Business Review*, 69(92): 176–190.

MALEY, J. (2009) The impact of the performance appraisal on the psychological contract of the remote subsidiary manager. *South African Journal of Human Resource Management*, (2): 63–73.

MALEY, J. (2011) The influence of various human resource management strategies on the performance management of subsidiary managers. *Asia Pacific Journal of Business*, 3(1): 28–46.

MALEY, J. (2014) Sustainability: The missing element in performance management. *Asia-Pacific Journal of Business Administration*, Special Edition 6(3): 3–3, ABDC-C.

MALEY, J. AND KRAMAR, R. (2007) Global performance appraisal: Policies, practices and processes in Australian subsidiaries of healthcare MNCs. *Research and Practice in Human Resource Management*, 15(2): 21–41.

MALEY, J. AND KRAMAR, R. (2014) The influences of global uncertainty on cross-border performance management. *Personnel Review*, 43(1): 2–2, ABDC-A.

MALEY, J. AND MOELLER, M. (2014) The effect of the performance appraisal system on trust for the inpatriate manager. *Journal of Business Research*, 67(1): 2803–2810, ABDC-A.

MALEY, J., MOELLER, M. AND HARVEY, M. (In Press) The contextualization of stressors on foreign assignments: An application to inpatriation. *International Journal of Intercultural Relations*.

MCPHAIL, R., FISHER, R., HARVEY, M. AND MOELLER, M. (2012) Staffing the global organization: 'Cultural nomads'. *Human Resource Development Quarterly*, 23(2): 259–276.

MILLIMAN, J., NASON, S., ZHU, C. AND CIERI, H. (2002) An exploratory assessment of the purposes of performance appraisals in North and Central America and the Pacific Rim. *Asia Pacific Journal of Human Resources*, 40(1), 105–122.

MOELLER, M., MALEY, J., HARVEY, M. AND KIESSLING, T. (2016) Global talent management and inpatriate social capital building: A status inconsistency perspective. *International Journal of Human Resource Management*, 27(9): 1–22.

MURPHY, K. (1993). *Honesty in the Workplace*. Belmont, CA: Wadsworth Inc.

MURPHY, K. AND BALZER, K. (1989) Rater errors and rating accuracy. *Journal of Applied Psychology*, 74: 619–624.

MURPHY, K. AND CLEVELAND, J. (1991) *Performance Appraisal: An Organisational Perspective*. Boston: Allywn and Bacon.

MURPHY, K. AND CLEVELAND, J. (1995) *Understanding Performance Appraisal*. London: Sage Publications.

MYLONI, B., HARZING, A. AND MIRZA. H. (2004) Human resource management in Greece: Have the colours of culture faded away? *International Journal of Cross-Cultural Management*, 1: 59–76.

NANKERVIS, A. AND COMPTON, R. (2006) Performance management: Theory in practice. *Asian Pacific Journal of Human Resources*, 44(1). 83–101.

NICKLESS, R. (2014) Prepare to fire the annual performance review. Available at: http://www.afr.com/news/policy/industrial-relations/prepare-to-fire-the-annual-performance-review-20140708-jgpac#ixzz3neAi16s5. Accessed 15 September 2015.

OTHMAN, R., DOMIL, A., SENIK, Z., ABDULLAH, A. AND HAMZAH, H. (2006) A case study of balanced scorecard implementation in a Malaysian company. *Journal of Asia-Pacific Business*, 7(2): 55–72.

PALMER, J. AND LOVELAND, J. (2008) The influence of group discussion on performance judgment accuracy, contrast effects and halo. *Journal of Psychology: Interdisciplinary and Applied*, 142(2): 117–130.

PAPALEXANDRIS, N., CHALIKIAS, J. AND PANAYOTOPOULOU, L. (2002) Societal culture and Human Resource Management: Exploring the mutual interaction in Greece. Paper presented at the 2nd International Conference, Human Resource Management in Europe: Trends and Challenges, Athens, Greece, 17–19 October.

PAUL, P. AND ELDER, L. (2008) The Miniature Guide to Critical Thinking Concepts and Tools. Foundation for Critical Thinking Press.

PERETZ, H. AND FRIED, Y. (2008) National values, performance appraisal and organizational performance: A study across 21 countries. Academy of Management Conference Proceeding. shrm.org. 2008.

PERKMANN, M. AND WALSH, K. (2007) University-industry relationships and open innovation: Towards a research agenda. Global Journal of Management Reviews, 9(4): 259–280.

PERLMUTTER, H. V. (1969) The tortuous evolution of the MNC. Columbia Journal of World Business, 4(1): 9–18.

PFAU, B. AND KAY, I. (2002) Does 360-degree feedback negatively affect company performance? Studies show that 360-degree feedback may do more harm than good. What's the problem? HRMagazine, 47(6): 54–60.

SCHULER, R., DOWLING, S., SMART, J. AND HUBER, V. (1992) HRM in Australia. Harper Educational Publishing.

SHEN, J. (2004) Global performance appraisals: Policies, practices and determinants in the case of Chinese multinational companies. Global Journal of Management, 25(6): 547–563.

SHIBATA, H. (2000) The transformation of the wage and performance appraisal system in a Japanese firm. International Journal of Human Resource Management, 11:294–313.

SNAPE, E., THOMPSON, D., Yan, F. K. C. and REDMAN, T. (1998) Performance appraisal and culture: Practice and attitudes in Hong Kong and Great Britain. International Journal of Human Resource Management, 9(5), 841–861.

SULLY DE LUQUE, M. AND SOMMER, S. (2007) The impact of culture on feedback seeking behaviour: an integrated model and propositions. Academy of Management Review, 25(4): 829–849.

TAORMINA R. AND GAO, J. (2009) Identifying acceptable performance appraisal criteria: A global perspective. Asia Pacific Journal of Human Resource Management, 47(1): 102–124.

TZINER, A. AND. KOPELMAN, R. (2002) Is there a Preferred Performance Rating Format? A Non-psychometric perspective. Applied Psychology, 51: 479–503.

ULRICH, D. (1997) Human Resource Champions. Boston: Harvard Business School Press.

VANCE, C. M. (2006) Strategic upstream and downstream considerations for effective global performance management. Global Journal of Cross-Cultural Management, 6(1): 37–56.

VARELA, O. AND PREMEAUX, S. (2008) Cross-cultural values affect multisource feedback dynamics? The case of high power distance and collectivism in two Latin American countries. Global Journal of Selection and Assessment, 16(2): 134–142.

VARMA, A., BUDHWAR, P. AND DE NISI, A. (2008) Performance Management Systems: A Global Perspective. New York: Routledge.

VARMA, A., PICHLER, S. AND SRINIVAS, E. (2005) The role of interpersonal affect in performance appraisal: Evidence from two samples – the US and India. Global Journal of Human Resource Management, 16(11): 2030–2043.

WRIGHT, P. M. AND MCMAHAN, G. C. (1992) Theoretical perspectives for strategic human resource management. Journal of Management, 18: 295–320.

10

REWARD MANAGEMENT

John Shields and Jim Rooney

LEARNING OUTCOMES

After reading this chapter, you should be able to:

➤ Appreciate the value of a constructively critical (pluralist) approach to understanding the theory and practice of reward management, particularly taking an employee-centred perspective
➤ Understand how reward strategies, programmes, and policies are structured in both domestic and international contexts
➤ Demonstrate a detailed awareness of the variety of financial and non-financial reward practices and of the different motivational and behavioural assumptions associated with particular types of reward
➤ Recognise the concepts, methods, and techniques associated with managing employee reward in both domestic and international contexts
➤ Demonstrate a detailed understanding of the differences and complementarities between each of the three main components of monetary reward for employees: base pay, benefits, and performance pay
➤ Understand the options and challenges involved in the application of theories, concepts, and practices related to reward
➤ Appreciate how social and cultural factors affect employees' perceptions of pay fairness and how these perceptions affect the design and effectiveness of pay programmes
➤ Examine the controversy surrounding the subject of executive remuneration, particularly regarding notions of pay equality, dispersion, and fairness
➤ Formulate practical solutions to the challenges of designing and implementing reward strategies, programmes, and policies that will support the organisation's needs to attract, retain, motivate, and develop domestic and international employees.

SUMMARY OF CHAPTER CONTENTS

➤ **Opening Case Study**: For Indian employees, money isn't everything
➤ Introduction
➤ Employee rewards: nature and purpose
➤ Intrinsic versus extrinsic rewards: which are more motivating?
➤ Taking a critical perspective on reward management
➤ Base pay
➤ Benefits plans
➤ Performance-related reward plans
➤ Reward communication

➤ Employment relations and reward management
➤ Executive remuneration
➤ International reward management
➤ Conclusion
➤ **End of Chapter Case Study**: The strategy and practice of rewards in Chinese MNCs
➤ For discussion and revision
➤ Glossary
➤ Further reading
➤ Web resources
➤ References

Opening Case Study   **For Indian employees, money isn't everything**

Globe Ground India (GGI), a subsidiary of the German airline Lufthansa, operates passenger and cargo handling for Lufthansa, as well as ground and ramp activities in Delhi, Mumbai, and a number of other Indian cities. In 2006, facing serious staff turnover and motivation problems, GGI conducted focus interviews with staff with a view to identifying ways in which the firm's reward system could be strengthened to improve staff retention and motivation.

The initial plan was to use the information gathered to develop a long-term incentive plan on top of the yearly bonus. However, one of the interview questions asked staff to nominate the 'highest incentive for you to increase your motivation', and the results were both unexpected and revealing. Staff rated 'money/higher wages' as third behind 'career/status' and 'job pleasure/enjoyment'. Clearly, intrinsic rewards and developmental opportunities were most salient for GGI's staff. Other studies confirm that career management, job design, benefits entitlements, and consistent salary adjustment are particularly important to employees in India.

After analysing the results, GGI developed and introduced a new 'total rewards' approach focusing not on long-term incentives but on meeting employees' developmental and job interest needs and on offering career pathways and prospects. This approach was then set out clearly and comprehensively in a new human resources manual.

This is not to suggest that money does not matter at all. As employees often queried the prior mode of salary adjustment and argued for seniority-based adjustment, the manual explains that salary increases are based on individual contribution and not on time of service alone.

The 2015 Gallup-Healthways ranking of wellbeing, based on 146,000 interviews of adults across 145 countries, reinforced this GGI analysis. This and similar studies indicate that financial well-being is likely to be more about earning enough money to balance your various needs, rather than the absolute amount of the financial rewards you receive (see: https://www.youtube.com/watch?v=sflXlpV7O-s).

Source: Adapted from Lang (2008); Krause-Jackson and Yoon (2015); Bloomberg (2015).

Questions

1   What could be possible explanation of Indian employees' preferences of 'career/status' and 'job pleasure/enjoyment' over 'money/higher wages'?
2   If the same choice is given to you, what would be your preference and why?

INTRODUCTION

Reward management is one of the most important yet most problematic of all human resource management (HRM) functions. It is not only one of the most technically demanding facets of HRM, but also one of the most complex and controversial in terms of the assumptions and debates surrounding the drivers of human motivation and work behaviour. Rewards are a 'red button' issue in the domain of people management.

As experienced human resources professionals know, reward management is very easy to do badly – but difficult to do well. An effective reward system has to be soundly designed and integrated. It also needs to be carefully implemented, communicated. and monitored. The obvious signs of reward mismanagement include perceived reward inequity (or unfairness), low motivation and effort on the part of employees, low job satisfaction, reduced commitment to the organisation, higher intention to

leave and increased staff turnover: in short, poor 'engagement' of employees with their job, their managers, their peers, their organisation and its customers.

This chapter presents an overview of the concepts, practices. and controversies associated with the reward management function. In doing this, it offers a constructively critical perspective on the main theories, tools and techniques for configuring effective reward systems for both domestic and international employees. First, we will consider the basic nature and purpose of remuneration and other rewards. We then proceed to explore one of the central debates in the field: the relative merits of extrinsic and intrinsic rewards. Next, we will consider the value of seeking to understand reward management from a constructively critical (pluralist) perspective. In particular, we acknowledge that employees are not simply 'resource' objects but, rather, are organisational stakeholders with their own distinct needs, expectations, and rights, as well as their own responsibilities and contractual obligations to their employer.

Attention then turns to the three main elements of monetary reward or remuneration – base pay, benefits, and performance-related rewards – and the types of pay plan associated with each of these. We will consider the general strengths and weaknesses of each major pay plan type, along with debates concerning both the effectiveness and the fairness of incentive plans and other performance-related reward practices.

As reward effectiveness is not simply a matter of system design but also a function of how clearly and consistently the system's principles and practices are communicated to the employees concerned, the next two sections of the chapter will examine both reward communications and the cognate and highly controversial matter of reward secrecy and transparency. The second of these two sections will examine the vexed question of executive remuneration systems as a special case of this important facet of HRM.

Finally, we will explore the special challenges associate with managing employee rewards in international contexts, noting the differences between 'home', 'host', and 'regional' approaches to reward configuration. This section also sets the stage for the chapter's major case study, which describes the additional challenges and options associated with the management of reward systems in an international context. Specifically, this case study of the reward strategies and practices of Chinese multinational corporations (MNCs) invites us to reflect on the complexities of reward management for line employees and expatriate reward management in host country contexts. As we shall see, the case highlights the dual approach to international reward practice favoured by firms headquartered in this rapidly emerging economic superpower.

However, before immersing ourselves in the details of domestic and international reward practice, it is important that we address the nature and purpose of rewards in general.

EMPLOYEE REWARDS: NATURE AND PURPOSE

A reward may be anything tangible (for example, pay) or intangible (for example, praise) that an organisation offers to its employees in exchange for their belonging to the organisation and for contributing work behaviours and results of the type that the organisation needs from its people in order to meet its strategic objectives, however these might be defined. A reward system has four primary objectives:

- To attract (or 'buy') the right people at the right time for the right jobs, tasks or roles.

- To retain the best people by satisfying their work-related needs and aspirations and recognising and rewarding their contribution.
- To develop (or 'build') the required workforce capabilities by recognising and rewarding employees' actions to enhance their knowledge, skill, and ability.
- To motivate employees to contribute to the best of their capability by recognising and rewarding high individual and group contributions towards meeting the organisation's strategic objectives.

At the same time, a well-designed and administered reward system has a number of important secondary objectives. In particular, it should seek to be the following:

- *Needs-fulfilling*: the rewards should be of value to employees in satisfying their relevant human needs.
- *Equitable or 'felt-fair'*: reward levels should be seen to be both commensurate with individual contributions and appropriate in comparison with the reward levels received by others.
- *Legal*: rewards should comply with relevant legal requirements regarding employees' rights and entitlements, including standards for mandatory minimum pay and benefits.
- *Affordable*: the rewards allocated, and any associated on-costs, should fall within the organisation's financial means.
- *Cost-effective*: there should be an appropriate 'return on investment' from total reward outlays.
- *Strategically aligned*: the reward system should be configured so as to support the organisation's strategic objectives.

There is, however, considerable potential for conflict between these objectives. For instance, tensions may arise between the goals of cost-containment and of offering rewards that are sufficient to attract and retain the right type and number of employees. From an organisational perspective, the optimal approach is not necessarily the cheapest. Rather, the optimal approach is the one that will maximise the returns to the organisation in comparison with the outlay made – and this takes us back to the vital matter of strategic reward management.

Class Activity

▸ Of the reward system objectives listed above, which would you nominate as the three most important, and why do you think these are the most important overall?

INTRINSIC VERSUS EXTRINSIC REWARDS: WHICH ARE MORE MOTIVATING?

Rewards can be divided into two broad categories: 'extrinsic' and 'intrinsic'.

Extrinsic rewards arise from factors associated with but external to the job that the employee does, that is, from the job context. Extrinsic rewards are of three main types:

- financial rewards;
- developmental rewards;
- social rewards.

Financial rewards – also referred to as 'pay', 'remuneration', or 'compensation' – are of three main types:

- base pay (the fixed component of the total remuneration);
- benefits, such as the employer's contributions to superannuation and personal health insurance;
- performance-related pay plans, including 'incentives', which vary with the performance measured.

Although pay may be the most obvious form of extrinsic reward, it is not the only form of reward, nor is it necessarily the most important in terms of influencing employees' attitudes, behaviour, and effort. *Developmental rewards* cover those rewards associated with personal learning, development and career growth, such as skills training and performance and leadership coaching. *Social rewards* are those associated with seniority and other forms of social esteem or status, a positive organisational climate, support for performance, quality of supervision, work-group affinity, and opportunities for enhanced work–life balance, such as flexible working time arrangements, staff sabbaticals, fitness and wellness programmes, and so on. In some cultures, developmental and social rewards may be more highly prized than rewards of a monetary nature. As the example in Box 10.1 suggests, employees in India may respond much more positively to having access to a clear career pathway than to being offered performance-related pay.

Intrinsic rewards arise from the content of the job itself, including the interest and challenge that it provides, task variety and autonomy, the degree of feedback, and the meaning and significance attributed to the job. One of the most important determinants of the level of intrinsic rewards in any organisation is thus the way in which its jobs are designed. The basic proposition here is that if you want the employees to do a good job, give them a good job to do.

One of the longstanding and animated debates in contemporary theory and practice in reward management concerns the relative merits of intrinsic and extrinsic rewards. Many commentators contend that extrinsic rewards in general, and performance-related pay in particular, are the most powerful motivators (see, for example, Gerhart et al., 2009; Gupta and Conway, 2013; Gupta and Mitra, 1998; Ledford, Gerhart and Fang, 2013; Shaw and Gupta, 2015). Others argue that intrinsic rewards provide the best basis for superior motivation and performance (see, for example, Deci and Ryan, 1985; Kohn, 1993a, 1993b; Pink, 2009).

Arguments that support incentive-based rewards derive either explicitly or implicitly from one or other of the main 'process' theories of work motivation. These theories, which include agency theory, reinforcement theory, expectancy theory, goal-setting theory, and equity theory, all emphasise the centrality of employees' cognitive processes in understanding and managing the relationship between rewards and task motivation (Shields et al., 2016):

- *Agency theory*, which assumes a potential conflict of interest between 'principals' (that is, owners) and self-seeking 'agents' (that is, hired employees), holds that performance-contingent pay is the most effective means of aligning employees' economic interests with those of employers/owners.
- *Reinforcement theory* posits that a timely reward for a given desired action will motivate employees to repeat the rewarded action, whereas punishment in the form of non-reward will extinguish any misbehaviour.
- *Expectancy theory* holds that an incentive is likely to motivate higher work effort if: (1) employees see the promised reward as personally valuable; (2) they expect that they can achieve the required level of performance; and (3) they trust the employer to deliver the reward in exchange for the achieved performance.
- *Goal-setting theory* suggests that employees will be motivated more strongly by performance targets that are specific, agreed, and challenging and by feedback that is precise and instantaneous.

A further common rationale for performance-related rewards is that they operationalise the 'equity' norm of distributive justice. *Equity theory* proposes, in part, that reward satisfaction stems from making employee reward outcomes (including pay level) commensurate with employees' individual inputs (Shields et al., 2016). In short, high performers should be paid more than low performers, with the inequality of the reward being proportional to the difference in individual performance. This is a common justification for performance-related pay. However, some motivation theorists question the claimed efficacy of extrinsic rewards and propose that rewards that are intrinsic to the job are the only true motivators.

Exponents of cognitive evaluation theory go further still, contending that the use of extrinsic rewards (and punishments) may destroy the intrinsic motivation that flows from inherent interest in the job. Also known as intrinsic motivation theory, *cognitive evaluation theory* posits that people are much more likely to act first and only evaluate, rationalise, and ascribe meaning and motive to what they have done after the event. The tendency is to confer motivational meaning on the behaviour – that is, to attribute meaning and purpose to it – only in retrospect. People are more likely to ask, 'Why *have* I done this?' than 'Why *should* I do this?' Cognitive evaluation theory suggests that individuals who have been deriving high intrinsic rewards for their work tasks may radically revise their self-attributed motives for doing the work once a financial incentive is offered to them (Gagne and Deci, 2005).

The point here is that the initial motivation to do something is likely to be implicit and intrinsic rather than premeditated and driven by the pursuit of some extrinsic reward. For this reason, Deci and Ryan (1985) argue that extrinsic rewards should not be applied to task performance, because these may very well dissipate the intrinsic motivation that may initially have driven the employee's performance. The perception of being 'controlled' extrinsically is assumed to be demotivating, a point embraced with some passion by several prominent opponents of performance incentives (Kohn, 1993a; Pink, 2009).

Nevertheless, cognitive evaluation theory is also open to challenge. As suggested in Box 10.2, it is by no means clear that intrinsic and extrinsic motivation are opposites; indeed, as critics suggest, the weight of evidence indicates that the two are, if anything, mutually reinforcing (Rynes et al., 2005). Furthermore, it is questionable whether most work behaviour is impulsive rather than premeditated, experience suggesting that both play a part in work behaviour. On the practical side, although cognitive evaluation theory may be quite appropriate for jobs and roles that are intrinsically motivating in the first instance, not all jobs will be intrinsically rewarding. In such cases, it will be necessary either to enrich the job content or to offer more in the way of pay or other extrinsic rewards.

TAKING A CRITICAL PERSPECTIVE ON REWARD MANAGEMENT

The debate over the relative influence of intrinsic and extrinsic motivational drivers and rewards also illustrates the value of adopting a constructively critical approach to the theory and practice of reward management. An ill-conceived reward system may not only fail to elicit the desired behaviour but may instead also encourage behaviour that is dysfunctional, deceptive, or even destructive; that is, it may give rise to endemic organisational misbehaviour. A critical approach to reward management may help to avert such problems.

A critical approach to reward management requires us to both question our assumptions about what employees may find rewarding and motivating and also to seek to interpret reward management from a multi-stakeholder (or 'pluralist') perspective – one acknowledging that employees have rights, interests, and expectations that are not wholly congruent with those of the employing organisation. As such, a critical approach moves away from the 'unitarist' or 'managerialist' assumption that the only relevant stakeholder interest is that of the employer and that employees are merely 'human resource' objects serving employer-determined ends (Watson, 2004). It also reminds us of the ethical importance and analytical value of adopting an employee-centred approach to understanding the nature and impact of reward management practice (Grant and Shields, 2006). What is a cost to the employer is income and economic security for employees and their dependents; what is a competitive level of pay to the employer may be seen as inequitable by the employee.

Box 10.2 Intrinsic versus extrinsic rewards – which are best?

The assumption that extrinsic and intrinsic factors are dichotomous rather than complementary is open to challenge. Some research suggests that extrinsic and intrinsic rewards can make a joint contribution to job satisfaction and other desired work attitudes and behaviour. Cameron and Pierce (1997) used a meta-analysis of a hundred studies of reward–performance effects to argue that intrinsic and extrinsic motivation combine in an additive way to produce an overall motivational force. They found that people generally enjoyed performing a task more rather than less when they received an extrinsic verbal or tangible reward. In particular, Cameron and Pierce highlighted that praise led to greater task interest and performance. The negative effects of extrinsic rewards, they suggested, were limited and easily prevented.

Exponents of the intrinsic rewards approach assume that it is possible to enrich all jobs when, in reality, this is not always so. For better or worse, many manufacturing and service organisations succeed quite effectively with job assignments that have limited skill content, a narrow task range, low autonomy, and close technical monitoring of work performance.

Building on these points, a critical pluralist approach also requires consideration to be given to the nature and significance of employees' 'voice', 'say', or 'representation' in determining rewards. How much influence do employees have, either collectively or individually, over the processes by which their monetary rewards are determined? In developed economies, trade unions have traditionally been seen as the chief vehicles of the collective voice in determining pay and conditions of employment, particularly by means of collective bargaining at the industry or enterprise level. In 'coordinated' market economies of the type typical of the Northern and Western Member States of the European Union, unions' influence in setting pay has traditionally been paralleled by government intervention and regulation designed both to protect low-paid workers and moderate pay increases for employees with greater bargaining power.

However, in developed economies, recent decades have witnessed a decline in union membership and union influence via collective bargaining, particularly in the private sector, along with a retreat from direct government intervention in pay regulation, and this has been accompanied by significant changes in employee voice. Such changes are sometimes taken as signifying the erosion of the employee's voice and a strengthening of 'managerial prerogative' in pay determination.

An alternative interpretation is that employee 'say in pay' has assumed new forms rather than necessarily diminishing. According to Lindrop (2009), new outlets for collective and individual employee voice have emerged. In countries such as the UK and Australia, the vacuum created by the decline in union collective bargaining has been filled, in part, by the rise of new institutions to determine pay, including occupational pay review bodies and tribunals changed with determining 'fair pay' standards for low-paid workers.

At an organisational level, suggests Lindrop (2009), the new voice mechanisms include collective mechanisms such as joint management–employee consultative committees and individually focused direct communication practices, for example direct employee attitude surveys; these are designed in part to inform improvements in reward system design and hence to strengthen employees' satisfaction with rewards, as well as their motivation and commitment to the organisation. As we shall see, various forms of 'financial participation' on the part of employees, such as employee share ownership and profit-sharing, may also be vehicles for employee voice and involvement. Yet the extent to which these new mechanisms do in fact support a genuine voice and influence, and a critical pluralist perspective, requires their consequences to be examined from the employees' frame of reference rather than simply from that of the employing organisation.

A critical approach also reminds us that the language of reward management – the 'discourse' or 'talk and text' – serves to influence ('construct') employees' and management's perceptions of themselves, each other, the nature of the employment relationship, organisational power inequalities and, indeed, organisational 'reality' itself.

Drawing on the work of French philosopher and historian, Michel Foucault, Barbara Townley (1993a, 1993b, 1994, 1998, 1999) argues that managers simultaneously empower themselves and subjugate those whom they are managing. They do this by means of discourses and practices that individualise, objectify, and discipline workers and shape their subjectivity and concept of self and work reality by means of complex regimes of classification, ordering and measurement. As such, the language associated with reward practices such as job evaluation, performance-related pay and competency-based pay can be understood as serving to shape employees' perceptions that differences in reward levels are natural, appropriate, and objectively determined. Recent research on this phenomenon in professional services industries such as accounting and law firms indicate that the importance of such power relationships is not simply a 'blue-collar' concern (for example, Costas and Grey, 2014; Mueller, Carter and Ross-Smith, 2011).

For our purposes, the key point here is that reward management is concerned with shaping employees' identities, attitudes, and behaviour through both language and practice. From a critical perspective, then, it is important that we appreciate the centrality of reward concepts, how these are communicated to employees by managers, and the meanings that employees attribute to these discursive concepts (Grant and Shields, 2006).

BASE PAY

Base pay is the foundational or 'fixed' component of remuneration and, for most employees, typically comprises the largest single component of total remuneration, with benefits and performance pay making up the remainder. In many countries, legislatures or tribunals have prescribed the payment of guaranteed minimum wage or salary levels. Base pay is generally regarded as the pay type best suited to addressing the objectives of attracting and retaining staff. Providing each employee with a guaranteed level of base pay demonstrates the employer's commitment to the employee, which in turn means that the employee is more likely to reciprocate. Base pay is also the pay component most closely involved in the setting and enforcement of minimum pay standards.

Although base pay systems can be very diverse, there are two broad approaches to building base pay:

- job-based pay;
- person-based pay.

As well as making different assumptions about what base pay can contribute to an organisation and how it can do so, these two approaches to configuring base pay entail distinct types of pay structure (that is, the formal 'architecture' of the base pay system) as well as different modes of evaluation (that is, the pricing of jobs and/or job-holders) and distinct modes of pay progression (that is, the 'rules' determining how each person's base pay level adjusts over time). Table 10.1 highlights the main points of difference between the job-based and person-based approaches.

Table 10.2 summarises the two main base pay options, including the structures, evaluation techniques, and modes of progression associated with each.

JOB-BASED BASE PAY

The traditional practice has been to fix base pay according to the 'size' or 'value' of the *job* or *position* occupied. Jobs of larger 'size' – that is, with a greater content of tasks, duties, and responsibilities – attract higher levels of base pay, and employees can increase their base pay chiefly by ascending a hierarchy of job-related pay steps incorporated into either a ladder-like pay scale or a stairway of narrow job grades.

A pay scale typically consists of a hierarchy of position-specific pay levels, each comprising a sequence of flat pay rates, steps or points. Traditionally, stepwise pay increments within each level were based on seniority or service, with the increase occurring automatically after each year of service.

A narrow grade (also known as a 'job grade') houses a group of jobs of similar size/value to the organisation and specifies a pay range for these jobs rather than a scale step or spot rate. Each grade will cover a group of jobs regarded as being of similar value to the organisation and therefore worthy of roughly the same range of base pay. Unlike simple pay scales, each grade allows for some variance in pay level based on the 'merit' of the individual job holder, but the range over which pay can vary is usually quite narrow, typically no more than 30 per cent, with the midpoint of the range serving as the pay rate for acceptable proficiency in the job (Perkins and White, 2011; Shields et al., 2016).

In job-based systems, there are two main techniques for pricing each job or position: market surveys and job evaluation.

Market surveys involve setting pay rates for particular jobs according to what other employers are paying for the same or similar jobs in external labour markets. Regular market surveys also allow organisations to monitor changes in market rates and adjust their own pay rates accordingly. As such, the approach emphasises 'external competitiveness' in determining the rate for the job. The organisation ascertains the range of amounts that other organisations are paying for jobs similar to its own and then makes a strategic choice about where it will position itself relative to its competitors. For this purpose, the market range for each position is commonly expressed as either percentile or quartile means (Shields et al., 2016).

Table 10.1 Job-based versus person-based base pay

Job-based base pay	Person-based base pay
Jobs add value	Individuals add value
Pay for job's worth	Pay for individual's worth
Pay for the 'size' of the job occupied	Pay for each individual's capacity to perform (that is, their KSAs)
Standard rate for the job, irrespective of KSA differences between job-holders	Different rates of pay depending on assessed capacity (KSAs)
Time-based payment according to time on the job	Time-based payment according to KSA levels
Direct external market pricing	Indirect external market pricing (disaggregated job pay rates)
Evaluation method: job evaluation	Evaluation methods: skill and/or competency assessment
Pay progression and promotion are based on seniority or merit	Pay progression is based on KSA development
Reinforces the promotional hierarchy	Reinforces KSA development

Table 10.2 Options for base pay

	Structures	Evaluation techniques	Modes of pay progression
Job-based pay	Pay ladders Narrow grades	Market surveys and/or job evaluation	Seniority and/or 'merit'-based increments and promotion
Person-based pay	Broad grades or job families Broadband systems	Skill assessment Competency assessment	Skill sets Competency zones or levels

Rather than undertaking the data-gathering themselves, many organisations use the market data provided by consulting firms specialising in remuneration.

Job evaluation, which is frequently seen as an alternative to reliance on market data, involves determining relative pay rates by relating them to the importance or relative value of the job to the organisation. This is achieved by comparing jobs on a number of factors thought to be important in determining job value, such as skill, effort, responsibility, or working conditions. The end result of job evaluation is a hierarchy of jobs in which all jobs of similar value to the organisation, no matter how different they might be in other respects, are placed at the same level in the job-based pay hierarchy. As such, job evaluation emphasises 'internal equity' in setting job-based pay rates rather than 'external competitiveness' per se (Perkins and White, 2011; Shields et al., 2016).

Job evaluation is thus a means of establishing and maintaining equitable differences in base pay between jobs within the organisation, particularly between jobs at different organisational levels. The degree of difference in pay level between jobs at the top and the bottom of an organisational hierarchy is also known as 'vertical pay dispersion', and there is considerable debate over whether a high degree of dispersion is preferable to a low degree of dispersion or vice versa (Bloom, 1999; Gupta and Delery, 2002). Critical Thinking 10.1 challenges you to frame your views about this important aspect of base pay structure.

? Critical Thinking 10.1 Pay dispersion

The term 'pay dispersion' refers to the degree of inequality in pay levels between jobs at the same organisational level (also called 'horizontal pay dispersion') and between jobs at different levels in the organisation (also known a 'vertical pay dispersion') (Gerhart and Rynes, 2003).

Questions

1 Is it better for an organisation to have a high degree of vertical pay dispersion or a low degree of vertical dispersion?
2 How might the appropriateness of high variability differ according to the company's social and cultural context?

The most widely used approach to systematic job evaluation is the points factor method. A points factor system typically has four main elements:

1 *'Compensable' factors*: job inputs (such as skill, knowledge, education, training, and experience), job

requirements (such as mental effort, physical effort, decision-making, and supervision), job outputs (such as product accuracy, consequences of error, and responsibility for cash and assets) and job conditions (work environment, hazards, and so on).
2 *Points-based rating scales* for these factors based how much of each factor is present.
3 *Factor weightings* reflecting the 'value-adding' importance of each factor for the organisation.
4 Assigning a monetary value to the total number of points assigned to each job.

As a means of valuing jobs and developing job-based pay structures, the points factor approach has much to commend it. It can introduce order, rationality, strategic focus, and consistency into potentially arbitrary pay structures by using transparent and clearly defined measures of job size and by offering a consistent means of measuring the relative size or value of the jobs involved. Furthermore, the points factor approach can also help to identify and eliminate inequities in the existing pay structure, as well as provide a rational basis for setting pay rates for new or changed jobs.

However, the points factor approach also has some weaknesses and drawbacks. In focusing on relative comparisons of job contents and on generic job content factors, it may downplay or even ignore critical strategic success factors related to the market, a point actually conceded by commentators who assert the continuing relevance of the approach to contemporary reward practice. According to Lawler (1988, 1990), points factor methods highlight job size over job-holder contribution, emphasise internal equity over external competitiveness, and reinforce bureaucracy and hierarchy. In practice, a well-managed system of job-based pay requires simultaneous attention to both internal equity and external competitiveness (Heneman and LeBlanc, 2002; Salimaki, Hakonen and Heneman, 2009).

✎ Class Activity

▸ When it comes to pricing jobs, what are the three main advantages of focusing on 'internal equity' considerations via the use of job evaluation?
▸ What are the three main disadvantages of such an approach to job pricing?

Job evaluation is sometimes seen as a means of correcting the gender-based pay inequality and distributive injustice (that is, unfairness in terms of reward outcome) evident in the wider labour market. Yet whether organisationally specific job evaluation can do much to further pay equity is a moot point. Indeed, some have argued that badly designed and badly implemented job evaluation may be a cause of continuing gender pay inequality rather than a reliable remedy (England and Kilbourne, 1991; Gupta and Jenkins, 1991).

Person-based base pay

More recently, the trend has been to configure base pay around the skills and competencies of the person rather than the 'size' of the job occupied and to couple this to very different base pay structures. Person-based pay can be configured according to the ('hard') technical knowledge and skills possessed by the individual employee, according to underlying ('soft') personal abilities or competencies, or in terms of a combination of both 'hard' and 'soft' attributes.

By recognising and rewarding the acquisition of technical skills and job-related knowledge, **skill-based pay** is said to facilitate functional flexibility through multiskilling and teamworking. Multiskilling allows employees to be redeployed quickly without delays for retraining and minimises the downtime arising from a lack of the required skills. By breaking down rigid job demarcations, it can in addition enable a more flexible utilisation of the workforce, as employees acquire a breadth and depth of relevant skills. Skill-based pay also lends itself to employees' involvement in system design and administration (Barrett, 1991; Ledford, 1991a, 1991b; Ledford and Heneman, 1999; Shields et al., 2016).

The basic building block for a skill-based system is the *skill set*. A skill set consists of a bundle of related tasks and activities – or 'skill elements' – the mastery of which constitutes a finite and verifiable unit of learning that can be used to develop and deliver training. Each skill set becomes a training module that must be completed successfully in order to warrant a further increase in the amount of base pay. In order to determine pay, associated skill sets are commonly housed in structures known as 'broad grades'. The pay range for each broad grade is typically 40–60 per cent, that is, some two to three times that of a narrow grade. Monetary values are attached to each skill set according to the estimated learning time required (Ledford, 1991b; Shields et al., 2016).

The combination of broad grades and skill-based pay is especially appropriate for roles with significant technical knowledge and skill requirements, such as process work, technical or paraprofessional roles, maintenance work, and administration. In such roles, technical skills are relatively easy to identify, impart, assess, and reward.

Some commentators suggest that a better means of configuring person-based base pay is to focus on assessing and rewarding deeply embedded abilities or 'competencies' such as leadership ability, motivation to achieve goals, persistence, composure, problem-solving ability, and so on. The appeal of the competencies approach lies chiefly in its focus on those personal attributes that are seen to be the most important and reliable drivers of high individual performance. The defining features of **competency-based pay** are:

- a system of competency assessment;
- a 'broadbanded' pay structure.

As such, the suggestion that *competency assessment* should apply not only to performance management and development but also to employee reward has intuitive appeal. Likewise, the competencies model is applicable to staff at all levels of the organisation and not just to skilled manual workers (Armstrong and Brown, 1998; Shields et al., 2016).

Broadbanding (also known as 'career banding') involves doing away with a large number of narrow jobs arranged in a steep hierarchy in favour of a much smaller number of job bands. Pay ranges are substantially wider – frequently 100–300 per cent – and the mode of pay progression is linked to either competency assessment or a combination of competency development and performance outcomes. A typical broadbanded structure will have between five and ten bands.

Progression within a given broadband may be linked either to competency assessment alone (that is, competency-*based* broadbanding) or to a combination of competency assessment and individual performance outcomes (that is, competency-*related* broadbanding). The latter approach is also known as 'contribution-related pay'. In purely competency-based systems, each broadband is divided into a small number of competency 'zones', each representing a successively deeper level of competency development. Pay increments are not automatic, and progression to the upper zones is not guaranteed. In fact, both in-zone and between-zone progression becomes increasingly difficult as competency requirements become more demanding (Perkins and White, 2011; Rosen and Turetsky, 2002; Shields et al., 2016).

Competency-based broadbanding promises employers an unprecedented degree of flexibility in determining individual base pay levels. Broadbanding has many potential advantages over traditional graded structures. By flattening job hierarchies, it can redirect employees' attention away from competition for jobs and promotion and towards individual and group contributions to organisational success. Uncoupling promotion from individual career development and base pay progression redefines career 'success' from a vertical to a horizontal trajectory. This means that individuals no longer have to aspire to a managerial role in order to further their careers and base pay. By linking career development and pay progression to capability and achievement in terms of individual performance, broadbanding also supports a more strategic approach to reward management. For these reasons, the competencies model is also especially applicable to high-performance knowledge work, managerial and executive roles. It is also applicable to service work roles (Shields et al., 2016).

Despite their promise, person-based approaches have a number of potential drawbacks (Canavan, 2008; Ledford, 2008; Murray and Gerhart, 2000; Shields et al., 2016):

- Paying for skills and competencies does not guarantee that the employee will apply them effectively.
- Skill and competency assessment is administratively complex and costly.
- Labour market values are still determined mainly by job 'size' rather than by the skills and competencies of individual job holders, so valuation remains problematic.
- 'Topping out': once employees have acquired all the skills or demonstrated all of the required competencies, their base pay will plateau. They may therefore lose task motivation and organisational commitment unless additional rewards, such as performance incentives, are made available.
- Obsolescence of skills and competencies: employees whose skills or competencies are no longer needed, for example because of changes to the product range or in terms of technology, may be exposed to a pay reduction or even redundancy.
- The wider pay ranges characteristic of person-based systems may create unrealistic expectations of opportunities for pay rises, and this can cause feelings of pay inequity, especially if these expectations remain unfulfilled.

For these reasons, the enthusiasm initially associated with skills- and competency-related pay has been replaced by a degree of caution (Heneman and LeBlanc, 2003; Hofrichter and McGovern, 2001), though the person-based approach still has its advocates (Gupta and Shaw, 2011; Zingheim and Schuster, 2012) and organisational adherents.

Table 10.3 summarises the incidence of base pay practices in UK organisations. Note the use of person-based methods, especially job-family and broadbanded structures and base pay progression based on competency and skill development, notwithstanding the continued preference for more traditional structures, market pricing and job-evaluation.

Table 10.3 Base pay practices in the UK, 2014–15

	Reward approaches	% of respondents using
Base pay structures	Individual rates/ranges/spot salaries	50
	Narrow graded	32
	Pay spines/service-related	31
	Job family	29
	Broad-banded	26
Base pay determination	Ability to pay	46
	Market rates (with JE)	30
	Market rates (without JE)	18
	Collective bargaining	7
Base pay progression criteria	Individual performance	74
	Competencies	84
	Market rates	61
	Skills	60
	Employee potential/value/retention	52
	Length of service	35

Source: Chartered Institute of Personnel and Development (2015: 4).

BENEFITS PLANS

Employee benefits are financial rewards that directly supplement the cash base pay and are generally focused on addressing the wellbeing and long-term security needs of employees and their dependants. As such, benefits are an increasingly heterogeneous phenomenon, ranging from employers' contributions to employee superannuation (that is, retirement savings) planning, health and medical insurance and paid holiday leave, to various work-related 'fringe benefits' – or 'perks', as they are also known - such as employer-funded mobile technology and travel.

Voluntary benefits

Although employers in most countries are obliged by law to make certain benefits available to employees (that is, 'mandatory benefits'), it is also open to employers to offer employees additional benefits as part of a strategic approach to reward management (that is, 'voluntary benefits'). In many developed countries, benefits comprise a growing proportion of total remuneration costs (Shields et al., 2016; Wright, 2009). Depending on the country involved, mandatory benefits may include employer-funded superannuation savings, life, health and disability insurance, worker compensation, various forms of paid leave (for example, annual, long-service, sickness, parental or carer leave), and severance pay.

Voluntary benefits can enhance the organisation's ability to attract and retain high-value employees and enable it to offer employees a more appealing 'value proposition'. As the workforce becomes more diverse and as the employees' level of education and expectation of reward rises, voluntary benefits are likely to assume an increasingly critical role in the ability of the reward management system to attract, retain, and motivate high-potential and high-performing employees.

Voluntary benefits include a wide range of rewards such as discount company loans, housing or mortgage subsidies, product or service discounts, company cars and/or free parking, self-education expenses, and the like. In addition to fringe benefits of a financial nature, many organisations now offer a range of voluntary non-monetary benefits carefully targeted at enhancing employees' work–life balance and wellbeing. These benefits include, among others, wellness programmes of various types. Examples include free medical check-ups, in-house gyms or subsidised gym membership, personal trainers, aerobics, yoga, Pilates and t'ai chi classes, in-office massages, stress reduction and relaxation sessions, ergonomic consultations, meditation rooms, staff health food canteens, nutrition seminars, weight control programmes and quit smoking programmes. As well as being inherently beneficial to employees themselves, health and fitness initiatives

such as these can make a significant contribution to reducing absenteeism and raising productivity (Shields et al., 2016). In part, these non-monetary plans are also targeted at reducing the costs associated with compulsory financial benefits, including statutory sick leave and stress leave entitlements.

Flexible benefits

The content of benefits packages may be either 'fixed' or 'flexible.' They may have a standard content, with the composition being determined by legal requirements and employer choice. Alternatively, they may be flexible in content, with employees having a degree of choice in how best to configure their package within a range of options made available voluntarily by the employer. The latter are also known as 'flexible' or 'cafeteria' benefits plans. The logic of flexible packages is that one size does not fit all. Differences in age, family responsibilities, financial circumstances, and lifestyle preferences mean that different employees will have different benefit needs, and the needs of any one employee will change considerably over time (Long, 2006; Shields et al., 2016).

Class Activity

▸ How might an a targeted approach to voluntary benefits be of value to an organisation wishing to attract, retain, and motivate high-calibre female professionals?

PERFORMANCE-RELATED REWARD PLANS

Performance-related reward plans, including incentives, cover rewards given on the basis of performance (that is, desired behaviour or results) delivered by employees either individually or collectively. An 'incentive' is a payment made on the basis of past performance in order to reinforce and enhance future performance. Performance pay is usually an overlay to base pay, and it varies according to the level of measured or assessed performance. In short, performance pay is contingent or 'at risk', rather than fixed or guaranteed.

Although there are many types of performance-related rewards, these can be classified according to four key variables: the *performance unit* involved (individual, work group, or whole organisation); the *performance criteria* used (behaviour, results, or both); the *time frame* over which performance is measured (short term or long term); and the *form of reward* (monetary, non-monetary, or company share equity) (Shields et al., 2016). Using these dimensions, we can identify three main categories of performance-related rewards:

- individual performance-related reward plans;
- collective short-term cash incentive plans;
- collective long-term equity-based incentive plans.

Table 10.4 summarises the specific reward practices within each of these three broad categories, and each of these practices will be examined in more detail below.

Individual performance plans

Schemes that reward individuals on the basis of formal performance appraisal scores are known generically as *merit pay* plans. In traditional merit pay plans, payments take the form of cumulative additions to base pay. These additions are termed 'merit raises' or 'merit increments.' These reward employees for appraised performance in a previous time period – typically one year – by raising their base pay to a higher level in the relevant job-based pay range.

From an organisational perspective, merit increments have a number of potential advantages. Since pay increments are linked to the individual performance achieved, the risk of the employer receiving no return on a pay increase is less than would be the case where pay is not directly performance related, as in a traditional structure involving seniority-based pay scales. Because they are a permanent addition to base pay, merit increments can also reinforce the attraction and retention of staff.

On the other hand, because merit increments combine performance pay and base pay, employees may fail to see a clear and objective 'line of sight' between performance and pay outcomes. Since each merit increment is a permanent addition to base pay, the resulting compound increase in base pay can over time compromise the cost-effectiveness of the pay system. The emphasis on individualism may also be problematic in national cultural contexts that place a high value on collectivism, as is the case throughout much of South-East Asia and Latin America.

An alternative approach is the *merit bonus* method, in which the appraisal-based payment does not roll into base pay but instead stands apart from it and does not become an on-going entitlement (Shields et al., 2016). The critical difference between this approach and traditional merit increments is that the payments made are conditional rather than cumulative. To be retained, the bonus must be must be re-earned. Motivation is driven by both the prospect of a higher bonus and the risk of loss of the bonus. Although this may be appropriate in many Western contexts, at-risk bonuses may be quite incompatible with cultures high on 'uncertainty avoidance' (see Chapter 1), such as those in Latin America, Eastern Europe, and Japan (Hofstede, 1984).

A simpler form of cash recognition is the discretionary bonus. These are irregular 'lump sum' awards for outstanding performance made at the discretion of the supervisor and/or senior management. Discretionary lump sum payments, being highly visible, can communicate a strong performance message. By the same token, the absence of formal performance assessment means that award allocation may be seen as being arbitrary and as having little clear link between performance and reward.

Incentives geared to measured individual results, or individual 'payment-by-results' plans, are among the oldest and most enduring of all performance pay plans.

Table 10.4 Performance-related reward options

Who? (= performance entity or unit) and when (= time frame for payout)	How? (= behaviour)	How much? (= results)
Individual performance reward plans	Merit raises or increments Merit bonuses	Piece rates Sales commissions Goal-based bonuses
	Discretionary bonuses Individual non-cash recognition awards	
Collective/group short-term incentives		Profit-sharing Gain-sharing Goal-sharing Team incentives Team non-cash recognition awards
Organisation-wide long-term incentives		Share grant plans Share purchase plans Share option plans Executive long-term incentive plans

A major attraction of results-based plans for employers is that they offer greater certainty, immediacy, and objectivity in the pay–performance relationship than are offered by other pay plans. Included in this category are piece rates, sales commissions, and bonus payments to individuals for goal achievement.

Piece rates were developed primarily for labour-intensive manufacturing jobs and had their heyday in the early to mid-twentieth century, when they lay at the forefront of innovation in reward theory and practice in industrialised economies. However, interest in individual output-based incentives of this type has waned with the relative decline in manufacturing activity in Western economies. Instead, sales commissions remain widely used in such sectors as consumer retailing, finance, insurance, and real estate, and goal-based individual reward plans have become an increasingly important feature of white-collar professional and managerial work. For these reasons, we shall focus here on commissions and goal-based bonuses.

In general, *commissions* have the attraction of being simple to set and measure. They institute automatic task clarity and provide instant feedback and reinforcement. However, they may also encourage aggressive, deceptive, or negligent selling practices, foster excessive competition among sales workers working for the same firm, and encourage sales staff to neglect important tasks, such as good record-keeping, after-sales follow-up and the training of new sales workers (Shields et al., 2016). Clearly, commissions are only applicable in sales roles.

Goal-based bonus plans, however, are capable of being adapted to virtually any role. In essence, these plans entail annual or quarterly bonus payments linked directly to individual goal setting. If the goals are financial in nature, such plans are self-funding, which means that they avoid one of the major shortcomings of traditional merit pay plans – budget underfunding. Even so, goal setting can be problematic. Where goals are either too loose/easy or too tight/hard, too few or too many, a goal-based bonus plan is unlikely to be effective. Rewarding only the hard, measurable results may encourage employees to ignore equally important but less quantifiable aspects of the job or role. For these reasons, individual results-based incentive plans tend to measure a range of parameters and are often built around a 'balanced scorecard' of weighted indicators and goals (Shields et al,. 2016).

Many organisations now use recognition of a non-monetary nature to reward individual performance. Non-cash rewards range from merchandise, shopping vouchers and retailer-specific debit cards to symbolic awards in the form of plaques, 'thank you' notes, pins, watches, pens and desk-sets, and the like. Such rewards are said to have the advantage of being personalised, immediate, and more enduring than cash (McAdams, 1999; Nelson, 1994). McAdams (1999: 245–251) asserts: 'It is easier and more effective to promote the excitement of a non-cash award than its cash equivalent. Non-cash awards have built-in excitement and recognition factors that cash simply doesn't have.' They are also likely to be less costly than cash. Conversely, non-cash recognition plans may create an atmosphere of 'winners' and 'losers' (when the same few employees repeatedly get the award) or, alternatively, of 'everyone a winner' (where everyone takes a turn at receiving recognition). They may also be demotivating where employees feel that the reward is tokenistic (Shields et al., 2016).

While the inspiration comes from US reward practices, as detailed in the media story in Box 10.3, cash and non-cash recognition plans ('perks') are also now assuming a prominent place in reward practices in Chinese firms.

In the News It's All in a Day's Perk at Chinese Tech Firms

Chinese technology companies have managed to attract talented employees because of the growth potential and generous bonuses they offer. This has lured talent away from Silicon Valley, and it is now increasingly difficult for multinationals to match up.

China's booming Internet companies routinely reward success not only through cash bonuses but also by organising cultural festivals and parties, such as the Lunar New Year, with lavish gifts to employees including expensive cars, ski trips, and generous cash payouts.

The companies, ranging from giants such as Internet search engine Baidu Inc. to smaller players such as Cheetah Mobile Inc., are known for thanking employees for good performance and continue to value employee happiness and retention.

However, in contrast to the stories of success and parties at the tech industry, the scenario in China's state-owned companies is characterised by austerity and moderate to low performance.

Search giant Baidu's annual party in 2015 was held at the Capital Stadium in Beijing. Featuring belly dancers and lingerie modelling, the stadium's capacity of 18,000 was clearly not enough for the company's 45,000 employees.

Meanwhile, white BMW X1 SUVs were gifted to the top ten employees at Cheetah Mobile. In the annual party of the company, the winners stepped onto a red carpet, each of them escorted by a young person of opposite gender. Their entrance was broadcast live to the nearly 2,000 employees inside the party venue.

Sheng Fu, chief executive of Cheetah Mobile, a mobile browser and security company, said. 'It is about showing the strength of our company and making our employees proud.'

In addition to the BMWs, Cheetah's top performers received annual bonuses equal to eight months' salary and company shares. Moreover, teams got free trips to Silicon Valley and ski vacations.

At Baidu, generous bonuses were distributed, with one top performer getting a bonus equal to 50 months' salary. Chinese traditionally give gifts of cash in red envelopes for the Lunar New Year, and executives at top tech firms try to outdo one another in their generosity.

However, not all companies have upped the ante this year. Some local as well as multinational companies saw their share price decline, cancelled their annual gala, and held lower-key celebrations. A manager at International Business Machines Corp. lamented that the top prize at its annual party in Shanghai was a sofa.

Overall, China's top Internet companies increased employee salaries by 10 per cent to 20 per cent on average in 2014 to boost employees' retention and motivation.

Source: Extract from Gu (2015).

Class Activity

▸ When it comes to recognising and rewarding individual performance, what are the three main advantages and three chief disadvantages of using non-cash recognition plans?

Collective performance plans

In certain contexts, rewarding group results may have decided advantages over individual performance rewards. The latter may be quite dysfunctional in organisations where work is organised on interdependent and cross-functional lines and where results are founded on a high degree of inter-employee cooperation. Interdependence of this type is one of the hallmarks of teamworking and high-involvement management.

In such organisations, it may be neither possible nor logical to attribute performance to specific individuals, since what counts is collective effort and contribution. Collective incentives may encourage employees to work collaboratively to achieve goals that require teamwork and cooperation. Accordingly, collective incentive schemes are more likely to elicit a greater degree of organisational citizenship behaviour than are schemes of an individual nature. Collective incentives may also be more appropriate in national cultural contexts where collectivism is valued above individualism, such as in most Asian countries and in Latin America (Hofstede, 1984). Workplace-wide collective plans are also likely to encounter less opposition from trade unions than are individual

incentive plans. Table 10.5 summarises the main advantages and disadvantages of collective incentives generally.

This is not to suggest that collective incentive plans are necessarily incompatible with individual performance pay plans. With careful planning, it is possible to combine the two approaches in such a way that they are mutually reinforcing. For instance, while the funding of a performance pay pool might be based on measures of an improvement in collective results, the distribution of payments from the pool could be based on an assessment of individual contribution (Heneman and Von Hipple, 1995; Merriman, 2009).

Table 10.5 Collective incentives – pros and cons

Advantages	Disadvantages
Provide an incentive for improving group performance.	Employees may feel that group reward undervalues individual contributions.
Self-funding; total labour costs vary with organisational 'capacity to pay'.	The bigger the group, the weaker the 'line of sight'.
	'Free-riding'/'social loafing'.
Can increase employees' understanding of the business.	Conflict over peer surveillance and peer pressure.
Self-monitoring reduces supervision costs.	Perverse sorting: everyone will want to belong to the group that gets the highest rewards.
Peer pressure on underperformers.	
Encourage organisational commitment and citizenship behaviour.	May encounter resistance from middle managers.

Most collective incentive plans fall into one or other of three plan types:

- profit-sharing;
- gain-sharing;
- goal-sharing.

Profit-sharing

A profit-sharing plan typically involves a formal arrangement under which bonus payments are made to eligible employees on a regular (usually annual) basis, based on a formula that links the size of the total bonus pool to an accounting measure of periodic (typically annual) profit, such as net profit (total income less operating costs) or net profit after tax. By allowing overall labour costs to be varied automatically according to the employer's 'capacity to pay', profit-sharing is seen as providing a form of organisational insurance against external contingencies, particularly fluctuations in demand and prices in the product market. As such, profit-sharing is wholly self-funding. It may also increase employees' identification with and understanding of the organisation's financial circumstances, enhance citizenship behaviour and reduce industrial conflict.

Conversely, because profitability is influenced by many variables that are beyond the employees' collective control, the line of sight between individual performance and reward is likely to be weak; that is, the 'instrumentality' (cause-and-effect) link between effort and reward, as prescribed by expectancy theory (see above), is at best very weak. For the same reason, profit-sharing may give rise to 'free-riding' or 'social loafing', especially where payments are allocated on an equal basis irrespective of individual contribution (Shields et al., 2016).

Gain-sharing

Gain-sharing is a form of collective performance-related pay in which management shares with all its employees in a particular production plant or business unit the financial gains associated with specific measures of improvement in the results achieved by that work group, as measured against a historical benchmark of the group's performance. Traditional gain-share plans emphasise 'hard' single-factor performance measures such as reductions in labour cost or improvement in labour productivity.

Like profit-sharing, such plans are self-funding, but gain-sharing also has a number of advantages over profit-sharing. Such schemes can be targeted to particular plants, departments, or divisions or to discrete business units in the wider organisation. This compares with profit-sharing, which is generally organisation-wide. Unlike profit-sharing, this approach can be applied in public sector and other

nonprofit organisations. It also seeks to reward only those results that are within the group's control. It can support a high-involvement culture through employee involvement programmes and devolution of decision-making. In addition, it is compatible with a unionised workforce and collective bargaining (Kim and Voos, 1997; Dalton, 1998).

The emphasis on continuous improvement means that gain-sharing is well suited to competitive strategies emphasising either cost containment, quality improvement, or both. However, traditional gain-share plans are a poor fit for highly dynamic contexts, since each change in technology, work organisation, and product type will require a recalibration of historical performance benchmarks. Cost-focused plans also ignore non-financial or 'soft' aspects of group performance, such as worksite safety, environmental compliance, and customer satisfaction (Shields et al., 2016).

Goal-sharing

Goal-sharing is the collective equivalent of individual goal-based bonuses (discussed above) and, like the latter, draws on the technique of goal setting. While goal-sharing resembles gain-sharing, it has several major differences. Goal-sharing is future-oriented, whereas gain-sharing is tied to retrospective performance benchmarks. This makes goal-sharing simpler to develop and more flexible, as well as wider in application and better placed to accommodate rapid changes in technology and product or service type. Goal-sharing generally includes both 'soft' performance factors, such as customer satisfaction and product quality, and financial targets. However, this means that goal-sharing is generally not self-funding, which in turn gives rise to the possibility of underfunding and of bonus payments that may not be seen as commensurate with the group's achievements (Shields et al., 2016).

Table 10.6 details the incidence of the main individual and collective performance reward practices in UK organisations. Note, in particular, the relatively high incidence of individual cash bonuses, merit raises, and individual non-cash recognition as well collective plans in the form of goal-sharing and profit-sharing. The high use of plans combining individual and collective performance measures also attests to the importance of using individual and collective incentives to moderate/complement each other.

Employee share plans

Organisation-wide, long-term incentive plans – more commonly known as employee share (or 'stock' or 'equity') plans, or ESOPs – allow eligible employees access to share ownership in the organisation that employs them and reward employees for improvements over time in the employing firm's share market performance (via an

Table 10.6 Performance pay practices in the UK, 2014–15

Individual performance-related schemes	Individual bonuses	57*
	Merit pay rises	51*
	Combination schemes	46*
	Individual non-monetary recognition awards	31*
	Sales commissions	29*
	Ad hoc/project-based schemes	24*
	Other individual-based cash incentives	22*
	Individual non-monetary incentive awards	16*
	Piece rates	3*
Group performance-related schemes	Goal-sharing	53†
	Profit-sharing	40†
	Group or team-based non-monetary recognition	30†
	Gain-sharing	21†
	Group or team-based non-monetary incentives	17†

*% of respondents indicating they operate an individual performance-related reward scheme.

†% of respondents indicating they operate a group performance-related reward scheme.

Source: Chartered Institute of Personnel and Development (2015: 5).

appreciation in share price) and operating performance (via share dividends and special bonus share issues).

As such, share plans are seen as having a long-term benefit by reinforcing employees' commitment to the success of the organisation. Because they stand to foster an 'ownership' mentality among employees, broadly based share plans (that is, plans in which many or most employees are eligible to participate) are particularly appropriate for organisations that embrace a high degree of employee involvement and participation (Kaarsemaker and Poutsma, 2006). Depending on how they are configured, share plans may also give employee-owners a genuine voice in management of the business and perhaps in managing other elements of the firm's reward system. However, the precise attitudinal and behavioural outcomes will depend on, among other things, the extent of employee eligibility and take-up and on the particular plan or plans involved.

Although share employee plans come in a wide variety of forms, most fall into one of three main types:

- share grant plans;
- share purchase plans;
- option plans.

Share grant plans

With share grant plans, employees receive a gift of fully paid shares in the firm. In some cases, the shares granted can be traded immediately, which means that the grant is technically 'unrestricted'. However, it has become increasingly common for share grants to have certain limitations attached, which generally means that ownership does not transfer ('vest') immediately and/or that the shares cannot be tradable immediately in the same way as 'common stock' (that is, ordinary shares held by external investors). Conditional share grants of this type are known as 'restricted' share plans: while employees are not required to outlay any of their own money, they usually cannot sell their shares until a specified minimum period has elapsed. For the company, share grants may encourage long-term employee commitment and membership behaviour, particularly where restricted shares and trust arrangements are involved.

From the employee's perspective, regular share grants can serve as a convenient means for employees to supplement their retirement savings, although employee shareholders may well have a far higher risk exposure than external shareholders, since the latter are more likely to have a diversified share portfolio covering a range of sectors, industries, and firms (Shields et al., 2016).

Share purchase plans

With share purchase plans, employees have the opportunity to purchase part or all of a specified quota of shares in the company. Employees typically pay a small deposit on the full share purchase price, with the balance of the purchase price repayable over a specified term. The plan typically includes favourable purchase terms, such as a purchase price that is set below the prevailing market value and/or a low- or zero-interest loan from the company to fund the purchase. Some schemes allow the share purchase loan to be repaid from dividends so that the repayment period is open-ended and there is no employee outlay from personal savings. Other schemes allow employees to fund their acquisition in a tax-effective way by means of a 'salary sacrifice', which allows the employees to quarantine the outlay from their taxable income. Some schemes involve employee savings plans and pay deductions to fund the purchase. Legal ownership of the shares vests to the employee over time as the loan is paid off.

As share purchases funded by a company loan mean that employees are indebted to the company for the duration of the loan, employees may thus be more accommodating of management initiatives. Also, where employees have had to pay for the shares, their motivation in terms of 'ownership' is likely to be considerably stronger and more enduring than would be the case where shares have been received as a gift.

By the same token, share purchase plans entail a greater risk all round than is the case with share grants. In particular, by their very nature, share purchase plans expose employees to greater financial risk. Employees committed to repaying the principal on a company loan at a fixed purchase price will experience severe financial difficulties if the share price collapses and the debt is not renegotiated or forgiven (Shields et al., 2016).

Employee option plans

A third type of share plan – employee option plans – gives employees the option of acquiring a specified quantity of company shares at a particular price on or after a designated future date. An option plan is a variant of share purchase in which the earliest date of purchase is set some time in the future. Such plans give the employee the right to buy a specified number of company shares at a predetermined price on a specified future date, such as the third anniversary of the option grant date. The price payable to exercise the option to acquire some or all of the shares – the 'strike price' – is commonly set at or below the market value of the shares at the time the option is granted.

Since the granting of an option does not confer an immediate ownership of equity, there will be no 'ownership' effect on motivation unless and until the option has been exercised. Until the options are exercisable, the main behavioural effects will be twofold. First, the restriction on exercising the options will reinforce staff retention, since the options are likely to be forfeited if the option-holder leaves the company. Second, during the holding period, the incentive effect will be largely extrinsic; that is, the holder will be motivated to improve the company's performance in order to strengthen market perceptions and increase the market share price, with a view to maximising any capital gain when it becomes possible for the employee to exercise the option to buy and sell the shares involved.

However, with option plans, the line of sight between the employee's effort and the financial reward is even more remote than is the case with share bonus and purchase plans, since there is a significant delay in realising any market-related rewards. In 'bull' share market conditions, in which most companies are experiencing share price appreciation, options may confer unearned ('windfall') gains on some option-holders. As with all equity plans, options are 'fair-weather' reward instruments: they may work well in times of share price growth but can also compound a firm's problems if the share price falls, say in a declining ('bear') share market, and the market price falls below the option strike price. Option plans may also encourage a speculative outlook among employees rather than an ownership mentality (Shields et al., 2016).

Criticisms of performance-related rewards

Performance-related rewards are among the most controversial facets of contemporary HRM practice, with some critics contending that they are doomed to fail because they rest on invalid assumptions about employee motivation. Others similarly argue that they are inherently unfair.

Those who argue that performance pay is dysfunctional tend to base their case on the premises underlying cognitive evaluation theory, discussed above, that extrinsic performance-related rewards are inimical to intrinsic motivation. One proponent of this view, US social psychologist Alfie Kohn (1993a, 1993b), asserts that incentive pay plans fail because they:

* undermine intrinsic interest in the job;
* motivate people to pursue the reward rather than do a good job;
* are instruments of behavioural manipulation and punishment;
* rupture cooperative work relationships;
* ignore or mask the reasons underlying work problems;
* discourage sensible risk-taking.

Kennaugh's (2015) recent article in the *Sydney Morning Herald* provides another version of this anti-incentive logic. Note the author's reference to Deci's contention, mentioned earlier in the chapter, that incentives erode intrinsic interest in the job. The author suggests that reward and punishment usually work when it comes to motivating people to do algorithmic tasks which are often monotonous and boring. However, when it comes to heuristic tasks where the outcome can be reached in a number of different ways, the individual needs to experiment for best results and may have to come up with something new based on personal experience and common sense. Here, reward and punishment are unlikely to work. The author emphasises that in such situations, the focus should be on 'fit'. When there is an appreciation of 'fit' and employees are in the right role and the right environment that honours their unique skills and values, then they are much more likely to be productive, creative and happy.

Although well-publicised instances of failing incentive plans lend support to such arguments (see, for example, Beer and Cannon, 2004), these criticisms are themselves open to challenge on both theoretical and empirical grounds (see, for instance, Gupta and Mitra, 1998; Gupta and Shaw, 1998). Research shows that, under certain conditions (such as those prescribed by expectancy theory), incentives can exert a positive influence on performance, at least in certain organisational and cultural contexts (Gerhart and Rynes, 2003; Gerhart et al., 2009).

As we have seen, the assumption that extrinsic and intrinsic factors are dichotomous rather than complementary is also open to empirical challenge (see, for example, Cameron and Pierce, 1997). Overall, the evidence for a positive incentive effect is stronger for results-based plans than for plans based on behavioural assessment. Citing US examples, Gerhart and Rynes (2003: 170–171, 175) note that there are 'compelling examples of the effectiveness of results-oriented plans' and that there is 'ample evidence that results-based incentive plans can greatly increase performance'. Furthermore, they suggest (2003: 195) that strong individual results-based incentives have not only a positive incentive effect, but also a potentially powerful 'job-sorting' effect, whereby poor performers are actively 'managed out' while high performing individuals actively seek out positions that offer high reward for high effort.

A further criticism of Kohn's case is that he underplays the distinction between individual and collective incentives (Bennett Stewart et al., 1993; Cumming, 1994; Evans et al., 1995). Kohn overlooks the fact that group incentives are consciously directed towards encouraging the very attitudinal, behavioural, and cultural characteristics that Kohn himself appears to endorse: teamwork, cooperation, shared effort and employee participation. Again, there is some evidence that appropriately designed group incentives can work (Gerhart et al., 2009) – what remains at issue empirically is the magnitude of the relationship.

So far we have only considered the arguments and evidence relating to the effectiveness of performance-related rewards in delivering the results and behaviours desired by the organisation, that is, to whether such plans can and do 'work'. From the employees' perspective, however, an equally important – if not more important – consideration is whether such plans are fair.

One of the most common rationales for performance-related pay is that it operationalises the 'equity' norm of distributive justice. To reiterate: equity theory proposes, in part, that reward satisfaction stems from establishing a good fit between an employee's inputs and outcomes. Reward relative to contribution – what could possibly be fairer? Yet there are those who argue that performance-related rewards can violate both distributive and procedural justice requirements. For instance, Heery (1996) argues that performance-related pay poses a threat to employee wellbeing because it contradicts employees' need for a stable and secure income, a need that is both economic and psychological. Without some level of guaranteed income, workers are likely to overwork and experience work-related stress and anxiety. Heery also suggests that performance-related pay tends to expose employees' pay to disproportionate risks. Shareholders may take calculated risks to reap a return, but employees have very different stakeholder needs, motives and expectations (Heery, 1996).

Critics also suggest that performance pay may also be procedurally unjust. According to Heery, such plans typically leave little scope for any independent representation of employees' interests, or 'voice'. Performance pay has also been questioned on the grounds that it may be especially disadvantageous to women employees. For instance, Rubery (1995) argues that women are likely to be worse off under performance-related pay, particularly where it takes the form of individual merit pay. In the context of the greater discretion available to line managers, the subjectivity inherent in behavioural assessment is likely to disadvantage women relative to men, especially in service work where supervisory positions tend to be male-dominated. Furthermore, where individual incentives apply, the individualisation of the employment relationship stands to weaken women's bargaining power further still. At least with job-based pay and job evaluation, the prospects for evening up the gender gap in pay and earnings are somewhat greater, partly because the process of pay determination is relatively open, transparent, and amenable to collective bargaining (Rubery, 1995).

So the question remains: 'What proportion of an employee's total pay should be 'at risk' against – or vary with – the performance?' Critical Thinking 10.2 invites you to formulate a considered position on the issue of 'pay variability'.

> ### ? Critical Thinking 10.2 Pay variability
>
> The term 'pay variability' refers to the degree to which pay outcomes for any given job or any given set of job-holders will vary by performance rather than being fixed or guaranteed (Gerhart and Rynes, 2003).
>
> **Questions**
>
> 1 Is it better for an organisation to have a high or a low level of pay variability?
> 2 How might the appropriateness of high variability differ according to the social and cultural context?

Perhaps the most meaningful conclusion to draw from these debates on the efficacy and fairness of performance pay is that such plans may have the potential to improve individual and group performance but that the effectiveness and felt-fairness of any such plan will be contingent on several factors: the mode of application, particularly the manner in which the pay–performance linkage is configured; how effectively this linkage is communicated and accepted; and how appropriate it is for the organisational context involved. In this respect, differences in social and cultural values are likely to be highly salient.

REWARD COMMUNICATION

Creating and maintaining employees' understanding and acceptance of the way in which they are rewarded is one of the most challenging yet important aspects of contemporary organisational communication. In a survey of UK reward professionals (Cotton and Chapman, 2010), poor rewards communication was ranked as the single greatest risk to the effectiveness of a reward system. Evidence suggests that reward communications practice looms as a potentially powerful but underutilised human resource tool (Shields et al., 2009). Even the most elegantly designed and contextually appropriate reward system will fail to attract, retain, and motivate employees unless it is understood and accepted by the managers and employees affected.

Clear communication of the philosophy and details underlying the reward system stands to increase employees' acceptance of the composition, structure, and level of the rewards, as well as to sharpen employees' line of sight between what they contribute and how they are rewarded. Two-way communication also has great potential here. Given the centrality of reward practice to achieving strong employee engagement, giving employees a say in how they are rewarded may be an effective outlet for both the individual and the collective voice. Regular attitude surveys are one way in which employees can be given a 'say in pay'. Other possibilities include focus groups and employee participation in job evaluation teams.

The other key stakeholder group in this respect comprises line managers. Without their 'buy-in', the line of communication between reward professionals and ordinary employees will be weak and unreliable. Given that such managers will also be pivotal to the administration and maintenance of the system, it is advisable that they are involved in the designing the reward process (Brown and Purcell, 2007).

However, reward communication does not necessarily equate with reward openness. The amount of pay information that should be shared with employees is a matter of longstanding debate, and a range of competing arguments have been advanced for both pay transparency and pay secrecy (Colella et al., 2007; Day, 2012, 2014). The case for transparency rests on the proposition that unless employees understand the pay system and how their individual rewards are determined, the system cannot contribute to the strategic goals of the firm or gain the trust of employees. Conversely, opponents argue that employee

privacy must be respected since knowledge of how others are being paid can foster jealousy, cause performance problems, and engender a cycle of 'catch-up' claims.

In determining the policy and practice of rewards communication, what, then, is the appropriate balance between disclosure and secrecy? Certainly, a policy of high transparency and regular employee attitude surveys would be more appropriate where a high-involvement management approach applies. Even here, though, it may be best to focus communication on the reward system 'rules' rather than on the details of pay outcomes for individual employees. Try your hand at addressing the issue of reward openness/secrecy by formulating responses to the questions posed in Critical Thinking 10.3.

> (?) **Critical Thinking 10.3 Reward secrecy and transparency**
>
> One approach to reward communication suggests that withholding from each employee details of the pay received by their fellow employees may restrain their demands for pay increases. In other words, revealing all may just encourage pay 'ratcheting', that is, employees in the same job or role demanding the same level of pay as that received by the highest paid employees in that role. The alternative approach proposes that pay secrecy of this type stands to violate the right of the employee to be treated with dignity and respect. Moreover, revealing more detail on reward levels, it is suggested, stands to reduce potentially counterproductive rumour and speculation about who has received what and why this might be so.
>
> **Questions**
>
> 1 In what circumstances might pay secrecy be appropriate or justified?
> 2 Can an organisation have too much pay transparency?
> 3 When and how should reward information be communicated to employees?

EMPLOYMENT RELATIONS AND EMPLOYEE REWARD MANAGEMENT

Although the main focus of decisions relating to reward system configuration may be the individual organisation or its constituent business units, determination of reward in general, and pay structure and level in particular, is also influenced by the context or contexts within which the organisation operates. These contextual factors include:

- the nature of the relevant product and labour markets;
- sociocultural norms and standards;
- the nature of government intervention and regulation;
- the contours of the prevailing employment relations system.

Key elements of the employment relations system include the nature of organisation and institutional power of the union and employer, the mode of industry-, regional-, and national-level bargaining, and the nature and extent of the government's regulation of pay and conditions of employment. As noted earlier in the chapter, the employment relations context also shapes the opportunities for and mechanisms of employee voice in the process of reward determination. Likewise, it can widen or constrain management choices regarding organisational pay structure and level.

Governments can have a major influence on reward processes and outcomes via a direct regulation of pay levels, equal pay legislation, industrial tribunals, pay review bodies, fair/minimum/low-pay bodies, centralised wage indexation, mandatory provision for works councils, and the like. However, the degree of government influence over setting pay varies significantly over time and between countries and sectors.

The nature of national- and industry-level bargaining systems may also exert a strong influence on reward practice at the organisational level. Traditionally, the mode and level of pay have been central issues in unions' collective bargaining at all levels: national, industry, occupational, and organisational. As we have seen, trade unions generally prefer some types of pay plan over others – job-based pay over person-based pay, fixed pay over variable pay, group incentives over individual incentives, for example (Long and Shields, 2009). The general decline of union influence in developed economies has undoubtedly influenced pay practices and levels. However, according to Katz and Darbishire (2000, cited in Perkins and Vartiainen, 2010: 179), the pattern of change in the European context has been non-uniform: within both the union and non-union sectors, the degree of variation in pay levels and practices has increased in recent decades.

The impact of changes in the level of government intervention and collective bargaining within the European Union is illustrative of these wider contextual influences on determining reward. As noted by Perkins and Vartiainen (2010: 178):

Across much of the European continent – and featuring explicitly in the taxonomy adopted by the European Union – an attempt has been made to socialise employment relations using the existence of intermediaries between employers and employees to act as a mechanism for regulating the pay issue and to attempt to codify working practices that employers may be able to adopt to secure a return on the payments that agree to make to employees, as laid down in statutory provisions resulting from collective bargaining.

This regime of 'social partnership' and reward regulation dates back many decades and includes a wide range of mandatory provisions. The Equal Pay Directive of 1975 required member countries of the then European Economic Community to adhere to and enforce the principle of 'equal pay for work of equal value', a requirement reiterated under the Treaty of Amsterdam, effective from 1999. In practice, this has been taken to mean that job evaluation systems should be free from discrimination.

Wage indexation is another characteristic feature of European employment relations systems. Indexation aims to preserve the real value of wages by adjusting them automatically for price inflation. Works councils and joint consultative committees, coupled with multi-employer collective bargaining, have also been prominent features of the European approach to pay determination. In addition, there has been a number of initiatives at the level of the European Union to encourage employee share ownership and other forms of financial participation such as profit-sharing. In the late 1990s, the proportion of business units with 200 or more employees that had broad-based share plans averaged 16 per cent, and in the decade that followed, Belgium, France, Germany, the Netherlands, and the UK all legislated to encourage greater share ownership on the part of employees (Pendleton, 2009).

However, there are now clear signs that these pillars of the model of the European 'coordinated' market economy are beginning to fragment. Although several countries still use indexation, a number (Denmark, France, Italy, the Netherlands, and Spain) abandoned this form of pay regulation out of a fear that indexation will actually fuel inflation (Robinson and Winning, 2011).

Pre-existing pay disparities between Eastern European countries and European Union countries also poses a pay equity dilemma for the European Commission itself. With workers from Poland and the Baltic States flocking to take up more highly paid administrative jobs in the Commission's headquarters in Brussels, the earnings of these employees far exceeds the pay levels available to even the most senior office-holders in their countries of origin. The Commission has come under pressure to peg salaries to the pay structure in these countries. However, doing so would mean that some Commission employees would be doing the same work as fellow workers but for vastly different rates of pay (Castle, 2011).

Trade liberalisation and exposure to international markets are also beginning to erode multi-employer collective bargaining within even the strongest coordinated economies in the European Union. The recent global crisis has impacted no less severely on the German employment model – until recently the exemplar of a 'coordinated market economy' and social partnership – than on those of less coordinated economies. Outcomes have included outsourcing, the rise of precarious employment, a growing low-wage sector, and the emergence of two-tier wage agreements under which unions agree to accept lower pay rates for non-union workers in exchange for the prospect of organising the latter and co-opting them onto works councils (Lehndorff et al., 2009; Haipeter, 2011).

In sum, as the European Union experience demonstrates, the changing nature of employment relations institutions and bargaining processes can exercise a powerful sway over pay structure and pay levels at the level of the individual organisation. One special case of interest here is the controversy surrounding executive pay, an example of the importance of individual bargaining and related power relations.

EXECUTIVE REMUNERATION

Whilst acknowledging similarities between the reward systems that have been implemented for executives and those of other employees, critical differences arise from both the scope and quantum of the objectives associated with executive remuneration systems. Corporate scandals from the 1980s onwards and the Global Financial Crisis (FSA, 2009) have escalated the public controversy over the levels of reward received by chief executive officers (CEOs)

and other top executives compared to other employees. For example, in a study of companies listed in the UK, the UK High Pay Commission found the following relationships between CEO remuneration and the average pay of employees and company directors at the same company (see Table 10.7 below).

The level of executive remuneration for listed companies in market-based economies has increased dramatically in absolute terms in recent decades (Jensen, Murphy and Wruck, 2004). Increased disclosure of the components and absolute amount of executive pay since 2000 has limited effect on this growth, prompting recent legislative action (see http://www.smh.com.au/business/banking-and-finance/putting-the-brakes-on-bosses-bonus-blowouts-20160816-gqtntr.html). Rather, it has heightened awareness of pay relativities amongst company executives, encouraging stronger informal control over boards of directors to 'match the market' in order to attract and retain the best executive talent (Bebchuk and Fried, 2004).

Executive Reward Disclosure

Corporate governance laws and regulations in many developed economies now require detailed disclosure of the reward package details of top executives in publicly listed companies.

Questions

1 What are the most persuasive arguments for mandatory disclosure of top- executive pay?
2 What are the most persuasive arguments against disclosure?
3 What is your view here?

Table 10.7 Reported remuneration of CEOs at selected FTSE companies, 1979–2011

Company Name	Director's pay 1979–1980	Lead executive actual total earnings 2009–2011	Total earnings increase 1980–2009/11	Top pay as multiple of average pay 1979–1980	Lead executive total earning as multiple of average pay 2009–2011
Lonmin	£224938	£1865342	729.3	44.1	113.1
BP	£143334	£4452624	3006.5	16.5	63.2
Barclays	£87323	£4365636	4899.4	14.5	75.0
GKN	£81000	£1534221	1794.1	14.9	47.7
Lloyds Banking Group	£79344	£2572000	3141.6	13.6	75.0
Reed Elsevier	£75209	£2028108	2596.6	13.3	38.4

Source: UK High Pay Centre (2012).

Renewed public outcry over seemingly excessive executive pay levels has prompted official inquiries, calls for statutory limits on top executive pay levels, and the introduction of statutory provision for binding shareholder voting on proposed pay packages for CEOs of public companies. It has even spawned public protest movements such as 'Occupy Wall Street' (Calhoun, 2013; Shrivastava and Ivanova, 2015). Debates on pay relativity and the existence of links between executive pay and firm performance have dominated this discussion (Ertuk et al., 2005; Hou, Priem and Goranova, 2014), prompting questions on the efficacy of corporate governance regulation to address these concerns (Yeoh, 2015).

For example, a review by the Australian Council of Superannuation Investors compared the fixed or base pay of executives in the Top 100 Australian listed companies with the average pay of workers over the decade ending in 2010. The comparison is summarised in Table 10.8 below.

Table 10.8 Comparison of executive and average worker base pay, Australia 2001–2010

Year	Average worker pay (Pa)	Average CEO base pay (pa)*	CEO pay multiple
2001	$42,645	$888,407	20.8 times
2002	$44,792	$984,045	22 times
2003	$47,543	$1,361,769	28.6 times
2004	$48,734	$1,416,877	29 times
2005	$51,766	£1,533,231	29.6 times
2006	$53,440	$1,795,658	33.6 times
2007	$56,108	$1,833,228	32.7 times
2008	$58,338	$1,947,350	33.4 times
2009	$61,911	$1,905,493	30.8 times
2010	$65,161	$2,048,892	31.4 times
2001–10	52.3%	130.6%	

Source: Executive salary figuree for 2001–2008 are drawn from CEO pay in the Top 100 Companies: 2009, Research Paper published by the Australian Council of Super Investors, September 2010; executive salaries for 2008 and 2010 are based on ACTU research of CEO salaries ASX/S&P 50 2010; Average worker pay from Australian Bureau of Statistics (catalogue no. 8302.0 May each year).

Source: ACTU Executive PayWatch, 2010

*CEO Salaries exclude News Corporation

Table 10.9 Comparison of executive and average worker base pay, United Kingdom 2001–2010

Year	Average FTSE 100 CEO salary/£	Increase in average salary	Ave employee pay/£	Increase	CEO salary as Multiple of average employee
2003	659,000	6%	24,767	2%	27
2004	672,000	2%	25,955	5%	27
2005	716,000	7%	27,254	5%	26
2006	711,000	−1%	30,828	13%	23
2007	755,000	6%	25,677	−17%	29
2008	810,000	7%	30,994	21%	26
2009	818,000	1%	32,521	5%	25
2010	825,000	1%	34,176	5%	24
2011	850,000	3%	35,744	5%	24
2012	862,000	1%	33,967	−5%	25

Source: High Pay Centre (2012: 16).

Analysis of the Top 100 UK listed firms highlight a similar story (see Table 10.9 below).

Gretchen Gavett, an associate editor at the *Harvard Business Review*, cited recent research on the ratio between executive and worker pay to highlight the difference between recent trends in executive pay and general expectations of the ideal ratio of executive/worker pay. One implication of this research is that if the 'ideal' ratio was to be realised without reducing current levels of executive pay, substantial increases in worker pay would be required in many countries, as Table 10.10 indicates:

Incentive plans have been the main drivers of the unprecedented growth in executive pay in advanced market-based countries since the early 1990s in both absolute terms and relative to the pay of ordinary wage and salary earners. Executive incentives are of two main types: short-term cash incentives and long-term equity-based incentives (such as option plans). In many Western liberal market economies, the relative contribution of **long-term incentives** to CEO total reward has risen substantially over the past two decades. Growth in

long-term incentives has also been the main drive of the unprecedented growth in total reward levels of CEOs and other top executives since the early 1990s. Studies of the components of CEO pay in a number of these countries confirm this trend. For example, a recent study in Australia, summarised in Table 10.11, provides a breakdown of the main components of the reported remuneration of ASX100 CEOs for 2014, as well as the total remuneration actually realised. On average, fixed pay comprised just 38.5 per cent of the reported total remuneration, while cash bonuses comprised 26.9 per cent and non-cash variable remuneration (i.e. share-related income) comprised 37.2 per cent. As these data show, the levels reported tend to understate the levels realised, a discrepancy due primarily to wealth derived from long-term incentives which continues to attract criticism from shareholder bodies.

International comparisons of CEO remuneration indicate that there are differences between market-based economies. For example, Table 10.10 below summarises the actual ratio of CEO pay to average unskilled worker pay as at 2012 in 16 different countries. It also reports

Table 10.10 International comparison of executive and average worker base pay

WHAT AVERAGE WORKERS SHOULD BE PAID

According to each country's ideal CEO-to-worker compensation ratios.

	RATIO		AVERAGE COMPENSATION		
	Actual	Ideal	CEO	Worker	Work at the ideal ratio
Australia	93	8.3	$4,183,419	$44,983	$502,012
Austria	36	5.0	1,567,908	43,555	313,582
Czech Republic	110	4.2	2,159,300	19,630	518,228
Denmark	48	2.0	2,186,880	45,560	1,093,440
France	104	6.7	3,965,312	38,132	594,794
Germany	147	6.3	5,912,781	40,223	946,045
Israel	76	3.6	2,189,104	28,804	601,998
Japan	67	6.0	2,354,581	35,143	392,430
Norway	58	2.3	2,551,420	43,990	1,093,481
Poland	28	5.0	561,932	20,069	112,386
Portugal	53	5.0	1,205,326	22,742	241,065
Spain	127	3.0	4,399,915	34,387	1,466,638
Sweden	89	2.2	3,358,326	37,784	1,511,262
Switzerland	148	5.0	7,435,816	50,242	1,487,163
United Kingdom	84	5.3	3,758,412	44,743	704,707
United States	354	6.7	12,259,894	34,645	1,838,975

Source: Gavett (2014).

Table 10.11 Reported and realised remuneration of CEOs of ASX100 companies, 2014

	Average	Median	Minimum	Maximum
Fixed pay and benefits	$1,929,122	$1,810,000	$343,573	$5,385,916
Cash bonus	$1,345,662	$1,065,009	$152,000	$7,766,336
Total cash	$3,146,136	$2,892,000	$657,073	$13,152,252
Reported total remuneration	$5,008,869	$4,195,278	$657,073	$22,088,011
Realised total remuneration	$5,626,235	$3,958,000	$657,073	$30,796,223

Source: Australian Council of Superannuation Investors (2015).

the results of survey data for these countries indicating the average desired or ideal ratio amongst respondents in each country. While the desired difference is far lower than the actual gap, Australian is something of an outlier in terms of tolerance for vertical pay disparity. Whereas the average desired gap across the countries is 4.6 times, Australian respondents said that they would prefer a ratio of 8.3 times.

In order to understand this trend, we need to examine the unique nature of executive short-term and long-term incentive plans, the unintended consequences of these plans, and the role of company directors as well as HR professionals. These will be discussed in turn.

Short- and long-term incentives plans for executives

Short-term incentive plans tend to take a form familiar to all employees with a combination of extrinsic and intrinsic rewards, with salary and bonuses being the usual form of financial payment. Whilst the relative amounts of these rewards generate significant discussion, the process to

design and manage these components is similar to those that apply to all employees. In contrast, it is the design and payment of executive long-term incentives that is the most problematic in terms of pay relativity and the impact on corporate performance. Consistent with an Agency Theory perspective, the aim of these incentives is to align the economic interests of executives with shareholders (Jensen and Murphy, 1990).

The aim is to encourage a longer-term focus through improved organisational performance, particularly in terms of total returns to shareholders. Such plans come in an almost limitless variety of forms, but most existing plans fall into one of the following categories: restricted share plans; performance shares (or zero-exercise price options); executive option plans; and share appreciation rights. Increasingly, such plans include both market-related performance targets and restrictions on the disposal of equity-based rewards. These plans are summarised in Table 10.12:

The following example (Box 10.4) illustrates the continued development of these executive long-term incentive schemes and the dissemination of US executive pay practices.

Table 10.12 Key long-term executive incentive plans

Plan Name	Description	Key Concepts/Terms
Restricted share plans	The executive receives shares free of charge once the target company performance has been achieved, but full shareholder entitlement is 'restricted' in some way.	'golden handcuff' 'vesting hurdles'
Performance shares	The executive takes up shares at no cost but only on condition of achieving a performance hurdle over a specific period.	'free grant'
Executive option plans	Similar to employee options plans except: 1. expensing of options costs; 2. dilution of existing shareholder returns and ownership (if options are material); 3. increasingly linked to performance hurdles.	Mandatory expensing of options; Performance hurdles; Total Shareholder Returns (TSR).
Share appreciation rights	Similar to employee options plans except: 1. they take account of dividend earnings as well as share price appreciation; 2. the executive is not required to take ownership of the shares.	Cash equivalent; Share price appreciation.

As highlighted earlier, how effective these executive incentive plans are in aligning executive reward with changes in ordinary shareholder wealth is a matter of on-going debate. In particular, plans seem to generate a material level of unintended consequences.

Unintended consequences

There is mounting evidence that executive incentives exacerbate rather than remedy the 'agency problem' – that is, executives have become more likely to act in their own economic self-interest and become 'self-fulfilling (Moran and Ghoshal, 1996; Pepper, Gore and Crossman, 2013). At the same time, the increasing agency cost associated with these long-term incentives plans are borne by the shareholders.

Executive excess can take many forms – from extravagant sign-on and termination payments to generous post-employment deals. Equity-based remuneration is intended to provide strong economic incentives to increase shareholder wealth. In practice, on the contrary, it has tended to create strong incentives to manage the share price, not the business. This can be seen in research that indicates that the relationship is less likely to be between executive pay and company performance but is, rather, between pay and company size (Tosi et al., 2000). Related research on the top 100 companies listed on the FTSE by Ertuk et al. (2005) indicates that 63 per cent of Total Shareholder Returns (TSR) are the result of general share-market increases rather than improved company earnings. Expressed in another form, at the same time

---

Box 10.4 WorleyParsons taps US for new executive bonus scheme

WorleyParsons chief executive Andrew Wood will benefit from a new share rights scheme if the company's stock rises. WorleyParsons has turned to the United States for new ideas on how to reward executives because its management team is missing out on bonuses on account of the engineering group's poor financial performance. WorleyParsons is believed to be the first company in Australia to adopt a new remuneration scheme that it calls 'share price performance rights' to attract and retain executives. The scheme, known in the US as 'market stock units', was recommended by US remuneration consulting group Frederic W. Cook.

WorleyParsons' head of investor relations Fran van Reyk said the new scheme was designed to allow executives to build holdings of equity and remain with the company during difficult periods, instead of taking jobs at competitors. 'We are competing in an international market for executives,' Ms van Reyk said. WorleyParsons hired Dennis Finn in 2014 from PwC to run its advisory business Advisian, and Filippo Abba in 2015 from Foster Wheeler Energy to run its project delivery and maintenance business. WorleyParsons executives did not receive short-term bonuses in fiscal 2015 because the engineering group, which reported a $39 million annual net loss, did not hit its profit targets. Equity grants included in long-term incentive plans have also not vested over the past three years because the company did not meet its shareholder return and earnings-per-share targets.

WorleyParsons' stock has also fallen sharply in recent years, losing 70 per cent of its value since October 2012 to close at $7.10 on Wednesday. WorleyParsons' remuneration committee had been evaluating the impact its pay structures have on 'the motivation and retention' of key people, especially during volatile periods, committee chairman John Green said in the company's annual report. The committee concluded that, while company performance should remain 'the driving force' in determining short-term incentives, it was also important to reward staff for 'significant achievements' in delivering strategy, Mr Green said.

Under the new scheme, executives will receive an annual grant of performance rights with a vesting period of two years. If WorleyParsons' stock price doubles over two years, the rights convert into twice the number of shares. If the stock price halves, the rights lapse. Between a potential halving of the stock price and a potential doubling, the rights vest on a proportional basis.

The Australian Shareholders Association, which notes WorleyParsons has been one of worst-performing stocks in the S&P/ASX 100 index over the past two years, describes the scheme as 'a real alignment with shareholders'. But proxy groups have raised questions over the company's decision to reward executives for poor performance – if the stock price goes down – and the fact it is not linked directly to individual performance. Still, proxy groups have recommended in favour of adopting the scheme, given WorleyParsons has not paid bonuses to executives in recent years and has reduced chief executive Andrew Wood's annual fixed pay of $1.6 million by 10 per cent from July 2015. ISS said its support for the scheme would depend on whether the company's board ensured that 'no materially misaligned and egregious outcomes' eventuated from the vesting of rights into shares.

Source: Wiggins (2015: 26).

as real TSR increased by 365 per cent, the pay to directors (including executives) increased by 523 per cent. In addition, whilst disclosure has increased in this period, a number of accounting and share price management techniques have gained popularity within boards of directors. These include share buybacks (effectively improving key finance ratios such as earnings per share by reducing the number of shares by which revenues, profit, and related accounting measures are calculated). Other accounting techniques such as mark-to-market and intangibles can also be managed for their effect on share price. Corporate restructuring activities such as mergers and demergers can also affect these forms of performance measurement to which incentive plans are linked. All of these can result in the over-pricing of shares as unintended consequences of executive incentive plans that have been adopted in the past (Jensen, Murphy and Wruck, 2004).

The overall result appears to be a disconnect between company performance (as reflected in its share price and executive pay in all of its forms. This can be illustrated in the following chart comparing from the UK High Pay Centre, showing that it is the increase 'in performance-related pay that is largely responsible for the near 400 per cent increase in executive pay over the past 15 years' (see Figure 10.1 below -Source: UK High Pay Centre, 2012: 20).

This would seem to lend some credence to Kohn's contention (see earlier in this chapter) that incentive plans are inherently dysfunctional. Incentives motivate the employee to get the reward, but that is all. So, what are the respective roles of company directors and HR professionals in this?

The role of company directors and HR professionals

Critics such as Bebchuk and Fried (2004) argue that the day-to-day power and knowledge at CEOs' command continues to allow them to manage their incentive plans to suit their personal economic interests. This suggests that company boards of directors, as representatives of the shareholders, need to be more vigilant and independent in linking executive reward to organisational performance. Indeed, in many corporate governance systems, accountability for decisions about executive pay level and composition has been tightened over a 30-year period from the Cadbury Committee Report in the UK, in which listed companies were encouraged to establish separate remuneration subcommittees of the main board in order to focus on this issue. The most recent of these changes allows shareholders to have a legislated right to a 'say on pay' in some countries, such as Australia and the USA, for top executives of companies in which they own shares (Shields et al., 2016). However, despite committees, executive remuneration experts, increases in the number of independent directors, and 'say on pay', concerns about executive pay continue.

So what role do and can HR professionals play?

Arguably, it is the responsibility of HR practitioners to alert boards to the effects on staff motivation and

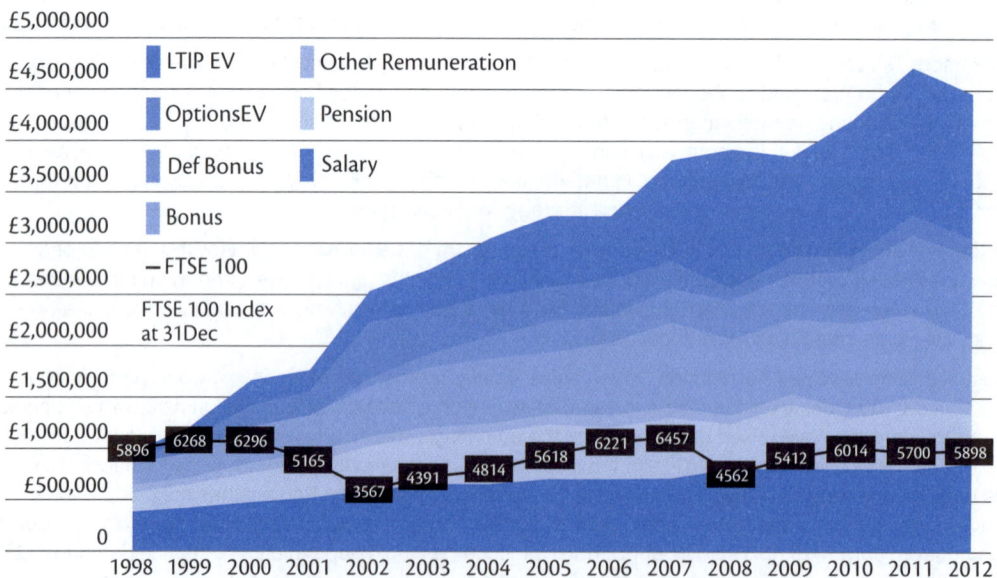

Figure 10.1 Comparison of executive pay and FTSE 100 Index, United Kingdom 1998–2012
Source: UK High Pay Centre (2012: 20).

perceived fairness arising from gaps between executive and nonexecutive rewards. This is essentially an organisational issue of perceived distributive injustice. For example, several studies have found that the greater the degree of vertical pay dispersion (i.e. the pay differential between lower-level employees and senior managers), the greater the degree of lower-level dissonance and the less the degree of lower-level commitment, cooperation, effort, and attention to quality (Byrne and Bongiorno, 1997). Given the published differentials between executive and nonexecutive remuneration (Kiatpongsan and Norton, 2014), HR professionals can no longer pretend that such matters are beyond their sphere of accountability. Executive pay has emerged as a pivotal ethical challenge for the HR profession. Executive misbehaviour has a profound effect on the motivation and wellbeing of other organisational employees and hence on the domain of the HR practitioner on both fairness and ethical grounds. This poses both a major challenge and a key opportunity for HR managers, since it involves engaging directors and senior executives in a critical dialogue about social responsibility and justice. Strategic reward management may well be another domain in which HR professionals can demonstrate significant organisational leadership.

This leads us to our final area of reward management interest, the international perspective.

INTERNATIONAL REWARD MANAGEMENT

Most of the reward concepts and tools that we have discussed so far have emerged in Western business contexts and are thus informed by Western assumptions about the nature of the employment 'deal'. Yet whether they are engaged in international joint venture operations with host country partners or in direct investment in subsidiaries in one or more host countries, firms with an international or multinational business focus – that is, MNCs – have to meet reward challenges that are often very different from those applicable to domestic employees. These cross-border differences are relevant to three main groups of employee:

- host-country nationals (HCNs) hired to work in the MNC's operations in the host country;
- home-country employees sent abroad (that is, 'expatriated') for periods of time to manage or work in operations in host countries;
- employees from other countries – third-country nationals (TCNs) – hired to work in either the home- or host-country operations.

Given the particular social, cultural, legal-institutional, economic and political context within which they live and their boundaries, HCN employees may have very different reward expectations from those in the firm's home base, as well as from expatriates and TCNs. For instance, in some countries, such as India and Indonesia, employees have a strong cultural respect for hierarchy and equally strong attachments to a stable, long-term employment relationship and to customary allowances and benefits. Managing base pay and benefits for HCN employees thus requires that the conditions and traditions of the host country be carefully taken into account.

In order to maintain reward consistency, some MNCs export the main elements of their home country reward practice to their subsidiary operations in other countries (an 'exporter' or 'ethnocentric' approach). Others seek to adapt to local or regional conditions (an 'adaptor' or 'polycentric' approach), while still others apply a blend of home and host practices at either a national level (a 'geocentric approach') or a regional level (a 'regiocentric' approach). This means not only being aware of the reward expectations and entitlements of HCNs but also having to make careful choices about how to reward local employees in order to establish and maintain a positive employment relationship (Bloom et al., 2003; Dowling et al., 2008).

Likewise, in configuring reward packages for expatriates, the MNC must decide whether it wishes to benchmark the level and mix of its rewards against parent country standards, host country standards, or a blend of home and host or home and regional standards.

On this basis, we can identify three broad approaches towards configuring expatriate rewards:

- the home-based or 'balance sheet' approach;
- the host-based or 'going rate' approach;
- the region-based approach.

Home-based approach

This approach, which remains the preferred approach in Western MNCs, aims to maintain a relativity of rewards against those of home country employees while providing a beneficial inducement to compensate for the employee's foreign assignment. In essence, the approach links the expatriate reward level to the home country pay structure and seeks to preserve home country purchasing power and living standards by means of a 'balance sheet' of compensatory financial adjustments.

The approach typically covers four main reward components:

> *Base salary*: the main component that serves as a benchmark for other components.

A foreign service inducement, relocation or 'hardship' premium: to attract home country employees to accept an expatriate assignment or to compensate them for any hardship associated with a foreign assignment.

Allowances: to compensate for any potential diminution in living standards relative to home standards, including cost of goods and services, housing expenses, and differences in income tax liabilities.

Benefits: including pension/superannuation contributions, health and medical insurance, social security, education expenses, and paid leave entitlements (Dowling et al., 2008).

While the balance sheet approach preserves an equitable relationship between expatriate reward levels and those remaining in the parent entity, the approach may create a considerable pay discrepancy between expatriates and HCNs performing similar roles. In low-pay countries, such as India and China, this may trigger internal perceptions of inequity/distributive injustice among HCNs (Dowling et al., 2008; Watson and Singh, 2005).

Host-based approach

Here, the base salary is linked to salary levels in the host country, partly with a view to maintaining an equitable relationship in reward levels between the parent firm and HCNs. In general, if prevailing pay rates in the host country are high by international standards, the firm may have little choice but to match the local market. Conversely, if local pay levels are low by international standards, as is the case in most developing countries, the firm will typically augment its employees' base pay with additional allowances and benefits in order to attract home country and third country expatriates (Dowling et al., 2008).

The 'going rate approach' is relatively uncomplicated, sets a common standard for expatriates from both the parent country and third countries, reinforces expatriates' identification with the host country, and institutes a degree of equality with HCN salaries. Conversely, a strict adherence to the going rate approach will make it difficult to attract expatriates to low-pay locations, while the prospect of major variations in pay level from one posting to the next may be equally damaging.

Region-based approach

In essence, this is the remuneration approach typical of a geocentric staffing strategy and is especially well suited to a staffing strategy emphasising labour mobility on a regional or a global scale and selection of the best person for the position, irrespective of nationality. With such an approach, remuneration levels will need to be expressed in a major global currency, such as the US dollar, or a regional currency, such as the Euro. The global approach also relies on the MNC developing a set of reward principles, policies, and practices that fits its global strategy, structure, and culture. The chief tenet of this approach is the marriage of competitiveness and flexibility of rewards at the local or regional scale, especially by allowing subsidiary managers the autonomy to configure the base pay, benefits, and incentives in line with local standards. There must also be consistency in the worldwide application of a set of 'core' reward principles, including, for instance, performance-based recognition and reward differentiation (Bloom et al., 2003; Watson and Singh, 2005).

Class Activity

▸ What are the three main differences between an 'exporter' and an 'adaptor' approach to managing the rewards of host country employees?

CONCLUSION

For many organisations operating within and between countries, employee rewards constitute the single largest operating expense. How – and how well – an employee reward system is designed, implemented, communicated, and maintained can make the difference between the success and failure of the organisation. Reward management is difficult to do well and easy to mismanage. The efficacy and fairness of reward practice is also the subject of an ongoing and robust debate.

This chapter has explored employee reward management from three perspectives: the critical, the applied, and the international. Each perspective invokes different assumptions regarding the role of rewards in the employment relationship; each also carries different implications regarding the efficacy and fairness of rewards.

The *critical approach* alerts us to the dangers of 'unitarist' assumptions about the nature, meaning, and influence of employee rewards. In essence, we have argued for a pluralist, or multistakeholder, framework for both understanding and 'managing' rewards. What is a cost to the organisation is income and economic security to the employee, and what is valued by the organisation may have little meaning or value for its employees.

In this sense, our exploration of the debate on the relative merits of extrinsic and intrinsic rewards serves to highlight the indeterminate nature of the relationship between the rewards on offer and the employees' reactions. Just as it is unsafe to assume that monetary rewards are invariably the primary motivator, so is it problematic to suppose that every employee is galvanised by the prospect of work that is inherently challenging and task-diverse. The key point here is that employees are not simply 'resource' objects but, rather, are organisational stakeholders with their own distinct needs, expectations, and rights, as well as responsibilities and contractual obligations to their employer.

A critical pluralist perspective also alerts us to the changing nature and significance of the employees' voice in how rewards are determined. As we have seen, this 'say in pay' may take various forms: individual or collective; union or non-union; formal or informal; direct or indirect. Indeed, it is erroneous to think of the structure, type, and level of rewards as being free of employee influence – that is, as being an artefact of unconstrained managerial discretion. Employee voice and agency continue to have an important bearing on setting pay, whether directly and collectively via the unions' collective bargaining activity, indirectly via minimum pay bodies and industrial tribunals, or by means of individual employees' choices about the worth and equity of the rewards on offer.

The *applied approach* draws attention to the vast variety of reward practices – and to the factors that should be taken into account in choosing between them. Here we have focused on the distinction between job- and person-based base pay, between fixed and flexible benefits plans, between individual and group performance pay plans, and between cash, non-cash, and equity-based plans. We have also considered the general strengths and weaknesses of each major pay plan type, as well as examining debates on both the effectiveness and fairness of

incentive plans and other performance-related reward practices. This has included an examination of the special case of executive remuneration plans. In essence, the chapter argues for an applied approach to reward management that favours 'best fit' over 'best practice'. In other words, the choice of plan type and structure of rewards, including horizontal and vertical pay dispersion and pay variability, should reflect the organisation's particular strategy, structure, and environmental circumstances rather than any supposed 'one best way' to configure the reward system.

The *international approach* draws attention to the wider context and the additional challenges and options associated with the management of reward systems in cross-border contexts. What works well in one country may be highly problematic in another country and national culture. Equally, however, this itself poses a major strategic challenge to MNCs based in home countries with strong national cultures: should their approach to international reward management simply reflect the home country practice, or should they seek to adapt to the practices of the host country and culture? Like the USA and Japan before it, China is now the archetypal instance of a strong home country culture. The end-of-chapter case study on the reward strategies and practices of Chinese MNCs accentuates the complexities of reward management for managing line employees' and expatriates' rewards in host country contexts that vary markedly from that of the parent entity's home country.

In sum, managing pay and other forms of reward is one of the most challenging and sensitive facets of contemporary HRM, while reward management itself is one of the most controversial areas of human resource practice. Perhaps more than with any other human resources process, it also allows human resources strategists to demonstrate their worth in terms of organisational effectiveness. Equally, effective reward management demands high-order competencies in organisational and behavioural analysis, as well as solid abilities in strategic decision-making, communication, and human resource leadership. For these reasons, it can also be immensely rewarding in its own right.

End of Chapter Case Study The strategy and practice of rewards in Chinese MNCs

The People's Republic of China now plays a central role in global economic growth and development, and Chinese state-owned enterprises and private firms are rapidly internationalising their operations in both developed and developing economies. China is a global economic power and yet a country that is still 'developing' rather than 'developed'.

Transition in Chinese domestic reward practices

Under China's old planned economy, Chinese domestic employment practices were based on long-term job security, lifelong social security, pay structures characterised by low dispersion/egalitarianism and group-based rather than individual incentives. The principal pay system was the national wage scales, which were determined by central legislation and regional government agencies and were configured differently for blue- and white-collar employees. Pay differences between low-skilled workers, skilled workers, and managers were minimal, and wage increases were infrequent and primarily took the form of nationwide grade promotions for all employees (Dowling et al., 2008). The combination of egalitarian pay structures and the 'iron rice bowl' model, which addressed workers' basic needs through free housing, schooling, and medical care, gave employees few extrinsic incentives to improve their performance or pursue promotion.

Since the 1980s, however, government controls have eased and firms have been given more autonomy to configure their own reward systems, albeit still within government guidelines. Job size has replaced age/seniority as the main determinant of reward level, and rising education levels have begun to influence pay differences. A performance-related reward approach in the form of an efficiency-based bonus has also been introduced to replace the grade-based system. Despite these changes, seniority and egalitarianism remain key characteristics of Chinese domestic reward practice, pay dispersion remains low, and enterprises tend to favour group bonuses over those of an individual nature.

International reward management in Chinese MNCs: A ten-company case study

How, then, do Chinese MNCs approach international reward management? Do they seek to export domestic practices or are they more adaptive and innovative in their cross-border approach? Does their approach emulate that of Western MNCs or do they take a different and perhaps uniquely Chinese path?

One of the few studies to date to have examined the reward practices of Chinese MNCs, that by Shen (2004), provides revealing evidence on these and related questions. Shen's study used a semi-structured, interview-based survey to collect data from ten Chinese MNCs with subsidiaries in the UK. Of these case study companies, seven were state-owned enterprises covering a variety of industries – from banking and technology importing to airlines and shipping – while the remaining three were share-issuing companies in the electronics and health products fields.

Shen's study found that the pattern of reward practice in the case organisations was company-specific rather than simply being a reflection of national or industry factors. An example of this pattern can be found in the technology industries where leading internationally focused Chinese technology firms have been able to attract and retain high quality employees, outbidding leading US rivals such as Google (Gu, 2015). On the basis of the evidence generated, Shen identified four different approaches to international reward management in the companies studied:

- host-based;
- home salary plus host-based;
- contract-based;
- diplomat-based.

Rewards for host-country nationals

All ten companies used the host-based approach for non-executive HCNs and a contract-based approach for HCN executives, with pay levels for HCNs commonly set quite high by UK standards. For HCN non-executives, the pay package generally included a fixed salary contract plus an individual merit bonus, typically of two to three months' additional salary based on an individual performance appraisal. The contract-based system applied to HCN executives differed from both home- and host-based practices in that the pay package was negotiated directly between the individual manager and the firm's headquarters, with payment based on a combination of individual capability, project importance, and divisional performance.

Expatriate rewards

For Chinese employees expatriated to a UK subsidiary, Shen's study identified three distinct reward approaches. In two firms, expatriates received a host-based salary plus their old home salary. One company adopted a negotiable contact-based approach identical to that applied to HCN executives; this emphasised individual capability, how important the project was, and the assignment location.

The other seven companies used a post-based approach for their expatriates, with the pay package including a fixed position-based salary, a post-based individual performance bonus, and a range of additional payments. The fixed component was much higher than for home-based employees. Bonuses were linked to divisional or departmental performance or to the status of the managerial post. This post-based approach, which accentuates hierarchy, originally used by the Chinese Foreign Ministry for international postings and now widely used by Chinese MNCs, is also commonly known as the 'diplomat-based' approach. In all cases, a uniform approach was applied to expatriate reward throughout all divisions within the subsidiary.

The Chinese dual model: The best of both worlds?

This heterogeneity is very different from the situation with domestic operations in Chinese enterprises, where companies tend to adopt a uniform approach to reward management. The contract and home-plus-host approaches are negotiable and based chiefly on individual capability and performance, compared with domestic reward practice under which pay is position-based and essentially non-negotiable. On this basis, Shen concluded that 'Chinese [international HRM] is more progressive than domestic HRM in adopting modern Western HRM concepts' (Shen, 2004: 23).

However, Shen's study showed in addition that this process of adaption also had uniquely Chinese characteristics, such that the firms involved could be seen as pursuing a 'dual' approach to international reward management. Even though the approaches taken were noticeably different from home-based reward practices, they also differed from the three standard approaches typically specified in the Western literature – host-based, home-based, and region-based. The firms involved adopted a 'best fit' approach that took account of both firm- and employee-specific factors, with reward practices tailored to employees' nationalities and their position in the organisational hierarchy. Under the dual model, HCN reward was either host-based or contract-based, whereas expatriate reward varied substantially from firm to firm. According to Shen (2004), the dual model reflected the 'dilemma' of Chinese MNCs wanting both to embrace international practices, in order to encourage an international transfer of talent, while at the same time maintaining close control over reward practices in their subsidiaries so as to limit the discrepancy between domestic practices and expatriate experience.

Factors influencing reward strategy and practice in Chinese MNCs

The study also showed that the reward strategies and practices adopted were influenced more strongly by some firm-level and contextual factors than by others. Reward strategies were shaped chiefly by the firm's international competitive strategy, its degree of reliance on international markets, and senior management's perception of the efficacy and appropriateness of the Chinese domestic reward system. However, inter-firm differences in actual reward practices, including reward structures and levels, were determined by a combination of three main contextual factors – legal, economic, and sociocultural – and by several firm-specific factors, most notably the industry in which the firm is involved.

Turning first to contextual factors, pay levels were generous by both Chinese and UK standards in order to attract high-quality home and host country managers and professionals. The firms studied also placed much weight on conformity to host country mandatory requirements, including minimum pay rates and paid leave entitlements. In a significant departure from home country practice, all companies also offered expatriates paid holiday leave, although, as Shen suggests (2004), the relatively high levels of base pay and benefits for HNCs need to be weighed against the fact that the firms studied offered HCNs almost no opportunity for development, promotion or transfer to the parent entity.

The dual approach to host- and home-sourced employees also reflected the cultural differences between China and the UK. Chinese practice is that the salary is non-negotiable, set according to position, level, seniority and the firm's overall performance, and not specified in the employment contract. However, with UK HNCs, the need to negotiate pay packages that would attract, retain and motivate local talent meant that this dual approach was embraced uniformly by all of the case companies, as was the use of individual performance bonuses. This host-based approach was also applied selectively to some expatriates, although egalitarianism remained the dominant consideration in relation to this group.

The study also highlighted the influence of a number of firm-specific factors. Regarding the impact of international HRM strategy generally, while two companies embraced a universal host-based approach to rewarding both HCN and expatriate employees, the majority of companies sought to retain control over expatriate reward expectations by means of diplomat- and contract-based approaches. Companies pursuing a polycentric approach to staffing were more likely to favour host-based reward practices, whereas those favouring ethnocentric staffing tended to adopt the diplomat-based approach.

The attitudes of senior management to home and host reward models were also influential. All firms judged the Chinese model to be unsuitable for HCN employees. However, there were differences in perceptions of the transferability of the Chinese model to expatriates, with some companies opting for a host-plus-home-based approach, and others preferring a more cautious contract-based solution. The nature of the industry itself also had an impact, with individual performance pay more likely to be applied to employees in trading enterprises and sales offices than elsewhere. In addition, reliance on and exposure to international markets was an important factor: firms with a relatively low reliance on international markets were more likely to prioritise egalitarianism over pay competitiveness, chiefly via the diplomat-based approach. Conversely, firms with a high reliance on international markets were more inclined to favour host-based standards.

Interestingly, Shen's study suggests that a range of firm-specific factors commonly assumed to influence reward practices – factors such as organisational structure, organisational culture, international experience and the size of international operations – appeared to have little impact in this sample of firms.

In sum, Shen's ten-firm case study highlights the dual approach to international reward management taken by these Chinese firms, the characteristically Chinese approach to the adaptor or 'host' strategy, the tension between the objectives of egalitarianism and competitiveness in reward practice, and the complex array of home country, host country and firm-specific factors that serve to shape strategies and practices related to international rewards. Although it remains to be seen whether further internationalisation will weaken the preference of Chinese MNC for a dual approach to international reward management, it is very likely that China's rapidly rising importance in the global economy will mean that Chinese firms will exercise far greater influence over global rewards in the decades to come.

Questions

1 Do you think that the 'dual' approach to international reward management preferred by Chinese MNCs is sustainable over the longer term as Chinese firms become progressively more integrated into the global economy?
2 If Chinese MNCs are to make greater use of HCNs in their staffing, how might they best modify their reward practices to support this change?
3 As China consolidates its position as an economic superpower, how might the reward practices preferred by Chinese MNCs influence trends in international reward management?

FOR DISCUSSION AND REVISION

Questions

1 Why should a firm use base pay at all?
2 Why do gender pay gaps persist, who is responsible for them, and what (if anything) can be done about them?
3 What makes for an effective employee share plan?
4 What are the obvious signs of failure of a performance and reward system?

Exercises

1 Break the class into pairs and allocate the following pay practices to a specific pair of students. Have each pair consider the pros and cons of their assigned pay practice as a means of furthering pay equity between the genders, and then have each pair report back to the full group. The practices are:
   - points factor job evaluation;
   - skill-based pay;
   - competency-based broadbanding;
   - flexible benefits;
   - merit raises;
   - discretionary bonuses.
2 As the human resources director of an MNC with a subsidiary operation in Indonesia, you have been asked to design a comprehensive reward system for the subsidiary's HCNs. What reward practices would you use?
3 Your UK-based organisation is planning to open a major facility (eventually employing 5,000 people) in Thailand, for which your team will be responsible. Senior management has asked you to assess the impact that cultural values will have on using traditional UK reward

practices for the HCNs there and to propose a comprehensive reward system for the new facility. Specifically, you are required to address the following issues:

- the pros and cons of replicating in the Thai context the large pay differences between more senior executives, mid-level managers, and the hourly workforce that apply in the UK context;
- the possibility of using incentive pay programmes driven by individual performance;
- identification of the benefits that employees will place a high value on, and those they will place a low value on;
- identification of work rules or traditions that may be different from those in the UK.

In making your assessment, you should refer to Hofstede's cultural dimension scores for the parent and host countries, which are available at: http://www.geert-hofstede.com/hofstede_dimensions.php.

GLOSSARY

Base salary: Pay received for a given work period, such as an hour or week, but not including additional pay, such as for overtime work. It is used as the basis for calculating other allowances and benefits.

Bonus: A reward or payment (either discretionary or non-discretionary) based on the performance of an individual, a group of workers, a business unit, or an entire workforce.

Motivation: The degree to which an individual wants and chooses to engage in certain specific behaviours.

Performance-related reward: Such schemes include incentives and rewards given on the basis of employee performance either individually or collectively. An 'incentive' is a payment made on the basis of performance in order to reinforce and enhance future performance.

Reward management: The formulation and implementation of strategies and policies that aim to reward people fairly, equitably, and consistently in accordance with their value to the organisation.

FURTHER READING

Books

ARMSTRONG, M. AND BROWN, D. (2006) *Strategic Reward: How Organisations Add Value through Reward*. London: Kogan Page.
A UK text with an applied focus and practical examples of innovative reward practices.

ARMSTRONG, M. AND MURLIS, H. (2007) *Reward Management: A Handbook of Remuneration Strategy and Practice* (revd 5th edn). London: Kogan Page and Hay Group.
The standard UK practitioner text in the rewards field, taking an applied rather than a critical focus.

GERHART, B. AND RYNES, S. (2003) *Compensation: Theory, Evidence, and Strategic Implications*. London: Sage.
A US text offering an excellent coverage of research and concepts related to reward management.

GOMEZ-MEJIA, L.R., BERRONE, P. AND FRANO-SANTOS, M. (2010) *Compensation and Organizational Performance*. New York: M.E. Sharpe.
A sophisticated coverage of reward-system design issues and reward-system influence on organisational performance.

GOMEZ-MEJIA, L. R. AND WERNER, S. (eds) (2008) *Global Compensation: Foundations and Perspectives*. London: Routledge.
Contains several solid chapters on the theory and practice of international rewards.

GREENE, R. J. (2010) *Rewarding Performance: Guiding Principles; Custom Strategies*. New York: Routledge.
Provides an insightful and practical coverage of performance pay practices.

GUTHRIE, J. P. (2015) Remuneration: Pay effects at work. In Boxall, P., Purcell, J. and Wright, P. (eds), *The Oxford Handbook of Human Resource Management*. Oxford: Oxford University Press, pp. 344–369.
An illuminating overview of theories and evidence on the effects of reward plans.

HENDERSON, R. I. (2006) *Compensation Management in a Knowledge-based World* (10th edn). Upper Saddle River, NJ: Prentice Hall.
A US text offering a solid coverage of applied aspects of reward management.

LONG, R. (2006) *Strategic Compensation in Canada* (3rd edn). Toronto: Thomson Nelson.
Provides both a solid coverage of Canadian reward practice and a clear and persuasive discussion of the relationship between reward practices and organisational strategy, structure, and management culture.

MARTOCCHIO, J. J. (2009) *Strategic Compensation: A Human Resource Management Approach* (5th edn). Upper Saddle River, NJ: Pearson/Prentice Hall.
A US text offering a solid coverage of applied aspects of reward management.

MILKOVICH, G., NEWMAN, J. AND GERHART, B. (2011) *Compensation* (10th edn). New York: McGraw-Hill Irwin,.
A leading US text in the rewards management field.

PERKINS, S. AND WHITE, G. (2011) *Employee Reward: Alternatives, Consequences and Contexts* (2nd edn). London: Chartered Institute for Personnel and Development.

Offers a fresh and an insightful treatment of reward theory and practice from a UK perspective.

RYNES, S. L. AND GERHART, B. (eds) (2000) *Compensation in Organisations: Current Research and Practice*. San Francisco: Jossey Bass.

A multiauthor text offering a detailed and sophisticated coverage of the strategic and psychological dimensions of employee rewards. Retains value despite its publication date.

SHIELDS, J., BROWN, M., KAINE, S., DOLLE-SAMUEL, C., NORTH-SAMARDZIC, A., MCLEAN, P., JOHNS, R., O'LEARY, P., PLIMMER, G. AND ROBINSON, J. (2016) *Managing Employee Performance and Reward: Concepts, Practices, Strategies* (2nd edn). Melbourne: Cambridge University Press.

Offers an integrated coverage of performance and reward management from a 'best fit' perspective.

WHITE, G. AND DRUCKER, J. (eds) (2009) *Reward Management: A Critical Text* (2nd edn). London: Routledge.

The second edition of a multiauthor text with chapters covering all key aspects of reward practice from various critical perspectives.

WorldatWork (2007) *The WorldatWork Handbook of Compensation, Benefits and Total Rewards*. New York: Wiley.

Offers an encyclopaedic coverage of rewards practices for line employees and executives. The text is informed by a unitarist rather than a critical perspective. WorldatWork is the leading US body representing reward professionals.

WRIGHT, A. (2004) *Reward Management in Context*. London: Chartered Institute of Personnel and Development.

Another useful UK text.

Journals

GERHART, B., RYNES, S. AND FULMER, I. (2009) Pay and performance: Individuals, groups, and executives. *Academy of Management Annals*, 3(1): 251–315.

Provides a provocative but circumspect and evidence-based argument in support of incentive plans for executives and line employees.

TREVOR, J. AND BROWN, W. (2014) The limits on pay as a strategic tool: Obstacles to alignment in non-union environments. *British Journal of Industrial Relations*. 53(3): 553–578.

A conceptual and empirical critique of the managerialist strategic alignment approach to reward configutation.

WERNER, S. AND WARD, S. (2004) Recent compensation research: An eclectic review. *Human Resource Management Review*, 14: 201–227.

A meticulous and high-level survey of rewards research and conceptual models for explaining the configuration and influence of reward systems. Particularly useful for framing research topics and models in the rewards field.

Web resources

Chartered Institute for Personnel and Development. Reward Management. Available at: http://www.cipd.co.uk/subjects/pay/default.htm.

A UK professional body website carrying information on rewards practices and strategies, including survey data.

E-Reward UK. About e-reward. Available at: http://www.e-reward.co.uk/about.asp.

A UK proprietary research organisation website providing information on reward practices, strategies, and case studies.

WorldatWork. Available at: http://www.worldatwork.org/waw/home/html/home.jsp.

A US professional body website carrying information on rewards practices and strategies, including survey data.

REFERENCES

ACTU Executive PayWatch (2010) Available at: http://www.actu.org.au/our-work/policy-issues. Accessed 18 November 2015.

ARMSTRONG M. AND BROWN D. (1998) Relating competencies to pay: The UK experience. *Compensation and Benefits Review*, May–June: 28–39.

Australian Council of Superannuation Investors (2015) *CEO Pay in ASX200 Companies*. Melbourne: ASCI.

BARRETT, G. V. (1991) Comparison of skill-based pay with traditional job evaluation techniques. *Human Resource Management Review*, 1: 97–105.

BEBCHUK, L .A. AND FRIED, J. (2004) *Pay without Performance: The Unfulfilled Promise of Executive Compensation*. Cambridge, MA, and London, England: Harvard University Press.

BEER, M. AND CANNON, M. D. (2004) Promise and peril in implementing pay-for-performance. *Human Resource Management*, 43(1): 3–20; critical commentaries 21–50.

BENNETT STEWART, G. III, APPLEBAUM, E., BEER, M., LEBBY, A. M, AMABILE, T. M., MCADAMS, J., KOZLOWSKI L. D., BAKER, G. P. III AND WOLTERS, D. S. (1993) Rethinking rewards. *Harvard Business Review*, 71(6): 37–49.

BLOOM, M. (1999), The performance effects of pay dispersion on individuals and 0rganizations. *Academy of Management Journal*, 42(1): 25–40.

BLOOM, M., MILKOVICH, G. AND MITRA, A. (2003) International compensation: Learning from how managers respond to variations in local host contexts. *International Journal of Human Resource Management*, December: 1350–1367.

Bloomberg (2015) Well-Being Rankings Prove Money Isn't Everything. Available at: http://www.bloomberg.com/news/videos/2015-06-26/well-being-rankings-prove-money-isn-t-everything.

BROWN, D. AND PURCELL, J. (2007) Reward management: On the line. *Compensation and Benefits Review*, 39(3): 28–34.

BYRNE, J. A AND BONGIORNO, L. (1997) How ordinary workers feel when fat cats get the cream. *Management Development Review*, 10(4/5): 164–165.

CALHOUN, C. (2013) Occupy Wall Street in perspective. *British Journal of Sociology*, 64 (1): 26–38.

CAMERON, J. AND PIERCE, D. (1997) Rewards, interest and performance: An evaluation of experimental findings. *ACA Journal/WorldatWork Journal*, 6(4): 6–15.

CANAVAN, J. (2008) Overcoming the challenge of aligning skill-based pay levels to the external market. *WorldatWork Journal*, 17(1): 18–25.

CASTLE, S. (2011) European Union salaries a haven for Eastern Europeans. *New York Times*, 8 March. Available at: http://www.nytimes.com/2011/03/09/world/europe/09latvia.html?_r=1. Accessed 20 January 2016.

Chartered Institute of Personnel and Development (2015) *Annual Survey Report: Reward Management 2014–15*. London: CIPD.

COLELLA, A., PAETZOLD, R. L., ZARDKOOHI, A. AND WESSON, M. J. (2007) Exposing pay secrecy. *Academy of Management Review*, 32(1): 55–71.

COSTAS, J. AND GREY, C. (2014). The temporality of power and the power of temporality: Imaginary future selves in professional service firms. *Organization Studies*, 35(6): 909–937.

COTTON, C. AND CHAPMAN, J. (2010) Rewards in the UK: Top 10 risks. *Workspan*, 53(1): 53–57.

CUMMING, C. (1994) Incentives that really do motivate. *Compensation and Benefits Review*, May–June: 38–40.

DALTON, G. (1998) The glass wall: Shattering the myth that alternative rewards won't work with unions. *Compensation and Benefits Review*, 30(6): 38–45.

DAY, N.E. (2012), Pay equity as a mediator of the relationships among attitudes and communication about pay level determination and pay secrecy. *Journal of Leadership and Organizational Studies*, 19(4): 440–454.

DAY, N. E. (2014) What the research says about pay secrecy. *WorldatWork Journal*, Fourth Quarter: 102–110.

DECI, E. L. AND RYAN, R. M. (1985) *Intrinsic Motivation and Self-determination in Human Behavior*. New York: Plenum Press.

DOWLING, P. J., WELCH, D. E. AND SCHULER, R. S. (2008) *International Human Resource Management: Managing People in a Multinational Context* (5th edn). Melbourne: Cengage Learning.

ENGLAND, P. AND KILBOURNE, B. (1991) Using job evaluation to achieve pay equity. *International Journal of Public Administration*, 14(5): 823–843.

ERTUK, I., FROUD, J., JOHAL, S. AND WILLIAMS, K. (2005) Pay for corporate performance or pay as social division? Rethinking the problem of top management pay in giant corporations. *Competition and Change*, 9(1): 49–74.

EVANS, E., HILLINS, J. F., MCNALLY, K. A., ZINGHEIM, P. K., BAHNER, R. R. AND WILSON, T. B. (1995) A series of essays about how rewards can succeed. *ACA Journal*, 4(2): 20–35.

FSA (Financial Services Authority) (2009) The Turner Review: A regulatory response to the global banking crisis, March. Available at: http//www.fsa.gov.ukpubsother-turner-review.pdf.

GAGNE, M. AND DECI, E. L. (2005) Self-determination theory and work motivation. *Journal of Organizational Behavior*, 26: 331–362.

GAVETT, G. (2014) CEOs get paid too much, according to pretty much everyone in the world. *Harvard Business Review Online*, 23 September. Available at: https://hbr.org/2014/09/ceos-get-paid-too-much-according-to-pretty-much-everyone-in-the-world/. Accessed 13 November 2015.

GERHART, B. AND RYNES, S. (2003) *Compensation: Theory, Evidence, and Strategic Implications*. Thousand Oaks, CA: Sage.

GERHART, B., RYNES, S. AND FULMER, I. S. (2009) Pay and performance: Individuals, groups, and executives. *Academy of Management Annals*, 3(1): 251–315.

GETTLER, L. (2010) Shares and share alike. *HR Monthly*, March: 29–33.

GRANT, D. AND SHIELDS, J. (2006) Identifying the subject: Worker identity as discursively contested terrain. In Hearn, M. and Michelson, G. (eds), *Rethinking Work: Time, Space and Discourse*. Melbourne: Cambridge University Press, pp. 285–307.

GU, W., (2015) The people's money: It's all in a day's perk at Chinese tech firms. *Wall Street Journal Asia*, 6 February: 1. Available at: http://search.proquest.com.ezproxy2.library.usyd.edu.au/docview/1651613157/F88E11338B2D42C7PQ/2?accountid=14757. Accessed 26 October 2015.

GUPTA, N. AND CONWAY, S. (2013) Evidence-based lessons about financial incentives and pay variations. *WorldatWork Journal*, Second Quarter: 7–16.

GUPTA, N. AND DELERY, J.E. (2002) Pay dispersion and workforce performance: Moderating effects of incentives and interdependence. *Strategic Management Journal*, 41: 511–525.

GUPTA, N. AND JENKINS, G. D. (1991) Practical problems in using job evaluation systems to determine compensation. *Human Resource Management Review*, 1(2): 133–144.

GUPTA, N. AND MITRA, A. (1998) The value of financial incentives: Myths and empirical realities. *ACA Journal/ WorldatWork Journal*, 7(3): 58–66.

GUPTA, N. AND SHAW, J. (1998) Let the evidence speak: Financial incentives are effective!! *Compensation and Benefits Review*, 30(2): 26, 28–32.

GUPTA, N. AND SHAW, J. D. (2011), A comparative examination of traditional and skill-based pay plans, *Journal of Managerial Psychology*, 26(4): 278–296.

HAIPETER, T. (2011) Works councils as actors in collective bargaining: Derogations and the development of code-termination in the German chemical and metalworking industries. *Economic and Industrial Democracy*. epub 22 February. doi: 10.1177/0143831X10393039.

HEERY, E. (1996) Risk, representation and the 'new pay'. *Personnel Review*, 25(6): 54–65.

HENEMAN, R. L. AND LEBLANC, P. (2002) Developing a more relevant and competitive approach for valuing knowledge work. *Compensation and Benefits Review*, 34(4): 43–47.

HENEMAN, R. L. AND LEBLANC P. (2003) Work valuation addresses shortcomings of both job evaluation and market pricing. *Compensation and Benefits Review*, 35(1): 7–11.

HENEMAN, R. L. AND VON HIPPLE C. (1995) Balancing group and individual rewards: rewarding individual contributions to the team. *Compensation and Benefits Review*, 27(4): 63–8.

High Pay Centre, (2012). One Law Who's Deciding For Them On Pay? How Big Companies Flout Rules The Make Up Of Remuneration Committees On Executive Pay. Available from: www.highpaycentre.org/pubs/one-law-for-them-how-big-companies-flout-rules-on-executive-pay [accessed 17 October 2015].

HOFRICHTER, D. AND MCGOVERN, T. (2001) People, competencies and performance: Clarifying means and ends. *Compensation and Benefits Review*, 33(4): 34–38.

HOFSTEDE, G. (1984) *Culture's Consequences*. London: Sage.

HOU, W., PRIEM, R. L. AND GORANOVA, M. (2014) Does one size fit all? Investigating pay-future performance relationships over the 'Seasons' of CEO tenure. *Journal of Management*, 20(10, 4): 1–28.

JENSEN, M. AND MURPHY, K. (1990) Performance pay and top-management incentives. *Journal of Political Economy*, 98(2): 225–264

JENSEN, M., MURPHY, D. AND WRUCK, E. (2004) Remuneration: Where we've Been, how we got here, what are the problems, and how to fix them. Papers SSRN.com.

KAARSEMAKER, E. AND POUTSMA, E. (2006) The fit of employee ownership with other human resource management practices: Theoretical and empirical suggestions regarding the existence of an ownership high-performance work system. *Economic and Industrial Democracy*, 27(4): 669–685.

KENNAUGH, W. (2015) The truth about incentives. *Sydney Morning Herald*, 31 October. Available at: http://www.smh.com.au/business/workplace-relations/the-truth-about-incentives-20151031-gknln9.html. Accessed 21 October 2015.

KIATPONGSAN, S. AND NORTON. I (2014) How much (more) should CEOs make? A universal desire for more equal pay. *Perspectives on Psychological Science*, November (9): 587–593.

KIM, D.-O. AND VOOS, P. (1997) Unionisation, union involvement, and the performance of gainsharing programs. *Industrial Relations/Relations Industrielles*, 52(2): 304–332.

KOHN, A. (1993a) *Punished by Rewards*. Boston: Houghton Mifflin.

KOHN, A. (1993b) Why incentive plans cannot work. *Harvard Business Review*, 71(5): 54–63.

KRAUSE-JACKSON, F. AND YOON, S. (2015) Money isn't everything: The 10 happiest countries in the world. Sydney Morning Herald, June 26. Available at: http://www.smh.com.au/printArticle?id=997606975.

LANG, J. M. (2008) Human resources in India: Retaining and motivating staff in a Lufthansa subsidiary. *Compensation and Benefits Review*, 40: 56–62.

LAWLER, E. E. (1988) What's wrong with pointfactor job evaluation. *Compensation and Benefits Review*, 18(2): 20–28.

LAWLER, E. E. (1990) *Strategic Pay: Aligning Organizational Strategies and Pay Systems*. San Francisco: Jossey-Bass.

LEDFORD, G. E. (1991a) Three case studies on skill-based pay: An overview. *Compensation and Benefits Review*, 23(2): 11–23.

LEDFORD, G. E. (1991b) The design of skill-based pay plans. In Rock, M. and Berger, L. (eds), *The Compensation Handbook: A State of the Art Guide to Compensation Strategy and Design* (3rd edn). New York: McGraw-Hill, pp. 199–217.

LEDFORD, G. E. (2008) Factors affecting the long-term success of skill-based pay. *WorldatWork Journal*, 17(1): 6–17.

LEDFORD, G., GERHART, B. AND FANG, M. (2013) Negative effects of extrinsic rewards on intrinsic motivation: More smoke than fire. *WorldatWork Journal*, Second Quarter: 17–29.

LEDFORD, G. E. AND HENEMAN, R. L. (1999) Pay for skills, knowledge and competencies. In Berger, L. A. and Berger, D. R. (eds), *The Compensation Handbook. A State-of-the-Art Guide to Compensation Strategy and Design* (4th edn). McGraw-Hill, pp. 143–56.

LEHNDORFF, S., BOSCH, G., HAIPETER, T. AND LATNIAK, E. (2009) The vulnerability of an export champion:

Upheaval in the German employment model. Paper presented at the Annual Congress of the International Industrial Relations Association (IIRA), Sydney, Australia, August.

LINDROP, E. (2009) Employee voice in pay determination. In White, G. and Drucker, J. (eds), *Reward Management. A Critical Text* (2nd edn). London: Routledge, pp. 41–45.

LONG, R. (2006) *Strategic Compensation in Canada* (3rd edn). Scarborough, ON: Thomson Nelson, pp. 187–213.

LONG, R. AND SHIELDS, J. (2009) Do unions affect pay methods of Canadian firms? A longitudinal study. *Relations Industrielles/Industrial Relations*, 64(3): 442–465.

MCADAMS, J. L. (1999) Non-monetary rewards: Cash equivalents and tangible awards. In Berger, L. A. and Berger, D. R. (eds), *The Compensation Handbook: A State-of-the-Art Guide to Compensation Strategy and Design* (4th edn). New York: McGraw-Hill, pp. 241–260.

MERRIMAN, K. K. (2009) On the folly of rewarding team performance, while hoping for teamwork. *Compensation and Benefits Review*, 41(1): 61–66.

MORAN, P. AND GHOSHAL, S. (1996) Bad for practice: A critique of the transaction cost theory. *Academy of Management Review*, 21(1): 13–47.

MUELLER, F., CARTER, C., AND ROSS-SMITH, A. (2011) Making sense of career in a Big Four accounting firm. *Current Sociology*, 59(4), 551–567.

MURRAY, B. AND GERHART, B. (2000) Skill-based pay and skill seeking. *Human Resource Management Review*, 10(3): 271–287.

NELSON, B. (1994) *1001 Ways to Reward Employees*. New York: Workman Publishing.

PENDLETON, A. (2009) Employee share ownership in Europe. In White, G. and Drucker, J. (eds), *Reward Management: A Critical Text* (2nd edn). London: Routledge, pp. 224–244.

PEPPER, A., GORE, J. AND CROSSMAN, A. (2013) Are long-term incentive plans an effective and efficient way of motivating senior executives? *Human Resource Management Journal*, 23(1): 36–51.

PERKINS, S. J. AND VARTIAINEN, M. (2010) European reward management? Introducing the special issue. *Thunderbird International Business Review*, 52(3): 175–187.

PERKINS, S. J. AND WHITE, G. (2011) *Employee Reward: Alternatives, Consequences and Contexts* (2nd edn). London: Chartered Institute of Personnel and Development.

PINK, D. (2009) *Drive: The Surprising Truth about What Motivates Us*. New York: Riverhead Books.

ROBINSON, F. AND WINNING, N. (2011) EU nations may only get stay of execution on indexation. *Wall Street Journal*, 7 March. Available at: http://online.wsj.com/article/BT-CO-20110307-710793.html. Accessed 20 March 2011.

ROSEN, A. S. AND TURETSKY, D. (2002) Broadbanding: The construction of a career management framework. *WorldatWork Journal*, 11(4): 45–55.

RUBERY, J. (1995) Performance-related pay and the prospects for gender pay equity. *Journal of Management Studies*, 32(5): 637–653.

RYNES, S. L., GERHART B. AND PARK, L. (2005) Personnel psychology: Performance evaluation and pay for performance. *Annual Review of Psychology*, 56: 571–600.

SALIMAKI, A., HAKONEN, A. AND HENEMAN, R. L. (2009) Managers generating meaning for pay: A test for reflection theory. *Journal of Managerial Psychology*, 24(2), 161–177.

SHAW, J. D. AND GUPTA, N. (2015) Let the evidence speak again! Financial incentives are more effective than we thought. *Human Resource Management Journal*, 25(3): 281–293.

SHEN, J. (2004) Compensation in Chinese multinationals. *Compensation and Benefits Review*, 36: 15–25.

SHIELDS, J., BROWN, M., KAINE, S., DOLLE-SAMUEL, C., NORTH-SAMARDZIC, A., MCLEAN, P., JOHNS, R., O'LEARY, P., PLIMMER, G. AND ROBINSON, J. (2016) *Managing Employee Performance and Reward: Concepts, Practices, Strategies* (2nd edn). Melbourne: Cambridge University Press.

SHIELDS, J., SCOTT, D., SPERLING, R. AND HIGGINS, T. (2009) Rewards communication in Australia: A survey of policies and programs. *Compensation and Benefits Review*, 41(6): 14–26.

SHRIVASTAVA, P. AND IVANOVA, O. (2015) Inequality, corporate legitimacy and the Occupy Wall Street movement. *Human Relations*. 68(7), 1209–1231.

TOSI, H. L., WERNER, S., KATZ, J. P. AND GOMEZ-MEJIA, L. R. (2000) How much does performance matter? A meta-analysis of CEO pay studies. *Journal of Management*, 26: 301–339.

TOWNLEY, B. (1993a) Foucault, power/knowledge, and its relevance for human resource management. *Academy of Management Review*, 18(3): 518–545.

TOWNLEY, B. (1993b) Performance appraisal and the emergence of management. *Journal of Management Studies*, 31(2): 221–238.

TOWNLEY, B. (1994) *Reframing Human Resource Management: Power, Ethics and the Subject at Work*. London: Sage.

TOWNLEY, B. (1998) Beyond good and evil: Depth and division in the management of human resources. In McKinlay, A. and Starkey, K. (eds), *Foucault, Management and Organization Theory*. London: Sage, pp. 191–210.

TOWNLEY, B. (1999) Nietzsche, competencies and Übermensch: Reflections on human and inhuman resource management. *Organization*, 6(2): 285–306.

WATSON, B. W. AND SINGH, G. (2005) Global pay systems: Compensation in support of a multinational strategy. *Compensation and Benefits Review*, January/February: 33–36.

WATSON, T. (2004) HRM and critical social science analysis. *Journal of Management Studies*, 41(3): 447–467.

WIGGINS, J. (2015) WorleyParsons taps US for new executive bonus scheme. *Sydney Morning Herald*, 14 October, p. 26.

WRIGHT, A. (2009) Benefits. In White, G. and Druker, J. (eds), *Reward Management. A Critical Text* (2nd edn). London: Routledge, pp. 174–191.

YEOH, P. (2015) Corporate governance in the UK: A time for reflection. *Business Law Review*, 36(4): 130–135.

ZINGHEIM, K. P. AND SCHUSTER, J. R. (2012) Skill pay successes: Managing the challenges. *WorldatWork Journal*, Third Quarter: 29–41.

TRAINING, DEVELOPMENT AND LEARNING

Peter A. Murray

LEARNING OUTCOMES

After reading this chapter, students should be able to:

➤ Understand the differences between training and learning
➤ Distinguish between the more classical approaches to training and more contemporary training and learning strategies
➤ Explore needs and person assessments in relation to building the human capital pool of an organisation in a global context
➤ Reflect on individual differences in training, development, and learning (TDL) and explore various training methods
➤ Apply organisational needs with performance capability matched to broader organisational and global strategies
➤ Analyse the relationship between knowledge and learning and ways to implement knowledge-sharing strategies
➤ Explore and apply different narratives in learning and their influence on performance
➤ Reflect on contemporary issues in learning such as digital and e-learning
➤ Specify how to solve training problems by analysing case study material.

SUMMARY OF CHAPTER CONTENTS

➤ **Opening Case Study**: Changying Precision Technology
➤ Introduction
➤ Training, development, and learning concepts
➤ Remaking history: from training to learning
➤ From classical to contemporary training methods
➤ Learning for international environments
➤ Conclusion
➤ **End of Chapter Case Study**: Ericsson
➤ For discussion and revision
➤ Glossary
➤ Further reading
➤ Web resources
➤ References

Opening Case Study **Changying Precision Technology**

Chinese factories such as Changying Precision Technology (CPT) raises interesting training dilemmas and hiring patterns for HRM practitioners in that country. The company has adopted Australian robotic technology called 'Sawyer', which is different from position-controlled robots employed in car companies in the USA. Since labour costs are increasing by 15per cent per year in China, and with millennial workers not interested in factory work, this has meant a combination of high turnover of 20–25 per cent a month coupled with high training and acquisition costs. Workforce realities has led companies such as CPT to shift the focus of work from leveraging people to leveraging robots. As we see in this chapter, this is high-quality situated learning in response to rapid innovation around competing markets. In China's case, the introduction of robotic technology conforms to the country's plan to become the global manufacturing leader by 2049. Interestingly, the exporter of the product from Australia, 'Rethink Robotics', suggests that 'as companies are deploying more and more of these robots, they're hiring people that are not roboticists, not automation engineers, but supervisors. Only now, their personnel on the production line are not just people; now they're people and robots. In many cases the people on the line are training. You don't program these robots; you show them what to do' (TechRepublic, 2015a; 2015b).

You will notice the links between this case and other chapters on human resource planning and recruitment and selection. In an emerging economy such as China, the training, development, and learning implications are significant. While traditional training is focused around on-the-job and off-the-job training, contemporary training and development is increasingly moving towards technology solutions, hard in terms of physical technology and soft in terms of social technology platforms such as Google, Twitter, LinkedIn, and others, plus the increasing functionality of Apps that create individual and organisational learning opportunities. At CPT, the robot might replace up to 20 people who performed tasks consecutively. Now, one supervisor simply shows the robot what to do, then says 'Go'. Previously, CPT had 650 workers however with the advent of new technology, this has reduced to 60 according to the company's General Manager (TechRepublic, 2015a; 2015b). Together with manufacturing technology, the rapid take-up of the internet in countries such as China because of low barriers to entry suggest that Internet-enabled offerings, including enterprise cloud services such as infrastructure as a service, platforms as a service and software as a service, make it possible for businesses to take advantage of advanced information technology capabilities while minimising upfront expenditures. For emerging countries, access to new technology (hard and soft) suggests that training agendas will change. External factors such as higher pay, the type of work on offer, and increasing familiarity around technology suggest that training and development priorities in China will move away from on-the-job coaching of hundreds of workers to fewer workers where learning priorities change on the basis of strategy and competition. Robots plus the rise of social technology platforms create future challenges (and opportunities) for HRM training and development.

Questions

1   How is computer technology changing the way people learn? The frequency of learning?
2   What demands for training and development will appear for workers in emerging economies? Why?
3   Massive workforces demand jobs, yet potential conflicts exist between technology platforms (hard and soft) and traditional work. How would you explain these conflicts in places of work?

INTRODUCTION

This chapter discusses and explores a number of critical issues related to training, development, and learning (TDL). It does this by highlighting the differences between the terms, reflecting on older, more classical approaches to training versus more contemporary and recent trends that are more situation- or context-specific. Such context-specificity means that the older approaches to training, although useful, have to be rethought. More recent trends in global organisations such as technological advances, human expectations of what constitutes a valuable job,

organisational expectations related to capabilities that match strategic business needs, and increased social interaction, have meant that the older approaches are now less valuable.

The discussion here explores the nuances and differences between individual and organisational learning including, but not limited to, developing versus recruiting workers, needs assessments linked to issues of training design and performance, various training and learning methods, the link between learning and knowledge, and critical issues within an international context. The chapter is designed to take readers from the existing normative and traditional views of TDL to a more critical creative viewpoint that is context-specific.

TRAINING, DEVELOPMENT, AND LEARNING CONCEPTS

First, there are differences between 'training', 'development' and 'learning' that should be noted. *Training* can be thought of as a kind of formal learning process provided in the workplace that might include training for a discrete job or role (Gibb, 2003). As we discuss later, however, training does not always lead to learning (Antonacopoulou, 1999), or to learning that can be applied in the workplace (Cortese, 2005; Izak, 2015).

Development is tied to training since organisations want to increase the capabilities and skills of their workers or 'develop' them in such a way that skill levels increase. The notion of development then extends to changing the whole person by helping people to grow (Gibb, 2003). However, this is not necessarily confined to skill enhancement. In fact, the original idea of human resources development came from the behavioural school of management in the 1930s and 1940s (Fulop et al., 1992). This was associated with a refocusing away from the more efficiency-driven approach of managing people at work (essentially seeing people at work as machines) to an approach developed in the 1920s by Elton Mayo (a Harvard Business School professor) that helped people excel in their workplace through better human relations and by recognising the power of social factors (Rose, 1975).

Learning is about a demonstrated change in the level of knowledge displayed by individuals (Gibb, 2008). However, it is also about recognising that individuals have different learning styles such that people 'learn' in different ways and at a different rate from other learners (Honey and Mumford, 1986, cited in Allinson and Hayes, 1996). In addition, learning incorporates, but is not limited to, narrative, storytelling and language (Dailey and Browning, 2014; Plesner and Gulbrandsen, 2015), adaptive and emergent learning (Espedal, 2008) and e-learning and digital learning (Peacock and Grande, 2016). For instance, the increasing focus on e-learning and digital learning represents a challenge for traditional classroom training techniques and social media are a rising phenomenon in this space. Consequently, organisations (and countries) can easily fall behind (McKinsey and Company, 2014a; Worly and Mohrman, 2014) in addressing skills gaps because of the pace of change and calls for new learning techniques. For the purposes of this chapter, 'learning' will closely follow what Antonacopoulou (2001: 328) describes as 'the liberation of knowledge through self-reflection and questioning' by developing a space through which common language and experiences can be observed. The nuances between the terms in TDL should be noted, but the important point is that one aspect cannot be useful without the others.

REMAKING HISTORY: FROM TRAINING TO LEARNING

Contrasting classical views of training

Think of imperatives or needs for training. Most countries have had similar needs for training within business enterprises, but the path and history of their experiences has been different. It is not the purpose of this section to trace the history of training country by country in a chronological way. However, it is useful to reflect on why the traditional, more standardised approaches to training that are common to different countries have had far-reaching implications for modern-day or contemporary training methods. We can do this by contrasting the classical and contemporary views of training by exploring four different themes.

In the first theme, we will examine the variation in training experiences between the UK and Australia. Although many differences are present, both countries have seen a similar evolution in terms of training and similar systems of governance. Although the discussion is limited to two countries, training methods as a means of increasing resources and capabilities are remarkably similar across all countries, meaning that training methods are somewhat universal in application; they may not be applied in exactly the same way, yet the foundations for training are almost identical. The development of the strategic human capital pool, for instance, is a worldwide phenomenon (Boxall and Macky, 2009; Clardy, 2008; Wright et al., 2001) in which training plays a key role.

In the second theme, we will analyse the external and internal organisational factors that drive training and learning and are common to all organisations irrespective of their geographical location. The factors that drive organisational change are for the most part the same factors that drive training agendas. Although the topics covered by the chapters in this book are integrated, job design and redesign are organisational factors that generally lead to a training needs analysis (TNA), suggesting that, in a world of fast-changing contexts, the stated intentions of training should be matched to the strategic needs of the business.

In the third theme, we will look at more recent research findings that influence training outcomes. We are particularly interested in organisational training consistent with the chapter's purpose of understanding what organisations should be doing with respect to TDL.

For the fourth theme, we will explore and contrast classical and contemporary training methods. Some questions to ask of this theme concern individual differences, social interaction and the generation of knowledge. That is, to what extent do the two approaches – classical and contemporary – contribute to a learner's ability to capture and share knowledge?

Classical views

Let's look at the first theme. From the early 1900s, the emphasis was mainly on establishing apprenticeships, meeting the skills requirements for all kinds of occupational persuasion from mechanical and building skills to engineering and architectural skills. The former, more 'blue-collar' occupations were typically confined to trade halls and institutional colleges around the globe, such as technical schools in the UK and technical and further education colleges in Australia. In comparison, training and teaching for professionals was always the domain of the universities. Many of the latter in the UK were established by counties, whereas in Australia these were Commonwealth institutions run by university councils and academic boards.

For technical training, priority was given to supervisory and technical staff, and most teaching occurred at night. It is useful here to point out that, for most of the twentieth century, training has been mostly focused on teaching a sell-and-tell, systematic and highly structured approach (Antonacopoulou, 1999). While the classical approaches will be outlined more clearly in theme four, training was typically thought of in terms of classroom instruction (university or technical), on-the-job (supervisor to worker), or off-the-job (attending a training course) learning. Training also occurred through vocational training or occupational or professional training for individuals (not always in a university but, for example, in a vocational college), and action learning (such as employees working in a cross-functional team). Out of these, classroom instruction was the most common.

Technical training did not extend to ordinary workers. Training for the latter depended on the organisational imperative for training, that is, the connection between business growth and training (Jones, 2004). Early approaches to skills were focused on just three skill types: technical, conceptual, and people. Generally, it was commonly thought that workers needed only technical skills, whereas managers required thinking ability related to conceptual and people skills. In terms of learning, with its simplistic attachment to skills, it is understandable why organisations advanced slowly in relation to connecting skills development with learning outcomes that matched organisational needs.

In the News   Capabilities for change

Many managers are good at budgeting, controlling, and carrying out shorter-term strategic change related to continuous learning or incremental learning; however, they are often not equipped with the capabilities required for large-scale change and learning. The questions for all managers (not just the HRM department) are how do we develop change skills; how do we train for them? These questions place a priority on managers to identify individuals with the right skills; another priority is to perform skills audits to identify the gaps and then provide training to meet these. The skills audits are not the sole responsibility of the HRM department. All managers now are expected to know what skills their workers require and to work with HRM to close skill gaps. One whole-scale misconception is that this is the responsibility of the HRM department. One can't be a manager unless one knows which capabilities and skills are needed at work. Now the HR department will assist with this plus help managers identify more skills, for example innovation and learning capability, that might be incorporated into a needs analysis of a staff skills audit. However, as noted in one of the Critical Reflection boxes, contemporary managers in 2016 and beyond need to think about the capabilities they require in an integrated way. Some key questions for managers to answer are: What kind of skills do I need in my department or SBU going forward? How can I match these to the overall strategies of the organisation? What specific training is required? And how do I develop an integrated approach? See the reference in this chapter to McKinsey and Company (2014a, 2014b).

As an aside, the training that occurred in organisations across much of the world through to the 1960s was very much efficiency driven and, as discussed earlier, focused more on occupational than individual needs (Fulop et al., 1992). In recognition of the latter, both the UK and Australia established a training system based on a national vocational qualification framework that has played an important role in increased skill development. This involves gaining nationally recognised qualifications that may or may not meet an organisation's needs (De Ceiri and Kramar, 2008); principally however, these national vocations systems have been designed to help people find work.

In terms of our first theme, the notion of training for ordinary workers was not really part of the earlier technical approaches, and tailored training for individual differences was not even considered. Training for the professions was mainly the domain of universities, where a qualification was more careers-focused. For individual learning, the earlier approaches were systematic and ad hoc (Antonacopoulou, 2006). In fact, technical-type instruction was generally considered poor (CIPD, 2009), and organisations considered this to be more of a cost than an investment (Smith, 2003).

In Australia, for instance, it was not until 1989 that a training reform agenda was established via a National Training Board, together with a new competency-based training system. These initiatives led to the training guarantee scheme in which enterprises with payroll costs in excess of A$200,000 were required to spend at least 1.5 per cent of their payroll on 'structured' training for their workers (Smith, 2003). These schemes have now been abandoned, and it is a matter of conjecture whether employing organisations spend enough on training. Recent research by Sheehan et al. (2006) of 1,372 senior human resources professionals found that only 54 per cent of managers felt that organisations were placing enough emphasis on developing training policies and practices to attract and retain talent.

In contrast, in the UK, some of these initiatives occurred much earlier through the Industry Training Act of 1964 and various training schemes. However, not dissimilar to the situation in Australia, industry training boards were replaced by enterprise councils, which in turn were replaced by sector skills councils (CIPD, 2009). In both countries, and indeed in much of the developed world, a benchmark or yardstick is often used to measure how much one country lags behind another in terms of its skills and the education of its workforce, including manufactured outputs. Here, both the UK and Australia show similar experiences, systems of reforms, and relative failures in educational investment.

Taken together, these older classical approaches and ideas for training remain dominant. Within the context of this chapter, they need to be contrasted with contemporary practices that are both critical and more reflective. Importantly, however, it is questionable whether the classical approaches are still relevant for the workers of today, who need greater flexibility and more socially interactive approaches to systems of instruction.

Overall, the classical approaches remain quite rigid, very systematic, highly structured and inflexible in terms of their scope and type of learning (Beckett and Murray, 2000). Even for most universities, it is questionable whether existing lecture theatres and halls familiar to baby-boomer and generation X professors are suitable for predominately generation Y learners and millennials who favour e-learning techniques and familiar discussion forums in which their peers participate (CIPD, 2008; Conway and Monks, 2008; Khanna and New, 2008). What this indicates for modern learners is that instructional preference has most probably shifted to a variety of training techniques that facilitate deeper learning and knowledge acquisition (see theme four below).

Needs assessment and discontinuous change

In moving to theme two, one can contrast the old classical approach to work and training needs with discontinuous markets. From earlier twentieth-century and post-war priorities for training, dramatic changes in the design of work became evident. This meant that training and learning changed fundamentally from about midway through the 1960s, moving from a more structured approach to a more holistic and flexible approach that valued workers' input into the actual design of programmes.

There are important lessons for trainers and managers to be learned from earlier failures. For the most part, older production failures point to inadequate needs assessments that were poorly articulated into training strategies. Understanding organisational and job needs is as important as understanding work design and redesign (see Chapter 7). Training and learning should be matched to strategic goals in such a way that training makes a real difference to learning outcomes. In fact, a useful question to ask is" if we separate the idea of developing skills and capabilities from the learning methods or training techniques that underpin them, what are we left with? Learning methods for instance have to be matched to strategy and strategy is always influenced by change. While we don't focus on change here in any significant way, some authors have indicated that the old ways of training for change are obsolete. For instance, Worly and Mohrman (2014) and suggest that the old ways of training for change (often called the old normal) had clear starts and ends; however, the new ways of training for change (or new normal) is more about taking stock of continuous, dynamic and shifting forces, similar to what companies are constantly facing related to discontinuities in existing systems (Malhotra and Hinings, 2015). The difference appears to be that these discontinuities and shocks are not punctuated 'every now and then', rather, they occur frequently meaning old theories and processes of learning and change may not be relevant for sustained competitive disequilibrium. For instance, Worly and Mohrman suggest that 'scholars have not provided organisations and the managers who run them with the frameworks to handle the pressure for more frequent fundamental change'. (2014: 216).

The strategic aspect of training is about structuring work in such a way that managers get the best out of their people (Antonacopoulou, 2006; Wright et al., 2001). In relation to these earlier approaches, it is useful to ask how structured learning was complemented by critical and creative thinking. To make training and learning really count, more efficient job design approaches focus on finding out about what is required for a job in the form of person, task and *organisational needs assessments* (Nankervis et al., 2008).

Before training can be articulated into training methods, some type of job analysis needs to occur. This requires trainers/managers to collect information related to a job description (lists of tasks, duties, and responsibilities), position descriptions related to work behaviours, work conditions and job characteristics, all linked to some way of measuring an employee's performance at a later date. For instance, graphic rating scales are used to measure performance (rating attributes from, for example, poor = 1 to distinguished performance = 5) for each employee; behavioural ranked scales (defined behaviours exhibited) can also be used, as can some mixture of these methods. Generally, an organisation uses a standardised graphic and behavioural scale to measure all employee performance. Performance outcomes are a critical part of training in the sense that training should be linked to performance in order to determine whether workers have transferred training knowledge into demonstrated skills (Khanna and New, 2008).

But, getting back to job assessment, a position analysis questionnaire (PAQ) analysis is critical:

> The job analyst is asked to determine whether each item (*such as those on a position description*) applies to the job being analysed. The analyst then rates the item on six scales: extent of use, amount of time, importance to the job, possibility of occurrence, applicability and special code (special rating scales used with a particular item). These ratings are submitted to the PAQ headquarters where a computer program generates a report regarding the job's scores on the job dimensions. (De Ceiri and Kramar, 2008: 193; emphasis added)

But before human resources managers or any other managers can develop people at work, they require a clear idea of what is expected of each worker. This generally refers to a *training needs analysis* (TNA). Note that the latter is different from a job analysis or position needs assessment. Whereas a PAQ, for instance, ascertains what skills, attitudes, and behaviours are required for each job, it is then the task of the trainer to assess whether existing workers can adequately demonstrate these.

In one sense, TNA is about the systematic gathering of data to highlight gaps in the existing skill levels, knowledge, and abilities of workers (CIPD, 2009; Nankervis et al., 2008). These gaps are then matched to changed job requirements that job analysts need to assess. That is, as

organisations increasingly compete through discontinuous information, technological and process and manufacturing changes, job requirements/position descriptions alter in such a way that trainers/managers have to assess the gaps and train workers to close them. Thus, old skills and abilities need to be rematched with the new skills and abilities needed for new job functions and processes. TNA could extend to the whole organisation (providing the right capabilities to meet organisational strategies) for a specific project (new ways of working or reorganisation) or just to individuals (tying personal development and individual capabilities to those of the business) (CIPD, 2009; Wright et al., 2001). Table 11.1 encapsulates the discussion here. Human resources managers also have to grapple with estimating the size and focus of the human capital pool, given that workers will leave and that training methods need to be sufficient to replace the skills lost.

Training in practice

For theme three, trends and the evidence from training outcomes in Australia are mixed. In the mid-1990s, a study of senior human resources managers was conducted by Kramar and Lake (1997). This study of 331 organisations, investigating the nature of human resources policies, found that in the organisations whose training expenditure was known, about 50 per cent of employees received internal or external training and another 20 per cent received some form of training. That is, according to data from the Australian Bureau of Statistics, approximately 80 per cent per cent of Australian workers received some form of training from their employer (Smith, 2003).

In research conducted in 2001, the amounts spent on training as a proportion of total salaries and wages had increased in most countries, for example in the UK (3.6 per cent) and Singapore (3.1 per cent), followed by Denmark and the Netherlands (3.0 per cent and 2.8 per cent, respectively). Australia was ranked fifth (2.5 per cent) and, interestingly, the USA sixth (1.9 per cent) (Brown et al., 2001). In comparison, however, a more recent survey conducted by Deloitte and the Australian Industry Group of 500 CEOs in businesses of all sizes found that, as a consequence of the 2008/09 global downturn, the overall expenditure on training was reduced by 4.1 per cent in 2009/10 (Australian Industry Group, 2009). In this survey, a third of businesses planned to cut their training budgets, with four in five reducing their training expenditure by up to 20 per cent. At the employee entry level, 36.8 per cent of companies employing apprentices expected to reduce the number of apprentices they would train during 2009/10.

This is in stark contrast to the situation in large manufacturers, who have been attracted to new business opportunities in emerging markets such as China and

Table 11.1 Position analysis and training needs assessment for a production controller

Job requirements using PAQ, January 2010	Job analysis using PAQ, July 2011	Gap analysis from PAQ, August 2011	Training needs analysis and training methods to use
1. Information: how does this worker get information? 2. Mental processes: reasoning, decision-making, planning and information processes. 3. Job context: mixture of physical and social contexts.	1. Reports directly to manufacturing manager and purchasing manager. 2. High-level thinking, regular planning meetings; communicates processes to other factory workers. 3. Must show skills lying between technical requirements and individual consideration/ people in factory.	1. Now reports only to purchasing. More knowledge of purchasing required. 2. High-level thinking; planning meetings with assistant; now trains workers in safety; must conduct quality meetings. 3. Requires a statement of the impact on workers of new roll-out process technology.	1. On the job. Issue report 12b to production controller. 2. Should attend safety training; needs updates on quality control and legislation changes. Off-the-job training. 3. On the job. Issue report 21c to controller on process technology. Needs to attend training course on new technology. Team training necessary.
Desired behaviours			
1. Performs in a cooperative manner. 2. Is a team player. 3. Makes clear decisions linked to goals. 4. Assigns production tasks in a timely way. 5. Understands and implements quality features. 6. Focuses on achieving controlling tasks. 7. Identifies and fixes control barriers.	Note: from performance appraisal (PAP), December: 1. PAP high. 2. Team skills average. 3. Tends to work by herself. 4. Very good. 5. Quality control high. 6. Very task-oriented. 7. Some new goals need to be set.	Gap analysis extracted from behavioural ranked scales in PAP: Main concern is team skills. Leadership gaps appear in instructional techniques and some social skill is lacking concerning other managers.	Should attend a leadership course run externally. Cross-functional team training is recommended, as well as attending an off-the-job team training seminar. Would also benefit from reflective instructional techniques, learning from workers and increased social interaction.

Source: PAQ, position analysis questionnaire.

India. In a global survey of 446 executives from manufacturing companies headquartered in 31 different countries, 63 per cent of executives stated that training was an important talent management strategy in emerging markets (Deloitte, 2007). Yet in a US survey of 325 employees of companies with an annual revenue of $500 million or more, only 32 per cent stated that training and retention were a top talent priority (Deloitte, 2009).

So what do these mixed survey results indicate? To a large extent, they suggest that the amount expended on training is context-specific from one country to the next and that in times of global crisis, companies tend to slash their training budgets to save costs. The results also suggest that training is very much tied to strategic business goals. For instance, in the 2007 Deloitte global survey, approximately one-quarter of the executives surveyed found it difficult to attract qualified workers in China, India, Latin America, and Eastern Europe. In a more recent survey in 2012, a report by McKinsey and Company of global leaders across the globe found that the priority for training was shifting towards developing leaders across their organisation. While many senior leaders felt that they were meeting their leadership targets, leadership remained their organisation's top priority. Overall, 73 per cent were actively implementing solutions, and 70 per cent claimed to be realising a positive impact. Importantly, 91 per cent of respondents suggested that their organisations were changing leadership competency models to reflect current and future realities, increasing their efforts to measure leadership performance measured against leadership competencies (McKinsey and Company, 2012: 28–29). This suggests that training, development and learning is shifting to key focus areas to meet emerging global needs and increasingly tied to performance measures (McKinsey and Company, 2014a).

Perhaps another way to interpret the results is by speculating on the type of training. Almost uniformly, surveys reflect training metrics for traditional forms of instruction

Refer to the report by McKinsey and Company called 'The State of Human Capital 2012'. Now turn to pages 28 and 29 of this report. Interestingly, we can see other points that we could add to our chapter heading 'Training in Practice'. What we see are a number of other key areas of developing leaders such as the need to 1) tell a compelling story, 2) inspire innovation and creativity/open-source, 3) lead with empathy, 4) model adaptability. Under point 3 lies a need to develop social and emotional intelligence and an understanding of their own and others' limitations. In many ways, this is tied to point 1 and the need to tell a compelling story. Since many leaders do not possess the skills of story-telling and often lack the ability to develop social and emotional intelligence in others – much less themselves.

Questions

1 In what ways can HR help with this process?
2 How can we encourage and develop more social skills, interactive skills?
3 How will this benefit a learning culture in any organisation?

such as in-house and external training, yet they seldom include learning from social forms of interaction and networking, story-telling and recalling narratives based on experience, self-reflection and electronic learning.

Apart from poor management practices, another reason why training outcomes do not translate into practice is the shift from an employee-centred focus to a strategic focus on the part of human resource management professionals. Modern human resources professionals work with management to analyse and devise solutions for organisational problems (Brown et al., 2009). Increasing pressure and an emphasis on strategic goals has meant a shift away from personnel managers, who focused more on the employee, towards human resource management professionals, who focus more on matching human capital to strategic goals.

Many researchers now talk more about human resources professionals building the human capital stock in such a way that it adds to the business's strategic advantage (Wright et al., 2001; Boxall and Macky, 2009). For some commentators, this has created a conflict between the ability of human resources professionals to see the world from the workers' perspective and the need to build customer and shareholder value from the employer's perspective (Peterson, 2004; Ulrich and Brockbank, 2005; Brown et al., 2009). Although the study by Brown et al. found that human resources professionals simply incorporated the older personnel functions into their strategic roles, many HR professionals still spend less than a third of their time on employee-centred activities (Brown et al., 2009), including training (Australian Industry Group, 2009). Increasingly, both HR professionals and managers need to spend equal amounts of time on employee-centred activities and linking these to activities that build shareholder value.

In comparison, the governments of both the UK and Australia have changed their perspectives on the value of internal training matched to external pressures. Public sector reforms have been based on three driving forces. The first of these concerns the reshaping of organisational structure and management through a better control of finances and the monitoring of performance (Rainbird and Munro, 2003). The second is that most federal, state, and local governments (boroughs and counties in the UK) now tender contracts on a competitive basis, leading to a third driving force: the need to mimic the competitive pressures of the private sector. In both the UK and Australia, the establishment of quite complex training registers is common, and competency or skill ladders consisting of a training matrix for worker progression (Table 11.2) are well known in both the public and the private sector. In the National Health Service in the UK, for example, people from a relatively low skills base can move up and across a skills escalator through training and development, which provides an impetus for innovative approaches to 'growing your own staff' (Rainbird and Munro, 2003: 31).

From classical to contemporary training methods

Questioning the logic of learning

Earlier, we briefly highlighted typical training and learning methods common in human resources development, including formal classroom training, on-the-job and off-the-job instruction, and others. Figure 11.1 highlights the various forms of traditional and mechanistic training methods. The most common are on-the-job, off-the-job, and the traditional classroom instruction that many learners experience in school classrooms. The point is that traditional methods of instruction perpetuate the myth that these approaches are good for learning. As Bratton and Gold (2007) ask, though, 'good for whom?'

Traditional methods conform to a 'one best way' approach and propagate the conflict between labour and capital (Rainbird and Munro, 2003) in which workplace learning is related to managerial strategies of labour control from one perspective and workers' resistance from another. This is not to say that these forms of training

Table 11.2 Career skills ladder for a bank manager

Levels	Leadership	Budgeting/finance	Team skills	Customer relations
Branch manager	Leads the entire team in the branch	Competencies within the entire branch reporting	Can design, implement and grow teams	Designs customer programmes
Relationship manager	Leads the sales and marketing team	Can complete full budgets and reports	Can develop full team and skill enhancement	Demonstrates superior customer skills
Support manager lending	Leads several groups by demonstrating strong leadership skills	Completes reports and analyses results	Practises team analytical skills	Principles of marketing course
Assistant support manager, lending	Leads one small group and demonstrates performance	Can complete budgetary documentation	Analyse team behaviour	Advanced customer programme
Front desk 2	Leadership course 2	Financial planning course	Team development course	Customer programme
Front desk 1	Leadership course 1	Learn budgeting techniques.	How to act in a team setting	How to deal with customers

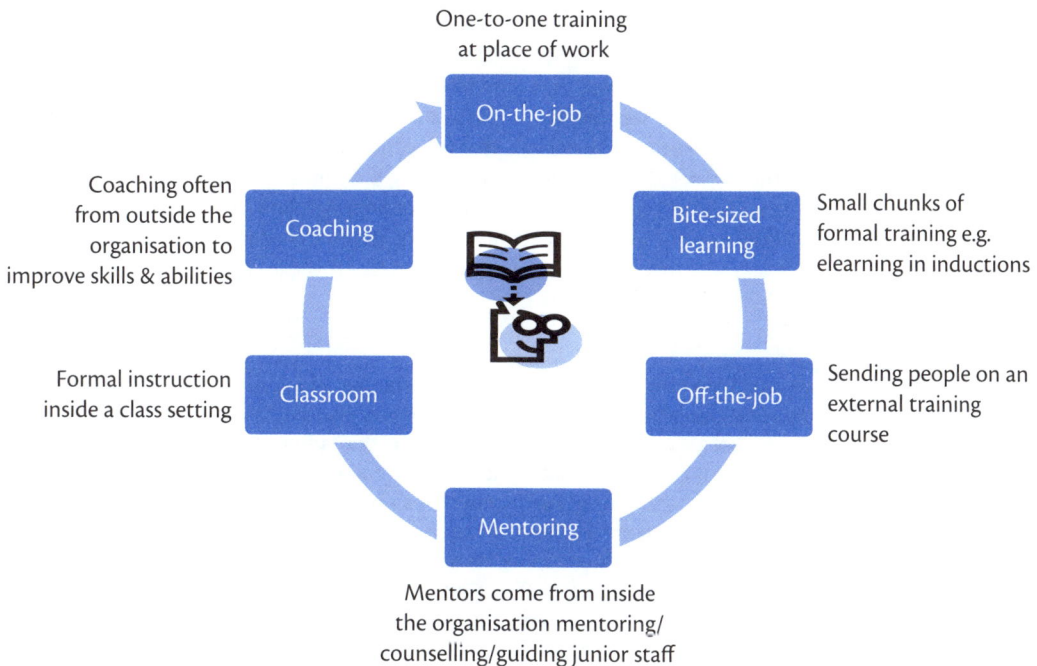

Figure 11.1 Typical traditional training methods

are outdated. Traditional or classical views still dominate learning in almost every university and college across the globe. However, it is becoming increasingly challenging for professors and organisational trainers to construct classroom learning in a way that young learners (generation Y) find interesting. So this begs the question of whether new learning should be challenging and much more reflective, as Bratton and Gold suggest:

It is increasingly being recognised that, rather than seeing organisations as single, unified and stable entities, a more pluralist and dynamic view needs to be adopted, composed of a set of ongoing activities and processes. It is within such activities and processes that people make sense of what they do and how work should occur, including what should and should not be learned ... *a learner may become aware that learning [from]* a *restructuring* has a cost and could undermine her or his collective relations with other employees. Employees may realise that the learning agenda belongs to management and that talk of corporate values, strategy and competencies is not neutral but rests on a dominant management ideology ... learning is about enhancing the ability of individuals and groups to learn. (2007: 337; emphasis added)

The flow of learning

Before we can explore different contemporary learning methods common to our fourth theme, let us for a moment note the difference between individual, group, and organisational learning, as well as the idea that every organisation has a culture for learning that reflects the dominant values and ideologies that we will call here the *learning climate*. Previous literature suggests that learning flows between different levels within the organisation (Crossan and Berdrow, 2003). A learning climate is the flow of beliefs between the individual, the group, and the organisational level. Individuals pass on their learning to teams, who in turn pass it on to the organisation (Crossan and Berdrow, 2003). In its turn, the organisation embeds the knowledge in its systems, processes and procedures before passing it back to new employees – and so the cycle of learning continues.

First, let's examine individual-level learning. According to Argyris and Schön (1978), individuals learn by engaging in a discover–choose–act cycle often called single-loop learning: they make choices from what they discover and then act on them. The problem here, however, is that no new learning occurs that challenges past assumptions. Think of a merchandising procedure within a retail store where the manager does all the training and possesses most of the knowledge. This may be satisfactory until he or she leaves and takes that knowledge away. The discovery process here might perhaps concern what other types of training are necessary to ensure that the knowledge is retained. The choice might be the manager passing on information in a traditional classroom setting. Several procedures and processes included in the training might, however, be challenged at a later date by other individuals, managers, or teams questioning the training methods and even the type of training conducted. This could lead to simple merchandising charts relating to particular merchandise that could be pasted onto the shop wall. This latter approach is one of double-loop learning. That is, individuals should be given the opportunity in the workplace to challenge, question and test the assumptions that drive most of the decisions they face. They do this by challenging a dominant or existent view, by questioning related assumptions, and by testing the old assumptions in a new conceptual model (Espedal, 2008; Hedberg, 1981; Kim, 1993;) (see the learning flows in Figure 11.2).

(?) **Critical Thinking 11.1**

In Chapter 2 of this book, we articulate how HRM is now more strategic. In addition to the narratives outlined by the chapter authors, strategic HRM can also be challenged by organisations that fundamentally see the HRM role as different from that of managers. For instance, let's examine this quote from Allen (2015: 1) 'executives and managers often think their job is to get financial results rather than to manage people. Second, when executives and managers neglect people management, the HR function worries about lapses and tends to "lean in" to right them itself. On the surface, this approach seems to meet an organisation's needs: management moves away from areas it views as unrewarding (and perhaps uncomfortable), while HR moves in, takes on responsibilities, solves problems, and gains some glory in the process' (TechRepublic, 2015a; 2015b). So what is going on here? HR managers and officers start to take on responsibilities that belong to business managers in other areas. On the one hand, the HRM function needs to be more strategic, but not so strategic that managers stop managing! The underlying pretext is that HRM officers might want to 'prove' their worth given debates about strategic human resource management (see Chapter 2). On the other hand, HRM officers are misinterpreting their role by trying to do the managers' work. If you asked questions about what role HR officers should occupy in comparison to a manager's role, how would they differ? The present chapter suggests that the underlying principle of HRM relates to training, development, and learning. Perhaps it is time for the HRM industry to rethink its role by becoming closer to human resource development practices rather than human resource management?

Questions

1   Should the HRM department develop and establish a company's leaders including determining how they lead? If not, why not?
2   Should the HRM department do the hard work of managing people? Develop a rationale for your answer.
3   HRM literature talks about 'managing up', but who should do this: managers or HRM executives/officers?

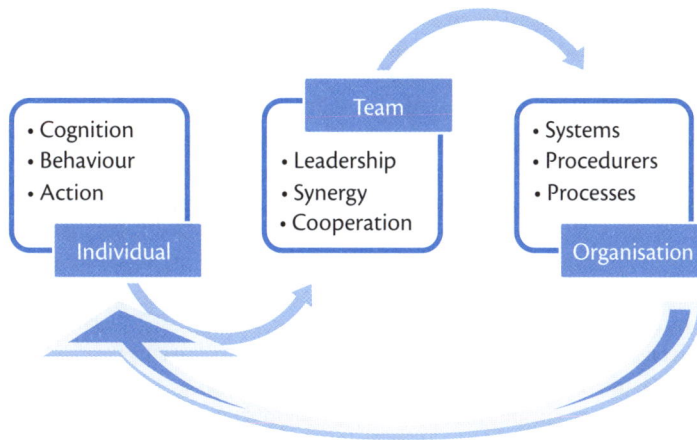

Figure 11.2 Flow of learning
Source: Adapted from Crossan et al. (1999: 524)

Another complementary idea is that individual learning is both a methodical and an emergent practice. Learning becomes standardised in organisational systems, methods and procedures, leading to *method-based* learning, that is, behaviour that enables a firm to constantly exploit its existing capabilities (March, 2006; Miller, 1996). This is lower-order learning associated with improving practices that are already known (Espedal, 2008). Conversely, the idea behind better learning is *emergent* learning, that is, higher-order learning associated with 'the changing of a logic of action that is known and experimentation with what is not known but might become known' (Espedal, 2008: 366). The latter is an extension of double-loop learning except that it has shifted to a more complex context, such as questioning existing decisions related to market development, for example, and whether these old decisions stand the test of time and competitive pressures in changing markets.

So from one perspective, individuals can be trained to think in double-loop terms, but so too can organisations through teamwork. Team members will most likely need training to understand how past decisions can be a stumbling block to new decisions that a team might have to negotiate. Organisations are only entities and of themselves do not learn; therefore they rely on individuals and teams to pass on learning in the form of existing knowledge or new knowledge learned. Now refer to the Stop and Reflect box 2 and the 'In the News Box' later in this chapter. The flow of learning is now dramatically influenced by social media and other applications. Importantly for trainers and managers, they can no longer separate constant virtual and digital forms of learning from these learning flows at the individual, team, and organisational

level. For instance, the influence of social media (software), smart-phones, and Big Data now co-constitute strategy. These new media forms are now being called *distributed strategy*. From a strategy and learning perspective, the environment is shrinking and subsequently challenging a managers 'control' over decision-making, including strategy. In contemporary organisations, social media is now challenging managerial control over strategic choice; software devices can enforce a 'particular form of collaboration' while 'hardware helps to enable third-party influence on company identity' (Plesner and Gulbrandsen, 2015: 156). Thus, rather than be constrained by forces outside the market, contemporary firms are using outside sources in different ways to help them develop strategic choices and identify what kind of learning should be matched to a firms external strategy. The point is that learning is not always something 'controlled' by internal trainers. These new forms of influence and learning are often described as a 'socio-technically constructed' approach because they cannot be avoided. An example would be creating online learning applications to encourage student and group learning (Peacock and Grande, 2016).

Social interaction in teams

The flow of learning is critical as noted; however, imagine that several staff have attended a valuable training course but the knowledge gained is tacit, held cognitively and not yet shared. Thus the flow of learning from the individual to the team will be interrupted. So how do trainers and managers facilitate a greater flow of knowledge between the two? If employees do not have an opportunity to share their tacit knowledge, then this knowledge will never be explained or demonstrated. For instance, Hu and Randel (2014: 215), contend that 'social capital within teams specifically involves resources such as access to information, mutual trust, and emotional support', meaning that these attributes are required for strong social relationships. What we are talking of here is social capital which can be thought of in one of three areas: 1) structural: the frequency of interaction among team members and the strength of ties among team members' 2) relational: trust, norms, obligations, and identification; and 3) cognitive: shared cognition such as transmitted information among team members. Hu and Randel suggest that 'social capital is more or less effective than extrinsic incentives in promoting knowledge sharing within a team', (214) most likely suggesting that social capital has an influence on team innovation.

Cognition and behaviour

Early theories of organisational learning fail to adequately address the relationship between cognitive structures (human thought processes) and the behavioural actions they give rise to (Hedberg, 1981). Many scholars suggest, for example, that changes in behaviour may occur without any cognitive development (Antonacopoulou, 2006; Cortese, 2005; Fiol and Lyles, 1985); conversely, the acquisition of knowledge – such as knowledge from a training course – may be gained without any accompanying change in behaviour (action that results from knowledge). This interplay between knowledge and behaviour means one of two things. That is, people might acquire knowledge but might not have the means to implement it; organisations might train people, for instance, but may not have the right workplace procedures available for people to practise the knowledge. Conversely, people might learn behaviours on the job but may not understand the reason why these behaviours are necessary, meaning that they will lack the knowledge to explain their actions. Creating change may be creating the illusion of learning such that management appears to be in control (Hedberg, 1981). Similarly, major behavioural change does not lead to a dramatic change in cognitive development. The creation of change may not be brought about by cognitive growth but merely by a need to do something (Antonacopoulou, 2001; Hedberg, 1981).

Carl Jung was one of the first theorists to try to make this connection by developing the idea of archetypes or cognitive patterns that structure thought and hence give order to the world (Jung, 1968; Morgan, 1997). Morgan explains how archetypes shape the way we 'meet ourselves' in encounters with the external world and are crucial for understanding links between conscious and unconscious aspects of the human psyche. Jung distinguished between two ways of perceiving reality (sensation and intuition) and two ways of judging (thinking and feeling):

- *Sensing–thinking* individuals tend, according to Jung, to make judgements and interpretations on the basis of 'hard facts' and logical analysis.
- *Sensing–feeling* individuals pay a great deal of attention to data derived from the senses, but arrive at judgements in terms of 'what feels right' rather than in terms of analysis.
- *Intuition–thinking* individuals tend to work their way through problems by thinking about the possibilities inherent in a situation. Their actions are guided by a combination of insight and feelings.
- *Intuition–feeling* individuals pay much more attention to values than to facts (Jung, in Morgan, 1997: 240–241).

The archetype patterns that guide thinking and action partly explain why managers find it difficult to link cognitive change with behavioural change. Managers often speak of frustration, for example, when trying to convert knowledge into action (Antonacopoulos, 2001). In trying to examine the archetypes from a workplace perspective, one can see that sensing–thinking individuals would be mainly concerned about the 'here and now' as hard facts would drive their decisions, whereas intuition–feeling individuals would relate more to concerns about the values and ideologies related to a problem.

A production manager who needs to meet targets knows exactly what she needs to do with her largely multicultural workers. However, a human resources manager who receives complaints about workplace conflict will want to analyse the problem based on values and individual differences. Whereas a production manager might solve the problem by 'getting on with it', the human resources manager wants to sit people down and talk about the problems. If a religious person is required to pray six times a day because of her religious practices, a sensor and pragmatist may say that this is not allowed and that all workers are only allowed three breaks in an eight-hour shift. A thinking–feeling manager, however, might see the logic in making a separate room available and allowing the worker to make up the time lost at a later date.

Honey and Mumford (cited in Allinson and Hayes, 1996) also suggest a complementary archetype system based on activists, reflectors, theorists and pragmatists:

- Similarly to Jung's classification, *activists* learn best when they use trial and error to discover something.
- *Reflectors*, however, learn best when given adequate time to digest, consider and prepare.

- *Theorists*, on the other, hand prefer a sound structure and a pattern or purpose, responding well to complex ideas that stretch their current thinking.
- Lastly, *pragmatists* learn best when given real-life practical issues to discuss.

Once again, the connection between cognition and behaviour should be noted. A manager may have several groups with different learning styles, and some groups will clearly learn more quickly than others. This is because the make-up of one group may consist of predominately sensors and pragmatists who want to make quick decisions based on 'facts'. However, this group may arrive at a decision prematurely without questioning the facts and assumptions. Another group, by comparison, may consist of both activists and theorists or some combination lying in between, allowing the group to question past actions and arrive at a better decision.

Kolb (1984) mixes the styles by suggesting a process loop in which concrete experience involves learning from the past. Learners then reflect on and observe their experiences, drawing from many perspectives (reflective observation) before integrating their thoughts into logically sound theories (abstract conceptualisation). Finally, they actively experiment with their decisions in light of the thinking process (active experimentation) (Bratton and Gold, 2007; Rylatt, 1994). Interestingly, in a class setting, have you ever wondered why some groups finish far earlier than others?

Knowledge management

Organisations have difficulty in dealing with knowledge sharing and knowledge conversion (Nonaka and Takeuchi, 1995) or even understanding what knowledge actually *is* and how it should be defined (Cook and Brown, 1999). Knowledge accumulation, knowledge sharing, and knowledge conversion are key resources in an organisation's capacity to turn capabilities into skills that make a difference in knowledge dissemination (Byosiere and Luethge, 2008; Eisenhardt and Martin, 2000). It is one thing to capture and store knowledge (Bassi, 1999) but quite another thing to share it so that its practical application is more evident throughout the organisation. While explicit and tacit knowledge is possessed by people, knowing is not about possession but about 'practice' and about interacting with the components of the social and physical world (Vera and Crossan, 2003: 126). As we discussed earlier, learning is valuable when the knowledge gained can be practised.

At the organisational level, knowledge is retained in systems, procedures, and policies by facilitating the formal articulation and codification of ideas (Arthur and Huntley, 2005). Learning behaviours will be required in practice to allow individuals and teams to express the 'know-what' and the 'know-how' by converting their knowledge into practice (Arthur

and Huntley, 2005; Brown and Duguid, 1991). One question is whether double-loop learning is evident in actions that allow individuals to convert the 'know-what' into 'know-how'. A second question concerns whether individuals themselves have acquired the right type of knowledge to make a significant contribution to the organisation. For knowledge to be useful for the organisation, individuals need to transform and challenge existing knowledge, often in groundbreaking ways that allow them to radically change and alter decisions (Crossan and Berdrow, 2003; Miller, 1996). Although learning is needed for knowledge conversion to occur, simple or basic training may not be enough to facilitate the knowledge conversion process (Byosiere and Luethge, 2008).

STOP AND REFLECT

Virtual learning models are growing in popularity in contemporary organisations. This seems partly due to the priority for learning and skill development priorities rapidly shifting in fast-change environments, the increasing speed of information technology and systems, and arising from this, the increasing pace of social media. According to the report by McKinsey and Company (2014b), millennials prefer social learning techniques to the more traditional learning face-to-face modes.

Questions

1 In these circumstances, how can contemporary organisations match the pace of learning?

2 How should their learning systems change and how can the HR department facilitate this?

3 If learners need to put into practise the knowledge they have acquired, how can organisational managers facilitate the process?

The knowledge conversion process can become a problem when not enough skills are in place through traditional training to convert knowledge into practice. For example, the conversion of tacit knowledge into explicit knowledge (externalisation), tacit knowledge into tacit knowledge (socialisation), explicit knowledge into tacit knowledge (internalisation), and explicit knowledge into explicit knowledge (combination) will require an approach to learning that may not be based on traditional learning practices. Rather, managers will need to reflect on how people learn, and to develop a range of learning methods that will allow knowledge sharing to occur. To externalise what they have learnt, there has to be some way for both individuals and teams to convert tacit knowledge into explicit knowledge. This might be achieved by many joint activities, face-to-face interactions over time, and 'managing by walking around' (Byosiere and Luethge, 2008). For example, knowledge communities or communities of practice (COPs) are a way of connecting experts or groups of people who have ideas to be shared. Typically, COPs acknowledge that learning is mostly informal and improvisational or situated within a context.

Building on earlier work by Lave and Wenger (1991), Brown and Duguid (1991) outline how COPs make a distinction between canonical and non-canonical practice, the former referring to what is supposed to be learned (as in traditional training), and the latter to what is actually learned (Bratton and Gold, 2007). At its most basic, a COP is organised as informal and self-organising around the needs of a situation, which is another form of conversion from knowledge into practice. It can be suggested that these conversion strategies are needed in far greater quantities in organisational contexts involving difficult strategic decisions. In a context of constant change, such as the computer industry, people will benefit from a variety of learning or multi-learning methods that enable tacit knowledge to be shared, or external knowledge (such as knowledge in a system) to be taught in such a way that workers relate to it. For externalisation, what is understood intuitively needs to be translated into a form that can be understood. Although traditional learning is clearly invoked where one learns the knowledge to the point at which it becomes second nature (Byosiere and Luethge, 2008), different behaviour through the use of metaphor, dialogues or analogies will be more useful for externalisation. This brings us to some other contemporary ideas for theme four related to learning in the workplace.

Learning from narrative and reflection

One can see from the flow of learning that explicit knowledge or knowledge communicated in some written form or spoken word can be independent of the individual so that it becomes organisational knowledge (Cortese, 2005). So an individual as described earlier as a learner who expresses a point of view of 'self' is only one agent of learning, and the self is always subjected to learning by others. Other agents could be students, instructors, mentors, experts, groups, or collective 'others'. For example, acquiring knowledge through concrete experiences (see Kolb's learning cycle) is only one medium from which a distinct learning style might emerge. In reality, a learner learns from multiple sources.

If managers, for example, always see learning as objectified, that is, what the learner learns must be right in his or her frame of mind or what the organisation or teacher teaches must be 'real', large gaps in knowledge may occur. Objectified learning is based on a realist assumption, blinding learners to one reality (either their own or someone else's) by restricting learning from multiple realities (Gergen, 1994; Ramsey, 2005). One can criticise Kolb's cycle for restricting learning to a closed lens – knowledge gained by an individual is also a communal joint production; experiences are not only constructed by one's self but by others. This means that an objectivist approach should be supplemented by a subjectivist or social constructionist approach (Gergen, 1991; Hosking, 1999) in which a learner such as a worker is tied to various on-going relations or experiences at work that enrich the learner's knowledge (see Mini Case Study 11.1).

(?) **Critical Thinking 11.2 Learning from narratives and experience**

Suzy Pakston had strong ideas from what she had learned in her marketing degree about how to build value into a products brand (branding). She often recounted her professor's words: 'Brands are built from capabilities by adding advantage to the product, by augmenting the product.' All her strategies related to this. This led to an objectivist state in which Suzy's own experiences dictated her view of the world.

But things changed when José was also hired as a brand manager – he had a conciliatory approach to building ideas related to a brand. He valued people's viewpoints and challenged his own on a consistent basis. Their two learning styles clashed dramatically. Suzy became frustrated by José's lack of clarity, while José viewed Suzy's views as one of many. This led to a major showdown in the general manager's office.

The general manager himself was sympathetic to Suzy's views, recounting his own experience as a product manager years earlier. He suggested that 'José get on with the job of management and leave managing people to the human resources department'. This greatly pleased Suzy, who left the meeting with a big grin. José, on the other hand, felt somewhat bemused and reflective, questioning his own methods.

On his way back to the office, he stepped in to see the marketing manager and had a quick chat. He began to explain his narrative of the meeting only to learn that Suzy had done the same 15 minutes earlier. José left a quarter of an hour later having heard the marketing manager's view that the answer lay somewhere in the middle. José later began to value the thought that collective others had influenced his ideas related to managing a brand. But there was still the problem of what to do with Suzy...

Questions

1 What approach would you take with Suzy if you were José?
2 Could Suzy learn anything from José? Or José anything from Suzy?

One way of understanding this is by linking the 'text' (such as a gesture, word or action, mannerism, acclamation or direction) to the context (the actual place, background or situation in which the text has occurred). If three workers are sent from the sales department to the factory floor to gain an appreciation of the factory's processes, it is highly likely that each will return with a different story based on the text–context relations. The first worker's narrative of his experiences retold later to, say, a manager is capable of communicating just as meaningfully but in a different way from that of the second or third worker, who expresses the narrative in a dissimilar way. Importantly, if all three sit down and retell their experiences, one worker will learn something from the others as their interpretations are different. Together, on-going and regular social relations have the potential to lead to a more enriched collective learning experience in which the perspectives of reality are treated as an on-going social performance in which knowing becomes simply a relational premise:

> What all these different language tools do is to tie the knower into on-going relations. From a relational perspective, text cannot be separated from context, act cannot be separated from supplement and self cannot be separated from other. These relational language tools invite a reflector to avoid being tied down to one particular account as if true. They prompt us to treat what people claim to know as saying as much about them as a situation. (Ramsey, 2005: 222)

With story-telling, understanding occurs not only in how the story is told but also in how it is received and interpreted, meaning that story-telling is a communal and not an individual activity. Our narratives are influenced by other narratives, which in turn reflect 'local realities' (see mini case study 11.1). Stories will be coordinated based on the context of what is occurring in practice, so although different managers will have different views about how goods are delivered once produced by the factory, communal stories will lead to joint action to ensure that customers are happy with the delivery process. What is interesting about Antonacopoulos's (2006) accounts

of stories of learning in the banking industry is that many managers believed that training was learning, yet later, in accounts to the researcher about the effectiveness of training, most managers reported text–context relations explaining why the training had not been effective: multiple realities reduced the ability of the learner to practise what he or she had learned.

Similarly, Cortese (2005), in a study of 24 middle and top managers about learning in their working life, collected 282 stories that described learning episodes. Out of these, 85 per cent of managers suggested that learning increased through the experience of others, through either observation, listening, or experimentation. For example, in support of a relational or highly interactive process, the teacher's own learning benefited from observation when a pupil pointed out a mistake in the teacher's demonstration. This led the teacher to question her own professional practice by adapting and rewriting her own internal manual of what she 'thought' she was demonstrating. Learning occurs by understanding that 'the other is different from me because I am different from him or her, in other words one succeeds in stepping back and observing oneself through the eyes of others' (Cortese, 2005: 102). It is important to note however that storytelling and narrative can not only be used to promote learning but also to destabilise learning. For instance, Dailey and Browning (2014) suggest that 'although certain stories are repeated to influence or exert power, other narratives may function to promote resistance'. Indeed, stories feed on differences and destabilise and disturb the order of 'reason' (2014: 28). So repeated narratives can be both positive and perhaps negative when they are used as a form of control and resistance related to the trade-off between stability versus change. Moreover, learning as narrative, as storytelling, as language, is both a socially situated process and an individual cognitive process that people use to make sense of their experiences (often called sense-making). These different sociological processes of learning replace the old ways of knowing through traditional learning. Some authors describe how language can be used as a process of linguistic improvisation (Bosma, Chia and Fouweather, 2016). Through semantic transformation and dialogue, fresh semantic spaces are 'creatively opened up, whereby new terms are coined and old ones broken up, combined, and/or redeployed in novel ways, in an effort to express the fresh circumstances experienced or new phenomena observed'. (2016: 16). These and other authors suggest that for learners, it is important to reconstitute our prevailing patterns of meaning, for example traditional norms that define our behaviour, by extending our horizons of comprehension that extend what we already know. This kind of transformation is probably related more too radical learning than incremental learning because it stretches the learners imagination.

📖 In the News   Leadership and training

Refer to the chapter heading 'Training in Practice' in McKinsey and Company and the survey they conducted in 2012. What is interesting here is that global leaders in 2012 found that there were many essential attributes of successful leaders. These were 1) to build trust; 2) to reflect and be thoughtful about what really matters; 3) influence is not about command and control; 4) be a T-shaped thinker (deep subject knowledge in one or more areas); 5) facilitate the possible, 6) be comfortable with ambiguity; and 7) build and manage networks. These kinds of leadership attributes and capabilities do not just happen. The question for HR managers - working with other Business managers – is how to make this happen? What kind of training would be needed? These capabilities are 'in the news' for a reason. Leadership skills here are identified as a basis from which to progress the organisation's overall strategic intent. To achieve these skills, contemporary organisations require a blend of traditional and e-learning techniques. For instance, a more recent report again by McKinsey and Company in 2014 found that contemporary global companies were spending the most resources related to learning and skill development on frontline employees and senior and executive leadership (McKinsey and Company, 2014a: 4), which matches executives' preference for higher-order leader skills. Interestingly, the most popular training and learning interventions in a sample of 1239 senior executives were on-the-job teaching (56 per cent), one-time internal course conducted in a classroom setting (34 per cent), formal or informal coaching (33 per cent), individual online course or exercises (32 per cent), and a series of internal courses or programmes conducted in a classroom setting (31 per cent). While on-the-job training remains the most popular, coaching is having a rapid rise from say 10 years ago. Coaching now extends not just to individuals, as it would be too costly to employ this intervention across the organisation. However, what we are seeing in global firms is specific coaching, either to senior or executive leaders and/or groups of leaders. The McKinsey report about building capabilities for performance also noted – which is an interesting counterpoint to our opening mini-case – that 'still fewer respondents report the use of more leading-edge learning methods, such as experiential environments (model factories or simulators, for example) or digital interventions beyond individual online classes, such as mobile learning exercises or group-based online courses' (2014b: 7). This suggests that digital learning and more contemporary learning methods have a slow take-up. What are the implications of the latter, and why are firms slow to adopt digital and e-learning techniques and applications?

Corporate social responsibility

For training and development purposes, corporate social responsibility (CSR) concerns two things:

- the demand for and supply of labour over a long period of time;
- socially responsible behaviour.

For example, in the hospital system in most countries, CSR is related to ensuring the survival of public health services in such a way that current generations will have the right type of health services available and that enough funding and provisions are made to ensure the survival of the health system for future generations. The latter goal extends to the lack of workers who would be available to fulfil these services if organisations did not make enough funds available for training and development purposes. As hospital services grow, governments need to ensure that enough funding is available to increase the number of workers (supply) to meet the demand of tomorrow's hospital systems. This takes us back to our earlier discussions on training. The question relates to whether organisations are spending enough on training to ensure the continued growth of their organisation.

The second point about CSR is global and local citizenship. This means that organisations should not emulate the circumstances leading to the collapse of energy company Enron and other similar corporations by not being responsible with shareholder funds. The situations of organisations that maintain a commitment to CSR on the one hand yet spend little in relation to TDL is an oxy-moron. That is, one cannot advance the ethics of being socially responsible, socially sustainable in the supply of labour, if one does very little in terms of TDL.

LEARNING FOR INTERNATIONAL ENVIRONMENTS

In their study of the Swedish telecommunications giant Ericsson, Hocking et al. (2007) found that expatriate work-ers had no pressing need to be bound to their host country sources for knowledge applications, even though gener-ally they were more likely to access their own expanded international networks in their home country. As we shall see, there are mixed realities surrounding this statement, because it suggests that the source of most knowledge for individuals on international assignments may well reside in the home country. In striving for greater knowledge, however, a kind of double-loop learning process enables individuals to expand their own (and others') knowledge, suggesting that expatriates will regularly consult individu-als with diverse backgrounds.

In terms of Kolb's learning cycles, expatriates' experien-tial learning is heavily influenced by local knowledge such as local personal networks and local culture. Drawing from the earlier point of narrative and reflection, learning from collective others and different narratives and tales from the field is an important source of learning. Learn-ing stems from observation, narratives, listening, and other opinions that challenge one's own worldview. This contrasts strongly with the approach that knowledge and learning is fundamentally an imperial and universal appli-cation of home country knowledge (Bartlett and Ghoshal, 1988) in which the application of knowledge in the host country is heavily influenced in advance of action. As we shall discuss below, social networks are important in deal-ing with significant cultural and social challenges.

It is not enough to send expatriates abroad only for them to rely on knowledge networks in their home coun-try, or only for them to learn from or form networks only in their host country. The issue here is that many employ-ees may not cope with or be able to adjust to the local network in the host country, much less learn from local colleagues. For instance, Tarique and Caligiuri (2009) suggest that cross-cultural adjustment does not always follow from cross-cultural training. In circumstances of poor adjustment, this may lead to early termination, lost business opportunities, low morale, anxiety and even depression.

Another issue is the type of training. Large companies appear to rely more on the classical training approaches

(such as pre-departure training) and one-off training events designed to 'equip' the expatriate with the cultural knowledge required. Although cross-cultural training, for example, has the potential to lead to better cross-cul-tural adjustment, recent research has been inconclusive (Littrell and Salas, 2005; Waxin and Panaccio, 2005). Some researchers contend that it is impossible to take as defini-tive the general consensus that such training is effective (Kealey and Protheroe, 1996). That is, many programmes are poorly designed and criticised for lacking theoretical justification.

Research by Tarique and Caligiuri (2009) found that knowledge (for example, cultural and procedural knowl-edge) should be established over time by expanding on the stock of existing knowledge. This approach to inter-national training is based on absorptive capacity, where memory development or the ability to put information into memory is self-reinforcing (Cohen and Levinthal, 1990). This means that accumulated prior knowledge, such as knowledge about objects, patterns, or concepts, is necessary for new knowledge to be recognised, assimi-lated, and utilised (see Bower and Hilgard, 1981; Cohen and Levinthal, 1990).

For instance, many researchers have found that, compared with pre-departure training, more frequent in-country cross-cultural training is likely to be more effective since expatriates increase their experiences and exposure to the host country's culture, beliefs, and values over time. The basis of absorptive capacity here is that the ability of an individual to adjust will depend on the magni-tude of prior accumulated cultural knowledge. The more cultural knowledge that has accumulated, the more likely it is that new cultural knowledge will be learned, leading to enhanced cultural adjustment.

Note that the importance of cultural adjustment is similar to the earlier point that training should be linked to performance outcomes to determine whether a worker has transferred training knowledge into demonstrated skill (Khanna and New, 2008). So the point of absorptive capacity relates to the sequencing and timing of train-ing. It suggests that how knowledge is accumulated and applied in the host country will depend on *different types of training activity* conducted at *different times* along an expatriates' journey.

The notion of absorptive capacity becomes more sali-ent with the rise of international and multinational cor-porations. The importance of transferring knowledge and maximising learning outcomes has become more critical in the face of the global financial crisis and increasing com-petition, and the challenge for training and development within this context has never been more focused. There are many issues here related to learning and knowledge, such as how to provide access to knowledge, different

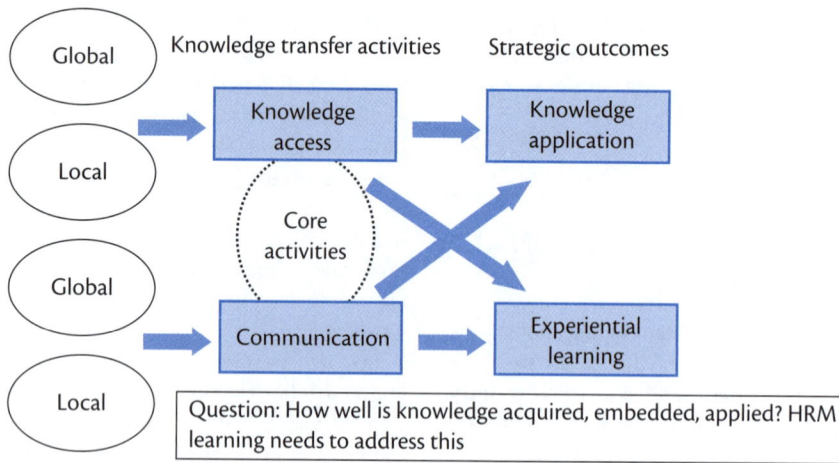

Figure 11.3 Making sense of knowledge transfer and outcomes
Source: Adapted from Hocking et al. (2007: 527).

knowledge applications and communication, as well as experiential learning (Hocking et al., 2007). The host country in which foreign nationals are to work will need to rely on the home country's stock of corporate knowledge, but host country nationals also have a habit of relying on their own experiences for local adaptation. The balance between global and local knowledge application, knowledge access, communication and experiential learning will be important here (Figure 11.3).

For the expatriate, knowledge application in the host country relies heavily on the headquarters and other global units. Here, expatriate managers access the deep stores of knowledge of organisational learning, as outlined in Figure 11.3. Expatriates, however, learn from local knowledge. As discussed, although cross-cultural training may be useful for expatriates, research suggests that context-generic knowledge gained by individuals is valuable when sourced from globally dispersed units (Hocking et al., 2007). As our previous description of the flow of learning indicates, corporate or organisational knowledge will also be enriched and embedded by adding more diversified knowledge, in this case from the host country and local managers.

In relation to Figure 11.3, the key for human resources practitioners is to balance global needs with local ones. Although corporate knowledge networks are critical for continued expatriate learning, local experiential learning and communication challenge corporate knowledge by balancing corporate needs with local contexts (see Chapter 3 for a detailed discussion of this).

In more recent times, research has not only focused on expatriates and how they learn, how they share knowledge and how they accumulate it. Instead, multinational companies in particular are beginning to understand the value of social capital and social ties in building networks of relationships that enhance both individual and organisational knowledge in international assignments. Individuals, for example, build social ties and networks through short-term assignments. Social ties provide access to information, reduce the costs associated with expatriation, enhance cross-border mobility and multilateral ties, and improve individual decision-making that can be used later to solve difficult international problems .

Social ties can be explained by the weak ties theory (Granovetter, 1973). This theory holds that distant and infrequent relationships (weak ties) are efficient for knowledge sharing as they provide access to novel information, whereas strong ties defined by the frequency of contact often lead to redundant information because they occur among smaller groups of actors. Strong ties may accordingly lead to redundant information since everyone knows what the others know (Van den Bossche et al., 2010). Recent research by Bozkurt and Mohr, for example, found that 'short-term assignments and business travel helped initiate cross-unit ties in large number of locations and with large numbers of partners' (2010: 150), confirming the value of social ties.

For organisations, however, challenges relate to mobility and to allowing individuals to accumulate a more superficial level of knowledge over a wider range of locations through business travel. Figure 11.3 might well be expanded by adding in a box related to social ties as a means of increasing social capital. The latter is also consistent with learning from narrative and reflection in which social ties expand narratives in ways that help managers to solve difficult problems.

CONCLUSION

This chapter has set out many issues related to TLD. The classical learning approaches were mainly concerned with training in classroom settings and short-course-type orientations. Common to these methods was that training was learning. Yet more recent contemporary research would suggest that training does not always lead to know-how or an application of learning in practice. Training might lead to an increase in cognitive knowledge, but only for a while. Without other learning experiences, knowledge will be forgotten. The key here is that knowledge learned must be practised so that cognition and behaviour work together.

The difference between individual and organisational learning is as pronounced as the difference between cognitive styles, learning styles, and how people 'actually' learn. The learning cycle put forward by Kolb is useful in advancing the notion of self-reflection, concrete experience, and learning from abstract conceptualisation in practice. However, as we discussed, this view of learning is restricted by the 'self'. Individualised accounts suggest that individuals can be objective about their personal reflection, yet individuals are only one agent of learning. Here, we discussed how multiple agents and realities potentially influence what a person learns and how she or he actually learns, the latter being related more to subjective or socially constructed learning, learning from narratives, and observation in practice. Unique styles and cognitions of learning need to be considered by managers. Whether individuals reflect one or two archetypes or cognitive patterns in the way people see reality should be considered. The chapter highlighted examples related to how sensing–thinking might act differently from sensing–feeling archetypes in practice.

One overriding theme to consider is the difference between single-loop and double-loop learning. It seems probable that organisations would consider multi-method learning in practice to allow workers and individuals to question and challenge long-held traditions so that new learning could be framed. Readers should also note the difference between learning and knowledge. Whereas learning typically describes 'flow', knowledge is embedded in systems and structures. Learning flows ultimately help learners to repudiate and challenge embedded knowledge. Accordingly, in developing the individual, learning plays a key role, not only in terms of what is learned but also by how the learning actually occurs; TDL should not occur in isolation from other human resources practices. For example, for needs and assessment purposes, TDL should be closely tied to performance management and to position and job descriptions. This is to ensure that TDL adopts an integrated approach to avoid the inevitable conflicts between general managers and human resources personnel over whether training is no more than a function needed for a specific time and place, but no longer.

Specific recommendations for learning ultimately depend on the organisation in its context. That is, text–context is a viable learning consideration, suggesting that a variety of texts should also be matched to the context. A case in point in the chapter is learning in the international environment, given that learners need to hear multiple voices and perspectives in order to expand their own. Although the traditional forms of learning should be noted, these are a form of text–context pattern that will work in some situations but not others.

End of Chapter Case Study Ericsson: Aligning training and learning with business transformation

As students we are frequent observers of different HR procedures and practices across global firms. If any of us, for instance, explored how different contemporary organisations develop their training and learning platforms, they would vary: some with more traditional training occurring in the classroom environment, others with a blend of on-the-job training and limited e-learning or digital learning. Often the latter is restricted to orientation and safety videos and off-the-shelf products. So if we examine a very large contemporary global firm such as Ericsson, how does such a large organisation align its training and learning priorities with its business strategies? First, there is no doubt that HR departments and functions need clear strategic guidance from senior management about the company's direction. As you have learned from previous chapters in this book, this can be a two-way street with HR executives playing a key role in any transformation. But let's focus on Ericsson. In 2010, the company moved away from its previous reliance on the consumer segment to reframing its strategies around telecom services, software and hardware by leveraging previous network-infrastructure and using this to develop new products for new markets, for example TV and media, cloud services and support software for communications infrastructure. Ericsson called this strategic shift 'Telecom IT solutions'. Importantly, the CEO and top HR managers knew that the only way to achieve this vision was to transform the skill sets and capabilities of its people. So how did they do this?

Similar to this chapter's emphasis on training needs analysis and other techniques, Ericsson found that 23 regional groups, each with a different set of processes and tools for developing and training people, could be consolidated into 10. Each of the new groups had a single people strategy that was closely linked to the new business strategy. In short, this would be similar to deciding what skills and capabilities are required for the whole firm, then performing a skills audit to see how these are linked to the broader strategy. The company also found that they needed an integrated HR platform, one that could be used by managers and workers with data centrally gathered and shared. Actual HR processes, systems, and policies were then matched to the globalised HR process which was simple, user friendly, and business focused. An online virtual portal was created called 'Ericsson Academy' which enabled employees to access global learning programmes from any location in the world. For the global strategy, then, it was critical for HR to create global learning programmes. Notice the emphasis here on e-learning and digital learning similar to a knowledge-based system that can be created to enable knowledge sharing and skill equipping through global training. Ericsson also developed data analytic techniques that helped them assess their recruitment processes, finding that more female candidates were applying for jobs posted by female managers. Importantly, the company spent a great deal of time communicating and sharing its common purpose around common people platforms and processes. In essence, this is a 'one size fits all' philosophy which can be achieved if a company has a unifying global strategy and is able to communicate this strategy so that its people requirements and capabilities are shared across key global regions (McKinsey Quarterly, 2016).

In terms of skills analysis, we can learn a lot from Ericsson's approach. For instance, in order to build a competency framework across the company, it was important first to map out its roles and the stages of each job, while laying out the competence and skills required for each of these. While this may seem a laborious process in any company, it helped Ericsson identify training and people requirement gaps linked to the annual strategic review. Overall, the process led to an aggregated capabilities map for the entire organisation. In any company, once these gaps are identified, this triggers demand signals for learning and recruitment, training and development, and when these skill demands need to be met. Knowing what type of learning programmes are required in advance greatly assists companies to continuously improve their training techniques by overhauling old ones. Earlier in this chapter we talked about the social constructionist approach and narrative as learning. So what we see here again in this example is an emphasis on collaborative tools. For instance, people want to learn in a collaborative way which led HR to create a video learning model where employees could upload their own videos and ideas similar to Facebook and other social learning platforms. Taken together, collaborative learning was included in mobile platforms allowing workers to learn whenever and wherever they liked, to effectively learn 'on-the-go'.

It is possible to contrast Ericsson's story of training, development, and learning with 'learning flows' as described in this chapter. The old Ericsson saw institutionalised learning embedded at the organisational level, for example in groups with different HR practices, processes, and systems, and how these systems were imposed on groups of workers. When such processes are not integrated across the firm, then the quality of feed-back learning to the individual is compromised. In addition, if such learning is not matched to the overall strategic direction, then the feed-forward aspect of learning from the individual to the team and to the organisation may not fit skill requirements. Hence, it would not be surprising that prior training needs analysis under the old system would have been inaccurate, leading to the development of skills not really relevant to busy managers. Since group learning is a key input in learning flows, overall group skills might not have been relevant to the company's direction. This is illustrated in the story of Ericsson and the need to rapidly transform how it learned. If, for example, one key learning capability was to equip groups with the skills to better interpret environmental signals and act on them, then this may have been less likely under the old training regime which was not correctly matched to the company's overall strategy. Ericsson's approach allows us to learn key lessons from global companies about how to develop and implement a global learning system that is tied to a company's strategic intent.

Questions

1   Choose three learning techniques/ideas from this chapter and discuss in groups how Ericsson's approach matches these.
2   Discuss in groups how training and development needs will be different for companies in five years' time and in ten years' time. How will learning needs change?
3   Explain how Ericsson's global learning approach seems to fit ideas related to learning as narrative. What are the key points?
4   Why is it important to link skill assessment and training needs analysis to the company's overall direction? Why can't the HR department develop these in isolation?

Class Activity

Imagine your class are employees of a sports car maker called 'The Invader'! There are three models; the A class Invader (attracted to a demographic of well-off single nest or retirees) with a V8 engine, the B class with a V6 engine, and the C class small Invader with a 4 Litre engine targeted specifically at 18–35-year-olds. The company does not make sedans, wagons, or SUVs. The cars are made by hand. No technological systems are used in the factory. Invader still use hand presses and hand drills to make and piece the car together; leather seats are made by hand, are very high quality, and are common across the range. Thus, there is high loyalty to the Invader brand, but sales are slow. Stories of how the company came into being are common, and these narratives are used to create the learning climate. Accordingly, you as the employee have learned by on-the-job training methods and narrative as learning. No other learning techniques have been used. Imagine though if Invader employed a highly skilled production and marketing manager from Toyota to revolutionise the brand. Based on less than perfect information, make additional assumptions and design a learning system to help the company improve its range of skills assuming you are the new manager.

▸ What will this look like?
▸ How will it be implemented?
▸ What conflicts might you envisage in designing the new training and development system?

Class Activity

As a new HR manager reporting to the HR Director, you have been placed in charge of all organisational development programmes in a global niche banking firm operating out of Brussels. The firm has over 5,000 employees who are mostly white-collar middle-class workers, with other 20 other branches spread across Europe as well as the Asia-Pacific Rim, taking advantage of emerging markets. What has become apparent in the bank is that each of the other branches has its own training and learning system to meet local and regional needs. When recently a worker from Singapore was transferred to Brussels, she had no idea about the learning climate and found it hard to adjust. In Singapore, work was more regulated and directed, with quite strict working hours, including seeking permission to make major trades and financial decisions.

In Brussels, she noticed this was the opposite. In addition, she felt she lacked many social skills found in the Brussels branch such that she found it difficult to communicate. As HR manager,

▸ How would you go about assessing current skills and capabilities?
▸ What would you try and tie this to?
▸ How could you solve these differences in learning and in knowledge applied in practice across branches?

FOR DISCUSSION AND REVISION

1 Contrast and compare traditional forms of learning with more contemporary forms. From a management perspective, what are the strengths and weaknesses and issues for reflection?

2 Think of any organisation whose text–context learning pattern could be influenced. In taking a narrative perspective, describe how text–context knowledge may change over time.

3 Collect at least five articles of research related to multi-methods of learning. Using this approach, discuss how organisational knowledge could be challenged and updated over time for an automotive firm such as a car retailer or manufacturer.

Action-oriented activities

1 Design a fictitious merchandising organisation that produces T-shirts and related apparel and has one factory outlet and a head office. The total size of the company should be 100 people, with generally one manager for every eight workers. The company is approximately 10 years old but is facing stiff competition in terms of better designs and merchandising, including electronic merchandising and selling. Sales have dropped by 15 per cent during the year, and workers are starting to fear for their jobs. Annual turnover has peaked at $10 million. Staff complaints are common, and the organisation relies on the design skills of two or three workers. Competencies and skills are often not matched to position statements, and there is no internal training/learning policy.

2 In outlining your design for the company, include a list of jobs and job functions most likely to be practised. Concentrate only on the managers. Perform a needs analysis followed by a position description and training plan. The latter should be focused on how the company can solve its immediate problems by concentrating on new management skills. Take about an hour in total for this exercise.

GLOSSARY

Active Learning: A learning principle that says participants learn more when they are actively involved in the process.

Case Study: A technique where the participants are asked to investigate a situation or problem and report their findings, causes and/or solutions.

Cognition: the mental action or process of acquiring knowledge and understanding through thought, experience, and the senses.

Competency: A knowledge, skill, ability, or trait that is needed to succeed at a particular task or job.

Competency-Based Training: An educational process that focuses on specific core competencies that have been clearly defined.

Core Competencies: Those things that are essential and 'must' be learned for an individual to accomplish the primary objectives of his/her job. The central, innermost or most essential part of what the trainee must know to do his/her job effectively.

Development: Training people to acquire new horizons, technologies, or viewpoints. It enables leaders to guide their organisations onto new expectations by being proactive rather than reactive. It enables workers to create better products, faster services, and more competitive organisations. It is learning for growth of the individual, but not related to a specific present or future job.

Knowledge Management: Capturing, organising, and storing the experiences of individual workers and groups within an organisation and making it available to others in the organisation.

Learning: Knowledge acquired by systematic study in any field. A relatively permanent change in behavioural potentiality that can be measured and that occurs as a result of reinforced practice; gaining knowledge, skills, or developing a behaviour through study, instruction, or experience.

Organisational Learning: the process of creating, retaining, and transferring knowledge within an organisation.

Skills: Application of knowledge in an effective and efficient manner to get something done. One notices skills in an employee by his/her behaviours.

Training: the transfer of defined and measurable knowledge or skills. Learning that is provided in order to improve performance on the present job.

Training Needs Analysis: A method of determining whether a training need exists and if it does, what training is required to fill the gap.

FURTHER READING

Journals

BINGHAM, C. B. AND DAVIS, J. P (2012) Learning sequences: Their existence, effect, and evolution. *Academy of Management Journal*, 55(3): 611–641.

BOZKURT, O. AND MOHR, A. T. (2010) Forms of cross-border mobility and social capital in multinational enterprises. *Human Resource Management Journal*, 21(2): 138–155.

GALAGAN, P. (2010) Disappearing act: The vanishing corporate classroom. *Training and Development*, 64(3): 29–31.

IZAK, M. (2015) Learning from a fool: Searching for the 'unmanaged' context for radical learning. *Management Learning*, 46, (1): 87–104.

MALHOTRA, N. AND HININGS, C. R. (2015) Unpacking continuity and change as a process of organisational transformation. *Long Range Planning*, 48: 1–22.

RAISCH, S., BIRKINSHAW, J., PROBST, G. AND TUSHMAN, M. L. (2009) Organisational ambidexterity: Balancing exploitation and exploration for sustained performance. *Organisation Science*, 20(4): 685–695.

TARIQUE, I. AND CALIGIURI, P. (2009) The role of cross-cultural absorptive capacity in the effectiveness of in-county cross-cultural training. *International Journal of Training and Development*, 13(3): 148–164.

TOMKINS, L. AND ULUS, E. (2015) 'Oh, was that "experiential learning"?!' Spaces, synergies and surprises with Kolb's learning cycle. *Management Learning*, doi: 10.1177/1350507615587451.

WEB RESOURCES

For training that incorporates e-learning and digital learning, see https://www.lynda.com/Web-training-tutorials/88-0.html

See how professional associations boost your development and opportunities for specific management training at http://www.managers.org.uk/.

Using your laptop or a class-based computer, log on to http://www.brainboxx.co.uk/A2_LEARNSTYLES/pages/roughandready.htm.

On this webpage, you will find a sample of Honey and Mumford's learning styles inventory. Go through the exercise (activist, pragmatist, theorist, reflector) in your tutorial or at home and bring your answers to share in class.

REFERENCES

ALLINSON, C. W. AND HAYES, J. (1996) The cognitive style index: A measure of intuition-analysis for organisational research. *Journal of Management Studies*, 33(1): 119–135.

ALLEN, P. L. (2015) Toward a new HR philosophy. Mckinsey Quarterly, April.

ANTONACOPOULOU, E. P. (1999) Training does not imply learning: The individual's perspective. *International Journal of Training and Development*, 3(1): 14–32.

ANTONACOPOULOU, E. P. (2001) The paradoxical nature of the relationship between training and learning. *Journal of Management Studies*, 38(3): 327–350.

ANTONACOPOULOU, E. P. (2006) The relationship between individual and organizational learning: New evidence from managerial learning practices. *Management Learning*, 37: 455–472.

ARGYRIS, C. AND SCHÖN, D. A. (1978) *Organizational Learning*. Reading, MA: Addison-Wesley.

ARTHUR, J. B. AND HUNTLEY, C. L. (2005) Ramping up the organisational learning curve: Assessing the impact of deliberate learning on organisational performance under gain sharing. *Academy of Management Journal*, 48(6): 1159–1170.

Australian Industry Group (2009) Business working hard to keep skilled workforce during downturn. Media Release, Corporate Affairs, Sydney.

BARTLETT, C. A. AND GHOSHAL, S. (1988) *Transnational Management: Text, Cases, and Reading in Cross-Border Management*. Chicago: Richard D. Irwin.

BASSI, L. (1999) Harnessing the power of intellectual capital. In Cortada, J. and Woods, J. (eds), *The Knowledge Management Yearbook 1999–2000*. Boston, MA: Butterworth Heinemann, pp. 422–431.

BECKETT, R. AND MURRAY, P. (2000) Learning by auditing. *TQM Magazine*, 12(2): 125–136.

BOSMA, B., CHIA, R. AND FOUWEATHER, I. (2016) Radical learning through semantic transformation: Capitalising on novelty. *Management Learning*, 47(1): 14–27.

BOWER, G. AND HILGARD, E. (1981) *Theories of Learning*. Englewood Cliffs, NJ: Prentice Hall.

BOXALL, P. AND MACKY, K. (2009) Research and theory on high-performance work systems: Progressing the high-involvement stream. *Human Resource Management Journal*, 19(1): 3–23.

BOZKURT, O. AND MOHR, A. T. (2010) Forms of cross-border mobility and social capital in multinational enterprises. *Human Resource Management Journal*, 21(2): 138–155.

BRATTON, J. AND GOLD, J. (2017) *Human Resource Management, Theory and Practice* (6th edn). Hampshire: Palgrave Macmillan.

BROWN, J. S. AND DUGUID, P. (1991) Organisational learning and communities-of-practice: Toward a unified view of working, learning and innovation. *Organisation Science*, 2(1): 40–47.

BROWN, M., METZ, I., CREGAN, C. AND KULIK, C. T. (2009) Irreconcilable differences? Strategic human resource management and employee well-being. *Asia Pacific Journal of Human Resources*, 47: 270–294.

BROWN, P. A., GREEN, A. AND LAUDER, H. (2001) *High Skills: Globalisation, Competitiveness and Skills Formation*. Oxford: Oxford University Press.

BYOSIERE, P. AND LUETHGE, D. J. (2008) Knowledge domains and knowledge conversion: an empirical investigation. *Journal of Knowledge Management*, 12(2): 67–78.

CIPD (Chartered Institute of Personnel and Development) (2008) *Training: A Measured Response*. London: CIPD.

CIPD (Chartered Institute of Personnel and Development) (2009) *Training: A Short History*. London: CIPD.

CLARDY, A. (2008) Human resource development and the resource-based model of core competencies: Methods for diagnosis and assessment. *Human Resource Development Review*, 7(4): 387–407.

COHEN, W. AND LEVINTHAL, D. (1990) Absorptive capacity: A new perspective on learning and innovations. *Administrative Science Quarterly*, 35: 128–152.

CONWAY, E. AND MONKS, K. (2008) HR practices and commitment to change: An employee-level analysis. *Human Resource Management Journal*, 18(1): 72–89.

COOK, S. AND BROWN, J. S. (1999) Bridging epistemologies: The generative dance between organisational knowledge and organisational knowing. *Organisational Science*, 10: 381–400.

CORTESE, C. G. (2005) Learning through teaching. *Management Learning*, 36: 87–115.

CROSSAN, M. AND BERDROW, I. (2003) Organisational learning and strategic renewal. *Strategic Management Journal*, 24: 1087–10105.

CROSSAN, M. M., LANE, H. W. AND WHITE, R. E. (1999) An organisational learning framework: From intuition to institution. *Academy of Management Review*, 24: 522–537.

DAILEY, S. L. AND BROWNING, L. (2014) Retelling Stories in organisations: Understanding the functions of narrative repetition. *Academy of Management Review*, 39(1), 22–43.

DE CIERI, H. AND KRAMAR, R. (2008) *Human Resource Management in Australia* (3rd edn). Sydney: McGraw-Hill.

DELOITTE (2007) *Innovation in Emerging Markets*. Annual Survey. Sydney: Deloitte's Global Manufacturing Industry Group.

DELOITTE (2009) Corporate leaders pre-emptively leaning into the recovery. Press release, 16 November, Sydney.

EISENHARDT, K. M. AND MARTIN. J. A. (2000) Dynamic capabilities: What are they? *Strategic Management Journal*, 21: 1105–1121.

ESPEDAL, B. (2008) In the pursuit of understanding how to balance lower and higher order learning in organizations. *Journal of Applied Behavioural Science*, 44(3): 365–390.

FIOL, C. M. AND LYLES, M. A. (1985) Organisational learning. *Academy of Management Review*, 10(4): 803–813.

FULOP, L., FRITH, F. AND HAYWARD, H. (1992) *Management for Australian Business: A Critical Text*. Melbourne: Macmillan.

GERGEN, K. J. (1991) *The Saturated Self*. New York: Basic Books.

GERGEN, K. J. (1994) *Realities and Relationships*. Cambridge, MA: Harvard University Press.

GIBB, S. (2003) Line manager involvement in learning and development: Small beer or big deal? *Employee Relations*, 25(3): 281–293.

GIBB, S. (2008) *Human Resource Development: Process, Practices and Perspectives* (2nd edn). Basingstoke: Palgrave Macmillan.

GRANOVETTER, M. S. (1973) The strength of weak ties. *American Journal of Sociology*, 78(6): 1360–1380.

HEDBERG, B. (1981) How organisations learn and unlearn. In Nystrom, P. C. and Starbuck, W. H. (eds), *Handbook of Organisational Design*. London: Oxford University Press, pp. 8–27.

HOCKING, B., BROWN, M. AND HARZING, A. W. (2007) Balancing global and local strategic contexts: Expatriate knowledge transfer, applications and learning within a transnational organization. *Human Resource Management*, 46(4): 513–533.

HOSKING, D. M. (1999) Social construction as process: Some new possibilities for research and development. *Concepts and Transformations*, 4(2): 117–132.

HU, L. AND RANDEL, A. E. (2014) Knowledge sharing in teams: Social capital, extrinsic incentives, and team innovation. *Group and Organization Management*, 39: 213.

JONES, J. (2004) Training and development, and business growth: A study of Australian manufacturing small- and medium-sized enterprises. *Asia Pacific Journal of Human Resources*, 42: 96–121.

JUNG, C. (1968) *The Archetypes and the Collective Unconscious*. Princeton, NJ: Bollingen.

KEALEY, D. AND PROTHEROE, D. (1996) The effectiveness of cross-cultural training for expatriates: An assessment of the literature on the issue. *International Journal of Intercultural Relations*, 20: 141–165.

KHANNA, S. AND NEW, J. R. (2008) Revolutionizing the workplace: A case study of the future of work program at capital one. *Human Resource Management*, 47(4): 795–808.

KIM, D. H. (1993) The link between individual and organizational learning. *Sloan Management Review*, Fall: 37–50.

KOLB, D. (1984) *Experiential Learning*. Englewood Cliffs, NJ: Prentice Hall.

KRAMAR, R. AND LAKE, N. (1997) *Price Waterhouse Cranfield Project on International Strategic Human Resource Management*. Sydney: Macquarie University.

LAVE, J. AND WENGER, E. (1991) *Situated Learning*. Cambridge: Cambridge University Press.

LITTRELL, L. AND SALAS, E. (2005) A review of cross-cultural training: Best practices, guidelines, and research needs. *Human Resource Development Review*, 4(3): 305–334.

MARCH, J. G. (2006) Rationality, foolishness, and adaptive intelligence. *Strategic Management Journal*, 27: 201–214.

MCKINSEY and Company (2012) The state of human capital 2012 False Summit: Why the human capital function still has far to go. Accessed online 15 February 2016.

MCKINSEY and Company (2014a) Building capabilities for performance. Accessed online 10 February 2016.

MCKINSEY and Company (2014b) Offline and falling behind: Barriers to internet adoption. October.

MCKINSEY Quarterly (2016) How Ericsson aligned its people with its transformation strategy: An interview with the chief HR officer Bina Chaurasia. January.

MILLER, D. (1996) A preliminary typology of organizational learning: Synthesizing the literature. *Journal of Management*, 22(3): 485–505.

MORGAN, G. (1997) *Images of Organisation*. London: Sage.

NANKERVIS, A., COMPTON, R. AND BAIRD, M. (2008) *Human Resource Management: Strategies and Processes* (6th edn). Melbourne: Cengage Learning.

NONAKA, I. AND TAKEUCHI, H. (1995) *The Knowledge-Creating Company*. Oxford: Oxford University Press.

PEACOCK, J. G., AND GRANDE, J. P. (2016) An online App platform enhances collaborative medical student group learning and classroom management. *Medical Teacher*, 38(2): 174–180.

PETERSON, R. B. (2004) A call for testing our assumptions. *Journal of Management Inquiry*, 13(3): 192–202.

PLESNER, U. AND GULBRANDSEN, I. T. (2015) Strategy and the new media: A research agenda. *Strategic Organisation*, 13(2): 153–162.

RAINBIRD, H. AND MUNRO, A. (2003) Workplace learning and the employment relationship in the public sector. *Human Resource Management Journal*, 13(2): 30–44.

RAMSEY, C. M. (2005) Narrative: from learning in reflection to learning in performance. *Management Learning*, 36(2): 219–235.

ROSE, M. (1975) *Industrial Behaviour: Theoretical Development since Taylor*. Harmondsworth: Penguin.

RYLATT, A. (1994) *Learning Unlimited*. Chatswood, Sydney: Business and Professional Publishing.

SHEEHAN, C., HOLLAND, P. AND DE CIERI, H. (2006) Current developments in HRM in Australian organisations. *Asia Pacific Journal of Human Resources*, 44: 132–152.

SMITH, A. (2003) Recent trends in Australian training and development. *Asia Pacific Journal of Human Resources*, 41: 231–244.

TARIQUE, I. AND CALIGIURI, P. (2009) The role of cross-cultural absorptive capacity in the effectiveness of in-county cross-cultural training. *International Journal of Training and Development*, 13(3): 148–164.

TechRepublic (2015a) Why China is scooping up robots from Rethink Robotics to solve its manufacturing problem. Available at: http://www.techrepublic.com/article/why-china-is-scooping-up-robots-from-rethink-robotics-to-solve-its-manufacturing-problem/. Accessed 7 February 2016.

TechRepublic, (2015b) Chinese factory replaces 90% of humans with robots, production soars. Available at: http://www.techrepublic.com/article/chinese-factory-replaces-90-of-humans-with-robots-production-soars/.

ULRICH, D. AND BROCKBANK, W. (2005) *The HR Value Proposition*. Boston, MA: Harvard Business School Press.

VAN DEN BOSSCHE, P., SEGERS, M. AND JANSEN, N. (2010) Transfer of training: The role of feedback in supportive social networks. *International Journal of Training and Development*, 14(2): 81–94.

VERA, D. AND CROSSAN, M. (2003) Organisational learning and knowledge management: Toward an integrative framework. In Easterby-Smith, M. and Lyles, M. (eds), *The Blackwell Handbook of Organisational Learning and Knowledge Management*. London: Blackwell, pp. 123–130.

WAXIN, M. AND PANACCIO, A. (2005) Cross-cultural training to facilitate expatriate adjustment: It works. *Personnel Review*, 34: 51–67.

WORLEY, C. G. AND MOHRMAN, S.A. (2014) Is change management obsolete? *Organisational Dynamics*, 43: 214–224.

WRIGHT, P., DUNFORD, B. AND SNELL, S. (2001) Human resources and the resource-based view of the firm. *Journal of Management*, 27: 701–721.

HRM and Contemporary Issues

12

TALENT MANAGEMENT: CRITICAL PERSPECTIVES

Stephen Swailes, Janet Handley, and Liz Rivers

LEARNING OUTCOMES

After reading this chapter you should be able to:

➤ Compare and critique definitions of talent management
➤ Explain the differences between talent management and human resource management
➤ Explain the reasons for the growth of corporate interest in talent management
➤ Discuss rational and critical approaches to talent management
➤ Discuss and critique the difficulties of identifying talent fairly and reliably.

SUMMARY OF CHAPTER CONTENTS

➤ **Opening Case Study**: Localisation in the Gulf States
➤ Introduction
➤ The rise of talent management
➤ Definitions of talent and talent management
➤ Identifying talent
➤ Theoretical perspectives
➤ Biasing factors
➤ Gender and talent management
➤ Conclusion
➤ **End of chapter case study**: Talent identification
➤ For discussion and revision
➤ Glossary
➤ Further reading
➤ References

Opening Case Study   Localisation in the Gulf States

As you will see in this chapter, 'talent' is interpreted in different ways across different organisations and cultures. Broadly speaking, it can mean exceptional skills relative to others, for example a talented sportswoman has better skills than others in her field, or it can mean the particular, idiosyncratic abilities that people have. This case leans towards the idea of talent as idiosyncratic rather than relative.

A serious economic problem facing the Gulf States is the employment of locals in place of migrants and expatriate workers. Gulf populations are young and growing. Young Saudis and Omanis, for example, want good jobs and a career, but the working populations of the Gulf States contain large numbers of foreign workers. The traditional way of finding jobs for locals has been to expand the public sector with cash from oil revenues. Public sector jobs are attractive to locals because they offer high status and are well paid and secure. But the public sectors in the Gulf cannot keep expanding – employing locals in the private sector is a priority.

To catalyse the employment of locals, Gulf countries and others have created localisation policies (e.g. Saudisation, Omanisation). In essence, these require employers to employ a percentage of locals in their workforce, with the percentage varying by sector and depending upon economic importance and past progress. So, we can see localisation as a particular form of talent management that focuses not on finding the best of the bunch but on deploying the talents of local people in decent jobs and laying the foundations for social and economic progress. But progress towards localisation has been slow. A key question therefore centres around the barriers to localisation: what are they and why do they persist?

Some barriers are well known. They include a lack of management and leadership training for locals, poor training, poor English language training, and negative perceptions of private sector employment by locals. New research, however, has revealed some more complex structural problems (Al Nahdi and Swailes, 2015). Bearing in mind that many foreign managers have influence over staffing decisions and that many private organisations are owned by locals, additional barriers to employing local talent include:

▸ Networking among expatriate managers suppresses the employment of locals.
▸ Local owners and managers preferring to employ foreign workers because they are perceived as being more productive.
▸ Inter-faith barriers – most foreign workers are not Muslim and observe different religious practices at work.
▸ Local owners and managers preferring to employ foreigners with whom they can maintain a greater social distance because of differences in language and customs.

Local talent therefore, in its broadest sense, is being suppressed by a lack of opportunity. Despite long-standing efforts by governments to increase the percentage of locals in the workforce, there are some deep-rooted barriers that impede progress. Some changes seem relatively easy, such as prioritising better language and management training, but some of these barriers will not be overcome in the short term. Foreigners prefer to employ foreigners because they are seen as more productive and easier to manage, and some locals who are owners and/or managers can control their businesses more easily through foreigners than through other locals by leveraging differences in language and culture.

Social barriers of this kind are not easily dismantled, and the case illustrates the sorts of issues that arise in talent identification and that can be extrapolated to talent management in organisations. Identifying talent is fraught with impressions, feelings, and biases.

Questions

1   Why can cash-rich governments not continue to expand the public sector to employ locals?
2   To what extent would you agree with the suggestion that foreign workers in the Gulf States are more efficient and productive than local workers?
3   What types of prejudices might exist against local workers in the Gulf and Middle East?

INTRODUCTION

A quick look through the management literature might suggest that talent management is a recent phenomenon. Most articles post-date 2000, and the starting point is often given as the influential book *The War for Talent* (Michaels, Handfield-Jones and Axelrod, 2001). The idea that corporations were fighting a war for talent and competing with each other for high-quality employees spread quickly through the boardrooms of corporate America and Northern Europe. Good people were in short supply; or so it was assumed.

However, although talk of 'talent' and 'talent management' in the context of everyday work was uncommon before 2000, the benefits of talented people to organisations and society had been recognised long before (Swailes, 2016). By the middle of the twentieth century, there was much interest in identifying promotable executives and the characteristics that gave them their promotability (Bowman, 1964; Randle, 1956). What is clear, however, is that there has been a shift in the emphasis that domestic and multinational organisations now put on managing talent.

An extensive study by the Boston Consulting Group (BCG, 2013) of executives across 34 countries found that while talent management was the most pressing HRM priority for companies, it was also the one in which their capabilities were the lowest. Similar findings came out of a large Pricewaterhouse Coopers survey of executives (PwC, 2014), which reported that 63 per cent of executives felt that skills shortages were a serious problem but only 34 per cent felt that their employee selection systems were 'well prepared' for the challenges that lie ahead.

Despite the heavy rhetoric about the importance of talent identification, many companies do not run talent programmes. Factors positively influencing the adoption of talent management in multinationals are size of the firm, whether products/services are standardised, whether the firm has a global HR approach, and whether the firm operates in relatively low technology sectors (McDonnell et al., 2010). There is no shortage of prescriptive advice on how to design and operate talent programmes, and we do not repeat that advice here. Instead, we set out a more critical analysis of talent management in an effort to better appreciate the practical operating problems that could arise when talent programmes are attempted.

DEFINITIONS

In common with other HR practices such as performance-related pay, organisations are free to choose whether they engage with talent management or not. If they do engage with it, then they are free to define it and to operate it in any way they wish to suit their own outlook on how people should be managed and their market position. An organisation might run a talent programme but prefer to call it something else that better fits with the organisation's language and culture. What this means is that organisations may run what they see as talent programmes but that do not match definitions used by academics.

Talent and talent management

First, what is talent? In the context of gifted children, Howe, Davidson and Sloboda (1998) argued that talent has five properties. These include: a partly innate and genetically transmitted component, that talent is something confined to a minority, and that talents are domain-specific, for example, music or dance. They refer to the genetic component as the 'talent account' but conclude that the main determinants of excellence are differences in early experiences, opportunities, training, and practice. Extending this theory to organisations suggests that:

- employees showing exceptional talent will make-up only a small proportion of the workforce;
- employees will need ample opportunities to hone and practice their talents; and,
- employees will use social capital accumulated in early life.

In relation to talent and giftedness in art, sport and other domains, 'talent' is often taken as meaning the top 10 per cent of an ability group compared to their age peers (Gagne, 2000). The link to age is important since, for example, it is inappropriate to compare the best pianists aged 16–18 with the best pianists aged 30–40 simply because the older group has more experience. A similar philosophy is usually applied in workplaces where talent might be sought across various levels of seniority and different operational areas.

The easiest way of looking at talent management is to see it as differentiating between current and potential employees in terms of their performance, contribution, and especially their potential; sorting the 'best from the rest'. Potential is a key factor because, although high performance is important, not all high performers are deemed to have the potential to go further in the organisation. This leads us to an exclusive or elitist view of a workforce and the labour markets that supply new employees; it is exclusive because most employees are excluded from the talent pool.

Following the elitist line, only a small proportion of employees will be deemed as talented. Although research on talent management has been impeded by a lack of consensus around a definition, the dust is starting to settle now and we suggest that, for elitist talent management, the definition provided by Collings and Mellahi (2009: 305) captures it well. As they see it, organisational talent management is the

> activities and processes that involve the systematic identification of key positions which differentially contribute to the organisation's sustainable competitive advantage, the development of a talent pool of high potential and high performing incumbents to fill these roles, and the development of a differentiated human resource architecture to facilitate filling these positions with competent incumbents and to ensure their continued commitment to the organisation.

Three things are emphasised in this definition: high potential people, sets of human resource management practices to leverage and further develop their potential, and fitting these people into key or pivotal roles where their skills will make the greatest impact on the organisation. This approach is unashamedly elitist. It assumes that some people are of more use than others and that some roles have more influence on organisational success than others. Pivotal roles are not just the most senior however; people in lower level, customer-facing roles can have big effects on organisational performance.

Class Activity

New research suggests that in sport and arts a small proportion of super-performers make a disproportionately high impact on organisational performance.

▸ To what extent might this result generalise to more traditional work sectors?
▸ Are there any characteristics of the nature of different types of work that make this finding more or less likely?

Global talent management

Global talent management is essentially the same philosophy and approach but applied across a much larger scale. Because of the larger scale, global talent management is more complex as it has to respond to an organisation's differing strategic priorities globally and be sensitive to cross-national and regional differences in beliefs about how people should be managed. Scullion and Collings (2011) give the following reasons for the emergence of global talent management as a key strategic issue for multinational corporations.

- A growing belief among executives that global business success rests on globally competent talent.
- A growing belief that there are shortages of management and leadership talent on an international scale while recognising that talented employees may be located (hidden) in complex global operations. Ways of surfacing the latent talent in a workforce are therefore a priority.
- Global talent searches are needed to identify the people who are capable of managing very diverse workforces brought about by rising gender diversity in the workplace and much easier mobility of labour within and across labour markets. Easier mobility also makes it easier for high potential people to work elsewhere – so retaining them has become more of a priority.
- The increasing shift to knowledge-based and service sectors in which human capital has more direct connections to organisational success because of the increasingly intellectual nature of work.

Inclusive talent management

As mentioned above, talent management is usually viewed through an elitist lens, but it can be approached in a variety of ways. Some organisations, perhaps because of sensitivity to possible criticism of elitism or perhaps because of genuine concerns about the morality of elitism, operate more inclusive strategies. Inclusive talent strategies appear to be much less common than elitist versions, however, and raise questions about how they might differ from good but standardised human resource management practices. To get a better understanding of what inclusive talent management could be like we need to appreciate how exclusive approaches differ from human resource management (see Table 12.1).

Human resource management focuses on all employees for the whole of their employment with the organisation.

Table 12.1 Talent management and human resource management

Dimension	HRM	Exclusive talent management
Scope	Covers all employees from recruitment through to termination of employment.	Focuses on a minority of employees for so long as they are in a talent pool.
Functions	Covers all HR remits (e.g. reward, employment relations and performance management) and compliance with employment law.	Focuses on identifying high potential employees and delivering a differentiated development experience. Emphasises career development and succession planning.
Purpose	Looks for consistency of experience across jobs, grades, and roles during the lifetime of employment.	Focuses on succession planning for key positions and filling key positions with high potential people.
Drivers	Visions of what employment with the organisation should be like. Includes strategies, policies, and practices unique to the organisation. Heavily influenced by the ways that line managers interpret and implement policies.	Talk of scarcity and competitive advantage. Closely linked to the resource-based view in choosing whom to develop. Conformance to sector and labour market expectations. Heavily influenced by senior managers, consultants, and a talent team in designing the approach.

It covers a wider range of functions than talent management and operates those functions across all roles and grades. The human resource management experience is heavily dependent upon the individual's relationship with his/her line manager, whereas the talent experience is overlaid with exposure to senior managers and other high potential people.

If inclusive talent management is to be more than a standard human resource management experience on offer to all employees, then it has to offer something different. Recent theoretical consideration of what inclusive talent management could entail (Swailes, Downs and Orr, 2014) proposes the following characteristics:

- Inclusive talent management has to focus on all (or at least most) employees.
- Talent in inclusive talent management in seen as an absolute characteristic of a person, not something that is relative to the talent of others.
- Organisations must try to identify and deploy the unique talents of all employees. Talent deployment on a larger scale requires greater organisational willingness to rotate people through jobs as a way of helping to discover where talents are best deployed.
- Where a person's talent cannot be effectively deployed in an organisation then reasonable efforts should be made to help the individual deploy their talents elsewhere.

In sharp contrast to the elitist definition, inclusive talent management has been defined as, 'the recognition and acceptance that all employees have talent together with the on-going evaluation and deployment of employees in positions that gives the best fit and opportunity (via participation) for employees to use those talents'. (Swailes et al., 2014: 533). This approach to talent management is unlikely to become widespread, however, because of the costs of implementing it. Nevertheless, it is in many ways a more accurate description of 'true' talent management since it recognises and tries to use the abilities, interests, and skills of an entire workforce rather than a small part of one. Indeed, Swailes and colleagues (2014) argued that conventional, elitist talent management is better seen as partial talent management since it only addresses part of the talent available to an organisation.

Questions

1 Of the forms of talent programme described above, which do you think has the strongest moral basis and why?
2 As an employee, which type of programme would you prefer to be part of?

THEORETICAL PERSPECTIVES

Strategic human resource management

Elitist approaches to talent management fit very well with classic theory around strategic human resource management. In particular, elitist talent management fits with and brings life to the idea of workforce differentiation (Huselid and Becker, 2011). In the differentiated workforce, not all employees are thought to contribute equally. Some jobs are assumed to be more important than others that, while they may be essential, do not add as much value to the organisation and may be easily staffed or contracted-out. Theory suggests that a differentiated workforce needs a differentiated human resource architecture to get the best out of it (Becker and Huselid, 2006). Failure to recognise differentiation impedes the organisation's competiveness and competitive advantage. The key question this poses is whether organisational competitiveness derives from the average performance of a majority of employees or the 'super' performance of a minority. New research is very clear that, in some sectors, employee performance is not normally distributed but follows a power distribution (Aguinis and O'Boyle, 2014; O'Boyle and Aguinis, 2012). Put simply, outstanding performance by a minority has a massive effect impact on organisational performance. Much more research is needed to test the extent to which this applies in other business sectors and cultures, however.

Talent management is a form of human resource development and, like most HRD, exists largely for the benefit of organisations not individuals. This is consistent with human capital theory and the resource-based view (Barney, 1991; Wright, Dunford and Snell, 2001) which assume that it is not worthwhile for organisations to develop employees unless it serves the organisation to do so – and even then they may leave (Bryson, 2007). Human capital theory has been influential in explaining why organisations should engage in HRD, and it recognises two types of skills: general and firm-specific. General skills are usable to other organisations whereas firm-specific skills, by definition, are not. From a human capital perspective, it only makes sense to run talent programmes that develop firm-specific skills as these give a higher return on investment. The resource-based view shifted explanations of competitive advantage away from external factors, such as social and economic trends, towards greater recognition of the role of internal factors. To give sustained competitive advantage, resources need to be rare, valuable, inimitable and integrated into the business (organised) and the more of these characteristics that a resource has the more useful it becomes. This makes sense because, for example, a resource that is easily obtained by competitors (not rare) and/or which is easily copied by competitors will not give competitive advantage for long.

Resources can be many things such as natural resources, capital, and inter-firm relationships, and we need to ask: what is the resource in talent management? At a simple level, it is the people named as talent who are the resource. We use 'named' here because in this context to say 'identified' as talent suggests that talent is objectifiable, something that can be identified with precision such that anyone not identified as talent is not talented. With that caveat in mind, the resource has to be more than simply the people and much more about what they bring. The resource is better seen as social structures that the 'talented' create and use to benefit the organisation. It is their relationships and their networks and their ability to use them effectively that lie at the heart of the true resource.

The distinctive social architecture that develops among people is rare in the sense that no other identical architecture or configuration exists and it is inimitable because other organisations cannot copy the same architecture. If this unique social structure is well organised, then the conditions for talent management to contribute a distinctive resource are met. There is some evidence for this theory from research on what happens to 'stars' when they move between organisations (Groysberg, Lee and Nanda, 2008; Groysberg, Nanda and Nohria, 2004). Groysberg and colleagues found that the performance of 'stars' dipped when they switched to another organisation, and this is explained by a loss or fracture of the networks that sustained the stars before switching. While some of a star's network remains in place, important aspects of it are lost and with it the ability to perform at the same very high level. This also explains why organisations often recruit whole teams, for example research and development teams or teams of traders. Recruiting a whole team improves the chances of preserving the social architecture that sustained the high performing team, and the chances of importing similar high levels of performance are maximised.

Now that we know why talent management should work, two related questions arise. First, are there other reasons why organisations pursue it? Second, why do some organisations not adopt it? Reasons for not adopting talent management include:

- Managers being satisfied with organisational performance to the extent that deliberate employee differentiation strategies are judged unnecessary.
- Managers believing that there are more pressing priorities to boost performance than talent management.
- Traditions of collectivism and equality in organisational cultures that would clash with the philosophy of elitist talent management. This explains why talent programmes occur less often in the public sector which tends to be sensitive to hard performance evaluation and explicit valuation of employee contributions,

accelerated promotion, and reward (Boyne, Jenkins and Pools, 1999).

- In large organisations, the sheer complexity of designing a fair international talent operation may be a disincentive.
- The (in)ability of senior HR managers to understand business needs to the extent that a useful talent system could be designed and operated.

> **? Critical Thinking 12.1** **Geographical variation in philosophy**
>
> Later in this chapter we refer to a 'dark side' to sum-up possible negative consequences of talent management. Think of the basics: A small number of employees is selected for special development aimed at accelerating their careers. The majority of employees are not. We would like you to think about possible dark-side effects and how organisations could minimise the risks of a dark side occurring. To help you do this:
>
> **Questions**
>
> 1 Organisation cultures are all different, so what types of culture could accentuate a dark side?
> 2 What features could organisations design into talent programmes to minimise the risk of a dark side?
> 3 How could organisations assess the extent to which a dark side is occurring?

Institutionalism

In relation to why organisations adopt or do not adopt talent systems, there is a compelling explanation over and above the resource-based view. In essence, some organisations adopt talent management because others do. This explanation relies on organisational institutionalism theory, which explains why organisations operating in the same sector are often very similar in the ways that they structure and operate. Think of banks and universities, for example. Every organisation operates in a field of organisations providing the same or similar products or services. In a field, organisations source new employees from the same labour markets, access the same supply chains and have similar stakeholder configurations. Fields create pressures for organisations to behave and function in the same or similar ways. Failure to conform to institutional pressures and look the same can be problematic for an organisation, as its reputation in the field could be tarnished by nonconformity.

Institutions are not organisations and should not be confused with them. An institution is, 'the more or less taken for granted repetitive social behaviour that is under-pinned by normative systems and cognitive understand-ings that give meaning to social exchange and thus enable self-reproducing social order'(Greenwood et al., 2008: 4).

Talent management arose in a particular corporate con-text in the United States. It fits with the American tradition of individualism and comparatively light unionisation and employment relations legislation. Organisations in Scandi-navia, Southern Europe, and South America, for example, operate in very different contexts. All countries operate dif-ferent social security systems and have different approaches to the role and extent of unionisation, worker involvement and collective bargaining. National-level factors like this have inspired the study of comparative human resource management, because of concerns over the generalisability of Anglo-American approaches to managing people.

Institutional environments come with a unique history shaped by culture and values, traditions, habits and inter-ests (Jafee, 2001). This means that organisations do not behave in rationally economic ways but conform to the social expectations of an institutional field. Organisational behaviour, such as choices about how to manage people, is not simply a response to market pressures but also insti-tutional pressures (Paauwe and Boselie, 2007). Conform-ing to the expectations of the field helps organisations to gain legitimacy and increases the likelihood of survival (Greenwood and Hinings, 1996).

In institutional theory, the mechanism that explains why organisations look alike is isomorphism (DiMaggio and Pow-ell, 1983), which manifests in three ways – coercive, mimetic, and normative isomorphism. Coercive mechanisms involve employment legislation and the role of government in busi-ness organisation. Recent government interest in the ways that banks operate is an example. Mimetic mechanisms refer to the imitation (miming) of competitors. A multina-tional corporation, for instance, that sees its competitors running talent programmes and whose current and pro-spective employees are looking for talent programmes will feel under pressure to respond even though there may not be a clear business case. To some extent, talent management could be a fashionable rather than a rational response. Nor-mative isomorphism is shaped by the influence of the pro-fessions on organisations. Different professions, for example finance, engineering, and law, have their own norms about how knowledge is created and transmitted and about career structures. Aspiring tax consultants or lawyers will have views about the career development that employers should be offering, and those views may push the organisa-tion towards some sort of talent strategy. Failure to respond would make the organisation look out of synch in the sector and tarnish its legitimacy.

Furthermore, all business sectors contain executives who move between firms and who meet at informal and formal events. As the network of interactions between people grows, then the occurrence of rationalised myths increases. These myths then diffuse throughout a sector through 'relational networks' (Greenwood et al., 2008: 3). What is deemed as rational, however, is set by the institu-tional context. What appears as rational in one sector is not necessarily seen as rational in another. Furthermore, while practices can differ widely between sectors, they can also differ widely within sectors when the same sector is viewed across national borders. Most developed countries have a university sector, for instance, but there are big dif-ferences in the ways that universities operate between countries and the differences are caused by political and cultural overlays.

Whether talent management has become an insti-tution is itself debatable. It perhaps has further to go before it becomes one, but in sectors where it is widely implemented without much thinking it is getting close to becoming one (Zucker, 1983). This insight from insti-tutionalism tells us that, in some sectors, talent man-agement, which is essentially an idea about how people should be managed, is probably adopted:

- to gain or maintain legitimacy;
- to appear rational and normal; and
- to offer something different from other organisations but also to conform with other organisations (Sahlin and Wedlin, 2008).

Class Activity

Look on the internet for examples of talent pro-grammes in multinational companies.

▸ What are the philosophies behind the programmes, what areas of the workforce are covered, and what development programmes are available to people in talent pools?

Celebrity society

Another critical view of the spread of talent manage-ment relies on ideas from the notion of celebrity society (van Krieken, 2012) and the ways that it has extended to organisations. Increases in the pay and rewards given to chief executives have outstripped those given to other employees, and alongside this many chief executives have sought and/or achieved corporate celebrity status. With constant pressure to deliver business improvements and a media hungry for stories, organisations are always looking out for success stories and individuality. Corporate insid-ers are often assumed to be too far steeped in problematic organisation cultures to risk at the top, and so outsiders are often preferred. Attracting attention, making bold decisions, publicising successes, winning prizes and awards are now an indispensible part of life at the top and have become part of what it means to be talented.

Alongside the increasing importance of celebrity, the management of large organisations has become more complex. International and global scale operations are more common, labour markets are much more fluid, capital is more easily available, and the power of investors is stronger. Talent management is a logical response to managing complex situations; find the smartest people and set them to work on taking the organisation forward. Those who pass the talent auditions and perform well will also become minor celebrities on the organisational stage and maybe, someday, a big 'star'. Talent pools symbolise what one has to do to be successful in an organisation. They are a touchstone, a reference point, for revealing one's identity in an otherwise large, complex and anonymous organisation.

Van Krieken (2012) argues that in celebrity society there is an oversupply of information and a scarcity of attention. Creating talent pools is a way of concentrating executive attention on a few people and interpreting performance through them rather than dealing with a multitude of employees and the countless interactions that occur between them. Talent management can be seen therefore as a way of helping to simplify the management of very complex situations.

STOP AND REFLECT

Think about the reasons for the growth and spread of talent management given above. Which reason(s) do you think is the most compelling and why? To help you do this, you might think about and discuss this statement: 'Talent management is much more about top managers playing-out their own visions of what high performers should be doing than it is about making a measurable difference to organisational performance.'

IDENTIFYING TALENT

Nine-box grids

Talent is usually seen as a combination of recent and current performance together with future potential. A common method of visualising a workforce on these dimensions is through a nine-box grid where the nine boxes are combinations of three levels of performance and

three levels of potential – see Figure 12.1. In a large organisation, the grids are completed at departmental and local levels and/or by functional areas. They are then aggregated upwards to provide talent analysts and planners with a picture of organisational talent across the organisation by level and area. The end-of-chapter case study shows how a large company used the nine-box approach and the systems that support it.

In Figure 12.1, each box is labelled according to the assessment of performance and potential based on the criteria used in the organisation. The implications of being located in a particular box depend on the organisation's HR policies. Only occupants of the 'superstar' box might be deemed 'talented' in a very elitist scheme. 'Stars' and 'future stars' might be included in a more inclusive but still elitist scheme. The majority of employees are likely to be located on the first and second rows.

Grids of this type can be problematic because individual performance can be erratic for reasons such as changing personal circumstances. Even though performance can be evidence based, it is also partially illusory, and underperformance is perhaps more likely to be recognised than excellent performance. In complex and fast-changing business conditions, assessments of high potential can be short-lived as environmental changes act to make them redundant. Effective grid use also requires open conversations with people, for example asking questions about their intent to leave the organisation.

The grid approach is highly managerial and performative. It utilises the concept of human value which in this instance assumes that different employees posses different values because they are capable of rendering different levels of service in the future. Borrowing directly from economics, the value of people is defined as the expected value of the services that they will deliver to the organisation in the future. Future services are a function of a person's productivity, their transferability, their promotability, and the likelihood that they will stay with the organisation (Flamholtz, 1999). In economic terms, the human value of an employee depends upon the value of what he/she could do in the coming year or two. Each of the four levels of service represents a 'service state' (Flamholtz, 1999: 180). For example, an employee who stays in his/her current position occupies one service state; an employee who is promoted to a higher position, and in theory who gives more value to the organisation, occupies a different service state. The nine-box grid is a qualitative way of capturing talent by scanning across a workforce and allocating employees to different service states according to their perceived value to the organisation.

Promotability timescale

	Uncertain	Medium term	Short term
High promotion potential	**Potential star** Combines under performance with high potential.	**Future star** Solid performance and shows high potential	**Superstar** Outstanding performance in all areas and shows high potential
Promotable	**Promising** Performance improvement needed to confirm potential.	**One to watch** Solid performance and shows some potential	**Star** Excellent performer and shows some potential
Not promotable	**Under performing** Performance management interventions needed.	**Reliable performer** Steady-state	**Excellent performer** Keep
	Underperforming	Good	Outstanding

Performance rating

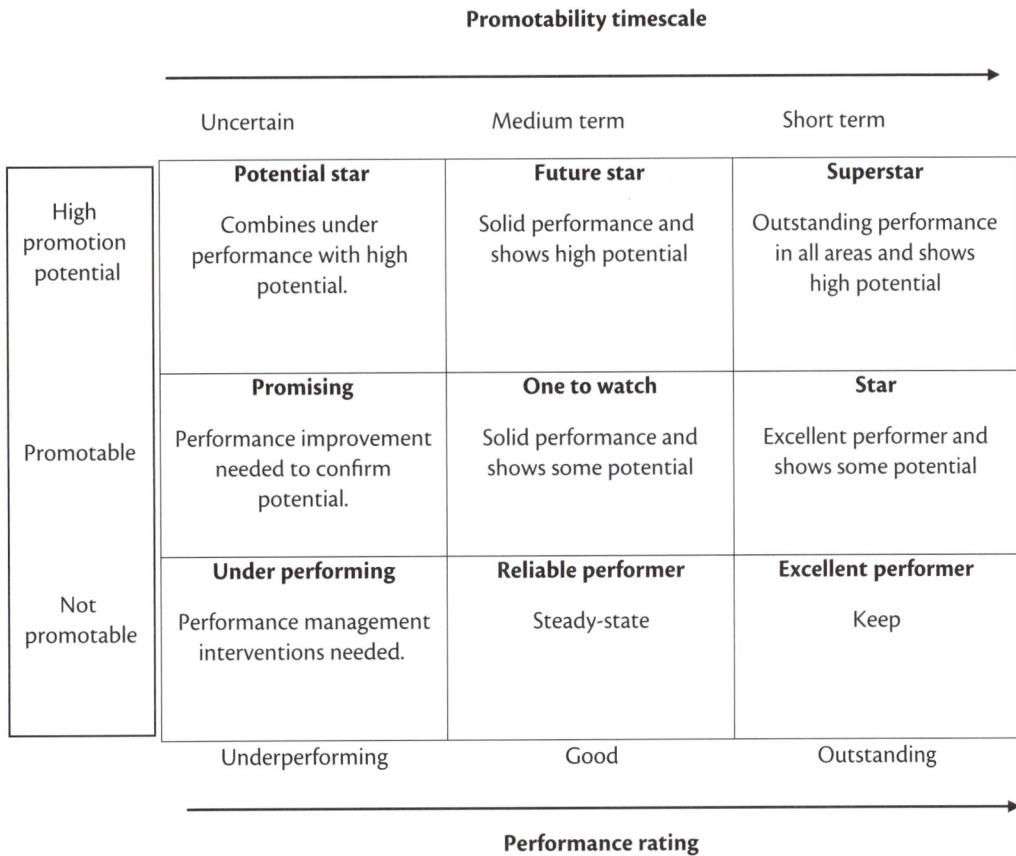

Figure 12.1 Example nine-box grid

Biasing factors in talent identification

A limitation of managerialist methods such as the grid is that they mask a lot of irrational behaviour that affects how employees are viewed. Sources of bias are summarised below.

Physical differences

A small but noticeable effect comes from personal attractiveness. Better-looking people tend to earn more than others. This does not apply everywhere, but it does in sectors where looks are more likely to enhance productivity, such as sales or consulting. Indeed, the best-looking people are more likely to self-sort into occupations where their looks will work to their advantage (Hamermesh and Biddle, 1994). Physical height also correlates with career success and higher earnings (Judge and Cable, 2004). This is explained by nutrition, which correlates with height and cognitive abilities (Schick and Steckel, 2015), although apparent height/earnings effects may be accentuated by

very short people sorting into low-pay occupations (Lundberg, Nystedt and Rooth, 2014).

Upwards influence and liking

A supervisor's ratings of promotability are affected by the upwards influence tactics used by subordinates such as reasoning, ingratiation, assertiveness, and bargaining. Trying to influence supervisors, however, is a risky game for subordinates because they do not know how supervisors will react (Thacker and Wayne, 1995). Upwards influence tactics are likely to vary across cultures and may be related to power-distance and individualism-collectivism (Terpstra-Tong and Ralston, 2002). Impression management is a closely related concept, and men and women have different approaches to the use of impression management, which leaves younger women in particular at a disadvantage (Singh, Kumra and Vinnicombe, 2002). Self-presentation is a powerful tactic in the workplace, and people who exhibit political skill will progress faster than those who do not (Blickle et al., 2012).

In addition to influence tactics, performance ratings are highly correlated with the extent to which raters like the people they are rating (interpersonal affect). Research shows a substantial overlap between rater liking and performance rating, although this is to some extent a reflection of true differences in ratee performance (Sutton et al., 2013; Varma and Pichler, 2007). A plausible explanation is that raters tend to like high performers more than others.

📖 **In the News   Class matters!**

Top law and accountancy firms in the UK are 'side-lining' working-class job applicants in favour of candidates from privileged backgrounds – according to a survey published in 2015. In their search for talent, firms used criteria such as the amount of travelling that candidates have done, their confidence, and a 'posh' accent. These and other factors were more likely seen in graduates from 'top' universities where recruitment was focused. Graduates from working-class backgrounds who are less likely to travel and be involved in prestigious social events were less likely to be recruited.

Read more at http://www.bbc.co.uk/news/education-33109052.

Gender

Gender is an important variable in leadership research and is a source of potential bias within talent management. Women continue to be disadvantaged at work (Acker, 2012; Calas and Smircich, 2006; Chartered Management Institute, 2014) and tend to lose out in terms of an enduring gender pay gap, an association with lower status and less stable part-time or flexible work (Durbin and Tomlinson, 2014; Wilson, 2013), and both horizontal and vertical segregation of jobs. Horizontally, men and women tend to be located in different types of work that become associated with a particular gender, typically to the detriment of work that is seen as largely populated by women. Vertically, there are far more men at the top of organisations and the professions than women. Even very senior women tend to lose out through political processes in organisations, which can became a double-bind since political behaviour is seen as congruent with a male norm and thus deemed inappropriate for women (Doldor, Anderson and Vinnicombe, 2013).

Acker (1990, 1992) suggested that inequality is inherent in organisations that are themselves gendered. Organisations are seen to have an inherent preference for male workers who are typically seen to be 'unencumbered' and thus ideal workers. Acker (1990, 1992) identified four key processes through which organisations remain gendered. The first, gender divisions, refers to notions of horizontal and vertical segregation noted above. The second refers to the manner in which 'symbols, images and forms of consciousness' (Acker, 1992: 253) produce and reproduce a gendered order. Thus, language and communication in organisations typically rely on notions of masculinity and making oneself heard, to the advantage of men. The third process, interactions between organisational stakeholders, works to reinforce 'images of gender' (Acker, 1992: 253) and ensures that hierarchies supporting and highlighting male dominance are maintained. The fourth process, 'internal mental work' (Acker, 1992: 253), relates to actions at both an individual and collective level that adhere to (or otherwise) gender-appropriate persona, with all four processes working together to reinforce a gendered organisation 'substructure' (Acker, 1992: 255). Women in modern organisations (fluid, focused on individual success) may be at an even greater disadvantage through these four processes, since career structures and ascendancy through the ranks are now less formalised and more subject to individual self-promotion and line manager sponsorship (Williams, Muller and Kilanski, 2012).

Such self- and line manager promotion is relevant to talent management that focuses on leadership talent and high leadership potential (De Vos and Dries, 2013). Talent identification processes, therefore, struggle to be gender-neutral (Farndale, Scullion and Sparrow, 2010) and are particularly prone to gender bias. The CIPD (2010) conducted a mixed-method study of talent management from the perspective of the talent managed and found that the manner in which talent is identified is increasingly reliant on opaque processes and aspects such as social networking. Other research supports this view and points to the central role of informal networks in talent progression decisions (Handley, 2014; Tansley and Tietze, 2013; Williams et al., 2012). However, women - particularly those in part-time employment (Durbin and Tomlinson, 2014) - do not benefit from mentors and networks to the same extent as men (Al Ariss, Cascio and Paauwe, 2014).

On the basis of in-depth interviews with 'high-potentials', Ibarra, Carter and Silva (2010) concluded that women are far less likely than men to benefit from mentoring, largely because their mentors tend not to be as senior and, therefore, are less influential and less likely to open up key network links for women. Linehan and Scullion (2008) identified similar difficulties facing senior female managers who were found to miss out on opportunities for promotion due to a lack of effective mentors and sponsors and a more limited access to powerful networks compared to male managers. The female managers in their study explicitly referred to difficulties in succeeding in a 'man's world' (Linehan and Scullion, 2008: 29) high-lighting the continuing relevance of Acker's (1990, 1992, 2012) model. Thus, women are less likely to benefit from mentoring and useful networks which may have a detrimental impact on their chances of being identified and included in talent pools and of progressing upwards.

As outlined above, talent management tends to focus on leadership or managerial talent. The notion of management or leadership itself, however, can be seen to be gendered because of an enduring notion of 'heroic' or masculine leadership (Billing, 2011; Broadridge and Simpson, 2011; Ford, Burkinshaw and Cahill, 2014), thus calling into question the equity of talent management approaches. Mäkelä et al. (2010) found evidence of two processes in global talent management; 'on-line' (characterised by recorded and demonstrated prior experience and feedback) and 'off-line' (more future-oriented) processes. The second, off-line, stage was seen to be particularly limited due to cultural distance between HQ and subsidiaries and homophily or similarity bias (the tendency to support or promote those who are similar to ourselves) and also because of network position (propinquity). People who were included in more central networks, who were closer or more visible to, and perceived as similar to, central decision-makers were more likely to be included in the talent pool. This has obvious implications for gender bias; women are less likely to benefit from powerful or central informal networks and, because they are less likely to comply with a masculine leadership construct, are more likely to be disadvantaged.

Acker's notion of the ideal masculine unencumbered worker permeates other aspects of the talent management process. Festing, Knappert and Kornau (2015), for example, after research across five countries, concluded that global performance management (one potential element of talent identification and selection) is more closely aligned with the preferences of male managers. Such processes are reinforced through the exposure of those included in talent pools to 'strategic language' and ways of talking to which the excluded are seldom if ever exposed. This can become a virtuous circle, whereby those identified as talented become perceived by others as ever more talented (as they are using strategic language) and, indeed, conduct identity work to reinforce this position (Tansley and Tietze, 2013). As women are less likely to be identified as talent and less likely to be senior managers, their exposure to such language will be restricted and their disadvantage potentially intensified.

Five aspects or elements of talent management that have an impact on the likely extent of gender bias have been observed in German media organisations (Festing, Kornau and Shafer, 2014). Gender bias was deemed *more* likely in an organisation that has:

- a prevailing masculine talent/management stereotype;
- hierarchical or vertical career orientation, with a model of linear career paths;
- greater focus on technical (rather than personal development) skills in talent development programmes;
- an elite (rather than inclusive) approach to talent management;
- a more 'discriminatory' talent management approach, for example male-dominated talent selection teams and opaque processes.

Thus, talent management, whilst potentially adding value for organisations, may have several unanticipated and potentially undesirable consequences for women.

> **(?) Critical Thinking 12.2**
>
> As you can see, there are some serious biasing effects that might be introduced into talent programmes simply because of a person's gender and the idea of the gendered organisation. We would like you to think about the following questions:
>
> **Questions**
>
> 1 To what extent do you think that gender is a real issue in the fairness of talent identification?
> 2 Do you think it is possible to overcome gender bias in talent management programmes?
> 3 What practices could organisations put in place to minimise gender bias?
> 4 Can you suggest any additional factors to the five identified by Festing and colleagues (2014) that would accentuate gender bias?

Talent identification in multinational companies

In addition to the general problems in talent identification, some issues arise specifically in MNCs. One obvious difference is the interaction of management styles emanating from the parent country and the host countries in which subsidiaries are based. Subsidiaries in different countries are influenced by different institutional effects (see above) that push towards isomorphism and in effect push to keep staffing systems apart. Vo (2009), for instance, found that US and Japanese MNCs operating in Vietnam followed different staffing policies. The American firm was more willing to employ locals in management roles and mirrored its home country practices by fast tracking high potential staff. In contrast, the Japanese MNC followed a traditional model of relying more on expatriate managers, long service and late promotion if justified. The Japanese firm also effectively restricted locals to going no further than middle management positions.

Analysing the British takeover of a French firm, Boussebaa and Morgan (2008) found major incompatibility problems. French managers saw the British approach of measuring performance and potential as leading to a 'rat race' in contrast to a much preferred *esprit de corps*. The whole philosophy of talent identification was different in France and grounded in the idea that a managerial elite is developed outside the firm in the *grand écoles* system. A British approach of seeking *potential* talent clashed with a French approach of employing *proven* talent.

Selection for talent pools in MNCs is, as well as performance, influenced by cultural differences, similarities (homophily) between high performing employees and the talent decision-makers, and the network position of staff such that higher visibility increases the chances of talent recognition (Mäkelä, Bjorkman and Ehrnrooth, 2010). Another specific barrier is the failure of MNCs to manage talent in subsidiaries, which is aggravated by managers in subsidiaries suppressing talented staff in an effort to keep them in the subsidiary (Mellahi and Collings, 2010).

Large and fast-moving economies

Large and fast-moving economies such as Brazil, Russia, India and China face a particular challenge arising from the type and availability of the human capital open to them. Concerns centre mostly around country-level effects such as the mobility of talented people (broadly defined as people with skills and qualifications). For India and China in particular, Doh et al. (2014) identified four underlying talent issues:

1 Population growth and shifts in the working age that will 'exacerbate generational differences within a workforce' (227). Expanding university education is producing more graduates, but companies face challenges responding to graduate expectations. Talent programmes will need to accommodate both local and expatriate ways of thinking about management.
2 Specialist skills could be in short supply despite rising university output.
3 The nature of work in India and China is changing, moving from labour-intensive to more capital-intensive and knowledge-based sectors. This requires far more interaction with other organisations and other countries, so cross-cultural competences will be at a premium.
4 Increasing interactions will push for convergence of HR systems, including talent management. Sharp differences in talent practices between Western and Eastern firms could be problematic.

One of the big debates in HRM is whether it actually makes any difference to organisational performance. Of course, many organisations assume that it does, but demonstrating a link empirically is very difficult partly for methodological reasons. However, the consensus now is that there are links between HR practices and organisational performance (Birdi et al., 2008; Crook et al., 2011). The question arises, however: will the same HR practices and architectures that work in the West migrate with the same effects to very different cultures and economic conditions? Or are different HR architectures required? What is becoming clear is that whatever HR systems are used, they have to be matched with quality (skills, expertise) of the local labour and the strategy of the firm (Li et al., 2015). Successful talent systems will also need to address local cultural norms such as cohesiveness and collaboration in China (Zhou et al., 2013); employees who can act as boundary spanners such as Japanese immigrants in Brazil (Furusawa and Brewster, 2015), and running separate HR practices for managerial and non-managerial employees where needed (Fey and Bjorkman, 2001).

A central question in cross-country studies of talent management is how the concept varies between countries. On what dimensions might ideas about talent differ? Inclusion versus exclusion seems an obvious one. Attitudes to age may differ – can older people still be recognised as talent? Expectations of the jobs that women should do and the roles that are appropriate for them may also differ starkly between West and East. Views towards sourcing talent from inside and outside may also vary. However, we suggest that differences within countries, wherever you look, will be greater than the differences between countries.

A comparative study of India and China found that both were comfortable with an elitist approach in common with the West; talent was seen in terms of young, promotable people, but the extent to which firms would see the need for distinctive programmes to manage talent may differ. Cooke et al., (2014) concluded that talent management has to be contingency-based such that the particular design of a programme will be contingent upon local customs, norms, and HR practices.

TALENT MANAGEMENT: THE DARK SIDE

Sources of bias in talent identification processes are one example of the 'dark side' of talent management. Figure 12.2 summarises some of the unanticipated consequences for employees who are included in or excluded from talent pools.

Included in the talent pool

- Disengagement if no challenging projects

- Self-fulfilling prophecy through exposure to better leadership and strategic language

Not included in the talent pool

- Insecurity, reduced performance

- Frustration

Both: dehumanisation

Process

- Silo mentality

- Elitist culture, teamworking difficult

- Political and obtuse

- Talent identification bias

Figure 12.2 The 'dark side' of talent management
source: Adapted from Handley (2014)

Potentially undesirable consequences for those who have not been identified as talent might include feelings of insecurity because they feel less valued, disappointment particularly if individuals have been rejected, or frustration, all of which could have a negative impact on their performance (Ford, Harding and Stoyanova, 2010). Those *included* in the talent pool might also experience negative consequences: they may feel that they are being treated simply as a 'resource' (and so dehumanised) or, alternatively, they may feel that promised opportunities have not materialised, causing individuals to become disengaged (Mellahi and Collings, 2010; Huang and Tansley, 2012; Vaiman et al., 2012).

The processes through which talent is identified and/or selected are a key contributor to such feelings through the biasing effects identified earlier in this chapter. In addition, team working may become problematic in elitist work cultures (Mellahi and Collings, 2010; Thunnissen, Boselie and Fruytier, 2013). Divisional, regional, or local managers may also have a vested interest in retaining their own talent and not putting their better performing or high potential people forward for central talent development (Farndale, Scullion and Sparrow, 2010). Political behaviour amongst those who might potentially be included in the talent pool, in addition to their line managers, may create significant barriers to effective implementation of talent

management and intensify unanticipated consequences for both the individual and the organisation (CIPD, 2010; Huang and Tansley, 2012; Malik and Singh, 2014).

CONCLUSION

Talent management is an evolving and complex field that is fraught with political overlays and interests. Some organisations have explicit talent programmes; others avoid explicit programmes but maintain 'hidden' talent lists of staff; and others avoid the practice altogether. The reasons why organisations adopt a particular approach are mired in assumptions about good leadership, what it looks like and how leaders should be developed, and each business sector has its own set of influencing factors that govern the extent and form of talent initiatives. Despite the investments that many organisations make in talent programmes, their effects on business performance are not well understood. For many organisations, talent programmes are an act of faith rather than a demonstrable influence on performance. The reasons why some people are identified as talent, the effects of talent programmes on performance, and the ways that organisations evaluate the success of talent programmes are important topics for future research.

End of Chapter Case Study Talent identification

This case relates to a large UK-based general merchandising, non-food retail company (RetCo) with 800 stores and over 25,000 employees. The context for RetCo's interest in talent management included competitive sector conditions, economic downturn, competition for skilled labour, and growing internet sales. The company encouraged internal promotions rather than new hires. The long-term challenge was to identify the type of people and skills needed in the future, understand the 'shape' of the current talent pool, and develop people in key areas.

Annual appraisal reviews of all personnel led to a performance grade based on achievement of objectives. A mid-year review process, known as a Management Development Review (MDR), was conducted to assess future potential with all management grades and optionally for clerical colleagues by exception where they are seen to have future potential to progress. The aim of the MDR was to look forward and identify the level of future potential in the business. Line managers completed documentation ahead of the MDR meeting classifying their direct reports' potential and providing a rating of risk and value to the business.

Individual talent data was transferred to a 'Mapping Document' for each function which plotted employee potential by grade against six levels of potential ranging from high to low. Where Senior Managers were rated as High Potential, line managers completed an additional checklist to validate against detailed criteria outlining what high potential meant. The purpose of this was to provoke thinking and discussion on the ratings for the MDR meeting. Individuals were then rated against a nine-box grid based on an assessment of their performance and future potential. Mid-year discussions held as an output of the MDR meeting were intended to be open and honest and convey the opinions of line managers and others about an employee's potential to ensure that individuals were clear about how the organisation saw them. Data were input to a talent management system that would feed data upwards so that regional managers could review talent data reports for their region.

While this talent system was elitist as it was grading people relative to each other as a prelude to selecting high achievers, it was to some extent inclusive given the large number of employees it covered. Structured talent programmes were designed for early career employees, developing people in their current role, and developing to the next level. This was supported by career profile documents by function, highlighting competency frameworks and leadership behaviours. Leadership programmes were designed for selected employees to develop three characteristics of high potential managers, Judgement, Drive, and Influence. New staff were given an introduction to the company's history and culture and told about the talent processes used. The company's commitment to employee development was evaluated through an annual engagement survey that asked staff to give their views towards career progress and a range of related concepts.

Line managers submitted their predicted ratings of an individual's performance prior to the formal appraisal meeting. These were collated by HR, and any unusual or contentious ratings were discussed with managers. Ratings were expected to fit a standard normal distribution, and inflated ratings could be downgraded – with possible adverse effects on the employee concerned. Employees also prepared for appraisal by self-rating their performance using a range of toolkits and documents to help them. Final performance ratings were linked to a sliding scale of pay increments; the better the rating the higher the increment.

MDR and appraisal discussions were documented separately but fed into a talent review system, for example an employee could be graded as ready for his/her next role within two years. To assess potential, employees were classified against six ratings of potential, each with descriptors explaining the criteria for each rating. In addition, value ratings related to the employee's value to the overall business, rated as critical, high, or standard. Risk ratings related to the risk of the employee leaving the business went from high if it was anticipated that he/she would leave within six months to low if it was anticipated he/she would not leave within eighteen months. A 'standard' rating, for example, meant that the employee had little impact on the business as a whole and that his/her skills could be replaced quite quickly. Documents were available to line managers describing the behaviours matching each rating. Although the risk and value classifications in particular were sensitive, it was suggested, though not mandatory, that line managers should share these ratings with employees.

When all data were entered into the review system, reports were prepared by HR for regional talent meetings attended by local managers, area managers, and regional managers. Review meetings aimed to calibrate talent decisions across the business. They were layered, in that different levels of management were considered at different meetings. Each employee was rated depending on his/her potential position and given an action plan depending upon his/her status: for example, to continue in his/her current role, to move across or upwards, or to deal with performance concerns. Line managers were asked to give feedback directly to employees on the MDR outcomes, though they were encouraged to avoid attaching 'labels' to their feedback for fear of 'pigeonholing' individuals.

To get consistency, HR staff trained line managers in how to conduct talent meetings, and they were given reference documents and advice on how to handle conversations with people, depending on their position on the grid. Examples of fictitious employees were used in an effort to get consistent interpretations of performance and potential. Question and answer routines, descriptors of the nine grid positions, and guidelines for appraisers were available, although there was less transparency in the information available to appraisees regarding the potential/MDR classifications.

Managing the annual talent meetings was a very busy time for HR staff. Because of the large scale of the talent process, HR business partners were collecting predicted grades, communicating review processes, training appraisers, preparing data and reports, and capturing the outcomes of talent meetings. Missing and suspicious data had to be checked before talent reports could be produced ahead of each review meeting. Alongside the review of most employees, data for the Executive MDR also had to be collated to review those having the potential to progress to Head of Function positions.

Employees nominated for progression to the next grade attended development centres to provide feedback on their performance and participated in structured leadership programmes, with development tailored around the skills and leadership behaviours required for the role. Additionally they were offered a range of development programmes including management skills, individual diagnostics, 360-degree feedback, internal mentoring, assessment and development centres, leadership, leading change, acting-up and secondment opportunities.

Questions

1   Given that the same talent identification strategy was intended for use across the business, what management problems might occur across the different regions?
2   How might employees react when they find out that they are located outside the top boxes in the nine-box grid? How do 'conversations' need to adjust to take account of grid position?
3   What political factors could influence the ways in which employees and managers 'play' the talent management system described in the case?

FOR DISCUSSION AND REVISION

1   What factors could executives and HR directors consider when designing a typical elitist talent programme for a multinational company?
2   Human resource metrics are used by organisations as a way of evaluating and measuring their human capital. What metrics (percentages, ratios, counts) could be used to help identify high-performing and high-potential employees.
3   What ethical issues, concerns, and problems could be considered in the design of talent programmes in a multinational company?
4   How might an organisation evaluate the effects, impacts, and success of a talent programme? Specifically, what factors could it evaluate?
5   What aspects of people and organisations make the fair and reliable identification of talent difficult?
6   How might employees excluded from talent pools react to their exclusion? What is the range of reactions that disaffected employees might display, and what factors could moderate or influence their reactions?

GLOSSARY

Institutionalism: Concerns the ways that organisations interact with society and are shaped by other organisations and government.

Strategic human resource management: Linking HR practices to the strategy of the organisation. This might seem obvious, but HR practices are often not closely linked to strategy.

Talent: 'Talent' is used to mean different things. Sometimes it is used as a synonym for 'employees'. More specifically, it refers to a small proportion of employees whom, by virtue of their high performance and high potential, an organisation is looking to transition into more senior roles.

Talent management: Talent management refers to systems and process that identify, develop, and deploy high-performing and high-potential employees to best effect in an organisation. Many organisations do not operate an explicit talent management programme.

Talent pools: Groups of employees marked out for their above average potential for promotion. Pools normally contain only a small fraction of a workforce, but pools may be created for junior, middle, and senior management and also for different functional areas in an organisation.

Unencumbered worker: Notionally, a worker available to meet all the demands of a job. Someone who is not constrained (encumbered) by children, dependents, or domestic responsibilities. Most are assumed to be male.

FURTHER READING

For more information on gendered organisations, see Acker, J. (1990) Hierarchies, jobs, bodies: A theory of gendered organizations. *Gender and Society*, 4(2): 139–158.

For more information on the idea of the 'glass cliff', see Mulcahy, M. and Linehan, C. (2014) Females and precarious board positions: Further evidence of the glass cliff. *British Journal of Management*, 25(3): 425–438.

For more information on the links between the corporate HR function and global talent management, see Farndale, E., Scullion, H. and Sparrow, P. (2010) The role of the corporate HR function in global talent management. *Journal of World Business*, 45: 161–168.

For a detailed review of global talent management, see Tarique, I. and Schuler, R. S. (2010) Global talent management: Literature review, integrative framework and suggestions for further research. *Journal of World Business*, 45: 122–133.

For a good summary of the psychology behind talent management, see Dries, N. (2013) The psychology of talent management: A review and research agenda. *Human Resource Management Review*, 23(4): 267–290.

For a good review of the different ways that organisations can approach talent management, see Sparrow, P., Scullion, H. and Tarique, I. (2014) Multiple lenses on talent management: Definitions and contours of the field. In Sparrow, P., Scullion, H. and Tarique, I. (eds), *Strategic Talent Management: Contemporary Issues in International Context*. Cambridge: Cambridge University Press, pp. 36–69.

REFERENCES

ACKER, J. (1990) Hierarchies, jobs, bodies: A theory of gendered organizations. *Gender and Society*, 4(2): 139–158.

ACKER, J. (1992) Gendering organizational theory. In Mills, A. J. and Tancred, P. (eds.), *Gendering Organizational Analysis*. California: Sage, pp. 248–260.

ACKER, J. (2012) Gendered organizations and intersectionality: Problems and possibilities. *Equality, Diversity and Inclusion: An International Journal*, 31 (3): 214–224.

AGUINIS, H. AND O'BOYLE, E. (2014) Star performers in twenty-first century organizations. *Personnel Psychology*, 67(2): 313–350.

AL ARISS, A., CASCIO, W.F. AND PAAUWE, J. (2014) Talent management: Current theories and future research directions. *Journal of World Business*, 49(2): 173–179.

AL NAHDI, Y. AND SWAILES, S. (2015) Towards job localisation in Oman: Drivers and barriers in the private sector. Paper given to the 4th EIASM Talent Management Workshop, Valencia, September.

BARNEY, J. (1991) Firm resources and sustained competitive advantage. *Journal of Management*, 17(1): 99–121.

BCG (2013) *Creating People Advantage 2013: Lifting HR Practices to the Next Level*. Boston: The Boston Consulting Group/European Association for People Management.

BECKER, B. E. AND HUSELID, M. A. (2006) Strategic human resource management: Where do we go from here? *Journal of Management*, 32(6): 898–925.

BILLING, Y. D. (2011). Are women in management victims of the phantom of the male norm? *Gender, Work and Organization*, 18(3): 298–317.

BIRDI, K., CLEGG, C., PATTERSON, M., ROBINSON, A., STRIDE, C., WALL, T. D. AND WOOD, S. J. (2008) The impact of human resource and operational management practices on company productivity: A longitudinal study. *Personnel Psychology*, 61: 467–501.

BLICKLE, G., DICKMANN, C., SCHNEIDER, P., KALTHOFER, Y. AND SUMMERS, J. (2012) When modesty wins: Impression management through modesty, political skill, and career success – a two-study investigation. *European Journal of Work and Organizational Psychology*, 21(6): 899–922.

BOUSSEBAA, M. AND MORGAN, G. (2008) Managing talent across national borders: The challenges faced by an international retail group. *Critical Perspectives on International Business*, 4(1): 25–41.

BOWMAN, G .W. (1964) What helps or harms promotability? *Harvard Business Review*, 42(1): 6–26 and 184–196.

BOYNE, G., JENKINS, G. AND POOLS, M. (1999) Human resource management in the public and private sectors: An empirical comparison. *Public Administration*, 77(2): 407–420.

BROADRIDGE, A. AND SIMPSON, R. (2011) 25 years on: Reflecting on the past and looking to the future in gender and management research. *British Journal of Management*, 22(3): 470–483.

BRYSON, J. (2007) Human resource development or developing human capability? In Bolton, S. C. and Houlihan, M. (eds), *Searching for the Human in Human Resource Management*. Basingstoke: Palgrave Macmillan, pp. 171–192.

CALAS, M. B. AND SMIRCICH, L. (2006) From the 'woman's point of view' ten years later: Towards a feminist organization studies. In Clegg, S. R., Hardy, C., Lawrence, T. B.

and Nord, W. R. (eds.), *The Sage Handbook of Organization Studies* (2nd ed.). London: Sage, pp. 284–346.

Chartered Management Institute (2014) *Women in Management: The Power of Role Models.* London: Chartered Management Institute.

CIPD (2010) *The Talent Perspective: What Does it Feel Like to be Talent-Managed.* London: CIPD. Available at: http:/www.cipd.co.uk.

COLLINGS, D. C. AND MELLAHI, K. (2009) Strategic talent management: A review and research agenda. *Human Resource Management Review,* 19(9): 304–313.

COOKE, F. L., SAINI, D. AND WANG, J. (2014) Talent management in China and India: A comparison of management perceptions and human resource practices. *Journal of World Business,* 49(2): 225–235.

CROOK, T. R., TODD, S. Y., COMBS, J. G. AND WOEHR, D. J. (2011) Does human capital matter? A meta-analysis of the relationship between human capital and firm performance. *Journal of Applied Psychology,* 96(3). 443–456.

DE VOS, A. AND DRIES, N. (2013). Applying a talent management lens to career management: The role of human capital composition and continuity. *International Journal of Human Resource Management,* 24(9): 1816–1831.

DIMAGGIO, P. J. AND POWELL, W. W. (1983) The iron cage revisited: Institutional isomorphism and collective rationality in organizational fields. *American Sociological Review,* 48(2): 147–160.

DOH, J., SMITH, R., STUMPF, S. AND TYMON, W. (2014) Emerging markets and regional patterns in talent management: The challenge of India and China. In Sparrow, P., Scullion, H. and Tarique, I. (eds), *Strategic Talent Management: Contemporary Issues in International Context.* Cambridge: Cambridge University Press, pp. 224–253.

DOLDOR, E., ANDERSON, D. AND VINNICOMBE, S. (2013) Refining the concept of political will: A gender perspective. *British Journal of Management,* 24(3): 414–427.

DURBIN, S. AND TOMLINSON, J. (2014) Female part-time Managers: Careers, mentors and role models. *Gender, Work and Organization.* 21(4): 308–320.

FARNDALE, E., SCULLION, H. AND SPARROW, P. (2010) The role of the corporate HR function in global talent management. *Journal of World Business,* 45(2): 161–168.

FESTING, M., KNAPPERT, L. AND KORNAU, A. (2015) Gender-specific preferences in global performance management: An empirical study of male and female managers in a multinational context. *Human Resource Management,* 54(1): 55–79.

FESTING, M., KORNAU, A. AND SCHAFER, L. (2014) Think talent – think male? A comparative case study analysis of gender inclusion in talent management practice in the German media industry. *International Journal of Human Resource Management,* 26(6): 707–732.

FEY, C.F. AND BJORKMAN, I. (2001) The effect of human resource management practices on MNC subsidiary performance in Russia. *Journal of International Business Studies,* 32(1): 59–75.

FLAMHOLTZ, E. G. (1999). *Human Resource Accounting: Advances in Concepts, Methods and Applications* (3rd edn). Boston: Kluwer Academic Publishers.

FORD, J., BURKINSHAW, P. AND CAHILL, J. (2014) *White Rose Women in Leadership Initiative: Absent talent in UK HEIs?* Available at: http://www.whiterose.ac.uk/wp-content/uploads/2014/11/White-Rose-Women-in-Leadership-Report-Sept-2014.pdf.

FORD, J., HARDING, N. AND STOYANOVA, D. (2010) *Talent Management in NHS Yorkshire and the Humber: The Current State of the Art.* Bradford: Bradford University School of Management.

FURUSAWA, M. AND BREWSTER, C. (2015) The bi-cultural option for global talent management: The Japanese/Brazilian Nikkeijin example. *Journal of World Business,* 50(1): 133–143.

GAGNE, F. (2000) Understanding the complex choreography of talent development through DGMT-based analysis. In Heller, K. A., Moncks, F. J. Sternberg, R. J. and Sabotnik, R. F. (eds), *International Handbook of Giftedness and Talent* (2nd edn). Elsevier: Oxford, pp. 67–79.

GREENWOOD, R. AND HININGS, C.R. (1996) Understanding radical organizational change: Bringing together the old and the new institutionalism. *Academy of Management Review,* 21(4): 1022–1054.

GREENWOOD, R., OLIVER, C., SAHLIN, K. AND SUDDABY, R. (2008) Introduction. In Greenwood, R., Oliver, C., Sahlin, K. and Suddaby, R. (eds), *The SAGE Handbook of Organizational Institutionalism.* London: SAGE, pp. 1–46.

GROYSBERG, B., LEE, L.-E. AND NANDA, A. (2008) Can they take it with them? The portability of Star knowledge workers' performance. *Management Science,* 54(7): 1213–1230.

GROYSBERG, B., NANDA, A. AND NOHRIA, N. (2004) The risky business of hiring stars. *Harvard Business Review,* 82(5): 92–100.

HAMERMESH, D. S. AND BIDDLE, J. E. (1994) Beauty and the labor market. *American Economic Review,* 84(5): 1174–1194.

HANDLEY, J. (2014) Gender, networks and talent management: Interim findings from a narrative inquiry. Paper presented at the 3rd EIASM Talent Management Workshop, Berlin, October.

HOWE, M. J. A., DAVIDSON, J. A. AND SLOBODA, J. A. (1998) Innate talents: Reality or myth? *Behavioral and Brain Sciences,* 21(3): 399–407.

HUANG, J. AND TANSLEY, C. (2012) Sneaking through the minefield of talent management: The notion of rhetorical obfuscation. *International Journal of Human Resource Management*, 23(17): 3673–3691.

HUSELID, M. A. AND BECKER, B. E. (2011) Bridging micro and macro domains: Workforce differentiation and strategic human resource management. *Journal of Management*, 37(2): 421–428.

IBARRA, H., CARTER, N. AND SILVA, C. (2010) Why men still get more promotions than women. *Harvard Business Review*, 88(9): 80–85.

JAFEE, D. (2001) *Organization Theory: Tension and Change*. Boston: McGraw-Hill.

JUDGE, T. A. AND CABLE, D. M. (2004) The effect of physical height on workplace success and income: Preliminary test of a theoretical model. *Journal of Applied Psychology*, 89(3): 428–441.

LI, X., QIN, X., JIANG, K., ZHANG, S. AND GAO, F.-Y. (2015) Human resource practices and firm performance in China: The moderating roles of regional human capital quality and firm innovation strategy. *Management and Organization Review*, 11(2): 237–261.

LINEHAN, M. AND SCULLION, H. (2008) The development of female global managers: The role of networking and mentoring. *Journal of Business Ethics*, 83(1): 29–40.

LUNDBERG, P., NYSTEDT, P. AND ROOTH, D.-O. (2014) Height and earnings: The role of cognitive and noncognitive skills. *Journal of Human Resources*, 49(1): 141–166.

MÄKELÄ, K., BJÖRKMAN, I. AND EHRNROOTH, M. (2010) How do MNCs establish their talent pools? Influences on individuals' likelihood of being labeled as talent. *Journal of World Business*, 45(2): 134–142.

MALIK, A. R. AND SINGH, P. (2014) 'High potential' programs: Let's hear it for 'B' players. *Human Resource Management Review*, 24(4): 330–346.

MCDONNELL, A., LAMARE, R., GUNNIGLE, P. AND LAVELLE, J. (2010) Developing tomorrow's leaders – evidence of global talent management in multinational enterprises. *Journal of World Business*, 45(2): 150–160.

MELLAHI, K. AND COLLINGS, D. G. (2010) The barriers to effective global talent management: The example of corporate elites in MNEs. *Journal of World Business*, 45(2): 143–149.

MICHAELS, E., HANDFIELD-JONES, H. AND AXELROD, B. (2001) *The War for Talent*. Boston: Harvard Business School Press.

O'BOYLE, E. AND AGUINIS, H. (2012) The best and the rest: Revisiting the norm of normality of individual performance. *Personnel Psychology*, 65(1): 79–119.

PAAUWE, J. AND BOSELIE, P. (2015) HRM and social embeddedness. In Boxall, P., Purcell, J. and Wright, P. (eds), *The Oxford Handbook of Human Resource Management*. Oxford: Oxford University Press, pp. 167–184.

PwC (2014) *17th Annual Global CEO Survey: The Talent Challenge*. Available at: www.pwc.com. Accessed 17 July 2015.

RANDLE, C. W. (1956) How to identify promotable executives. *Harvard Business Review*, 34(3): 122–134.

SAHLIN, K. AND WEDLIN, L. (2008) Circulating ideas: Imitation, translation and editing. In Greenwood, R., Oliver, C., Sahlin, K. and Suddaby, R. (eds), *The SAGE Handbook of Organizational Institutionalism*. London: SAGE, pp. 219–242.

SCHICK, A. AND STECKEL, R. (2015) Height, human capital and earnings: The contributions of cognitive and noncognitive ability. *Journal of Human Capital*, 9(1): 94–115.

SCULLION, H. AND COLLINGS, D.C. (2011) *Global Talent Management*. London: Routledge.

SINGH, V., KUMRA, S. AND VINNICOMBE, S. (2002) Gender and impression management: Playing the promotion game. *Journal of Business Ethics*, 37(1): 77–89.

SUTTON, A., BALDWIN, S., WOOD, L. AND HOFFMAN, B. (2013) A meta-analysis of the relationship between rater liking and performance ratings. *Human Performance*, 26: 409–429.

SWAILES, S. (2013) The ethics of talent management. *Business Ethics: A European Review*, 22(1): 32–46.

SWAILES, S. (2016) The cultural evolution of talent management: A memetic analysis. *Human Resource Development Review*, 15(3): 340–358.

SWAILES, S., DOWNS, Y. AND ORR, K. (2014) Conceptualising inclusive talent management: Potential, possibilities and practicalities. *Human Resource Development International*, 17(5): 529–544.

TANSLEY, C. AND TIETZE, S. (2013) Rites of passage through talent management progression stages: An identity work perspective. *International Journal of Human Resource Management*, 4(9): 799–815.

TERPSTRA-TONG, J. AND RALSON, D. A. (2002) Moving toward a global understanding of upward influence strategies: An Asian perspective with directions for cross-cultural research. *Asia Pacific Journal of Management*, 19: 373–404.

THACKER, R. A. AND WAYNE, S. J. (1995) An examination of the relationship between upward influence tactics and assessments of promotability. *Journal of Management*, 21(4): 739–756.

THUNNISSEN, M., BOSELIE, P. AND FRUYTIER, B. (2013) A review of talent management: 'Infancy or adolescence?' *International Journal of Human Resource Management*, 24(9): 1744–1761.

VAIMAN, V., SCULLION, H. AND COLLINGS, D. (2012) Talent management decision making. *Management Decision*, 50(5): 925–941.

VAN KRIEKEN, R. (2012) *Celebrity Society*. London: Routledge.

VARMA, A. AND PICHLER, S. (2007) Interpersonal affect: Does it really bias performance appraisals? *Journal of Labor Research*, 28(2): 397–412.

VO, A. N. (2009) Career development for host country nationals: A case of American and Japanese multinational companies in Vietnam. *International Journal of Human Resource Management*, 20(6): 1402–1420.

WILLIAMS, C. L., MULLER, C. AND KILANSKI, K. (2012) Gendered organizations in the new economy. *Gender and Society*, 26(4): 549–573.

WILSON, F. (2013). *Organizational Behaviour and Gender* (2nd edn). Aldershot: Ashgate

WRIGHT, P. M., DUNFORD, B. B. AND SNELL, S. A. (2001) Human resources and the resource-based view of the firm. *Journal of Management*, 27(6): 701–721.

ZHOU, Y., HONG, Y., AND LIU, J. (2013) Internal commitment or external collaboration? The impact of human resource management systems on firm performance and innovation. *Human Resource Management*, 52(2): 263–288.

ZUCKER, L. G. (1983) Organizations as institutions. *Research in the Sociology of Organizations*, 2: 1–47.

13

INTERNATIONAL ASSIGNMENTS

Jawad Syed and Andrew Jenkins

LEARNING OUTCOMES

After reading this chapter, you should be able to:

➤ Understand the role of international human resource management in multinational corporations
➤ Understand how international assignments are different from domestic assignments
➤ Evaluate the nature and evolution of expatriation
➤ Assess the impact of staffing policies on expatriation
➤ Understand the motives of international assignees
➤ Outline the international assignment process
➤ Understand the antecedents of successful expatriation
➤ Critically engage with international assignment issues through examples, questions and case studies.

Opening Case Study Global mobility and its challenges

On the surface, an expatriate appears to have a glamorous life and career. However, the attraction of foreign destinations may fade in the face of local sociocultural norms, laws and economic realities, which may be very different from those found in the expatriate's country of origin. While the reward packages for expatriates are no longer as lucrative as they used to be two or three decades ago, organisations still need to have expatriates to realise their strategic vision and objectives. In an ever-increasing globalised and technologised world, international assignments continue to thrive. The *Managing the Global Mobility Function 2014* report (FEM, 2014) reveals that while 51 per cent of assignments are still long term, there is an upward trend in the use of 3–12 months short-term assignments in organisations. The FEM report reveals that 20 per cent of assignments are short term while 5 per cent are commuter assignments and 6 per cent are business trips. The report also shows that some organisations send several employees, one after the other, on six-month assignments instead of sending one person on a long-term expatriate assignment. There is also an increase in the use of business travellers, who frequently travel to foreign destinations often once a fortnight or even weekly – depending upon the distance and time of travel – as a part of their job. Given the increasing need and use of expatriates by organisations, there has emerged a new industry of global mobility professionals and advisers who have the skill and knowledge to smooth out expatriation and repatriation. Their services range from visa and travelling arrangements to the issues of language and taxation. Their services are vital to 'support the assignee so the assignment is a success, and to help get the right talent to the right place quickly' (O'Donovan, 2014: para.9).

Questions

1 How is the attraction of global destinations compromised by contextual challenges?
2 Refer to a real life MNC and identify the contextual challenges facing its expatriate employees.

INTRODUCTION

International assignments are a key part of human resource management in the current global era. Employees as well as organisations benefit by gaining international experience, in terms of professional growth and enhancing business outreach and performance. With businesses increasingly operating globally and making inroads in emerging markets, organisations are sending more employees on international assignments. At the same time, employees are expected to be more culturally aware and mobile than ever. In addition to a means to organisational control and bilateral transfer of knowledge, it is equally important to avoid misunderstandings caused by a lack of knowledge of the local culture and context. This chapter explains the notion of international assignments, in relation to HRM in a global context, and also discusses how international assignments are different from domestic staffing. It critically examines the nature and evolution of international assignments, which are also enabled by advances in transport and communication technologies. It further examines the range of options available to organisations in terms of deployment of expatriates or local employees. It discusses the issues of expatriate selection and adjustment and also identifies some of the competencies, along with antecedents, needed for successful expatriation. The chapter provides a number of

examples, from different countries and organisations, to illustrate the theoretical discussion.

GLOBALISATION, INTERNATIONAL FIRMS AND INTERNATIONAL HUMAN RESOURCE MANAGEMENT (IHRM)

In the twenty-first century, many businesses operate on a global basis. The globalisation of business is the result of a number of factors including advances in communications and technology, ease of travel, increasing competition worldwide, and the development of free trade areas such as the European Union (EU), the ASEAN Free Trade Area (AFTA), the North American Free Trade Agreement (NAFTA), and the Southern African Development Community (SADC). Companies are seeking new markets for their goods and services, looking beyond domestic boundaries, with many pursuing external growth strategies using cross-national acquisitions, mergers and joint ventures (Foot, Hook and Jenkins, 2016). The sale of goods and services internationally requires the development of an international infrastructure requiring, for example, the development of distribution networks and the establishment of manufacturing plants. Companies that are pursuing a low-cost strategy may decide to transfer their manufacturing production to countries where labour is less costly. However, globalisation is not only about domestic firms pursuing business opportunities overseas. It is also concerned with foreign firms seeking to invest in domestic markets. Most governments actively encourage inward investment as a means of supporting employment, increasing the tax base, and breaking down the barriers to conducting business.

There are a number of terms that are frequently used to describe businesses that operate in different countries. Rugman and Collinson (2012: 7) define a multinational enterprise (MNE) as 'a company headquartered in one country but having operations in other countries' whilst Shim, Siegel and Levine (2013) state that a Multinational Corporation (MNC) is a firm that operates in two or more counties. According to Bartlett and Ghoshal (1998), Multinational companies or enterprises have reasonably independent operations in a number of different countries where they establish their own approach, usually responding to local requirements. According to Daniels, Radebaugh and Sullivan (2015) a multinational company or enterprise is sometimes referred to as a Transnational company (TNC). However, Bartlett and Ghoshal (1998) claim that a TNC is not an existing type of company but, rather, an ideal towards which companies need to strive in order to survive in an ever-more complex and competitive environment. Some authors, such as Brake (1999) state that, as a company becomes more global, it progresses from being an international firm to a multinational firm and then to a global firm, but other authors, such as Aggarwal, Berrill, Hutson and Kearney (2011), point out that the different terms such as multinational company (MNC), multinational enterprise (MNE), and transnational corporation (TNC) are often interchangeably used by international business (IB) writers.

In terms of the HRM implications for the organisational types discussed above, writers often refer interchangeably to global perspectives and international issues or allude to the differing organisational needs rather than the typology of organisations (Sparrow, 1999). In assessing the characteristics needed for their ideal transnational organisation, Bartlett and Ghoshal (1998) conclude that HRM on an international basis is basically HRM in general but with added levels of complexity, namely, flexibility, diversity, commitment, and a unitarist approach.

INTERNATIONAL ASSIGNMENTS DEFINED

An international assignee is a term used to refer to an employee assigned by his or her employer to work in a country other than his/her home country for a fixed period of time. The term 'expatriate' is often used when describing and discussing international assignments. Peng and Meyer (2011: 8) define an expatriate assignment as 'a temporary job abroad with a multinational company', whilst Plourde et al. (2014) comment that an expatriate is an employee who shifts from headquarters to work in foreign subsidiaries. Similarly, McEvoy and Buller (2013) refer to expatriates as home-country nationals who are sent by the parent company to work temporarily in a different country. Ahlstrom and Bruton (2010) state that an expatriate is an individual from one country who works and resides in another country, but they do not provide a time-frame for the assignment. Initially, expatriates were differentiated into two distinct groups: those sponsored by companies and those taking the initiative themselves, although the boundaries between these groups have become increasingly blurred (Doherty, Richardson and Thorn, 2013). International assignments vary according to their duration. The CIPD (2013a) has identified three types of international assignment: a business trip of less than 31 days duration for a single trip; a short-term assignment of more than 31 days but less than 12 months; and a long-term assignment of two years or more. An international assignment lasting between 12 months and two years is, rather confusingly, not covered by the above-mentioned CIPD classification.

The need for organisations to develop global direction, identity, and control and the growth of international business ventures has prompted a massive rise in global mobility, expatriate employment and international assignments. There are many reasons why organisations use international assignments, and these are examined in the next section.

MOTIVES FOR INTERNATIONAL ASSIGNMENTS

As stated in the previous section, there are different types of international assignment relating to the duration of the assignment and who initiates the assignment. The use of an international assignment will also depend on the organisation's strategic and Human Resource objectives and the countries the organisation operates in. According to the CIPD (2013a), an expatriate may be considered for an international assignment where there is a lack of local qualified staff, to train local staff to replace expatriates, to transfer technical expertise, to provide international experience to managers, to develop employees, to share knowledge between different parts of the organisation and to create an international corporate culture. Howse (2015) states that the main reasons why organisations use international assignments are to introduce a new initiative, to ensure cover for an expatriate's period of leave, to undertake a specific project for a limited time, and to develop a business in another country.

International assignments are used by businesses to achieve a number of objectives. In addition to those stated by the CIPD (2013b) and Howse (2015) above, these include corporate control/coordination and the delivery of superior financial results, two-way transfer of know-how and organisational development, to fill positions with qualified competent staff, to build greater corporate loyalty and to facilitate management development by increasing global awareness and ensuring career development for high-potential staff. It should also be remembered that international assignments do not just relate to individuals but whole teams may be relocated where collective knowledge is required (Bonache and Brewster, 2001).

EXPATRIATE RECRUITMENT AND SELECTION

A number of recruitment methods commonly used to attract candidates for international assignments include internal promotion, cross-national advertising, headhunting, international graduate programmes, and local recruitment (CIPD, 2013b). Commonly used selection methods for assessing the suitability of candidates for an international assignment include interviews, assessment centres, and psychological testing (CIPD, 2013b). Selection of expatriates is different from routine or domestic staffing, because selection decisions are more complex in terms of job description, person specification, and actual issues and challenges involved in performing expatriate roles and duties.

Potočnik et al. (2014) propose a holistic four-stage process model for recruiting and selecting international employees. The competencies of the HR managers who will be responsible for the international recruitment and selection will be determined in Stage 1. In Stage 2 international recruitment takes place of parent-country nationals,

host-country nationals, and third-county nationals. International selection will take place in Stage 3, taking into account the person's capacity for cultural adjustment, international experience, family situation, linguistic ability, knowledge, skills and competencies, personality traits, and the person-organisation fit. In Stage 4 the international recruitment and selection process will be evaluated to determine the extent to which it was successful.

In selecting expatriates for an international assignment, a number of factors will need to be considered. These include:

1 **The organisation's strategic goals**
   There are a number of generic strategies that companies may choose to follow (growth, stability, and retrenchment), and there are a number of ways of pursuing each of these strategies (Millmore et al., 2007). The type of generic strategy followed will affect the firm's Human Resource Management strategy, including its use of expatriates. Caligiuri, Tarique and Jacobs (2009: 258) comment that 'firms differ on the extent to which international assignees are central to their global business strategy and, in turn, whether selection for international assignments is a strategic priority'.

2 **The technical competencies required for the job**
   Technical competencies refer to the knowledge and skills required to successfully undertake a task or a job. Causin and Ayoun (2011) comment that the firm's need for technical competence results in the tendency to use expatriates in countries where management talents are not readily available. This may be especially the case in developing countries. However, in selecting expatriates for international assignments, it should be remembered that those with the best technical competencies are not necessarily those with the best cross-cultural management and adjustment skills (Ibrahim et al., 2002).

3 **The personal traits or relational abilities required for the job**
   Many researchers have found a positive correlation between the expatriate's personality and the likelihood of the expatriate succeeding in his or her international assignment (for example Caligiuri, Tarique and Jacobs, 2009; Downes, Varner and Hemmasi, 2010). Relational abilities refer to creating and maintaining trusting relationships across boundaries (Dotlich and Noel, 1998), and these abilities are considered to be a crucial international competence for the expatriate (Jordan and Cartwright, 1998).

4   The nature of the assignment

There are many different types of international assignment. Examples include establishing a branch office overseas, an International Joint Venture (IJV), knowledge transfer from headquarters to a subsidiary, or the introduction of new processes, products or services. Meyskens et al. (2009) discuss alternative forms of international assignment such as frequent flyer assignments, short-term assignments, commuter assignments, transfers, localisations, intra-regional, developmental, and virtual assignments.

5   The expatriate's ability to cope with a different culture

The ability of the expatriate to deal with cross-cultural adjustment (CCA) is a key consideration in the selection process. CCA is complex and multidimensional (Koveshnikov, Wechtler and Dejoux, 2014) and relates to 'the process of adaptation to living and working in a foreign culture' (Okpara and Kabongo, 2011: 24). Black and Gregersen (1991) identified three components of CCA: work adjustment, interaction adjustment, and general adjustment. If the employee has successfully completed an international assignment in the past, then it is likely that the person is able to adjust to a different culture, but past performance is not always an indicator of future performance. Irrespective of whether the employee has experience of international assignments, pre-departure training can help the expatriate adjust to a different culture.

6   The expatriate's family situation

An expatriate family will face more challenges than the solo expatriate (Haslberger and Brewster, 2008). Family adjustment is a key factor in the success of an international assignment. Cseh and Rosenbusch's (2012) research into the relationship between the flexibility of the expatriate's family in a US-based multinational corporation and their cross-cultural adjustment found that 'the components of family flexibility (roles, rules, assertiveness, and leadership) played a key role in the cross-cultural adjustment of the expatriate, spouse and children' (61). In research examining why international assignments fail, based on findings from 64 expatriate families who had prematurely returned from an international assignment, Cole and Nesbeth (2014) found that the most common reason for assignment failure from the perspective of the families involved is lack of organisational support during the assignment, with family issues mentioned as the second most frequent cause of failure.

7   Legal issues pertaining to the host country

Each country has its own laws and regulations concerning work. Some governments have 'localisation programmes' in place where expatriates are replaced by local workers. This is the case in countries within the Gulf Cooperation Council (Scurry, Rodriguez and Bailouni, 2013). Work-permits and visas are also used by most countries to control foreign labour. Paetkau (2009) assesses the dilemma for US firms sending expatriates to Saudi Arabia, as this country would refuse to process work visas for young, single women, openly gay people, disabled employees, Jewish employees, and anyone aged over 50.

8   Other factors

The industry in which the firm is located is important because some industries, such as financial services, rely on expatriate labour, particularly for management-level positions, whereas other industries, such as food manufacturing, do not. The host country's level of economic development, education, and political stability will also affect if and how expatriates are used. The 'cultural toughness' or 'cultural distance' of a country will need to be considered. This relates to the dissimilarities between the home and host cultures and the physical distance between them. More specifically, Froese and Peltokorpi (2011: 50) state that cultural distance refers to 'differences between any two countries with respect to the level of development, education, business and everyday language, cultural values, and the extent of connections between these countries'. The larger the cultural distance, the more difficult the adaptation process for the international assignee. Company characteristics such as organisational structure, age of the firm, and growth strategy will also influence the nature of international assignments.

In relation to selecting and training Scandinavian expatriates for international assignments, Björkman and Gertsen (1993), in a survey of 146 Scandinavian firms, found that the following criteria were used to select expatriates for international assignments: technical/other professional qualifications (mentioned by 80.1 per cent of respondents); previous achievements (45.9 per cent); motivation (34.2 per cent); managerial talents (27.4 per cent); independence (24.7 per cent); communicative talent (21.9 per cent); language skills (20.5 per cent); ambitions/commitment (19.2 per cent); international experience (18.5 per cent); flexibility (10.3 per cent) and adaptability of the family (2.7 per cent). Briscoe, Schuler and Tarique (2012) state that the most important selection criteria for an international assignment are job suitability, cultural adaptability, and the desire to undertake an international assignment.

The costs of not selecting the right employee for an international assignment can be considerable. The concept of 'expatriate failure', usually defined as premature return from an international assignment, is widely discussed in the literature although Harzing and Chris-tensen (2004) state that the concept is of little value and should be abandoned in favour of using Human Resource theories on labour turnover and employee performance. Expatriate failure can be costly for the organisation and the individual. With reference to the hotel industry, Avril and Magnini (2007) claim that a large proportion of expatriate manager assignments end in failure, resulting in additional direct and indirect costs. According to Yea-ton and Hall (2008), the most common causes of failure of international assignments are the selection process, the pre- and post-departure training, inadequate knowl-edge of the host country's culture, and poor repatria-tion efforts. While many of the managers used by MNCs in their overseas operations are expatriates, mastering cultural differences and overcoming other expatriation related challenges is crucial for successful individual and organisational performance. Expatriate recruitment and selection is often left to good luck instead of sound judge-ment and is affected by ethnocentrism, stereotyping, and irrational decisions.

EXPATRIATES AND THE PSYCHOLOGICAL CONTRACT

Sims (1994: 375) defines the psychological contract as 'the set of expectations held by the individual employee that specify what the individual and the organisation expect to give to and receive from each other in the course of their work relationship'. The psychological contract is different from a legal contract in that much of it will be assumed and not written down. It represents the reality of work as perceived by the organisation and the employee and may have greater influence on how people behave in the workplace than the formal written contract (Foot, Hook and Jenkins, 2016). Managing employees' psychological contracts is a major challenge for managers in all organisa-tions (Pate and Scullion, 2009), and this is also the case in relation to expatriates and international assignments. In their research into the influence of psychological con-tracts on adjustment and organisational commitment of expatriates on business assignments in Taiwan, Chen and Chiu (2009: 810) found that 'the fulfilment of expatri-ates' psychological contracts has a positive and significant influence on both their psychological and sociocultural adjustment to a foreign environment. Moreover, the fulfil-ment of psychological contracts has a positive influence on their organisational commitment.' Thus, managers overseeing international assignments need to ensure that the organisation's human resource management policies and practices are able to meet expatriates' expectations concerning the fulfilment of their psychological contracts.

PHASES OF AN INTERNATIONAL ASSIGNMENT

An international assignment will typically incorporate three stages: pre-departure, including recruitment, selec-tion, briefing, and training; the actual assignment, involv-ing adjustment, performance, and dealing with issues of culture shock and stress; and post-assignment, includ-ing repatriation, transfer, and issues concerning reverse culture shock and the psychological contract (Peng and Meyer, 2011). Collings et al. (2011) also refer to three stages of an international assignment: pre-, during, and post-assignment. In their 2009 paper, Cerdin and Pargneux propose an integrative model of international assignment success related to the phases of pre-expatriation, expa-triation, and repatriation. The authors claim that 'interna-tional assignment success is more complex than what the literature usually proposes' (2009: 7) and suggest that suc-cess is measured in terms of the individual's career, the job, and development. Cerdin and Pargneux further propose that international assignment success is measured at the organisational level during the second and third phase by assessing performance, network and relationship building, the transfer of expertise, and the retention of employees.

Culture shock is a concept used to describe the differ-ent emotions felt by the expatriate upon entry to a foreign country (Sims and Schraeder, 2004) and is 'character-ised by the absence of familiar signs and symbols, often resulting in anxiety and frustration' (Friedman, Murphy and Dyke, 2009: 253). Culture shock represents a stage in Oberg's (1960) 'U-curve model'. The initial stage of the U-curve is the honeymoon stage, followed by a period of 'culture shock' involving disillusionment and frustration (the lowest point of the 'U'), culminating in the adapta-tion and mastery stage (Friedman, Murphy and Dyke, 2009). Evidence supporting the existence of a U-curve for expatriates is mixed (Black and Mendenhall, 1991), with Selmer (1999) claiming that not all expatriates experience the honeymoon stage or 'culture shock'. Furthermore, Haslberger (2005) criticises the concept of 'culture shock' as being not clearly defined and being composed of many different aspects.

ENSURING A SUCCESSFUL INTERNATIONAL ASSIGNEE EXPERIENCE

In order to ensure that the international assignment is a success, a full analysis of the job requirements – techni-cal requirements, managerial responsibilities, cultural requirements – should be undertaken. In common with a domestic assignment, a job description and person specification will need to be written (Foot, Hook and Jenkins, 2016). An analysis of the country of assignment, including culture, standard of living, and physical environment, would need to be established using, for example, the PESTEL framework of analysis that divides environmental influences into six categories: political, economic, social, technological, environmental, and legal (Johnson et al., 2014). The candidate would be evaluated according to specified criteria such as job suitability, cultural adaptability, desire for foreign assignment, abilities, personality, career status, and language skills. The successful candidate will need to be prepared for the assignment by means of pre-departure training and informed of the compensation and reward package. In addition, where the employee intends taking his/her spouse, children or other dependents, orientation will need to be provided to all those affected by the assignment. Finally, a successful international assignment will not end when the assignment finishes but when the person (and his/her family) returns home and when the employee is re-integrated into the organisation. There is a danger, however, that, having returned to the home country, the expatriate does not stay with the organisation, resulting in a failure to capitalise on the benefits provided by the expatriate's individual talent (Reiche, Kraimer and Harzing, 2011). In their examination of the determinants of success for international assignees in terms of knowledge transfer, Bonache and Zárraga-Oberty (2008) established that transfer success will be affected by the abilities and motivation of international staff, the abilities and motivation of local staff, and the relationship between international and local staff.

INTERNATIONAL MANAGEMENT COMPETENCIES

In order to be successful in his or her international assignment, the expatriate will need to have a number of competencies. Relational abilities are a key determining success factor as developing and maintaining close personal contacts with foreign managers is critical to the success of the assignment (Causin and Ayoun, 2011). The expatriate will need to be culturally sensitive, especially where the home- and host-country cultures are very different, as home- and host-country differences will directly influence the cross-cultural adjustment of the expatriate (Froese and Peltokorpi, 2011). In addition to adapting to the new business and cultural environment, the international manager may have to deal with a different language (Miao, Adler and Xu, 2011). Learning a foreign language is rarely straightforward and requires dedication, patience,

and hard work. Some languages are notoriously difficult to learn. Russian, Mandarin, and Arabic, for example, are considered very difficult languages for native English speakers to learn, although this will depend on the individual's background, education, and experience. The expatriate will also need to be able to deal with stressful situations, potentially leading to 'burnout' (Silbiger and Pines, 2014). Working overseas, being exposed to a different culture, and attempting to speak a foreign language can be stressful. By its very nature, taking on an overseas assignment can lead to increased levels of stress (Holopainen and Björkman, 2005).

Van der Zee and van Oudenhoven (2000, 2001) identify five personality traits required for success in an intercultural context: cultural empathy, open-mindedness, social initiative, emotional stability, and flexibility. These traits are important in dealing with a different culture and adjusting to that culture. In addition, many international assignments involve the expatriate being a member of, or managing, a multicultural team. This requires the expatriate to have a number of intercultural competencies, namely 'sufficient cultural knowledge, skilled actions, and suitable motivation or personality orientation of a member of a multicultural team' (Matveev and Milter, 2004: 106).

A comparative study of Indian expatriates in Oman and Indian employees in their home country by Deosthalee (2002) revealed that Indian females working in Oman experience more stress than their counterparts working in India; expatriates with postgraduate qualifications working in Oman experience more stress than their counterparts working in India; and Indian expatriates over the age of 45 working in Oman experience more stress than their counterparts working in their home country. The threat of terrorism is likely to be an additional source of stress for the expatriate (Bader and Berg, 2014). Some international assignments are located in 'high risk' countries where the threat of terrorism is more likely, although a feature of terrorism in the twenty-first century is that almost nowhere is immune from its effects.

Class Activity

▸ Browse mainstream media or the internet to identify two or three successful international managers. What are their core competencies?

CROSS-CULTURAL TRAINING

Cross-cultural training, also known as intercultural training, can assist in developing intercultural competencies (Graf and Mertesacker, 2009). Morris, Savani and Roberts

(2014) claim that, in learning about a different culture, training can help the individual gain native-like fluency in another culture. There are different levels of intercultural training. Zamor (2008) identifies two levels: the 'cognitive' which transmits facts about the culture's cultural values and political and economic situation, and the 'experiential' where the participant, through simulation, learns how to behave in the foreign culture. According to Chien (2012), most intercultural training programmes employ at least one of six different approaches: information training, attribution training, cultural awareness, cognitive-behaviour modification, experiential leaning, and interaction. Mendenhall, Dunbar and Oddou (1987) offer a number of recommendations for firms wishing to improve their cross-cultural training programmes. These include: getting top management support, both politically and financially; quantifying the financial cost of a failed international assignment; covering the key areas of productivity and acculturation; designing the training based on the degree of integration required and, where the family is involved in the international assignment, involving them in the training. Offering intercultural training is important in preparing an employee for an international assignment, and should be provided prior to departure, but it should be remembered that training can never totally remove the stress and anxiety associated with cross-cultural contact (Zakaria, 2000).

In the News Global shortage of healthcare workers

The world today faces a major shortage of health workers. Disasters such as the 2004 Indian Ocean earthquake and tsunami, the 2010 Haiti earthquake, and the 2014 Ebola outbreak in West Africa highlighted the need for well-trained health care workers across the world. A 2013 WHO report estimated that the shortage of health care workers across the world amounted to about 7.2 million, a number that has nearly doubled since 2007. More than 70 per cent of that deficit is in resource-poor locations in Asia and Africa (UCSF News, 2015).

TYPES OF INTERNATIONAL ASSIGNEES USED BY MNCS

MNCs can deploy staff for international assignments from three groups: parent-country nationals (PCNs), third-country nationals (TCNs), and host-country nationals (HCNs) (Nickson, 2013). There are advantages and disadvantages of each, but it is likely that the firm will use a combination of the three. Multinationals may decide to first use PCNs but, over time, employ more TCNs and particularly HCNs (Nickson, 2013). According to Rofcanin, Imer and Zingoni (2014), PCNs are employees who are citizens of the country where the firm's headquarters is based; HCNs are employees who are citizens of the country where the firm's subsidiary is located; and TCNs are employees who are citizens of a country other than the country where the firm is headquartered or where the firm's subsidiary is located. Nickson (2013) identifies three principal motives for sending employees overseas: to take up a position where a HCN is unavailable or difficult to train; to develop managers by giving them international experience; or to develop a more geocentric attitude to staffing in the organisation.

It is possible that some PCNs share the same culture as the host country in which the subsidiary is located. Whilst they are permanently located in the firm's home country, they belong culturally to the host country. They can therefore be considered as a hybrid type of employee, combining the benefits of a PCN and a HCN. Srinivasan et al. (2009) refer to these people as 'expatriates of host-country origin' (EHCO). Based on a survey and in-depth interviews of human resource managers of 15 MNCs with operations in India, Srinivasan et al. (2009) conclude that EHCOs are more willing to accept expatriate assignments than parent-country nationals (PCNs) but their success depends on the breadth and depth of their experience, both in the parent and host countries.

Another type of international assignee used by MNCs is the 'inpatriate'. Whilst expatriates are sent from the host country to the overseas subsidiary, inpatriates, on the other hand, represent a group of managers who are transferred to the parent country of the organisation on a permanent or semi-permanent basis (Harvey, Reiche and Moeller, 2011). Although both expatriation and inpatriation are forms of overseas assignment, each requires 'distinct types of socialisation processes to ensure performance conducive to the organisation's goals' (Moeller, Harvey and Williams, 2010: 172). Inpatriates may be used by the MNC to enhance the 'global mind-set' of its managers by increasing the cultural diversity of its management cadre.

PERLMUTTER'S MODEL OF INTERNATIONAL ORIENTATIONS

Based on Perlmutter's typologies of organisations, Rugman and Collinson (2012) identify three types of organisation: ethnocentric, polycentric, and geocentric. Ethnocentric firms are dominated by managers from the parent country where processes and leadership styles are transferred from headquarters to the subsidiary. The ethnocentric firm believes that its approach to management in the home country is superior and, therefore, key positions anywhere in the world should be filled by managers from the home country (Nickson, 2013). Polycentric firms act like a federation of semi-autonomous businesses with strict reporting structures but some delegation of business activities to the subsidiary (Rugman and Collinson, 2012). With this approach, local staff are employed in key positions and enjoy relatively high levels of autonomy (Nickson, 2013). Geocentric firms are more collaborative in that the headquarters and subsidiaries share power and responsibility with promotion being based on ability rather than nationality and managers sharing worldwide interests rather than focusing on specific markets (Rugman and Collinson, 2012). In reality, very few multinationals will fit perfectly to Perlmutter's orientations. The firm's headquarters, for example, may have different orientations to different subsidiaries. In addition, a firm may change its orientation due to the performance of its subsidiaries or the growth of the business through the development of new products and services (Mahmood, 2015).

Class Activity

Divide your class into three groups. Each group should be able to define ethnocentric, polycentric, and geocentric firms respectively and provide examples form real-life organisations. Each group should also discuss the implications of the firm's international orientation for international assignments.

REPATRIATION OF INTERNATIONAL ASSIGNEES

Repatriation is the process concerning the return of an expatriate from an international assignment. Issues concerning repatriation will have to be addressed if employers wish to recruit and retain talented employees or persuade them to accept an international assignment. Peng and Meyer (2011) identify two key challenges concerning repatriation: in relation to professional re-entry, the individual may be anxious about his/her career, be concerned about work adjustment and fear loss of status and pay and, in relation to the expatriate's private life, friends and family may have moved on and the individual's spouse and children may find it difficult to adjust to life back home. Peng and Meyer (2011) also state that the returning international assignee may be affected by 'reverse culture shock' because of changes that have taken place in

the home country, the company, or within the expatriate him/herself.

Repatriation is a complex issue to address, but many organisations do not have policies and procedures for the return of employees from international assignments (Yeaton and Hall, 2008). Dissatisfaction with repatriation can lead to higher levels of staff turnover amongst expatriates returning from international assignments. It is important that companies have appropriate repatriation policies, as returning expatriates may leave an organisation if they perceive that there are a lack of practices to reward and utilise the expatriate's newly acquired knowledge and skills (Nery-Kjerfve and McLean, 2012). In a study focusing on Korean expatriates and spouses working in Australia, Cho, Hutchings and Marchant (2013) found that repatriation was largely influenced by requests from superiors; traditional expatriate training and mentoring were no longer seen as necessary given technological development; and decisions regarding repatriation were affected by how this affected their children's education.

Shen and Hall (2009) relate the concept of job embeddedness to research on international assignments to help explain how the processes of repatriation might lead to strengthened person-organisation fit or career exploration. The straightforward assumption that the authors make is 'the stronger employees' ties are to their job and to the people, the organisation, the community, and other factors associated with it – that is, the greater their job embeddedness – the more likely they are to remain in that job' (794). In this context, Shen and Hall (2009) recommend using shorter international assignments, carefully designing re-entry and career planning, strengthening links to the firm by emphasising the cost of leaving, offering developmental support to the expatriate, spouse and family, and ensuring that Human Resource managers responsible for expatriates have international assignment experience.

Kraimer, Shaffer and Bolino (2009) examined the retention of expatriates from a career advancement perspective, analysing the effects of expatriate experiences and organisational career support on career advancement upon return to the home country. Based on data collected from a sample of 84 recently repatriated employees to five US-based multinational firms, the results reveal, somewhat counterintuitively, that the number of international assignments had a negative relationship with career advancement upon repatriation. Thus, expatriates did better upon their return to the home country when they had only completed one international assignment. Results also showed that expatriate assignments that were developmental in nature were positively related to career advancement while those expatriate assignments focusing on the acquisition of managerial skills were negatively related to career advancement.

According to a recent report in Saudi media, it was noted that migrant domestic workers have made a significant role in contemporary Saudi society. 'Their contribution could be seen in various aspects of Saudi way of life,' said Dr Mohsin Shaikh Al-Hassan, well-known Islamic scholar and TV host. He said that 30 years ago, Saudi women did the household chores, but now they go to work at 6:00 in the morning and return home at 5:00 p.m. 'In their absence, domestic helpers do the work at home like cooking, cleaning, washing clothes and preparing food for the family,' he said. They also need, he said, nannies to look after their children while they're away from home (Estimo Jr, 2016).

Question

1   Do you see any ethical dilemma in above example? Critically discuss.

CRITICAL DISCUSSION

Research on international assignments and global careers has received limited attention from a critical management perspective (for exceptions see, e.g. Hassard, Morris, and McCann, 2012; Pringle and Mallon, 2003; Scurry, Blenkinsopp, and Hay, 2013). Yet increasingly a global career is being acknowledged as valuable, a form of symbolic capital that can help individuals to accrue career capital and advance their careers (Doherty and Dickmann, 2009; McKenna and Scurry, 2015).

In their study into the effects of international assignments on global careers, Dickmann and Harris (2005) consider the dual dependency of such assignments and global careers by contrasting individual and organisational perspectives. In particular, their study highlights the importance of informal norms and the impact of international assignments on the career capital of individuals.

International assignments are often portrayed as a glamorous opportunity for young and ambitious employees (Dickmann and Baruch, 2011), yet such assignments are also subject to significant constraints and boundaries (Costas, 2013). It is important to investigate the personal and psychological costs that may arise due to international postings as well as to recognise the potential power asymmetries that may shape the diverse experiences of expatriates and local workers. When thinking about global assignments, there is also a need to consider how an individual's social position and values have roots in nationally bounded social structures as well as transnational arrangements of social practices (Pries, 2001). While scholarship has highlighted the personal 'dark sides' of global careers and global working, it is equally important to understand more the broader organisational and societal 'dark sides' of international assignments (Richardson and Zikic, 2007; Shaffer and Harrison, 1998; McKenna and Scurry, 2015).

Fechter and Walsh (2010) note that vast amount of knowledge about the lives of European colonials and settlers can be held in stark contrast with relative dearth of studies of those who might be regarded as their modern-day equivalents, i.e., contemporary 'expatriates', or citizens of 'Western' nation-states who are involved in temporary migration processes to destinations outside 'the West'. These contemporary expatriates, and the privileges available to them, are rarely considered through a postcolonial framework. From an intersectional lens, it is important to investigate international assignments from viewpoints of class, race, sexuality and gender. Thus, illegal immigrants, asylum seekers and temporary immigrants are all understood in some way to be pursuing an 'international career' although their circumstances and opportunities may not be comparable to those of expatriates and skilled migrants. There is therefore a need to encourage a broader, more critical investigation of marginalised groups and whether they can be considered to have a 'career' at all (McKenna and Scurry, 2015).

Critical thinking 13.1

Theoretically, any person going to work outside of his or her country of citizenship would be described as an expatriate, regardless of the person's colour of skin or nationality. In common usage, the term is often used in the context of professionals or skilled workers sent abroad by their companies (Castree et al., 2013). However, in many countries in Asia, Africa and the Middle East, in practice an 'expat' is a term reserved exclusively for Western white people going to work abroad. In contrast, mixed-race or black people from Africa, Asia and Arab countries are described as immigrants. Europeans are considered by some people as 'expats' because they are somehow considered to be more knowledgeable than people from other backgrounds, whereas an immigrant is a term set aside for 'inferior races' (Koutonin, 2015).

Question

1   Why are white people considered as 'expats' when non-white people are thought of as 'immigrants'?

In conclusion, there are a numbers of options available to MNCs in terms of international assignments. Also there are different motives for expatriation from organisational and individual perspectives. Depending upon the nature of industry and market cycle, there are different types of international assignment available.

Notwithstanding the multitude of motivations and options, staffing methods should focus on international competencies. Such methods should be based on a job analysis, job description, person specification, and a competency profile. Moreover, there is a need to facilitate integration and adjustment of expatriates in host countries. Equally important is the necessity to consider issues of repatriation and to develop policies to deal with these issues.

CONCLUSION

The chapter highlighted the relevance of international assignments to HRM in a global context and also explained how international assignments are different from domestic assignments. It critically evaluated the notion and its evolution in diverse contexts, such as the contrasting notions of expatriates versus migrant workers. The chapter also discussed the impact of HRM policies on expatriation and examined the motives of international assignees.

The examples and the discussion pointed towards the difficulties and challenges related to expatriation and also identified features and antecedents of successful expatriation. The chapter critically engaged with international assignment issues through organisational examples, reports, questions, and case studies from diverse global and industrial contexts. The chapter has shown that international assignees are very diverse in terms of their individual characteristics and the nature of assignment, for example gender, race, nationality, and skill as well as assignment length, transfer direction, and different levels at which the assignment is initiated. Increased communication and transports links have facilitated globalisation of organisations and workforce. However, depending upon the context as well as organisational orientation, the global workforce remains segmented and hierarchical, for example different treatment of Western 'expats' versus 'immigrants' from other countries. The various forms of assignment provide MNCs with a resource to address the challenges of globalisation and enhance their ability to expand and conduct their international operations. In this respect, international assignments may be seen as a source of strategic competitive advantage. The key challenge for MNCs is to capitalise upon the experiences and skills that their employees develop during international assignments in the long run.

End of Chapter Case Study Chinese expats in India

The Chinese community in India comprises immigrants from China and Indian-born people of Chinese ancestry. In the late eighteenth century, Chinese immigrants came to India to work at the Calcutta (Kolkata) port and Madras port. In 1962, the Indo-China border dispute resulted in a war leading to mistrust and frictions between the two neighbours. However, the situation started to normalise when India and China resumed diplomatic relations in 1976. The ethnic Chinese in India have contributed to many areas of social and economic life; they have engaged in manufacturing and trade of leather products as well as beauty parlours and restaurants. Today, there are thousands of Chinese living in Kolkata, Mumbai, and other cities in India. Many Chinese companies, entrepreneurs, and managers are operating in India in fields as diverse as telecommunications, power, construction, heavy machinery, and pharmaceuticals.

Chinese investors

In recent years, the Indian government has been encouraging foreign companies to set up manufacturing units in India under its 'Make in India' programme (Ribeiro and Kan, 2015). China is now the world's largest economy (by output), producing 16 per cent of all goods and services, whereas India accounts for 7 per cent (IMF, 2105). In 2014, Indo-China trade was estimated to be about $72 billion (BI, 2015). In the aftermath of economic liberalisation policies of India since 1991, there has been an influx of not only Western but also Chinese investors and companies. Investors from mainland China as well as Taiwan have started operating in India, at times also relocating their skilled employees and managers. One such example is Foxconn Technology Group (Hon Hai Precision Industry Co., Ltd.,) a multinational electronics contract manufacturing company headquartered in New Taipei, which is estimated to be the third-largest information technology company by revenue. In August 2015, Foxconn entered into a memorandum of understanding with the Indian state government of Maharashtra and announced that, as a part of its plan to set up 12 manufacturing facilities in India by 2020, the company will invest US$5 billion in a large electronics factory and other facilities in the India. The investment is likely to create employment for at least 50,000 people (Ribeiro and Kan, 2015). For the contract manufacturing company (Foxconn) which makes a variety of products for various companies, including the iPhone, India presents an opportunity to build products such as smartphones both for the booming local market and for global customers. The company already employs over a million workers in China, where it has factories across the country.

In recent years, the company has faced labour shortages in China as many workers are looking for the highest wages possible and are happy to leave for better jobs. To expand its manufacturing base, Foxconn is looking at setting up factories in India and Indonesia. In a statement, Foxconn said that the investments in Maharashtra will be in the areas of manufacturing, research, and development, and other strategic capabilities, to tap into the pool of local talent in the technology and manufacturing sectors (Ribeiro and Kan, 2015).

In the aftermath of Prime Minister Narendra Modi coming to power in 2014, many Chinese companies are finding the confidence to step into the Indian market. While Lenovo, Huawei, and Xiaomi are already household names in India, new entrants such as Gionee and Oppo are equally active. More companies such as Shandong Tiejun Electric Power Engineering, Xian Electric Engineering, and Shanghai Urban Construction are charting out India plans after the Indian government cleared these companies in 2015 (BI, 2015).

India remains a difficult terrain for Chinese expatriates

Chinese manufacturing companies, including mobile phone makers, are expanding into India, utilising human and other resources available in the local market. With Chinese firms setting up their factories and offices in India, they have brought with them Chinese high-ranking officials. While some Chinese expatriates adjust to the Indian culture, most of them find it difficult to adjust to the local culture, and some Chinese expatriates may find it difficult to absorb the culture shock of India's many chaotic festivals, elections, cuisines, and languages (Mandavia, 2015).

Most of the 5,000–7,000 Chinese expatriates living in India prefer to remain isolated from Indian culture (BI, 2015). The Chinese expatriates form close communities within themselves. Many of them live together and interact together while very few mingle with the local Indian community. The number of Chinese expatriates in India has doubled over the past two years, as a result of hundreds of Chinese nationals moving to India in search of business (Mandavia, 2015). Most of them choose to stay secluded from Indians due to language and cultural barriers and their inherent shyness. A Chinese expatriate, Pan Xuan, who has been in Gurgaon for six years, said his 'talkative' Indian colleagues helped him adjust to the diverse country to a great extent by taking him out for biryani or inviting him for Holi and Diwali celebrations (BI, 2015). Most Chinese expatriates live in Gurgaon, Mumbai, and Bengaluru and often avoid public transport. Many return to China after two to three years on the completion of their assignment. It is tough to get work visas, Chinese expatriates complain, and they have to go back home periodically to comply with regulations (BI, 2015).

Mandavia (2015) reports the case of Shengyu Yang, an Oppo employee, who is in India to help the Chinese phone maker make inroads into a fiercely competitive handset market. The 29-year-old Yang lives with his wife in Powai, an upcoming hub for Chinese expatriates in Mumbai. Despite his affection for India, Yang reports certain teething problems, such as the difference in work cultures. 'It is not easy to manage teams here. Indians also understand time differently. It is stretchable for them,' he laughs. His wife Jessie and himself, like most other expatriates from China, spend weekends socialising with others from their home country or engaging in sports. Most Chinese expatriates don't find it easy to mix with locals. Yang's wife Jessie is trying to learn Hindi to feel more at home. But she is still not comfortable with the idea of venturing too far outside Mumbai without her husband. 'When I came to India, I didn't leave home without my husband for one-and-a-half months. In China, we had a negative view about safety in India. Only now I know Mumbai is safe, but we have not travelled much outside' (Mandavia, 2015).

A 2014 Pew Research Centre survey found that only 30 per cent of Chinese hold a favourable view of India (Pew, 2014). For that to change, Chinese investors and expatriates may consider that despite all the misgivings about the Indian culture and economy, there's opportunity, especially for IT professionals and producers. Learning Indian culture and Hindi, in addition to English, may improve their prospects substantially (Mandavia, 2015). Equally, the Indian government and local business partners may consider relaxing working visa regulations as well as opportunities for Chinese expatriates to learn the local culture and language while also ensuring their safety and wellbeing.

Questions

1 What are some of the key difficulties facing Chinese expatriates in India?
2 What can (a) MNCs (b) host country do to address the challenges facing Chinese expatriates in India?
3 What factors should Chines MNCs consider in (a) recruiting and selecting and (b) training managers and other employees for international assignments in India?

FOR DISCUSSION AND REVISION

1 What role does international human resource management play in multinational corporations?
2 What are 'international assignments' and why do multinational corporations use them?
3 What are the key issues in recruiting and selecting staff for international assignments?
4 What is meant be the term 'Psychological Contract' and how does this affect the international assignment?
5 What can a multinational do to ensure the success of an international assignment?
6 What competencies do international assignees need in order to succeed?
7 What different types of international assignees are used by multinationals?
8 What factors need to be considered when an international assignee is repatriated to the organisation's 'home' country?

FURTHER READING

BUCKLEY, P. J., AND GHAURI, P. N. (2015) *International Business Strategy: Theory and Practice*. London: Routledge.

CHRISTOPHER, E. M., (2012) *International Management: Explorations across Cultures*. London: Kogan Page Ltd.

DANIELS, J. D., SULLIVAN, D. AND RADEBAUGH, L. H. (2015) *International Business: Environments and Operations*. Boston: Pearson.

GRIFFIN, R. W., AND PUSTAY, M. W. (2015) *International Business: A Managerial Perspective*. Boston: Pearson.

HILL, C. W. L. (2014) *International Business: Competing in the Global Marketplace*. New York: McGraw-Hill Education.

VAIMAN, V. AND HASLBERGER, A. (2013) *Talent Management of Self-Initiated Expatriates: A Neglected Source of Global Talent*. Basingstoke: Palgrave Macmillan.

WEB RESOURCES

http://britishexpat.com/.

This UK-based website contains information about living and working overseas. There is a forum where users can interact with one another, and users are able to sign-up for a free monthly newsletter.

http://www.canuckabroad.com/.

This is a web-based resource for Canadian travellers and expatriates and includes information on almost every country in the world. It also includes a forum for exchanging information.

http://www.easyexpat.com/.

This website provides expatriates with information about the major cities to which expatriates are posted. The site contains a blog and a number of useful tools.

http://www.expatwoman.com/.

This Dubai-based website provides resources to help support women and families taking on new expatriate challenges, especially in relation to the Middle East.

http://www.shanghaiexpat.com/.

A website that provides information for expatriates living and working in Shanghai. The resource includes social events, online forums, and venue listings.

http://www.singaporeexpats.com/.

A website that provides information for expatriates living and working in Singapore. The resource includes social events, property listings, and transport information.

REFERENCES

AGGARWAL, R., BERRILL, J., HUTSON, E. AND KEARNEY, C. (2011) What is a multinational corporation? Classifying the degree of firm-level multinationality. *International Business Review*, 20(5): 557–577. doi:10.1016/j.ibusrev.2010.11.004.

AHLSTROM, D. AND BRUTON, G. (2010) *International Management*. London: South-Western Cengage Learning.

AVRIL, A. B. AND MAGNINI, V. P. (2007) A holistic approach to expatriate success. *International Journal of Contemporary Hospitality Management*, 19(1): 53–64.

BADER, B. AND BERG, N. (2014) The influence of terrorism on expatriate performance: A conceptual approach. *International Journal of Human Resource Management*, 25(4): 539–557.

BARTLETT, C. A. AND GHOSHAL, S. (1998) *Managing across Borders: The Transnational Solution* (2nd edn). London: Random House/Business Books.

BI (Business Insider) (2015) India isn't the favourite place on earth for Chinese expats! They'd rather live elsewhere. *Business Insider*, August 28. Available at: http://

www.businessinsider.in/India-isnt-the-favourite-place-on-earth-for-Chinese-expats-Theyd-rather-live-else-where/articleshow/48710251.cms.

BJÖRKMAN, I. AND GERTSEN, M. (1993) Selecting and training Scandinavian expatriates: Determinants of corporate practice. *Scandinavian Journal of Management*, 9(2): 145–164.

BLACK, J. S. AND GREGERSEN, H. B. (1991) Antecedents to cross-cultural adjustment for expatriates in Pacific-Rim assignments. *Human Relations*, 44: 497–515.

BLACK, J. S. AND GREGERSEN, H. B. (1999) The right way to manage expats. *Harvard Business Review*, 77 (March–April): 52–63.

BLACK, J. AND MENDENHALL, M. (1991) The U-curve adjustment hypothesis revisited: A review and theoretical framework. *Journal of International Business Studies*, 22: 225–246.

BOLTON, S. C. AND HOULIHAN, M. (2007) *Searching for the Human in Human Resource Management*. London: Palgrave Macmillan.

BONACHE, J. AND BREWSTER, C. (2001) Knowledge transfer and the management of expatriation. *Thunderbird International Business Review*, 43(1): 145–168.

BONACHE, J. AND ZÁRRAGA-OBERTY, C. (2008) Determinants of the success of international assignees as knowledge transferors: A theoretical framework. *International Journal of Human Resource Management*, 19(1): 1–18.

BOXALL, P., PURCELL, J. AND WRIGHT, P. (2015) *The Oxford Handbook of Human Resource Management*. Oxford: Oxford University Press.

BRAKE, T. (1999). The HR manager as global business partner. In Joynt, P. and Morton, B. (eds), *The Global HR Manager*, London: Institute of Personnel and Development, 59–86.

BRISCOE, D. R., SCHULER, R. S. AND TARIQUE, I. (2012) *International Human Resource Management: Policies and Practices for Multinational Enterprises*. London: Routledge.

CALIGIURI, P., TARIQUE, I. AND JACOBS, R. (2009) Selection for international assignments. *Human Resource Management Review*, 19(3): 251–262.

CASTREE, N., ROGERS, A. AND KITCHIN, R. (2013) *A Dictionary of Human Geography*. Oxford: Oxford University Press.

CAUSIN, G. AND AYOUN, B. (2011) Packing for the trip: A model of competencies for successful expatriate hospitality assignment. *International Journal of Hospitality Management*, 30(4): 795–802.

CERDIN, J. AND PARGNEUX, M. (2009) Career and international assignment fit: Toward an integrative model of success. *Human Resource Management*, 48(1): 5–25.

CHEN, H. AND CHIU, Y. (2009) The influence of psychological contracts on the adjustment and organisational commitment among expatriates: An empirical study in Taiwan. *International Journal of Manpower*, 30(8): 797–814.

CHIEN, T. (2012) Intercultural training for Taiwanese business expatriates. *Industrial and Commercial Training*, 44(3): 164–170.

CHO, T., HUTCHINGS, K. AND MARCHANT, T. (2013) Key factors influencing Korean expatriates' and spouses' perceptions of expatriation and repatriation. *International Journal of Human Resource Management*, 24(5): 1051–1075.

CIPD (Chartered Institute of Personnel and Development) (2013a) *International Mobility*. CIPD factsheet available at: www.cipd.co.uk. Accessed 18 March 2015.

CIPD (Chartered Institute of Personnel and Development) (2013b) *International Resourcing and Recruitment*. CIPD factsheet available at: www.cipd.co.uk. Accessed 18 March 2015.

COLE, N. AND NESBETH, K. (2014) Why do international assignments fail? Expatriate families speak. *International Studies of Management and Organization*, 44(3): 66–79.

COLLINGS, D. G., DOHERTY, N., LUETHY, M. AND OSBORN, D. (2011) Understanding and supporting the career implications of international assignments. *Journal of Vocational Behavior*, 78(3): 361–371.

COSTAS, J. (2013) Problematizing mobility: A metaphor of stickiness, non-places and the kinetic elite. *Organization Studies*, 34(10): 1467–1485.

CSEH, M. AND ROSENBUSCH, K. (2012) The cross-cultural adjustment process of expatriate families in a multinational organization: A family system theory perspective. *Human Resource Development International*, 15(1): 61–77.

DANIELS, J. D., RADEBAUGH, L. H. AND SULLIVAN, D. P. (2015) *International Business*. Harlow: Pearson Education.

DEOSTHALEE, P. G. (2002) Are Indian expatriates in the sultanate of Oman under stress? *Journal of Managerial Psychology*, 17(6): 523–528.

DICKMANN, M. AND BARUCH, Y. (2011) *Global Careers*. New York, NY: Routledge.

DICKMANN, M. AND HARRIS, H. (2005) Developing career capital for global careers: The role of international assignments. *Journal of World Business*, 40(4): 399–408.

DOHERTY, N. AND DICKMANN, M. (2009) Exposing the symbolic capital of international assignments. *International Journal of Human Resource Management*, 20(2): 301–320.

DOHERTY, N., RICHARDSON, J. AND THORN, K. (2013) Self-initiated expatriation and self-initiated expatriates. *Career Development International*, 18(1): 97–112.

DOTLICH, D. AND NOEL, J. (1998) *Action Learning: How the World's Top Companies Are Recreating Their Leaders and Themselves*. Jossey-Bass: San Francisco.

DOWNES, M., VARNER, I. I. AND HEMMASI, M. (2010) Individual profiles as predictors of expatriate effectiveness.

Competitiveness Review: An International Business Journal, 20(3): 235–247. doi:10.1108/10595421011047424.

DOWNES, M., VARNER, I. I. AND MUSINSKI, L. (2007) Personality traits as predictors of expatriate effectiveness: A synthesis and reconceptualization. *Review of Business*, 27(3): 16–23.

ESTIMO JR, R. C. (2016) Expat workers 'play key role' in Saudi society. *Arab News*, January 17. Available at: http://www.arabnews.com/saudi-arabia/news/866296.

FECHTER, A.-M. AND WALSH, K. (2010) Examining 'expatriate' continuities: Postcolonial approaches to mobile professionals. *Journal of Ethnic and Migration Studies*, 36(8): 1197–1210.

FEM (Forum for Expatriate Management) (2014) Managing the Global Mobility Function, 2014 Report. Available at: http://totallyexpat.com/fem-reports/.

FOOT, M., HOOK, C. AND JENKINS, A. (2016) *Introducing Human Resource Management*. Harlow: Pearson.

FORSTER, N. (2000) Expatriates and the impact of cross-cultural training. *Human Resource Management Journal*, 10(3): 63–78.

FRIEDMAN, P., MURPHY, S. A. AND DYKE, L. S. (2009) Expatriate adjustment from the inside out: An autoethnographic account. *International Journal of Human Resource Management*, 20(2): 252–268.

FROESE, F. AND PELTOKORPI, V. (2011) Cultural distance and expatriate job satisfaction. *International Journal of Intercultural Relations*, 35(1): 49–60.

GRAF, A. AND MERTESACKER, M. (2009) Intercultural training: Six measures assessing training needs. *Journal of European Industrial Training*, 33(6): 539–558.

GREY, C. AND WILLMOTT, H. (2005) *Critical Management Studies: A Reader*. Oxford: Oxford University Press.

HARVEY, M., REICHE, B. S. AND MOELLER, M. (2011) Developing effective global relationships through staffing with inpatriate managers: The role of interpersonal trust. *Journal of International Management*, 17(2): 150161.

HARZING, A., AND CHRISTENSEN, C. (2004) Expatriate failure: Time to abandon the concept? *Career Development International*, 9(7): 616–626.

HASLBERGER, A. (2005). The complexities of expatriate adaptation. *Human Resource Management Review*, 15(2): 160–180.

HASLBERGER, A. AND BREWSTER, C. (2008) The expatriate family: An international perspective. *Journal of Managerial Psychology*, 23(3): 324–346.

HASSARD, J., MORRIS, J. AND MCCANN, L. (2012) 'My Brilliant Career'? New organizational forms and changing managerial careers in Japan, the UK, and USA. *Journal of Management Studies*, 49(3): 571–599.

HOLOPAINEN, J. AND BJÖRKMAN, I. (2005) The personal characteristics of the successful expatriate: A critical review of the literature and an empirical investigation. *Personnel Review*, 34(1): 37–50.

HOWSE, M. (2015) Making a success of long-term international assignments. Available at: www.xperthr.co.uk. Accessed 18 March 2015.

IBRAHIM, D., GOBY, V., ANNAVARJULA, M., AHMED, Z. and Osman-Gani, A. (2002) Determinants of expatriate success: An empirical study of Singaporean expatriates in the People's Republic of China. *Journal of Transnational Management Development*, 7(4): 73–88.

IMF (International Monetary Fund) (2015) *World Economic and Financial Surveys, World Economic Outlook Database*. Available at: http://www.imf.org/external/pubs/ft/weo/2015/01/weodata/index.aspx.

JOHNSON, G., WHITTINGTON, R., ANGWIN, D., REGNER, P. and Scholes, K. (2014) *Exploring Strategy: Text and Cases*. Harlow: Pearson Education.

JORDAN, J. AND CARTWRIGHT, S. (1998) Selecting expatriate managers: Key traits and competencies. *Leadership and Organization Development Journal*, 19(2): 89–96.

KOVESHNIKOV, A., WECHTLER, H. AND DEJOUX, C. (2014) Cross-cultural adjustment of expatriates: The role of emotional intelligence and gender. *Journal of World Business*, 49(3): 362–371.

KOUTONIN, M. R. (2015) Why are white people expats when the rest of us are immigrants? *Guardian*, 13 March. Available at: http://www.theguardian.com/global-development-professionals-network/2015/mar/13/white-people-expats-immigrants-migration.

KRAIMER, M. L., SHAFFER, M. A. AND BOLINO, M. C. (2009) The influence of expatriate and repatriate experiences on career advancement and repatriate retention. *Human Resource Management*, 48(1): 27–47.

KYRIAKIDOU, O. (2012) Recruitment, selection and retention. In KRAMAR, R. AND SYED, J. (eds.), *Human Resource Management in a Global Context: A Critical Approach*. London: Palgrave Macmillan, pp.175–210.

LEGGE, K. (1995) *Human Resource Management: Rhetorics and Realities*. London: Palgrave Macmillan.

LEOPOLD, J., HARRIS, L. AND WATSON, T. J. (2005) *The Strategic Management of Human Resources*. London: FT Prentice Hall.

MAHMOOD, M. (2015) Strategy, structure, and HRM policy orientation: Employee recruitment and selection practices in multinational subsidiaries. *Asia Pacific Journal of Human Resources*, 53(3): 331–350.

MANDAVIA, M. (2015) Why India remains a difficult terrain for 7,000 Chinese expatriates living in the country. *Economic Times*, August 28. Available at: http://economictimes.indiatimes.com/articleshow/48703439.cms.

MATVEEV, A. V. AND MILTER, R. G. (2004) The value of intercultural competence for performance of multicultural teams. *Team Performance Management: An International Journal*, 10(5/6): 104–111.

MCEVOY, G. M. AND BULLER, P. F. (2013) Research for practice: The management of expatriates. *Thunderbird International Business Review*, 55(2): 213–226.

MCKENNA, S. AND SURRY, T. (2015) Critical perspectives on global careers: Special issue call for papers from critical perspectives on international business. Available at: http://www.emeraldgrouppublishing.com/products/journals/call_for_papers.htm?id=5954.

MENDENHALL, M. E., DUNBAR, E. AND ODDOU, G. R. (1987) Expatriate selection, training and career-pathing: A review and critique. *Human Resource Management*, 26(3): 331–345.

MEYSKENS, M., CLARKE, L., WERTHER, J., WILLIAM B. AND VON GLINOW, M. A. (2009) The paradox of international talent: Alternative forms of international assignments. *International Journal of Human Resource Management*, 20(6): 1439–1450.

MIAO, L., ADLER, H. AND XU, X. (2011) A stakeholder approach to expatriate management: Perceptions of hotel expatriate managers in China. *International Journal of Hospitality Management*, 30(3): 530–541.

MILLMORE, M., LEWIS, P., SAUNDERS, M., THORNHILL, A. and Morrow, T. (2007) *Strategic Human Resource Management: Contemporary Issues*. London: Financial Times Prentice Hall.

MOELLER, M., HARVEY, M. AND WILLIAMS, W. (2010) Socialization of inpatriate managers to the headquarters of global organizations: A social learning perspective. *Human Resource Development Review*, 9(2): 169–193.

MORRIS, M. W., SAVANI, K., MOR, S. AND CHO, J. (2014) When in Rome: Intercultural learning and implications for training. *Research in Organizational Behavior*, 34: 189–215.

MORRIS, M. W., SAVANI, K. AND ROBERTS, R. D. (2014) Intercultural training and assessment: Implications for organizational and public policies. *Policy Insights from the Behavioral and Brain Sciences*, 1(1): 63–71. doi:10.1177/2372732214550404.

NERY-KJERFVE, T. AND MCLEAN, G. N. (2012) Repatriation of expatriate employees, knowledge transfer, and organizational learning: What do we know? *European Journal of Training and Development*, 36(6): 614–629.

NICKSON, D. (2013) *Human Resource Management for Hospitality and Tourism Industries*. London: Routledge.

OBERG, K. (1960) Cultural shock: Adjustment to new cultural environments. *Practical Anthropology*, 7: 177–182.

O'DONOVAN, D. (2014). The right talent in the right place. *Telegraph*, 29 October. Available at: http://www.telegraph.co.uk/expat/before-you-go/11194906/The-right-talent-in-the-right-place.html.

OKPARA, J. O. AND KABONGO, J. D. (2011) Cross-cultural training and expatriate adjustment: A study of western expatriates in Nigeria. *Journal of World Business*, 46(1): 22–30.

PAETKAU, T. M. (2009) When does a foreign law compel a US employer to discriminate against US expatriates? A modest proposal for reform. *Labor Law Journal*, 60(2): 92–103.

PATE, J. AND SCULLION, H. (2009) The changing nature of the traditional expatriate psychological contract. *Employee Relations*, 32(1): 56–73.

PENG, M. AND MEYER, K. (2011) *International Business*. London: South-Western Cengage Learning.

Pew (2014) How Asians rate China, India, Pakistan, Japan and the US, global attitudes and trends. *Pew Research Centre*. July 11. Available at: http://www.pewglobal.org/2014/07/14/global-opposition-to-u-s-surveillance-and-drones-but-limited-harm-to-americas-image/pg-2014-07-14-balance-of-power-4-01/.

PINNINGTON, A., MACKLIN, R. AND CAMPBELL, T. (2007) *Human Resource Management: Ethics and Employment*. Oxford: Oxford University Press.

PLOURDE, Y., PARKER, S. C. AND SCHAAN, J. L. (2014) Expatriation and its effect on headquarters' attention in the multinational enterprise. *Strategic Management Journal*, 35(6): 938–947.

POTOČNIK, K., NAVARRO, M., DERELI, B. AND TACER, B. (2014) Recruitment and selection in the international context. In ŐZBILGIN. M., GROUTSIS, D. AND HARVEY, W. (eds), *International Human Resource Management*. New York. Cambridge University Press USA, pp. 67–92.

PRIES, L. 2001. The approach of transnational social spaces: Responding to new configurations of the social and the spatial. In Pries, L. (ed.), *New Transnational Social Spaces: International Migration and Transnational Companies in the Early Twenty-First Century*. Abingdon: Routledge, pp. 3–33.

PRINGLE, J. K. AND MALLON, M. (2003) Challenges to the boundaryless career odyssey. *International Journal of Human Resource Management*, 15(4): 839–853.

REICHE, B. S., KRAIMER, M. L. AND HARZING, A. (2011) Why do international assignees stay? An organizational embeddedness perspective. *Journal of International Business Studies*, 42(4): 521–544.

RIBEIRO, J. AND KAN, M. (2015) Foxconn to invest $5B to set up first of up to 12 factories in India. *IT World*, August 9. Available at: http://www.itworld.com/article/2968375/android/foxconn-to-invest-5b-to-set-up-first-of-up-to-12-factories-in-india.html.

RICHARDSON, J. AND ZIKIC, J. (2007) The darker side of an international academic career. *Career Development International*, 12(2): 164–186.

ROFCANIN, Y., IMER, H. AND ZINGONI, M. (2014) Global trends in international human resource management. In Ozbilgin, M., Groutsis, D. and Harvey, W. (eds), *International Human Resource Management*. New York: Cambridge University Press USA, 6–22.

RUGMAN, A. M. AND COLLINSON, S. (2012) *International Business*. Harlow: Pearson Education.

SCURRY, T., BLENKINSOPP, J. AND HAY, A. (2013) Global Careers: Perspectives from the United Kingdom. In REIS, C. AND BARUCH, Y. (eds), *Careers without Borders: Critical Perspectives*. London: Routledge, 31–54.

SCURRY, T., RODRIGUEZ, J. K. AND BAILOUNI, S. (2013). Narratives of identity of self-initiated expatriates in Qatar. *Career Development International*, 18(1): 12–33.

SELMER, J. (1999). Culture shock in China? Adjustment pattern of western expatriate business managers. *International Business Review*, 8(5–6): 515–534.

SHAFFER, M. A. AND HARRISON, J. A. (1998) Expatriates' psychological withdrawal from international assignments: Work, nonwork, and family influences. *Personnel Psychology*, 51(1): 87–118.

SHEN, Y. AND HALL, D. T. T. (2009) When expatriates explore other options: Retaining talent through greater job embeddedness and repatriation adjustment. *Human Resource Management*, 48(5): 793–816.

SHIM, J., SIEGEL, J. AND LEVINE, M. (2013) *The Dictionary of International Business Terms*. Hoboken: Routledge.

SILBIGER, A. AND PINES, A. M. (2014) Expatriate stress and burnout. *International Journal of Human Resource Management*, 25(8): 1170–1183.

SIMS, R. H. AND SCHRAEDER, M. (2004) An examination of salient factors affecting expatriate culture shock. *Journal of Business and Management*, 10(1): 73–87.

SIMS, R. R. (1994) Human resource management's role in clarifying the new psychological contract. *Human Resource Management*, 33(3): 373–382.

SPARROW, P. (1999) Abroad minded. *People Management*, 20 May: 40–44.

SRINIVASAN, V., VALK, R., THITE, M. AND HARVEY, M. (2009) Expatriates of host-country origin: 'Coming home to test the waters'. *International Journal of Human Resource Management*, 20(2): 269–285.

SYED, J., HAZBOUN, N. G. AND MURRAY, P. A. (2014) What locals want: Jordanian employees' views on expatriate managers. *International Journal of Human Resource Management*, 25(2): 212–233.

UCSF News (2015) HEAL Initiative Aims to Address Global Shortage of Health Care Workers. University of California San Francisco. August 6. Available at: https://www.ucsf.edu/news/2015/08/131211/heal-initiative-launches-global-health-boot-camp.

VAN DER ZEE, K. I. AND VAN OUDENHOVEN, J. P. (2000) Psychometric qualities of the Multicultural Personality Questionnaire: A multidimensional instrument of multicultural effectiveness. *European Journal of Personality*, 14: 291–309.

VAN DER ZEE, K. I. AND VAN OUDENHOVEN, J. P. (2001) The multicultural personality questionnaire: Reliability and validity of self- and other ratings of multicultural effectiveness. *Journal of Research in Personality*, 35: 278–288.

WHO (World Health Organisation) (2010). *User's Guide to the WHO Global Code of Practice on the International Recruitment of Health Personnel*. Geneva: World Health Organisation.

YEATON, K. AND HALL, N. (2008) Expatriates: Reducing failure rates. *Journal of Corporate Accounting and Finance*, 19(3): 75–78.

ZAKARIA, N. (2000) The effects of cross-cultural training on the acculturation process of the global workforce. *International Journal of Manpower*, 21(6): 492–510.

ZAMOR, C. (2008) *Intercultural Trainings for German Expatriates Going to China*. Hamburg, Germany: Igel Verlag.

14

HRM, PRODUCTIVITY, AND EMPLOYEE INVOLVEMENT

Amanda Pyman

LEARNING OUTCOMES

After reading this chapter, you should be able to:

➤ Explain the link between strategic human resource management and employee involvement, and why productivity is a better measure of the impact of human resource management practices than profitability
➤ Define employee involvement using human resource management and employment relations lenses; identify channels used to facilitate employee involvement and their potential challenges
➤ Distinguish between employee involvement and employee participation
➤ Identify the major trends in employee involvement in Anglo-American and European countries and the major drivers of these trends
➤ Identify and critically discuss the objectives and effectiveness of employee involvement
➤ Identify good practices in employee involvement and participation for organisations, managers, employees and policy-makers.

SUMMARY OF CHAPTER CONTENTS

➤ **Opening Case Study**: Health and safety in the workplace
➤ Introduction
➤ SHRM and employee involvement
➤ Theories and concepts of employee involvement: Human resource management versus employment relations
➤ Employee involvement and productivity: examples from Europe
➤ Critical summary of employee involvement
➤ Employee involvement in a global context: macro-environmental influences
➤ A critical analysis of employee Involvement
➤ Benefits of studying HRM from a critical perspective for managers
➤ Conclusion
➤ **End of Chapter Case Study**: Employee involvement at Paper Co
➤ For discussion and revision
➤ Glossary
➤ Further reading
➤ Web resources
➤ References

Opening Case Study **Health and safety in the workplace**

Health and safety are critical issues in the workplace. An issue often forgotten within the domain of health and safety is workplace cleanliness. How can employee involvement, HRM, and productivity be examined in relation to workplace cleanliness? Let us examine the Department of Business and Administration, a renowned business school in a leading public sector University in Pakistan.

The department is large, offering undergraduate and graduate educational programmes with more than 2,000 students enrolled in the courses on offer. In a busy department, health and safety can always raise its head as an issue. In fact, the department occasionally receives complaints about cleanliness, despite employing nine full-time and four part-time sanitary workers.

In recent times, cleanliness has been a strongly contested issue in the department, following the receipt of complaints from students and faculty members regarding the unhygienic state of bathrooms, classrooms, and the cafeteria. One mechanism by which complaints were raised was through suggestion schemes, whereby stakeholders submitted their complaints in physical boxes located in the main hall and cafeteria within the department. How would the director of the department respond to such complaints and seek to resolve these issues?

In seeking to respond to and resolve these issues, the director first made a decision about the problem: he deemed the cleanliness issues to be of strategic importance to all stakeholders. Therefore, a combined faculty and administrative staff meeting was called. The director believed that by calling a department-wide meeting to discuss and determine remedial actions, organisational performance would be improved and, ultimately, employees would take greater ownership of the solutions and their implementation in the workplace.

Through a series of department-wide meetings aimed at problem identification, the department realised, among other things, that the cleanliness problems stemmed from the fact that too many sanitary workers reported to a chief administrative officer alongside other workers (the span of control in an organisational reporting sense was too large) and that there was no rotation of sanitary workers; instead, they were constantly undertaking repetitive tasks. As a result of the meetings and proactively addressing the problem, the department implemented the following measures: a full-time health and safety officer was appointed and all sanitary workers reported to this position; a 'clean work environment' engagement survey was developed and administered to all staff as a means to measure the cleanliness of office spaces, bathrooms, stairwells, corridors, classrooms, grounds and the cafeteria; faculty staff were assigned to a roster as 'duty officers' to undertake independent daily audits of workplace cleanliness; job rotation was implemented for sanitary workers; and, at a strategic level, a workplace cleanliness policy developed. As a direct result of these collective interventions, the outcomes for the department were outstanding: reduced complaints and enhanced employee satisfaction. As cleanliness improved over time, the department was able to disband the roster of duty officers (using academic staff), and the workplace cleanliness policy was taken over by the health and safety officer as an administrative-focused strategic and operational task in the organisation.

Questions

1 How is occupational health and safety linked with employee productivity?
2 Identify and discus examples from organisations in your own city or country where health and safety measures have had a positive effect on employees.

Source: Saba Nasir, Doctoral Candidate, Monash University

INTRODUCTION

The term 'employee voice' has been used to cover a variety of processes and structures, including employee involvement, that enable and at times empower employees, both directly and indirectly, to contribute to and/or participate in a firm's decision-making (Boxall and Purcell, 2003). Within the strategic human resource management (SHRM) literature, employee involvement is afforded a central role in high-commitment and high-performance work systems, with such models advocating that high levels of involvement, along with other bundles of human resource practices, are linked to improved productivity and profitability of the firm (Marchington, 2007; Richardson et al., 2010). This assumption is based on the notion that employees are a major source of competitive advantage, and thus employee involvement practices increase the stock of ideas and contributions, enhancing employee commitment and engendering cooperative, high-trust relations (Marchington, 2007). The assumption is also based on the notion that employee involvement and participation in the strategic direction of the organisation are elements of a successful organisational culture, whereby there is a relationship between employee involvement, organisational productivity, performance and commitment (Phipps et al., 2013).

The aim of this chapter is to critically evaluate the relationship between human resource management (HRM), productivity, and employee involvement. The chapter begins by considering the link between SHRM and employee involvement. This section is followed by a review of the theories and concepts of employee involvement, distinguishing four types. The distinction between the different types of employee involvement is followed by a consideration of the relationship between employee involvement and productivity and a critical analysis of the utility of different forms of employee involvement.

Employee involvement is then discussed in a global context, emphasising the importance of situating involvement in a broader political, social, and legislative framework. Students are directed to consider a comparative analysis of employee involvement in Australia and Britain; then they have the opportunity to apply this knowledge by considering the importance of the regulation of employee involvement in Australia vis-à-vis Britain. A case study of employee involvement in a British site of a multinational corporation (MNC) follows. The chapter concludes with a critical analysis and summary of employee involvement, identifying the benefits to managers of studying HRM from a critical perspective and identifying good practice and recommendations for organisations, managers, employees, and policy-makers.

SHRM AND EMPLOYEE INVOLVEMENT

The rise of SHRM has led to a focus on the way in which human resources practices are linked with, and impact upon, organisational performance and productivity. As Kaplan and Norton (1992) identify, human resource variables such as employees' skills, commitment, and satisfaction levels are performance-drivers in all firms. However, profit and labour productivity are also core elements of the causal chain within an organisation and are influenced by human resource strategies.

Boxall and Purcell (2003) argue that HRM ought to be concerned with three goal domains that contribute to a firm's viability:

- productivity;
- flexibility;
- legitimacy.

Superior performance equates to the attainment of successful outcomes across all three domains. For organisations, the key concern is adopting a cost-effective set of human resource practices that underpin profitable and productive relations in the firm, while simultaneously achieving flexibility and legitimacy (Boxall and Purcell, 2003). In strategy terms, this would normally include a blend of human resource practices concerned with hiring and developing employee skills, motivating appropriate performance and providing leadership and opportunities for employees to be involved and participate in organisational decision-making. This blend of human resource practices is commonly referred to as the abilities (A), motivations (M) and opportunities (O) model [AMO model] (Boxall and Macky, 2009). Similarly, the resource-based view identifies employee skills, knowledge and technical systems as organisational competencies (Leonard, 1998).

Boxall and Purcell (2003) argue that labour productivity is a better measure of HRM in firms than profitability, as labour productivity is solely concerned with people management. Labour productivity is defined as the value of labour outputs proportional to the cost of labour inputs, the objective being that HRM is cost-effective (Boxall and Purcell, 2003). Cost-effectiveness is a core requirement of the overarching HRM system and strategy within a firm. All firms need to assess what human resource practices are needed to ensure cost-effectiveness within the context in which they operate. Employee involvement has been advocated as one human resource practice, among others, that can enhance labour productivity.

THEORIES AND CONCEPTS OF EMPLOYEE INVOLVEMENT: HUMAN RESOURCE MANAGEMENT VERSUS EMPLOYMENT RELATIONS

Employee involvement can be explored, in theoretical terms, from a human resource management lens and/or an employment relations lens. According to HRM theory, the rationale for employee involvement is to increase performance through individual forms such as focus groups or an open door policy. The philosophy underpinning employee involvement is managerial or unitarist; that is, a frame of reference that assumes an identity of interest between employers and employees (Boxall and Purcell, 2003). Thus, employee involvement is used to engender loyalty to the organisation and enhance performance (Wilkinson et al., 2015). This lens contrasts with an organisational behaviour lens, whereby the rationale for involvement is job design through both individual and groups forms, such as teamwork and speaking up programmes (Wilkinson et al., 2015). The philosophy underpinning organisational behaviour is also unitarist, yet in comparison to HRM it is focused on engagement and commitment (Wilkinson *et al.* 2015). Finally, employee involvement can be explored from an employment relations lens. Given the multidisciplinary nature of employment relations, there are several different theoretical strands from which to explore employee involvement. The first is the political science tradition whereby involvement is representative for the purpose of creating citizenship. The philosophy of involvement is therefore legalistic and rights-based, intended to enable democracy (Wilkinson *et al.* 2015). The second strand is labour process theory. Here, involvement is collective and is achieved through collective bargaining, works councils, and partnership between employers and unions (Wilkinson et al,. 2015). The overarching philosophy is pluralist: involvement is intended to facilitate power-sharing in the employment relationship, by acting as a countervailing power to managerial prerogative (Wilkinson et al., 2015). The final strand, transaction cost economics, entails the application of economics to employment relations (Wilkinson et al., 2015). Under this approach, involvement is representative, whether through union or non-union forms or a combination of the two. The philosophy is utilitarian; involvement is a means of generating transaction efficacy through cost switching between involvement options/channels (Wilkinson et al,. 2015).

As can be seen from the above discussion, there are a wide range of theoretical perspectives within HRM and ER that have been utilised to explore employee involvement. Each theoretical lens examines the forms or practices of involvement in the organisation slightly differently, based on different rationales for involvement and different ideological or philosophical underpinnings (Wilkinson et al., 2015). Despite these differences, employee involvement is often characterised as direct or indirect (representative-based). Direct channels are defined as two-way mechanisms of employee communication and involvement. Examples are team briefings, quality circles, and suggestion schemes (Marginson et al., 2010). Indirect voice (involvement and participation) is achieved through representative arrangements, which may include union structures, JCCs (union or non-union based), or non-union structures (company councils/associations). The variety of direct and indirect involvement channels include:

- regular meetings;
- suggestion schemes;

- employee attitude surveys;
- quality circles;
- task forces;
- semi-autonomous work groups/self-managed teams;
- off-line teams;
- joint consultative committees (JCCs);
- works councils;
- financial involvement;
- team briefings; and
- grievance procedures.

From a SHRM perspective, employee involvement is management-initiated and management-led and has a number of objectives, as summarised in Box 14.1. These objectives are not mutually exclusive: management may introduce employee involvement for a variety of reasons, with an overarching objective of improving labour productivity and organisational competitiveness through a positive impact on the psychological contract.

Employee involvement systems became prominent in the 1980s as external environmental changes exacerbated the need for organisational flexibility and the proactive management of human resources. Prior to the 1980s, involvement was framed in broader terms under the umbrellas of employee participation and industrial democracy (see, for example, Brewster et al., 2007;

Box 14.1 The objectives of employee involvement

▸ To enhance employees' skills, abilities and motivation.
▸ To enhance the meaning of work for employees, their job satisfaction and morale.
▸ To enhance employees' commitment and loyalty.
▸ To enhance employees' performance.
▸ To enhance employees' cooperation and engagement.
▸ To create relational capital: networks among employees.
▸ To allow employees to express complaints or grievances to management and reduce industrial conflict.
▸ To tap into and release employees' skills, creativity, knowledge and ideas, and to incorporate these contributions into management decision-making.
▸ To empower employees and encourage discretionary behaviour.
▸ To enhance organisational operations and performance.

Source: Boxall and Purcell (2003); Marchington (2007); Richardson et al. (2010); Maden (2015), Wilkinson et al. (2015).

Marchington, 2007). The differences in terminology are in part related to the decline of trade unions and representative forms of participation and to the rise of direct, management-led forms of involvement, which have become the norm. These trends are discussed later in the chapter.

Leopold (2004) defines employee involvement as management-initiated and -inspired structures designed to secure the direct involvement and contributions of individual employees in decision-making, in an attempt to secure employees' commitment, motivation and loyalty (see also Chapter 1). The purpose of employee involvement is to contribute to the achievement of organisational goals and objectives of increased efficiency, productivity, and customer service, as part of a larger strategy to achieve and sustain a competitive advantage.

According to SHRM, employee involvement takes place within the context of a strict management agenda, and therefore the incidence of employee involvement varies, dependent upon managerial choices and the organisational context. Dundon and Gollan (2007) categorise the micro-organisational dimensions that impact upon employee involvement as follows:

- management strategies towards trade unions and leadership styles in the organisation (Pihlak and Alas 2012);
- occupational identity and group solidarity;
- autonomy;
- trust; and
- power and influence.

Class Activity

Choose one of the micro-organisational dimensions that impact on employee involvement as specified by Dundon and Gollan (2007). Using a company you know, and your knowledge and experience, explain how this dimension affected employee involvement.

Marchington and Wilkinson (2002) identify four categories of employee involvement: *downward communication, upward problem-solving, task participation,* and *financial involvement*. These categories are summarised in Table 14.1.

Table 14.1 Categories of employee involvement

Objectives	Potential problems
Downward communication	
1. Informs and educates employees directly on management's plans. 2. Formal or informal 3. Regular or irregular	1. Lack of commitment to implement employee involvement mechanisms in practice. 2. Lack of line management skills and/or cynicism and suspicion among employees (Townley, 1994; Leopold, 2004). 3. Acts as a threat to or may marginalise unionised mechanisms of communication in the workplace (Fiorito, 2001; Leopold, 2004; Wood and Fenton-O'Creevy, 2005).
Upward problem-solving	
1. Allows management to draw on employees' knowledge, skills and expertise within their jobs, for example with respect to diversity (see also Chapter 4). 2. Individual or group level 3. Increases the 'stock' of ideas in an organisation to encourage cooperative relationships and legitimate change. Examples include suggestion schemes, virtual teams, quality circles, two-way briefings and lean management (see also Chapter 11). 4. Improves quality and customer service within the organisation.	1. Employee competence is a precondition for effective decision-making (Marchington, 2007). 2. Employees may not see the added value of such schemes and/or may be resentful of the level of involvement required relative to the potential gains 3. May lead to work intensification for employees (Godard, 2001; Green, 2004). 4. Supervisors and/or line managers may feel threatened by employees' ideas and the practice of sharing information. This may lead to feelings of resentment or marginalisation in the managerial chain of command (Marchington, 2007). 5. Rewarding staff through upward problem-solving initiatives undermines the assumption that continuous improvement should be an objective for all staff and for the organisation (Leopold, 2004). Upward problem-solving may also increase organisational performance without a commensurate increase in employees' rewards. 6. Upward problem-solving may be used to achieve improvements in productivity that will result in job losses (Marchington, 2007).

(Continued)

Objectives	Potential problems
Task participation	
1. Encourages employees' to extend the range and types of tasks they undertake. Examples include job restructuring (job enrichment, job redesign) and teamworking. 2. Counteracts alienation among employees 3. Increases employees' commitment and satisfaction and their responsiveness to change (see also Chapter 11). 4. Improves levels of quality, productivity and customer service, and therefore enhances the organisation's competitive advantage. 5. Horizontal or vertical	1. Work intensification for employees, or perceptions of increased control by employers over the labour process. 2. An actual increase in managerial control and the subsequent dilution of employees' autonomy (Marchington, 2007).
Financial involvement	
1. Links individual employees' rewards to the success of a department/unit of the larger organisation. Examples include profit-sharing, share/incentive plans, employee share ownership schemes and employee share ownership plans (see also Chapter 10)	1. Financial involvement exposes employees to the vagaries of the share market 2. In times of financial difficulty, and in extreme cases of corporate collapse, organisations may be unable to provide employees with rewards, undermining the whole premise of this mechanism and violating notions of fairness and legitimacy 3. Employees can free-ride: if they only care about their personal pay-offs, group-based incentive schemes can be rendered ineffective (Kalmi et al., 2005)

Sources: Marchington (1992, 2007) and Marchington and Wilkinson (2002)

(?) Critical Thinking 14.1

The notion of partnership agreements between employers and trade unions has gained popularity in Britain. One well-known example of a partnership agreement is between Tesco (one of the big four supermarkets) and the Union of Shop Distributive Allied Workers (USDAW).

Questions

1 A partnership agreement is an agreement between an employer and trade union. What are the benefits of a partnership agreement between an employer and union from a human resource management perspective?
2 What are the potential drawbacks of a partnership agreement from the perspective of employees in the employment relationship at the individual workplace? Use the example of an employee at a supermarket checkout to think critically about the drawbacks of a partnership agreement.

Despite the different categorisations of employee involvement examined above, common elements can be identified (Brewster et al., 2007; Cox et al., 2006; Wilkinson et al., 2015). These include:

▸ *Actors*: the different parties or players involved at the individual, group, workplace, or institutional levels. For example, employees, employers, trade unions, employer associations, works councils (Marchington 2015a).
▸ *Level of involvement*: the level at which employees are involved, for example the individual, work group/team, or organisational level.
▸ *Scope of involvement*: the workplace subjects or issues in which employees are involved, for example task-/job-related issues, operational issues, and/or strategic organisational issues (see, for example, Knudsen, 1995).
▸ *Breadth of involvement*: the number of mechanisms (employee involvement channels) operating in the workplace (Marchington, 2007, 2015b).
▸ *Depth of involvement*: the frequency of meetings, the opportunities employees have to raise issues with managers, and the degree of influence employees feel they have over decisions (Marchington, 2007, 2015b).

The typology shown in Table 14.1 is just one classification of employee involvement. A range of different typologies are advocated in the literature (see for example, Dundon et al., 2004; Leopold, 2004; Marchington, 2007). For instance, Dundon et al. (2004) categorise employee involvement differently from Marchington and Wilkinson (2002) yet also identify four types: articulation of individual dissatisfaction; expression of collective organisation; contribution to management decision-making; and demonstration of mutuality and cooperative employment relations. These four types have different purposes and involvement practices. Articulation of individual dissatisfaction aims to rectify a problem with management or prevent a deterioration in employment relations. Involvement takes place through a complaint mechanism to a line manager or a grievance procedure; akin to upward communication (see Table 14.1). Expression of collective organisation aims to provide a countervailing source of power to managerial prerogative through trade union representation, using mechanisms such as collective bargaining and industrial action (Dundon et al,. 204; Wilkinson et al., 2015). Contribution to management decision-making is self-evident: employees seek to improve work organisation, quality, and productivity. Such intentions are akin to upward communication described in Table 14.1 and would entail practices such as problem-solving groups, quality circles, suggestion schemes, attitudinal surveys and self-managed teams (Dundon et al., 204; Wilkinson et al., 2015). Demonstration of mutuality and cooperative relations is intended to achieve long-term viability for the organisation and its employees. Employee involvement practices are centred around partnership agreements between employers and trade unions, joint consultative committees and/or works councils (Dundon et al,. 2004; Wilkinson et al., 2015). The different categorisations of employee involvement discussed above reinforce the differences between a SHRM lens and an employment relations lens when examining the relationship between HRM practices, productivity, and employee involvement, as described earlier.

The key learning points arising from the discussion of the objectives and categories of employee involvement are summarised in Box 14.2.

Class Activity

Consider your own experiences of employee involvement within a job and organisation.

▸ Using Marchington and Wilkinson's (2002) typology (Table 14.1), how were you involved in your job/organisation?
▸ What channel(s) of involvement did you find most effective in your job/organisation? Why?

Box 14.2 Key learning points: The objectives and categories of employee involvement

▸ The scope, level and nature of employee involvement vary across organisations.
▸ The actors captured by employee involvement differ across organisations.
▸ Employee involvement can take place over decisions at the corporate/organisational level, the plant level, the team level, or the individual level. The location at which decisions take place can be distinguished in terms of power-centred decisions, ownership-centred decisions, and task-centred decisions (Marchington and Wilkinson, 2002) or job-related and/or strategic-related issues.
▸ The level at which employee involvement takes place will be linked to the objectives of employee involvement within the organisation and the organisational setting itself.
▸ Employee involvement can coexist with or replace employee participation in an organisation. The extent to which the two are used simultaneously will be related to management's objectives and to the strength and level of employee participation in the organisation.
▸ Employee involvement will have different degrees of influence within organisations. The extent to which employees believe that their views are listened to and that they have a genuine influence on decision-making will be important in determining employees' overall evaluations and judgements of the effectiveness and fairness of employee involvement mechanisms within the organisation, and of management in general (Boxall and Purcell, 2003).

STOP AND REFLECT

One issue that has attracted increasing attention in workplaces is the capacity of new technologies to enhance employee involvement and in turn, productivity and performance. However, the many different faces of technology and its myriad capabilities mean that adverse consequences are possible too. For instance, there have many recent cases of dismissals related to social media usage (e.g. Beachboard, 2014). For human resource professionals, social media have become an important tool for 'investigating' potential employees in the recruitment process.

Question

1   To what extent is it right to fire an employee for posting nasty/derogatory comments about work/an organisation on Facebook?

EMPLOYEE INVOLVEMENT AND PRODUCTIVITY IN A GLOBAL CONTEXT

While organisations adopt employee involvement schemes for many different reasons, one of the main drivers is increased productivity. The notion of employee involvement leading to increased productivity is derived from the resource-based view of the firm, which focuses on the relationship between 'bundles' of HRM practices and organisational performance outcomes (Poutsma et al., 2003, 2006). Employee involvement is one HRM practice that can be linked to improved productivity and organisational performance. For example, direct involvement schemes such as upward problem-solving and task participation may be used to improve communication and cooperation between management and employees, to coordinate employees' tasks without supervision and/or to facilitate joint problem-solving. These objectives can lead to increased employee commitment, trust and information flows, organisational learning and efficiency, and in turn, reduced turnover (Hardy and Adnett, 2006; Poutsma et al., 2006; Wheeler, 2008). Financial involvement may also be used to align employees' interests to the organisation, by linking rewards to organisational outcomes, thus engendering greater employee commitment, reduced absenteeism and improved productivity (Kalmi et al., 2005; Poutsma et al., 2006). However, as Hardy and Adnett (2006) note, there is a trade-off between increased employee involvement which can provide greater information and innovation, and the costs of delay and lower short-term employment growth that may result from increased employee involvement.

Evidence suggests that different forms of employee involvement and participation can complement each other, further enhancing organisational performance effects (Kalmi et al., 2005; Poutsma et al., 2006). For example, financial participation can provide an incentive for employees to share information, complementing direct involvement schemes that encourage a cooperative corporate culture, thereby contributing to the effectiveness of work teams and quality circles (Poutsma et al., 2006). In fact, research indicates that financial participation has even more beneficial impacts on performance when other forms of participation are present (see Poutsma et al., 2006). Evidence from listed companies in Finland, Germany, the Netherlands, and the UK however, finds a lack of complementarity between financial participation and other forms of involvement.

There has been increased interest in financial participation, profit-based pay, and employee share ownership plans in many European economies (Poutsma et al., 2003; Kalmi et al., 2005). In Western Europe, financial participation has been part of the social policy agenda of the European Community (Wheeler, 2008) and is central to the Lisbon and European Employment Strategies, which seek to transform the performance of the European economy to create the most competitive and knowledge-based economy in the world (European Commission, 2001). While European labour laws introduced since the 1970s have sought to strengthen employers' consultation with the workforce, workplace democracy remains at the fore of the European Social Policy Agenda (Hardy and Adnett, 2006).

A study by the European Foundation for the Improvement of Living and Working Conditions conducted between 1999 and 2004, for example, reported active engagement with financial participation across Europe. According to this study, financial participation was increasingly common among large European companies and had the potential to deliver tangible benefits for employees, organisations, and national economies alike (European Foundation for the Improvement of Living and Working Conditions, 2005). In particular, this study found:

- Profit-sharing was the most prevalent form of financial participation, but there was variation among countries.
- Worker ownership via share ownership plans was common in countries with legislation and tax breaks that supported such schemes.
- Small and medium-sized enterprises confronted significant difficulties in adopting share ownership plans due to the high costs and administrative detail involved.
- Companies that had share ownership plans in place, compared with those that did not, tended to communicate better with their employees.

(*Source*: European Foundation for the Improvement of Living and Working Conditions, 2005: 1).

Diversity in employee share ownership and profit-sharing schemes is also supported by Poutsma and de Nijs (2003). They found that the spread of different forms of financial participation in European countries was strongly linked with promotional measures taken by governments. Where macroeconomic policy explicitly encouraged incentives and financial advantages, systems of financial participation were stronger (Poutsma and de Nijs, 2003). The data also revealed that financial participation was more commonly found in dynamic workplaces with participative work structures; in addition, contextual factors, including national institutional patterns, were more important than company-specific characteristics in shaping the spread and use of financial participation schemes (Poutsma and de Nijs, 2003) (see also the section on macro-environmental influences below).

Survey evidence from 151 organisations in France, Germany, Spain, the Netherlands, Finland, and the UK further identifies considerable variation across European Member States (Poutsma, 2006). While 32 per cent of firms had share acquisition plans for all or most of their employees, such plans were most common in Germany (40 per cent), France (54 per cent), and the UK (91 per cent), and relatively rare in Spain (16 per cent), the Netherlands (14 per cent), and Finland (12 per cent) (Poutsma, 2006). With respect to profit-sharing, 37 per cent of firms used such schemes for all or most of their employees, but stock options were generally limited to managerial employees (Poutsma, 2006). Participation rates were approximately 80 per cent in profit-sharing plans, but only 60–65 per cent in share plans (Poutsma, 2006). The incidence of profit-sharing plans also varied considerably between countries, being most common in France (52 per cent), Finland (52 per cent), and the Netherlands (45 per cent) (Poutsma, 2006). Important conclusions identified from Poutsma's (2006) study were:

- Profit-sharing plans and share-related plans were broadly based in those organisations where they existed, had varied participation rates, and were more common in participative organisations.
- The main objectives of financial participation were to increase employees' motivation and demonstrate that employees were valued by the organisation.
- The main obstacles to financial participation were restrictive and complicated legal frameworks, as well as insufficient tax breaks.

(?) Critical Thinking 14.2

China, an emerging market economy, stands in contrast to the Anglo-American countries. China, once based on a state socialist system, has undergone rapid reform, moving to a market-based system that has entailed dramatic changes to human resource management. For example, state-owned enterprises have declined, state-controlled unions have been diluted, and industrial conflict has increased.

Questions

1 Given the labour market reforms that have taken place in China and the opening up the economy, why might employee involvement and participation take different forms from the practices in Europe and Anglo-American countries?

2 How might forms of employee involvement in China, particularly in multinational or private enterprises, converge, or look similar to, employee involvement practices in the Western model?

A more recent study by Guery (2015) of the relationship between employee share ownership and employer-provided training found that there is a complementarity between the two, supporting the notion of high-performance work systems and the bundling of HR practices. However, this study did recognise that complementarity is tenuous and complex when training expenditures increase, reinforcing the importance of micro-organisational dimensions in shaping employee involvement.

CRITICAL SUMMARY OF EMPLOYEE INVOLVEMENT

The utility of different forms of employee involvement and participation have increasingly attracted widespread attention within the academic literature (see, for example, Wood and Fenton-O'Creevy, 2005; Brewster et al., 2007; Charlwood and Terry, 2007), yet are often Anglo-American centric. There is a great need for more in-depth empirical studies of employee involvement in emerging economies.

Trends in employee involvement and participation have been one of the drivers underlying increased interest in the utility of different forms of employee voice. In most Anglo-American economies, the decline of trade union membership and representation, increasing globalisation and the rise of neoliberal economic policies focused on labour market flexibility, individualism and decollectivisation have spawned the growth of employee involvement, and at the same time a decline in participatory mechanisms (through elected union representatives particularly) (see, for example, Boxall and Purcell, 2003; Brewster et al., 2007; Dundon and Gollan, 2007; Gollan, 2006; Purcell and Georgiadis, 2007; Wood and Wall, 2007). Indeed, the use of employee involvement by employers became the dominant approach in the latter decades of the twentieth century, illustrating the impact of macroeconomic factors, beliefs, and values on the structures of HRM.

Despite the common assumption that employee involvement substitutes for union representation, a growing body of empirical literature reveals that a combination of employee involvement and participation is most effective for employers and employees (see, for example, Bryson, 2004; Charlwood and Terry, 2007; Gollan, 2006; Wood and Fenton-O'Creevy, 2005). For instance, Sako (1998), in a study of the impact of employee voice in the European car components industry, found that a combination of direct and indirect forms had the strongest effect on performance in this sector.

These findings have been reinforced by a large-scale European survey of participation in the mid-1990s, which found that the greater number of participatory forms that were used, the more likely managers were to report benefits from increased output and declining absenteeism (Boxall and Purcell, 2003). In Australia, Pyman et al. (2006) also found that the combination of direct and indirect voice mechanisms was a stronger predictor of employees' perceived control over their jobs and their influence over job rewards than a single voice channel alone. Despite favourable evidence for the complementarity or coexistence of direct and indirect voice channels, the decision of an employer to utilise direct or indirect mechanisms will be strongly influenced by the environment in which the firm operates and the nature of its operations (Brewster et al., 2007).

MACRO-ENVIRONMENTAL INFLUENCES ON EMPLOYEE INVOLVEMENT IN THE GLOBAL CONTEXT

Previous sections of this chapter have identified the importance of organisational and workplace (internal) factors in shaping employee involvement mechanisms. It is important to understand, however, the strategic goals and impact of HRM and employee involvement in a broader sense, because employee involvement relates to a range of stakeholder interests (Marchington, 2007). Boxall and Purcell (2003) refer to this as the 'social legitimacy' element of the causal chain, and this chain identifies the human resources practices that are required to underpin legal, ethical, and socially responsible employment relationships in the firm, addressing issues such as minimum employment standards and human rights.

Social legitimacy is a necessary feature of SHRM and should not be understated (Boxall and Purcell, 2003). Therefore, it is important to examine employee involvement through the lens of social legitimacy and ethics, and not just performance and productivity, because voice mechanisms are bound by other systemic social and economic features (Hyman 2005). Similarly, Marchington (2007) argues that voice is the area of HRM in which tensions between organisational and employees' goals and between shareholder and stakeholder interests are most apparent, because it connects with the question of managerial prerogative and social legitimacy. A recent study by Mellat Parast (2013) of the effect of top management

In the News   Employee involvement goes wrong!

What happens when management-initiated employee involvement goes horribly wrong? The recent Volkswagen (VW) scandal highlights this scenario perfectly. Volkswagen has been hit financially and publicly by a recent scandal that has seen the company forced to engage in an extremely costly recall. The scandal arose due to Volkswagen's installation of cheat devices in diesel cars to pass emissions tests. Essentially, the company knowingly installed devices that rig the pollution emissions of their vehicles in the US market. After the scandal was uncovered, tests showed that VW models contravene the emissions regulations by as much as 40 times permitted levels; results confirmed by the Environmental Protection Agency. So what does this case illustrate about employee involvement, productivity, and human resource management?

Five days after the scandal was made public, CEO Martin Winterkorn resigned. Yet, in the days after the scandal, the CEO maintained publicly that he had not done anything wrong. The resignation of the CEO came after public apologies and serious threats to the brand; threats that transpired in the financial markets and saw a dramatic decline in the company's share price. In his resignation, the CEO recognised that it was he who had to accept responsibility for the shortcomings of the company, as a way to rebuild trust in the brand; yet, that he was stunned that misconduct was possible on such a large scale within the Volkswagen Group. The CEO will not be the only scalp to go in the midst of this scandal. In the wake of lawsuits within countries and from individual motorists, a declining share price and declining consumer confidence, the board has made it clear that all employees involved in the misconduct that resulted in immeasurable harm for Volkswagen will be subject to full consequences.

The Volkswagen scandal is interesting for many reasons. First, is it possible that the CEO had no knowledge of the installation of emissions cheating devices? Second, what is the responsibility of the engineers at the shopfloor (factory) level in installing defeat devices: was such a practice of their own volition, or was it a management direction? What does the Volkswagen scandal teach us about ethics and morality versus control and power, thinking about power both at the organisational and management level. What should be the appropriate sanctions/punishments, for Volkswagen as a company and the employees involved, for intentionally misleading regulators and consumers?

(*Source*: Telegraph 2015).

support and corporate social responsibility on employee involvement and performance demonstrates the interrelationship between social legitimacy and ethics, finding that the implementation of CSR can have a positive effect on the formation of 'moral capital' in the firm through enhancing employee involvement.

As the Volkswagen scandal illustrates, employee involvement is one human resource practice that is directly shaped by industry and by societal, legal and political forces (Boxall and Purcell, 2003). More specifically, Dundon and Gollan (2007) and Marchington (2007) identify the following macro-environmental factors that together with organisational/workplace factors shape involvement:

- market influences (product and labour markets, industrial relations, and competitive pressures);
- technology, skills and staffing levels;
- structural influences (organisational size, sector and nationality or ownership);
- the regulatory or policy environment and financial system (including legislation and the national business system).

Marchington (2015a) has argued that there is an important omission in the above list of factors: the role of employers' organisations, professional associations, and other specialist organisations that operate as intermediary forces between the state and individual employers to shape employee involvement and participation. He finds that these 'soft' institutional and intermediary forces are more likely to shape employee involvement and participation, because they allow employers choice and flexibility and are designed as interventions that align with the national business system and government priorities. Nevertheless, soft and hard institutional forces impact on managerial decision-making at the level of the organisation, and these forces are in turn shaped by the origin and structure of employment relations systems and wider social institutions, as well as by their pathways of evolution in different countries. For example, the UK, a liberal market economy, is often criticised on the basis that weaker labour market regulation allows employers more freedom and choice over their management of the employment relationship. In the case of employee involvement, this has led to a preoccupation with task-based structures that fail to challenge managerial dominance or enable genuine empowerment; this is also known as the low-road or low-commitment approach to SHRM (Brewster et al., 2007; Wood and Fenton-O'Creevy, 2005). Therefore, as Boxall and Purcell (2003) note, although legislation can dictate the form taken by some involvement and participation systems, it can never specify *how* organisations manage or

deal with such structures in practice. It is always the case that if management does not wish to engage in a meaningful dialogue with its employees and their representatives, it can render legislatively imposed systems of involvement and participation largely insignificant. Organisations and managers retain discretion, even in the presence of legislation; therefore involvement can range from a strategic, organisational-wide, embedded initiative to the rendering of employee involvement as a trivial nuisance or 'bolt-on' that becomes an additional burden or simply a means of perfunctory compliance for line managers (Boxall and Purcell, 2003). Legislation, in order to be effective, must have a catalytic effect on beliefs and values, especially on those who are required to share power and be accountable to their subordinates within organisations (Boxall and Purcell, 2003).

Employee involvement systems that are 'empty shells' (Noon and Hoque, 2004), that is, disconnected from organisational life and decision-making, will have a short lifespan and will fail to provide effective or meaningful channels for employee influence and empowerment (Marchington, 2007). For employee involvement to be effective and meaningful, the 'social contract' (Walton et al., 1994) must be centred upon commitment and cooperation, with employee involvement being legitimate and actively encouraged and promoted by managers and employees in practice. The beliefs and values of the society in which organisations, managers and employees operate are a crucial added dimension.

Practical examples of the differences in employee involvement across countries arising from the influence of both macro-and micro-determinants can be seen in *What Workers Say: Employee Voice in the Anglo-American Workplace* (Freeman et al., 2007). This book was based upon an international comparison of employees' voices in six countries: the USA, Canada, Britain, Ireland, Australia, and New Zealand. The country researchers adopted a common methodology: a set of surveys based upon the 1994–1995 Worker Representation and Participation Survey in the USA (Freeman and Rogers, 1999) and the 2001 British Worker Representation and Participation Survey (Diamond and Freeman, 2001).

Employee involvement in a global context and the important influence that regulation and national origin have on employee involvement mechanisms in practice can be further illustrated by developments in the European Union (EU). As previously noted, attempts to regulate employee participation and industrial democracy in Europe have been on the EU agenda since the early 1990s (Hall, 2005; Waddington, 2003). In 2002, representing one of the most significant interventions with regard to employee representation, the EU Information and Consultation Directive was enacted. This Directive established a general framework of minimum requirements for employees' rights to information and consultation. The Directive (Gollan and Wilkinson, 2007: 1146) required organisations in all Member States to:

- Share information on the recent and probable development of the undertaking's or the establishment's activities and economic situation;
- Inform and consult on the situation, structure, and probable development of employment and on any anticipatory measures envisaged, in particular where there is a threat to employment; and
- Inform and consult, with a view to reaching an agreement, on decisions likely to lead to substantial changes in work organisation or in contractual relations. Information means the provision of data on the business to employees and/or their representatives, whether over workplace or strategic issues, with a view to allowing employees to participate in dialogue. Consultation is defined as the exchange of views between employers and employees, with a view to the establishment of dialogue; yet, management ultimately retains decision-making power.

The impact of the EU Directive on Information and Consultation has been varied across Member States owing to the different statutory systems and national influences that exist (Gollan and Wilkinson, 2007; Marginson et al., 2010). This variation is consistent with evidence of variation in financial participation schemes in Europe. Differences in information and consultation can be illustrated by recent research undertaken by Marginson et al. (2010), which shows that MNCs have distinct preferences regarding the structures for employee representation and the form that arrangements for employees' voice take, based on the different countries of origin in which they are based. This research is summarised in Box 14.3 (see also Mini Case Study 14.1).

A contrasting example to the Anglo-American countries is China. In a study of the effects of employee involvement and participation on subjective wellbeing in Urban China, Cheng (2014) found that some elements of employee involvement and participation are significantly associated with employees' self-perceived satisfaction with work, life, protection of rights and benefits, and state sector reform. Cheng (2014) concluded that some employees who are willing to participate in higher-level decision-making might be unable to find adequate institutional channels to materialise their ambitions and, therefore, that potential exists to further develop employee involvement and participation as a more effective means to improve urban Chinese employees' wellbeing and their workplace conditions.

In summary, Marginson et al. (2010) concluded that there was evidence for country of origin influences on the patterns of employee representation and consultative voice in MNCs but that these influences were also shaped by other factors, including sector and method of growth.

Box 14.3 Employee representation and consultative voice in MNCs operating in Britain

The research by Marginson et al. (2010) was based on a survey of employment practices and a structured interview with a senior human resources executive in 302 MNCs in the UK. Focusing on the results for indirect and consultative voice mechanisms, the findings showed that:

▸ meetings of senior management and the entire workforce were used in 76 per cent of MNCs;
▸ team (briefing) groups were used in 76 per cent of MNCs;
▸ problem-solving or continuous improvement groups were used in 77 per cent of MNCs;
▸ formally designated teams with delegated responsibility were used in 73 per cent of MNCs;
▸ in summary, 99 per cent of MNCs had one or more direct consultative voice mechanisms in operation.
▸ In terms of differences between the MNCs' consultative voice policies, the research revealed the following:
▸ Japanese-based MNCs were significantly more likely than US MNCs to emphasise indirect forms of consultation, as were those MNCs based in the rest of Europe.
▸ MNCs from the UK did not significantly differ from US MNCs regarding their consultative voice policy: both emphasised direct forms.
▸ Sector had an influence on the practices of MNCs, with service sector MNCs, in comparison with MNCs involved in manufacturing, emphasising direct rather than indirect channels.
▸ MNCs that had been operating in the UK only over the past five years were less likely to emphasise direct channels compared with longer-established companies.
▸ MNCs that had grown by acquisition emphasised direct over indirect channels.

Mini Case Study A comparative analysis between Australia and Britain

Compare the legislative and political environments in Australia and Britain to consider the importance of the regulation of employee involvement and the subsequent implications for the parties involved in the employment relationship and for HRM.

Australia

The election of a federal Labor government in 2008 brought about a significant change in industrial relations and HRM in Australia. Replacing a hostile, conservative neoliberal government that had been perceived to tip the balance of industrial relations regulation in favour of employers (Cooper and Ellem, 2008), the Labor government introduced the Fair Work Act (Cth) in 2009. This Act significantly changed industrial relations in Australia. The major object of the Fair Work Act 2009 (Cth) (Division 2, Section 3) is to provide a balanced framework for cooperative and productive relations that promotes national economic prosperity and social inclusion for all Australians by:

▸ providing workplace relations laws that are fair, flexible for businesses and promote productivity and economic growth;
▸ ensuring a guaranteed safety net of fair, relevant and enforceable minimum terms and conditions;
▸ ensuring that the above conditions cannot be undermined by individual employment agreements;
▸ assisting employees to balance their work and family responsibilities;
▸ enabling fairness and representation at work and the prevention of discrimination, providing protection against unfair treatment and discrimination, providing access to effective procedures to resolve grievances and disputes, and providing effective compliance mechanisms;
▸ achieving productivity and fairness through a focus on enterprise-level bargaining underpinned by good faith obligations and clear rules;
▸ acknowledging the special circumstances of small and medium-sized businesses.

Questions

In light of the objectives of the Fair Work Australia Act 2009 (Cth), consider the following questions:

1   How can you relate the objectives of the new legislation to the objectives of employee involvement as described by theory?
2   What are the likely future outcomes for employee involvement in Australia, given the objects and focus of the legislation introduced in 2009?

UK

The Information and Consultation of Employees Regulations (ICE) in the UK establish a general statutory framework giving employees a right to be informed and consulted by their employers over a range of business, employment and restructuring issues (Hall, 2005). The legislation, established in 2005, was implemented over three years, and stems from the EU Information and Consultation Directive introduced in 2002. The legislation has applied since April 2005 to large undertakings with at least 150 employees, since April 2007 to those undertakings with at least 100 employees, and since April 2008 to companies with at least 50 employees. The Regulations diverge from the EU Information and Consultation Directive (2002) by providing considerable flexibility for employers in their response and therefore enabling the adoption of information and consultation arrangements that are organisation-specific. There has been increased research evaluating the impact of the Regulations and of management's approach to information and consultation in the UK (see, for example, Hall, 2005; Hall et al., 2007, 2009; Gollan and Wilkinson, 2007; Wilkinson et al., 2007).

Questions

In light of the introduction of the ICE Regulations (2005) in the UK, consider the following questions:

1   Why might employees value information and consultation that is imposed by legislation?
2   What are the benefits for organisations of informing and consulting employees?
3   What factors are likely to influence a company's strategy towards information and consultation in the workplace?

A CRITICAL ANALYSIS OF EMPLOYEE INVOLVEMENT

Employee involvement is management-initiated and management-driven. The shortcomings of management-controlled employee involvement are manifold. First, there is potential for contradictory and competing objectives and initiatives between senior and line managers. For example, where line managers play a critical role in the delivery and implementation of employee involvement with front-line staff, it is possible that line managers may prioritise operational production and service issues over and above investment in employee involvement initiatives (Boxall and Purcell, 2003). Anglo-American models of corporate governance, which promote short-termism, management-driven capitalism, and returns to shareholders at all costs, may also serve to undermine longer-term investment in potentially costly employee involvement initiatives (see, for example, Brewster et al., 2007). Line managers may also lack adequate training in employee involvement or lack an understanding of why investing in such initiatives is important and/or may benefit the organisation.

Any contradictions between senior and line management, or between espoused and actual employee involvement policies and initiatives within an organisation, will be noticed by employees. Such contradictions will mean that the penetration of employee involvement will be weak and may therefore have adverse consequences for employees' job satisfaction, commitment and loyalty (Boxall and Purcell, 2003). In order to facilitate employee involvement, line managers and senior managers must create a strong and supportive environment by exhibiting trust, encouraging development and the sharing of concerns, communicating, listening, acting in a genuine manner, and being transparent, honest and open with their employees. Managers must collectively demonstrate enthusiasm and respect employees' views by asking them what matters and by devolving autonomy (Robertson, 2010a, 2010b).

Second, the very notion of employee involvement, from a theoretical perspective of unitarism, assumes that there is an identity of interest between employers and employees. However, the very purpose and objective of employee involvement is to create commitment and loyalty, meaning that, in practice, a common identity of interest between employers and employees may simply be a fallacy (Boxall and Purcell, 2003). Ultimately, as Boxall and Purcell (2003) note, the justification for employee involvement is an end value in its own right. As such, it is always contentious and subject to reinterpretation, as employers and employees in the organisation and the wider political system have to deal with changing industrial and ethical problems (Boxall and Purcell, 2003).

The constantly changing and contradictory nature of employee involvement therefore underscores the importance of trust between employers and employees and the maintenance and sustainability of trust over time. For example, Kessler and Purcell (1996), in a study of joint working practices, found that the level of trust between employers and employees markedly increased when employees and/or their representatives were involved in all stages of a change process overseen by a joint working party. Management also reported greater benefits to the organisation when such employee involvement took place.

Third, the presence of employee involvement initiatives is not in itself enough to secure favourable outcomes for the employee and employer. It is not the mere presence of employee involvement that guarantees quality or favourable outcomes. Rather, it is the systems, processes, values, and degree of embeddedness of employee involvement initiatives that determines their success in practice, suggesting the need for complementary human resources practices alongside employee involvement (see, for example, Brown et al., 2009; Cox et al., 2006; Dundon et al., 2004; Gollan, 2006; Marchington, 2005, 2007; Richardson et al., 2010; Wilkinson et al., 2007). Indeed, research evidence shows that where employee voice arrangements are established by law and are socially embedded, they are more successful and durable over time (Boxall and Purcell, 2003; Richardson et al., 2010). Marchington (2015b), however, recognises that while legislation, government action, and intermediary bodies do have an influence on employee involvement, the way in which management interprets immediate organisational forces remains significantly more important in determining the embeddedness of employee involvement within organisations. So, while legislation can dictate the forms that employee involvement or participation can take, it can never specify how organisations manage or deal with these structures at an organisational level. As a result, the contextual factors within the individual firm and the strategic choices of the individual company are critical in shaping and driving employee involvement and participation. As Boxall and Purcell (2003) note, it is always the case that if management does not wish to engage in a meaningful dialogue with employees and/or their representatives, it can render legislatively imposed voice systems largely trivial.

It is likely, therefore, that the solutions and means to achieve employee involvement are different for each firm, influenced by institutional, societal, sectoral, industrial, and organisational factors. For instance, evidence shows marked differences in the strategies of small firms, which favour informal and direct employee involvement, compared with the more formalised processes of employee involvement in larger firms (Gilman et al., 2015; Wilkinson et al., 2007). Employers are more likely to adopt sophisticated methods of employee involvement where:

- they are competing in a sector that requires innovative investment in human resources due to capital-intensive production systems;
- they are using sophisticated technology; and/or
- there is a clear pay-off to the employees and the firm of doing this, with regard to employees' skills, abilities, motivation and training (Boxall and Purcell, 2003).

STOP AND REFLECT

Compare the supermarket and university sectors.

Questions

1. What are the human resource management characteristics of each sector?
2. To what extent do these sectors utilise employee involvement?
3. How might employee involvement be improved in each of these sectors?

Despite the assumed benefits of employee involvement for organisational productivity and performance, there are numerous difficulties in substantiating the performance effects of employee involvement systems in practice (see, for example, Boxall and Purcell, 2003; Dundon and Gollan, 2007; Richardson et al., 2010). One key problem arises due to the individual contingencies and context of the firm acting as a determinant of employee involvement initiatives, meaning that a vast array of different schemes are used in practice. It is therefore very difficult to tease out the impact of individual practices across different contexts (Boxall and Purcell, 2003). In addition, empirical research tends to be cross-sectional rather than longitudinal, meaning that causation cannot be determined. Much of the research also relies on managers' interpretations of the perceived impact of employee involvement on performance, thus ignoring employees' perceptions (Dundon and Gollan, 2007; Marchington, 2007; Richardson et al., 2010).

Related to the issue of causation is the difficulty of measuring the embeddedness of employee involvement initiatives and how they shape and change behaviours (Boxall and Purcell, 2003). More longitudinal research is needed to evaluate the embeddedness of employee involvement and how this influences and changes the behaviour of employers and employees over time. Despite the difficulty of proving the performance- and productivity-enhancing effects of employee involvement, there is substantial empirical evidence to support the notion that employee involvement

can have benefits for employees and the organisation, particularly in terms of increased employee job satisfaction, loyalty and commitment (see, for example, Cox et al., 2006; Holland et al., 2011; Pyman et al., 2010).

Class Activity

▶ What behaviours should managers employ to facilitate employee involvement in the workplace?

BENEFITS OF STUDYING HRM FROM A CRITICAL PERSPECTIVE FOR MANAGERS

It is important to study employee involvement, as part of HRM, from a critical perspective, because it allows practising managers to evaluate both employers' and employees' perceptions and judgements of the operation and the effectiveness of employee involvement initiatives. This duality is fundamental, given that both parties will have different interests and will therefore utilise different effectiveness criteria. It is the goal of practising human resource managers to maximise both parties' interests and outcomes, in order to generate favourable outcomes for both the individual and the organisation.

Being aware of and understanding the different interests of employers and employees is also critical for human resource managers, in order to appreciate the importance of the nature and quality of the underlying relationship between the parties, and in particular the levels of trust between them. It is the understanding and management of trust by human resource practitioners that is key to ensuring a genuine and beneficial exchange for employers and employees, in both an economic and a psychological sense. With respect to employee involvement, trust needs to be carefully managed by human resources practitioners over the long term, as trust and justice are potential outcomes of employee involvement and are also likely to influence the way in which employee involvement develops internally (Cox et al., 2006).

Given evidence suggesting that it is the degree to which employee involvement mechanisms are embedded within the organisation that will determine the success and durability of involvement initiatives (see, for example, Dundon et al., 2004), management of trust in the implementation and operation of employee involvement over time is critical. As Gollan (2006) argues, only by establishing mechanisms that enable employees to have a legitimate voice and allow differences to emerge will managers be able to channel such differences into productive outcomes.

CONCLUSION

Employee involvement is argued to be a core ingredient in high-performance work systems that can subsequently lead to improvements in the organisation's performance and productivity by enhancing employees' contributions, satisfaction and commitment, leading, in turn, to a sustainable competitive advantage. The level and scope of employee involvement systems varies enormously, with decisions ranging from those on task-related issues to strategic, power-centred issues. The locus of decision-making will influence the type and scope of employee involvement systems adopted, as will organisational and national context. Since the 1980s, there has been a shift away from indirect, union-based forms of involvement and participation, to increased use of direct, task-based forms of involvement, such as regular meetings, suggestion schemes, and team briefings. This shift has been visible in most advanced market economies, and there remains a lack of research on emerging economies.

The development of employee involvement systems granting employees access to, and participation in, managerial decision-making has been heralded as a means of empowerment and mutual gains. However, empowerment and mutual gains are not guaranteed by the presence of an employee involvement system – it is how employee involvement systems operate in practice that will determine outcomes for employers and employees. Although legislation remains an important influence on employee involvement and participatory systems, particularly the degree to which they are viewed as legitimate, it is the process of managing people and how this is undertaken at the level of the organisation that remains an ethical and social choice for managers. The choices that managers make fundamentally shape the outcomes gained from employee involvement systems, and organisational and managerial empowerment initiatives must be situated and integrated within the larger work environment, because isolated initiatives will not achieve their intended outcomes (Leopold, 2004) (see In the News).

As Gallie and White (1993) also note, involvement is of fundamental importance in shaping employees'

attitudes to the organisation in which they work. It is strongly related to the way they respond to changes in work organisation and to their perception of the overall quality of the relationship between management and employees. Employee involvement systems must therefore be integrated, meaningful, and effective in the eyes of employees in order to have tangible effects on job satisfaction, organisational commitment, and discretion and, in turn, favourable impacts on organisational performance and labour productivity. A central debate within the literature therefore centres on the degree to which employee involvement systems are illustrative of a passing fad or, alternatively, represent socially embedded structures that enable more cooperative and effective ways of managing people and attaining good organisational performance.

The degree to which employee involvement systems are socially embedded within an organisation is critically dependent on senior and line managers and the degree of importance and purpose they attach to such systems, in addition to the means and extent to which they support and activate them. Just because employee involvement is present does not mean that it will be effective. Therefore, where employee involvement systems are embedded, legitimate, and morally accepted activities, strongly supported and activated by managers in practice, they will produce positive, sustainable, added value outcomes for the company and its employees. A supportive organisational climate and culture of involvement, and high levels of trust between employers and employees, are seminal design elements allowing employee involvement to take root and prosper in an organisation in practice (Boxall and Purcell, 2003). Positive outcomes, in terms of performance and labour productivity, are achieved for employers and employees, reinforcing how important it is to address both parties' evaluations and perceptions of the effectiveness of employee involvement systems, given the complex, multifaceted nature of the employment relationship.

The key learning points from this chapter, areas of good practice and recommendations for key stakeholders are summarised in Box 14.4.

Box 14.4 Key learning points: Good practice and recommendations for employers, employees, and policy-makers

▸ Employee involvement varies according to institutional, organisational, and workplace contexts. In this respect, the ideologies of policy-makers, employers and employees will shape the nature and success of such mechanisms.

▸ Managers need to consider the rationale for employee involvement, the implementation of employee involvement, the influence of broader social systems, and employees' expectations.

- For employees, changes at the work-group level can make a significant difference within the organisation and to their experience of work.
- Employee involvement needs to be embedded within the workplace, as much depends on how employee involvement is implemented and sustained. The regularity and thoroughness with which employee involvement practices are applied can have a significant impact on their quality. To be effective, employee involvement must operate in a strong, supportive organisational climate and be underpinned by the principles of consistency, fairness, and legitimacy. The lifespan of employee involvement mechanisms will also determine their quality and effectiveness. Employee involvement mechanisms that are deeply embedded within the workplace, are legitimised as valued aspects of organisational routines, and cover a wide range of employees will be more effective for managers and employees and will have a more positive impact on employees' perceptions.
- The effectiveness of employee involvement mechanisms also depends on whether they are used individually or in isolation. Combinations of direct (employee involvement) and indirect (participation) mechanisms have the strongest relationship with workers' commitment, satisfaction, and discretion. Employee involvement mechanisms must link with other components of HRM. The greater the degree of 'fit' between employee involvement and the overarching human resources system, the greater added value
- Most research focuses on intended employee involvement practices within a workplace, rather than on those experienced by employees. Research must be sensitive to the complexities of voice and examine employees' experiences in greater detail in addition to voice in emerging/developing economies.
- The impact of employee involvement mechanisms on bottom line performance and labour productivity is contested. Employers always retain some degree of choice over whether or not they implement employee involvement and other voice systems. Employee involvement will have a positive impact on performance and labour productivity if the relevant channels are embedded within the workplace.

(See, for example, Boxall and Purcell 2010; Cheng, 2014; Marchington, 2015a; Richardson et al., 2010; Wilkinson et al., 2015 ; Pyman et al., 2016).

End of Chapter Case Study Employee involvement at Paper Co

Paper Co is a large, multisite manufacturing organisation that is a joint venture between two blue-chip MNCs (Swedish and Anglo-American). Paper Co supplies recycled newsprint paper to regional and national publishers and printers in Western Europe and the USA. The company employs a total of 370 staff, two-thirds of whom are manual shift workers. The company is unionised, with a union density of approximately 40 per cent, but this density has been declining on an annual basis.

Paper Co operates 24 hours a day, 7 days a week, 365 days a year. The production process is highly automated, and two paper machines produce 400,000 tonnes of paper per annum. Its annual turnover is approximately £130 million. Operations at Paper Co have not, however, escaped the effects of globalisation and the economic downturn. Increased global competition and rising energy prices have continued to threaten the profitability and competitiveness of the UK paper-making industry, an industry that collectively employs over 10,000 workers across 60 mills (Carley, 2007) . Over the last decade, paper production has fallen by over a quarter, with the closure of over 35 paper mills across the UK (Confederation of Paper Industries, 2008). The domestic market for paper, including newsprint, has contracted, but the collection of recovered paper has continued to rise. The industry has thus witnessed a rapid expansion in the export of recovered paper to the Far East and Europe. In October 2008, due to rising costs and a decline in profits, Paper Co announced 37 redundancies below management level.

Notable features of the company's culture are its longstanding commitment to health and safety, product quality and communication and consultation, in which employee voice comprises union and non-union (direct and indirect) channels. Union voice within the company, and the paper-making industry in general, is a longstanding feature, and industry-wide bargaining arrangements continue to set pay, terms, and conditions. In May 2007, the national agreement was modernised through the launch of a national partnership agreement between the Confederation of Paper Industry, Amicus, the Transport and General Workers Union, and the GMB (Carley, 2007). Similar to the partnership agreement found in the printing industry, the 'Papermaking Partnership' encourages stakeholders to 'work together, grow together, and stay together' in order to improve the industry's competitiveness.

Despite the continuation of national collective bargaining, the locus of consultation and negotiation at Paper Co is mainly at plant level. Consultation occurs through an elected 'Operating Council', established in 1994, which represents all production workers for the purposes of information and consultation. The formal purpose of the Operating Council is to promote the efficient and profitable development of Paper Co and all its employees, the safety, education, and welfare of operations personnel, and the quality of communication and cooperation within the operations.

Critical incident The establishment of a new employee involvement channel

Alongside union voice within Paper Co, a Joint Consultation Forum (JCF) was established in early 2005. This forum extended consultation rights to the non-manual workforce. The JCF operates in parallel with the Operating Council. The JCF and the Operating Council are supplemented by a variety of other direct involvement and communication channels, including monthly team briefings, a quarterly magazine, a company intranet, and notice boards.

The establishment of the JCF within Paper Co was management-driven at the level of the organisation. The rationale for establishing the JCF was twofold:

▸ to pre-empt the ICE Regulations, which came into effect on 6 April 2005 and legally mandated the provision of information and consultation in UK workplaces;
▸ the human resources manager deemed information and consultation to be an indicator of best practice, particularly in light of the history and successful involvement of the Operating Council in the paper mill's operational issues.

Therefore, the establishment of the JCF was important in order to ensure equal treatment of non-manual workers.

The structure and implementation of the JCF

A consultation committee comprising of a cross-section of managers and supervisors and four employee representatives (from the non-manual workforce) was charged with developing the JCF. These employee representatives were management-appointed rather than elected, based on whom the human resources manager felt could meaningfully contribute to the consultation exercise. Three consultation meetings followed to determine the structure, the constituency, that is, the body of employees to be covered, the method of selecting employee representatives, and the scope of the forum. The consultation committee also drafted the JCF constitution. The structure of the forum dominated the committee's discussions, and a number of possibilities were considered, including the extension of the Operating Council to cover non-unionised employees. However, the consultation committee decided that the most appropriate course of action was to form a separate body, the JCF, that would sit alongside the Operating Council.

During the consultation process, employee representatives had very little input into the structure and content of the constitution, since it was management that decided to implement the JCF. For the most part, human resources developed the constitution with reference to the formal provisions of the ICE Regulations and in light of the constitution of the Operating Council. The objectives of the JCF emphasised the business case for involvement, promoting the efficient and profitable development of Paper Co and the safety and development of its employees. A formal election process, including a secret ballot, was used to fill the representative positions on the JCF and was supervised by the consultation committee. Non-manual staff employed on a permanent or temporary contract of employment were eligible to stand as representatives. Once the elections had been concluded, the constitution was signed by management and the JCF representatives during a joint meeting between the consultation committee and the JCF members. The consultation committee was subsequently abandoned.

On the JCF, provision is made for the appointment of five employee representatives from the non-manual workforce, who tend to be office based. The average representative load is 30 employees per representative. Representatives serve a two-year term and are allowed to stand for re-election; there is no limit on the number of terms that a representative may serve. On the management side, the finance director is the chair of the JCF, and the operations director is a permanent member of the JCF. The senior human resources advisor is the JCF secretary. UNITE (as the representative union) has not been assigned a formal seat on the JCF, but rather an observational role. In practice, however, union representatives participate in JCF discussions. Non-union representatives on the JCF are sceptical of the presence of union representatives and question whether they add any value to the consultation process. For example, union representatives do not always attend meetings owing to their shift patterns being inconsistent with the timing and dates of JCF meetings, and it is felt that union representatives tend to raise issues that relate only to their members.

The scope of the JCF is fairly broad. As Box 14.5 shows, issues relating to the workplace, the economic situation, employment prospects, and work organisation all fall within the ambit of the forum. However, the constitution is vague in terms of what information and consultation entails in practice: these terms are not formally defined. There is also no reference to the timing of consultation or the extent to which managers involve employees in the issues listed in Box 14.5.

Box 14.5 The scope of the JCF at Paper Co

Issues included:

▸ the workplace;
▸ the economic situation of the business;
▸ employment prospects within the business;
▸ training and development;
▸ decisions likely to lead to substantial changes in work organisation or contractual relations;
▸ social and welfare facilities.

Issues excluded:

▸ matters related to pay, terms and conditions of employment, and individual employee issues beyond the scope of the JCF.

The constitution provides for quarterly meetings to be conducted in a positive and constructive atmosphere, where individual contributions are to be encouraged and respected and considered in terms of the effect on all parts of the business. Parties to the JCF are reminded that some subjects may be highly sensitive and should thus be treated as private and confidential. However, although no confidentiality agreements exist, management has also not provided representatives with any information that they have asked to be kept confidential in practice. Rights to time off and training are addressed within the constitution. Representatives are given 'reasonable' time to carry out their representative duties and the right to attend any training felt necessary for their development. The training of representatives so far has been conducted by the Involvement and Participation Association (IPA). The IPA facilitated a one-day training session for all management and employee representatives at the inception stage of the JCF, and additional training took place two years later for those representatives who had joined the forum within this period.

The operation of the JCF

The senior human resources advisor is responsible for compiling the JCF agenda and e-mails representatives two weeks in advance of each meeting for suggestions. Employee representatives rely on e-mail and informal interaction in their search for agenda items. In practice, however, few employees put forward suggestions to their representatives.

Networking between the representatives is fairly formalised. Although the constitution does not provide for formal pre-meetings of representatives, with management's consent non-union employee representatives meet formally before the agenda is finalised. These meetings are used by the representatives to clarify any issues that employees propose to the JCF, and to discuss what information the representatives should seek from management at the next meeting. The finance director and senior human resources advisor also meet once a week before JCF meetings to discuss the agenda. After each meeting, the minutes of the JCF are posted on the intranet and on office notice boards. However, employee representatives do not formally report back to employees what happened at the JCF, either face to face or as a collective group.

Issues raised and impact on decision-making

All parties to the JCF are content with the frequency of meetings and the relaxed manner in which these are conducted. Nevertheless, a general sentiment among the human resources manager, senior human resources advisor, and employee representatives is that the nature of the JCF is to provide information rather than being for consultation. The agenda is also seen as one-way, weighted towards employee-initiated rather than management-initiated issues. Issues voiced by representatives are largely 'office-based' and concern organisational welfare issues rather than strategic matters applicable to the larger mill. Examples of employees' suggestions made to the JCF have encompassed dress-down Fridays, on-site maintenance and transport, car parking, showers, site access cards, health and safety, and canteen facilities.

Despite the preoccupation of the JCF with welfare issues, the scope of issues considered has broadened, particularly since the IPA's second training session in 2007. This development of the JCF has heightened employees' confidence in and expectations of information and consultation. Examples of higher-level issues considered by the JCF since 2007 include flexible working practices and individual performance-related pay for non-manual employees. Some representatives do, however, feel that the potential impact of IPA training, in terms of advancing the scope of the JCF, has been weakened by the lack of participation of management and existing representatives. Despite the fact that higher-level issues have been raised by the JCF, employees have also reported that these were not discussed or considered in depth by management. For example, the prospect of introducing performance-related pay for non-manual employees was rejected outright, generating scepticism and distrust among employees regarding the level of employee involvement provided in practice.

The representatives' perceptions of how management treats employees' suggestions and ideas (the extent of management buy-in) varied. On the positive side, there was a sentiment that meetings were conducted in a relaxed and sociable manner and that management were genuine in their efforts to discuss matters raised within the JCF. Tangible changes have also resulted from the issues raised on the JCF. Examples include the cycle-to-work scheme, a healthcare plan, and changes to the inside and exterior of the mill. Nevertheless, there was a conception among representatives that the finance director was reluctant in his role as chair of the JCF and that management were not fully engaged, evidenced by the fact that they were selective in the information they provided to employees, particularly regarding Paper Co's future plans. Nevertheless, at each meeting, management provides an overview that includes the company's financial situation, sales figures, news items, and a summary of the issues raised at the previous meeting. Some employees feel however, that this does not provide added value over and above the information already available on the intranet.

The JCF has been used for consultation. Examples include the implementation of policies regarding bullying and harassment, smoking legislation, the company pension scheme, and redundancies. Separate subcommittees were established to handle these issues individually, yet the ability of employees to influence management's final decision was limited, demonstrating a reactive approach to consultation by management. Management's reluctance to share decision-making power has been largely evidenced by the stage at which consultation has taken place. The human resources manager and the majority of representatives perceived that consultation has tended to happen too late in the decision-making process. The JCF is therefore seen as a 'toothless beast'. One example was during a redundancy process in which management was seen to pay only lip service to employees' suggestions for alternative ways in which management could reduce costs, in order to subsequently reduce the number of redundancies.

Impact and effectiveness of the JCF

Senior managers and employee representatives believe that the JCF is a good initiative within the company, despite some cynicism that the scope and influence of the JCF are trivial. For managers and employee representatives, the JCF is perceived as an important upward communication tool, enabling employees to understand the progress and situation of the company, in addition to providing a channel to raise issues of concern. This channel allows management to take advantage of employees' initiatives and ideas and to develop better solutions and make better, more informed decisions. For employees, the beneficial outcomes include increased levels of trust, involvement and engagement.

Despite these common views, the scope and impact of the JCF, in terms of delivering genuine employee involvement and acting as a driver of change, is less clear. This lack of impact is illustrated by the wider lack of interest in the JCF among employees, which acts as a source of frustration for representatives. It is also important to note that Paper Co has not reviewed the effectiveness of the JCF since its introduction. Nevertheless, the JCF is seen as an effective mechanism operating alongside the Operating Council, particularly with regard to organisation-wide issues such as redundancies.

Despite the successful coexistence of union and non-union voice mechanisms in Paper Co, albeit for different sections of the workforce and different areas of the business, there is a sentiment among employees that communication from senior and line management has deteriorated as company profitability has fallen, prompting a suggestion that management inform and consult only in the 'good times'. A new CEO has also been seen to lack visibility and presence among the employees, particularly at the lower organisational levels. These perceptions reinforce among employees a view of a lack of leadership, varied management styles and selective distribution of information. Employees have also reported that interdepartmental communication has been lacking. Regardless of these criticisms, employees have also reported that Paper Co is a good place to work due to the existence of close working and social relationships, good working conditions, varied shift patterns, staff development opportunities, a family feel and a strong culture of safety.

Source: Dr Elaine Bull.

Questions

1 Utilising Marchington and Wilkinson's (2002) typology, how would you classify the JCF in Paper Co?
2 What are the strengths and weaknesses of the JCF in Paper Co?
3 To what extent do management at Paper Co exhibit a lack of buy-in or commitment to employee involvement?
4 Employee representatives on the JCF reported a lack of interest among employees. What factors might explain the indifference of employees to the JCF?
5 The CEO of Paper Co has asked you to advise on how the JCF can be developed in order to be more effective in the future. Identify and justify your recommendations for the JCF.

FOR DISCUSSION AND REVISION

1 How does employee involvement link to SHRM?
2 How do you distinguish employee involvement from a human resource management lens versus an employment relations lens?
3 Why is labour productivity a better measure of the impact of human resources practices than profitability?
4 Distinguish three categories of employee involvement.
5 Discuss the differences between direct and indirect employee involvement.
6 Identify two major trends in employee involvement since the 1980s. What have been the implications of these trends for managers, employees, and trade unions?
7 What are the limits of legislated employee involvement systems?
8 Why is it important for employee involvement systems to be socially embedded within an organisation?
9 How can an organisation achieve socially embedded employee involvement systems?
10 Why is it difficult to establish a causal link between employee involvement systems and performance and productivity?

GLOSSARY

Employee involvement: how employees are involved in issues and decisions that impact them at work.

Employee participation: how employees participate in issues and decisions that impact them at work.

Employee voice: an umbrella term that describes how employees are informed, involved, and participate in issues and decisions that impact them at work.

Direct employee involvement: a type of employee involvement that depicts two-way communication in the absence of a third party.

Indirect employee involvement: a type of employee involvement that entails involvement and participation through an intermediary or third party such as a trade union.

Labour productivity: the value of labour outputs proportional to the cost of labour inputs.

FURTHER READING

BOXALL, P. AND MACKY, K. (2007) High-performance work systems and organisational performance: Bridging theory and practice. *Asia Pacific Journal of Human Resources*, 45(3): 261–270.

This paper explores the meaning and significance of high-performance work systems, in which work reforms designed to increase employee involvement are seen as a core underpinning. This paper argues that practices such as employee involvement need to be adapted to industry and occupational conditions and considers the managerial and governance processes in which they are embedded. The paper concludes by reaffirming the value of evaluating both management practices and employee responses to organisational outcomes, as a means to bridge the gap between theory and practice.

BOXALL, P. AND MACKY, K. (2009) Research and theory on high-performance work systems: Progressing the high involvement stream. *Human Resource Management Journal*, 19(1): 3–23.

This paper critically analyses the notion of a high-performance work system and its companion terminology: high-involvement work systems and high-commitment management. The major models proposed in the literature are reviewed, and it is argued that research should be dedicated to examining the processes that underpin employees' experiences of high-involvement management systems and their subsequent links to employee and operational outcomes. The paper is useful in critiquing the existing HRM literature and theory which assume that employee involvement is a core component of a high-performance/high-commitment and/or high-involvement work system. The paper also makes robust recommendations for advancing theory in this field.

BROWN, M., GEDDES, A. AND HEYWOOD, J. S. (2009) The determinants of employee-involvement schemes: Private sector Australian evidence. *Economic and Industrial Democracy*, 28(2): 259–291.

This paper utilises data from the Australian Workplace Industrial Relations Survey to examine the determinants of four different types of employee involvement scheme: autonomous groups, quality circles, JCCs, and task forces. The authors found that employee involvement is associated with employees who are expected to stay in their jobs for longer and with higher attachment to the labour force. Complementary human resources practices such as formal training and incentive pay are also associated with the increased use of employee involvement, as are unionisation, workplace size, and the extent of competition. The paper is useful in providing an up-to-date perspective on the nature and scope of employee involvement systems in private sector organisations in Australia.

BUDD, J., GOLLAN, P. AND WILKINSON, A. (2010) New approaches to employee voice and participation in organisations. *Human Relations*, 63(3, Special Issue): 303–310.

This special issue of *Human Relations* extends existing knowledge on employee voice and participation by capturing a variety of different contemporary streams of research on the topic, including institutional, behavioural, and strategic approaches. The articles extend our current knowledge and understanding by examining new organisational forms and the practices and processes affecting the nature and structure of employee voice and participation within organisations.

CHENG, Z. (2014) The effects of employee involvement and participation on subjective wellbeing: Evidence from urban China. *Social Indicators Research*, 118: 457–483.

This paper uses data from a Chinese General Social survey to examine the relationship between employee involvement and participation and subjective wellbeing in the transitioned economy of China. Using econometric analysis, the paper finds that some elements of employee involvement and participation are significantly associated with employees' self-perceived satisfaction with work, life, protection of rights and benefits, and state sector reform. The elements of employee involvement and participation that are associated with subjective wellbeing include: participative and consultative management, freedom of expression and effective discussion between employees and their supervisors, and better understanding of an participation in workplace reforms.

HOLLAND, P., PYMAN, A., COOPER, B. AND TEICHER, J. (2011) Employee voice and job satisfaction in Australia: The centrality of direct voice. *Human Resource Management*, 50(1): 95–111.

This paper examines the relationship between employee voice and job satisfaction, utilising data from the Australian Worker Representation and Participation Survey (2007). Regression analyses suggest that direct voice appears to be central in underpinning employees' job satisfaction. This paper is useful for considering the design of direct employee involvement schemes with the objective of enhancing employees' job satisfaction.

MARCHINGTON, M. (2015a) The role of institutional and intermediary forces in shaping patterns of employee involvement and participation in Anglo-American countries. *International Journal of Human Resource Management*, 26(20): 2594–2616.

This paper addresses an important gap in studies of employee involvement: the role of employers' organisations, professional associations, and other specialist organisations as intermediary forces between the state and individual employers in shaping employee involvement and participation. The paper compares the role of these different forces in the UK, Ireland, Australia, and New Zealand. The comparative study reveals that these soft intermediary forces are more likely to shape employee involvement and participation for two reasons: they allow employers choice and flexibility in implementation and fit with national business systems in these countries. However, these interventions are voluntary and are therefore susceptible to change if government priorities change or if employers are continually attracted by management fads.

PYMAN, A., HOLLAND, P., TEICHER, J. AND COOPER, B. (2010) Industrial relations climate, employee voice and managerial attitudes to unions: An Australian study. *British Journal of Industrial Relations*, 48(2): 460–480.

Using data from the Australian Worker Representation and Participation Survey (2007), this paper examines how employee voice arrangements and managerial attitudes to unions shape employees' perceptions of the industrial relations climate. Regression analyses demonstrate that employees' perceptions of the industrial relations climate are more likely to be favourable if they have access to direct-only voice arrangements. Where management is perceived by employees to oppose unions (in unionised workplaces), the industrial relations climate is more likely to be reported as poor.

WEB RESOURCES

Engage for Success: http://www.engageforsuccess.org/.

Engage for success is a movement that has grown out of the UK and is the idea that there is a better way to work: a way that enables personal and organisational growth and growth for Britain. It is a movement focused on 'unlocking' the capability and potential of people at work. The aim of the movement is to increase awareness of the power and potential of employee engagement and to provide individuals and organisations with examples and evidence of its importance and practical tools as to how it works in practice to drive performance and productivity. The movement is widely supported across the UK by public, private, and third sector organisations.

REFERENCES

BEACHBOARD, J. L. (2014) Question and answer: Dismissal of employees and right of privacy in employment. *HR Specialist: California Employment Law*, 8(8): 8.

BOXALL, P. AND MACKY, K. (2009) Research and theory on high-performance work systems: Progressing the high-involvement stream. *Human Resource Management Journal*, 19(1): 3–23.

BOXALL, P. AND PURCELL, J. (2015) *Strategy and Human Resource Management*. Basingstoke: Palgrave Macmillan.

BOXALL, P. AND PURCELL, J. (2015) An HRM perspective on employee participation. In Wilkinson, A., Gollan, P., Marchington, M. and Lewin, D. (eds), *The Oxford Handbook of Participation in Organizations*. Oxford: Oxford University Press, 29–51.

BREWSTER, C., CROUCHER, R., WOOD, G. AND BROOKES, M. (2007) Collective and individual voice: Convergence in Europe? *International Journal of Human Resource Management*, 18(7): 1246–1262.

BROWN, M., GEDDES, L. A. AND HEYWOOD, J. S. (2009) The determinants of employee-involvement schemes: Private sector Australian evidence. *Economic and Industrial Democracy*, 28(2): 259–291.

BRYSON, A. (2004) Managerial responsiveness to union and nonunion worker voice in Britain. *Industrial Relations*, 43(1): 213–241.

BRYSON, A. AND FREEMAN, R. B. (2007) What voice do British workers want? In Freeman, R. B., Boxall P. and Haynes, P. (eds), *What Workers Say: Employee Voice in the Anglo-American Workplace*. Ithaca, NY: Cornell University Press, pp. 72–96.

CARLEY, M. (2007) Partnership deal agreed in papermaking industry. *European Industrial Relations Observatory*. Available at: http://www.eurofound.europa.eu/eiro/2007/08/articles/uk0708019i.htm. Accessed 18 January 2016.

CHARLWOOD, A. AND TERRY, M. (2007) 21st-century models of employee representation: Structures, processes and outcomes. *Industrial Relations Journal*, 38(4): 320–337.

CHENG, Z. (2014) The effects of employee involvement and participation on subjective wellbeing: Evidence from urban China. *Social Indicators Research*, 118(2): 457–483.

Confederation of Paper Industries (2008) 2008 Annual Review. Confederation of Paper Industries. Available at: http://www.paper.org.uk/information/annualreviews/2008review.pdf. Accessed 10 January 2016.

COOPER, R. AND ELLEM, B. (2008) The neoliberal state, trade unions and collective bargaining in Australia. *British Journal of Industrial Relations*, 46(3): 532–554.

COX, A., ZAGELMEYER, S. AND MARCHINGTON, M. (2006) Embedding employee involvement and participation at work. *Human Resource Management Journal*, 16(3): 250–267.

DIAMOND, W. AND FREEMAN, R. B. (2001) *What Workers Want from Workplace Organisations: A Report to the TUC's Promoting Trade Unionism Task Group*. London: Trades Union Congress.

DUNDON, T. AND GOLLAN, P. (2007) Re-conceptualizing voice in the non-union workplace. *International Journal of Human Resource Management*, 18(7): 1182–1198.

DUNDON, T., WILKINSON, A., MARCHINGTON, M. AND ACKERS, P. (2004) The meanings and purpose of employee voice. *International Journal of Human Resource Management*, 15(6): 1150–1171.

European Commission (2001) *EU Employment and Social Policy 1999–2001: Jobs, Cohesion, Productivity*. Luxembourg: Office for Official Publications of the European Communities.

European Foundation for the Improvement of Living and Working Conditions (2005) *Employee Financial Participation in the European Union*. Dublin: European Foundation for the Improvement of Living and Working Conditions.

FIORITO, J. (2001) Human resource management practices and worker desires for union representation. *Journal of Labor Research*, 22(2): 335–354.

FREEMAN, R. B., BOXALL, P. AND HAYNES, P. (2007) *What Workers Say: Employee Voice in the Anglo-American Workplace*. Ithaca, NY: Cornell University Press.

FREEMAN, R. B. AND ROGERS, J. (1999) *What Workers Want*. Ithaca, NY: Cornell University Press.

GALLIE, D. AND WHITE, M. (1993) *Employee Commitment and the Skills Revolution*. London: Policy Studies Institute.

GILMAN, M., RABY. S. AND PYMAN, A. (2015)The contours of employee voice in SMEs: The importance of context. *Human Resource Management Journal*, 25(4): 563–579.

GODARD, J. (2001) High-performance and the transformation of work? The implications of alternative work practices for the experience and outcomes of work. *Industrial and Labor Relations Review*, 54: 776–805.

GOLLAN, P. (2006) Editorial: Consultation and non-union employee representation. *Industrial Relations Journal*, 37(5): 428–437.

GOLLAN, P. AND WILKINSON, A. (2007) Implications of the EU Information and Consultation Directive and the regulations in the UK: Prospects for the future of employee representation. *International Journal of Human Resource Management*, 18(7): 1145–1158.

GREEN, F. (2004) Why has work effort become more intense? *Industrial Relations*, 43(4): 709–741.

GUERY, L. (2015) Why do firms adopt employee share ownership? Bundling ESO and direct involvement for developing human capital investments. *Employee Relations*, 37(3): 296–313.

HALL, M. (2005) Assessing the information and consultation of employees regulations. *Industrial Law Journal*, 34(2): 103–126.

HALL, M., HUTCHINSON, S., PARKER, J., PURCELL, J. AND TERRY, M. (2007) *Implementing Information and Consultation: Early Experience under the ICE Regulations*. Department for Business, Enterprise and Regulatory Reform, Employment Relations Research Series No. 88. London: Department for Business Enterprise and Regulatory Reform/CIPD/ACAS.

HALL, M., HUTCHINSON, S., PURCELL, J., TERRY, M. AND PARKER, J. (2009) *Implementing Information and Consultation:* *Evidence from Longitudinal Case Studies with 150 or More Employees*. Department for Business Innovation and Skills, Employment Relations Research Series No. 105. London: Department for Business Innovation and Skills.

HARDY, S. AND ADNETT, N. (2006) 'Breaking the ICE': Workplace democracy in a modernized social Europe. *International Journal of Human Resource Management*, 17(6): 1021–131.

HOLLAND, P., PYMAN, A., COOPER, B. AND TEICHER, J. (2011) Employee voice and job satisfaction in Australia: The centrality of direct voice. *Human Resource Management*, 50(1): 95–111.

HYMAN, R. (2005) Whose (social) partnership? In STUART, M. AND MARTINEZ LUCIO, M. (eds), *Partnership and Modernisation in Employment Relations*. Oxford: Routledge, pp. 251–265.

KALMI, P., PENDLETON, A. AND POUTSMA, E. (2005) Financial participation and performance in Europe. *Human Resource Management Journal*, 15(4): 54–67.

KAPLAN, R. S. AND NORTON, D. P. (1992) The Balanced Scorecard – measures that drive performance. *Harvard Business Review*, (January – February): 71–9.

KERSLEY, B., ALPIN, C., FORTH, J. et al. (2005) Inside the workplace: First findings from the 2004 Workplace Employment Relations Survey (WERS 2004). Available at: http://cw.routledge.com/textbooks/0415378133/first-findings/report.asp. Accessed 21 December 2015.

KESSLER, I. AND PURCELL, J. (1996) The value of joint working parties. *Work, Employment and Society*, 10(4): 663–682.

KNUDSEN, H. (1995) *Employee Participation in Europe*. London: Sage.

LEONARD, D. (1998) *Wellsprings of Knowledge: Building and Sustaining the Sources of Innovation*. Boston, MA: Harvard Business School Press.

LEOPOLD, J. (2004) Employee participation, involvement and communications. In Leopold, J., Harris L. and Watson T. (eds), *The Strategic Managing of Human Resources*. Harlow: Pearson Education, pp. 434–460.

MADEN, C. (2015) Linking high involvement human resource practices to employee proactivity. *Personnel Review*, 44(5): 720–738.

MARCHINGTON, M. (1992) *Managing the Team*. Oxford: Blackwell.

MARCHINGTON, M. (2005) Employee involvement: Patterns and explanations. In HARLEY, B., HYMAN J. AND THOMPSON P. (eds), *Participation and Democracy at Work: Essays in Honour of Harvie Ramsay*. Basingstoke: Palgrave Macmillan: pp. 20–37.

MARCHINGTON, M. (2007) Employee voice systems. In BOXALL, P., PURCELL, J. AND WRIGHT, P. M. (eds), *The*

Oxford Handbook of Human Resource Management. Oxford: Oxford University Press, pp. 231–250.

MARCHINGTON, M. (2015a) The role of institutional and intermediary forces in shaping patterns of employee involvement and participation (EIP) in Anglo-American countries. *International Journal of Human Resource Management*, 26(20): 2594–2616.

MARCHINGTON, M. (2015b) Analysing the forces shaping employee involvement and participation at organization level in liberal market economies (LMEs). *Human Resource Management Journal*, 25(1): 1–18.

MARCHINGTON, M. AND WILKINSON, A. (2002) *People Management and Development: Human Resource Management at Work* (2ⁿᵈ edn). London: Chartered Institute of Personnel and Development.

MARGINSON, P., EDWARDS, P., EDWARDS, T., FERNER, A. AND TREGASKIS, O. (2010) Employee representation and consultative voice in multinational companies operating in Britain. *British Journal of Industrial Relations*, 48(1): 151–180.

MELLAT-PARAST, M. (2013) Quality citizenship, employee involvement and operational performance: An empirical investigation. *International Journal of Production Research*, 51(10): 2805–2820.

NOON, M. AND HOQUE, K. (2004) Equal opportunities policy and practice in Britain: Evaluating the 'empty shell' hypothesis. *Work, Employment and Society*, 18(3): 481–506.

PHIPPS, S. T. A, PRIETO, L. C. and NDINGURI, E. N. (2013) Understanding the impact of employee involvement on organizational productivity: The moderating role of organizational conflict. *Journal of Organizational Culture, Communications and Conflict*, 17(2): 107–120.

PIHLAK, U. AND ALAS, R. (2012) Leadership style and employee involvement during organizational change. *Journal of Management and Change*, 29(1): 46–66.

POUTSMA, E. (2006) *Changing Patterns of Employee Financial Participation in Europe*. Nijmegen: Nijmegen School of Management.

POUTSMA, E. AND DE NIJS, W. (2003) Broad-based employee financial participation in the European Union. *International Journal of Human Resource Management*, 14(6): 863–892.

POUTSMA, E., DE NIJS, W. AND POOLE, M. (2003) The global phenomenon of employee financial participation. *International Journal of Human Resource Management*, 14(6): 855–862.

POUTSMA, E., KALMI, P. AND PENDLETON, A. (2006) The relationship between financial participation and other forms of employee participation: New survey evidence from Europe. *Economic and Industrial Democracy*, 27(4): 637–667.

PURCELL, J. AND GEORGIADIS, K. (2007) Why should employers bother with worker voice? In FREEMAN, R. B., BOXALL, P. AND HAYNES, P. (eds), *What Workers Say: Employee Voice in the Anglo-American Workplace*. Ithaca, NY: Cornell University Press, pp. 181–197.

PYMAN, A., COOPER, B., TEICHER, J. AND HOLLAND, P. (2006) A comparison of the effectiveness of employee voice arrangements in Australia. *Industrial Relations Journal*, 37(5): 543–559.

PYMAN, A., HOLLAND, P., TEICHER, J. AND COOPER, B. (2010) Industrial relations climate, employee voice and managerial attitudes to unions: An Australian study. *British Journal of Industrial Relations* 48(2): 460–480.

PYMAN, A., GOLLAN, P.J., WILKINSON, A., XU, C. & KALFA, S. (EDS.) (2016) 'Introduction: Employee Voice in Emerging Economies: Charting New Territory", in Employee Voice in Emerging Economies, Advances in Industrial and Labor Relations, Volume 23: pp. ix - xiii. DOI: HTTP://DX.DOI.ORG/10.1108/S0742-618620160000023002

RICHARDSON, M., DANFORD, A., STEWART, P. AND PULIGNANO, V. (2010) Employee participation and involvement: Experiences of aerospace and automobile workers in the UK and Italy. *European Journal of Industrial Relations*, 16(1): 21–37.

ROBERTSON, R. (2010a) Employee. *Stakeholder Magazine*, February: 24–27.

ROBERTSON, R. (2010b) Workforce 2010. Employee section. *Stakeholder Magazine*, May: 24–27.

SAKO, M. (1998) The nature and impact of employee 'voice' in the European car components industry. *Human Resource Management Journal*, 8(2): 6–13.

TEICHER, J., HOLLAND, P., PYMAN, A. AND COOPER, B. (2007) Australian workers: Finding their voice? In FREEMAN, R. B., BOXALL, P. AND HAYNES, P. (eds), *What Workers Say: Employee Voice in the Anglo-American Workplace*. Ithaca, NY: Cornell University Press, pp.125–144.

Telegraph (2015) VW boss Martin Winterkorn quits and says 'I did nothing wrong'. Available at: http://www.telegraph.co.uk/finance/newsbysector/industry/11886523/VW-boss-Martin-Winterkorn-quits-and-says-I-did-nothing-wrong.html.

TOWNLEY, B. (1994) Communicating with employees. In Sisson, K. (ed.), *Personnel Management: A Comprehensive Guide to Theory and Practice in Britain* (2ⁿᵈ edn). Oxford: Blackwell, pp. 595–633.

WADDINGTON, J. (2003) What do representatives think of the practices of European works councils? Views from six countries. *European Journal of Industrial Relations*, 9(3): 303–325.

WALTON, R. E., CUTCHER-GURSHENFELD, J. E. AND MCKERSIE, R. B. (1994) *Strategic Negotiations: A Theory of Change in Labor–Management Relations*. Boston, MA: Harvard Business School Press.

WHEELER, H. N. (2008) A new frontier for labor: Collective action by worker owners. *Labor Studies Journal*, 33(2): 163–178.

WILKINSON, A., DUNDON, T., DONAGHEY, J. AND FREEMAN, R. B. (eds.) (2015) *Handbook of Research on Employee Voice*. Edward Elgar: UK.

WILKINSON, A., DUNDON, T. AND GRUGULIS, I. (2007) Information and consultation: Exploring employee involvement in SMEs. *International Journal of Human Resource Management*, 18(7): 1279–1297.

WOOD, S. J. AND FENTON-O'CREEVY, M. P. (2005) Direct involvement, representation and employee voice in UK multinationals in Europe. *European Journal of Industrial Relations*, 11(1): 27–50.

WOOD, S. J. AND WALL, T. D. (2007) Work enrichment and employee voice in human resource management performance studies. *International Journal ofHuman Resource Management*, 18(7): 1335–1372.

WORK–LIFE BALANCE IN THE TWENTY-FIRST CENTURY

Nicolina Kamenou-Aigbekaen and Yu Fu

LEARNING OUTCOMES

After reading this chapter, you should be able to:

➤ Understand the changing nature of the workplace and its effects on work–life balance in a global context
➤ Review the changing nature of employment in relation to issues of work–life balance for different social groups, focusing on gender, age, disability, ethnicity, religion, and sexuality
➤ Outline the range of work–life balance initiatives and flexible working practices
➤ Outline the legislative context for work and family balance, as well as key equality legislation
➤ Evaluate the societal and economic benefits and costs in relation to balancing work and life
➤ Outline key current debates on work–life balance issues in a global context
➤ Acknowledge, and engage in debates relating to, cultural specificity and variation across countries and regions in terms of issues of work–life balance
➤ Critically engage with key work–life balance issues through examples, questions and an end-of-chapter case study.

SUMMARY OF CHAPTER CONTENTS

➤ **Opening Case Study**: Balancing work and life in a non-Western economy
➤ Introduction
➤ The changing face of employment
➤ Work–life balance initiatives and flexible working arrangements
➤ The legal framework
➤ Employee wellbeing and health
➤ International and contextual considerations in work–life balance debates
➤ Conclusion
➤ **End of Chapter Case Study**: Work and wellbeing in a Chinese multinational
➤ For discussion and revision
➤ Further reading
➤ Web resources
➤ Glossary
➤ References

Opening Case Study Balancing work and life in a non-Western economy

Ewere woke up at 5:15 a.m. and quickly got ready as she wanted to avoid the hectic Lagos traffic jam. At this time, it would only take her 20 minutes to reach the office, but if she set off any later, it could take more than two hours to cover the short distance. She was already dreading another long day; the return journey would be quicker if she stayed at work till about 7 p.m. Her husband, Osagie, was also up and getting ready for work but their two daughters were still peacefully asleep. She was very thankful to her parents, especially her mother, for all their help and support with the girls. She couldn't help feeling guilty, however, for missing out on her children's daily activities. Comments from both her parents that she never has the time to fulfil her home responsibilities didn't help the tension she constantly felt when at work.

When she arrived in the office, her boss, Mr Adebayo, was standing by her desk with a large pile of staff apprais-als. She needed to review and countersign them by lunchtime, he mentioned on his way out. After the consolida-tion of Nigerian banks a few years before, competition had increased in the industry, and senior managers in her bank kept reminding staff 'how lucky' they were to have a job. Ewere felt that everyone was out for themselves and wanted to showcase their own individual achievements.

Staff always seemed so busy and focused on their work. She could tell, however, that they were not necessarily productive, although they were very keen to be 'seen to be working'. It was clear that her boss expected every-one, men and women, to be committed to the organisation, and he would often be overheard saying 'we need to put the company first'. Flexibility or flexible policies were never discussed as an option at the bank. When you were hired, it was assumed you would work full time – although it often felt like she working two days in one, from 6:30 a.m. to 7:30 p.m. There was never any acknowledgment or explicit appreciation of her hard work and the long hours she put in.

Ewere was almost half way through the appraisal forms. It was 10:30 am and she was already exhausted. She had four meetings scheduled in the afternoon and still had to prepare for two of them, but her mind was else-where. Her mum had told her the previous night that she and her father were 'too old to be full-time parents for the second time'. She had ambitions to progress further, but she also felt she was missing out on so much at home.

Ewere left work at 7:15 p.m. that evening and made it home at 8:00 p.m. The girls were already asleep. She could hardly hold a conversation with her husband and parents over dinner. She could feel her mum's disapprov-ing stare on her but tried to ignore it. She and Osagie got up, said goodnight to her parents, and went to bed exhausted, knowing that the next day would be very similar to the one she had today.

Questions

1 What are the key issues Ewere is facing at work and at home?
2 Is she receiving support from her organisation? Is she receiving support from her family?
3 What areas could be improved at work to help her better balance her work and personal life demands?

INTRODUCTION

Globalisation, increased competition, a long-hours work-ing culture, people living longer, changes in family struc-tures and evolving legal provisions related to employment and working conditions have a direct effect not only on individuals' workplace experiences but also on their pri-vate and social life experiences.

This chapter engages in key debates on work–life bal-ance (WLB) by taking a global perspective, acknowledging national and cultural differences in how WLB is perceived and how flexible working arrangements are negotiated, and noting diverse legal frameworks and workplace practices dealing with work and employment, rights for parents, carers, and so on. The experiences of social groups, including among others women, older workers, and ethnic minority groups, in relation to WLB issues are also explored. A range of WLB organisational initiatives and flexible work-ing types are presented, together with the legal protection associated with these practices. A discussion of the social and economic benefits of a healthy, fulfilled workforce is presented, as is an evaluation of the costs of inaction on the part of organisations and the government, such as the costs of high absenteeism and work-related stress. Key con-cepts will be evaluated, and examples and exercises will be provided throughout the chapter, along with an end-of-chapter case study, in order to help readers engage with critical issues and debates on WLB in varied contexts.

Changing demographics, such as the ageing population trend experienced in most developed economies, the increasing number of women in the labour market, renegotiated social roles, the rise in single-parent families, and an increased awareness of diversity and legislative changes, have had an impact on WLB and governmental and organisational initiatives related to WLB. The increased importance placed on the public image of organisations and the drive to engage in corporate social responsibility initiatives indicate an understanding from the employers' view of the need to engage with wellbeing and WLB initiatives. Coupled with legal regulation and an acknowledgment of the business case argument – that is, the argument that treating employees with respect, providing flexible working arrangements, and acknowledging external-to-work responsibilities can be linked to increased productivity and commitment – this makes a compelling case for treating WLB initiatives as key to organisational success. *The Sunday Times* 100 Best Companies to Work For, a large-scale survey that focuses on best practice initiatives in relation to people management, includes as some of its key areas 'wellbeing', which relates to WLB, and 'giving something back', which focuses on whether the organisation contributes to its local community and society (http://www.bestcompanies.co.uk, as cited in Bolton and Wibberley, 2007).

It should be noted at this point that the term 'balance' is often deceiving as it implies distinct lives that can be experienced as finite and separate from each other. A central critique, therefore, of discussions of WLB consistently focused on the problematic notion that a well-balanced approach between paid work and life outside work is assumed to be feasible (Sparrow and Cooper, 2003). The term 'balance' assumes a trade off between work and life, whereas in reality there is great overlap between these two worlds, with 'no clear-cut distinction between the world of work and the work of family, friends and social networks and community' (Taylor, 2002: 17).

Despite this critique, as well as discussions of wide-ranging issues in WLB, most debates in the area have typically assumed a naive view of the 'life' aspect of the WLB equation (Kamenou, 2008). The focus has typically been placed on working mothers and family-friendly policies, but more recently the experiences of fathers and their 'contribution to the home' have been gaining increasing attention (see, for example, Clarke and O'Brien, 2003; Featherstone, 2003). Discussions of juggling work and personal demands have typically ignored issues faced by other groups, for example disabled or older workers or the carers of older or disabled people (Gardiner et al., 2007). With few exceptions (see, for example, Bradley et al., 2005; Dale, 2005; Healy et al., 2004; Kamenou, 2008; Rana et al., 1998), issues around ethnicity, culture and religion have

also been absent from the majority of discussions around WLB debates and initiatives.

One cannot assume that employment experiences are universal across the world or, indeed, universal within a country or region. Economic, sociopolitical and cultural factors, education systems, and family structures will have an effect on individuals' experiences in the workplace, on the centrality of work in people's lives, on how work and family responsibilities are negotiated, and on how childcare responsibilities are divided.

The following sections will engage with key issues in relation to work and life, and will critically review changing trends in employment in relation to a number of social groups who have been historically disadvantaged in the labour market. Key equality legislation for the protection of each group will also be cited. Readers are advised to refer to Chapter 4 on 'Diversity Management' for a more detailed discussion of diversity issues and equality approaches.

Class Activity

Form groups of three to four people, and research and discuss the questions below.

▸ Choose one local company and list its WLB policies and practices.
▸ Choose one multinational company and identify WLB programmes of the company.
▸ Explore and compare the core values of the WLB systems of these two companies.

THE CHANGING FACE OF EMPLOYMENT

Gender

The number of women entering employment has been steadily increasing since World War II, with the male participation rate slowly falling. This trend is predicted to continue, and some argue that the number of women in the labour market will be higher than that of their male counterparts in the next decade. Syed and Murray (2009) have also argued that statistics that indicate that the participation rates of mothers in the workplace have been increasing, give a positive message in terms of recognising that women can meet the requirements of top management positions.

There has also been a rise in the number of single-parent families, with most of these families being headed by women rather than men. The number of dual-career couples is increasing, and this trend makes the effort to 'balance' work and personal life more challenging. It is argued that today's fathers are more 'hands-on' than their own fathers and grandfathers were and are more willing to share childcare responsibilities. Interestingly, some recent research has indicated that, in dual-career households where women earn the same as or more than their male counterparts, men are willing to help with childcare but are reluctant to support their partners with domestic work (Crompton and Lyonette, 2009). Research indicates that women typically do three-quarters of the domestic work even when they are in paid employment: they do an average of 18.5 hours a week, whereas their male counterparts typically undertake 6 hours a week of domestic work (Kan, 2001).

As stated earlier, the majority of discussions on WLB have focused on women, mainly working mothers. Although this should be acknowledged as a shortcoming in the literature as the experiences of other social groups have, in the majority, been absent, it has to be recognised that gender is a key component of WLB debates – women in the workplace still face disadvantage in employment and career progression and are still subjected to stereotypical gendered assumptions.

Some seminal research in the UK in the 1990s brought to the forefront the shortcomings of existing organisational cultures in relation to family-friendly policies and WLB issues. Lewis (1997) and Liff and Cameron (1997) argued that there is an underlying assumption that women are not as committed to work and to their careers as their male counterparts, and women are often seen as 'the problem' (Liff and Cameron, 1997). The writers have argued that notions of commitment are therefore gendered, commitment being assessed on male standards such as hours of work and a linear career path with no career breaks. This ignores the unequal distribution of domestic and childcare responsibilities and focuses on inputs (that is, hours at work) rather than outputs (that is, productivity and end results). Moreover, Lewis (1997) argued that two main barriers to effective family-friendly policies are a low sense of entitlement to these policies by employees who do not feel they can utilise them, and organisational discourses of time, which:

> obscure the advantages of alternative ways of working, for the organisation as well as for individual employees and their families, and perpetuate organisational structures which interfere with family life, and help to maintain gender inequalities. (Lewis, 1997: 21)

More recent work by Herman, Lewis and Humber (2013), exploring the experience of mothers working

in science, engineering, and technology sectors in three European countries, found that female professionals' careers are not only influenced by their corporation culture but also shaped by specific national policies and provisions within which they live and work. Furthermore, Sullivan (2015) revealed that a discursive approach to explicating constructions of work–life balance and working motherhood has been used in the articles from the highest circulating UK women's magazines: 'women are told not to feel guilty about 'Bad Mum Guilt' in the same sentence as being explicitly told that they must reduce their work hours and take steps to solve the problem' (Sullivan, 2015: 296). It is indicated that both social policy in the UK and wider discourses positioning women as struggling individuals need to be examined in social and political context. Slaughter (2012) places the focus on the need for a cultural shift where it is acknowledged that it is not women who have to adapt so as to be seen as committed to their career but it is organisations that need to move away from a discriminatory masculine culture.

In the UK, a statutory Gender Equality Duty had been enforced from 2007, which required all British public authorities to actively promote gender equality and to eliminate unlawful discrimination and harassment. Recent developments, such as the UK Equality Act 2010 and International Development (Gender Equality) Act 2014, combine previous equality legislation, including the Sex Discrimination Act 1975. Recently, the GREAT Initiative and Plan UK (2015) evaluated the implementation of the International Development (Gender Equality) Act 2014 and found that the Department for International Development (DFID) has placed great emphasis on meaningful engagement with the Act.

It has been argued that some countries have made further progress in renegotiating traditional gender roles. Scandinavian countries are often cited as best-practice examples of employment practices, welfare systems, and initiatives on wellbeing. For example, Lamb (2009) contended that gender roles have successfully changed at work and home in Sweden. Swedish social policies presume that couples adopt the dual breadwinner model, which then places the onus on the government and organisations to enable both men and women to be part of the labour force. Through a number of cultural or societal changes, Lamb argues that Sweden has redefined the notion of a 'good father' by emphasising the need for men to be involved in their children's care. Critical Thinking 15.1 explores some key issues in relation to WLB and fathers in Britain in some more detail, including some questions for readers to consider.

(?) Critical Thinking 15.1 Fathers and WLB

An Equality and Human Rights Commission (EHRC) Report has highlighted the tensions that British fathers experience in attempting to balance work and family. It touches on the lack of confidence of many fathers to request flexible working as they fear this would have a negative effect on their career as they could be perceived to be less committed to their organisation.

Andrea Murray, Acting Group Director of Strategy from the EHRC has stated:

> Two-thirds of fathers see flexible working as an important benefit when looking for a new job. This highlights an opportunity for British businesses to use flexible working as an incentive for attracting and retaining the most talented of employees. [Such policies have been associated with] increased productivity, reduction in staff turnover, reduced training costs and an ability to respond better to customer requirements.

Questions

1   What are the longer-term implications of fathers not spending time with their children? Think of the impact this situation can have for both home life and organisations.
2   Imagine you are an human resources manager. Your organisation has well-developed policies on WLB initiatives and flexible working arrangements, but you are aware that the 'take-up' of these initiatives is much lower for male than female staff. You will head a group meeting to discuss ways to encourage all staff who might benefit from these initiatives to utilise them. What would be your main recommendations? What barriers could you envisage facing?

Source: Equality and Human Rights Commission (2009), cited in wired.gov.

Age

WLB is central to all individuals and should not always be equated with balancing work with family or childcare demands. As discussed earlier in the chapter, developing economies are faced with an ageing population, and this has a profound effect on issues to do with care, retirement and pensions. It is predicted that by 2030 more than a quarter of the population will be over 65 (Torrington et al., 2008).

With the age structure of the population changing, the competition for young employees can intensify, and the increase in the group of 35-year-olds and older will increase demand for WLB policies as men and women in this group are likely to have family commitments (Bunting, 2004). With the removal of the compulsory retirement age, the proportion of people over 60 who stay economically active will also increase, and Bunting (2004) argues that this group includes individuals who are disillusioned with work and experience low job satisfaction:

> Meanwhile, those at the beginning of their working lives will increasingly have to consider how they can maintain the intensity of work over the long haul; retirement no longer beckons at sixty, but at seventy or even beyond. (Bunting, 2004: 305)

There are age-related stereotypes labelling older workers as less able to learn and adapt to technology and younger workers as unmotivated and not experienced. Torrington et al. (2008) argue, however, that, in relation to older workers, there is evidence that people over the age of 50 can perform well and be highly motivated if the appropriate systems and support structures are in place. It is argued that the availability of flexible working arrangements, training, clear performance targets, and proactive avoidance of discriminatory practices are central factors in older workers having a positive employment experience, accompanied by job satisfaction and high productivity. Platman (2002)'s study investigated the adoption of 'portfolio' careers as a means in retaining older workers in organisations. The research investigated portfolio careers in the media industry for people over the age of 50, the findings suggesting that this type of career is seen as attractive to this age group as it provides high flexibility in terms of hours and type of work, and does not impose a retirement threshold.

There is legal protection against age discrimination in the European community through the European Union's (EU) Framework Directive for Equal Treatment in Employment and Occupation (2000). This was adopted in the UK in 2006 as the Employment Equality (Age) Regulations. These Regulations cover workers of all ages and all employers, encompassing employment and vocational training, flexible working, retirement, redundancy and pay. Through this legislation, there is now no official retirement age in the UK. The 'standard' or 'default' age is 65, but this is not mandatory. The EU Directive, and subsequently the UK legislation, is seen as a response to the trend of an ageing population and therefore as capitalising on the available pool of candidates, as well as addressing concerns about labour shortages and about age discrimination in the labour market. Interestingly, protection for age discrimination in the USA, through the Age Discrimination in Employment Act (1967) only protects individuals who are 40 years of age or older.

Disability

Despite extensive policies and initiatives in the UK focusing on disability, mainly developed under the Labour government, discrimination and disadvantage are still faced by people with disabilities. A lack of understanding and engagement with the varied forms of disability has been exacerbating the marginalisation of disabled people. People who have a disability are a highly disparate group in that their disability can vary in terms of its severity, stability, and type (Woodhams and Danieli, 2000) and may also include mental health issues, learning difficulties, and sensory impairments.

Legal protection against disability discrimination was formalised in the UK with the Disability Discrimination Act in 1995 (extended in 2005), which placed the onus on employers to have to make 'reasonable adjustments' to the workplace environment and working arrangements in order to accommodate people with disabilities. Since 2006, the public sector has had specific responsibilities through the Disability Equality Duty. This duty requires employers in public sector organisations to proactively promote equality for disabled people and to carry out equality impact assessments on their policies. Disability discrimination is now covered as part of the New Equality Act 2010, mentioned above.

In terms of the need to balance work and personal life demands, it is important for employers to recognise the needs of staff with a disability or impairment. Staff who have health problems, especially long-term illnesses, are 'in particular need of working practices that facilitate a balance between work demands and life needs' (Hogarth et al., 2001: 253).

Sexual orientation

Falling outside the heterosexual (and male, white, able-bodied) norm is still a challenging situation for lesbian, gay, bisexual, and transgender (LGBT) people in employment and society. Discrimination based on sexual orientation is often difficult to identify and challenge, as members of the LGBT community may not disclose their sexuality due to fear of exclusion and discrimination. There is legal protection in EU Member States, and the UK's sexual orientation regulations give effect to the requirement in the Equal Treatment Framework Directive through the Employment Equality (Sexual Orientation) Regulations 2003.

The USA does not have federal legislation in place to protect LGBT people on sexual orientation grounds (Sargeant, 2009), despite a long-running campaign for national legislation. States and municipalities have the option to enforce legislation at that level, but they also have the option not to; 15 states actually have anti-gay partnership laws in place (Howenstine, 2006).

Sargeant (2009: 639) argued that lesbians, gay men, bisexuals, and transgender people are placed in one category mainly for convenience in terms of identifying 'the discriminatory treatment that they jointly suffer as a result of not conforming to the expectations of a heterosexist society'. The author argues that the life experiences and discrimination faced by the 'LGBT group' are not identical and that there is a distinction in law between lesbians, gay men, and bisexuals as a group and transgender people as a separate group. Sargeant's (2009) paper explored issues of LGBT elders from a UK and a US perspective. There is very limited research on LGBT elders, and this paper argues that this group experience particular discrimination that is unique and different from the experiences of elders in general and heterosexual elders in particular.

There is little academic research on lesbian and gay parents and their experiences in the workplace and society. A report by the American Psychological Association (2005) cited research comparing the children of lesbian and gay parents with the children of heterosexual parents and indicated that common stereotypes of the effect of gay parenting on children's sexuality and development were not supported. Early studies focused on middle-class, well-educated families, but recent research has taken differences in terms of ethnicity, socioeconomic status, and regions into account and still found no support for the stereotypes (American Psychological Association, 2005).

Race, ethnicity, culture, and religion

Protection from race discrimination in the UK came in the form of the Race Relations Act 1976 and the Race Relations (Amendment) Act 2000, and there is now protection through the Equality Act 2010. The UK public sector also has specific responsibilities through the Race Equality Duty. In terms of religion or belief, the EU's Employment Equality (Religion or Belief) Regulations 2003 provide protection for groups or individuals on the grounds of their religion or belief. An important effect of this legislation is the fact that religious groups who do not share a common ethnicity are now protected from discrimination.

As mentioned earlier in this chapter, when engaging in debates on WLB, an understanding of the diversity of forms of life and life experiences is crucial. Factors such as race, religion and culture may have an effect on how individuals conceptualise and experience key issues in terms of both their work and their personal life. Issues such as religious responsibilities, caring for extended families, and priorities in different regions and countries in relation to WLB are very important to consider. At the same time, one should not generalise and assume that specific ethnic or religious groups would behave in a specific way – the main point is that diversity should be acknowledged both within and across groups.

An area that has been receiving more attention in recent years is the impact of the interaction of gender with race, culture, and religion on work and societal experiences. This section will present some key literature and key arguments in relation to ethnic minority women, focusing on their experiences in terms of work and life.

In relation to domestic labour and household structures, Gardiner (1997) has proposed that there are different experiences across racial and ethnic groups. Carby (1982) argued, for example, that the experiences of African American and Black Caribbean women were shaped by the history of slavery and colonialism. Gardiner (1997) also contended that full-time motherhood was never dominant for this group of women as there was a necessity to work full time to support their families. More recent data support these views, with Duncan and Irwin (2004: 394) suggesting that Caribbean mothers are more likely to see 'substantial hours in employments as a built-in component of good mothering' and to accept that they have the primary responsibility for childcare and domestic responsibilities as well as taking the necessity to work for granted.

Bhopal (1997: 4) contended that South Asian women's experiences may be different from those from African and Caribbean communities in that 'the specific cultural norms and standards of South Asian families may be reinforced through different forms of patriarchy experienced by women'. In addition, South Asian women may experience oppression 'by the form of marriage they participate in, the giving of dowries, participating in domestic labour and the degree of control they have in domestic finance'. She argued that although South Asian communities are diverse, there are similarities that place them in a different setting from white communities: 'there is the primacy of family over the individual...with emphasis on child rearing and family interaction patterns for both males and females' (Bhopal, 1997: 7).

Research supports the contention that a major factor of stress for ethnic minority women is their perception of living two separate lives (Bell, 1986; Denton, 1990; Davidson, 1997; Kamenou, 2008). Thomas and Aldefer (1989: 135) define this as 'bicultural stress': 'the set of emotional and physical upheavals produced by a bicultural existence'. Bell et al. (1993: 118–119) have argued that 'circumstances often dictate that, for women of colour to be successful managers, they must adopt a new identity and abandon commitment to their old culture [of racial or ethnic community]'. The bicultural stress can be intensified by the fact that the ethnic minority women's own communities may perceive them as 'traitors' when they try to fit in the white dominant culture of their organisations (Bell et al., 1993).

It is important, therefore, to acknowledge the diversity of experiences when focusing on work and life debates, as placing all women – and men – in predetermined groups, regardless of their ethnicity, socioeconomic status, age, or other factors, assumes a naive understanding of the different societal and work experiences. Acknowledging different forms of life is crucial in order to engage in a realistic analysis that can inform organisational policy and practice (Kamenou, 2008).

STOP AND REFLECT

Questions

1 What issues do women – and men – face in employment today in relation to balancing work and personal life commitments?

2 There may be additional concerns for other social groups (that is, people with disabilities, ethnic minority groups, and so on) in relation to balancing work and life. Discuss.

Critical Thinking 15.2 engages in a key discussion on the interaction between choice and structural constraints in the context of employment and career development.

(?) Critical Thinking 15.2 All about choice?

There have been on-going debates on the importance of agency and the strategies that women and other social groups employ in determining their own career path. Hakim (1991, 1995, 2004) has argued that agency is central to women's choices in terms of decisions on whether they focus on their job or career or whether they choose to focus on their family. Hakim has been heavily criticised for assuming that everyone can make free choices without acknowledging structural constraints (Devine, 1994; Ginn et al., 1996; McRae, 2003). Later, Hakim (2008) argued that social and family policy must be gender-neutral, but should cater for diversity in lifestyle preferences. For example, Pinker (2008) found that paid sabbatical leave is available to both men and women in Belgium. The sabbatical leave can be used for childcare, further education, or any other purpose. Thus, staff with or without children or other dependants could take advantage of this policy. However, some evidence indicated that the gender-neutral policies may increase differences between working men and women, as men often used this leave to update or extend their qualifications, while women normally used it for family purposes (Ibid.). Recently, Beddoes and Pawley (2014) conducted in-depth interviews with STEM (science, technology, engineering, and mathematics) faculty members and highlighted a discourse of choice framing the challenges faced by female academics in particular.

On the other side of the debate, some writers analysing women's position in the labour market have focused on the limitations imposed by structures for women's opportunities and advancement (see, for example, Walby, 1983, 1986; Bhopal, 1997). Walby's theory of patriarchy (1983, 1986) has been criticised for its indifference to the practices and motivation of individuals. As Collinson et al. (1990: 48) have argued, Walby is 'unable to explain how these social structures are constituted, and this inevitably results in a theory of patriarchy which is heavily deterministic as well as economistic'.

A number of writers have argued that an acknowledgement of the interaction of structure and agency, as well as culture, is needed when examining the impact of gender on employment (see, for example, Devine, 1994; Evetts, 2000) and of ethnicity and gender on career development (see, for instance, Kamenou, 2002, 2008).

Questions

1 In the context of the agency versus structure debate, reflect on key issues discussed in this chapter in relation to WLB. How important to do you think women's and men's choices are in relation to balancing work and life?
2 What would you consider to be the key constraints in taking up flexible working and other WLB initiatives offered in organisations?
3 Do you think there are issues or concerns that may affect some social groups more than others? Extend your discussions beyond a focus on gender, to include other groups such as ethnic minority or disabled groups.

WORK–LIFE BALANCE INITIATIVES AND FLEXIBLE WORKING ARRANGEMENTS

The chapter now turns to a review of a number of WLB initiatives and flexible working arrangements.

The majority of WLB initiatives focus on arrangements to help parents or carers with children or older and disabled family members. These initiatives typically include a number of flexible working arrangements, as discussed below, as well as the possibility of on-site crèche facilities and childcare allowances. There is, however, a trend, mainly for larger organisations, to provide programmes that can benefit all of their employees; these typically centre around wellbeing, reducing stress and providing support. Free or subsidised health club memberships are now common in larger organisations, as are health insurance provisions. Some organisations also provide opportunities for counselling for staff who may be facing work and also personal problems. There is a wide range of flexible working arrangements, the most common being:

- part-time work;
- flexible hours;
- job-sharing;
- career breaks;
- working from home/working remotely (teleworking);
- seasonal hours;
- term-time work;
- shift-swapping;
- compressed working time;
- unpaid leave/unpaid sabbatical.

Box 15.1 provides an insight into WLB policies at the Royal Bank of Scotland (RBS).

Box 15.1 Wellbeing and WLB policies at RBS

The Royal Bank of Scotland Group (RBS) is one of the world's leading financial institutions. It serves customers and employs staff in Europe, Asia, the Middle East, and North America. RBS was ranked in the top five leading companies in the Business in the Community (BITC) Employee Engagement and Wellbeing Public Reporting benchmark in 2014. It continues to develop and support more wellbeing and WLB policies, such as:

▸ Bank-wide training: the training aims to help employees recognise and combat unconscious bias; it continued throughout 2015.

▸ Employee-led networks: as stated on the IBM website, the networks are focused on specific diversity and inclusion issues. Their employee-led networks are:

　▸ Focused women;
　▸ RBS Multicultural Network;
　▸ Enable - the disability network;
　▸ Families and Careers Network;
　▸ Rainbow Network;

▸ The Lifematters Helpline: this employee assistance programme has been delivering wellbeing packs to support both the practical and emotional aspects of redundancy, stress awareness guides for line managers and employees, and learning spotlights on stress management and work–life balance.

Source: RBS website, working at RBS. Available at: http://www.rbs.com/sustainability/working-at-rbs.html. Accessed November 2015.

Dieckhoff and Gallie (2007) cite flexible working arrangements as being high on the EU agenda of economic inclusion and adaptability. The UK government policy on flexible working focuses on the business case argument; that is, the focus is on the benefits to employers and business. Policy and practice in relation to WLB and flexible working in EU countries have in the main focused on the parents of young children, but as discussed earlier in the chapter, there has been more attention recently on other groups, such as older workers and carers.

'Flexible work' is typically seen as work outside the 'standard' arrangements of permanent, fixed daytime work of between 30 and 48 hours a week and working 'on site' (Tomlinson and Gardiner, 2009). Booth and Frank (2005), as cited in Tomlinson and Gardiner (2009), found that only two-fifths of male and female employees have 'standard' jobs in the UK. As a number of writers have argued (see, for example, Lewis, 1997; Liff and Cameron, 1997), the notion of 'standard' work assumes a male model of work characterised by continuous employment with no career breaks. There is, however, a gender dimension, as research indicates that women are less likely to have this linear career model and more likely to work on a casual basis or in part-time contracts, to have career breaks and to work from home. Tomlinson and Gardiner (2009) also argue that there are gender differences in terms of the requests for flexible working. Men typically request 'flexi-time', while women more often request a reduction in hours, be it permanent or temporary.

Existing research alerts us to the dangers of flexible working arrangements, as they often reinforce gendered working patterns rather than challenge them. The rhetoric, therefore, of flexible working assuming more engagement from a wider talent pool, and consequently increased productivity and commitment, may be conflated by the reality of employers using arrangements that suit them and their business, with no real impact on the gendered culture of organisations.

Guest's (1987, 1989) normative model of human resource management (HRM), based on four key dimensions (strategic integration, commitment, flexibility – numerical and functional – and quality) has been criticised in relation to equality. HRM appears to promote equality as the emphasis is on attracting, retaining, and fostering the commitment of the 'best people' for the job, regardless of irrelevant characteristics such as gender or race. The critique focuses on the argument that, in reality, HRM may be a barrier to equality as individuals may foster their own interests, there are power relations at play, and there may be a desire to maintain the status quo of inequality in order to utilise people for the benefit of the organisation. For example, organisations may benefit from a system in which peripheral labour is cheaper and available on demand, with fewer benefits for individuals working at lower levels of the organisation or on casual or fixed-term contracts. Such a system reinforces existing inequalities and horizontal and vertical segregation.

It is also worth noting that the research interests in relation to the development of WLB in China have been increasing. For example, Russell (2008) found that work–life balance has not been seen as a critical issue in most Chinese organisations. It is argued that although there is an emerging acceptance of the value of the flexible working option, many WLB programmes have just been simply adapted from (or are the same as) those already implemented by parent multinational companies (Russell, 2008). Ren and Foster (2013) argued that work rather than family characteristics has a greater impact on work–family conflict for women working in a Chinese airline company. Moreover, the authors highlight the role of the Chinese State when developing and promoting WLB policies and practices (Crompton et al., 2005). Furthermore, Zhang et al. (2013) argued that work-to-family conflict is negatively associated with life-satisfaction among Chinese married couples. Their findings suggest that it is important to examine the work–life interface from a cultural viewpoint, as national cultural values can influence how people perceive their work and family roles. The issue of WLB is still new in China, and there is as yet no law reinforcement from the government. More research needs to be conducted to explore and investigate the WLB policies and practices in the fast developing economy.

In the News Work–life balance support at Colgate-Palmolive

Colgate-Palmolive is a multinational corporation based in New York, dealing in household, healthcare and personal products worldwide. In a Forbes list on the best companies for work–life balance, Colgate-Palmolive was at the top.

The company identifies 'encouraging a healthy balance between work and personal responsibilities' as a priority area for its employees and mentions facilities such as nearby childcare centres; tuition assistance; emergency in-home care for dependents; and health, legal, and financial counselling services as a part of employee compensation and benefits.

With the worldwide economic growth and the tightening of the labour market, companies are exploring new ways to attract and retain top talent. One way to achieve this is by providing a good work–life balance to their employees.

Source: http://www.forbes.com/sites/kathryndill/2014/07/29/the-best-companies-for-work-life-balance/#451b1da16d86.

Mini Case Study Work-life balance in a Swiss university

Suzan, the head of the management department and a 55-year-old Canadian, has been working at a Swiss university with an international reputation for over 20 years. Due to budget-cutting and restructuring activities, Suzan's current main responsibility involves merging the departments of Management with Economics and Social Science into one Business School.

Since this was a public university in Switzerland, the associate professors and professors had secure and permanent positions. Thus, Suzan's proposal to cut down the personnel budget was to reduce the number of the teaching assistants within the departments. All teaching assistants had five-year contracts, and they also needed to undertake their doctoral studies as one of the requirements in their contracts. There were twelve teaching assistants in both departments, and four of them would be finishing their contracts and graduating this summer. Suzan was planning to hire only two new assistants from the coming semester, because she thought the assistants could manage to deliver all seminars across the whole newly merged school. When Suzan announced her plan during the departmental meeting, all teaching assistants and professors strongly opposed it.

The teaching assistants complained that they were highly stressed and exhausted by being overloaded with heavy teaching hours, as well as their PhD research. Two of the assistants had serious burnout last year, and they took three months sick leave. The rest of the assistants had to share their workload. Some of them only had 30-minutes lunch breaks between two seminars, and all of them had to work during weekends to catch up with their PhD studies. Most of them did not use their annual leave last year. They argued that they would be unable to deliver the seminars that Suzan was proposing.

The professors also emphasised that students had been complaining that the assistants just uploaded the solutions online without detailed explanations, and they were not happy with the limited office hours the assistants could offer. The assistants argued that they were unable to deliver quality teaching and research when they were so overloaded.

Suzan could totally empathise with all the problems raised by the assistants, as she had been experiencing similar issues herself over the last few years in terms of feeling overloaded and unable to cope. She was extremely busy with her administrative duties and research tasks, and she had to work overtime nearly every day, including weekends. Her husband had been supportive and he took care of most home issues. Sometimes he joked with Suzan telling her she was married to her job and not him!

Researching WLB initiatives in your country

▸ You can work individually, or work in a group for this exercise.
▸ Are you aware of any legislation in relation to WLB in your home country? If yes, please identify the legislation(s). If no, you can now do some research and find out related legislations.
▸ Analyse the development of the legislations.
▸ Explore the current implementation and impact of the legislations in your country.

THE LEGAL FRAMEWORK

The legal framework has been developing in the area of employment and work practices, and legislation has been a key driver for developing organisational policies on family-friendly policies and, more widely, on WLB. UK legislation has been mostly driven by EU Directives, and a number of legal provisions were significantly extended in April 2003. The UK government introduced a 10-year strategy for childcare in 2004, which included proposals to extend existing statutory provisions on maternity and paternity leave. These provisions resulted in the Work and Families Act 2006, mostly effective from April 2007 onwards.

In May 2011 the UK government launched a consultation on plans to introduce a new system of flexible parental leave and an extension of the right to request flexible working to all employees (BIS 2011). The response to this consultation was published in November 2012 and the measures are being taken forward through the implementation of the Children and Families Act 2014 (Box 15.2).

Continental Europe provides more comprehensive and equitable childcare arrangements than the UK. France, Denmark and Sweden offer publicly funded childcare, which has an effect in increasing female participation rates. The provision of parental leave is higher than in Britain, with three years offered in France, Sweden, and Denmark, and with higher levels of pay. In Norway, a component of parental leave is only available to fathers in order to encourage men to take it up. Bunting (2004)

Box 15.2 Children and Families Act 2014

The Children and Families Act was passed in March 2014 and aims to improve services for children and young people and their families. It makes some big changes to laws about how education, health and social care services must support children and young people with special education needs (SEN) and disabilities, including:

▸ Making sure education, health, and social care services work together to support children and young people with SEN and disabilities.
▸ Making assessments and care planning for those with the most complex needs quicker and more joined up by replacing Statements of SEN with Education Health and Care plans (EHC plans).
▸ More of a focus in the new EHC plans on outcomes and getting ready for adult life. The new EHC plans can go up to age 25 for those who stay in education and have complex needs.
▸ Giving families with an EHC plan more choice and control about the services they access and how the budget for their care is spent.
▸ Making sure children and young people with SEN and disabilities and their families have more of a say about the services they access and about how services are developed locally.
▸ Better information for families about services in their area – such as our Local Offer webpages.

Source: Leeds City Council (2014).

cites a remarkable rise in the take-up rate of this, which increased from a mere 2 per cent in 1990 to 85 per cent in 2000. The author also cites examples from Italy, Spain, and Belgium, where parents have the flexibility to spread out parental leave over a number of years.

EMPLOYEE WELLBEING AND HEALTH

The implications of a long-hours culture in which commitment is often linked to inputs rather than outputs can have a negative effect on employees. As Noon and Blyton (1997) have argued, individual working hours do not always equate to an organisation's operating hours, and more flexibility is demanded to serve a '24/7 society'. There is wide evidence of work intensification over the last couple of decades and of increased levels of stress. Stress is now seen as a common phenomenon in the workplace, with wide-ranging negative implications

for both workers and employers. Studies have indicated that individuals in employment have been suffering from anxiety and have been experiencing work overload, loss of control, and insufficient personal time (Holbeche and McCartney, 2002).

Other writers have argued that employers will occur 'costs of inaction' (see, for example, Liff and Cameron, 1997; Sparrow and Cooper, 2003) if they do not attempt to challenge the long-hours, input-driven work cultures. Some of these costs include poor health, overwork resulting in stress and stress-related illnesses, dissatisfaction, family conflicts, higher absenteeism, lower productivity, and high staff turnover. Existing work cultures implicitly demand that work takes priority over everything else, including family. Bunting (2004), in her book *Willing Slaves: How the Overwork culture Is Ruling Our Lives*, warns about the dangers of the British overwork culture (Box 15.3) and its negative effects on our own health and the health of our children, as well as the negative impact on relationships between parents and their children.

Box 15.3 Working hours: Overly committed or overly stretched?

In 2007 Coats argued that the UK government needed to adopt an interventionist stance and reconsider its position in relation to the EU Working Time Directive (1993) and the UK's Working Time Regulations 1998. Coats contended that the UK government should consider a phased approach to the removal of the opt-out from the 48-hour maximum working week that the EU Working Time Directive advocates. He argued that this initiative was adopted in the Republic of Ireland with no adverse impact on economic growth or employment.

Bunting (2004: 304) argued that, in many European countries, long hours at work are considered as 'a sign of inefficiency or incompetence, rather than of commitment as it is in overwork cultures'. A number of the UK's neighbours, such as Austria, Finland, Spain, and Sweden, have limits of 39- or 40-hour weeks.

Bunting also cited Australia and New Zealand as countries with an 'overwork culture' and stated this is mainly due to the deregulation of the labour market: 'the number of male employees working more than eleven hours a day jumped from one in eighteen to one in eight between 1974 and 1997' (2004: 302).

INTERNATIONAL AND CONTEXTUAL CONSIDERATIONS IN WORK–LIFE BALANCE DEBATES

Throughout the chapter, examples were cited in countries outside the UK, mainly in Europe and in the USA, in relation to their involvement with work and life issues. This section will provide further discussion and some illustrations of key issues in different contexts, including non-Western societies such as Africa, India, and Japan, as well as issues facing employees, including expatriates, in multinational corporations (MNCs) around the world.

Within international HRM research, issues are intertwined with the theories and practices of cross-cultural management and diversity management. As Özbilgin (2005: 164) argues 'the international level, by definition, embodies a greater level of diversity than the national level'. At the international level, Stephens and Black (1991), as cited in Özbilgin (2005), noted the significance of WLB issues in a study of 67 American expatriate managers and argued that recognising the career aspirations of the expatriates' spouses and partners was an important area to consider within international HRM.

Shaffer et al. (2001) explored the impact of perceived organisational support and of work–family conflict on the psychological withdrawal of expatriates and identified that both these factors have a direct effect on their decision to quit international assignments. These two studies highlight the importance of a better understanding of work–family issues and of the needs of family members accompanying expatriates on international assignments. This understanding of and sensitivity to key issues can provide organisations with an important insight into the issues faced by international staff and, in turn, lead to higher chances of the international assignments being successfully completed.

De Cieri and Bardoel (2008), in their study of 13 MNCs, identified key tensions in relation to the management of work–life issues. Participants in their research, mainly human resources and diversity managers, contended that WLB was important for talent management and for developing a high-performing workforce. As the authors state (31): 'Managers and employees are beginning to recognise the strategic role of global work–life policies and practices in managing a global workforce; this presents several challenges for the [human resources] function in MNCs.'

As stated earlier in the chapter, it is important, when engaging with debates on balancing work and personal life, to recognise the diversity of experience in terms of regions, culture and nationality. Lewis et al. (2007) argue, however, that the WLB concept originated in a Western, neoliberal context, particularly in the USA and the UK. This is not to argue that issues and tensions in balancing work and family/personal lives are not universal concerns. However, the context in which one operates should be kept in mind when attempting to understand these concerns, as a model based on a Westernised, developed economy setting, with a reliance on market forces, may not be applicable to a developing, non-Westernised emerging economy. In the latter situation, other issues, such as rapid industrialisation, security, and efforts to maintain traditional family structures may be at play (Box 15.4). Recent work on the negotiated self and work identities of Indian call-centre workers has highlighted WLB tensions and stress for these workers, in the context of global outsourcing (see, for example, Aryee et al., 2005; D'Cruz and Noronha, 2008).

Box 15.4 WLB in non-Western economies

Lewis et al.'s (2007) study of WLB tensions involved interviews with participants in seven countries, including India, South Africa, and Japan. They argue that work intensification is becoming a global phenomenon, in which long hours are equated with commitment in the context of a 'new economy'. The authors cite a participant in a South African country meeting as stating: 'You work long hours, and then you are seen as really making a difference.' An Indian management consultant is also cited as arguing that the long-hours culture 'has become so entrenched…especially in the new economy…we've got to work hard and … literally give up our personal lives' (Lewis et al., 2007: 366). There is increasing attention to work–life balance challenges in Japan, partly due to the context of very low birth rates, and there are on-going debates on how to further engage men in domestic and childcare work. One female participant argued, however, that:

There is a two-tier workforce in Japan. One, which is very highly career orientated, which is described as full-time work and is largely dominated by men. The second is part-time work, which lacks any of the benefits associated with full-time work and is largely dominated by women. [Men] are seen as the breadwinners and they are desperate to get jobs that enable them to provide economically for current or future families. (Lewis et al., 2007: 364)

STOP AND REFLECT

Questions

1 Explore and discuss the real cases regarding to the WLB systems in emerging economies.

2 Compare the main differences between the systems that have been implemented in developed and emerging economies.

CONCLUSION

This chapter has critically reviewed key WLB theories, debates, and pertinent issues. It has been argued that most WLB debates have assumed a naive view of the 'life'

aspect, and this chapter has attempted to provide a more balanced perspective on key issues. It has engaged with changing trends in the workplace, acknowledging the diversity of experiences across social groups and across regions. It has been highlighted throughout that both researchers and managers should be sensitive to this diversity and should not attempt to prescribe a 'one-size-fits-all' approach when offering suggestions and solutions to balancing work and personal life demands.

The chapter reviewed the changing nature of employment in relation to work–life balance issues and flexible working arrangements, examining this through the lens of diversity and looking at gender, age, disability, ethnicity, religion and sexual orientation.

Some areas emerging through the discussions have focused on the dangers of equating commitment and productivity with a long-hours culture, where input is considered as more important than output. The Work Foundation (CIPD, 2003) contends that managers need to shift the way they measure staff, focusing on performance and outputs. A shake-up of the existing organisational cultures and a shift to a more supportive environment, where all individuals are valued irrespective of characteristics such as gender, race, and age, is crucial. In addition, the involvement of human resources as well as line managers in supporting this change and leading by example cannot be overestimated.

Glynn et al. (2002) suggest a range of management skills needed in promoting and managing flexibility, including planning, delegating fairly, understanding the capacity and skills of their staff, and being able to resist pressure from other parts of their organisation when demands are deemed unrealistic. In addition to these skills, there is a need to identify a business case for WLB initiatives, as this should provide organisations and staff with a clear rationale for the benefits to themselves and, in the latter case, their employers. Adapting policies to operational needs, monitoring progress, and highlighting success stories are also positive steps that organisations can take in the quest for a better balance between work and life (whatever form that life may take).

As indicated through international examples, managers should be aware of differences in terms of priorities and perspectives in different regions across the world. An understanding of socioeconomic, political, and cultural settings is fundamental in devising and implementing appropriate WLB policies that employers and employees can embrace and benefit from.

End of Chapter Case Study Work and wellbeing in a Chinese multinational

It was another hot, humid and smoggy day in Beijing, and Ailing was waiting for the company shuttle bus to go to work. She had stopped hoping for better weather at least three weeks ago. Ailing was a 42-year-old Chinese woman with a teenage son, and she had been working in a state-owned multinational energy company for more than 14 years. Her husband also worked in the same company, and he had been working as an expatriate in Sudan over the last five years. Before moving to the human resource (HR) department, Ailing had worked in the marketing department and was responsible for public relations. Her main responsibility was to act as a consultant in communication matters. Due to restructuring activities in the company, Ailing had been assigned to the HR team as a manager five years ago. She had a bachelor's degree in business management. She was also doing an MBA degree in human resource management in one of the top universities in Beijing during weekends, in order to keep her knowledge up to date. The new task of the HR team was to update the work–life balance (WLB) system throughout the organisation in China.

It was not only the weather that got to Ailing but also the fact that many things would be changing within the HR department in the next few months. She did not have time to sit in the employee canteen and to enjoy the free breakfast buffet provided by the company. She ordered an egg sandwich and a cup of green tea for take-away and quickly finished her breakfast while going through all her work emails.

The main purposes of creating and establishing a WLB system were to develop and promote a healthy working environment, as well as positive employee relations. Ailing and her team members had been working on the system over the past two years. By learning from other Western multinational competitors, Ailing's company had also developed various programmes to support total quality of life for their employees. For example, apart from providing free company shuttle bus and free meals at their staff canteen, the company also rented a fully equipped sport centre every Sunday morning. All employees, as well as two of their family members could access all the facilities at that time. Moreover, vouchers for cinemas and bookshops were also generously provided for employees every six months.

Ironically, Ailing, the HR manager who developed these programmes, was too busy to take advantage of all these wellness benefits herself. The only programme she could benefit from was the tuition and education support, as her MBA study was fully reimbursed by the company. In addition, since her husband worked as an expatriate, their son's tuition fee for a private bilingual boarding school had also been partially paid by the company. Ailing and her husband were planning to send their son to study in the USA for his Bachelor's and Master's degrees, and both of them had to work hard in order to have enough put aside. Although the company would also reimburse the fees of higher education for their son, the living expenses in the United States were still much higher than in Beijing.

Ailing's son could only come home during weekends, when she had to attend lectures in the university. The only periods Ailing could spend with her son were Friday and Saturday evenings, then she had to drive him back to the school which was outside the city every Sunday afternoon. Due to the time difference, she was only able to have short video chats with her husband in the evenings while he was taking his lunch breaks in Sudan. She couldn't help feeling guilty, though, for missing out on her son's and husband's everyday lives. Ailing herself, always felt stressed and frustrated, as she had few people to talk to. She loved her job, she knew she was really good at it, and she prided herself in being known as professional and reliable. She wanted to progress further within her organisation but constantly felt guilty about not spending enough time with her family. Her husband often said he felt the same way but this was the way it had to be if they wanted to provide the best for them and their son.

A new email just popped into her computer screen. It was about the gala dinner next Friday night for the middle and senior managers in the company. She really didn't have the energy to attend, and it would be one of the few nights she could spend with her son. In addition, as a Muslim woman, Ailing did not feel very comfortable when there was alcohol around, and at these functions people tended to drink a lot. Most of her colleagues were aware of Ailing's religion, but she always felt they wouldn't be willing to change their habits just because she was there. This was also a key reason Ailing did not normally eat in the staff canteen, as there was no halal food and only a few vegetarian options. Despite all these thoughts in her mind, she still accepted the invitation to the gala dinner. She didn't want to be perceived as an outsider.

Questions

1   What are the main issues Ailing is facing at work and at home?
2   Do you think Ailing is receiving enough support from her company?
3   How could she better balance her work and personal life demands?
4   Could the nature of her job have an impact on Ailing's relationship with her husband and son? In what ways?
5   Could there be any cultural/religious elements that readers need to be sensitive to when offering their suggestions?

FOR DISCUSSION AND REVISION

1   What areas do WLB debates seem to be focusing on?
2   Would you consider this to be limiting? If so, in what way?
3   What can be the costs of an 'overwork' culture to both employees and organisations?
4   What key legislation can you cite that protects social groups from discrimination?
5   What legislation can you cite in relation to employment and work and life?
6   Highlight key differences in how employers and employees may be dealing with WLB in different regions. Think of examples in the Western, developed economies and also in non-Western, emerging markets.
7   If you were a senior human resources manager in an MNC who has been transferred to the Chinese office, how would you attempt to implement the flexible working arrangements and family-friendly policies designed at the parent company? What issues would you need to consider?

GLOSSARY

Diversity: It is important to acknowledge that diverse employees (in terms of social group but also individual differences) may have different work–life balance needs.

Employee wellbeing: Linked to being happy, healthy, and satisfied at work; and these factors are said to be influenced by workplace interventions. In reality it is hard to separate wellbeing at work and wellbeing outside of work as one's overall health and wellbeing are also heavily determined by external, non-work factors.

Family-friendly policies: Organisational policies that focus on supporting employees who are also carers (to young children, elderly parents, disabled family members, etc.). It has been argued however that 'family friendliness' should be a subset of work–life balance, as everyone and not just carers need to balance work and non-work lives.

Flexible working: Forms of working that allow for flexibility in terms of hours of work, type of work, location of work, etc. Some definitions include benefits such as workplace crèches, childcare vouchers, career breaks, etc.

Work–life balance: A concept that implies or assumes a comfortable equilibrium between our work and personal lives. In reality, these two spheres overlap, and it is often challenging to achieve a balance between work and life outside work.

FURTHER READING

Books

BURKE, R. J. AND COOPER, C. L. (2008) *The Long Hours Culture: Causes, Consequences and Choices*. Bingley: Emerald Group.

An edited collection of chapters on key issues of WLB, divided into three sections of causes, consequences, and choices.

CIPD (Chartered Institute of Personnel and Development) (2000) *Getting the Right Work–Life Balance*. London: CIPD.
This research report by M. Coussey from the University of Cambridge engages with a number of real-life case studies focusing on work and life and family-friendly practices.

FELSTEAD, A. AND JEWSON, N. (1999) *Global Trends in Flexible Labour*. London: Macmillan Business.
An edited book with chapters from numerous authors on flexible work and non-standard forms of employment. It includes discussions and research from European countries, such as Germany, Spain, Sweden, and the UK.

HEERY, E. AND SALMON, J. (2000) *The Insecure Workforce*. London: Routledge.
An edited collection of chapters focusing on the 'insecurity thesis' and looking at this in a variety of contexts, such as the public sector, 'gendered employment', the psychological contract, trade unions, and so on.

HOUSTON, D. M. (2005) *Work–Life Balance in the 21st Century*. Basingstoke: Palgrave Macmillan.
An edited collection of chapters on a wide range of WLB issues including gender, careers, fatherhood, job insecurity, ethnicity, and organisational cultures.

WEB RESOURCES

Readers are also encouraged to utilise the following relevant websites that provide numerous articles, statistics and information on WLB issues:

The Chartered Institute of Personnel and Development (CIPD): www.cipd.co.uk.

The Equality and Human Rights Commission (EHRC): http://www.equalityhumanrights.com/.

The HRM guide: http://www.hrmguide.co.uk/.

REFERENCES

American Psychological Association (2005) *Lesbian and Gay Parenting*. Washington: APA.

ARYEE, S., SRINIVAS, E. S. AND TAN, H. H. (2005) Rhythms of life: Antecedents and outcomes of work–family balance in employed parents. *Journal of Applied Psychology*, 90(1): 132–146.

BEDDOES, K. AND PAWLEY, A. L. (2014) 'Different people have difference priorities': Work–family balance, gender, and the discourse of choice, *Studies in Higher Education*, 39(9): 1573–1585.

BELL, E. L. (1986) The power within: Bicultural life structures and stress among black women. Unpublished PhD dissertation, Case Western Reserve University.

BELL, E. L., DENTON, T. C. AND NKOMO, S. (1993) Women of color in management: Towards an inclusive analysis. In Larwood, L. and Gutek, B. (eds), *Women in Management: Trends, Issues, and Challenges in Managerial Diversity*. CA: Sage.

BHOPAL, K. (1997) *Gender, 'Race' and Patriarchy: A Study of South Asian Women*. Farnham: Ashgate.

BIS (2011) Consultation on Modern Workplace. BIS.

BOLTON, S. C. AND WIBBERLEY, G. (2007) Best companies, best practice and dignity at work. In Bolton, S. C. (ed.), *Dimensions of Dignity at Work*. Burlington: Butterworth-Heinemann, pp. 134–153.

BOOTH, A. L. AND FRANK, J. (2005) Gender and work–life flexibility in the labour market. In Houston, D. M. (ed.), *Work–Life Balance in the 21st Century*. Basingstoke: Palgrave Macmillan, pp. 11–28.

BRADLEY, H., HEALY, G. AND MUKHERJEE, N. (2005) Multiple burdens: Problems of work–life balance for ethnic minority trade union activist women. In Houston, D. (ed.), *Work–Life Balance in the 21st Century*. Basingstoke: Palgrave Macmillan, pp. 211–229.

BUNTING, M. (2004) *Willing Slaves: How the Overwork Culture Is Ruling Our Lives*. London: HarperCollins.

CARBY, H. V. (1982) White women listen! Black feminism and the boundaries of sisterhood. In Centre for Contemporary Cultural Studies. *The Empire Strikes Back: Race and Racism in 70s Britain*. London: Hutchinson, pp. 212–235.

CIPD (2003) Managers obstruct flexibility. *People Management*, 9(18): 9.

CLARKE, L. AND O'BRIEN, M. (2003) Father involvement in Britain: The research and policy evidence. In Day, R. and Lamb, M. (eds), *Reconceptualising and Measuring Fatherhood*. Mahwah, NJ: Lawrence Erlbaum, pp. 34–52.

COATS, D. (2007) Respect at work: Just how good are British workplaces? In Bolton, S. C. (ed.), *Dimensions of Dignity at Work*. Burlington: Butterworth-Heinemann, pp. 53–70.

COLLINSON, D., KNIGHTS, D. AND COLLINSON, M. (1990) *Managing to Discriminate*. London: Routledge.

CROMPTON, R., BROCKMANN, M. AND LYONETTE, C., (2005) Attitudes, women's employment and the domestic division of labour: A cross-national analysis in two waves. *Work, Employment and Society*, 19(2): 213–234.

CROMPTON, R. AND LYONNETTE, C. (2009) Partners' relative earnings and the domestic division of labour. Paper presented at the Gender Inequalities in the 21st Century conference, Queen's College, Cambridge, 26–27 March.

DALE, A. (2005) Combining family and employment: Evidence from Pakistani and Bangladeshi women. In Houston, D. (ed.), *Work–Life Balance in the 21st Century*. Basingstoke: Palgrave Macmillan, pp. 230–245.

DAVIDSON, M. J. (1997) *The Black and Ethnic Minority Woman Manager: Cracking the Concrete Ceiling*. London: Paul Chapman.

D'CRUZ, P. AND NORONHA, E. (2008) Doing emotional labour: The experiences of Indian call centre agents. *Global Business Review*, 9: 131–147.

DE CIERI, H. AND BARDOEL, E. A. (2008) Tensions for HR: Who takes responsibility for work–life management in multinational corporations? Final Report to the Society for Human Resource Management (SHRM) Research Foundation. Based on a paper presented to the Academy of International Business Annual Conference, June 30–July 4, Milan, Italy.

DENTON, T. C. (1990) Bonding and supportive relationships among black professional women: Rituals of restoration. *Journal of Organizational Behavior*, 11: 447–457.

DEVINE, F. (1994) Segregation and supply: Preferences and plans among 'self-made' women. *Gender, Work and Organization*, 1(2): 94–109.

DIECKHOFF, M. AND GALLIE, D. (2007) The renewed Lisbon strategy and social inclusion policy. *Industrial Relations Journal*, 38(6): 480–502.

DUNCAN, S. AND IRWIN, S. (2004) The social patterning of values and rationalities: mothers' choices in combining caring and employment. *Social Policy and Society*, 3(4): 391–399.

Equality and Human Rights Commission (2009) Fathers struggling to balance work and family: Working dads want more time with their children. Available at: http://www.wired-gov.net/wg/wg-news-1.nsf/0/B82B5A1686C97C9680257655005A2729?OpenDocument. Accessed 18 February 2016.

EVETTS, J. (2000) Analysing change in women's careers: Culture, structure and action dimensions. *Gender, Work and Organization*, 7(1): 57–67.

FEATHERSTONE, B. (2003) Taking fathers seriously. *British Journal of Social Work*, 33: 239–254.

Forbes (2015) The best companies for work–life balance. Available at: <http://www.forbes.com/sites/kathryndill/2015/07/17/the-best-companies-for-work-life-balance-2/. >. Accessed November 2015.

GARDINER, J. (1997) *Gender, Care and Economics*, Basingstoke: Macmillan.

GARDINER, J., STUART, M., FORDE, C., GREENWOOD, I., MACKENZIE, R. AND PERRETT, R. (2007) Work–life balance and older workers: Employees' perspectives on retirement transitions following redundancy. *International Journal of Human Resource Management*, 18(3): 476–489.

GINN, J., ARBER, S., BRANNEN, J., DALE, A., DEX, S., ELIAS, P. et al. (1996) Feminist fallacies: A reply to Hakim on women's employment. *British Journal of Sociology*, 47(1): 167–174.

GLYNN, C., STEINBERG, I. AND MCCARTNEY, C. (2002) *Work–Life Balance: The Role of the Manager*. Horsham: Roffey Park Institute.

GREAT Initiative and Plan UK (2015) One year down the road, the impact of the International Development (Gender Equality) Act 2014. The GREAT Initiative and Plan UK, May 2015.

GUEST, D. E. (1987) Human resource management and industrial relations. *Journal of Management Studies*, 24(5): 503–521.

GUEST, D. E. (1989) Personnel and HRM: Can you tell the difference? *Personnel Management*, January: 48–51.

HAKIM, C. (1991) Grateful slaves and self-made women: Fact and fantasy in women's work orientations. *European Social Review*, 7(2): 102–121.

HAKIM, C. (1995) Five feminist myths about women's employment. *British Journal of Sociology*, 46(3): 429–455.

HAKIM, C. (2004) *Key Issues in Women's Work: Female Diversity and the Polarisation of Women's Employment*. London: Glass House Press.

HAKIM, C. (2008). Is gender equality legislation becoming counter-productive? *Public Police Research*, September–November: 133–136.

HEALY, G., BRADLEY, J. AND MUKHERJEE, N. (2004) Inspiring union women – black and minority ethnic women in trade unions. In Healy, G., Heery, E., Taylor, P. and Brown, W. (eds), *The Future of Worker Representation*. London: Palgrave, pp. 103–126.

HERMAN, C., LEWIS, S. AND HUMBERT A. L. (2013) Women scientists and engineers in European companies: Putting the motherhood under the microscope. *Gender, Work and Organization*, 20(5): 467–478.

HOGARTH, T., HASLUCK, C., PIERRE, G. WINTERBOTHAM, M. AND VIVIAN, D. (2001) *Work–Life Balance 2000: Results from the Baseline Study*. Norwich: Department of Education and Employment Institute for Employment Research with IFF Research.

HOLBECHE, L. AND MCCARTNEY, C. (2002) *The Park Management Agenda*. Horsham: Roffey Park Institute.

HOWENSTINE, D. W. (2006) Beyond rational relations: The constitutional infirmities of anti-gay partnership laws under the equal protection clause. *Washington Law Review*, 81(2): 417–446.

KAMENOU, N. (2002) Ethnic minority women in English organisations: Career experiences and opportunities. Unpublished PhD thesis, Leeds University Business School, University of Leeds.

KAMENOU, N. (2008) Reconsidering work–life balance debates: Challenging limited understandings of the 'life' component in the context of ethnic minority women's experiences. *British Journal of Management*, Special Issue on Gender in Management: New Theoretical Perspectives, 19(S1): S99–109.

KAN, M. (2001) *Gender Asymmetry in the Division of Domestic Labour. Who Does the Housework?* Report. Colchester: University of Essex Institute for Social and Economic Research.

LAMB, M. (2009) Mothers, fathers, or parents at home and at work. Paper presented at the Gender Inequalities in the 21st Century conference, Queen's College, Cambridge, 26–27 March.

Leeds City Council (2014) Children and Families Act 2014. Available at: http://www.leeds.gov.uk/residents/Pages/Children-and-Families-Act.aspx. Accessed November 2015.

LEWIS, S. (1997) 'Family friendly' employment policies: A route to changing organizational cultures or playing about at the margins? *Gender, Work and Organization*, 4(1): 13–23.

LEWIS, S., GAMBLES, R. AND RAPOPORT, R. (2007) The constraints of a work–life balance approach: An international perspective. *International Journal of Human Resource Management*, 18(3): 360–373.

LIFF, S. AND CAMERON, I. (1997) Changing equality cultures to move beyond 'women's problems'. *Gender, Work and Organization*, 4(1): 35–46.

MCRAE, S. (2003) Choice and constraints in mothers' employment careers: McRae replies to Hakim. *British Journal of Sociology*, 54(4): 585–592.

NOON, M. AND BLYTON, P. (1997) *The Realities of Work*. London: Macmillan Business.

ÖZBILGIN, M. (2005) *International Human Resource Management: Theory and Practice*. London: Palgrave Macmillan.

PLATMAN, K. (2002) Matured assets. *People Management*, 8(24): 40–42.

PINKER, S. (2008) *The sexual paradox: Men, women and the real gender gap*. New York: Scribner.

RANA, B. K., KAGAN, C., LEWIS, S. AND ROUT, U. (1998) British South Asian women managers and professionals: Experiences of work and family. *Women in Management Review*, 13(6): 221–232.

REN, X. AND FOSTER, D. (2013) Women's experiences of work and family conflict in a Chinese airline. *Asia Pacific Business Review*, 17(3): 325–341.

RUSSELL, G. (2008) *Work and Life in China*. Chestnut Hill, MA: Boston College Centre for Work and Family.

SARGEANT, M. (2009) Age discrimination, sexual orientation and gender identity: UK/US perspectives. *Equal Opportunities International*, 28(8): 634–645.

SHAFFER, M. A., HARRISON, D. A., GILLEY, K. M. AND LUK, D. M. (2001) Struggling for balance amid turbulence on international assignments: Work–family conflict, support and commitment. *Journal of Management*, 27(1, January–February): 99–121.

SLAUGHTER, A.-M. (2012) Why women still can't have it all. *The Atlantic*, June 13. Available at: www.theatlantic.com/magazine/archive/2012/07/why-women-still-cant-have-it-all/309020. Accessed 10 March 2015.

SPARROW, P. R. AND COOPER, C. L. (2003) *The Employment Relationship: Key Challenges for HR*. Oxford: Butterworth-Heinemann.

STEPHENS, G. K. AND BLACK, S. (1991) The impact of spouse's career orientation on managers during international transfers. *Journal of Management Studies*, 28: 417–428.

SULLIVAN, C. (2015) 'Bad Mum Guilt': The representation of 'work–life balance' in UK women's magazines. *Community, Work and Family*, 18(3): 284–298.

SYED, J. AND MURRAY, P. (2009) Combating the English language deficit: The labour market experiences of migrant women in Australia. *Human Resource Management Journal*, 19(4): 413–432.

TAYLOR, R. (2002) *The Future of Work–Life Balance*. Swindon: Economic and Social Research Council.

THOMAS, D. A. AND ALDEFER, C. P. (1989) The influence of race on career dynamics: Theory and research on minority career experiences. In Arthur, M., Hall, D. T. and Lawrence, B. S. (eds), *Handbook of Career Theory*. Port Hope, ON: Cambridge University Press, pp. 133–158.

TOMLINSON, J. AND GARDINER, J. (2009) Organisational approaches to flexible working: Perspectives of equality and diversity managers in the UK. *Equal Opportunities International*, 28(8): 671–686.

TORRINGTON, D., HALL, L. AND TAYLOR, S. (2008) *Human Resource Management*. Harlow: Prentice Hall.

WALBY, S. (1983) Patriarchal structures: The case of unemployment. In Gamarnikow, E., Morgan, D., Purvis, J. and Taylorson, D. (eds), *Gender, Class and Work*. London: Heinemann.

WALBY, S. (1986) *Patriarchy at Work*. Oxford: Polity Press.

WOODHAMS, C. AND DANIELI, A. (2000) Disability and diversity – a difference too far? *Personnel Review*, 29(3): 402–17.

ZHANG, M., FORLEY, S. AND YANG, B. (2013) Work–family conflict among Chinese married couples: Testing spillover and crossover effects. *International Journal of Human Resource Management*, 24(17): 3213–3231.

MANAGING GLOBAL AND MIGRANT WORKERS

Chris Brewster, Michael Dickmann, Liisa Mäkelä, and Vesa Suutari

LEARNING OUTCOMES

After reading this chapter, you should be able to:

➤ understand the different forms of international work
➤ be familiar with benefits and problems involved with each type of international work both from an individual and an organisational perspective
➤ understand the issues involved in the management of different types of international work within international organisations.

SUMMARY OF CHAPTER CONTENTS

➤ **Opening Case Study**: Cool International
➤ Introduction
➤ International business travel
➤ Short-term assignments
➤ Assigned expatriates
➤ Self-initiated expatriates
➤ Global careerists
➤ Migrant workers
➤ Global work and the use of knowledge and networks
➤ Work-life balance related issues facing expatriates
➤ Conclusion
➤ **End of Chapter Case Study**: Management of short-term project mobility within a Finnish company
➤ Glossary
➤ Further reading
➤ Web resources
➤ References

The international workforce has existed since slaves built the pyramids. But international work has been increasing substantially in recent decades. With it, the interest in how to manage international workers, their talent and global careers has grown. In this chapter we are exploring key forms of international work. We use the length of international assignment as our template and concentrate on international business travellers (IBTs); short-term assignees, company-sponsored long-term expatriates (AEs), self-initiated expatriates (SIEs) and global careerists. We also discuss immigration related mobility of labour. Throughout the text we will investigate contextual, strategic, operational and individual influences and will put a particular focus on how organisations can manage their international workers.

Opening Case Study **Cool International**

Cool International is a UK-based multinational that has expanded rapidly into European, Asian, and South American markets over the past two decades through acquisitions and joint ventures. Their global strategy envisaged a rapid growth in the BRIC countries – Brazil, Russia, India, China – as well as other emerging markets. As a result, the character of the company was fundamentally altered, and it now has far more business by turnover and profit from international activities than in the UK.

Due to the very rapid growth in the pace of internationalisation, shortages of international managers emerged as a significant problem. The implementation of the global strategy was increasingly constrained by these shortages which threatened corporate efforts to expand abroad. As a result the company undertook a strategic review of the requirements of resourcing key positions in international operations. This review suggested that the company should shift away from a reliance on traditional expatriate assignments and towards a more flexible form of resourcing international assignments through the introduction of shorter-term assignments, international commuter assignments (staff commute from home base while family remains at home), and international business travel [see below for details of these forms of international work]. Increased localisation and the establishment of a truly global talent management approach were also considered.

The changes in their global mobility approach were broadly successful and facilitated the company's continued global expansion, and the contribution of international operations to revenues continues to expand. Corporate executives indicate that they feel this success would have been constrained without the introduction of more flexible international staffing arrangements. However, the key problem that Cool International encountered was not related to these workers but to their difficulties in encouraging their managers to accept traditional, long-term foreign assignments. One former expatriate – returning from Rio de Janeiro – put a potential problem into words: 'When I returned, people asked me "How was it on the beach?" And I had worked so hard in Brazil. Now, it seems, I have to prove to my new colleagues and my new boss that this was not just a "jolly". I feel that my career chances have definitely taken a turn for the worse.'

Questions

1   More flexible international staffing may save the company money. Are there any downsides?
2   Why do you think the issues arose with the traditional long-term expatriates?
3   How should the company handle returning expatriates to make them feel that their time abroad has been valued?

INTRODUCTION

International work appears in many different forms within international organisations. Due to the globalisation of business life, increasing numbers of professionals and managers have international responsibilities requiring international travel or work in foreign affiliates of multinational enterprises (MNEs) for shorter or longer periods of time. International organisations need to manage, coordinate, and integrate their activities across borders, transfer knowledge and best practices between units and across borders, and serve customers across the world. At the same time, job markets are becoming increasingly international due to increased mobility of individuals. Professionals are increasingly internationally oriented due to their international travel, study exchanges, and job experiences abroad. Thus, international job markets may offer increasingly interesting job options for many looking for new experiences and development opportunities in an international environment. In many economies, there are also reports of

increasing need for migrant workers, in the context of skill shortages, aging population, and decreasing fertility rates (Al Ariss and Özbilgin, 2010). Thus international work appears in many different forms across different organisational levels, and organisations increasingly utilise international, mobile workforces in their staffing. In the light of these developments, we will next discuss different forms of international work and the management of these different types of individuals within organisations. We will start by looking at international business travel as an important and currently under-researched phenomenon.

INTERNATIONAL BUSINESS TRAVEL

International business travel has increased substantially during the past few decades due to geographically expanded markets and business networks and increases in multinational companies with subsidiaries and globally dispersed projects (Gustafsson, 2012) – facilitated by technological capability increases in the air transport industry. Though technical solutions such as web conferences and online meetings make communication without the need to be physically present possible, meeting people in person is important for trust creation, relationship building, and the enhanced transfer of tacit knowledge. Advanced transportation connections around the globe have enabled international business travel to increase (Collings, Scullion, and Morley, 2007; Faulconbridge and Beaverstock, 2008; Ramsey et al., 2011), perhaps partly replacing the traditional multiyear assignments abroad. The objective is to provide cost control for companies and varied career opportunities for employees, since it is argued that there may be a reluctance to expatriate (Gripenberg et al., 2013). International business travellers (IBTs) have become an important and increasing part of the international workforce, with their work involving continual visits to foreign markets, units, and projects abroad. The duration of their visits ranges from days to weeks depending on the task required of them (Welch, Welch and Worm, 2007).

According to reports focusing on business travel trends in the USA, significant increases in international outbound travel were expected involving many millions of dollars (Global Business Travel Association, 2014) a pattern expected to be replicated around the world (Travel and Tourism Council, 2014). There remains an un-researched, perhaps un-researchable, question about whether this is money well spent. Business travel may not reduce costs as much as anticipated: the costs of the travel, hotels, entertaining, etc., is high in itself. Costs are transferred from central expatriation budgets to decentralised line or project budgets, so comparisons are not easy. Of all forms of international experience, HRM departments have least control over business travel (Brewster, Harris and Petrovic, 2001). And the benefits side of the equation is even more difficult to assess. Do these managers and specialists act as a sort of 'flying glue', passing messages between parts of the organisation and helping it to work effectively, or are they a set of mavericks, flying into contexts they don't understand, making decisions in circumstances that they cannot fully appreciate, and leaving the locals to 'mop up' after they have flown out? Because of the costs and the benefits, managing international business travel is important (Welch et al., 2007), but the amount of empirical research on international business travellers from a human resource management perspective remains severely limited (Collings et al., 2007; McKenna and Richardson, 2007).

So far, the studies that we have on international business travelling can be divided into two main categories, one focusing on the organisational perspective and travel management and another examining the travellers themselves (Gustafsson, 2012). When business travel has been studied from the perspective of the organisation, it has mostly adopted the concept of 'travel management', studying the organisation's policies and regulations concerning business travel (Holma, 2012). Research related to the employees who do international business travelling as a part of their job has mainly been conducted within the field of travel medicine, focusing on physical or psychological disorders of travellers caused by travelling (Patel, 2011).

For companies, managing international business travelling is not an easy task since it involves different stakeholders (e.g. travellers, travel managers, decision-makers, suppliers, and travel agencies) with different interests. The main purpose of 'travel management' in companies is clearly economic: to control and reduce the costs of travels (Holma, 2009). Studies focusing on travel management have examined compliance with corporate travel policies (Douglas and Lubbe, 2009), stakeholder values and preferences relating to the travel management process (Gustafsson, 2012), corporate travel as a purchasing operation (Holma, 2012) and environmental aspects of travel (Hoyer and Næss, 2001). A subsidiary objective for company travel management departments is to ensure the security of business travellers and decent working conditions for them. That is important as their job involves IBTs spending a lot of time in airplanes and airports, working long hours, and undertaking complex tasks, often in challenging or even dangerous environments.

One essential job demand is the intensity of travelling, in particular, how often one needs to travel and how long the trips last (Burkholder et al., 2010; Mäkelä et al., 2014). Studies have provided evidence that increasing the frequency and duration of trips increases the risk of ill health among travellers, linked with such symptoms as increased alcohol consumption, sleep deprivation, and feelings of insecurity about the traveller's ability to keep pace with the workload (Burkholder et al., 2010). Earlier research showed that increased trip frequency and/or duration is related to dissatisfaction with travelling, greater stress, work–family conflict, and problems maintaining social networks (Jensen, 2013; Mäkelä, Bergbom, Tanskanen and Kinnunen, 2014; Mäkelä, Kinnunen and Suutari, 2015; Mäkelä, Bergbom, Saarenpä and Suutari, 2015; Westman, Etzion, and Chen, 2008). Very frequent international business trips also have a negative effect on the well-being of travellers' families (Espino et al., 2002). Moreover, there are job demands related to the risks involved in working in different locations around the globe that can jeopardise IBTs' wellbeing: including health and safety issues, changing time zones (jet lag), and stress caused by use of a foreign language (Badera and Berg, 2014; Ivancevich et al.,

2003). In addition to all that, the greater the climatic and cultural contrast between the traveller's country of origin and the travel destination, the greater is the risk of illness (Patel, 2011). Beside these very concrete job demands, psychological demands are important and, for instance, the pressures of planning the trip, trip logistics, health concerns, and cultural issues are found to create stress for the business traveller (DeFrank et al., 2000).

Researchers have also identified positive factors related to international business trips including, for instance, variety of tasks, life-style, personal development (Demel and Mayrhofer, 2010; Welch, Welch and Worm, 2007) and possibilities for respite (Westman and Etzion, 2002).

The importance of the support gained from organisation during the business travel has been recognised (Collings et al., 2007; Harvey et al., 2010; Mayerhofer et al., 2004). Among the studies focusing on the consequences of international business travel for individual IBTs, there are some crucial organisational aspects. First, control over travel, that is, employees' ability to decide when they travel and how much they travel, has been found to be negatively related to burnout and work-to-family conflict (Jensen, 2013). Another job resource is organisations' restitution culture, which refers to organisations' attitudes to the employees' need for rest after long periods of travelling and whether they are willing to accept, for instance, flexibility in working hours. A restitution culture reported being negatively related to both burnout and work-to-family conflict (Jensen, 2013).

STOP AND REFLECT

Questions

1 Would you want to be a frequent business traveller?

2 How do you weigh the excitement, the interest sense of importance, and the expense account against the stress, the health issues and the risks?

3 How long do you think it is possible for someone to be a frequent international business traveller?

SHORT-TERM ASSIGNMENTS

Another area that has been around as long as international business has existed, but that appears to be growing, is short-term assignments, usually defined as assignments that last between a month and a year (Collings, Scullion and Morley, 2007: Tahvanainen, Welch and Worm, 2005) but in most cases lasting much less than that, anything from a few weeks to six months. In most countries, assignments of more than six months require a local contract

in the host country (with associated tax implications). Absence from the country for less than six months means that people stay in the taxation, social security, and pensions systems of their home base, so such assignments are much simpler to administer (Tahvanainen, 2003).

Salt and Wood (2012) summarise the evidence about the trends in short-term assignments. They cite a series of consultancy reports that indicate the desire on the part of their clients to increase the amount of short-term assignments and some academic authors who have claimed that it is growing (Collings, et al., 2007; Fenwick 2004; Mayrhofer, Sparrow and Zimmermann, 2008; Minbaeva and Michailova 2004). As good academics, however, they point out that this evidence is thin – we have no real baseline to start measuring from and little solid data to show any growth. Nor is there much evidence about variations between MNEs, or between host locations, or between established and new production centres or markets, which require different strategies for each. We note, too, that there is little evidence about the variation between types of short-term assignments (Suutari et al., 2013).

Easier and cheaper travel and improvements in communications technology have made the option of short-term assignments more feasible in recent years and, as with the use of the other cheaper, non-standard forms of international experience, the economic crisis that began in 2008 has undoubtedly added to the pressure to use of short-term assignments. In some cases the roles that such assignments play are the same as those played by long-term expatriation: to fill immediate gaps in the labour force until someone more permanent can take over, for example. However they are less likely to be about co-ordination and control and perhaps more likely to be about training and development (Jie and Lang, 2009). Where such assignments bring short-term expatriates into the headquarters operation for this purpose, they are sometimes referred to, from an ethnocentric perspective, as in-patriates (Cerdin and Sharma, 2014; Reiche, Kraimer and Harzing, 2009) Short-term assignments may be used to help build new international markets (Findlay et al., 2000; Millar and Salt, 2006). Short-term assignments can offer access to specialised talent in other countries (Hocking, Brown and Harzing, 2004; Minbaeva and Michailova, 2004) and/ or can be used as training assignments to develop specific knowledge and skills in the transferees (Salt and Wood, 2012: 439).

A frequent use of short-term assignments is by organisations that operate on a project basis (Suutari et al., 2013). It has been argued that project assignments came to prominence in the 1970s when the oil and gas industries sent engineers to build refineries and wellheads. Today, such short-term assignments are widely used by industries such as construction, consulting and IT. They are typically characterised by the assignees' technical skills and the limited duration of assignments. The assignment is seen as part of getting the project completed and hence is controlled by the project manager and not by the HRM department (Brewster, Harris and Petrovic, 2001), and is usually classified in the organisation as distinct from standard expatriation assignments.

Compared to the standard expatriate, short-term assignees are more likely to be recruited from outside the organisation, more likely to leave their families at home, more likely to have their salary paid on an 'at home' basis (plus expenses) and less likely to receive generous benefits (Starr and Currie, 2009). Otherwise, they may not be so different: the host country will invariably treat the short-term assignee like an expatriate, requiring visas and immigration documents, in some cases imposing tax obligations, and often restricting his or her activities in various ways (Suutari et al., 2013).

There are obvious advantages for the organisation in having this cheaper, more focused and more flexible resource. The downsides are limited and only operate in certain circumstances: for example, difficulties in building up effective relationships with local employees and customers (Tahvanainen et al., 2005) may be irrelevant to someone doing a highly technical job or only there to learn about an aspect of the business. For the expatriates too there are advantages: the chance to learn with less commitment than a long-term assignment, a quick burst of improved income with little chance for them to spend it, and the satisfaction of contributing to the completion of a project. On the other hand, they experience many of the same problems that occur with long-term standard expatriation: short notice of the move, little preparation, plus, in this case, separation from the family, which may only be for a few months but even so can create strains (Starr, 2009). In addition, the short-term assignee has little opportunity to get 'into' the local community, often ends up working long hours, and may find the time of work lonely and depressing.

ASSIGNED EXPATRIATES

Long-term assigned expatriates (AEs) are supported by their employers to legally work in a country outside their country-of-origin generally for a duration of more than one year (Andresen et al., 2012. Research on AEs has been at the centre of academic attention for several decades (Adler, 1984; Black et al., 1991; Brewster and Scullion, 1997; Edström and Galbraith, 1977; Harvey, 1989) and the number of AEs is increasing over time (Brookfield, 2014; RES-Forum, 2014). A multitude of topics have been explored, including (but not restricted to) demographics, personality, gender, location, remuneration, benefits, tax and social

security issues, legal and labour law context, motivations to go, selection, cross-cultural adjustment, health and wellbeing, hostile environments, host teams and wider host country context, training and development, global careers, performance (including return on investment and broader company benefits), repatriation and retention. The most common perspectives were organisational or individual, at times investigated using a dual dependency approach (Larsen, 2004). In this section we investigate the management of international workers so that the expatriate cycle (Sparrow, Brewster and Harris, 2004) – distinguishing a pre-selection, international work, and return phase – is a useful concept to structure our discussion. We will start by exploring strategic and motivational aspects in the pre-selection stage.

There are a multitude of reasons why expatriates are sent by their organisations to their international assignments. These include controlling the MNEs' foreign subsidiaries, coordinating softer aspects such as organisational culture, developing (and testing) the potential global leaders of the future, or simply providing expertise and staffing a position when this does not seem possible from the local labour market (Edström and Galbraith, 1977). More recently, drivers such as knowledge transfer, innovation, and broader global talent management have become more prominent (Cerdin and Brewster, 2014; Collings, 2014). Key is that organisations are conscious about what the primary driver of a particular assignment is in order to shape their approaches to selection, remuneration, development, careers, and retention. Sending an individual to a country to fill a skills gap, or 'fire-fighting' as it is sometimes known, means that the AE needs to learn to perform in the new environment very rapidly and that the 'value-add' is being accumulated while the expatriate is 'out there'. In contrast, global leadership development has far less need for the AE to perform quickly and has much longer 'return on investment' times. There are manifold implications for expatriate management, career and retention planning with some organisations starting to tailor their expatriate packages to the assignment drivers (RES Forum, 2014).

In turn, AEs also pursue their individual motivations when working abroad. Research has shown that AEs are strongly career orientated, valuing a range of developmental opportunities in relation to their job-related skills and abilities, leadership competencies, as well as the promotion prospects, more highly than individuals who are not sent by their company (see section on SIEs below) (Doherty et al., 2011; Andresen et al., 2013). Thus, employers need to pay high attention to the global career aspects of their AEs. Selection can also take account of the different drivers of AEs with the goal to find a strong congruence of organisation and individual objectives.

The recommendations for expatriate selection include that organisations should seek individuals who have a strong emotional and cultural intelligence, i.e. they have an extensive inter-personal orientation, good communication skills, have a global mind-set, demonstrate behavioural flexibility, are inquisitive, can live with high degrees of uncertainty, are resilient, have a high willingness to learn about different national cultures and diverse business contexts, have high self-confidence and optimism (Caligiuri, 2013; Thomas and Inkson, 2004). Beyond the actual selection criteria, organisations have a choice whether to use open or closed as well as formal or informal approaches. There is a general sense in the literature that global selection in most organisations could be more sophisticated with companies often using closed and informal approaches (Harris and Brewster, 1999) as well as limited criteria, mostly centred around the willingness of people to move and performance on the job. Involving the expatriate's partner/family and the host organisation in the actual decision whether to work in this particular location is also seen as important for the willingness to embark on the foreign sojourn and the friendliness of reception (Dickmann et al., 2008; Dowling et al., 2008). Allowing 'look–see visits' or giving the prospective expatriate the opportunity to have work-relevant insights into the host environment can improve the eventual adjustment (Sparrow et al., 2004; Takeuchi et al., 2005). Providing the expatriate (and the assignee's family) with some pre-departure training is seen to facilitate adjustment – however, the actual spend on it by organisations is relatively low (Doherty and Dickmann, 2012).

This moves our discussion into the time when AEs work abroad. Research has been devoted to investigating factors that make the successful adjustment – or at least coping – of expatriates to their host environments more likely. Much of the attention has been on the conceptualisation of adjustment, the cognitive, emotional, and behavioural aspects of living abroad, and which individual and organisational characteristics may improve individual adjustment (Black et al., 1991; Haslberger et al., 2013).

Adjustment is improved when family and dual career issues that are important to AEs and their families are factored into the costs and support that expatriates receive (Harvey, 1997). The administrative and logical support of the organisation for the physical move of the AE and his/her family is important to the expatriate and can determine how much time and effort the AE is able to spend on the organisation's work in the first weeks of the assignment (Dowling et al., 2008).

Generally, the individual's interaction with the host team (Toh and DeNisi, 2005) and his/her family's reaction to their new context are seen as having an impact on the emotional, cognitive, and behavioural reaction of the AE

to the foreign environment. Local 'buddies' can help AEs to support partners to carve out meaningful roles in the host country and to design integrative approaches so that the expatriate is not seen as an outsider who has the role to control locals (on behalf of the HQ).

While the degree of adjustment needed by the AE depends on many factors – in some ways the organisation often wants the assignee not to completely become local. This is the case especially for control and coordination driven global postings, for instance when the host environment is characterised by a high degree of bribery or highly ineffective work or negotiation practices (Briscoe and Schuler, 2004). However, in most cases organisations do want their assignees to adjust to a large degree to their host environments as this is argued to be good for both employers and individuals (Black et al., 1991). A new conceptualisation of the dimensions of adjustment (Haslberger et al., 2013) argues that the behavioural adequacy of AEs increases over time though they may initially suffer from culture shock. Their affective comfort with living in the new country will go up and down but over time should also increase, as, hopefully, will their ability to apply locally effective behaviour. The process takes time (Bhaskar-Shrinivas et al., 2005; Hippler, Brewster and Haslberger, 2015). We lack the empirical evidence to investigate the work effectiveness of people who are suffering because they have failed to adjust. It still seems prudent to recommend that organisations seek to draw up policies and practices that aim to support expatriates to either avoid culture shock or to help them cope with it successfully.

MNEs may have performance and reward management practices that are globally integrated to a high extent (Dickmann et al., 2009). This is likely to encourage a better global–local cooperation, understanding and transfer of knowledge (Ferner, 1997; Edwards et al., 2007). AEs are likely to understand the sending organisation and the effects of their international HRM policies and practices on their career prospects over time. AEs benefit from international moves in terms of their remuneration and career progression (Andresen et al., 2013).

Repatriation is one of the biggest challenges for organisations (Suutari and Brewster, 2003). In a world with perfect knowledge, MNEs would understand the drivers, strengths and weaknesses of their expatriates, would have chosen an assignment that increased the benefits of their assignees in tune with corporate objectives, would be in a position to design a long-term career and return plan, etc. However, knowledge is not perfect and the competitive context as well as their staff resources are highly dynamic. The determinants of repatriate career success (Lazarova and Cerdin, 2007) include the characteristics of the international experience (how long was it, how successful was it, was it developmental, and how important was the assignment unit?). In addition, the global strategic configuration (Dickmann and Müller-Camen, 2006; Bartlett and Ghoshal, 1999) and top management experience are important. The more highly integrated the organisation and the more international experience is valued, the more likely repatriate career success is. Moreover, management practices with respect to career development plans, repatriation assistance and international connectivity mechanisms also impact long-term career success (Lazarova and Cerdin, 2007). Research indicates that while repatriate churn is high in the period immediately after return, over the longer term retention figures of repatriates and non-expatriated peers are similar (Doherty and Dickmann, 2012). Further recommendations for organisations to manage their international workforce through the difficult repatriation phase include early communication about the next career step with the expatriate (which may include the management of repatriate expectations), coherent and consistent execution of global career policies and practices, and symbolic career systems that value international experience (Briscoe and Schuler, 2004; Doherty and Dickmann, 2009; Dowling et al., 2008; Sparrow et al., 2004). In addition, job choice 'at home' that does not reduce responsibilities and autonomy would be important, thereby implicitly recommending an evaluation of whether the repatriate can be promoted. We will now explore the issues involved in the management of members of the international workforce who were not sent abroad by their employer but made their own way there.

Class Activity

▸ Discuss the benefits and disadvantages of short-term and long-term assignments from the point of view of the organisation and of the expatriates. Construct a four-box chart showing these clearly.

SELF-INITIATED EXPATRIATES

As we have said, the early research on expatriates was conducted on the people sent abroad by their employers (AEs) and that has been the case since. However, several studies suggest that there is, perhaps, a more or less equal number of people working in foreign countries as expatriates, that is, intending to move on from that country before the end of their careers, who are not assigned there by their employer, and are not employed on expatriate terms and conditions, but have made their own way to the country (Cerdin and Le Pargneux, 2010; Jokinen, Brewster and Suutari, 2008; Peltokorpi and Froese, 2009). These individuals, first identified only in 2000 (Suutari

and Brewster, 2000), have become known as self-initiated expatriates (SIEs). SIEs have found international jobs on their own initiative, changed their employer, and moved abroad. These are part of the internationally experienced and capable labour force and offer an alternative staffing possibility for organisations looking for such professional staff. Their use may be increasing, because of increased use of online recruitment tools and the growth in numbers of people who have different kinds of international experiences through education, travel and, in some cases, previous work in other countries. SIEs take foreign jobs with employment contracts that match either other international employees or local employees; they do not get expatriate salaries or benefits.

SIEs differ from AEs not just in the employment contracts but in a number of other ways. SIEs are typically recruited to lower-level jobs than assigned expatriates, even if these are still managerial or expert roles (Cerdin and Le Pargneux, 2010): the costs of the latter generally mean that they are only used for higher-level posts and more challenging tasks in the foreign affiliates. Since, see above, the costs of moving employees with their families to foreign locations are so high, the contribution has to be commensurately high in order to be economically reasonable. When costs are high, companies typically aim to reduce them, in this case to reduce the need for assigned expatriates with full expatriate compensation packages. SIEs offer one option for recruiting people with quite similar capabilities, often very internationally oriented professionals, but with different, cheaper, kinds of contracts and related salary benefits than AEs. Because SIEs are normally recruited locally on local, host country contracts, they do not get typically get the extra support, allowances or insurances than AEs receive – though on rare occasions more experienced SIE may be able to negotiate some similar benefits into their contracts. Due to their personal interests, international orientation, and type of their contract, SIEs on average stay longer in their assignments than AEs with shorter and fixed-term contracts, so employers benefit from the services of SIEs for longer.

The SIE-population is very diverse and different groups within it have different motives for working abroad (Suutari and Brewster, 2000). The population includes early career professionals who are looking for international experience and new adventure or language skills immediately or soon after their graduation, typically working in lower-level jobs in local organisations. At the other end of the career continuum, we find internationally experienced senior managers who have spent much of their career internationally and thus operate in senior management jobs, often within large MNEs. Some SIEs are so-called localised professionals who have first worked abroad as assigned expatriates but after a long stay, their contract has been changed to a local contract by employers who are not prepared to pay expatriate salaries for people who have chosen to stay in the foreign country and will do so even without the expatriate uplift. Sometimes expatriates have found other local options and thus have move to other employers within the host country. Often there are family reasons behind such overall life decisions of staying permanently abroad. Another common type of SIEs is partners of dual-career couples in which the other partner is working as an assigned expatriate and the partner looks for work in the same country. A distinct category is that of people working for the international organisations (the UN, the EU, etc.) who have applied for posts in those organisations, taken examinations and been appointed – to an office outside their own home country. They earn the same as all other employees of the international organisations. From the international staffing perspective all kinds of SIEs offer different possibilities for organisations looking for specific professional expertise in combination with an international orientation.

In order to gain full advantage from self-initiated expatriates, organisations must try to smooth their transfer from one country to another (Howe-Walsh and Schyns, 2010) and be active in their induction processes. SIEs, by definition, can be supported only after appointment and arrival in the host country. Less experienced SIEs and their families might benefit from training (e.g. cross-cultural training, language training, professional training, induction to the new organisation) and overall support (e.g. living arrangements, health care systems, taxation and local regulations, partner job search assistance, social connections, social activities).

(?) Critical Thinking 16.1

What are the advantages for organisations of employing self-initiated expatriates? Usually such expatriates are employed on local terms and conditions without any of the enhanced salaries, or payments of housing costs, education costs and travel advantages. Are they being exploited? Could organisations exploit them (take advantage of their skills and knowledge) more?

Question

1 Why would an assigned expatriate want to become a self-initiated expatriate? Why would a self-initiated expatriate want to become an assigned expatriates?

GLOBAL CAREERISTS

An increasing proportion of international professionals have a succession of international jobs. These global talents have developed an ability to apply skills and transfer knowledge quickly and efficiently and to lead foreign and cross-cultural teams and activities abroad. Organisations need internationally experienced and mobile employees, particularly at managerial level, who are ready to assume responsibilities in global or regional headquarters or to open and manage new international operations in different contexts. One archetype of such internationally mobile employees is that of the 'global careerist', a manager with a long-term global career (e.g. Cappellen and Janssens, 2005; Dickman and Harris, 2005; Herman and Tetrick, 2009; Stahl and Cerdin, 2004; Suutari, 2003; Suutari, Tornikoski and Mäkelä, 2012). For example, between 40 per cent and 70 per cent of existing European expatriates have already had previous international experience; and among self-initiated expatriate samples the figure is at the top end of that (Stahl and Cerdin, 2004, Jokinen et al., 2008; Cerdin and Le Pargneux, 2010). Patterns vary – some organisations have 'foreign staff' who only work outside their home country, while many other global managers sometimes also work periodically in the home country. Some of them change between AE and SIE positions when they transfer to other MNEs or to local companies.

Due to their mobile nature, these experienced global careerists are important assets to international organisations. The globalisation of business life means that an increasing proportion of companies need to develop international competence when opening or expanding their international operations. The developmental nature of international work experiences means that, over the course of their careers, these professionals assume various challenging roles in a number of different international environments, so their competencies develop considerably (Suutari and Mäkelä, 2007). They have strong global management capabilities and social networks as well as high levels of self-awareness and self-confidence, which they can utilise in their next international jobs.

However, their very mobility may cause challenges for companies in retaining such individuals (Evans, Pucik, Bjorkman, 2011). They are likely to be headhunted and may receive indirect job offers through their wide international professional and social networks. Such departures represent losses for the organisation, not only in terms of talent, skills and knowledge but also in terms of the previous investment in the development of the departing individual and the cost of finding someone else. Thus the importance of successful talent management of such global professionals becomes crucial (Cerdin and Brewster, 2014; Collings, 2014; Suutari, Wurtz and Tornikoski, 2014). Such talent management refers to the HRM activities that aim to attract, develop, and retain individuals with high levels of global competencies (Schuler and Tarique, 2012).

In order to succeed in attracting and retaining such experienced global managers, it is important to understand what kinds of career motives they have and how organisations should support them. Global careerists clearly value the nature and characteristics of their job over the financial compensation involved (Stahl and Cerdin, 2004; Suutari, Tornikoski and Mäkelä, 2012;) and look for meaningful, strategic jobs in which they can fully utilise their experiences and skills, in order to develop those further. To gain the attention of global careerists, organisations should thus focus on the job itself, the competencies required and the developmental challenges involved. Global careerists enjoy working in challenging and culturally diverse job environments and so are attracted to challenging new roles in the international business environment. Given that their international jobs often involve a high level of managerial autonomy in combination with wide responsibilities, it is also likely that global careerist finds narrow and restrictive job descriptions less interesting. It is also important to recognise that, typically, experienced global careerists are headhunted or get job offers through their wide professional networks, rather than actively seeking jobs on the open market, so different recruitment approaches may be necessary.

Global managers, and their families, develop valuable coping skills in dealing with the challenges involved with frequent relocations and related adjustment issues (Mäkelä and Suutari, 2011), but they have also learned to value and expect the organisational support offered to them and their families. Corporate support is expected for practical arrangements such as accommodation, school and day-care arrangements, and health care. Family concerns are perceived as important due to constant adjustment pressures on the family, and thus family training and support (e.g. language training, cross-cultural training, spouse career support and support in building social connections locally) may be valued by the global careerists. Long working days and frequent international travel mean that the global careerists in turn value flexibility from their employers in arranging their schedules and also securing adequate time for staying with the family. In order for them to stay in touch with extended family and friends at home country, companies often offer paid travel back to the home country during vacations. The complexity of their personal and family situation means that global careerists often needed assistance too with practical matters provided by legal counsellors, pension specialists, insurance advisors, investment and tax consultants. Since International job are often on fixed-term contracts and since global careerists see less attraction in staying in a certain job and location more permanently, career support and planning becomes crucial: companies find that career discussion with their international professionals periodically helps to retain them during the transition stages when, typically, they analyse the external options as well.

📖 **In the News Religious frictions**

In the area broadly defined as the Middle East and amongst migrants in other countries and regions from the Middle East there has been, at least amongst a minority of people, a growth in commitment to a militant and aggressive form of Islamism. At the same time, a continuing series of military interventions in local conflicts in the region by Western powers over a couple of decades led, in 2015 and 2016, to a massive surge of migration into Europe from the region, which caused huge political debates. What to do with the migrants? How would governments be able to filter out the militants, hiding amongst these desperate people as a way into their 'enemy' countries, from genuine refugees? There were active debates between those who felt a duty to assist people forced from their homes and countries in terrible circumstances – and who noted that historically refugees and immigrants are more entrepreneurial and have been an engine of economic growth – and those who felt that they would change social structures forever, including some who felt that Muslims would never assimilate into Christian Europe and would put extra pressure on already stretched housing, social care, health, and educations systems. Could they all be fed and housed and looked after? And then, how were they to be integrated into local labour markets? How were they to find jobs? Would people want to live with, or to work with, people from a different religion and culture? And from a human resource management point of view, how do you assess for work applicants who have no paperwork and who cannot prove their qualifications or their credentials; and what can you do to integrate them with the existing workforce?

MIGRANT WORKERS

In many economies, there is an increasing need for migrants, in the context of skill shortages, aging population, and decreasing fertility rates (Al Ariss and Ozbilgin, 2010). Migrants tend to be more entrepreneurial, more active, and prepared to do unpopular jobs, which means that they are often seen as a key means to keep economies moving forward. Indeed the last few decades have seen migration – a feature of the world population for thousands of years – expanding considerably. Historically, migration changed in character after the First World War with the widespread introduction of passports as governments tried to keep control of who entered and left their territories. The total number of migrants is now estimated as almost a quarter of a billion people (UN, 2013). Most migrants work: they are, especially the skilled ones amongst them, now an important part of the global talent pool (Guo and Al Ariss, 2015).

They are not necessarily a well-managed part of the global talent pool. In many cases their skills are under-utilised (Al Ariss and Syed, 2011; Al Ariss, et al., 2012); it is not uncommon to hear tales of medically qualified doctors having to work as taxi drivers in countries with a shortage of medical staff. Migrants often face problems of discrimination (Dietz, 2010; Turchick Hakak and Al Ariss, 2013) and consequent lack of opportunities. How well they adapt to the new working environment often depends on their motivation for migration in the first place (Cerdin, Abdeljalil-Diné and Brewster, 2014): those expatriates who have looked forward to a new life in their adopted country are more likely to adapt well than those who have been driven from their home and have no great attachment to their new place of residence. For the former, in particular, the overlap with the self-initiated expatriate category may be considerable. The main difference seems to be intent to stay – migrants intend to stay for a long time, maybe for the rest of their lives: expatriates for a shorter time. But some expatriates stay on until they die and some migrants return home within a short time. Here too there may be prejudice: Al Ariss and Crowley-Henry (2013) show that those who move from developed Western countries are usually referred to as expatriates; those who come from the less-developed countries are often called migrants.

Human resource management of migrants is a 'hidden aspect' of the subject (Guo and Al Ariss, 2015: 1290). The existing research indicates that migrants may be discriminated against in selection or promotion processes or in daily management practices by supervisors, due to them being seen as 'different', so diversity/ cross-cultural training is often needed to support the equal treatment of employees in the workplace when the diversity of the workforce increases. Due to their different backgrounds, immigrants also often need more in-depth and longitudinal initiation to the workplace and the work itself in order to succeed as expected. Due to the ever greater globalisation of the workforce, MNCs increasingly develop diversity management policies and practices to help to deal with possible problems and, in turn, to fully utilise the benefits that such diversity may offer (Sippola and Smale, 2007). Clearly, employers can either hinder or facilitate the process of migrants getting work permits, having their qualifications recognised, gaining a job that utilises their skills to the full and offers a good salary, and fitting in with the rest of the workforce.

Class Activity

Imagine you have just arrived in a country as a new immigrant with a Master's degree in engineering but no papers to prove it – these were lost in the journey – and only a rudimentary knowledge of the local language. A distant cousin finds you a job in a factory packing wine into boxes. The pay is far more than you earned as an engineer in your own country but you know that with the higher costs of living in your new country it will be of less value.

▸ Do you take the job? Justify your decision.
▸ Assume you do take the job, what support would you expect from your employer? From your workmates?
▸ What would you do in these circumstances?

Critical Thinking 16.2

Is migration a good thing in general or does it create more problems than it solves? From whose point of view? What role does migration play in ensuring that work opportunities and workers are likely to be found in the same place? Can societies survive without migration? And, from an HRM point of view, does the kind of migrant matter? What can organisations do to best utilise the skills and capacities that migrants bring with them?

GLOBAL WORK AND THE USE OF KNOWLEDGE AND NETWORKS

One of the modern career approaches frequently used in expatriation research is the intelligent careers framework (DeFillippi and Arthur, 1994). It argues that individuals need to maximise their investment (and accumulation) of three forms of career capital (Inkson and Arthur, 2001): their knowledge, skills and abilities (knowing how), their social networks (knowing whom), and the energy and motivation that they bring into the world of work (knowing why). Each of the three 'knowings' is interconnected, and the general idea is that the usefulness of the intelligent career for individuals depends on the transferability of acquired career capital. In terms of acquiring transferable skills, insights, and abilities, a thorough understanding of the competencies of the host unit is important and how these would fit into the long-term careers of individuals within their organisational setting (cf. Shaffer et al., 2012). Where career systems are not strongly enacted, social networks are highly important for expatriates (Dickmann and

Doherty, 2008), especially at the point of return. Career capital considerations have strong impacts on how individuals behave and what choices they are likely to take. For instance, AEs may prefer to go to a centre of excellence as this may increase the chances of knowledge and skills transfer to their following location. In addition, in organisations with informal career systems, they may network more strongly, especially if they know that their 'return ticket' to a meaningful position could be assured through social connections.

The successful acquisition, transfer, and use of skills, knowledge, capabilities and social capital during and after international work is highly important not only for individuals but also for their employers (Al Ariss and Syed, 2011). Edström and Galbraith (1977) in a classic work outlined why this was crucial for organisations. Amongst their predominant drivers for expatriation we can find situations in which locals do not have the capabilities to fill certain positions successfully. Therefore, skills gaps and the need to rapidly fill positions when local talent is not available are one key driver of expatriation and, often, lead to knowledge transfer towards the host unit (Dickmann and Baruch, 2011; Bonache and Dickmann, 2008). In addition, another key driver is the development of future leaders for the organisation which, in essence, means knowledge and experience acquisition in the host unit to be used in the long term, mostly in further stages of individuals careers which may well mean in their home countries (Dickmann and Baruch, 2011). In addition, it becomes more and more common that expatriates have the explicit goal to rear a local successor – this embodies a major effort to transfer explicit knowledge, skills, and insights to the host unit. Moreover, the coordination aim outlined by Edström and Galbraith (1977) incorporates the attempt to transfer cultural norms, values, and behaviours from the head office to the local unit.

It is clear that the transfer of knowledge upon the return of expatriates can be highly valuable for organisations and that their talent management would be seriously impaired if such a transfer did not happen (Farndale et al., 2010). Furthermore, individuals strive to maximise (Inkson and Arthur, 2001) and transfer (Lamb and Sutherland, 2010) their social capital. With respect to social work contacts, expatriates are likely to build valuable structural and relational networks (Burt, 1997) during their time abroad. After repatriation, they may experience network advantages in comparison to non-expatriated peers, as they tend to interact with more central, powerful business actors (Burt, Kilduff and Tasselli, 2013; Doherty and Dickmann, 2012). It is likely that returning migrants and self-initiated expatriates also attempt to utilise their international networks to their and their employers' advantage (Andresen, Al Ariss and Walter, 2013).

STOP AND REFLECT

Questions

1 How could companies widen the perspectives they use to think about the different types of jobs involving an international element?

2 How would they find and implement new ideas and turn them into practice?

3 Can international work be used to improve employees' wellbeing in the future?

WORK-LIFE BALANCE RELATED ISSUES FACING EXPATRIATES

International work often leads employees and their families to leave their home country and move to another country, some doing that only once and some doing that several times in a row. Even if the job does not require relocating the whole family, it may lead to distant relationship and regular absences from home due to travel and/or short-term assignments. Thus, it is evident that this kind of job and career is not only having an effect on employee him- or herself but is also having impacts on the whole family (Haslberger and Brewster, 2008). Global trends such as the increased number of women in positions involving international responsibilities and dual-career couples (see for a review Kierner, 2015) have made work–family issues more predominant in the context of international work. Moreover, different types of expatriate jobs and the jobs of international business travellers are often found to be very challenging, for instance because of broadness of responsibilities, high levels of autonomy, and a need to adjust in new work environment. These kinds of job demands are not helping international employees to balance their work and family lives. From that perspective it is not surprising that work–family interface is among the main challenges faced by people working in international work environment (Mäkelä and Suutari, 2011; Suutari, 2003).

Among expatriates, family reasons have been found to be among the main reasons for expatriate failure, and family adjustment has been found to impact negatively on expatriate performance. Also divorces among expatriate couples are quite common (McNulty, 2012. Expatriate careers may also limit the possibilities to even start a family life (Mäkelä, Suutari and Mayerhofer, 2012), and this can lead to loneliness and feelings of unbalance between work and personal life. Among international travellers research has not been very intensive so far, but nevertheless, already the findings from such studies have indicated that frequent international travelling causes work–life balance problems (Westman, Etzion and Chen, 2008; Mäkelä, Kinnunen and Suutari, 2015; Mäkelä et al., 2014) which, in turn, may lead to health problems, such as sleep problems (Mäkelä et al.,

2014) or burnout (Jensen, 2013). It has also been found (Mäkelä et al., 2015) that parental responsibilities increase the risk of work–family conflict and the risk is the most severe for mothers who travel very intensively (compared to non-parent travellers and father travellers). On the other hand, positive experiences also exist and an international environment is seen to offer an interesting, stimulating, and developmental working and living environment both for international professionals and their families (Mäkelä and Suutari, 2011; Suutari, 2003). Moreover, family members can also be a source of social support and thus provide important backing for international employee (Mäkelä, De Cieri and Mockaitis, 2015). However, it is important that companies employing an international workforce create and implement policies and practices to help people to combine their work and personal lives, for instance helping their expatriates with accommodation and children's school arrangements. They should also provide flexi-time and time for recovery after business trips. These kinds of policies and practices are likely to improve employees'

wellbeing and, through that, lead to better organisational outcomes (De Cieri and Bardoel, 2015**).**

Class Activity

Work–life balance

Think about your current life situation. What kind of international work would suit you now? How would your personal life affect your chances of succeeding in that kind of international work? After that, imagine your ideal life situation in five to ten years from now. What kind of international work would suit you then? What was the role of your imaginary life situation in your thoughts? For instance, if you thought that different international work would suit you in present situation compared to the situation in a future, why was that? What kinds of work–life balance policies and practices would you expect from your employer in these two situations? Discuss about your thoughts in groups of three to five peers.

In the News Decreasing cost, increasing wellbeing?

In 2013 a Finnish news and picture agency released the information that work previously done during the Finnish night time (night shifts) will be done in future literally on the other side of the world, in Sydney, Australia. This decision was made after benchmarking other European media houses which already had relocated their night-shift employees in Sydney.

The company said that they had two reasons to do that. First, the company justified the decision on the grounds of cost savings; night shifts are expensive and the cost savings of this solution will be approximately one journalist person-year salary. They also said that Sydney as a location is far from the cheapest option but that the infrastructure, climate, and cultural environment make it very tempting. Second, the company highlighted that this arrangement will provide improvements for their personnel's wellbeing because, due to the time difference between Australia and Finland, the hours that were nightshift in Finland are normal day hours in Australia. In general, shift work has been found to have many negative consequences for employees' physical and psychological wellbeing.

In practice, the company did not provide generous benefits for their employees moving abroad – that is, they were not sent as traditionally defined expatriates and needed, for instance, to find and pay for their accommodation themselves. Company representatives defined these international jobs as a possibility for job-rotation and an opportunity to work in their office in Sydney, contracts lasting one to two years. The company opened four positions to be advertised internally. They selected the first team of 'kangaroo-shifters', as they call their employees working in Sydney. After all practical arrangements, such as working visas, had been made, one woman and three men moved to Sydney, the first ones in May 2014. Two of the recruited employees were dual-career couple with two children, and they said that the children's grandmother moved with them in order to help them with childcare and daily chores. Two other men were in their 30s. the new team of journalists moving to Sydney was announced at the end of 2014, and they moved to Sydney when earlier team members' contracts ended or when new replacement people were needed for some other reason.

This kind of open-minded solution to make use of benefits provided by new technologies and people willing to work abroad seems have led to positive outcomes. The 'kangaroo-shifters' themselves have said that doing the work during the day time is much more efficient compared to when they worked nightshifts. They also said that when there is no need to be awake during the night, you feel much better in general. It seems that the company has been satisfied with these arrangements, as it has not given any sign of closing the Sydney site.

CONCLUSION

This chapter has explored the importance and difficulty of managing the international workforce, recognising that contextual and strategic influences will affect the strategic management of international mobility. The different options presented here are not mutually exclusive: an individual member of the labour force can belong to different categories (being a short- or long-term assignee *and* self-initiated, for example). Further, people move between these options over time, being an inpatriate at one point in their career, a frequent flyer at another, and a standard expatriate at a third. In between they may be members of a local workforce. MNEs need to think about all of their internationally experienced and capable human resources comprehensively and coherently: focusing just on standard expatriates may mean that they are not effectively managing all their global workforce. The overlap between the current attention to expatriates and global talent management has been noted (Collings, 2014; Farndale, Scullion and Sparrow, 2010; Furusawa and Brewster, 2014), but the full range of talents open to an MNE goes well beyond expatriates or even those on the organisation's high-flyers list.

There is a clear and obvious need for more focus on and more research into all forms (summarised in e.g. Andresen, Al Ariss, and Walther, 2013; Mayrhofer, Reichel and Sparrow, 2012; Suutari and Brewster, 2009), and researchers are beginning to catch up with this requirement. As tabulated in Suutari and Brewster (2009: 134–136), each of these forms comes with a built-in set of advantages and disadvantages for the organisation and the individual. However, there is relatively little empirical research to confirm these suggestions. Long-term, standard expatriation is usually managed by the international human resource department through the mechanism of organisation-wide policies. However, there is much less clarity about short-term assignments – are they also managed as if they are one form, or are there separate groups within the category? We have even less information about frequent flyers or about global careerists or migrants and how they fit into the global workforce. By whom are these assignments managed, how that is done and what are the organisation-level co-ordination and control mechanisms for such projects, if there are any?

Most of all, there is a research gap in identifying the full range of international experience available within an MNE, the advantages and disadvantages for all concerned in each of the forms and the extent of, and how, they ensure that they are able to co-ordinate the appropriate mix of different forms of international experience in a more effective manner that will enable them to take full advantage of the expertise that they have available.

Class Activity

Before coming to the class, search different virtual communities (e.g. LinkedIn group, Facebook group, discussion forum, etc.) consisting of international employees. What kinds of communities were available and what kinds of international employees were part of those communities? What were the main topics covered in the discussions? Share your findings with your peers and discuss in small groups: first, what do the virtual communities reveal about the current situation of the international work environment; second, discuss how the virtual communities, social media, and advanced communication technologies in general have changed the work and life of international employees.

End of Chapter Case Study Management of short-term project mobility within a Finnish company

The company is a leading global provider of process solutions, technologies and services for its business segment. It employs over 2,000 people, more than half work of whom work in foreign subsidiaries. The first International assignments in the company took place in the 1960s and since then the number of employees working abroad has grown steadily. As is typical in many companies, it has already created good assignment policies concerning long-term international assignments, while a need to develop better policies for managing increasing numbers of short-term assignees, and in particular project assignees, has emerged.

So, a project concerning the development of new policies was launched involving interviewing assignees, line managers, and HRM-professionals. Among the different types of assignments, *project assignment* was clearly the most common type In the company. From an organisational perspective, the key benefit of short-term assignments was flexibility in human resource planning with shared utilisation of individual work and short-term transfers of human resources to fulfil urgent or short-term staffing needs. Project-based international mobility was expected from employees also, since technical assistance and support is included within each sale. Short-term staff transfers were seen to enhance the communication and knowledge-sharing between units – an issue that was seen to be of increasing importance. Thus, the assignments were seen to support the strategic aim of increased global integration. Close contact with customers was also stressed, since the assignees got a lot of feedback for their services and products which could then be utilised in R&D and marketing.

From the individual perspective, the positive characteristics involved the development opportunities the international projects offered assignees. This involved seeing different ways of doing things across units, formation of personal relationships across organisational and national borders, in-depth learning of environments in which customers operate, an opportunity to see how technological solutions operate in the field, as well as contacts with foreign customers and the understanding of their specific needs. International project work typically also included challenges such as tight schedules and intensive working, often in pressured or even dangerous circumstances. The main challenges faced by project assignees involved distance from family – sometimes with limited communication possibilities due to working in difficult environments or different time zones and also the intensive nature of the work. Due to the limited length of stay in each location, it was difficult to get adjusted to any specific place. Due to the intensive group form of working during projects, individual problems caused challenges for the wellbeing and performance of the whole group.

The company lacked guidelines on how to deal with these kinds of problem situations and often they were not dealt with early enough. The other concerns faced by the HRM specialists were related to challenges in developing fair assignment policies that would apply in a multitude of different circumstances and the sensitivity and complexity of handling family-related concerns. The assignees called for more support from HRM.

The company is trying to clarify its policies on these short-term assignments. Separate policies were determined for short-term assignments (as opposed to the policies for more traditional expatriate assignments) because the management processes are very different. Previously, everything up to three months had been classified as a business trip. More recently the company has developed a separate policy for project assignments to cover all assignments lasting more than a month. Assignments between three and six months have been administered with something called *the memo* in which terms and conditions have been specified. Assignments over six months involved more detailed contracts, and in many countries such a contract is required in the host country as well. Assignees with shorter contracts receive their salary in their home country, whereas for longer stays salary arrangements may differ. Employees may, with company support, move their family when assignments are more than four months long. The company also started to arrange visits and informal guidance on these issues for the whole family before the assignment.

It was also felt that the selection of project assignees was not systematic enough. Assignees argued that not all employees are suitable for such assignment and stressed the need for more careful selection. Project assignees tended to get the posts because of their personal relationships with the project manager. Senior managers either confirm the selected group, which is formed by the project leader, or jointly plan the recruitments so that the best people are allocated to different projects. A new selection process for project assignees was created. In this new process, the project management initiates recruitment, and candidate selection is completed together with the line manager. A need for more systematised processes, including a pre-selected pool of candidates available for transfers, was identified. Also, the development of better tools for screening people was raised.

Contract negotiations had been conducted up to now on a case-by-case basis. Contract and compensation negotiations were very time consuming for the HRM specialists – the amount of time being dependent on the length of the assignment, the need for insurance briefing, the need to involve family issues, and the type of the assignment. The contract negotiations took place between the assignee, his or her supervisor/line manager/project manager and the HRM manager. When the assignee works for the host subsidiary, the latter covers the compensation, so the assignee's superior there will also be included in the negotiations. In a new policy, flexibility in project assignment compensation is being reduced as increasingly strict project budgets give guidelines for negotiations. Overall, the HRM department saw a need to standardise the process in order to cut time spent on negotiations and to create fairness.

The new policy also includes new guidelines for training. The project managers were made responsible for organising training, as they know the project, the location and the related training needs best. With regard to performance management (PM), assignees felt that the standard process was problematic, as their supervisors had little knowledge about their performance during the project assignment. They also felt that, overall, they did not get much feedback on their performance. The whole process was seen to be too dependent on a single supervisor: it was seen that the PM process must involve additional discussions at the end of the assignment (even if informally conducted), besides the annual PM process.

For further information see Suutari et al. (2013).

Questions

1 Analyse the advantages and disadvantages of flexible alternative forms of international assignments.
2 Many organisations tend to have a 'one size fits all' international mobility policy. Why do they do that? How would you manage international workers in the different categories? Would you design diverse policies?
3 What can you do as an individual and as an organisation to counter the impression that expatriates go to exotic locations to have a 'jolly' time in which they simply relax and enjoy their lives?

GLOSSARY

Assigned expatriates: Employees who are supported by their employers to legally work in a country outside their country of origin, generally for a duration of more than one year and less than five years.

Career capital: The knowing how, knowing whom, and knowing why, built up over a succession of jobs and available for the next one.

Global careerists: Internationally oriented professionals with a long-term global career involving different types of international work during their careers.

Intelligent careers: Consciously using the value of knowledge, skills, contacts, and understanding built up during the course of a career to get closer to the position wanted.

International business travellers: People travelling frequently to different parts of their company or to clients or prospective clients for visits ranging from days to weeks depending on the task required of them.

International commuters: People living in one country and working in another – usually for a limited period of time.

Expatriates: People working outside their own country for what they anticipate will be a limited period of time.

Migrants: People moving from their original home country to another country in the expectation that they will spend the rest of their lives in the new country.

Multinational enterprises: Organisations (usually, but not only, multinational corporations) that have operations in, and employ people in, more than one country.

Self-initiated expatriates: People working abroad for what they intend to be a limited, even if quite long in some cases, period, who have made their own way to the country on their own initiative.

Short-term assignments: for a period of less than a year (usually less than six months) where the expatriate, even if he or she has a family, leaves them behind and goes on their own.

Work–life balance: The process of ensuring a relationship between work and non-work aspects of life that satisfies the individual, his or her family, and his or her employer.

FURTHER READING

AKRAM, A. (ed.) (2015) *Global Talent Management - Challenges, Strategies, and Opportunities*. London: Springer.

COLLINGS, D., CALIGIURI, P. AND WOOD, G. (eds) (2015) *Routledge Companion to International HRM*. London: Routledge.

DICKMANN, M. AND Y. BARUCH (2011) *Global Careers*. New York, Milton Park: Routledge.

HASLBERGER, B., BREWSTER, C. AND HIPPLER, T. (2014) *Managing Performance Abroad: A New Model for Understanding Expatriate Adjustment*. London: Routledge.

MÄKELÄ, L. AND SUUTARI, V. (eds) (2015) *Work and Family Interface in the International Career Context*. London: Springer.

VAIMAN, V. AND HASLBERGER, A. (eds) (2013) *Managing Talent of Self-Initiated Expatriates: A Neglected Source of the Global Talent Flow*. London: Palgrave Macmillan.

WEB RESOURCES

Global Business Travel Association. Available at: http://www.gbta.org.

REFERENCES

ADLER, N J. (1984) Women do not want international careers: And other myths about international management. *Organizational Dynamics* 13(2): 66–79.

AL ARISS, A. AND CROWLEY-HENRY, M. (2013) Self-initiated expatriation and migration in the management literature: Present theorizations and future research directions. *Career Development International*, 18(1): 78–96.

AL ARISS,A., KOALL, I ÖZBILGIN, M. AND SUUTARI, V. (2012) Careers of skilled migrants: Towards a theoretical and methodological expansion, *Journal of Management Development*, 31(2): 92–101.

AL ARISS, A. AND ÖZBILGIN, M. (2010) Understanding self-initiated expatriates: Career experiences of Lebanese self-initiated expatriates in France. *Thunderbird International Business Review*, 52(4): 275–285.

AL ARISS, A. AND SYED, J. (2011) Capital mobilisation of skilled migrants: A relational perspective. *British Journal of Management*, 22(2): 286–304.

ANDRESEN, M., AL ARISS, A. AND WALTHER, M. (eds.) (2013) *Self-Initiated Expatriation: Individual, Organizational, and National Perspectives*. London, New York: Routledge

ANDRESEN, M., BERGDOLT, F., MARGENFELD, J. AND DICK-MANN, M. (2014) Addressing international mobility confusion: Developing definitions and differentiations for self-initiated and assigned expatriates as well as migrants. *International Journal of Human Resource Management*, 25(16): 2295–2318.

BADER, B. AND BERG, N. (2014) The influence of terrorism on expatriate performance: a conceptual approach, *International Journal of Human Resource Management*, 25: 539–557.

BARTLETT, C. A. AND GHOSHAL, S. (1999) *Managing across Borders: The transnational solution* (vol. 2). Boston, MA: Harvard Business School Press.

BHASKAR-SHRINIVAS, P., HARRISON, D. A., SHAFFER, M. A. AND LUK, D. M. (2005) Input-based and time-based models of international adjustment: Meta-analytic evidence and theoretical extensions. *Academy of Management Journal*, 48(2), 257–281.

BLACK, J. S., MENDENHALL, M. AND ODDOU, G. (1991) Toward a comprehensive model of international adjustment: An integration of multiple theoretical perspectives. *Academy of Management Review*, 16(2), 291–317.

BONACHE, J. AND DICKMANN, M. (2008) Transfer of strategic HR know-how in MNCs: Mechanisms, barriers and initiatives. In Dickmann, M. Brewster, C. and Sparrow, P. (eds), *International Human Resource Management: A European Perspective*. London: Routledge, pp. 67–84.

BREWSTER, C., HARRIS, H. AND PETROVIC, J. (2001) Globally mobile employees: Managing the mix. *Journal of Professional HRM*, 25: 11–15.

BREWSTER, C. AND HIPPLER, T. (2013) The dimensions of expatriate adjustment. Human Resource Management, 52(3): 333–351.

BREWSTER, C. AND SCULLION, H. (1997) A review and agenda for expatriate HRM. *Human Resource Management Journal*, 7(3): 32–41.

BRISCOE, D. R. AND SCHULER, R. S. (2004) *International Human Resource Management: Policy and Practice for the Global Enterprise* (vol. 5). London: Psychology Press.

Brookfield Global Relocation Survey (2014) *Global Relocation Trends: 2014 Survey Report*. Woodridge, Illinois: Brookfield Global Relocation Services.

BURKHOLDER, J., JOINES, R., CUNNINGHAM-HILL, M. AND XU, B. (2010) Health and well-being factors, associated with international business travel. *Journal of Travel Medicine*, 17: 329–333.

BURT, R. S. (1997) The contingent value of social capital. *Administrative Science Quarterly*, 22(2): 339–365.

BURT, R. S., KILDUFF, M. AND TASSELLI, S. (2013) Social network analysis: Foundations and frontiers on advantage. *Annual Review of Psychology*, 64(1): 527–547.

CALIGIURI, P. (2013) *Cultural Agility: Building a Pipeline of Successful Global Professionals*. San Francisco: Jossey-Bass.

CAPPELLEN, T. AND JANSSENS, M. (2005) Career paths of global managers: Towards future research. *Journal of World Business*, 40: 348–360.

CERDIN, J.-L., ABDELJALIL-DINÉ, M. AND BREWSTER, C. (2014) Qualified immigrants' success: Exploring the motivation to migrate and to adjust. *Journal of International Business Studies* 45(2): 151–168.

CERDIN, J.-L. AND BREWSTER. (2014) Talent management and expatriation: Bridging two streams of research and practice. *Journal of World Business*, 49(2), 245–252.

CERDIN, J.-L. AND LE PARGNEUX, M. (2010) Career anchors: A comparison between organization-assigned and self-initiated expatriates. *Thunderbird International Business Review*, 52(4): 287–299.

CERDIN, J.-L. AND SHARMA, K. (2014) Inpatriation as a key component of global talent management. In Al Ariss, A. (ed.), *Global Talent Management: Challenges, Strategies and Opportunities*. Heidelberg: Springer, pp. 79–92.

COLLINGS, D. G. (2014). Integrating global mobility and global talent management: Exploring the challenges and strategic opportunities. *Journal of World Business*, 49(2): 253–261.

COLLINGS, D. G., SCULLION, H. AND MORLEY, M. J. (2007) Changing patterns of global staffing in the multinational enterprise: Challenges to the conventional expatriate assignments and emerging alternatives. *Journal of World Business*, 42: 198–213.

DE CIERI, H. AND BARDOEL, A. (2015) A framework for work–life management in multinational corporations. In Mäkelä, L. and Suutari, V. (eds), *Work and Family Interface in the International Career Context*. London: Springer Science and Business Media, pp. 197–216.

DEFILLIPPI, R. J. AND ARTHUR, M. B. (1994) The boundaryless career: A competency-based perspective. *Journal of Organizational Behavior*, 15(4), 307–324.

DEFRANK, R. S., KONOPASKE, R. AND IVANCEVICH, J. M. (2000) Executive travel stress: Perils of the road warrior. *Academy of Management Executive*, 14(2): 58–71.

DEMEL, B. AND MAYRHOFER, W. (2010) Frequent business travelers across Europe: Career aspirations and implications. *Thunderbird International Business Review*, 52(4): 301–311.

DICKMANN, M. (2013) Why do they come to London? Exploring the motivations of expatriates to work in the British capital. *Journal of Management Development*, 31(8): 783–800.

DICKMANN, M. AND BARUCH, Y. (2011) *Global Careers*. London: Routledge.

DICKMANN, M. AND DOHERTY, N. (2008) Exploring the career capital impact of international assignments within distinct organisational contexts. *British Journal of Management*, 19(2): 145–161.

DICKMANN, M., DOHERTY, N., MILLS, T. AND BREWSTER, C. (2008) Why do they go? Individual and corporate perspectives on the factors influencing the decision to accept an international assignment. *International Journal of Human Resource Management*, 19(4): 731–751.

DICKMANN, M. AND HARRIS, H. (2005) Developing career capital for global careers: The role of international assignments. *Journal of World Business*, 40: 399–408.

DICKMANN, M. AND MÜLLER-CAMEN, M. (2006) A typology of international human resource management strategies and processes. *International Journal of Human Resource Management*, 17(4): 580–601.

DICKMANN, M., MÜLLER-CAMEN, M. AND KELLIHER, C. (2009) Exploring standardisation and knowledge networking processes in transnational human resource management. *Personnel Review*, 38(1): 5–25.

DIETZ, G. (2010) Introduction to the special issue on employment discrimination against immigrants. *Journal of Managerial Psychology*, 25 (2): 148–158. Doherty, N. and Dickmann, M. (2009) Exposing the symbolic capital of international assignments. *International Journal of Human Resource Management*, 20(2): 301–320.

DOHERTY, N. AND DICKMANN, M. (2012) Measuring the return on investment in international assignments: An action research approach. *International Journal of Human Resource Management*, 23(16): 3434–3454.

DOHERTY, N., DICKMANN, M. AND MILLS, T. (2011) Exploring the motives of company-backed and self-initiated expatriates. *International Journal of Human Resource Management*, 22(3): 595–611.

DOWLING, P., FESTING, M. AND ENGLE SR, A. D. (2008) *International Human Resource Management: Managing People in a Multinational Context*. London: Thomson Learning.

EDSTRÖM, A. AND GALBRAITH, J. R. (1977) Transfer of managers as a coordination and control strategy in multinational organizations. *Administrative Science Quarterly*, 22(2): 248–263.

EDWARDS, T., COLLING, T. AND FERNER, A. (2007) Conceptual approaches to the transfer of employment practices in multinational companies: An integrated approach. *Human Resource Management Journal*, 17(3), 201–217.

ESPINO, C. M., SUNDSTROM, S. M., FRICK, H. L., JACOBS, M. AND PETERS, M. (2002) International business travel: Impact on families and travellers. *Occupational and Environmental Medicine*, 59: 309–322.

EVANS, P., PUCIK, V. AND BJÖRKMAN, I. (2011) *The Global Challenge: International Human Resource Management* (2nd edn). New York: McGraw-Hill.

FARNDALE, E., SCULLION, H. AND SPARROW, P. R. (2010) The role of the corporate HR function in global talent management. *Journal of World Business*, 45(2): 161–168.

FAULCONBRIDGE, J. AND BEAVERSTOCK, J. (2008) Geographies of international business travel in professional service economy. In Hislop, D. (ed.), *Mobility and Technology in the Workplace*. London: Mobility and Technology in the Workplace, pp. 87–102.

FENWICK, M. (2004) On international assignment: Is expatriation the only way to go? *Asia Pacific Journal of Human Resources*, 42(3): 365–377.

FERNER, A. (1997) Country of origin effects and HRM in multinational companies. *Human Resource Management Journal*, 7(1), 19–37.

FINDLAY, A. M., LI, F. L. N., JOWETT, A. J. AND SKELDON, R. (2000) Skilled international migration and the global city: A study of expatriates in Hong Kong. *Applied Geography*, 20(3): 277–304.

FURUSAWA, M. AND BREWSTER, C. (2014) The bi-cultural option for global talent management: The Japanese/ Brazilian *Nikkeijin* example. *Journal of World Business*, 50(1): 133–143.

Global Business Travel Association. (2014) GBTA BTI Outlook – United States. Prospects for Domestic & International Outbound Business Travel 2013–2014.

GRIPENBERG, P., NIEMISTÖ, C. AND ALAPETERI, C. (2013) Ask us equally if we want to go: Evolving gender implications in international assignments among Finnish business graduates. *Journal of Global Mobility: The Home of Expatriate Management Research*, 1(3): 287–311.

GUO, C., AND AL ARISS, A. (2015) Human resource management of international migrants: Current theories and future research. *International Journal of Human Resource Management*, 26(10): 1287–1297.

GUSTAFSSON, P. (2012) Travel time and working time: What business travellers do when they travel, and why. *Time and Society*, 21: 203–222.

HARRIS, H., AND BREWSTER, C. (1999) The coffee-machine system: How international selection really works. *International Journal of Human Resource Management*, 10(3): 488–500.

HARVEY, M. (1997) The impact of the dual-career expatriate on international human resource management. *Journal of International Management*, 3: 251–290.Harvey, M. G. (1989) Repatriation of corporate executives: An empirical study. *Journal of International Business Studies*, 20(1): 131–144.

HARVEY, M., MAYERHOFER, H., HARTMANN, L. AND MOELLER, M. (2010) Corralling the horses' to staff the global organization of the 21st century. *Organizational Dynamics*, 39: 258–268.

HASLBERGER, A. AND BREWSTER, C. (2008) The expatriate family: An international perspective. *Journal of Managerial Psychology*, 23(3): 324–346.

HOLMA, A.-M. (2012) Interpersonal interaction in business triads: Case studies in corporate travel purchasing. *Journal of Purchasing and Supply Management*, 18(2): 101–112.

HERMAN, J. L. AND TETRICK, L. E. (2009) Problem-focused versus emotion-focused coping strategies and repatriation adjustment. *Human Resource Management*, 48(1): 69–88.

HIPPLER, T. (2009) Why do they go? Empirical evidence of employees' motives for seeking or accepting relocation. *International Journal of Human Resource Management*, 20(6): 1381–1401.

HIPPLER, T., BREWSTER, C. AND HASLBERGER, A. (2015) The elephant in the room: The role of time in expatriate adjustment. *International Journal of Human Resource Management* 26(15): 1920–1935.

HOCKING, J. B., BROWN, M. AND HARZING, A.-W. (2004) A knowledge transfer perspective of strategic assignment purposes and their path-dependent outcomes. *International Journal of Human Resource Management*, 15(3): 565–586.

HOWE-WALSH, L. AND SCHYNS, B. (2010) Self-initiated expatriation: Implications for HRM. *International Journal of Human Resource Management*, 21(2): 260–273.

HOYER, K. AND NÆSS, P. (2001) Conference tourism: A problem for the environment, as well as for research? *Journal of Sustainable Tourism*, 9(6): 451–470.

INKSON, K. AND ARTHUR, M. B. (2001) How to be a successful career capitalist. *Organizational Dynamics*, 30(1): 48–61.

IVANEVICH, J. M., KONOPASKE, R. AND DEFRANK, R. S. (2003) Business travel stress: A model, propositions and managerial implications. *Work and Stress*, 17(2): 138–157.

JENSEN, M. (2013) Exploring business travel with work-family conflict and the emotional exhaustion component of burnout as outcome variables: The job demands-resources perspective. *European Journal of Work and Organizational Psychology*, 23(4): 497–510.

JIE, S. AND LANG, B. (2009) Cross-cultural training and its impact on expatriate performance in Australian MNEs. *Human Resource Development International*, 12(4): 371–386.

JOKINEN, T., BREWSTER, C. AND SUUTARI, V. (2008) Career capital during international work experiences: Contrasting self-initiated expatriate experiences and assigned expatriation. *International Journal of Human Resource Management*, 19(6): 978–998.

KIERNER, A. (2015) Dual-income and dual-career couples in international context. In Mäkelä, L. and Suutari, V. (eds), *Work and Family Interface in the International Career Context*. London: Springer Science and Business Media, pp. 95–116.

LAMB, M. AND SUTHERLAND, M. (2010) The components of career capital for knowledge workers in the global economy. *International Journal of Human Resource Management*, 21(3): 295–312.

LARSEN, H. H. (2004) Global career as dual dependency between the organization and the individual. *Journal of Management Development*, 23(9): 860–869.

LAZAROVA, M. B. AND CERDIN, J. L. (2007) Revisiting repatriation concerns: Organizational support versus career and contextual influences. *Journal of International Business Studies*, 38(3): 404–429.

MÄKELÄ, L., BERGBOM, B., SAARENPÄÄ, K. AND SUUTARI, V. (2015) Work–family conflict faced by international business travellers: Do gender and parental status make a difference? *Journal of Global Mobility*, 3(2): 155–168.

MÄKELÄ, L., BERGBOM, B., TANSKANEN, J. AND KINNUNEN, U. (2014) A longitudinal mediation model on the relationship between international business travel and sleep problems via work–family conflict. *Career Development International*, 19(7): 794–812.

MÄKELÄ, L., DE CIERI, H. AND MOCKAITIS, A. (2015) International Business Traveler, Is Work Always on Your Mind? An investigation of the relationship between sources of social support and satisfaction with work-related international travel: The moderating role of over-commitment. In Mäkelä, L. and Suutari, V. (eds), *Work and Family Interface in the International Career Context*. London: Springer Science and Business Media, pp. 181–196.

MÄKELÄ, L., KINNUNEN, U. AND SUUTARI, V. (2015) Work-to-life conflict and enrichment among international business travellers: The role of international career orientation. *Human Resource Management*, 54(3): 517–531.

MÄKELÄ, L., AND SUUTARI, V. (2011) Coping with work–family conflicts in the global career context. *Thunderbird International Business Review*, 53(3): 365–375.

MÄKELÄ, L., SUUTARI, V. AND MAYERHOFER, H. (2011) Lives of female expatriates: Work-life balance concerns. *Gender in Management: An International Journal*, 26(4): 256–274.

MAYERHOFER, H., HARTMANN, L. C., MICHELITSCH-RIEDL, G. AND KOLLINGER, I. (2004) Flexpatriate assignments: A neglected issue in global staffing. *International Journal of Human Resource Management*, 15(8): 1371–1389.

MAYRHOFER, W., REICHEL, A. AND SPARROW, P. (2012) Alternative forms of international working. In Stahl, G. K., Björkman, I. and Morris, S. (eds), Handbook of Research in International Human Resource Management (2nd edn). Cheltenham: Edward Elgar, pp. 300–327.

MAYRHOFER, W., SPARROW, P. AND ZIMMERMANN, A. (2008) Modern forms of international working. In Brewster, C., Sparrow, P. and Dickmann, M. (eds), International Human Resource Management. London: Routledge, pp. 219-239.

MCKENNA, S. AND RICHARDSON, J. (2007) The increasing complexity of the internationally mobile professional. Cross Cultural Management: An International Journal, 14(4): 307–320.

MILLAR, J. AND SALT, J. (2006) The mobility of expertise in trans-national corporations. Migration Research Unit, Working Paper, University College London.

MINBAEVA, D. B. AND S. MICHAILOVA (2004) Knowledge transfer and expatriation in multinational corporations: The role of disseminative capacity. Employee Relations, 26(6): 663–679.

MCNULTY, Y. (2012) 'Being dumped in to sink or swim': An empirical study of organizational support for the trailing spouse. Human Resource Development International, 15(4): 417–434.

PATEL, D. (2011) Occupational travel. Occupational Medicine, 61(1): 6–18.

PELTOKORPI, V. AND FROESE, F. J. (2009) Organizational expatriates and self-initiated expatriates: Who adjusts better to work and life in Japan? International Journal of Human Resource Management, 20(5): 1096–1112.

RAMSEY, J. R., NASSIF LEONEL, J., ZOCCAL GOMES, G. AND RAFAEL REIS MONTEIRO, P. (2011) Cultural intelligence's influence on international business travelers' stress. Cross-Cultural Management: An International Journal, 18(1): 21–37.

REICHE, S., KRAIMER, M. L. AND HARZING, A.-W. K. (2009) Inpatriates as agents of cross-unit knowledge flows in multinational corporations. In Sparrow, P. R. (ed.), Handbook of International Human Resource Management: Integrating People, Process and Context. Chichester: John Wiley and Son, pp. 151–170.

RES-Forum (2014) Key Trends in Global Mobility. RES Forum, UniGroup Relocation Network and Equus Software. Report authored by M. Dickmann, 102 pages, London.

RES-Forum (2015) The RES Forum Annual Report: Global Mobility and the Global Talent Management Conundrum, RES Forum, UniGroup Relocation Network and Equus Software. Report authored by M. Dickmann, 108 pages, London.

SALT, J. AND WOOD, P. (2012) Recession and international corporate mobility. Global Networks, 12(4): 425–445.

SCHULER, R. AND TARIQUE, I. (2012) Global talent management: Theoretical perspectives, systems, and challenges. In Björkman, I. and Stahl, G. (eds), Handbook of Research in IHRM. London: Edward Elgar Publishing, pp. 385–404.

SHAFFER, M. A., KRAIMER, M. L., CHEN, Y. P. AND BOLINO, M. C. (2012) Choices, challenges, and career consequences of global work experiences: A review and future agenda. Journal of Management, 38(4): 1282–1327.

SIPPOLA, A. AND SMALE, A. (2007) The global integration of diversity management: A longitudinal case study. International Journal of Human Resource Management, 18(11): 1895–1916.

SPARROW, P., BREWSTER, C. AND HARRIS, H. (2004) Globalizing Human Resource Management. London: Routledge.

STAHL, G. K. AND CERDIN, J.-L. (2004) Global careers in French and German multinational corporations. Journal of Management Development, 23(9): 885–902.

STARR, T. L. (2009) Repatriation and short-term assignments: An exploration into expectations, change and dilemmas. International Journal of Human Resource Management, 20(2): 286–300.

STARR, T. L. AND CURRIE, G. (2009) Out of sight but still in the picture: Short-term international assignments and the influential role of family. International Journal of Human Resource Management, 20(6): 1421–1438.

SUUTARI, V. (2003) Global managers: Career orientation, career tracks, life-style implications, and career commitment. Journal of Managerial Psychology, 18(3): 185–207.

SUUTARI, V. AND BREWSTER, C. (2000) Making their own way: International experience through self-initiated foreign assignments. Journal of World Business, 35(4): 417–436.

SUUTARI, V. AND BREWSTER, C. (2003) Repatriation: Evidence from a longitudinal study of careers and empirical expectations among Finnish repatriates. International Journal of Human Resource Management, 14(7): 1132–1151.

SUUTARI, V. AND BREWSTER, C. (2009) Beyond expatriation: Different forms of international employment. In Sparrow, P. (ed.), Handbook of International Human Resource Management: Integrating People, Process and Context. Chichester: Wiley, pp. 131–150.

SUUTARI, V., BREWSTER, C., RIUSALA, K. AND SYRJAKARI, S. (2013) Managing non-standard international experience: Evidence from a Finnish company. Journal of Global Mobility, 1(2): 118–138.

SUUTARI, V. AND MÄKELÄ, K. (2007) The career capital of managers with global careers. Journal of Managerial Psychology, 22: 628–648.

SUUTARI, TORNIKOSKI C. AND MÄKELÄ, L. (2012) Career decision-making of global careerists. International Journal of Human Resource Management, 23(16): 3455–3478.

SUUTARI, V. WURTZ, O. AND TORNIKOSKI, C. (2014) How to attract and retain global careerists: Evidence from Finland. In Al Ariss, A. (ed.), *Global Talent Management*. London: Springer, pp. 237–249.

TAHVANAINEN, M. (2003) *Short-Term International Assignments: Popular Yet Largely Unknown Way of Working Abroad*. Helsinki: HeSE Print.

TAHVANAINEN, M., WELCH, D. AND WORM, V. (2005) Implications of short-term international assignments. *European Management Journal*, 23(6): 663–673.

TAKEUCHI, R., TESLUK, P. E., YUN, S. AND LEPAK, D. P. (2005) An integrative view of international experience. *Academy of Management Journal*, 48(1): 85–100.

THOMAS, D. C. AND INKSON, K. (2004) *Cultural Intelligence: People Skills for Global Business*. San Francisco, CA: Berrett-Koehler.

TOH, S. M. AND DENISI, A. S. (2005) A local perspective to expatriate success. *The Academy of Management Executive*, 19(1): 132–146.

TURCHICK HAKAK, L. AND AL ARISS, A. (2013) Vulnerable work and international migrants: A relational human resource management perspective. *International Journal of Human Resource Management*, 24(22): 4116–4131.

Travel and Tourism Council. (2014) Travel & Tourism. Economic Impact 2014. Available at: http://www.wttc.org/-/media/files/reports/economic impact research/regional reports/world2014.pdf. Accessed April 15, 2015.

UN (2013) *Population Facts*. New York: Department of Economic and Social Affairs, Population Division, United Nations

WELCH, D., WELCH, L. AND WORM, V. (2007) The international business traveller: A neglected but strategic human resource. *International Journal of Human Resource Management*, 18(2): 173–183.

WESTMAN, M. AND ETZION, D. (2002) The impact of short overseas business trips on job stress and burnout. *Applied Psychology*, 51(4): 582–592.

WESTMAN, M., ETZION, D. AND CHEN, S. (2008) Crossover of positive experiences from business travellers to their spouses. *Journal of Managerial Psychology*, 24(3): 269–284.

17

SUSTAINABLE HRM

Robin Kramar

Sustainable HRM challenges the logic embedded in Strategic HRM by acknowledging the importance of recognising the impact of management, particularly HRM practices, on a broad range of outcomes resulting from organisational activities. A key to the understanding of Sustainable HRM is an interpretation of the term Sustainable. This interpretation has been shaped by the Brundtland Commission's report on Sustainable Development and the national context in which organisations operate. Although the literature on Sustainable HRM is diverse, it can be categorised into three groups which have a unifying characteristic. This characteristic is capability reproduction. The major characteristics of the evolving area of Sustainable HRM include the impact of HRM practices on individual, social, organisational, and ecological outcomes and the tensions associated with these outcomes. The recognition of these outcomes has implications for the measurement and reporting of organisational activities and the capabilities required of managers. These issues are explored in this chapter.

Opening Case Study Sustainable HRM

Sustainable HRM has a broad reach. It moves beyond only considering HRM practices for employees and includes the practices used for all people within the supply chain. Organisations in many industries outsource aspects of the production of goods and services to suppliers in emerging, low-cost economies. Economists who subscribe to the theory of comparative advantage argue that international trade will make all stakeholders better off (Meyerson, 1997), even when working conditions in low cost economies are sub-standard by Western standards. These economists claim that people in low-cost economies have better lives than when they are working in subsistence farms or other less desirable work, such as prostitution (Chen, 2011).

However, there is evidence that these low-cost countries want to attract foreign direct investment, and in order to maintain low labour costs, they allow breaches in human rights in workplaces in their countries (Lauwo and Otusanya, 2014). Although there are a number of codes and standards that protect the rights of people working in the workplaces in these developing countries, multinational companies (MNCs) operating in these countries are complacent with regard to these codes or find it difficult to implement them in the context of these countries (Barrienbtos and Smith, 2007). A study of information disclosure of information disclosure by companies with global value chains reveals that these companies recognised the importance of maintaining a positive social image on human and labour rights. However, the reality was different (Müller-Camen et al., 2013).

Examination of the Global Reporting Initiative (GRI) Sustainability Reports of 250 companies revealed that although companies claimed to disclose information on human and labour rights for their internal and external workforces, the quality of the information did not indicate comprehensive, accurate disclosure. In these reports companies paid little attention to human rights aspects such as child labour, nor did they provide detailed information on their internal and external workforces and the systems and procedures implemented. Companies over-reported on irrelevant factors, claimed full disclosure, and reported that their suppliers complied with the standards because they complied with the rules, laws, and regulations operating in their countries (Parsa, Roper, Muller-Camen and Szigetvari, 2014).

The issue of child labour engaged by suppliers is an important aspect of Sustainable HRM. Child labour is widespread in developing countries, with almost 12 per cent of 5–14-year-old children being involved in paid labour (UNICEF, 2015). India has a large percentage of children in the workforce, with official statistics revealing 435,530 children being employed in 2011 (www.labour.nic.in). It is worth noting that between 2004 and 2005 the number of children aged between 5 and 14 years who were working halved because of government legislation providing for child protection. Most of the children who are employed are in the garment industry. These children are engaged by small producers of garments. Retailers, such as Wal-Mart and JC Penney, brand fashions, such as Gap, and athletic footwear companies, such as Reebok, typically design and market garments but outsource the manufacture of the garments to these small companies. There are considerable cost advantages to these large companies in outsourcing the manufacture of garments to companies employing children (Chen, 2011).

The principles embedded in a broad view of Sustainable HRM extend beyond the standards and outcomes applying to employees. It extends beyond the regulations and legal compliance requirements of a national context. It extends beyond the focus on results for the owners of the organisation and raises many of the tensions involved by recognising these complexities.

INTRODUCTION

For more than 30 years Strategic HRM has been the dominant approach to people management. However, in the last decade an alternative approach, Sustainable HRM, has emerged. The literature on Sustainable HRM first developed in a European context, and its interpretation varies in different national contexts. A wide variety of terms have been used to capture the essence of Sustainable HRM.

White the emphases of the literature vary, there are common unifying themes. These themes focus on

capability development, the requirement to recognise a wide range of outcomes resulting from management practices and a long-term perspective. The diversity of interpretations and literature on Sustainable HRM can be categorised into three groups: Capability Reproduction; Promoting Social and Environmental Health; and Connections. Sustainable HRM recognises the tensions associated with interpretations of sustainability and the difficulties associated with the implementation of HRM policies.

The broader view of HRM promoted by Sustainable HRM has implications for the measures and reporting indicators for organisations. There are a number of frameworks and systems that enable organisations to capture the processes and outcomes of management and organisational practices. A framework has been developed that captures the shadow side of HRM, the negative impacts of HRM on employees and their families. Sustainable HRM also has implications for the capabilities required of organisational members.

THE DEVELOPMENT OF SUSTAINABLE HRM

The development of Sustainable HRM represents an emerging formal recognition of the detrimental impact organisational activities have on people and the ecology of the world. This impact has increased exponentially as developments such as globalisation of the economies and cultures, populations growth in different economies occurring at differential rates, and the disparity between the rich and poorer nations were recognised. This section discusses the factors leading to the emergence of ideas about Sustainable HRM.

The concept of sustainability is derived from a Latin word 'sustinere' which means 'to hold up' or in more colloquial terms to endure (http://dictionary.reference.com/browse/sustainability). This notion of endurance is central to an understanding of sustainability at all levels and arenas. These levels include the macro-, organisational, and micro-levels and the ecological, social/human, and economic arenas. These levels and arenas are not mutually exclusive but are interdependent.

The World Commission on the Environment and Development (WCED) under the Chairmanship of Gro Harlem Brundtland (The Brundtland Commission) was established by the United Nations (UN) in recognition of competing macro-economic developments that were having a detrimental impact on ecological and social outcomes. During the 1980s, ideas based on neoliberalism informed economic policies and institutions promoting economic globalisation. This globalised economic growth was accompanied by ecological degradation and a decline in the relative social wellbeing between developed and developing nations.

The Brundtland Commission Report (The Report) and its paper *Our Common Future* was a watershed in the understanding of sustainability. The Report developed the term 'sustainable development'. This term extended previous notions of sustainability and development by acknowledging that the environment was a broad context, of which the ecology was only one part. It recognised that the environment and development are interdependent and that they have long-term consequences. 'Sustainable development' is a complex concept, with at its core the idea that development meets the needs of the present generation without compromising the ability of future generations to meet their own needs.

Sustainable development therefore requires a long-term, global perspective. This perspective acknowledges the needs of various stakeholders, including the needs of the world's poorest people and the boundaries imposed by factors such as technology and social organisation on the ability to meet the needs of current and future generations. This approach to sustainable development reflected the Commission's concern for the degradation of the environment and the social impact and waste of human resources resulting from the prevailing nature of economic growth and development (Brundtland, 1987).

The Commission identified three pillars of sustainable development which operated at the macro level. These were economic growth, environmental protection, and social equality. These pillars have been used as the basis of outcomes at the organisational level. The triple bottom line (TBL) accounting framework explicitly measures the performance of an organisation in the ecological/environmental, the social, and the economic arenas internally and externally (Elkington 1997). The TBL acknowledges the responsibility of an organisation to a variety of stakeholders, not just its responsibility to shareholders as proposed by Friedman (1970). The notion of responsibility to future generations as propounded by the Brundtland Commission has been used to extend the TBL. The quadruple bottom-line (QBL) includes a fourth pillar, which sets out long-term outcomes, such as intergenerational equity (http://cambridgeleadershipdevelopment.com/quadruple-bottom-line).

Although the concept of sustainable development and the TBL extended the criteria for measuring organisational outcomes and performance, during the last 20 years strategic human resource management (SHRM) has increasingly sought to demonstrate its contribution to economic and financial outcomes. The importance of organisations ensuring their economic future, meeting their financial obligations, remaining viable in their chosen market, and securing financial backing (Boxall and Purcell, 2011) has influenced this emphasis. 'Virtually all SHRM research takes the managerial/organisational perspective with an emphasis on the consequences for organisational performance' (Lengnick-Hall et al., 2009, 76–77). There has been particular concern that HRM make a positive contribution to financial outcomes and that HRM practitioners add value to organisational results (Ulrich et al., 2012).

The direct and indirect contributions of HRM to financial outcomes have been frequently demonstrated. HRM has been shown to contribute to reduced turnover, increased positive social outcomes, productivity, improved job satisfaction, trust and increased commitment (Arthur, 1994; Boxall and Macky, 2009; Brammer et al., 2007; Collins and Clark, 2003; Evans and Davis, 2005; Huselid, 1995; Macky and Boxall, 2008; Pattersen et al., 1997; Petersen, 2004; Richard and Johnson, 2001). HRM can therefore contribute to improved cost efficiencies through lower salaries and savings from lower recruitment and training costs, lower turnover and improved productivity (Bachaus et al., 2002; Petersen, 2004).

Early models of SHRM, such as the Harvard model (Beer et al., 1984) recognised that HRM practices were influenced by external factors such as legislation and varying stakeholder interests. The Harvard model also explicitly acknowledged that HRM practices could have positive outcomes on employee behaviour and longer-term outcomes on employee wellbeing. Unlike neoliberalism economies (LMEs), for instance in the USA, Australia, and the United Kingdom, which focus on the importance of shareholder value, many European and Scandinavian countries recognise the interdependence between businesses and their local community (Avery 2005). These economies, which have been called 'co-ordinated market economies' (CMEs), acknowledge the diversity of stakeholder interests in the economy and society.

Interest in Sustainable HRM emerged from the European context. At the beginning of the twenty-first century Zaugg et al. (2001) explored Sustainable HRM practices in eight European countries (Germany, Italy, France, Spain, Austria, Great Britain, the Netherlands, and Switzerland). A variety of terms are included under the banner of Sustainable HRM. These include terms such as sustainable work systems (SWSs) (Docherty et al., 2002), HR sustainability (Gollan, 2000), sustainable management of HRM (Ehnert, 2006, 2009, 2011), sustainable leadership (Avery, 2005; Avery and Bergsteiner, 2010) and Sustainable HRM (Mariappanadar, 2003, 2012; Kramar, 2014). Sustainable organisation has been used to refer to organisations that recognise the relationship between HRM practices and positive ecological and environmental outcomes. In addition, literature is emerging under the banner of Green

HRM. This literature does not include the term 'sustainable'; however, it is concerned with the impact of HRM on broader ecological/environmental outcomes (Renwick, Redman and Maguire, 2011; Jackson et al., 2011).

These terms are concerned with a variety of aspects of Sustainable HRM. They include the longevity or endurance of HRM systems, the positive and negative impact of HRM practices on the wellbeing of employees, their families and communities, the impact on ecological, social/human and financial outcomes of an organisation's activities, and meeting the needs of a variety of stakeholders in the present and also in the future. In the USA (Jackson et al., 2011) and the United Kingdom (Renwick et al., 2011), a body of literature that is concerned with the way HRM could contribute to positive ecological outcomes has developed. All the terms identified in this paragraph and the previous paragraph are subsumed under the label of Sustainable HRM.

Economies in other regions traditionally displayed characteristics that do not conform to the LME or CME characteristics. In the Asian region, sociocultural influences were shaped by the values of creeds and ideologies such as Confucianism, Buddhism, and Islam. These creeds and ideologies emphasised values such as social harmony, respect for authority, conflict avoidance and the importance of personal connections. These values were reflected in the operation and perception of the role of Asian firms and the responsibilities of employers and employees. Mutual loyalty was an integral part of the management of Asian organisations and this was reflected in an expectation of guaranteed lifetime employment for permanent employees (Debroux 2014).

This positive social and human outcome coexisted with less favourable working arrangements for employees in small organisations and for the contingent workforce. Employment conditions and wage rates were significantly different from those for permanent employees. These different approaches indicated contradictions in the way different people were managed in the economy.

In addition, the characteristics of Sustainable HRM are challenged 'by the simultaneous surge of requests for higher efficiency, social fairness and environmental

---

Mini Case Study Sufficiency economy

In Thailand, His Majesty King Bhumibhol Adulyadej espoused a philosophy of 'Sufficiency Economy' as a means of dealing with some of the challenges produced by globalisation. The principles of this philosophy consist of the three components of moderation, reasonableness, and the requirement to deal with shocks from internal and external changes. The two conditions necessary to achieve this philosophy are knowledge and morality. This 'Sufficiency Economy' philosophy is regarded as a guide to behaviour in all spheres of life, including the operation of business. Following the increasing number of bankruptcies during the Asian Economic Crisis, this philosophy was emphasised as a means to recovery.

Studies indicate that the 'Sufficiency Economy' principles have been successful in sustaining business performance in some organisations in Thailand. These principles are consistent with the 19 principles of Sustainable Leadership evident in organisations in the Rhineland. Research into the Siam Cement Group and the Bathroom Design Company reveal that these 19 principles are grouped into six groups in these two organisations.

These groups are:

▸ adopting a long-term perspective;
▸ developing leaders from within the business;
▸ establishing a strong organisational culture;
▸ supporting incremental and radical innovation;
▸ acting socially responsible;
▸ practicing ethical behaviour.

The Siam Cement Group has been in business for more than 100 years. One of the primary core values of the Group is ethical behaviour which is represented in its Code of Conduct and Corporate Governance. This is a basis for the organisational culture and the radical and incremental innovations in product development in the Group. The second core value is that of social responsibility. This is reflected in the practice of investing in the training of all employees, establishment of self-governing teams, and the provision of scholarships to attend universities. It is also reflected more broadly in the sponsorship of many projects that further environmental and social responsibility and in the decision to expand foreign business rather than sell Baht for American dollars during the Asian Financial Crisis.

Similarly, the Bathroom Design Company Ltd demonstrates the same six groups of principles as the Group discussed above. This company also has a strong organisational culture, which is characterised by ethics, social responsibility, and innovation, as well as diligence and perseverance. Employees are also paid more than the industry standard, as is the case in the Group. The culture is strengthened by the Company encouraging employees to follow the five Buddhist commandments:

▸ Abstain from taking life.
▸ Abstain from what is not given.
▸ Abstain from sexual misconduct.
▸ Abstain from false speech.
▸ Abstain from intoxicants causing heedlessness.

Thus, in Thailand it is possible to observe some of the characteristics of Sustainable HRM operating even during periods of economic crisis and growing globalisation of the economy. The national cultural and religious context of the country reflected in the 'Sufficiency Principle' and Buddhist values provides a reference point for management and HRM practices in some Thai organisations.

Sources: Kantabutra, 2012; Kantabutra and Avery, 2011; Kantabutra, 2006; Avery, 2005.

---

awareness especially from major customers in the USA and Europe' (Debroux, 2014: 319). Following the Asian economic crisis many organisations in Asia adopted the characteristics of people management that were consistent with those of SHRM. However, at the same time they retained some of the features associated with Sustainable HRM (Kramar and Parry, 2014).

CATEGORIES OF SUSTAINABLE HRM

The writings on Sustainable HRM are diverse and piecemeal. There is no one precise definition of the term. The writings differ in terms of the emphasis given to particular internal and external outcomes. For instance, the term has been used to refer to human and social outcomes that contribute to the continuation of the organisation in the long term through the development of human capabilities. The term has also been used to refer to positive social and human outcomes for their own sake, not just for their contribution to financial outcomes and the achievement of organisational strategy. Another body of literature, labelled Green HRM, refers to the Sustainable HRM literature that focuses on the contribution of HRM to positive ecological outcomes.

The literature on Sustainable HRM can be categorised into three groups. These groups are not mutually exclusive, but they provide a simple means of drawing out the major distinctions between the various writings on Sustainable HRM. The categories are labelled Capability reproduction, Promoting Social and Environmental Health, and Connections.

Capability Reproduction refers to the literature (Browning and Delahaye, 2011; Clarke, 2011; Ehnert, 2009; Wells, 2011) that links HRM practices to internal outcomes, in particular the endurance of the organisation, and therefore to economic outcomes. According to these writers, the concept of Sustainable HRM is an extension of SHRM and it represents a new, holistic approach to people management. Writers (Clarke, 2011; Ehnert, 2009; Wilkinson et al., 2001) in this group argue that HRM practices are essential for the development of human capabilities required to operate in a context of environmental, demographic, and social pressures. They claim that HRM practices need to develop and regenerate human and social capabilities at least as fast as the organisation 'consumes' the capabilities.

Human and social capabilities are 'consumed' when employee abilities, knowledge and skills are not developed. This failure to develop employee capabilities has been referred to as depreciation of employee capabilities. A culture and work environment that is not supportive of employees and fails to develop collaboration and motivation also 'consumes' capabilities.

A wide variety of HRM practices have been found to contribute to positive human outcomes and the development of capabilities. These include collaborative HR development (Browning and Delahaye, 2011), organisational structures that facilitate employee participation and direct communication with employees (Donnelly and Proctor-Thomson, 2011), and work roles and performance evaluation that focus on building employee strengths and facilitating performance (Wells, 2011). Some of the literature in this category appears to resemble HRM packages such as high performance work systems (HPWS), rather than a new approach to HRM. However, Sustainable HRM differs from HPWS because it explicitly focuses on long-term social/human outcomes. This is expressed by Wilkinson et al. (2001: 1498–1499) when they argue that HR sustainability requires a 'shift from short-term corporate survival to long-term business success' and a focus on positive social outcomes.

The second group of writers (Branco and Rodrigues, 2006; Collinson et al., 2007; Mariappanadar, 2003, 2012; Orlitzky et al., 2003) labelled 'Promoting social and environmental health', focuses on the relationship between HRM and external outcomes. These outcomes are typically representative of corporate social responsibility (CSR) and the TBL. Much of this literature identifies the way in which social/human outcomes and/or environmental outcomes contribute to economic and financial outcomes. For instance research (Walsh, Weber and Margolis, 2003) demonstrates that the majority (100 out of 121 papers) of research papers that empirically examined the relationship between CSR and corporate financial performance 'attach CSR to an economic rationale'

(868). Therefore many, but not all, of these writers reflect the efficiency approach to sustainability. The different approaches to sustainability are discussed in more detail in the next section.

Within this group other writers (Docherty et al., 2002; Docherty et al., 2009; Kira, 2002; Mariappanadar, 2003, 2012) focus on the negative impact of HRM on externalities, as well as on the individual, organisational, and societal levels. They acknowledge that HRM practices such as work intensification, temporary employment, excessive performance standards, and ambiguous job roles have a detrimental impact on an organisation's human and social capital, individual wellbeing, family and community health, satisfaction, and organisational culture.

The third group 'Connections', examines the relationships between management, including HRM practices, and organisational outcomes, including environmental, social, and financial outcomes. Implicit in these writings is a moral concern with organisations behaving responsibly towards a variety of stakeholders. As discussed in an earlier section, national context has an influence on management practices, and this is explored in the literature on Sustainable Leadership (Avery, 2005; Avery and Bergsteiner, 2010). Avery and Bergsteiner (2010) explain that sustainable leadership 'refers to achieving futures in which humans live within their ecological and social means without exploiting other parties' (30). They claim that this approach is dominant in European countries that adopt the Rhineland approach to economic theory, which is based on a stakeholder model. They acknowledge that approaches to HRM and leadership are influenced by national institutional and social contexts but claim that Sustainable leadership can be adopted in a variety of contexts.

A comprehensive study (Zaugg et al., 2001) found that organisations in Switzerland consider Sustainable HRM as part of their traditions. The study found there was a belief in a 'Swiss tradition of harmonious co-existence of employees, corporations and society' (Ehnert, 2006: 8). Consequently employees were regarded as equal partners with management. It is therefore assumed that they participate in decision-making and take responsibility for their careers. Three practices are regarded as particularly significant: employee development, reward systems, and the integration of sustainability into company strategies, goals, and culture (Ehnert 2006).

Other literature concerned with Sustainable organisations (Dunphy et al., 2007) argues that environmental and human/social outcomes are interrelated and contribute to organisational sustainability. Dunphy et al. (2007) reveal that in order for organisations to contribute to positive ecological/environmental outcomes they need to manage their staff in particular ways. They claim that organisations with strong corporate values, senior executive support, flexible structures, HRM practices that build capabilities of the workforce, participative decision-making, diversity management, high levels of workplace health and safety, and performance indicators that reflect ethical concerns are best able to achieve these positive environmental/ecological outcomes.

The Green HRM literature focuses on drawing out the relationships between environmental management and HRM (Jabbour and Santos, 2008; Jackson et al., 2011). It expands SHRM so it includes sustainability issues (Kramar, 2012; Osland and Osland, 2007) and also addresses the role of HRM on preventing negative environmental outcomes such as pollution (Bunge et al., 1996; Jackson et al., 2011; Renwick et al., 2011). Positive environmental outcomes have been found to result from a variety of HRM policies relating to attracting and selecting, training and development, performance management, pay and reward systems, and especially employee involvement and employee empowerment and engagement. These HRM policies are able to create cultures, climates, and capabilities necessary for desirable environmental outcomes.

The writers (Clarke, 2011; Wilkinson et al., 2001) in these three categories of Sustainable HRM understand HRM and its relationship to sustainability in different ways. The group 'Capability Reproduction' focuses on internal outcomes and emphasises economic outcomes and the creation of 'sustainable competitive advantage' through the development of human and social capability. The group 'Promoting Social and Environmental Health' emphasises broader external outcomes including ecological/environmental outcomes (Mariappanadar, 2003; Orlitzky, Schmidt and Rynes, 2003; Collinson, Cobb, Power and Stevenson, 2007). The group 'Connections' moves beyond just HRM practices. Writers in this group (Avery, 2005; Avery and Bergsteiner, 2010; Dunphy et al., 2007; Jackson et al., 2011) examine the interrelationships between management practices, including HRM and organisations, that include the broader outcomes of environmental/ecological outcomes. This literature acknowledges the influence of national contexts on management practices (Avery, 2005) and the interrelationships between ecological/environmental outcomes and HRM practices (Dunphy et al., 2007).

The literature in these three groups indicates that a novel approach to HRM is emerging. Although the writings on Sustainable HRM are diverse and do not represent a coherent body of literature, the focus on the development of human capital as an essential outcome of HRM does represent a different focus from that of SHRM. SHRM focuses on the achievement of business outcomes. The next section explores the major characteristics of Sustainable HRM and describes a model that captures these characteristics.

MAJOR CHARACTERISTICS OF SUSTAINABLE HRM

Sustainable HRM represents a novel approach to the management of people. Unlike SHRM, which is concerned with the contribution of HRM practices to economic outcomes, Sustainable HRM is concerned with a broader range of outcomes that are consistent with the achievement of TBL outcomes as well as the prevention of negative human, social, and ecological outcomes. A great strength of the Sustainable HRM approach is its acknowledgement of the competing interpretations of sustainability and the tensions that arise as a consequence of these interpretations. Ehnert (2009) captures these tensions in a paradox framework that identifies the HRM contradictions that can occur simultaneously when trying to reconcile these tensions. In addition, when a model takes into account the factors necessary for the effective implementation of HRM practices, some insights can be gained into the endurance of an HRM system.

A recent definition of Sustainable HRM includes these characteristics. It can be defined as 'the pattern of planned or emerging HRM strategies and practices intended to enable the achievement of financial, social and ecological goals while simultaneously reproducing the HR base over a long term. It seeks to minimise the negative impacts on the natural environment and on people and communities and acknowledges the critical enabling role of CEOs, middle and line managers, HRM professionals and employees in providing messages which are distinctive, consistent and reflect consensus among decision makers' (Kramar, 2014: 1084).

Figure 17.1 provides a framework that captures some of the factors operating at the macro- and organisational level. It also displays the tensions associated with sustainability interpretations and the some of the impacts of HRM on organisational, social, individual, and ecological outcomes. This figure is a development of earlier models developed by Ehnert (2009) and Kramar (2014).

Factors operating in the macro-environment are identified as influences on the stock of human capital in the labour market and on organisational strategy and practices. These factors include socioeconomic, ecological, institutional, technological, demographic, legislative, political, religious, and cultural factors. The state plays an influential role in HRM in terms of the law, as a public sector employer, and as an economic, social and environmental policy-maker, although this has in the main been neglected by the SHRM literature (Matinez Lucio and Stuart, 2011). Institutional analysis argues that institutions and social structures within a particular national context shape the actions and choices made by organisations and individuals (DiMaggio and Powell, 1983).

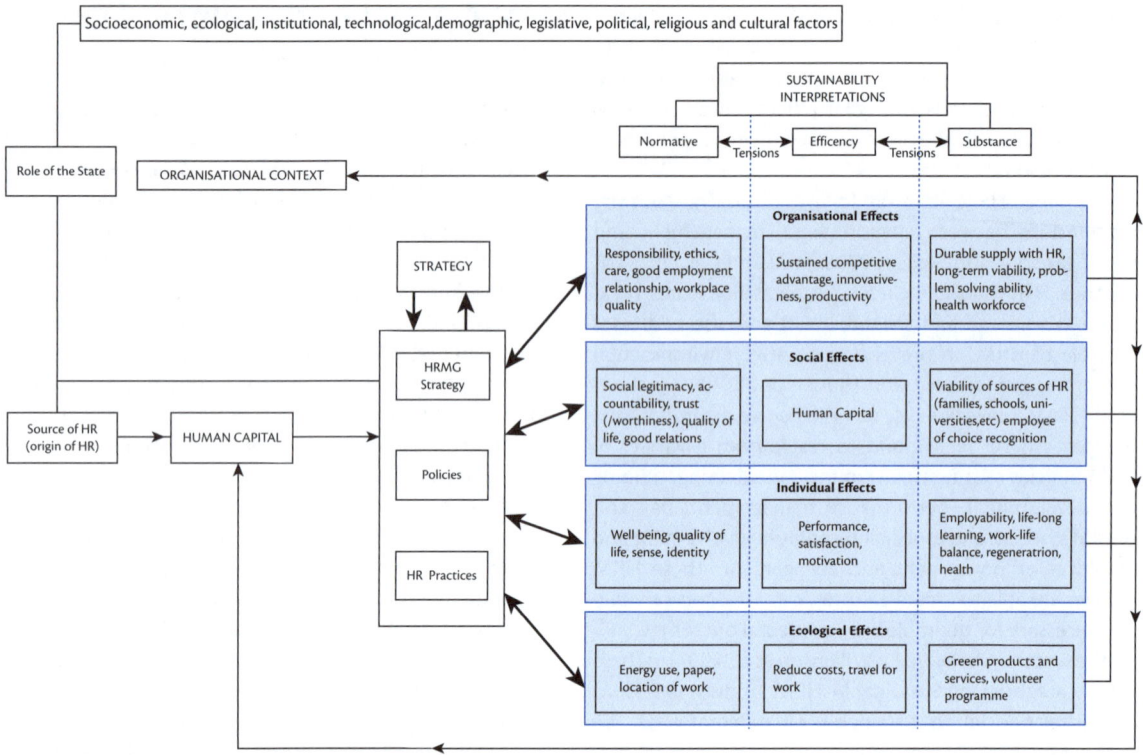

Figure 17.1 Conceptual Framework.
Adapted from Kramar 2014

The stock of capital available in the labour market has an influence on the human capital available in an organisation. The availability of human capital in an organisation and in the labour market is also influenced by an organisation's HRM strategy, HRM policies, and HRM practices. Expenditure on training, development, and employee learning by an organisation will influence the capabilities available in the present and in the future internal and external labour markets.

Unlike SHRM, the model of Sustainable HRM (Figure 17.1) identifies the complexities associated with the interpretations of sustainability. Organisations in LMEs are viewed as having a dominant approach to sustainability that reflects the efficiency/innovation interpretation. This interpretation reflects the Friedman's view of sustainability. The objective of the efficiency/innovation interpretation is to reduce consumption (and costs) or to increase the efficiency of resource exploitation (and value creation) via innovation (Ehnert, 2009). Although this interpretation is framed in terms of a 'win-win', the focus is on achieving economic outcomes.

However, many organisations are concerned with efficiency outcomes but at the same time concerned with behaving as responsible corporate citizens. The

responsible interpretation of sustainability is underpinned by the Brundtland Commission definition of sustainable development. According to this interpretation, particular management practices are adopted because of a sense of responsibility to a variety of stakeholders. According to this interpretation, the performance of an organisation would be measured in terms of a variety of performance outcomes such as employee wellbeing, community wellbeing, and quality of life. As discussed previously, this is a common dominant interpretation of sustainability in European countries.

The third interpretation of sustainability is the substance approach. This interpretation seeks to maintain and develop the HR capability and human capital of the organisation, so that the relative consumption and reproduction of human resources enable the organisation to survive in the future. Using this interpretation, organisations are required to acknowledge the value and quality of people within the organisation. Education and training institutions that are external to the organisation play a role in influencing the quantity and quality of people available to the organisation.

Figure 17.1 reveals the tensions associated with the normative, efficiency/innovation interpretations of sustainability and the efficiency/innovation and the substance interpretations. The identification of these tensions is very revealing about HRM practices. Many organisations experience these tensions simultaneously and as a consequence develop contradictory HRM practices. For instance, work–life balance initiatives and flexible working arrangements are available in many organisations; however, high performance expectations and customer requirements can make it difficult to access these policies.

Unlike SHRM, this Sustainable HRM figure identifies the organisational, social, individual, and ecological effects of HRM. There are tensions associated with the competing outcomes necessary for the endurance or sustainability of an organisation. These outcomes are identified within the organisational context; however, organisations are open systems and the outcomes identified in the figure include impacts beyond the organisation. They include social outcomes such as family outcomes and quality of life, individual outcomes in the labour market, such as an individual's employability, ecological outcomes, such as energy and resource consumption, and the capabilities required by an organisation to work effectively.

This figure explicitly acknowledges that organisations seek outcomes that are inconsistent with each other. This challenges the rational view of organisations and the strategic management process that informs the SHRM literature. The Sustainable HRM approach to HRM identifies that organisations want to be seen as and behave as responsible corporate citizens, yet they are required to achieve sustainable competitive advantage and operate more efficiently and also to ensure they have the necessary human and social resource base. The objectives of sustainable HRM are therefore '(1) to balance the ambiguities and duality of efficiency and sustainability over a long-lasting calendar year; (2) to sustain, develop and reproduce an organisation's human and social resource base, for example help the mutual exchange relationships; and (3) to evaluate and assess negative effects of HR activities on the HR base and sources of HR' (Ehnert, 2006: 14).

Consider the bundles of HRM practices that have been labelled High Performance Work Practices (HPWP) or High Performance Work Systems (HPWS). These practices have been widely discussed in the literature. Consider the practices adopted in the organisations discussed in Thailand and reflect on whether Sustainable HRM is just another label for HPWP/HPWS.

MEASURING THE OUTCOMES OF SUSTAINABLE HRM

When broader outcomes such as social, human, and ecological outcomes are identified as important as financial outcomes of organisational performance, it would follow that management would report on measures covering these outcomes. There are a number of systems that measure a wide range of organisational outcomes. These include the Global Reporting Initiative (GRI), Account-Ability, Standard AA1000 and Integrated Reporting supported by the Integrated Reporting Council (The IIRC). The GRI standards are regarded as the global standard for sustainability reporting (Ehnert et al., 2015).

The GRI provides a variety of organisations with G4 Guidelines based on principles. These Reporting Principles include the:

- Materiality Principle;
- Sustainability Context Principle.

A Sustainability Report to the GRI is required to follow the Reporting Principles and report on three categories of sustainability: economic, social, and environmental. Six groups are identified as indicators of issues associated with sustainability. These groups are economic, environmental, social, product responsibility, human rights, and labour practices and decent work (GRI, 2015). Within these groups/categories there are sub-categories and within the Social category the four sub-categories are Labour Practices and Decent Work', 'Human Rights', 'Society' and Product Responsibility'.

Two of these categories are directly related to HRM (Ehnert et al., 2015). These are the 'Labour Practices and Decent Work' and 'Human Rights' categories. Labour Practices and Decent Work' is based on a number of internationally recognised universal standards and the ILO Decent Work Agenda (AGENDA). The aspects covered by the sub-category of 'Labour Practices and Decent Work' are broad ranging and include Employment, Labour/Management Relations, Occupational Health and Safety, Training and Education, Diversity and Equal Opportunity, Equal Remuneration for Women and Men, Supplier Assessment for Labour Practices, and Labour Practices Grievance Mechanisms (GRI, 2015: 9).

Some of the guidelines for reporting on these sub-categories include 'Total number and rates of new employee hires and employee turnover by age group, gender and region' (GA-LA1); 'Minimum notice periods regarding operational changes, including whether these are specified in collective agreements' (GA-LA4); 'Workers with high incidence or high risk of diseases related to their occupation' (GA4-LA7); and 'Average hours of training per year per employee by gender and by employee category (GA4-LA9). Similarly the 'Human Rights' sub-category includes reporting on ten processes pertaining to HRM. These include non-discrimination (GA4-HR3); 'Child Labour' (GA4-HR5); Indigenous Rights (GA 4-HR8); and 'Forced Compulsory Labour (GA4-HR6).

Class Activity

Go to the IKEA website and review IKEA's position on Sustainability and the aspects that are consistent with Sustainable HRM. The GRI website will have a copy of the IKEA Sustainability Report. Review this report and make a judgement about how well IKEA's Sustainability Report reflects its stated position on Sustainability in the areas that could be regarded as part of Sustainable HRM.

When a broad view of Sustainable HRM is taken, the Society, Environmental, and of course the Economic categories are also an indirect outcome of Sustainable HRM. For instance, within the Society category aspects such as the impact on local communities and grievance mechanisms for this impact are measures of outcomes that are influenced by HRM processes. As discussed earlier, a range of research in the area of strategic HRM demonstrates how HRM processes influence economic outcomes.

Sustainable HRM explicitly takes into account the positive and negative outcomes of HRM policies. These positive and negative outcomes can occur within the organisation or they may be external to the organisation. Sustainable HRM explicitly takes into account the positive and negative outcomes of HRM policies. The positive outcomes are widely reported in the academic literature (Arthur, 1994; Boxall and Macky, 2009) and in literature from consulting companies (BCG, 2012; Gallup Consulting, 2010).

A number of frameworks have been developed to identify the HRM processes that contribute to positive human outcomes, such as positive emotions, the reproduction of capabilities, and human capital. Some of these frameworks, such as the Watson Wyatt *Human Capital Index*, the Boston Consulting Group (BCG) and World Federation of People Management Associations (WPFMA) research, and the Gallup organisation's employee engagement surveys, reveal that developing human capital, such as strong leaders, retaining talented people and developing high and emerging potentials, tracking performance (BCG, 2012), retaining high performers (Baron and Armstrong, 2007), and developing intangibles such as employee engagement (Gallup Consulting, 2010) contribute to the maintenance of human capital. These frameworks measure the impact of HRM practices on these social and human outcomes and also the financial, quality, and other outcomes of management practice.

Human capital has also been defined as 'systems by which people are managed'. When this is done the focus is on identifying and reporting to internal and external stakeholders on the HRM practices in place. Models for this approach include those developed by Dunphy et al. (2007), Boedker (2005), Royal and O'Donnell (2005), and O'Donnell et al. (2009). One example the Star model (O'Donnell et al., 2009) identifies the system of HRM policies that contribute to human capital outcomes such as creativity and adaptability, capabilities required for organisational renewal, retention of talent for the longer term through career planning and succession planning, and efficient employee behaviour. Figure 17.2 describes this model.

Two other systems such as the Balanced Scorecard and the Society for Knowledge Economics' *The Australian Guiding Principles to Extended Performance Management* also provide frameworks for identifying the practices that can be used to develop human capital. The Balanced Scorecard identifies measures that contribute to future development of human capabilities using the category of learning and growth (Kaplan and Norton, 1996). The research and index developed by the Society for Knowledge Economics (SKE) indicates that innovative and high financially performing workplaces have high scores on aspects such as leadership (including authentic and developmental leadership), perceptions of fairness (including procedural and distributive fairness), and employee outcomes (such as satisfaction and wellbeing) (SKE, 2011).

The negative consequences of HRM are wide ranging. The negative impacts of retrenching and making staff redundant are harmful to employees and their families (Armstrong-Stassen and Cameron, 2003; Eliason and Storrie, 2009; European Expert Group in Health in Restructuring [HIRES], 2009; Pfeffer, 2010: 38) They also have a detrimental impact on those employees who survive the downsizing and remain in the organisation (survivors) (Baran et al., 2009; Cascio, 2002). In circumstances when employees are required to expend high amounts of work effort, work long hours, and do not have the opportunity to recover from this effort, there are negative impacts on employees (Sparks et al., 1997).

Mariappanadar has developed a conceptual framework of negative externalities that can occur as a consequence of HRM practices. He defines the harm of negative externalities of HRM practices as 'the profound, incomprehensible and negative impact on employees' and their family members' reduced personal outcomes, social and work related well-being that are caused by work practices used by organisations to extract maximum skills, abilities and

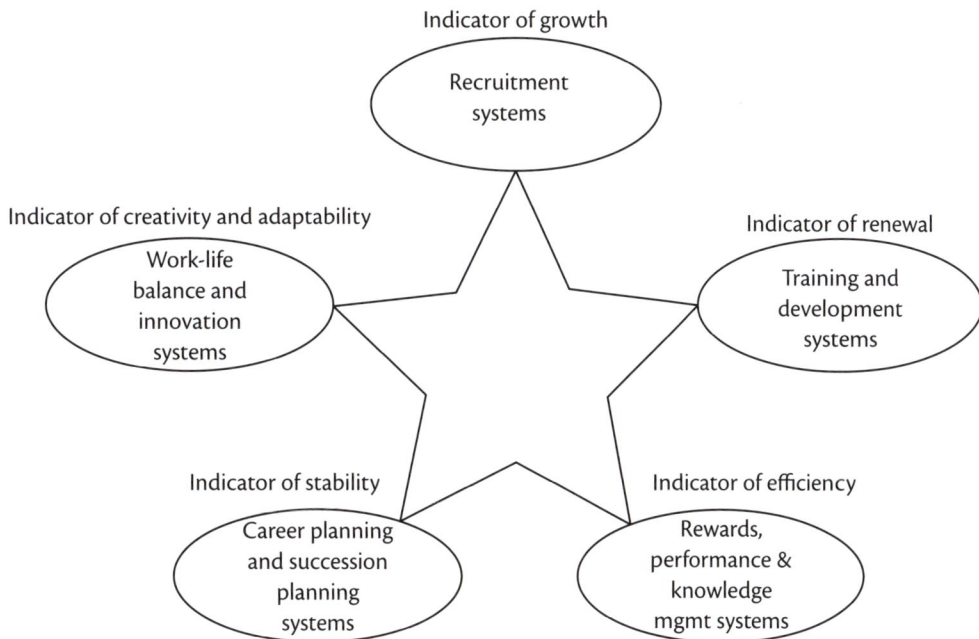

Figure 17.2 Star model of HRM

motivation of employees to achieve highly effective and efficient performance' (Mariappanadar, 2014: 187).

Mariappanadar's framework (2014) identifies four attributes of negative externality:

- the level of risk or severity of harm;
- the manifestation of harm;
- the impact of harm; and
- the avoidability of harm.

These attributes of negative externalities of HRM practices have an impact on employees, their families and their communities. The impacts are categorised into three clusters with a variety of indicators. These clusters are psychological, social, and work related. The indicators in psychological could be negative wellbeing, job-related suicide, and psychological injury. The indicators in the social category include family breakups/divorce, work–family conflict, and domestic violence. While indicators in the work-related health aspect are stress-related illnesses, depression, alcohol/drug abuse and rehabilitation. Mariappanadar (2014) proposes each of these attributes has a polarity of characteristics:

- low and high risk or severity of harm;
- avoidable or unavoidable characteristics;
- temporary and time-lagged manifestations; and
- temporary or enduring characteristics.

One of the advantages of this framework is that it identifies moderating influences on the four attribute identified above. These moderating influences include individual differences such as personality, gender, cultural values, and ability, which impact coping mechanisms. Other moderating influences include HRM practices that could be designed to lessen HRM negative impacts such as retrenchments, work intensification, and lack of training and development. These moderating HRM practices could include job redesign, support and employee care services during retrenchments and downsizing, and the provision of training and development to build employee and organisational skill bases. Figure 17.3 depicts this framework on the negative externalities resulting from HRM.

This framework contributes to an understanding of Sustainable HRM. In circumstances where managers are concerned with preventing or limiting the negative impact of HRM practices, such as retrenchments and work intensification, they could make decisions based on information and research to prevent or correct these negative impacts on employees, families, and communities. These negative impacts can be reduced by investing in and encouraging survivors to develop and acquire additional skills so they maximise their productivity (Mariappanadar, 2003, 2014). Services that provide assistance with outplacement, psychological and career counselling and transition advice to members of organisations who are retrenched or made redundant can also reduce the negative impacts (Mariappanadar, 2014).

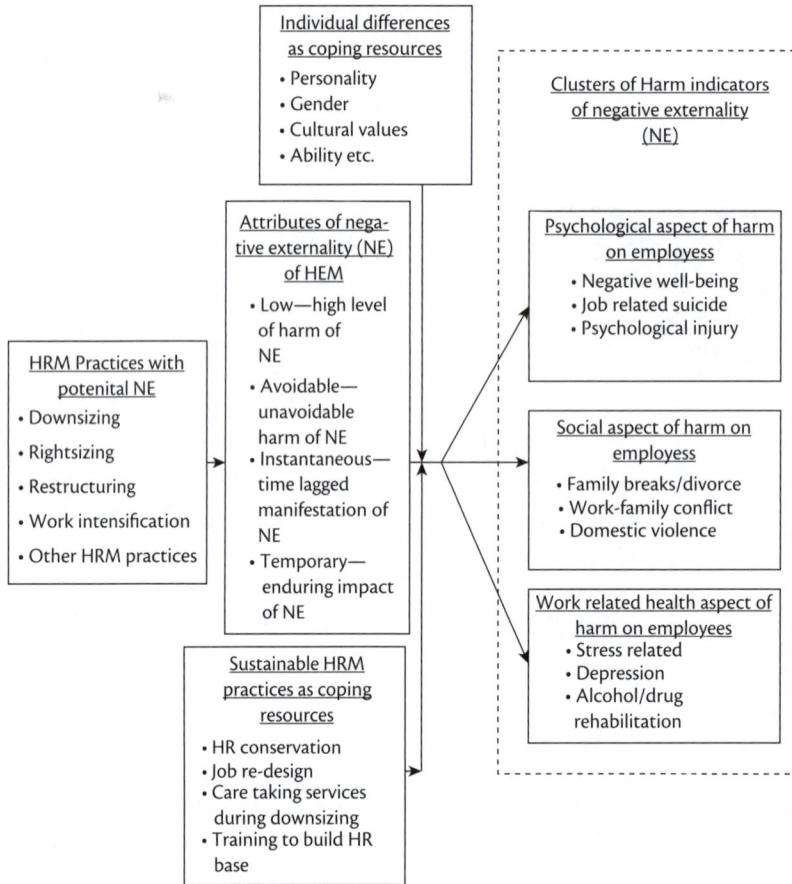

Figure 17.3 Harm indicators of negative externalities

Class Activity

▸ Consider a workplace you are familiar with and identify some of the HR practices that could result in employee and social harm. Discuss this with your class mates.

Question

1 As discussed in the previous section, a number of measurement systems and frameworks have been developed to measure the outcomes of a variety of organisational outcomes. Do you think that if organisations are 'ecologically responsible' and 'socially responsible' they can continue to do business in their usual manner?

SUSTAINABLE HRM AND THE REALITY OF HRM

The SHRM literature fails to adequately address the inconsistency of HRM practice in organisations, the execution of HRM policies in the workplace, and the tensions between competing desirable organisational outcomes. HRM practice involves ambiguities, paradoxes, dualities, and dilemmas (Hampden-Turner and Trompenaars, 2000). It is not a matter of managers choosing one set of HRM practices as proposed by contingency (Schuler and Jackson, 1987) and the universalistic theorists (Pfeffer, 1998); rather 'layering' of policies occurs as organisations respond to tensions arising from the movement between the dualities associated with implementation (Hampden-Turner, 1990; Evans, 1999, 328). The Sustainable HRM approach is able to take into account this layering by acknowledging the tensions associated with the different outcomes desired by the management of organisations.

One of the many mysteries of HRM practices is the failure of managers and employees to implement and execute policies as intended. One of the models of Sustainable HRM recognises this by acknowledging that the execution and implementation of HRM practices are not neutral processes but involve political aspects (Bartram et al., 2007; Kramar, 1992; Sheehan et al., 2007) and social, cultural, and power factors (Kramar, 1992). The practice of HRM, rather than HRM policy, cannot be explained by rational choice because people involved in developing and implementing HR policies operate in a context of conflicting pressures.

It has been found that CEOs, middle and line managers play an essential role in the implementation of HRM policies (Mayrhofer et al., 2004; Purcell and Hutchinson, 2007). The CEO provides legitimacy for the enactment of HR policies, commits resources, and ensures group agreement within the organisational hierarchy (Bartram et al., 2007; Bowen and Ostroff, 2004; Stanton et al., 2010). Similarly middle and line managers are essential. They are required to develop employee commitment and encourage their acceptance of the policies. They need to behave in ways that are consistent with the policies and the values of the organisation and have this behaviour reciprocated by employees.

If implementation of HR policies is to occur, employees need to perceive HR policies as fair and viable and appreciate that their implementation will contribute to economic, social, and ecological outcomes. Employees also need to understand the policies and acknowledge what they mean for their behaviour. It is also important that there is a perception of consistency between decision-makers and employees and that managers receive consistent messages about HR policies.

Sustainable HRM provides insights into the capabilities and skills required by members of organisations to formulate, implement, and execute HRM policies that contribute to positive economic, social/human, and ecological outcomes. One of the key features of Sustainable HRM is an acknowledgement of the ambiguities and tensions associated with desirable organisational outcomes and

how these differ for various stakeholders of an organisation. Employees and managers at all levels of the organisation therefore require the ability to conduct dialogue with each other. The process of dialogue is a communication and sense-making process that requires individuals to have concern for the group (Piaget, 1962). It therefore provides a link between the individual and collective groups.

Dialogue involves two or more groups working together in a collaborative way to come to a common understanding. Dialogue requires skills such as listening, the ability to understand different points of view and reflect on these different points of view. It also requires that employees and managers have the ability to critically reflect on their assumptions, their values and preconceived ideas about how an organisation should operate and what its desirable outcomes and goals should be (Boud, Cressey and Docherty, 2006).

The ability to engage in dialogue and develop the skills to undertake this process requires people to be open-minded and believe that other people with other points of view can enhance understanding about particular issues. This requires open-mindedness and an ability and willingness to change. The process of dialogue can be time-consuming and therefore requires patience. This has implications for the development of managers and employees. Individuals will need to learn skills and develop knowledge of themselves, their values, and assumptions if they are to engage in dialogue.

Another skill central to Sustainable HRM is the ability to think systemically. Systemic thinking involves relational, holistic thinking. This requires more than simple problem-solving and focusing on 'cause and effect'. It requires recognising the many dimensions and dynamic nature of issues. It also recognises that many factors interact to create issues and that decisions have a number of consequences (Sterling, 2004). These factors will need to be taken into account when considering HRM policy formulation and implementation. For instance, decisions to reduce labour costs by cutting the size of the workforce by retrenching people have implications for the people who are retrenched, for their families and, as discussed previously, for those who remain in the organisation. Consequently, when systemic thinking is applied to the reduction of labour costs in an organisation, it would follow that a variety of ways of reducing costs generally, a number of different ways of doing this, and the consequences of each of each decision would be considered. The process of systemic thinking is enhanced by engaging a variety of stakeholders by information sharing and participating in the formulation of a variety of alternatives and the identification of the possible consequences of the various decisions.

? Critical Thinking 17.1

Identify some of the difficulties associated with Line Managers implementing some of the HRM practices that could be regarded as consistent with Sustainable HRM. Consider some of the actions that could be taken to limit these difficulties.

In the News 7-Eleven

7-Eleven is the largest retail convenience chain in Australia. In late 2015 an investigation by a television network, the ABC, and the Fairfax Media exposed socially unsustainable HRM practices. They found 69 per cent of stores had payroll compliance issues and falsification of records and rosters. International students on student visas are only permitted to work 40 hours per fortnight; however, in a number of 7-Eleven stores franchisees were requiring students to work more hours, paying them half the legal award rate of pay, and falsifying records sent to head office. If the students did not comply, they were threatened with notifying authorities about their contravention of visa requirements.

The Fair Work Ombudsman is the regulator that monitors compliance of legal wage rates and conditions. They have conducted audits on a number of stores and found 60 per cent were underpaying staff. They also discovered that this level of underpaying was double the rate of non-compliance in an audit undertaken previously. The regulator has taken legal action against three franchisees. Other franchises have given an undertaking to pay employees at the legal minimum wage rate.

Incoming Chairman of 7-Eleven Michael Smith denies that the 7-Eleven business model forced franchisees to look for ways to cut costs. However, the Board will be discussing ways of changing the business model to ensure that employees are treated fairly. Smith claims the company should have known about these practices. 7-Eleven thought they were running a very professional company and were using high calibre auditors.

Many students studying in Australia have poor English skills and find the cost of living expensive. During the investigation students reported that they feared risking their visas and believed they needed to accept the lower wages. There is also evidence of franchisees withholding passports and driver's licences.

On the other hand, some franchisees claim they face many difficulties. For instance, many don't have appropriate accounting skills, and engaging accountants is expensive. Wage costs are a major expense, and when these costs and interest payments are included, the income received by the franchisees is under pressure. In order to reduce labour costs some franchisees work on the weekends when wages are more expensive.

This incident demonstrates the tension between the interpretations of sustainability from a 'normative' perspective and from an 'efficiency' perspective. It also raises the issues of the importance of external regulators in protecting those employees who have little power and are vulnerable. It highlights the relationship between strategy and HRM practices.

Sources: http://www.abc.net.au/news/2015; http://www.sbs.com.au; http://www.smh.com.au/business.

CONCLUSION

Sustainable HRM has evolved from the SHRM approach that emerged during the 1980s. Just as SHRM evolved, so now is Sustainable HRM evolving. Sustainable HRM has key characteristics but also a varying range of interpretations from different writers. International reporting frameworks provide insights into aspects of the breadth of Sustainable HRM in an international, global market; however, as with the implementation of HRM practices, the reality of the practice occurring in organisations is a challenge.

The development of Sustainable HRM has implications for the models adopted by business and the expectations of various stakeholders. The formulation and implementation of HR practices consistent with Sustainable HRM require a variety of additional capabilities. Sustainable HRM will also require a rethinking of HR processes and purpose. As an approach to management that highlights the inconsistencies and contradictions in the processes and practices, it challenges many of the commonly held views about management and business.

End of Chapter Case Study HRM in Brunei's public sector

W. L. Gore and Associates provides an example of a company that displays some, but not all, of these characteristics of Sustainable HRM. It is an international company making 1,000 products and located in more than 50 countries. It is known for its innovative products and for being one of the '100 best companies to work for'. When the company was established in 1958, its founder, Bill Gore, did not have a well-established business plan; however, he did have a strong desire to innovate and to manage the company's people so that they felt safe, valued, engaged, and that they were making a contribution. He believed these social and business outcomes were best achieved by creating a 'unique, non-hierarchical culture which fosters the innovative spirit of individuals and small teams'.

The culture is informed by four guiding principles:

▸ Fairness to each other and everyone with whom we come in contact;
▸ freedom to encourage, help, and allow other associates to grow in knowledge, skill, and scope of responsibility;
▸ the ability to make one's own commitments and keep them; and
▸ consultation with other associates before undertaking actions that could impact the reputation of the company.

These principles also serve as a reference point for employee behaviour and decisions. The principles are reflected in the selection process of new recruits, which involves teams of associates; the deployment of staff, which involves staff volunteering for jobs; the appointment of leaders, which often involves teams of associates; the maximum size of a facility, which cannot exceed 200 associates; and the requirement for consultation and associate involvement. The principles also underpin the pursuit of the company's strategy which focuses on innovation, growth, and differentiated and quality products that exceed the needs of customers.

W. L. Gore is a private company and is therefore not required to answer to external shareholders. The company is constantly growing through processes such as acquisitions and the development of new products internally. The HR processes encourage the transfer of knowledge, the pursuit of new ideas, the development of capabilities, and a recognition of the value of tangible and intangible resources.

The processes of consultation, involvement in decision-making, and sharing knowledge can be time -onsuming processes; however, it is believed that once a decision is made, associates are keen to execute the decision. Individual performance assessments are based on team-member evaluations, and rewards are based on these evaluations. Performance pay reflects individual performance, and arrangements exist for profit-related pay, the provision of stock, and free private health care. There are no hierarchical structures or formal channels of communication, and the company seeks to maximise individual potential by having sponsors assist associates to develop their potential and contribute to the organisation. Positive social outcomes include associate satisfaction and retention. The various business units within W. L. Gore and Associates are concerned about their impact on the environment. The organisation has an Environmental Responsibility Statement which is set out below.

A Legacy of Responsible Innovation

Gore's respect for the environment is a natural outgrowth of our legacy of responsible innovation. Throughout our history, we've applied the principles of sound science to create products that improve the quality of life, including products that solve difficult environmental problems. As a company and as individuals, we are committed to achieving a positive economic impact while being environmentally responsible. We will use the best scientific understanding available to guide us in our actions.

At Gore, we have an ongoing commitment to meeting all applicable health, safety, and environmental regulations and standards. We carefully consider the effects of our products and operations on the environment, as well as on the health and well-being of people. We strive to be good stewards of air, water, and energy resources, and in our management of waste.

As an innovative company, we are often in the forefront of technological breakthroughs where we assume added responsibilities. We will draw upon our unique knowledge, and the knowledge of others, to advance the understanding of the interaction of our products and processes with the environment. In all of our efforts, we will take a holistic approach that considers both the short- and long-term implications of our decisions and the prosperity of future generations.

W. L. Gore and Associates

The organisation states that it is committed to meeting the needs of customers through its innovative, reliable products and to improving the communities in which the organisation operates and the associates live. W. L. Gore has a continuing commitment to a legacy of taking a long-term view and seeks to make decisions that are consistent with this principle. The human resource practices and 'lattice structure', which is an integral part of building the culture and supported by human resource practices, are intended to provide a basis for responsible decisions and behaviour with regard to human, social, ecological, and community outcomes.

Questions

1 Discuss the reasons for the development of the Sustainable HRM approach.
2 Explain in what ways Sustainable HRM is different from SHRM.
3 Explain the reasons for the development of reporting frameworks on the practices of organisations and their impact on a broad range of outcomes. Assess the effectiveness of these frameworks in shaping management practice.
4 Discuss the implications of Sustainable HRM for HRM policy and practice.
5 What factors do you consider will shape the future of the management of people in business organisations?

Class Activity

The first part of the chapter indicates the importance of a number of national characteristics, such as values, religious beliefs and the state of the economy. These influence an organisation and are considered when formulating strategy and HRM policies. Figure 17.1 provides a framework that illustrates this.

▸ Are there particular external influences in countries in the Arabian Peninsula/Gulf States that impact HRM policies and create particular issues with respect to social responsibility and sustainable HRM?

GLOSSARY

Coordinated Market Economies (CMEs) are those economies that acknowledge the diversity of stakeholder interests in the economy and society. These interests can be reflected in arrangements such as government regulations and worker representatives on Workers Councils within organisations.

Dialogue involves two or more groups working together in a collaborative way to come to a common understanding.

Global Reporting Initiative (GRI) establishes Reporting Principles for organisations that wish to report on three categories of sustainability: economic, social, and environmental. Six groups are identified as indicators of issues associated with sustainability. These groups are economic, environmental, social, product responsibility, human rights, and labour practices and decent work.

Green HRM focuses on drawing out the relationships between environmental management and HRM.

Harm of negative externalities of HRM practices is defined as the profound negative impact on employees' and their family members' reduced personal outcomes, social and work related wellbeing that are caused by work practices used by organisations to extract maximum skills, abilities, and motivation of employees to achieve highly effective and efficient performance. (Mariappanadar 2014, 187).

Liberal Market Economies (LMEs) are economies that are based on the principles of neoliberalism and focus on the importance of shareholder value and on enabling the market to operate without restrictions such as regulations.

Sustainability Central to the concept of sustainability is endurance at the macro-, organisational, and micro-levels and in the ecological, social/human and economic arenas. These levels and arenas are not mutually exclusive but are interdependent.

Sustainable development according to the Brundtland Commission refers to economic growth, environmental protection, and social equality.

Sustainable HRM can be defined as the pattern of planned or emerging HRM strategies and practices intended to enable the achievement of financial, social, and ecological goals while simultaneously reproducing the HR base over a long term. It seeks to minimise negative impacts on the natural environment and on people and communities and acknowledges the critical enabling role of CEOs, middle and line managers, HRM professionals, and employees in providing messages that are distinctive and consistent and reflect consensus among decision-makers.

Triple bottom line is an accounting framework that explicitly measures the performance of an organisation in terms of ecological/environmental, social, and economic outcomes.

FURTHER READING

AVERY, G. AND BERGSTEINER, H. (2010) *Honeybees and Locusts: The Business Case for Sustainable Leadership*. St. Leonards: Allen and Unwin.

EHNERT, I. AND HARRY, W. (2012) Recent developments and future prospects on sustainable human resource management: Introduction to the Special Issue. *Management Revue* 23(3): 221–238.

EHNERT, I., PARSA, S., ROPER, I., WAGNER, M. AND MULLER-CAMEN, M. (2015) Reporting on sustainability and HRM: A comparative study of sustainability reporting practices by the world's largest companies. *International Journal of Human Resource Management*, http://dx.doi.org.10.1080/09585192.2015.1024.157.

JACKSON, S. AND SEO, J. (2010) The greening of strategic HRM scholarship. *Organization Management Journal* 7(4): 278–290.

MARIAPPANADAR, S. (2012) The harm indicators of negative externality of efficiency-focused organisational practices. *International Journal of Social Economics*, 39: 209–220.

REFERENCES

ARMSTRONG-SASSEN, M. AND CAMERON, S. J. (2003) Nurses' job satisfaction and turnover intentions over a six-year period of hospital downsizing and amalgamation. *International Journal of Public Administration*, 26: 1607–1620.

ARTHUR, J. B. (1994) Effects of human resource systems on manufacturing performance and turnover. *Academy of Management Journal*, 37(3): 670–687.

AVERY, G. (2005) *Leadership for Sustainable Futures: Achieving Success in a Competitive World*. Cheltenham: Edward Elgar.

AVERY, G. AND BERGSTEINER, H. (2010) *Honeybees and Locusts: The Business Case for Sustainable Leadership*. St. Leonards: Allen and Unwin.

BACHAUS, K., STONE, B. AND HEINER, K. (2002) Exploring the relationship between corporate social performance and employer effectiveness. *Business and Society*, 41(3): 319–344.

BARAN, M., KANTEN, P., KANTEN, S. AND YASHOGLU, M. (2009) An empirical research on the relationship between job insecurity and employee health and safety. *Ege Academy Review*, 9: 969–976.

BARRIENTOS, S. AND SMITH, S. (2007) Do workers benefit from ethical trade: Assessing codes of practice in global production of systems. *Third World Quarterly*, 28(4): 713–719.

BARTRAM, T., STANTON, P., LEGGAT, S., CASIMIR, C. AND FRASER, B. (2007) Lost in transition: Exploring the link between HRM and performance in healthcare. *Human Resource Management Journal*, 17(1): 21–41.

BCG (Boston Consulting Group and WFPMA) (2012) *Realizing the Value of People Management*. www.bcgperspectives.

BECKER, B. E. AND HUSELID, M. A. (2006) Strategic human resource management: Where do we go from here? *Journal of Management*, 32(6): 898–925.

BEER, M., SPECTOR, R., LAWRENCE, P., QUINN MILLS, D. AND WALTON, R. (1984) *Human Resource Management: A General Managers Perspective*. Glencoe, IL: Free Press.

BOEDKER, C. (2005) Australian guiding principles on extended performance management: A guide to better managing, measuring and reporting knowledge-intensive resources (DRAFT), Society for Knowledge Economics, Australia.

BOUD, D., CRESSEY, P. AND DOCHERTY, P. (eds) (2006) *Productive Reflection at Work*. Oxford: Routledge.

BOWEN, D. E. AND OSTROFF, C. (2004) Understanding HRM-firm performance linkages: The role of 'strength' of the HRM System. *Academy of Management Review*, 29: 203–221.

BOXALL, P. AND MACKY, K. (2009) Research and theory on high-performance work systems: Progressing the high-involvement stream. *Human Resource Management Journal*, 19(1): 3–23.

BOXALL, P. AND PURCELL, J. (2011) *Strategy and Human Resource Management*. Hampshire: Palgrave Macmillan.

BRAMMER, S., MILLINGTON, A. AND RAYTON, B. (2007) Exploring the relationship between corporate social responsibility to organisational commitment. *International Journal of Human Resource Management*, 18(10): 1701–1719.

BRANCO, M. AND RODRIGUES, L. (2006) Corporate social responsibility and resource-based perspectives. *Journal of Business Ethics*, 69(2): 111–132.

BROWNING, V. AND DELAHAYE, B. (2011) Enhancing workplace learning through collaborative HRD. In Clarke, M. (ed.), *Readings in HRM and Sustainability*. Melbourne: Tilde University Press, pp. 36–50.

BRUNDTLAND, G. (ed.) (1987) *Report of the World Commission on Environment and Development: Our Common Future*. Oxford: Oxford University Press.

BUNGE, J., COHEN-ROSENTHAL, E. AND RUIZ-QUINTANILLA, A. (1996) Employment participation in pollution reduction: Preliminary analysis of the toxic release inventory. *Journal of Cleaner Production*, 4: 453–470.

CASCIO, W. F. (2002) *Restructuring: Creative and Productive Alternatives to Layoffs*. San Francisco: Barrett-Koehler.

CLARKE, M. (ed.) (2011) Sustainable HRM: A new approach to people management. In *Readings in HRM and Sustainability*. Melbourne: Tilde University Press, pp. 1–7.

COLLINS, C. J. AND CLARK, K. D. (2003) Strategic human resource practices, top management teams social networks, and firm performance: The role of human resource practices in creating organizational competitive advantage. *Academy of Management Journal*, 46(6): 740–751.

COLLINSON, D., COBB, G., POWER, D. AND STEVENSON, L. (2007) The financial performance of the FTSE4 good indices. *Corporate Social Responsibility and Environmental Management*, 15(1): 14–28.

DEBROUX, P. (2014) Sustainable HRM in East and Southeast Asia. In EHNERT, I., HARRY, W. AND ZINK, K. J. (eds), *Sustainability and Human Resource Management: Developing Sustainable Business Organizations*. Heidelberg: Springer-Verlag.

DIMAGGIO, P. J. AND POWELL, W. W. (1983) The Iron Cage revisited: Institutional isomorphism and collective rationality in organizational fields. *American Sociological Review*, 48: 147–160.

DOCHERTY, P., FORSLIN, J., (Rami) Shani, A. B. and Kira, M. (eds.) (2002) Emerging work systems: From intensive to sustainable. In *Creating Sustainable Work Systems: Emerging Perspectives and Practice*. London: Routledge, pp. 3–14.

DOCHERTY, P., KIRA, M. AND SHANI, A. B. (2009) What the world needs now is sustainable work systems. In

DOCHERTY, P., KIRA, M. AND SHANI, A. B. (eds), *Creating Sustainable Work Systems: Developing Social Sustainability* (2nd ed.). London: Routledge, pp. 1–21.

DONNELLY, N. AND PROCTOR-THOMSON, S. (2011) Workplace sustainability and employee voice. In CLARKE, M. (ed.), *Readings in HRM and Sustainability*. Melbourne: Tilde University Press, pp. 117–132.

DUNPHY, D., GRIFFITHS, A. AND BENN, S. (2007) *Organization Change for Corporate Sustainability* (2nd ed.). London: Routledge.

EHNERT, I. (2006) Sustainability issues in human resource management: Linkages, theoretical approaches, and outlines for an emerging field. In *21st EIASM SHRM Workshop*, Aston, Birmingham, March 28–29.

EHNERT, I. (2009) *Sustainable Human Resource Management: A Conceptual and Exploratory Analysis from a Paradox Perspective*. Berlin: Physica-Verlag.

EHNERT, I. (2011) Sustainability and human resource management. In WILKINSON, A. AND TOWNSEND, K. (eds), *The Future of Employment Relations*. Hampshire: Palgrave Macmillan, pp. 215–237.

EHNERT, I. AND HARRY, W. (2012) Recent developments and future prospects on sustainable human resource management: Introduction to the Special Issue. *Management Revue*, 23(3): 221–238.

EHNERT, I., PARSA, S., ROPER, I., WAGNER, M. AND MULLER-CAMEN, M. (2015) Reporting on sustainability and HRM: A comparative study of sustainable reporting practices by the world's largest companies. *International Journal of Human Resource Management*, http://dx.doi.org/10.1080/0985192.2015.1024157.

ELIASON, M. AND STORRIE, D. (2009) Does job loss shorten life? *Journal of Human Resources*, 44: 277–302.

ELKINGTON, J. (1997) *Cannibals with Forks: The Triple Bottom Line of the 21st Century*. Oxford: Capstone.

European Expert Group in Health in Restructuring (2009) *Health in Restructuring (HIRES): Innovative Approaches and Policy Recommendations*. Munich: Rainer-Hampp.

EVANS, P. A. L. (1999) HRM on the edge: A duality perspective. *Organization*, 6(2): 325–338.

EVANS, P. AND DAVIS, W. D. (2005) High performing work systems and organisational performance: The mediating role of internal social structure. *Journal of Management*, 31(5): 758–775.

FRIEDMAN, M. (1970) The social responsibility of business is to increase profits. *New York Times Magazine*, September 13, 32–33.

Gallup Consulting (2010) *The State of the Global Workplace: A World-Wide Study of Engagement and Well-Being*. Washington, DC: Gallup 1-200.

GOLLAN, P. (2000) Human resources, capabilities and sustainability. In DUNPHY, D., BENEVISTE, J., GRIFFITHS, A. AND SUTTON, P. (eds), *Sustainability: The Corporate Challenge of the Twenty-First Century*. Sydney: Allen and Unwin, pp. 55–77.

GRI (2015) About GRI. Retrieved from https://www.globalreporting.org/information/about-gri/pages/default.aspx.

HAMPDEN-TURNER, C. (1990) *Charting the Corporate Mind: Graphic Solutions to Business Conflicts*. New York: Free Press.

HAMPDEN-TURNER, C. AND TROMPENAARS, F. (2000) *Building Cross-Cultural Competence: How to Create Wealth from Conflicting Values*. Chichester: Wiley.

HUSELID, M. A. (1995) The impact of human resource management practices on turnover, productivity and corporate financial performance. *Academy of Management Journal*, 38(3): 635–670.

JABBOUR, C. A. AND SANTOS, F. C. A. (2008) The central role of HRM in the search for sustainable organisations. *International Journal of Human Resource Management*, 19(12): 2133–2154.

JACKSON, S., RENWICK, D., JABBOUR, C. J .C. AND MULLER-CAMEN, M. (2011) State-of-the-art and future directions for green human resource management: Introduction to the Special Issue. *German Journal of Human Resource Management*, 25(2): 99–116.

JACKSON, S. AND SEO, J. (2010) The greening of strategic HRM scholarship. *Organization Management Journal*, 7(4): 278–290.

KANTABUTRA, S. (2006) Relating vision-based leadership to sustainable business performance: A Thai perspective. *Kravis Leadership Institute Leadership Review*, 6: 37–53.

KANTABUTRA, S. (2012) Putting Rhineland principles into practice in Thailand: Sustainable leadership at Bathroom Design Company. *Global Business and Organizational Excellence*, July/August: 6–19.

KANTABUTRA, S. AND AVERY, G. (2011) Sustainable leadership at Siam Cement. *Journal of Business Strategy*, 32(4): 32–41.

KAPLAN, R. S. AND NORTON, D. P. (1996) *The Balanced Scorecard: Translating Strategy into Action*. Boston: Harvard Business School Press.

KIRA, M. (2002) Moving from consuming to regenerative work. In Docherty, P., Forslin, J. and (Rami) Shani, A. B. (eds), *Creating Sustainable Work Systems: Emerging Perspectives and Practice*. London: Routledge, pp. 29–39.

KRAMAR, R. (1992) Strategic human resource management: Are the promises fulfilled? *Asia Pacific Journal of Human Resource Management*, 32(1): 1–15.

KRAMAR, R. (2009) Human resources. In Staib, R. (ed.), *Business Management and Environmental Stewardship*. Hampshire: Palgrave Macmillan, pp. 97–117.

KRAMAR, R. (2012) Human resources: An integral part of sustainability. In Jones, G. (ed.), *Current Research in*

Sustainability. Melbourne: Tilde University Press, pp. 153–178.

KRAMAR, R. (2014) Beyond strategic HRM: Is sustainable HRM the next approach? *International Journal of Human Resource Management*, 25(8): 1069–1087.

KRAMAR, R. AND PARRY, E. (2014) Human resource management in the Asia Pacific region: Similarities and difference. *Asia Pacific Journal of Human Resources*, 52(4): 400–419.

LAUWO, S. AND OTUSANYA, O. J. (2014) Corporate accountability and human rights disclosures: A case study of Barrick Gold Mine in Tanzania. *Accounting Forum*, 38(2): 91–108.

LENGNICK-HALL, M. L., LENGNICK-HALL, C. A., ANDRADE, L. A. AND DRAKE, B. (2009) Strategic human resource management: The evolution of the field. *Human Resource Management Review*, 19: 64–85.

MACKY, K. AND BOXALL, P. (2008) High involvement work processes, work intensification and employee well-being: A study of New Zealand worker experiences. *Asia Pacific Journal of Human Resources*, 46(1): 38–55.

MALEY, J. AND KRAMAR, R. (2014) The influence of global uncertainty on the cross-border performance appraisal: A real options approach. *Personnel Review*, 43(1): 2–20.

MARIAPPANADAR, S. (2003) Sustainable human resource strategy: The sustainable and unstainable dilemmas of retrenchment. *International Journal of Social Economics*, 30(8): 906–923.

MARIAPPANADAR, S. (2012) The harm indicators of negative externality of efficiency-focused organisational practices. *International Journal of Social Economics*, 39: 209–220.

MARIAPPANADAR, S. (2014) The model of negative externally for sustainable HRM. In EHNERT, I., HARRY W. AND ZINK, K. J. (eds), *Sustainability and Human Resource Management: Developing Sustainable Business Organisations*. Berlin, Heidelberg: Springer-Verlag.

MATINEZ LUCIO, M. AND STUART, M. (2011) The state, public policy and the renewal of HRM. *International Journal of Human Resource Management*, 22(18): 3661–3671.

MAYRHOFER, W., MULLER-CAMEN, M., LEDOLTER, J., STRUNK, G. AND ERTEN C. (2004) Devolving responsibilities for human resources to line management: An empirical study about convergence in Europe. *Journal for East European Management Studies*, 9(2): 123–146.

MÜLLER-CAMEN, MICHAEL, SZIGETVARI, EVA, PARSA, S, ROPER, I. (2013) Human Rights in the supply chain: Assessing multinationals' social reporting. 'Sustainability and HRM' Workshop, Louvain-la-Neuve, Belgien, 02.09.–03.09.

MYERSON, A.R. (1997) In principle, a case for more 'sweatshops'. *The New York Times*, June 22. Available at: http://www.nytimes.com/1997/06/22/weekinreview/in-principle-a-case-for-more-sweatshops.html.

O'DONNELL, L., KRAMAR, R. AND CADIZ DYBALL, M. (2009) Human capital reporting: Should it be industry specific? *Asia Pacific Journal of Human Resources*, 47(3): 358–373.

ORLITZKY, M., SCHMIDT, F. AND RYNES, S. (2003) Corporate social financial performance: A meta-analysis. *Organizational Studies*, 24(3): 403–441.

OSLAND, A. AND OSLAND, J. S. (2007) Aracruz Cellulose: Best practices icon but still at risk. *International Journal of Manpower*, 8: 435–450.

PATTERSON, M. G., WEST, M. A., LAWTHORN, R. AND NICKELL, S. (1997) *Impact of People Management Practices on Business Performance* (Issues in People Management 22). London: Institute of Personnel and Development.

PETERSON, D. K. (2004) The relationship between perceptions of corporate citizenship and organizational commitment. *Business and Society*, 43(3): 296–319.

PFEFFER, J. (1998) Seven practices of successful organizations. *California Management Review*, 40(2): 96–124.

PFEFFER, J. (2010) Building sustainable organizations: The human factor. *Academy Management Perspective*, 24: 34–45.

PIAGET, J. (1962), *Comments on Vygotsky's Critical Remarks Concerning the Language and Thought of the Child and Judgement and Reasoning in the Child*. Cambridge, MA: MIT Press.

PURCELL, J. AND HUTCHINSON, S. (2007) Front-line managers as agents in the HRM-performance causal chain: Theory, analysis and evidence. *Human Resource Management Journal*, 17(1): 3–20.

RENWICK, D. W .S., REDMAN, T. AND MAGUIRE, S. (2011) Green human resource management: A review and research agenda. *International Journal of Management Reviews*, 15: 1–14.

RICHARD, O. C. AND JOHNSON, N. B. (2001) Strategic human resource management effectiveness and firm performance. *International Journal of Human Resource Management*, 12(2): 299–310.

ROYAL, C. AND O'DONNELL, L. (2005) Embedding human capital analysis in the investment process: A human resources challenge. *Asia Pacific Journal of Human Resources*, 43(1): 117–136.

SCHULER, R. S. AND JACKSON, S. E. (1987) Linking competitive strategies with human resource management practices. *Academy of Management Executive*, 1(3): 207–219.

SCHULER, R. S. AND JACKSON, S. E. (2005) A quarter-century review of human resource management in the US: The growth in importance of the international perspective. *Management Revue*, 16(1): 1–25.

SHEEHAN, C., COOPER, B., HOLLAND, P. AND DE CIERI, H. (2007) The relationship between HRM avenues of political influence and perceived organizational performance. *Human Resource Management*, 46(4): 611–629.

SKE (Society of Knowledge Economics) (2011) *Leadership, Culture and Management Practices in High Performing Workplaces in Australia*, A report commissioned by the Department of Education, Employment and Workplace Relations, Sydney.

SPARKS, K., COOPER, C., FRIED, Y. AND SHIROM, A. (1997) The effects of hours of work on health: A meta-analytic review. *Journal of Occupational and Organizational Psychology*, 70(4): 391–408.

STANTON, P., YOUNG, S., BARTRAM, T. AND LEGGAT, S. (2010) Singing the same song: Translating HRM messages across management hierarchies. *International Journal of Human Resource Management*, 21(4): 567–581.

STERLING, S. (2004) *Linking Thinking*. Perthshire, Scotland: WWF.

ULRICH, D. (1997) *Human Resource Champions: The Next Agenda for Adding Value and Delivering Results*. Boston, MA: Harvard Business School Press.

ULRICH, D. AND BROCKBANK, W. (2005) *The HR Value Proposition*. Boston, MA: Harvard Business School Press.

ULRICH, D., YOUNGER, W., BROCKBANK, W. AND ULRICH, M. (2012) *Competencies for HR Professionals, Working Outside-In*. Provo, Utah: RBL Group.

UNICEF (2015) An estimated 150 million children worldwide are engaged in child labour. Available at: https://data.unicef.org/topic/child-protection/child-labour/.

WALSH, J., WEBER, K. AND MARGOLIS, J. (2003) Social issues and management: Our lost cause. *Journal of Management*, 29(6): 859–881.

WELLS, S. (2011) HRM for sustainability: Creating a new paradigm. In Clarke, M. (ed.), *Readings in HRM and Sustainability*. Melbourne: Tilde University Press, pp. 133–146.

WILKINSON, A., HILL, M. AND GOLLAN, P. (2001) The sustainability debate. *International Journal of Operations and Production Management*, 12(12): 1492–1502.

ZAUGG, R. J., BLUM, A. AND THOM, N. (2001) *Sustainability in Human Resource Management: Evaluation Report*. Bern: IOP-Press.

INDEX